The Moving Picture Book

The Moving Picture Book

BY WILLIAM KUHNS
Assisted by Raymond Groetsch and Joe McJimsey

Design: William Kuhns with Linda Matthews

Art Director: Dan Johnson

Pflaum
Dayton, Ohio

Photo Credits

Grateful acknowledgment is made to the following for permission to use material in this book.

Excerpts from *Film As Art* by Rudolph Arnheim. Originally published by the University of California Press; reprinted by permission of The Regents of the University of California.

Andrew Sarris on *The Man Who Shot Liberty Valance,* from *Film Culture* No. 25, Summer, 1962/*The Primal Screen: Essays on Film and Related Subjects,* Simon & Schuster: New York, 1973. ©1962, 1973; used with permission of Andrew Sarris.

From *Fun in a Chinese Laundry: An Autobiography* by Josef von Sternberg. Macmillan: New York, 1973. Used with permission.

From *Hitchcock* by François Truffaut. Copyright ©1967 by François Truffaut and Helen Scott. Reprinted by permission of Simon & Schuster.

From *The Comic Mind* by Gerald Mast, copyright ©1973 by Gerald Mast. Reprinted by permission of the publisher, The Bobbs-Merrill Company, Inc.

"The Evolution of the Western," from *What Is Cinema? Vol. II* by André Bazin, selected and translated by Hugh Gray. Originally published by the University of California Press; reprinted by permission of The Regents of the University of California.

From *Deeper Into Movies* by Pauline Kael, by permission of Atlantic-Little, Brown and Co. Copyright ©1972 by Pauline Kael. This material originally appeared in *The New Yorker.*

Review of *The Treasure of the Sierra Madre* from *Agee on Film,* Vol. I, by James Agee. Copyright 1948, ©1958 by James Agee Trust. Reprinted by permission of Grosset & Dunlap, Inc.

Excerpts from "The Gimp," reprinted from *Commentary,* by permission; copyright ©1952 by the American Jewish Committee.

Excerpt from *Notes of a Film Director* by Sergei Eisenstein. Dover Publications, Inc., New York.

From *Theory of the Film* by Béla Balázs. Dover Publications, Inc., New York.

Library of Congress
Catalog Card Number 75-6381

ISBN 0-8278-0054-1

Following are the motion pictures represented in this book by photos. The (d) director, copyright holders and/or producers are identified, as are the 16mm. distributors of the films. Additional sources of photos, including their page numbers, are listed also. In many cases these photos are not from films but are of persons, production scenes, or miscellanea. Discrepancies in dates given for movies in the copyright notices, in photograph identification, and in the text illustrate a difficulty in "dating" films. It is not generally agreed how a film should be dated, whether by copyright date, completion of production, or release for public showing. Distributors and photo sources are identified by code letters as follows:

A./Gene Andrewski
B./Lloyd Montreuil
C./Contemporary Films/McGraw-Hill
CA./Canadian Film Archives Stills Library
CF./Creative Film Society
D./Walt Disney Productions
F./Films Inc.
G./Brother Alexis Gonzales, FSC
I./Ivy Films
IF./International Film Bureau
K./Richard Koszarski
L./Learning Corporation of America
M./Macmillan Audio Brandon
MMA./Museum of Modern Art/Film Stills Archive
P./Pyramid Films
PC./Private collection
T./Twyman Films
U./United Artists 16
W./Warners 16

COVER: The film sequences used on the cover are from Charles Braverman's **An American Time Capsule** (1968) and are used with the permission of David Adams, president of Pyramid Films, distributor of the film.

African Queen, The (d) John Huston/©1950 Horizon Enterprises, Inc./T. **All the King's Men** (d) Robert Rossen/©1950 Columbia Pictures Corp./T. **Allures** 1964 Jordan Belson/P.

Bananas (d) Woody Allen/1971 United Artists; Charles Joffee, producer/U. **Battle of the Century, The** (d) Hal Roach/from *The Golden Age of Comedy*©1957 by Ro-Co Productions, Inc., released by Distributors Corp. of America/T. **Battleship Potemkin, The** (d) Sergei Eisenstein/1925 USSR, Goskino/T. **Ben Hur** (d) Fred Niblo/from *Hollywood: The Dream Factory* **Betty Boop's Desert Isle**/Max Fleischer/I. **Big House, The** (d) George Hill/©1930 by Metro-Goldwyn-Mayer Distributing Co./F. **Big Store, The** (d) Charles Reisner/©1941 by Loew's, Inc./F. **Birds, The** (d) Alfred Hitchcock/1963 Universal/T. **Birth of a Nation, The** (d) D. W. Griffith/©1915 Epoch Producing Corp./M. **Blood of a Poet** (d) Jean Cocteau/1930 Vicomte de Noailles/M. **Bonnie and Clyde** (d) Arthur Penn/1967 Warner Brothers, A Tatira-Hiller Production./T. **Bringing Up Baby** (d) Howard Hawks/©1938 RKO Radio Pictures, Inc./M. **Bus Stop** (d) Joshua Logan/©1956 20th Century-Fox Corp./M.

Catalog 1971 John Whitney; Motion Graphics, Inc./P. **Chromophobia** 1968 Raoul Servais/I. **Citizen Kane** (d) Orson Welles/©1941, 1968 RKO Radio Pictures, Inc./F. (Films Inc., non-theatrical) and Janus (theatrical). **Crowd, The** (d) King Vidor/©1928 Metro-Goldwyn-Mayer Distributing Co./F.

Dante's Inferno (d) Harry Lachman/©1935 20th Century-Fox Corp./F. **Daydreams** (d) Buster Keaton/©1922 Buster Keaton Productions, Inc./M. **Dead End** (d) William Wyler/©1937 Samuel Goldwyn/M. **Dead Reckoning** (d) John Cromwell/©1947 Columbia Pictures Corp./M. **Duck Soup** (d) Leo McCarey/©1930 Paramount Productions, Inc./T.

Ersatz 1961 Zagreb Studio, Yugoslavia/C. **Experiments in Motion Graphics** 1968 John Whitney; Motion Graphics, Inc./P. **Eye Hears, The Ear Sees, The** (d) Norman McLaren/1970, National Film Board of Canada/L.

Felix Makes Whoopee ©Pat Sullivan/C. **Flowers and Trees** ©1932 Walt Disney Productions, Ltd./M. **Fly, The** 1970 Zagreb Studio, Yugoslavia/C. **For a Few Dollars More** (d) Sergio Leone/1965 United Artists/U. **Forbidden Planet** (d) Fred Wilcox/©1956 Loew's Inc./F. **Foreign Correspondent** (d) Alfred Hitchcock/©1940 by Walter Wanger/F. **Frame by Frame** 1973 Paul Burnford and Jerry Samuelson/P. **French Connection, The** (d) William Friedkin/1971 20th Century-Fox/F.

General Line, The (Old and New) (d) Sergei Eisenstein/Grigori Alexandrov/1929 Sovkino/M. **Gertie the Dinosaur** ©1914, Winsor McCay/M. **Gold Diggers of 1935** (d) Busby Berkeley/©1935 by First National Pictures, Inc., and the Vitaphone Corp./U. **Golden Age of Comedy, The** (d) Robert Youngson/©1957 by Ro-Co Productions, Inc., released by Distributors Corp. of America/T. **Goldframe** 1969 Raoul Servais/I. **Grand Hotel** (d) Edmund Goulding/©1932 Metro-Goldwyn-Mayer Distributing Corp./F. **Grand Prix** (d) John Frankenheimer/©1967 Metro-Goldwyn-Mayer, Inc./F. **Grapes of Wrath, The** (d) John Ford/©1940 by 20th Century-Fox Film Corp./F. **Great Train Robbery, The** (d) Edwin S. Porter/©1903 Edison/M. **Greed** (d) Erich von Stroheim/©1925 Metro-Goldwyn-Mayer Pictures Corp./F.

Hallelujah, I'm a Bum! (d) Lewis Milestone/©1933 by

Feature Productions, Inc./M. **Hobby** 1968 produced by Featurette Studio, Lodz, Poland/C. **Hollywood: The Dream Factory** 1972 Renox Documentary/Metro-Goldwyn-Mayer/F.

I Am a Fugitive From a Chain Gang (d) Mervyn LeRoy/ ©1932 Warner Brothers Pictures, Inc./U. **Informer, The** (d) John Ford/©1935 RKO Radio Pictures, Inc./F.

Jetée, La (d) Chris Marker /1962 produced by Argos Films/R.T.F./P. **Johnny Belinda** (d) Jean Negulesco/ ©1948 Warner Brothers Pictures, Inc./U. **Jupiter's Thunderbolts** (d) Geo. Méliès/©1903 Geo. Méliès/M.

K-9000: A Space Oddity 1971 Haboush Productions/C.

Labyrinth 1966 produced by Short Film Studio, Warsaw/C. **Lady From Shanghai, The** (d) Orson Welles/ ©1948 Columbia Pictures Corp./M. **Last Laugh, The** (d) F. W. Murnau/©1925 Ufa Films Inc./M.

M (d) Fritz Lang/©1933 Foremco Pictures Corp. and Nassau Films, Inc./M. **Macbeth** (d) Orson Welles/ ©1948 Literary Classics Productions/M. **Machine** 1966 Wolfgang Urchs/P. **Magic Lantern** (d) Geo. Méliès/©1903 Geo. Méliès/M. **Magnificent Ambersons, The** (d) Orson Welles/©1942 RKO Radio Pictures, Inc./F. **Manchurian Candidate, The** (d) John Frankenheimer/©1962 United Artists Corp./U. **Man Hunt** (d) Fritz Lang/©1941 20th Century-Fox Film Corp./F. **M*A*S*H** (d) Robert Altman/1970 20th Century-Fox/F. **Mask of Dimitrious, The** (d) Jean Negulesco/©1944 by Warner Brothers Pictures Corp./U. **Matrix** 1971 John Whitney; Motion Graphics, Inc./P. **Medium Cool** (d) Haskell Wexler/1969 Paramount/F. **Monkey Business** (d) Norman Z. McLeod/©1931 by Paramount Publix Corp./U. **My Darling Clementine** (d) John Ford/©1946 20th Century-Fox Film Corp./F.

Never Give a Sucker An Even Break (d) Edward Cline/ ©1941 Universal Pictures Co., Inc./M. **Nine Variations on a Dance Theme** (d) Hilary Harris/1966 Hilary Harris/Film Images.

North by Northwest (d) Alfred Hitchcock/©1959 Loew's, Inc./F.

Occurrence at Owl Creek Bridge, An (d) Robert Enrico/1962 Robert Enrico/C. **October (Ten Days That Shook the World)** (d) Sergei Eisenstein/1927 Sovkino/ M. **Odd Man Out** (d) Sir Carol Reed/1947 Rank/Universal-International/C. **Olympia(d)** (d) Leni Riefenstahl/1938 Leni Riefenstahl Tobias-Filmkunst/M. **One-Eyed Jacks** (d) Marlon Brando/1961 Paramount/ F. **Pas de Deux** (d) Norman McLaren/1967 National Film Board of Canada/L. **Pather Panchali** (d) Satyajit Ray/1955 Government of West Bengal/M. **Point Blank** (d) John Boorman/1967 Metro-Goldwyn-Mayer/F.

Pretty Poison (d) Noel Black/1968 20th Century-Fox/F. **Psycho** (d) Alfred Hitchcock/©1960 Paramount Pictures Corp./T. **Pulse** Peter Spoecker, B.Y.M. Productions/C.

Red River (d) Howard Hawks/©1948 Monterey Productions/U. **Roaring Twenties, The** (d) Raoul Walsh/ ©1939 Warner Brothers Pictures, Inc./U.

Saboteur (d) Alfred Hitchcock/©1942 Universal Pictures Co., Inc./T. **Sahara** (d) Zoltan Korda/©1943 Columbia Pictures Corp./M. **Seconds** (d) John Frankenheimer/1966 Paramount/F. **Set-up, The** (d) Robert Wise/©1949 RKO Radio Pictures,Inc./F. **Sherlock Jr.** (d) Buster Keaton/©1924 Joseph M. Schenck/M. **She Wore a Yellow Ribbon** (d) John Ford/©1949 Argosy Pictures Corp./M. **Snow White (Betty Boop)** (d) Max Fleischer/©1933 Paramount Productions, Inc./C. **Spellbound** (d) Alfred Hitchcock/©1945 Vanguard Productions/M. **Start the Revolution Without Me** (d) Bud Yorkin/1969 Warner Brothers; producer, Norbud Films/ W. **Steamboat Willie** ©1928 Walter E. Disney/M. **Street Musique** (d) Ryan Larkin/1972 National Film Board of Canada/L. **Strike** (d) Sergei Eisenstein/ 1928 Goskino/Proletkult/M.

Take the Money and Run (d) Woody Allen/1969 Palomar Pictures; Cinerama Releasing/F. **Tamer of Wild Horses** 1967 Zagreb Studio, Yugoslavia/C. **There They Go-Go** Warner Brothers/M. **Thin Man, The** (d) W. S. VanDyke/©1934 Metro-Goldwyn-Mayer Corp./F. **Time Piece** (d) Jim Henson/1965 produced by Jim Henson/C. **Tomorrow** (d) Joseph Anthony/1972 Filmgroup Productions/Filmgroup (35mm.). **Touch of Evil** (d) Orson Welles/©1952 Universal Pictures Co., Inc./T. **Trial, The** (d) Orson Welles/1962 Paris Europa/FI-C-IT/Hisa Films/M. **2001: A Space Odyssey** (d) Stanley Kubrick/1968 Metro-Goldwyn-Mayer/CA.

Walkabout (d) Nicholas Roeg/1972 20th Century Fox/ F. **Wall, The**/1965 produced by Zagreb Film Studio, Yugoslavia/C. **Westerner, The** (d) William Wyler/ ©1940 Samuel Goldwyn/M. **White Heat** (d) Raoul Walsh/©1949 Warner Brothers Pictures, Inc./U. **Wild Boys of the Road** (d) William A. Wellman/©1933 First National Pictures, Inc./U. **Wild Bunch, The** (d) Sam Peckinpah/1969 Warner Brothers/W. **Wild Orchids** (d) Sidney Franklin/from *Hollywood: The Dream Factory*/F. **Wind, The** (d) Victor Seastrom/©1928 Metro-Goldwyn-Mayer/F. **Wizard of Oz, The** (d) Victor Fleming/from *Hollywood: The Dream Factory*/F.

ADDITIONAL PHOTO SOURCES

PAGE **19** Orson Welles/CF. & K. **20** *Citizen Kane*/ Blum Theatre Collection, State Historical Society of Wisconsin. **22** Black Maria/Wide World. **23** Eadweard Muybridge/MMA. **24** Toys/C. W. Ceram, *Archaeology of the Cinema* (Harcourt, Brace & World, Inc.). **27** D. W. Griffith/P.C. **28** Spectacle/G. **32** *Citizen Kane*/MMA. **32** *Spellbound*/MMA. **33** *Our Little Girl*/ CF. **33** *Golden Earrings*/CF. **34** Edison Studio/ MMA. **35** *Sands of Iwo Jima*/CF. **36** Film Stock/Alan Rogers. **38-44** *Pretty Poison* Production Exhibits/Noel Black. **46** *The Cabinet of Dr. Caligari*/CF. **54** *Youngblood Hawke*/A. **57** *Dr. Strangelove*/MMA. **59** *The Madwoman of Chaillot*/G. **61** *Dr. Glas*/CF. **77** *October*/MMA. **82** *Giant*/G. **83** *The Loneliness of the Long Distance Runner*/PC. **86** *The Graduate*/B. **87** *The Third Man*/A. **87** *The Secret of Santa Vittoria*/G. **87** *Solo*/P. **90** *The Sea of Grass*/A. **94** *M*/CF. **94** *Midnight Cowboy*/B. **96** *The Gang That Couldn't Shoot Straight*/G. **112** *The Cabinet of Dr. Caligari*/CF. **125** *La Jetée*/CA. **151** *Monte Carlo*/CF. **152** *La Strada*/ PC. **164** Orson Welles/MMA. **165** *Catch 22*/K. **166** Sergei Eisenstein/Dover Publications, Inc. **166** *The General Line*/MMA. **168** *The Long Gray Line*/CF. **170** *Spellbound*/PC. **171** Alfred Hitchcock/CF. **173** *Sabotage*/PC. **181** *Rear Window*/G. **186** *Psycho*/ Donald Wigal. **188** Cave Drawing/American Museum of Natural History. **192** *Snow White and the Seven Dwarfs*/D. **192** Walt Disney/PC. **193** *Snow White and the Seven Dwarfs*/D. **206** *Pas de Deux*/CF. **209** *Five Film Exercises*/CF. **233** *High Noon*/PC. **233** *Little Caesar*/PC. **233** *2001: A Space Odyssey*/MMA. **233** *Son of Frankenstein*/PC. **233** *Hello Dolly!*/UPI. **233** *The Circus*/PC. **236** *The Life and Times of Judge Roy Bean*/G. **238** *Bonnie and Clyde*/MMA. **239** *Little Caesar*/MMA. **241** *Point Blank*/CA. **242** *A Trip to the Moon*/CF. **242** *The Thing From Another World*/ PC. **242** *Them!*/PC. **243** *Metropolis*/CF. **243** *2001: A Space Odyssey*/MMA. **243** *The Beast From 20,000 Fathoms*/PC. **244** *Frankenstein*/Edison. **244** *Frankenstein*/PC. **244** *The Curse of Frankenstein*/PC. **244** *Dracula*/PC. **245** *Phantom of the Opera*/CA. **245** *The Hunchback of Notre Dame*/PC. **245** *Abbott and Costello Meet Dr. Jekyll and Mr. Hyde*/PC. **246** *Gold Diggers of 1935*/PC. **246** *Carefree*/F. **246** *An American in Paris*/F. **246** *Singin' in the Rain*/PC. **247** *A Day at the Races*/F. **247** *Fiddler on the Roof*/PC. **247** *Hello Dolly!*/John P. Lowe. **247** *Anchors Aweigh*/F. **248** *The Circus*/PC. **248** *Harold Lloyd's World of Comedy*/American Film Institute. **248** *At the Circus*/ CF. **248** Laurel and Hardy/PC. **249** *M*A*S*H*/G. **249** *Dr. Strangelove*/MMA. **252** *Bringing Up Baby*/PC. **253** Buster Keaton/MMA. **253** Woody Allen/G. **256** *The Birth of a Nation*/G. **256** *King Kong*/PC. **256** *Gold Diggers of 1935*/PC. **256** *Gone With the Wind*/ G. **257** *The Wizard of Oz*/CF. **257** *To Have and Have Not*/PC. **257** *Singin' in the Rain*/PC. **257** *Easy Rider*/ PC. **262-3** MGM Stars/G.

Acknowledgements

This book would have been impossible without the assistance of many people, but foremost among them the 16mm film distributors whose cooperation was generous and unstinting. At Contemporary Films/McGraw-Hill, thanks to Peter Schillaci; at Creative Film Society, to the late Bob Pike, and to Angelina Pike and Lois Werth; at Film Images, to Art Brown; at Films Incorporated to Charles Benton and Gail Livingood and Nell Watts and Doug Lemza and Jack Strouss, but particularly to Estelle Redd, whose help throughout was invaluable; to Anne Hebert of the International Film Bureau; to Ann Clementi of the Learning Corporation of America; to Myron Bresnick of Macmillan Audio Brandon, and especially to Carol Crowder there; to David Adams of Pyramid Films, always of considerable help; to Ray Swank of Swank Motion Pictures; to Allen P. Twyman of Twyman Films, extremely helpful; to Donald Krim of United Artists 16; to Christopher Wood of United World Films; and to David Sussman of Warner Brothers 16. The contribution of these people and these companies to the book is inestimable.

The preparation of this book involved exhausting, continuous and demanding work of many people, primarily of Raymond Groetsch and Joe McJimsey; of Georges Cordona; and of Siri Lambourne—these four people bore the brunt of work involved in developing this book and worked with a diligence and commitment that shows in these pages. Thanks also to Ronald Weinberg and Maggie Causey and Jack Boasberg; and to Paul McGuff and Lloyd Montreuil and Dr. Michael Ellis; all of them of invaluable help in various ways, with ideas or suggestions or encouragement.

And, for their help in locating and obtaining stills, thanks to Jana Vosikovska and Jim Forrester of the Canadian Film Institute in Ottawa; to Brother Alexis Gonzales, FSC, for some of the best stills in the book; to the late Bob Pike, and Angelina Pike, of the Creative Film Society; to Gene Andrewski, to Donald Wigal; to Mary Corliss of the Museum of Modern Art film stills archive; to Joe Dispenza, and to Mike Renov.

Yet others, of help in a variety of ways: many thanks to Noel Black, for making available his files on *Pretty Poison,* and his reminiscences; to Alan Rogers, who provided the strips of film used in the production section; to Ann Whitley, who helped organize the final section of manuscript; to Marleen Keeley, who typed the manuscript; and especially to Peter Morris, whose shrewd eye in editing the Sadoul film dictionaries proved itself shrewd again in his painstaking and extremely beneficial reading of this book to catch errors both minute and glaring.

Finally, I wish to thank the people at Pflaum Publishing, who not only coped with a book of this nature, but improved on it considerably. I would never have undertaken such a book without the support and knowledge of Jack Heher, editor at Pflaum, whose instincts in publishing are the most trustworthy I've ever encountered as a writer; and to Dan Johnson, whose stunning design of my earlier *Movies in America* gave me the courage and faith to attempt a book of such difficult layout and design problems, with never a single doubt that it would come to rest in the very best of hands. Ultimately though I must simply congratulate Linda Matthews, who has worked solely with this book for many months, improving on virtually every layout and taking many of my ideas even further, if in the same direction.

—W. K.

Books and Writers

In lieu of a bibliography there are books and writers I would like to acknowledge and at the same time recommend. Foremost is *Theory of the Film* by Béla Balázs (Dover), the Hungarian critic who wrote with an acute, unparalleled sense of the psychological nuances possible in such film techniques as the closeup or camera angle. Balázs, who wrote much of this book in the early thirties, was supremely conscious of the human tensions and contradictions that could be explored in faces or moving hands. His chapter on the soundtrack is an eloquent manifesto of the potential of the sound film, as valid today as when he wrote it forty years ago.

Invaluable as references, to me—and to anyone interested in film—are the two dictionaries by Georges Sadoul, *Dictionary of Films* and *Dictionary of Film Makers,* translated, edited, and updated by Peter Morris (University of California Press). These books are not only scholarly and accurate, but they make fascinating reading. Sadoul and Morris have captured the themes and textures and significance of major films, and their directors.

On *Citizen Kane,* I can't recommend too highly *The Citizen Kane Book,* by Pauline Kael and Herman J. Mankiewicz and Orson Welles (Atlantic-Little, Brown). Kael's essay "Raising Kane" is a splendid piece of scholarship mingled with reminiscence and gossip, and captures the atmosphere of those months before and during the shooting of *Kane.* The shooting script itself makes wonderful reading; reading the lines you can virtually hear the voices of Welles and Joseph Cotten and Everett Sloan. Also helpful on *Kane* are *Focus on Citizen Kane,* edited by Ronald Gottesman (Prentice-Hall), with essays by Borges, Bazin and Truffaut, as well as Bernard Herrmann (who scored the film) and Gregg Toland (who photographed it); and *The Films of Orson Welles,* by Charles Higham (University of California Press), a well-researched, if often salty and vehemently opinionated study of Welles' films.

On the early films I am indebted to Lewis Jacobs' classic, *The Rise of the American Film* (Teachers College Press) and Kevin Brownlow's *The Parade's Gone By* (Ballantine). Of the many books on Griffith my favorite is *Billy Bitzer, His Story* (Farrar, Straus & Giroux), a tantalizing autobiography by Griffith's cohort and cameraman, and a marvelous portrait of the master. Robert M. Henderson has written two books on Griffith—*D. W. Griffith, The Years at Biograph* (Noonday), and *D. W. Griffith, His Life and Work* (Oxford)—which I found lively and helpful.

Film aesthetics, the subject more or less of chapters three to seven, can be controversial terrain; my guides, beyond Béla Balázs, were Rudolf Arnheim (*Film as Art,* University of California Press), André Bazin (*What Is Cinema?, I* and *II,* University of California Press), and to some extent the great Russian theorists Sergei Eisenstein (*Film Form, The Film Sense,* Harcourt, Brace & World; and *Notes of a Film Director,* Dover), and V. I. Pudovkin (*Film Technique and Film Acting,* Bonanza). Recommended also: *The Cinema as Art,* by Ralph Stephenson and J. R. Debrix (Penguin) and Ernest Lindgren, *Art of the Film* (Macmillan). The classic single book on editing remains today, as twenty years ago, *The Technique of Film Editing* by Karel Reisz and Gavin Millar (Hastings House).

Of innumerable books on directors I would like to single out Andrew Sarris' *The American Cinema* (Dutton), a book that always engenders some response; and one of the best of the many anthologies, *Film Makers on Film Making,* edited by Harry M. Geduld (Indiana University Press). Two books on Hitchcock proved supremely helpful: *Hitchcock* by François Truffaut—one of the most intelligent and articulate statements ever made by a director; and Robin Wood's *Hitchcock's Films* (Paperback Library), an always fascinating and frequently brilliant analysis of Hitchcock's later films.

There is a dearth of strong literature on animation. Ralph Stephenson's *The Animated Film* (A. S. Barnes) remains the best overview. Richard Schickel's *The Disney Version* (Simon and Schuster) should be read in connection with the lavish but uncritical *The Art of Walt Disney* by Christopher Finch (Abrams). There is a superb issue of *Film Comment* (Vol. 11, No. 1) on the Hollywood cartoon which will hopefully appear in book form. On the graphic film artists, the best introduction to date is Gene Youngblood's *Expanded Cinema* (Dutton), which includes interviews with Jordan Belson and the Whitneys.

Beyond the critics reprinted in chapter 10, there are others to be recommended, and the best introduction may be through anthologies. Stanley Kauffmann with Bruce Henstell have done *American Film Criticism, from the Beginnings through Citizen Kane* (Liveright), a splendid collection of early criticism including writings by Edmund Wilson, Gilbert Seldes, and Otis Ferguson. More recently, the National Society of Film Critics has published several volumes of annual reviews (*Film 67/68,* etc., Simon and Schuster) that contain writings by many of the best critics writing in English.

On genre there is relatively little; Stuart Kaminsky's new *American Film Genres* (Pflaum), though uneven, marks a beginning. The best introduction remains Robert Warshow's classic essays on "The Westerner" and "The Gangster as Tragic Hero," in *The Immediate Experience* (Atheneum). And on Hollywood . . . ? Three books I've found to be lively excursions into Hollywood, via anecdote: *The Wit and Wisdom of Hollywood,* by Max Wilk (Warner Paperback Library); *Hollywood at Sunset,* by Charles Higham (Saturday Review Press), and Lillian Ross' classic *Picture* (Avon Books), the story of the making of the movie *The Red Badge of Courage.*

For teachers who are teaching film, three books that have stood me in good stead in my own teaching: *Perspectives on the Study of Film,* edited by John Stuart Katz (Little, Brown and Company), a provocative anthology; *Guidebook to Film,* by Ronald Gottesman and Harry Geduld (Holt, Rinehart and Winston), a fine if all too brief guide to the services and sources in film study; and the best quickie reference to film titles I've found yet, Leonard Maltin's *TV Movies* (Signet).

—W. K.

Contents

Introduction

The Moving Picture Book is an introductory text for high school and early college students. It began as a revision of a film primer I had written in 1967, *Exploring the Film*. In the intervening years I had taught enough film courses (in some discouraging cases, to students who only a year or two earlier had used my text) to discover that any textbook in film is inadequate. The central resource of film study are the films themselves. A text can only comment on the films, and most often these are films the students don't see. They are asked to learn not from the film, but from the authority of the teacher or textbook writer.

I have tried to design and write a book in which the films can communicate something of themselves directly from the printed page. There are two purposes in this book. One is to provoke students into making their own recognition and reaching their own understanding about various terms and techniques and possibilities in movies. The other purpose is to whet appetites. If nothing else, an introductory text in film should awaken and invigorate the desire to see more movies, and older movies, and unfamiliar movies.

This book is as much a tribute as a text. I've tried to suggest a few of the riches in what film has accomplished, moments that belong solely to the movies and to no other art. Hopefully this book can give the beginning student not only a flickering understanding of what movies are, and have been, but some feeling for the movies, and what they can be.

WILLIAM KUHNS

CHAPTER ONE

'Citizen Kane'

'Citizen Kane'

The opening shot of *Citizen Kane* fixes on a harsh NO TRESPASSING sign pinned to a barred iron fence. Then we see a heavy, wrought iron insignia, the letter K and in the background, fogged in a mist, a palace atop a hill. Glimpses of caged monkeys, forests, moats, the grounds of what now appears to be almost a castle: then a window with the lights flashing on, off, on again. And inside: a huge bed, on which a man lies, silhouetted against the dawn. The screen fills with snow; a tiny cottage with figures; and, as the camera pulls back, we recognize that it is a water-filled glass paperweight, and the man in the bed is holding it in his hand. There is a brief, enormous closeup of the man's lips; they mutter the word "Rosebud." The glass paperweight rolls to the floor and shatters. A nurse enters the room and slips the sheet over the dead man's head.

A brief preface in which a man's life ends, yet already suggesting the contours and themes of an extraordinary movie. The mood created by the opening shots is dense, chilly, foreboding; and we're given to suspect that somehow so was the man's life. The snowy landscape that becomes something in his dying hand suggests more about him, though it's oblique, uncertain, as though in his last few moments this was the only world he saw. When the glass drops and shatters and the landscape becomes a soil on the floor, we're left with a potent feeling of something expansive having suddenly, jarringly ended. And the vast closeup of two lips, muttering "Rosebud." Suddenly we're involved in a kind of puzzle. What is Rosebud? Who is this man?

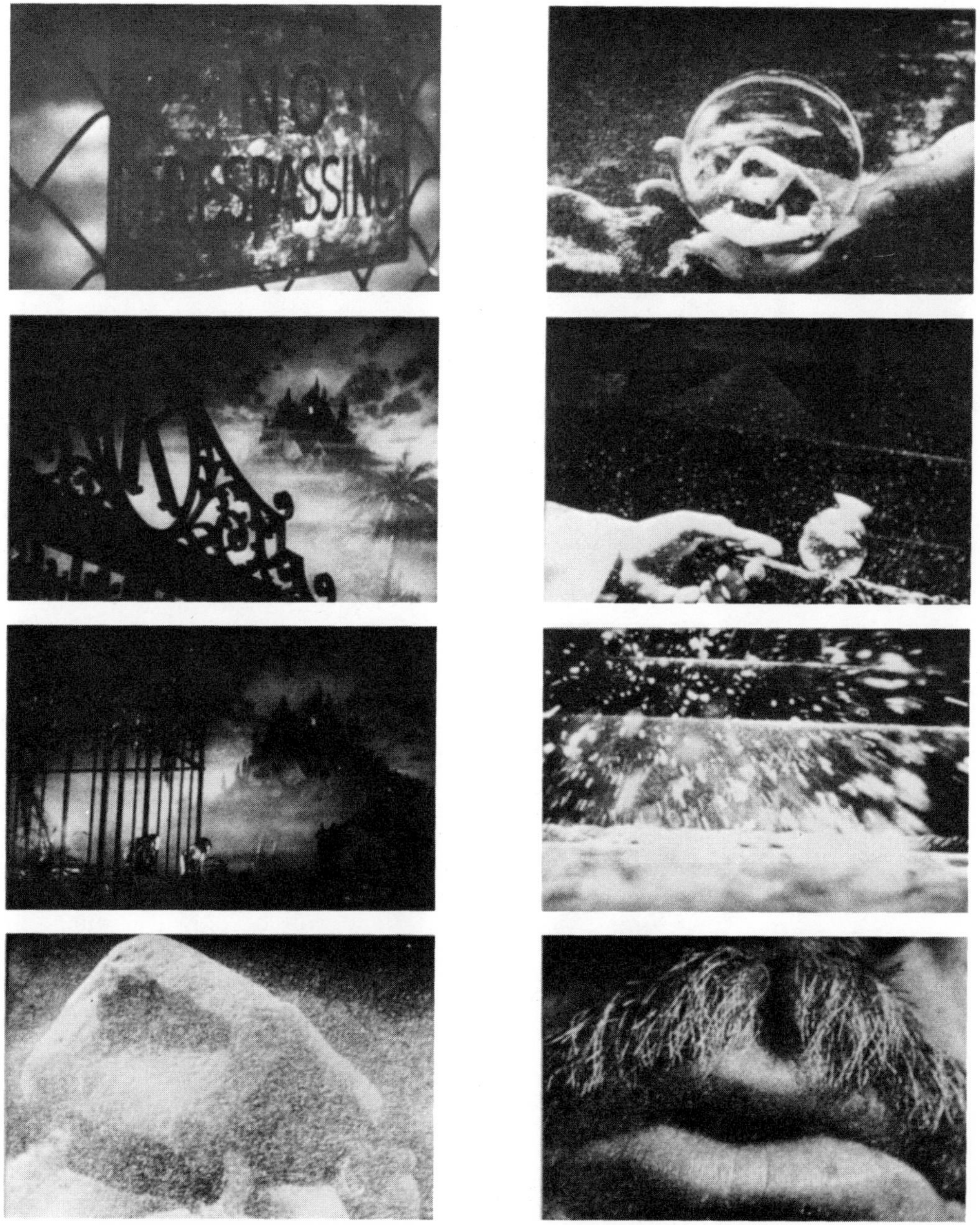

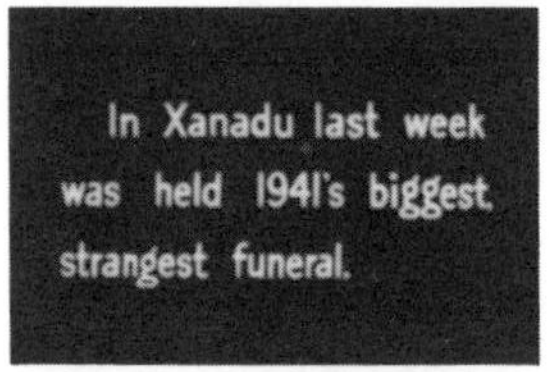

Abruptly the music changes to a violently loud, brazen, strident tune; a newsreel begins: "News on the March!" In the whirlwind, gusty manner of the "March of Time" newsreels of the thirties and forties, we're taken on a wildly swift tour of the life of Charles Foster Kane, ". . . more newsworthy than the names in his own headlines. . . . greatest newspaper tycoon of this or any other generation." We see his fabulous mansion, Xanadu, ". . . world's largest private pleasure ground"—an estate of thousands of acres, encompassing "the largest private zoo since Noah . . . the loot of the world." The cost? "No man can say." The newsreel wends through Kane's life with almost no regard for chronology: the Kane empire of newspapers, paper mills, gold mines; the passionate, controversial newspapers, guided by Kane's staunch opinions on everything; Kane's beginnings and his early life in a boarding house in Colorado; the first newspaper which he ran himself, the *New York Enquirer;* the fiery accusations against Kane—that he's a mudslinger, a Communist, an anarchist; and Kane's reply, "I am, have been, and will be only one thing—an American." Kane was married twice, once to the niece of a President; again, to a singer, Susan Alexander, whose ill-fated opera career he prompted. His one attempt to run for political office was buried in scandal and defeat. Gradually, as the Depression overcame the country, Kane newspapers began to fold; Kane retreated to his mountain palace, Xanadu. Then, "as it must to all men, death came to Charles Foster Kane."

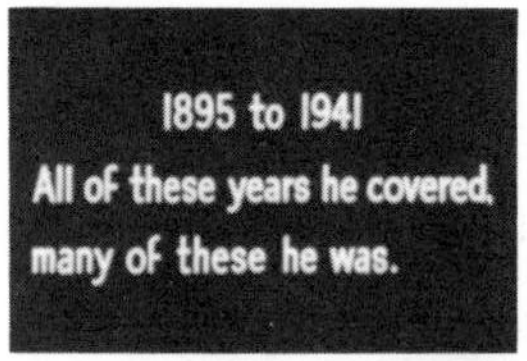

The "News on the March" logo flashes on the screen, then grinds to a slow halt, as if the projector had given out. Several men stand in a darkened screening room and discuss Kane; unsatisfied with the newsreel, they figure to investigate Kane further; they need an "angle." His dying word, "Rosebud," intrigues the producer Rawlston, and a reporter, Thompson, is sent to visit the people who knew Kane best to find out what the dying word meant.

Here we see already established the intricate structure of *Citizen Kane:* not a simple story of a man's life, with a beginning, middle and end; but a structure that will reveal Kane *as others knew him:* a man seen through the distinct and shifting biases, prejudices, attitudes of others. The newsreel has already swept through his life, suggesting the major landmarks; we already sense a disproportionate stature and grandiloquence about Kane; and already—though it's not from "Rosebud" —some sense of mystery. Indeed, the device of the newsreel is doubly shrewd; it does away with our normal expectations for "What happens next?"—in a way we already know; it prepares us instead for the movie that *Citizen Kane* really is—a psychology of this majestic figure: beneath the public success, who was this man?

The newsreel also created, particularly for the audiences of 1941, when the movie was released, a jarring sense of somebody else—the man after whom Kane was modelled and who tried to have the movie stopped, even destroyed, once it had been made. The parallels between Kane's life and that of William Randolph Hearst, magnate of the Hearst publishing empire, are revealing. Hearst began with one newspaper *(The San Francisco Examiner);* like Kane, he raided rival newspapers to build a staff; like Kane he practiced (some say invented) the species of reporting known as "yellow journalism": stories written at a fever pitch, with more regard to effects than facts; as Kane says, "If the headline is big enough, it *makes* the news big enough." Hearst's newspapers were probably responsible for the Spanish-American War in 1898—as were Kane's; Hearst was politically ambitious and though (unlike Kane) he did win two elections, he lost (like Kane) in the race for governor of New York. But the most striking—and damning—parallels between Kane and Hearst are to be found in Susan Alexander, Kane's singer girlfriend; and Xanadu, Kane's vast, tomblike palace. During the late twenties and thirties, Hearst was enchanted by a girl he discovered in Ziegfeld's chorus line, Marion Davies; he built a Hollywood acting career for her which, while she did have charm and a native acting ability, was probably wrong for her: heavy romantic roles that were out of character with Marion Davies, indeed, out of character with the style of thirties movies. Kane falls in love with Susan Alexander, a would-be singer for whom he builds a three-million-dollar opera house and whom he forces, with her lungs of tin, to face audiences that rightly find her singing a disaster. So with Xanadu. Hearst's magnificent estate at San Simeon (now a museum operated by the state of California) is luxurious, immense, crowded with the artistic history of Europe. In its heyday, the twenties and the thirties, it was a grand court for the major figures of Hollywood and statesmen and writers and artists from all over the world. Kane's Xanadu is as plush, as regal, without, however, the sparking vitality and the grace of San Simeon: it seems like nothing so much as a vast echo chamber; a hollow, statue-populated tomb. In both parallels, *Citizen Kane* not only creates vivid similarities to Hearst, it uses them as indicting matter in caricaturing and finally condemning Hearst.

The fact that *Citizen Kane* mirrors so explicitly a powerful figure of its age suggests an important dimension of the film: it was touched with danger. The men who made *Citizen Kane*—Herman Mankiewicz, who wrote most of the screenplay; Orson Welles, who starred and directed; Welles' Mercury Theatre group, who comprised the majority of actors; Gregg Toland, the amazing cameraman; and the technicians—all were involved in a project that was in a sense *more* than simply a movie: something with bite, something that would startle and rock the jaded, "there's-nothing-left-to-show-us" movie audiences of 1941. As Pauline Kael points out so well in her splendid *New Yorker* essay, "Raising Kane," it was precisely this daring, this edge of danger, that gave the production much of its excitement and fervor—and, no doubt, its shaggy ideas and wild inventiveness.

Indeed, from the beginning the men who made *Citizen Kane,* particularly Welles, stood at an enormous advantage over most Hollywood filmmakers of the time. Welles and his Mercury Theatre Players had established an impressive reputation in the late thirties doing theatre and radio; and when, on a radio show Halloween eve, 1938, Welles did a contemporary version of H. G. Wells' *War of the Worlds* (in which a newscaster kept cutting in on ballroom music and in which the entire story was told as if it were a bona fide newscast), thousands of people across the country believed the threat to be real; cars collided on a New Jersey highway, trying to avoid the supposed landing place; a general panic was created by the single stunt, giving Welles an overnight international reputation—and bringing him to the attention of Hollywood.

At first he didn't appear interested in making a movie: there were theatre performances, radio shows; but when the then-struggling RKO turned to the protean young Welles (he was only 24 at the time) and offered him a contract that gave him sole creative control of three feature films—a contract unheard-of in Hollywood till that time—Welles visited the studio and agreed.

His first project was to be an adaptation of Joseph Conrad's novel *The Heart of Darkness;* that project, and a few others that followed, never materialized, and so he and scriptwriter Herman J. Mankiewicz turned to the concept of *Citizen Kane* (originally entitled, significantly, *American*).

Welles didn't go after Hollywood talent except in those areas where he needed their technical expertise: on camera, lighting, set design, special effects. Shrewdly, he tapped some of the best professionals in the business—men who had labored on stock movie productions for years and who, given the creative edge that Welles not only permitted but encouraged, were eager to try ideas and possibilities pent up for a long time. Gregg Toland, for example, the cameraman, already had a substantial reputation in Hollywood. By the end of his life he was to become the highest-paid of Hollywood cameramen. Welles told him that he wanted kinds of effects never before included in the movies: ceilings, for instance, should be visible in the shots. Toland didn't tell Welles (as perhaps most other cameramen would have) that it wasn't done that way, that it was simply impossible. He found a way to do it, to make it work. This spirit and excitement inflamed the entire project.

Likewise, Welles shrewdly used his own Mercury Theatre players for his cast, and since they were fresh to Hollywood, they were capable of making a new kind of movie without complaining that you don't do things that way. As actors, they are stunning: Joseph Cotten, Everett Sloane, George Coulouris, Ray Collins, Ruth Warrick, Erskine Sanford—many of them went on to become screen actors on their own after *Kane*. The music, including the spoof opera "Salammbo" was done by Bernard Herrmann, a Mercury Theatre musician who went on later to score some of the better films to emerge from Hollywood in the fifties and sixties: such as Hitchcock's *Psycho, Vertigo,* and *North by Northwest*. Even the film editor, Robert Wise, at the time himself a beginner, went on to become the director of features like *West Side Story, Haunting,* and *The Sound of Music.*

In effect, *Citizen Kane* was born of a rare opportunity, a rare confluence of talent: beginners and professionals working in Hollywood, yet totally apart from the standard Hollywood working conventions and expectations, free to make the movie they wanted the way they wanted, free to suggest, to try out new techniques and ideas, free to challenge every established rule of the Hollywood movie making process they wanted.

And what they created was a clear triumph: a movie of incredible energy, of dazzling technical ingenuity and—as time would prove—of revolutionary significance; a film that kept the screen burgeoning with a life of its own. The camera is more than an observer in *Kane,* as the lights are more than simple light sources and the sets more than settings: everything in *Kane,* it seems, becomes magnified, takes on proportions that have never been glimpsed in a movie before. Structurally, in its transitions and its dramatizations, in its use of sound and imagery and editing, *Kane* is simply one of the most inventive movies ever made.

Beyond its technical and narrative virtuosity, *Kane* has all the shaggy richness and resonance of a distinctly American masterpiece. "We can get Kane out of our heads," William Whitebait has commented, "but not Kane's dream." The energy, the sense of fervent activity, the jutting movement in *Kane* all are thoroughly, specifically American; as is Kane himself, and the characters that surround him. *Citizen Kane* may not be, finally, the most profound movie made about the American Dream, but it is quite possibly the most indigenous and authentic; as though the process of making the film itself were some kind of realization of that Dream for those who made it. Even today, the picture has not aged the sense of an empire mounting, of people engaged in an enterprise that's capable of achieving something—the excitement hasn't ebbed, and still remains with the viewer over the distance of more than thirty years.

Indeed, watching the film itself is a process that requires us to provide some of the excitement ourselves; just as it requires us to work at seeing and catching its nuances and transitions and darting changes. Writes the critic Herman G. Weinberg: "In Orson Welles' films the spectator may not sit back in his seat and relax, on the contrary he must meet the film at least halfway in order to decipher what is happening, practically every second; if not everything is lost." With its revolutionary technique of deep focus, which involves our eyes as never before in the frame; with its movement through time and place as sudden as a darting insect; with its subtle soundtrack and even more subtle play of light and shadow, *Citizen Kane* requires that we recreate it as we see it; that we discover ourselves the richness and excitement of the film as though retracing the same psychological steps of the men and women in the process of making it. *Citizen Kane* isn't simply a movie you watch; it's an excursion you take into some of the richest and most exciting possibilities of movies themselves.

A Jigsaw Structure

One of the most poignant shots in *Citizen Kane* shows Susan Alexander, Kane's second wife, hunched over a crossword puzzle in Xanadu. The jigsaw configuration of that puzzle seems almost a visual motif in *Kane,* where fragments and multiple things abound. Even the structure of the film is a kind of jigsaw: after the newsreel ends and the newsmen gather to talk, one reporter—Thompson—is sent in search of the "meaning" of Kane's life, implicit, so the reporters think, in his last spoken word, "Rosebud." Thompson checks five sources—the memoirs of the banker Thatcher, and four interviews—and the flashback recounting of these five sources provides the structure, the point of view, and the bit-by-bit piecing together of the idea we get of this man called Kane.

It is an extraordinary structure, not only because it permits varied points of view, but as well because it assumes that no one point of view can fully and accurately capture Kane: we are never really permitted to know Kane as an authoritative omniscient narrator tells us he is, but only (as it would be in real life) as others knew him, with always that overlapping of opinions and reactions, always that inescapable hint of prejudice. And so, when events are depicted from two viewpoints, we do catch subtle differences: Susan's opera career, for example, is depicted by Kane's friend Jed Leland as a staged farce; by Susan Alexander as a solo performance for a single clapping man in the audience—Kane. For banker Thatcher, Kane's newspaper career was a spectacle of scandal-mongering and rigged wars; for the more loyal Bernstein it was a dedicated effort; or at least it began that way. Point of view shades and creates perspective for everything in *Citizen Kane:* like the angled camera, the harsh contrasting lighting.

FACELESS MEN

End of the newsreel, and against two shafts of light we see the reporters talking. We never see their faces, now or throughout the film: a sly reference to the notorious anonymity of the Luce (TIME-LIFE) journalists.

FIVE POINTS OF VIEW

The five people from whom we learn Kane's story. Note the reporter Thompson: always present, always faceless.

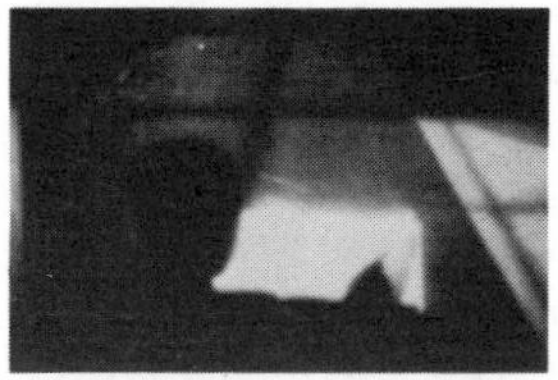

Reading Thatcher's Memoirs

Interviewing Bernstein

Interviewing Leland

Interviewing Susan

Interviewing Raymond

The Camera

When the word was known, legend has it, among the Hollywood professionals that Orson Welles had been given free rein to make a movie for RKO, he received a letter from Gregg Toland asking to work on the project. Toland was at the time one of the crack cinematographers in Hollywood—a cameraman known to be capable of achieving difficult effects with limited light or problematic sets. He had worked (and later continued working) for one of the highest regarded professionals, William Wyler, and his photographic style was clean and richly hued, and had already—prior to working on *Kane*—shown a tendency toward shooting "in depth": capturing an engaging sense of depth within the frame.

Welles gave Toland considerable latitude in shooting *Kane*. As Toland puts it, "Welles was insistent that the story be told most effectively, letting the Hollywood conventions of movie-making go hang if need be." The result was one of the most ambitious and revolutionary uses of the camera in film history.

In most movies the camera is a kind of impartial observer, and for all purposes invisible to the audience. Not in *Kane*. For one thing, the camera rarely used the standard shots: the face-on medium shot, the closeup; instead, it angled toward the characters, often from a low or high angle, usually to emphasize a point of view. And, a seemingly small thing, but revolutionary, the camera showed ceilings. Previously in Hollywood sets were built without ceilings for the sake of moving lighting equipment, sound booms, etc. Welles constructed sets with ceilings, which gave a natural sense of spatial enclosures to the scenes. Camera movement, used sparingly but expressively, emphasized the beginnings and ends of major sequences, as a means of adding a slight emotional touch, like a leitmotif in a musical score.

ANGLE

Susan's tantrum:
high and low angle serve to isolate and reduce Susan, and make Kane even more imperious and implacable.

CEILINGS

The presence of ceilings throughout *Citizen Kane* not only marked a "first" for Hollywood studios, but gave the sets a more convincing, more encompassing feeling: we are always conscious of places in *Kane*, and of the subtle force of a place upon the characters.

MOVING CAMERA

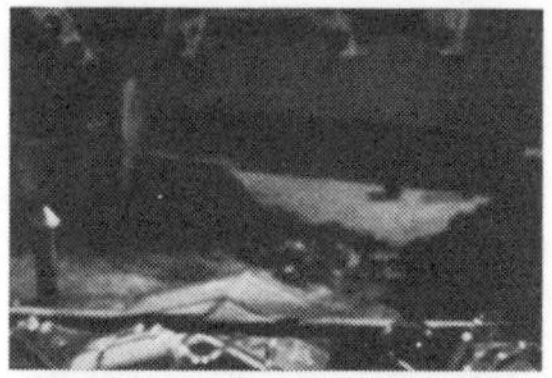

The famous approach to Susan Alexander's nightclub—a dolly shot in toward the skylight, then a subtle dissolve through it.

Other effects, related to the camera, are no less striking—and often revolutionary—examples of Toland's genius: superbly framed images; the use of reflection to underscore dialogue or mood; shots that emphasize a distinct feeling, as the isolation in Susan's opera premiere.

But it's with lighting—types of lighting previously considered taboo in Hollywood—that Toland gives *Kane* much of its gothic, theatrical flavor. Rarely is the whole set lit in *Kane:* more often we see only pools of light, and the characters step in and out of the light, creating distinct ideas of their relation to the action. Toland shot into bright harsh spotlights; he backlit figures so we couldn't see their faces, only their dark outlines; he blotted out figures in a scene so that their presence took on a taut dramatic quality; he used lighting to isolate, to relate, to separate. For perhaps the first time in a Hollywood film, lighting became itself distinctly expressive, not a mere tool of the camera.

Just before the separation from his mother a camera movement in closeup from the mother to the young Kane.

FRAMING

POOLS OF LIGHT

REFLECTION

BLOTTING

ISOLATION

BACKLIGHTING

In the sequence where Kane and his wife go to Susan Alexander's apartment to face Gettys, lighting becomes a means of changing our sympathy from Kane to Gettys: note how the scene at first darkens Gettys' face, then gradually Kane's.

A Revolution in the Technique: Deep Focus

Citizen Kane shattered conventions, used camera and lighting as active parts of a dramatic whole; but in one drastic sweep, by daring the limits of a technique, it transformed the history of cinema, much as Griffith's intercutting in *The Birth of a Nation* had affected every film to follow it.

The technique is deep focus: shooting the image so that *both* the foreground and the background are in focus, and thereby giving dramatic play to the very space within the frame itself. Previously most shots in most films focused on a single field: a face, a group of people—in fact, a cameraman would have told you that's the only way the camera can work. Toland, experimenting with a new lens and "pushing" the film beyond its normal speed, found a way to shoot with a far greater depth of field, and he and Welles agreed that was the way that *Kane* was to be shot.

Deep focus is revolutionary because it forces the film viewer to use his eyes as never before: he must select, roam the frame, spot and anticipate the action within the frame—rather than have it visually flung at him, as in previous manners of shooting. Critics like Bazin consider deep focus more "realistic"—providing a more honest and accurate depiction of the three-dimensional world than techniques like editing or montage. But ultimately deep focus—particularly as Welles and Toland used it in *Kane*—gives dramatic life to dead space: provides a way of dramatizing and clarifying relationships by the simple physical spacing of characters (or characters and things) within a shot.

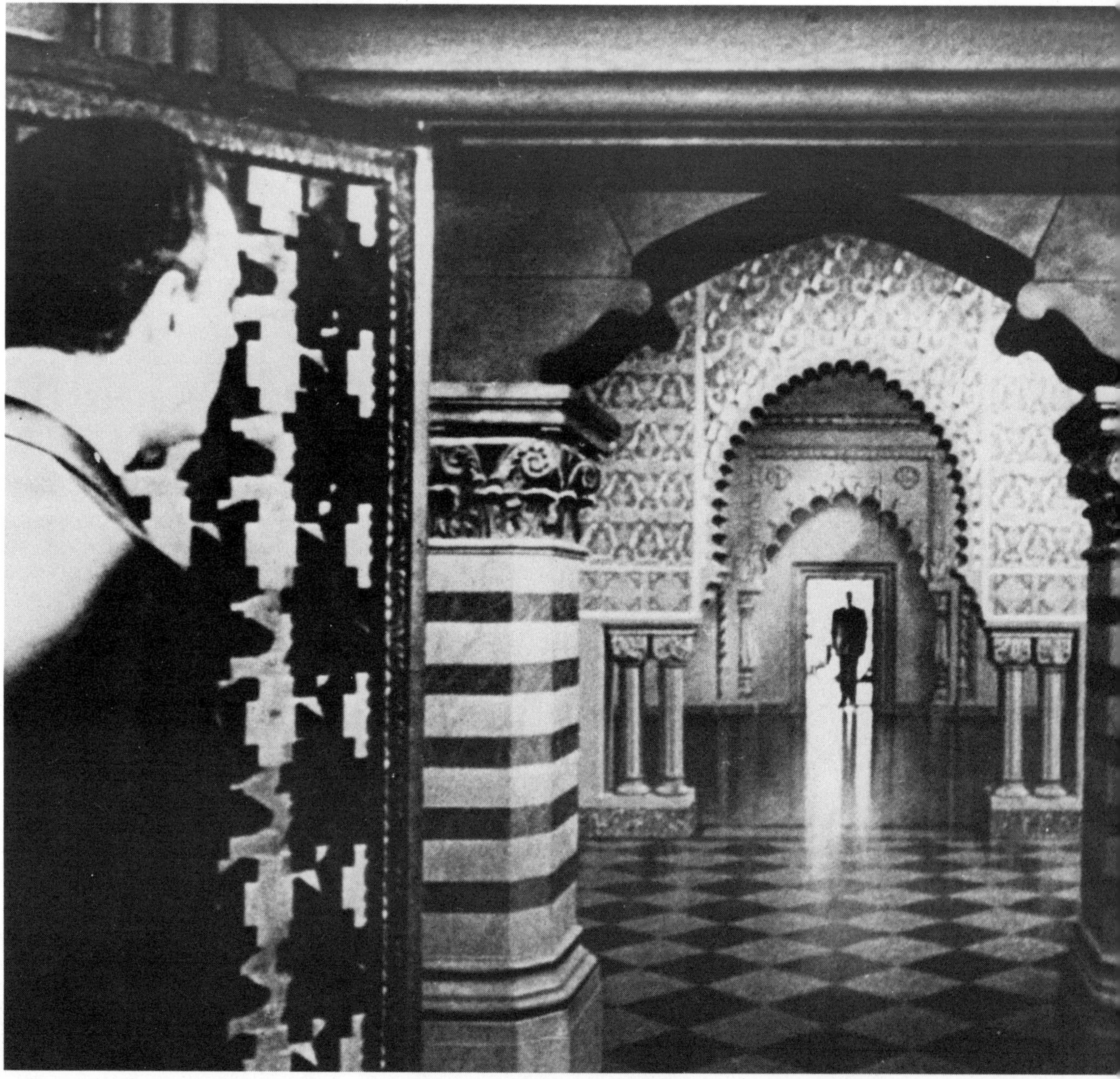

Raymond, the butler at Xanadu, watches as Kane approaches through a series of corridors. Actually, this is a "process" shot which involved matting a tiny replica of the hallways to the figures of Raymond and Kane: many of the deep-focus shots in *Citizen Kane* are similarly made.

"Depth of field is not just a stock in trade of the cameraman like the series of filters or of such-and-such a style of lighting, it is a capital gain in the field of direction—a dialectical step forward in the history of film language."

—André Bazin, "The Evolution of the Language of Cinema" in *What Is Cinema?*

A SENSE OF 3 DIMENSIONS

Deep focus anticipated the "three-dimensional" movies of the fifties by creating a vivid sense of space in which action could be propelled forward within the screen. When Kane tosses his jacket to Leland at the newspaper party, it flies right at us: a vivid sense of real movement, not simply a two-dimensional replica of movement.

FOREGROUND VS. BACKGROUND

Three shots from Xanadu, in which the camera plays Susan, in the foreground, against Kane, deep in the background. Deep focus can charge spaces with dramatic meanings by just such a tension between foreground and background action.

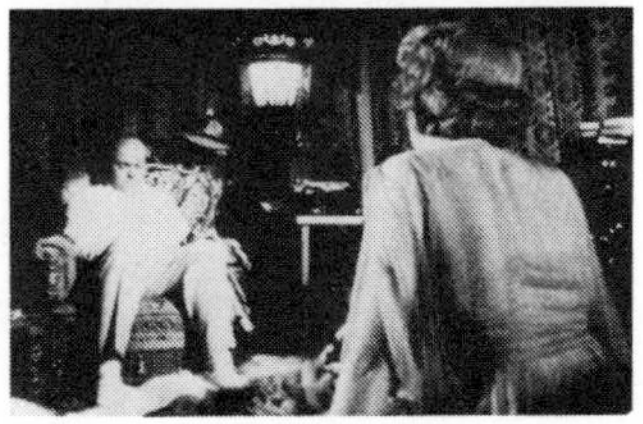

IMMOBILE CAMERA

The bedroom scene: in the first frame spoon, glass and uncorked medicine bottle in the foreground; Susan lies in darkness, but the door—where we hear pounding—is lit. Other frames show Kane, the doctor's bag—all from the same perspective.

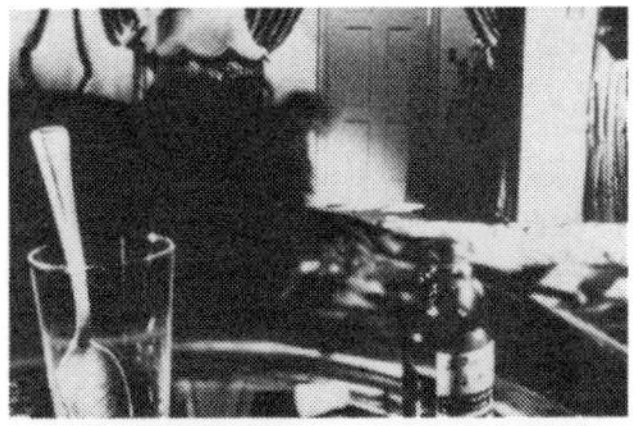

ECONOMY

When Leland and Kane meet amidst the wreckage of the campaign office, the mere presence of that wreckage serves as a potent and economical way of reminding us of Kane's defeat.

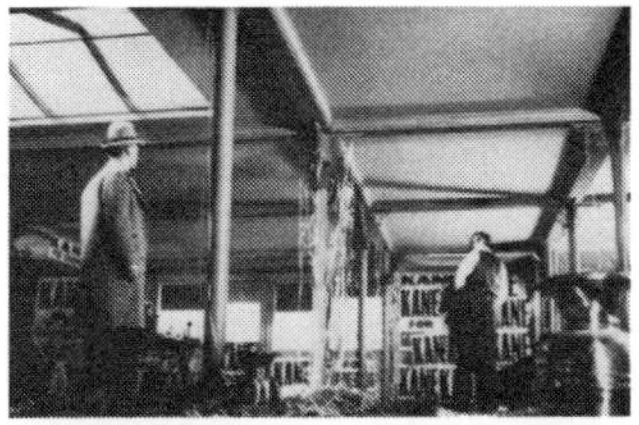

A MANNER OF FRAMING

Three examples of deep focus framing using a "triangle" structure: note the effect in each frame of the simple presence of a third party in the background—how the action takes on a further perspective by our awareness of somebody else's relationship to it.

OVERLAPPING SOUND

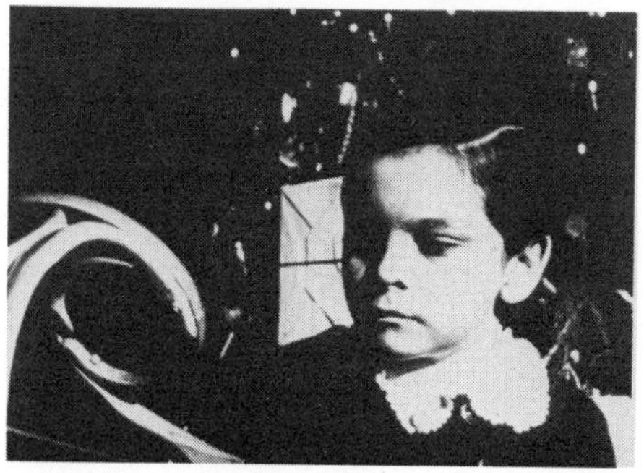

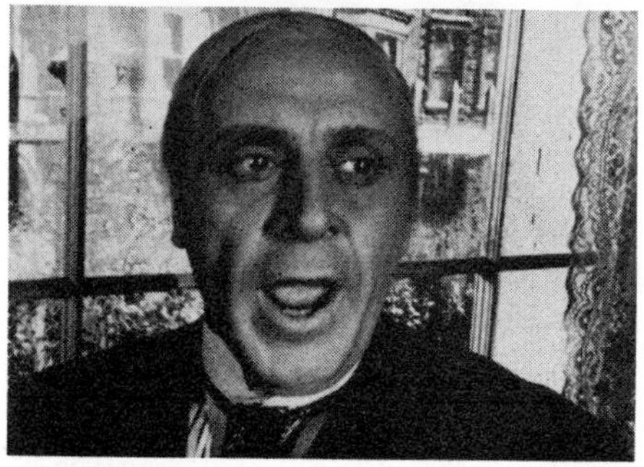

A Genius for Sound

Orson Welles (and most of his players and his musical scorer Bernard Herrmann) came to *Citizen Kane* from radio; indeed, Welles' Mercury Theatre Players had been one of the most imaginative and creative forces in radio. Given their background in and fascination with sound, it is not too unexpected that few films of the sound era—before or after *Kane* —use sound so resourcefully, so freshly, so effectively. In *Kane* sound becomes far more than the synchronized voices of its actors; sound is contrapuntal, contrasts with the image, undermines or amplifies the image.

Often Welles uses *overlapping* sound to give fresh coherence and suggestive power to a transition. When the camera fades out on the young Kane's sled (left) and fades in on a white package that he unwraps, it next travels up, where a tall, stiff-faced man says, "Merry Christmas . . ." and cuts to the banker Thatcher, saying, ". . . and a happy New Year"—going on to mention in the next breath that Kane is now 25, and ready to take responsibility for his considerable empire. The transition is so slickly handled that such a passage of time (usually difficult to handle) becomes immediately apparent.

(Another, even more famous, use of overlapping sound takes place during the breakfast table sequence between Kane and his first wife, discussed later in this chapter under Transition.)

Sound often accentuates and amplifies the actions in *Kane,* giving them a convincing resonance. When at the beginning Kane dies, the slow furtive music wears down, as though a phonograph had been suddenly turned off with the needle yet in the tracks: a blunt, effective suggestion that Kane—and perhaps even something beyond Kane—has ended. On the steps of Susan Alexander's apartment, Kane shouts at Gettys, who has just wrecked his political career, "I'm going to send you to Sing Sing, Gettys!"—words that echo hollowly, intimating Kane's shattered emotional condition at that moment. Echoes figure elsewhere throughout *Kane:* in the Thatcher Library,

A PHONOGRAPH WINDING DOWN

Kane's death: as the nurse fits the sheet over his head, the music grinds down like a recording that somebody turned off.

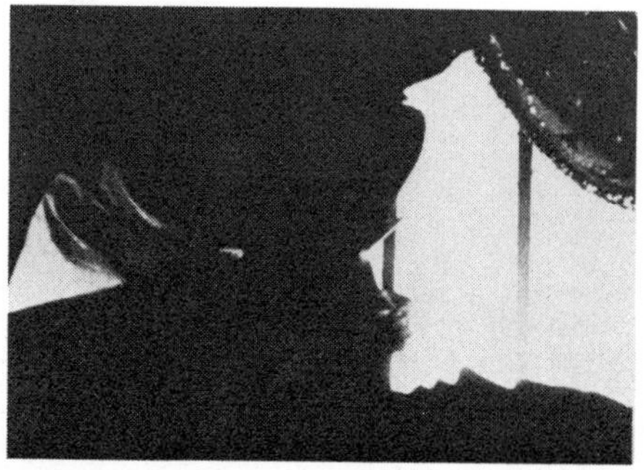

OTHER ECHOES

Xanadu: a hall of echoes that emphasizes the tomblike, deathly emptiness of Kane's life.

"Going to send you to Sing Sing, Gettys." "Gettys, Gettys, Gettys . . ." echoed brassily: Kane's desperation felt aloud.

with its massive tomblike spaces; in the cluttered storage area at the end of the film; but particularly at Xanadu, where they become a convincing underscoring of its hollow desolation.

Sound makes up for an absence of visual imagery in *Kane:* true to the adage of radio (which Welles must have known intimately), the proper sounds can make us imagine something with more force and conviction than if we see it. There is no real opera-sized audience for Susan's operas: she and we face glaring spotlights—but the soundtrack creates the effect of an audience. The same is true of Kane's political rally, where the clapping on the soundtrack is enough to suggest the presence of thousands.

Sometimes sound is used jarringly to create a mood, anticipate an event, as the screech of a cockatoo at the opening of Raymond the butler's flashback on Kane: a shrill, grotesque sound—followed immediately by Kane's stalking into Susan's room and tearing it up in a fit of consummate anger. The opening to the opera sequence as recalled by Susan suggests a similar effect: a shattering, off-key note, followed by the rising crescendo of the orchestra—no doubt that we're at an opera, no doubt that it's going to be a disaster.

Even the background music becomes highly significant in Kane. There are several themes interwoven through the film, identified with Susan, with Kane, with Xanadu, that recur at various times, often with ironic force. When Kane and Susan argue over their marriage at the picnic, a singer croons in the background, "It can't be love . . ." adding a further ironic dimension to the scene.

'IT CAN'T BE LOVE'

The picnic sequence, where Kane and Susan argue over their marriage; and the background song becomes a further commentary.

THE OPERA

Quick cuts: Susan, her coach, and a tumultuous mood created by the rising music.

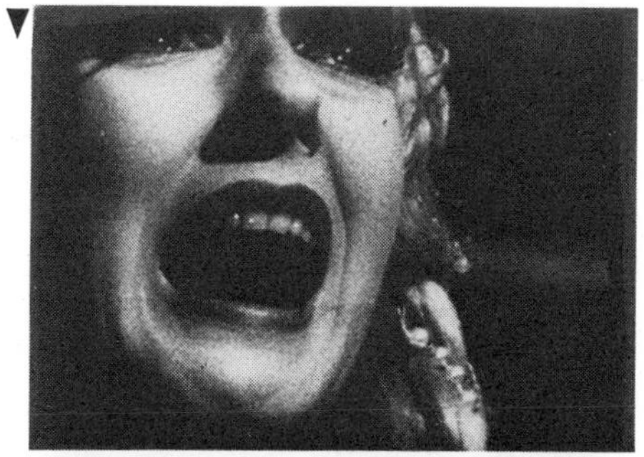

WHAT SOUND CAN HIDE

The political rally: convincing, not from the crowds we *see* (we don't), but from the crowds we hear.

A SCREECHING BIRD

The opening shot in Raymond's flashback about Kane: a startling, vivid way of capturing Kane's state of mind just after Susan has left him.

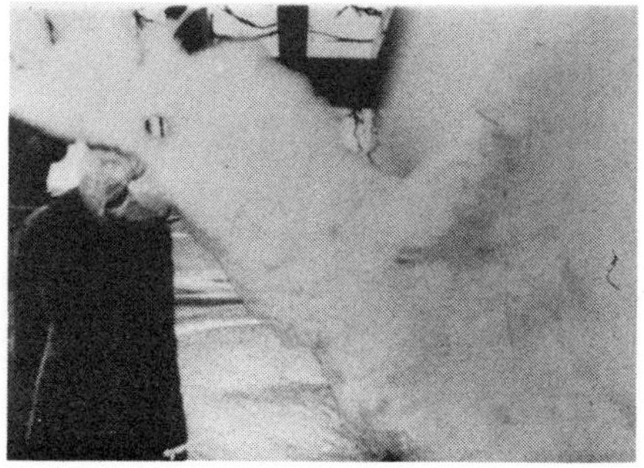

Atmosphere and Imagery

Citizen Kane has a curious flavor for being the story of a modern newspaper mogul: the style is high gothic—sets and camera angles that might better befit the prince of Transylvania. Yet the style fits, if only because it becomes a kind of visual counterpoint to the story. As a result of the style, we tend to become highly conscious of Kane's failures as a man: his isolation, his heightening contempt, his naked presence in a world that seems scaled to his bigger-than-life proportions.

The gothic quality abounds in the sets: the vast, pillared newspaper room; the huge poster of Kane (as if giving visual identification to his political ambitions) at the rally; Thatcher's library, haunted with dead space; and of course Xanadu—massive, still, a cavern that visually echoes Kane's despondency, his growing solitude.

The film is rich in images that act much like atmosphere and sets in reflecting Kane. Obviously the most familiar are the newspapers that appear throughout in a variety of contexts: as in the twin mirrors at Xanadu, Kane is reflected, repeated, echoed to the world in newspapers, his own as well as others.

Other images—of all manner—are used throughout *Kane:* the screaming bird at Xanadu; the Declaration of Principles that Leland sends Kane and Kane shreds; the picture puzzles and piled crates of never-opened, perhaps never glimpsed statues; the glass replica of a snowscape that Kane drops from his hand at the movie's beginning; and, of course, the sled: images almost invariably of things shattered or fragmented or incomplete.

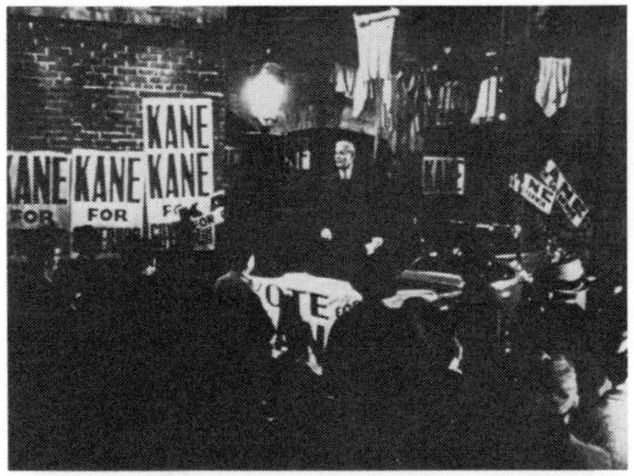

THE THATCHER LIBRARY

One of the most gothic sets in the film: a vast barren room, illuminated by a single broad shaft of sunlight.

THE POLITICAL RALLY

One of the most auspicious and stunning sets in *Citizen Kane:* a vast poster of Kane, against which he speaks; the poster not only reflects his ambitions and ego, it also helps draw our attention away from the dummies that made up the crowd.

XANADU

The block lighting and Gregg Toland's cinematography give Xanadu interiors a sense of vast, haunted spaces: Kane's presence there tends to be statuesque, rigid, without a tinge of spontaneity.

NEWSPAPERS:
AMPLIFYING KANE

In *Citizen Kane* newspapers are not only the linchpin of Kane's career; they become as well visual echoes of every achievement and setback in Kane's life—a convincing way of reflecting Kane's prominence and fame, and of maintaining the newspaper motif throughout the film.

SUSAN'S ROOM

Playthings: baroque, yet amidst Xanadu's gloom, strangely cheerful.

'SHAPES OF MULTIPLICITY AND DIVERSITY . . .'

Writes Jorge Luis Borges: "In astonishing and endlessly varied ways, Orson Welles exhibits the fragments of the life of the man, Charles Foster Kane, and invites us to combine and reconstruct them. Shapes of multiplicity and diversity abound . . ." *Citizen Kane* is visually replete with such fragmentary images: jigsaw puzzles, piled newspapers, assembled statuary—hints everywhere of fragmentation, incompleteness.

Transition

Citizen Kane spans a lifetime, and darts between times and places and points of view with amazing agility and vigor—a freedom made possible largely by the film's creative and unusual transitions.

Certainly the most stunning—and one of the most memorable transitions in film history—is Jed Leland's recapitulation of Kane's first marriage. "It was a marriage, just like any other marriage," he begins, on the dissolve to Kane and his wife chatting warmly, closely, at a breakfast table. The talk is cozy, affectionate, continuous; only as a swish pan changes the scene to a few years later—now they're sitting a little further apart—does the tone in the conversation change, but without any abrupt shift in the dialogue itself. The scene continues, dialogue and distances growing, but throughout there is no noticeable break in the conversation, only a growing tone of impatience, anger, and finally hostility; in the last image, they aren't even speaking—they sit at some distance from one another now, and Kane reads the *Enquirer* while his wife reads the rival newspaper, the *Chronicle*. The scene takes only a few minutes and yet firmly, tactfully, brilliantly covers the geography of a ruined marriage.

Other transitions are as effective, if possibly not as memorable. At Xanadu, we get a profound sense of passing time in a montage of Susan completing a host of different jigsaw puzzles (representing, tellingly, different seasons of the year). When Kane and Bernstein and Leland stand outside the *Chronicle* office admiring the photograph of the *Chronicle* staff ("With them fellows on the *Chronicle*, it's no trick to get circulation," says Bernstein), the camera closes in on the photograph, holds, and a moment later Kane steps before them, a camera and flash go off, and the men begin to move.

EROSION OF A MARRIAGE ▼

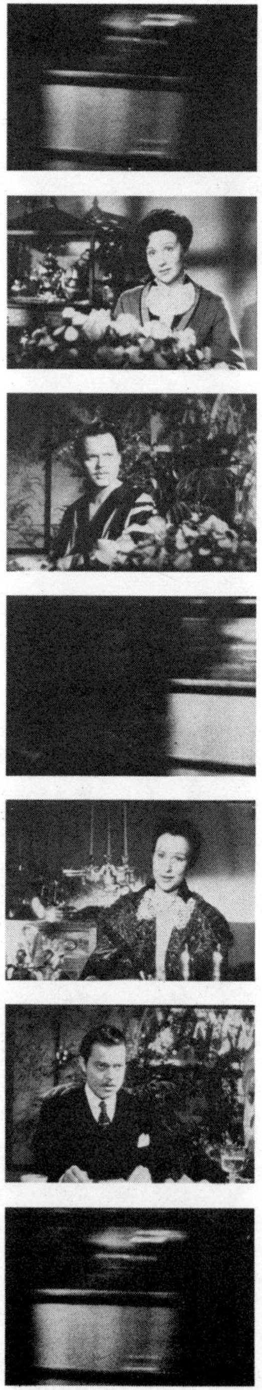

One of the most famous montages in film history: dialogue throughout the sequence is unbroken, creating firm continuity through flexing images.

SUSAN AT XANADU. The seasons of how many years?

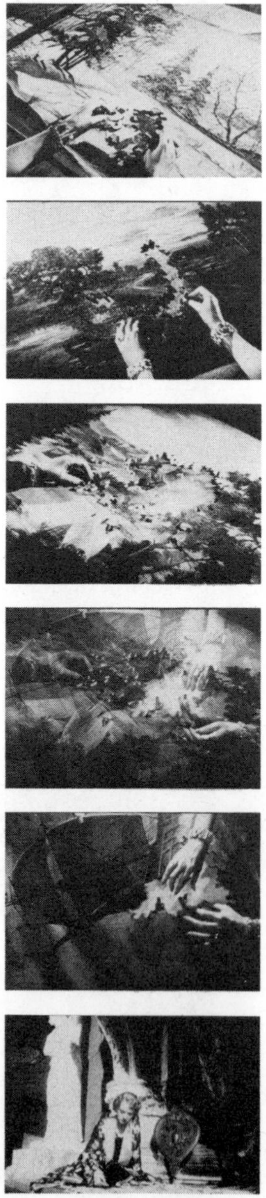

A PICTURE COMES ALIVE

. . . and becomes another picture: one of the cleverer and more revealing transitions in *Citizen Kane,* as Kane hires off the prize staff of the *Chronicle,* the rival newspaper.

A SUBTLE SHIFTING OF TIME AND PLACE

►

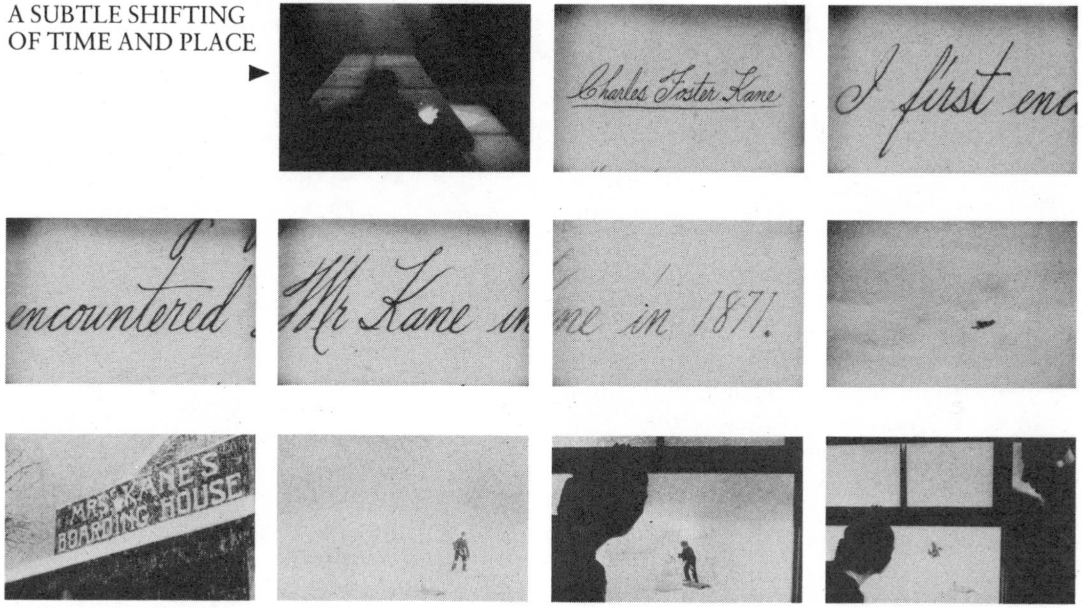

TWO TECHNIQUES, TWO TRANSITIONS

From the words in Thatcher's memoirs, a dissolve to the Colorado boarding house of Kane's childhood: then, on a shot of the boy Kane, the camera pulls back into the window, revealing his mother and Thatcher.

WHAT A TRANSITION CAN ESTABLISH

The two newspaper headlines—and the choice of the second one—tell us Kane lost the election; that newspaper, lying on the ground as Leland passes to enter the election headquarters, becomes less humorous and sets the mood for the coming scene between Kane and Leland.

Who Was Kane?

In a film replete with images of puzzles and piled boxes and all manner of incompletely assembled things, the most incomplete of all, finally, is Kane himself—an enigma whose stature and authority and power we never for a moment doubt, yet whose deepest motives and desires are left to speculation, though there are hints.

Indeed, each of the five narrators provides some hint about Kane. In Thatcher's memoirs the reporter Thompson comes across a scene involving the aging Kane, an even more aging Thatcher, and Bernstein. Thatcher asks Kane what he would like to have been: Kane glares directly at him, states coldly, "Everything you hate."

Bernstein, Kane's manager, speaks of Kane in a manner tinged with regret, but still curiously loyal. "You take Mr. Kane," he tells the reporter. "It wasn't money he wanted." And later, about Rosebud: "Maybe it was something he lost. Mr. Kane was a man that lost almost everything he had." Again, barely hints, but the suggestion of a man driven by something, losing much—maybe all—in the process.

We are led to believe that Jed Leland knew Kane better than anyone; and indeed, Leland's narrative is the longest in the film, and depicts the turning point in Kane's life: the end of his first marriage, his affair with Susan, and the shattered political campaign. Leland's comments on Kane seem to strike with more force as well: "He never gave himself away. . . . He never gave anything away. He just left you a tip. . . . He had a lot of opinions, but he didn't believe in any of them. He didn't believe in anything except Charlie Kane."

Susan depicts Kane as a strangely affectionate grotesque: a man who seems estranged from her and yet who clings to her, driving her into the debacle of her singing career. "I told you he was really interested in my voice," she

ALWAYS, AS OTHERS KNEW HIM

THATCHER, THE BANKER:

the insolent young Kane, the hateful older Kane:

BERNSTEIN, HIS MANAGING EDITOR:

remembering the best times—the early days of running the *Enquirer*:

JEDEDIAH LELAND:

Kane's best friend, recalling Kane's failures: a failed marriage, a failed election, a failed friendship:

SUSAN ALEXANDER KANE:

Kane as a towering figure, imposing, forcing her through a disastrous opera career, the single man clapping in the audience:

RAYMOND, THE BUTLER AT XANADU:

Kane after Susan has left him; alone in the bleak mansion, a figure lost in the empty spaces and timeless depths of Xanadu's great halls:

tells Thompson. "What do you think he built that opera house for? I didn't want it. I didn't want to sing. It was his idea—everything was his idea—except my leaving him."

Raymond, Kane's butler at Xanadu, is more oblique; he seems the kind of man who will give nothing without some return. He describes Kane at Xanadu much as we see him there: strange, distant, "a little gone in the head. . . . He said all kinds of things that didn't mean anything." A further sense of incompleteness, of Kane as an enigma of shattered, unassembled parts.

And what of the image of Kane we ourselves see in the film? The boy Charles, taken from his parents at the Colorado boarding house; the vigorous young newspaper publisher, attacking the trusts and bankers and announcing his high-sounding Declaration of Principles ("You don't wanta make any promises, Mr. Kane, you don't wanta keep," says Bernstein prophetically); the curiously tender, amusing Kane when he meets and does shadow play for Susan (perhaps the least convincing scene in the film, for that reason); the bombastic, voice-shaking politician Kane; and, with Gettys, with the later Susan, and at Xanadu, an increasingly distant, isolated figure, whose moods all seem to some degree hostile.

Rosebud is little help: even when we do discover that it was the childhood sled, we're left with an inkling of a ruined childhood, little more. "It's a gimmick, really, and rather dollar-book Freud," Welles has said of Rosebud. Finally, Kane resists analysis for us as he did for those who knew him: a puzzle never completed.

WELLES' KANE

There is little doubting that much of the authority and personal power that we associate with Charles Foster Kane comes from Orson Welles' superb performance—a feat of acting that remains impressive today, for its range, its subtle eloquence and its totally convincing character. Much of the power comes from Welles' voice: a deep, heavy voice that had charged radio with a ring of dramatic authority, used in *Kane* to heighten our fascination with this man, to give each line something beyond simple inflection—a kind of resonance that further clarified and empowered Kane's presence for us. The Kane depicted by Welles is a man of subtle moods, of hidden intentions, of too easy a smile, too flashy a grin: someone we're invited to respect, if never quite admire; to want to like, if never quite be able to like. As there are vast distances within the stone walls of Xanadu, Welles implies distances within Kane: as though there are moods and realms within him that don't know of one another, as though Kane himself—and Welles' basso voice further suggests this—were a kind of human echo chamber, resonating with distant sounds unheard to anyone but him.

THE FACES OF KANE

Orson Welles' portrayal of Kane is remarkable not only in that we see him age perceptibly throughout the film, but, as Pauline Kael has pointed out, because we see the same personality evolving, and quite convincingly. The older Kane may be a little *too* stiff and arrogant; but we never doubt that this is the same man, nor is there any question in the vacillation of his moods.

Where Credit Is Due

CITIZEN KANE

RKO Radio Pictures, 1940-41, A Mercury Production. Time: 119 minutes. Filmed from 30 July to 23 October, 1940 in RKO Studios, Hollywood. Press showing 9 April 1941 in New York and Los Angeles. Premieres: 1 May 1941, Palace Theatre, New York; 8 May 1941, El Capitan Theatre in Hollywood.

CAST

Charles Foster Kane	ORSON WELLES
Jedediah Leland	JOSEPH COTTEN
Susan Alexander Kane	DOROTHY COMINGORE
Kane's mother	AGNES MOOREHEAD
Emily Norton Kane	RUTH WARRICK
James W. Gettys	RAY COLLINS
Mr. Carter	ERSKINE SANFORD
Mr. Bernstein	EVERETT SLOANE
Thompson, the reporter	WILLIAM ALLAND
Raymond, the butler	PAUL STEWART
Walter Parks Thatcher	GEORGE COULOURIS
Signor Matisti	FORTUNIO BONANOVA
Headwaiter	GUS SCHILLING
Rawlston	PHILIP VAN ZANDT
Miss Anderson	GEORGIA BACKUS
Kane, Sr.	HARRY SHANNON
Kane's son	SONNY BUPP
Kane at age eight	BUDDY SWAN
Hillman	RICHARD BAER
Georgia	JOAN BLAIR

SCREENPLAY	Herman J. Mankiewicz and Orson Welles (assisted by Joseph Cotten and John Houseman)
PRODUCTION AND DIRECTION	Orson Welles
PHOTOGRAPHY	Gregg Toland
EDITING	Robert Wise (and Mark Robson)
ART DIRECTION	Van Nest Polglase and Perry Ferguson
COSTUMES	Edward Stevenson
DECORS	Darrell Silvera
MUSIC	Bernard Herrmann

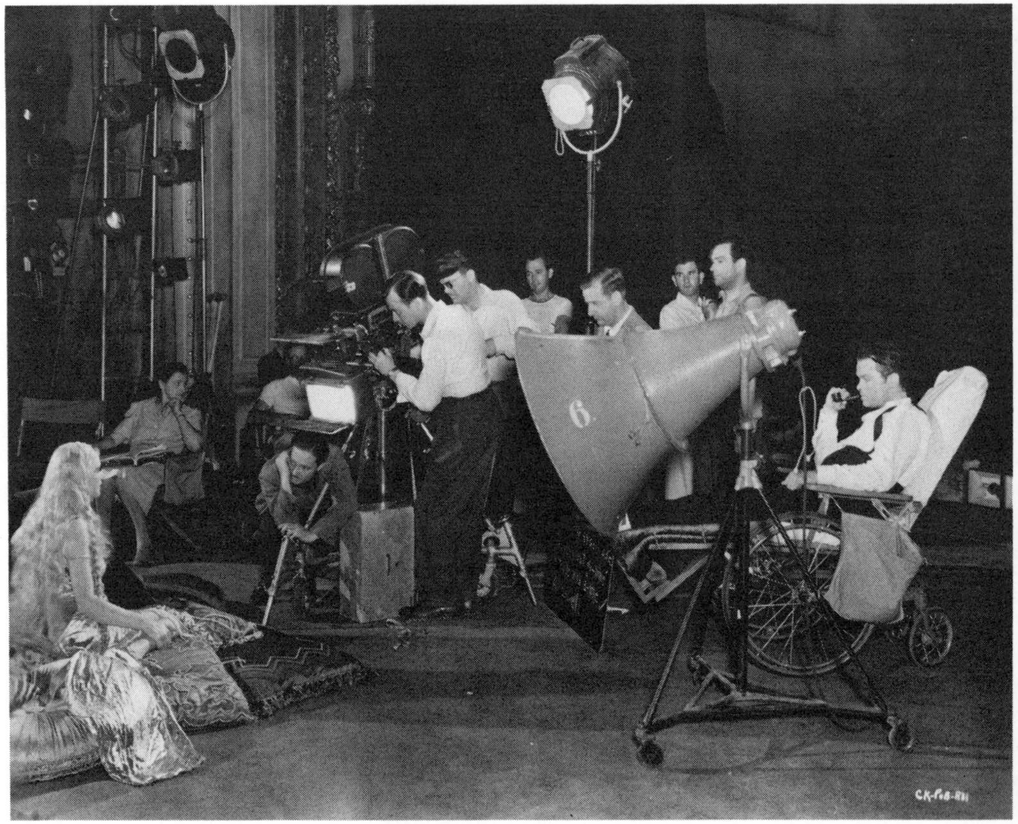

Gregg Toland (under the camera), director of photography, Orson Welles (in the wheelchair while an injured ankle heals), and crew members on the *Citizen Kane* set focus on Dorothy Comingore in a rehearsal for an opera scene. Comingore was that cliché of Hollywood movies, a "young unknown" picked by Welles for this starring role in a film that made her "immortal."

History and Production

CHAPTER TWO

History

". . . for many centuries it was the first chance to observe, with the naked eye so to speak, one of the rarest phenomena of the history of culture: the emergence of a new form of artistic expression, the only one born in our time, and in our society and therefore the only one with the material, intellectual and spiritual determinants of which we are entirely familiar. It would have been worth while to seize this opportunity because—if for no other reason—knowledge of the evolutionary process of this new form of artistic expression would per amalgam *have provided a key to many secrets of the other arts."—Béla Balázs,* Theory of the Film.

Poetry, painting, music, sculpture, dance and drama—the arts that have lifted man's spirit throughout history—were probably born before history. Their origins are rooted in man's dimly remembered past. The first poet, for example, may have been a tribal hunter who leaned over the fire one night and began telling a story—possibly mostly in grunts and gestures—but who absorbed and fascinated his companions, enough that they encouraged him to do it again, and again. A new art, one suspects, is not born as an art: it emerges from a need for people to entertain and delight one another, from a desire to share and tease and enliven and excite.

Movies began from much the same initial impulse: not as the new major art of our time, but as a bit of sideshow gimmickry, a tease for the eyes. Historians are still disputing inventions and influences, but movies in their infancy—40- and 50-second-long strips of film in which a man sneezed or a train chugged into a railway station—were created and sold and promoted by entrepreneurs who wanted to give people a new kind of thrill for a nickel. Even the one Olympian artist of the early film, D. W. Griffith, could not quite take this new "art" all that seriously. "The motion pictures," he said, "give a man someplace to go besides a saloon."

The movies—like the steam engine and the cannon and the airplane—evolved from a series of toys. Whether sophisticated toys for bored rich folk like the Lampascope or Phantasmagoria of the 19th century; or simple, unsophisticated toys for children, like the Zoetrope or Vivascope, or the popular, penny-cost Thaumatrope (a round bit of paper with pictures on both sides and strings you tug to make the paper twirl and unify the two images): toys all the same, gimmicks that create the illusion of movement by spinning or rolling or sweeping past faster than the human eye can detect.

Toward the latter part of the 19th century a handful of men, in the U.S. and England and France—mostly working independently from one another—began to experiment with motion picture photography. Eadweard Muybridge, commissioned to photograph a moving horse to determine whether all four legs ever left the ground together, developed a technique using a battery of cameras which photographed figures in motion at split-second intervals. J. A. R. Rudge built a mechanism in 1875 that projected moving slides on a rotating cylinder. Ottomar Anschütz built a gadget called the Tachyscope in 1887 which flashed dozens of images in rapid succession through a peephole. By 1880 a Frenchman, Etienne Marey, had developed a gun that "shot" small film negatives instead of cartridges, the first true harbinger of the motion picture camera.

But the most notable advance was made by an assistant of Thomas Alva Edison, and only after nine slow years of research and experiments. W. L. Dickson essentially invented the celluloid strip of film and a shutter and movement mechanism that enabled the film to pass through camera or projector. By the early 1890's Dickson and Edison had built Kinetoscopes—peepshow boxes—for showing these movies, and in 1893 began a studio for shooting movies.

Elsewhere others were at work on the same problems and came up with similar solutions: Louis Aimé Augustin Le Prince (who disappeared under strange circumstances in 1890) invented a movie camera that also projected; and the Lumière brothers in Paris went a step further than Dickson and Edison by using Dickson's camera to develop a projector which could show films to a large audience and not simply one-at-a-time as did the peepshow Kinetoscope. In Paris, on December 28, 1895, the first "movies" were shown publicly: girls frolicking on a beach; Auguste Lumière and his wife feeding their infant daughter; and the arrival of a train in a station. Edison, confounded by the success of projected movies in Europe, teamed up with another American inventor, Thomas Armet, to launch an American projector, and in 1896 the first movies were projected in New York in a former shoe store.

The birth of a technology—but not yet the birth of an art. It would take later minds, less of a mechanical than an imaginative bent, to shape this new tool into the powerful, expressive language that film has since become.

The first U.S. motion picture studio was built in West Orange, N.J., in 1893. It was officially known as *The Kinetographic Theatre* but was nicknamed *Black Maria* (by the Edison Company workers) after the slang term for police van, because it was portable. Black inside and out, it was mounted on a turntable so that its skylight could face sunlight all day.

Studies in motion, by Eadweard Muybridge, circa 1875: a bet as to whether all four feet of a galloping horse left the ground helped to stimulate experimental work that would become a forerunner of motion picture photography.

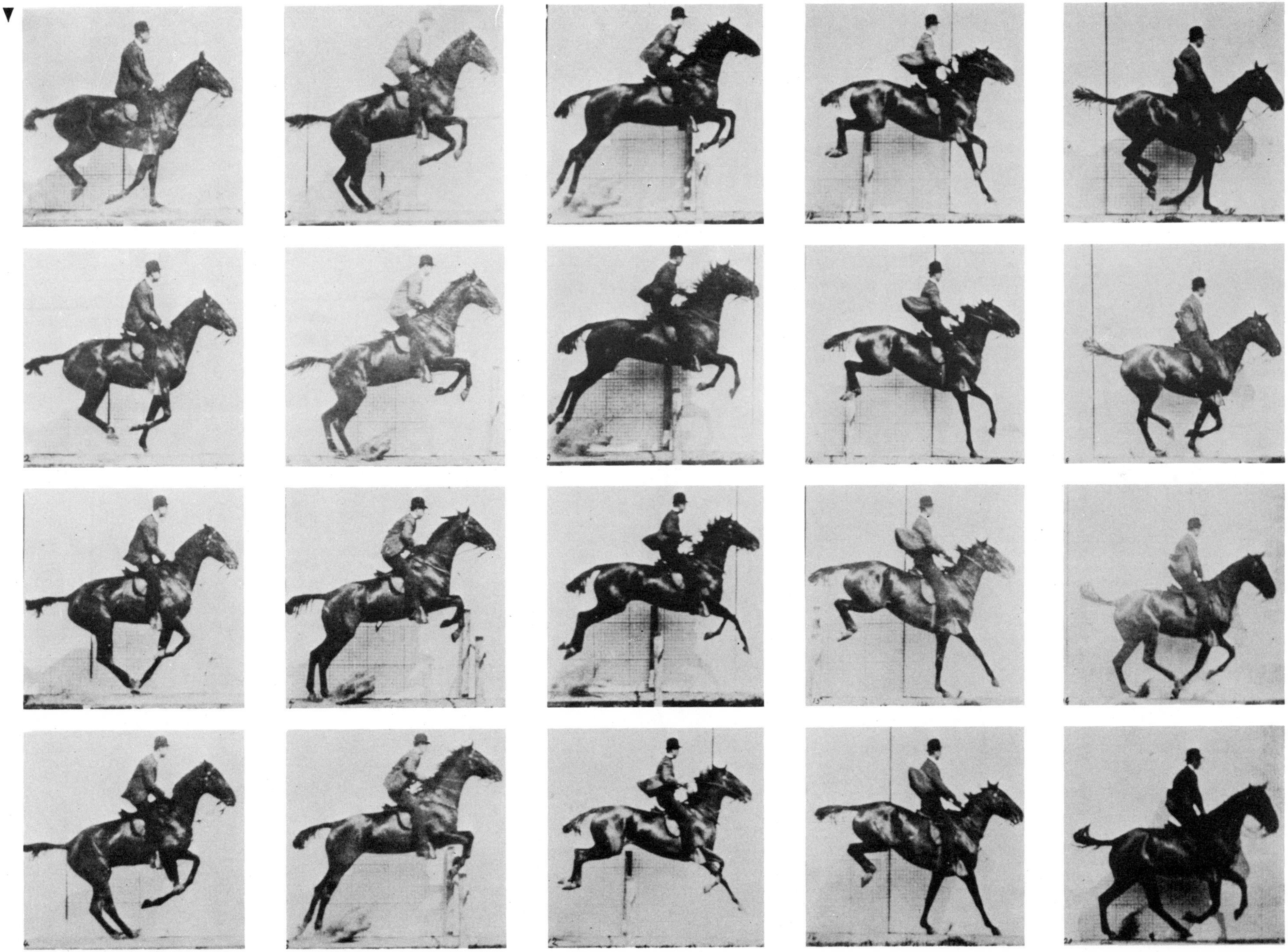

Born of a Toy

All these toys that anticipated the movies—and the movies themselves—would have been impossible but for a single quirk of the human eye: the tendency for an impression to remain on the retina for a fraction of a second. None of these toys—or the motion picture projector itself—truly reproduces movement. They flash a series of slightly changing images past, and at such a speed that the retinal impressions blur into one another, so that the brain cannot distinguish the separation between each one—and what we "see" is movement.

This phenomenon is called persistence of vision, and it underlies and explains why a flickering spate of single, separate images can seem to move. The images never truly move, but if they shoot past our eyes fast enough (generally fourteen or so per second), our eyes interpret movement. (This also explains the slightly jerky "flickering" quality of 8mm films—which move past at 16 frames per second—as against the more fluid, convincing movement of 16mm or 35mm film, which runs through a projector at 24 frames per second.)

ZOETROPE

The metal drum spins, and the viewer watches through the slits as the figures on the strip inside seem to move. 1834.

PRAXINOSCOPE

A little "theatre" in which the viewer peeks through an open rectangle to watch the images move.

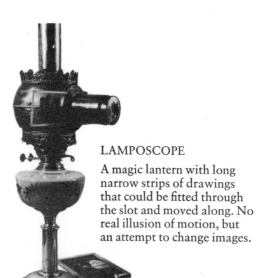

THAUMATROPE

Pull the string taut and the two sides spin, creating the illusion of being one image: invented by Dr. John Ayrton in Paris, in 1825, it was the simplest and easiest to make of the toys that preceded movies.

LAMPOSCOPE

A magic lantern with long narrow strips of drawings that could be fitted through the slot and moved along. No real illusion of motion, but an attempt to change images.

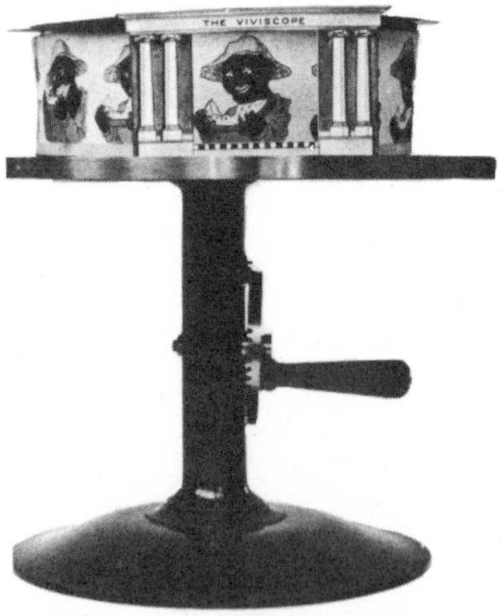

VIVISCOPE

Like the Zoetrope, a mounted drum that spins; only here the strip itself spins alone, and there is a frame that anticipates the movie screen.

The Movies as Magic Show: Georges Méliès

Pioneers are men who blaze trails that become six-lane highways. We're so used to traveling those highways that we find it hard to believe that at one time it was wilderness, unknown.

Georges Méliès was a practicing magician in Paris, and it should strike us as no coincidence that the first man to recognize the potential of film was a master entertainer in the arts of magic and shrewd audience trickery. When Méliès saw one of the Lumière movies, he immediately bought a camera from Lumière and began shooting. But he didn't shoot normal, ordinary life as Lumière had; he created fantasies, and in pursuing the possibilities of those fantasies invented much of the language of film that we know today: the cut, the dissolve, double exposure, fades, fast motion, slow motion, matting, even animation.

The films of Méliès were theatrical; the camera was set in a fixed position; but the subjects alerted audiences—and Méliès himself—to the possibilities of film. In *An Impossible Voyage* (1904) a train draws up a steep mountain and continues on into space. In *A Trip to the Moon* (1902) a rocket blasts from earth and smashes into the eye of the Man in the Moon—at once a visual joke and a feat of impressive special effects.

DISAPPEAR, REAPPEAR

In *Jupiter's Thunderbolts* (1903), Méliès makes his figures disappear and reappear in various places by the "magic" of stopping and restarting his camera.

SPLIT SCREEN

Magic Lantern (1903) uses both a second matted image and the dissolve (note the center frame) to spoof Méliès' own newfound art, the movies.

CONVERSATIONS WITH HIMSELF

A favorite Méliès technique: setting himself in the frame twice, at different scales; the use of his head alone marks a forerunner of the closeup.

A Movie Is the Sum of Its Parts:

Edwin S. Porter

Edwin Porter began as a cameraman for Edison's Black Maria studio, and upon seeing Méliès' vivid, exultant fantasies, argued with Edison that it was possible to make more than everyday pictures that moved. He began to experiment, and realized that movies could tell a story, something that only Méliès to the time had done.

Using some stock footage from Edison's files, and shooting some fresh footage, Porter made a brief film called *The Life of an American Fireman.* By jumping from one scene to another, Porter was the first to edit a film and create a fresh whole from a variety of parts. Moreover, his technique *dramatized* the story. Audiences thrilled to the film because there were characters they could identify with and a story, dramatically told, with a beginning, middle and end.

Porter's triumph was his next film, *The Great Train Robbery*—the film that has been known to generations as (though it really isn't) "the first movie." *The Great Train Robbery* is the first well-told movie story using techniques of cross-editing, and employing the oldest and favorite cinematic device of them all: the chase. Only later, with D. W. Griffith, would the possibilities of film, particularly editing, take on more development and sophistication after *The Great Train Robbery*.

"You may be next."

THE GREAT TRAIN ROBBERY

Among the first films to use the technique of cross-editing (moving between one action and another); but more important, the first film to excite audiences to the possibility of movies as a narrative art. Not surprisingly, *The Great Train Robbery* is a Western, an action movie (note the fight atop a moving train) and ends with a touch of "You may be next" movie morality. This shot, by the way, is the first real use of the closeup.

A Movie Is More Than the Sum of Its Parts:

D. W. Griffith

"Hollywood was his invention," wrote the critic James Agee. Chaplin had said, "The whole industry owes its existence to him." Eisenstein and virtually every other director to follow considered him their master, teacher and mentor. Yet—such are the cruelties of Hollywood—by 1948, when he died, he was impoverished, unknown, ill-treated and had not directed a film of his own for almost two decades.

David Wark Griffith took what was till his time a sideshow amusement and refashioned it into a living, expressive art. The techniques that he and his cameraman Billy Bitzer invented—from the closeup to sophisticated uses of parallel and cross-editing—were to change the face of the movies forever, setting down as though in a code the laws that bound an audience to the dramatic events being unfurled on the screen.

Griffith was born in 1875 on a farm in Kentucky. He wanted above all to be a writer, and even after international renown as *the* artist of film, he looked upon the entire enterprise with a slightly jaundiced eye. (When a friend asked him what he thought after he had seen his first moving picture show as a young man, Griffith has recalled remarking, that "any man who enjoys such a thing should be shot at sunrise.")

He entered movies as an actor, but soon came to direct them, and once he had begun to direct, movies would never again be the same. For Griffith saw film much the way a good dramatist might look upon words, as the raw material with which one can express and intensify life itself. Searching for a way to locate and focus on the selected detail, he invented the closeup. (Other inventions, and they were myriad, were often accidents: Billy Bitzer tells how a lucky accident created the first fade-out. "We couldn't cut abruptly—that would be crude," said Bitzer. "The fade-out gave a really dignified touch; we didn't have a five-cent movie anymore.")

There was always something outsized and disproportionate about Griffith: when he was making two-reelers between 1909 and 1915, much as everyone else in the infant film industry, he felt a gnawing urge toward something bigger. Finally, in 1914, he began production on a film that would be scaled far more ambitiously than the films he had been working on—or those everyone else was working on. It would be an epic, the first film epic, and would center on that period that Griffith as a Southerner felt had become totally the property of Northern interpretation: the Civil War and the Reconstruction in the South that followed.

Griffith had made ambitious films previously: the most recent, *Judith of Bethulia,* was itself near-epic in scale and ambition. But what he was attempting, as he himself commented, was to redefine for audiences what movies were all about. And he hadn't the slightest doubt that he could do it.

"Most people considered a motion picture drama a ten-cent proposition. They measured everything by the standard of price. It was not surprising they overlooked the fundamentals of the case and were unprepared to pass judgement upon the undertaking. But, in all truth, there was neither daring nor venturesomeness in this move. You see, we knew what we had."

What he had was a movie that in a stroke transformed the struggling infant industry of cheap entertainments into the major art of our century. Its name was *The Birth of a Nation.*

D. W. Griffith, 1921.

'Like Writing History in Lightning'

THE BIRTH OF A NATION

When President Woodrow Wilson saw *The Birth of a Nation,* he said, "It is like writing history in lightning." It was that—and more.

It cost $100,000, in 1915 an unheard of sum for a movie. It depicted an era with greater authenticity and scale and vitality than any movie previously—more than most since. Most importantly, *The Birth of a Nation* was the first movie to use the full dramatic potential of the screen to tell a story. With it Griffith created the rule book that has guided directors since: matching closeups and long and medium shots; pacing the editing; intercutting to heighten the dramatic momentum; using camera movement, fades, and dissolves, not only as methods of transition and to denote changes in time and space, but for their emotional effect. Actors move through the film with restraint: not the lugubrious, overworked expressions they had inherited from the stage of the time. Places remembered from history were recreated with authentic detail. The movie was meant to be a masterpiece, judged by the standards even of the future.

The story itself, based on Thomas Dixon's novel, *The Clansman,* involves a complex set of relationships between a Northern family, the Stonemans, and a Southern family, the Camerons. It was criticized in its day (and still is) for its biased, racist image of blacks—a criticism that is valid; Griffith was, after all, trying to rewrite history. Yet the film remains a remarkable achievement, its drama momentous and trenchant over fifty years later.

Spectacle

SCALE

In its use of hundreds of extras, its vast terrains and sets, *The Birth of a Nation* outstripped all films before it—American and European—in creating life on a vast scale within the screen.

HISTORIC REPRODUCTION

Griffith and his assistants studied old Matthew Brady photographs to be able to recreate sets that not only looked, but were authentic: his careful designs have rarely been matched since for accuracy.

Dramatic Force

NUANCES

The emotional quality of *The Birth of a Nation:* Ben's return home from war, hugging his sister Elsie.

CHARACTERIZATION

Lynch, the mulatto, mistreating a dog; Elsie kissing a bird: brief, totally visual ways of telling audiences who these people are.

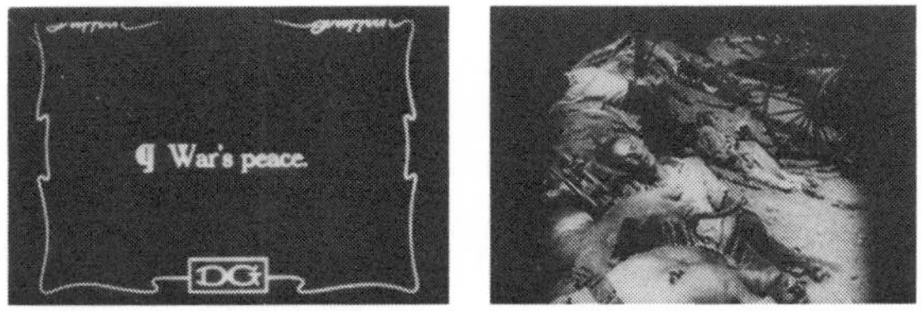

IRONY

Touches like this lull in battle give the film a tautness, help override its sentimental tone.

Technique

IRIS

By closing down the camera's diaphragm, Billy Bitzer could darken much of the screen, highlighting one action.

CAMEO

John Wilkes Booth, seen before he assassinates Lincoln: the cameo, like the iris, has gone out of style, but was common throughout the silent era.

SUPERIMPOSITION

Used to create a split-screen effect: the ravage of war is seen in a double perspective.

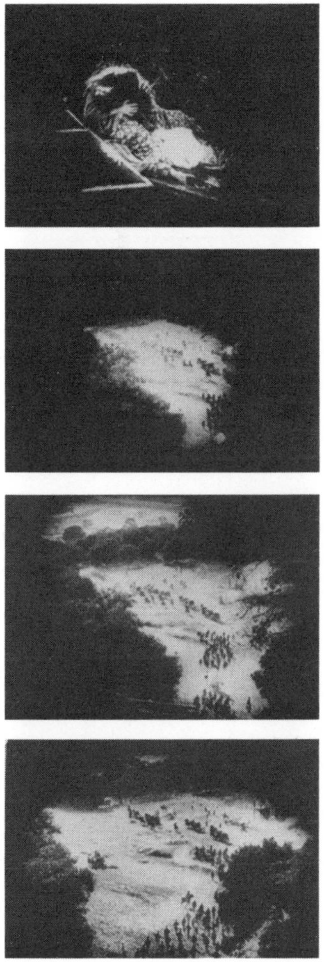

MOVING CAMERA

One of the most famous shots in film history: opening with an iris close shot of a huddled, displaced family, Griffith moves the camera to show Sherman's march to the sea, establishing in one fluid shot the effects and scale of war.

A Story Told to the Eyes

NARRATIVE EDITING

Griffith's early ambition had been to write novels and plays; he considered movies little more than a sideshow attraction, even as he was devising the language that enabled them to transcend the sideshow forever. Griffith was not a theorist, but a brilliantly talented man attempting to use this new medium to unfold a narrative at its most dramatic pitch. It was this passion for storytelling that led Griffith, almost by instinct, to develop the techniques of cutting and intercutting which would, from *The Birth of a Nation* on, dominate film-making.

Griffith used shots to create, as the critic Gilbert Seldes put it, "a whole far greater than the sum of its parts." In the Lincoln assassination sequence, for example, he skillfully intercuts between the large theater in long shot, individuals like Lincoln, his bodyguard, and Booth in medium shot, and provides critical closeups: such as Booth's pistol. The effect is to enlarge, heighten, intensify our feeling of the drama; we're crucially *aware* of what's going to happen in an agonizing way. This suspense is taken even further in the sequence where the Negro Gus chases Flora in the woods; here Griffith not only intercuts, but builds the momentum of the sequence by shortening each shot so that the physical action itself seems to go faster, become more violent.

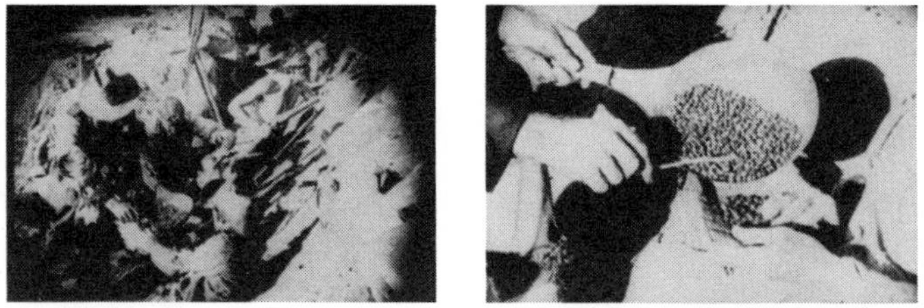

MORE THAN AN INSERT

Griffith referred to closeups as "inserts" and remarked once in a disparaging way that they are simply a mechanical trick and of little use to anyone. This is hardly true in his use of closeups in *The Birth of a Nation*. When the troops eat, a closeup reveals the dry parched corn they eat; when Cameron looks into a locket, the camera looks with him, sees what he sees. In both cases the dramatic flow is heightened, intensified by the two-shot combination.

INTERCUTTING

Two gatherings: a ball for the soldiers, and across town, the Negroes at a more tumultuous, even violent display, as they riot.

FLASHBACK

When Phil proposes to Margaret, Griffith cuts to an image of her brother being killed by Northerners: clarifying what's in her mind, and why she refuses.

LEAPS IN TIME

A scene in the state legislature during Reconstruction, in which Griffith cuts from the empty seats to the same scene, with the seats now occupied.

THE CHASE: HEIGHTENING SUSPENSE

One of the first chase scenes ever filmed, the sequence in which Flora goes into the woods and is chased by the Negro Gus achieves—even today—potent suspense through Griffith's deft intercutting. Once Griffith has established the chase between Gus and Flora, he cuts back to the house, where Ben, aware that Flora is gone, begins to look for her, introducing a third element and charging the sequence with even greater tension.

ASSASSINATION OF LINCOLN

Griffith builds to the assassination sequence by situating us in the theater, focusing on the audience, the drama, and finally the arrival of Lincoln, whom the audience rises to cheer. Through vignette episodes, Griffith shows the bodyguard leaving his post to watch the play; and John Wilkes Booth outside the President's box—emphasizing Booth's intentions by a closeup of the gun; and finally the shot and Booth's escape to the stage below. The cutting is organized solely to recount and dramatize narrative.

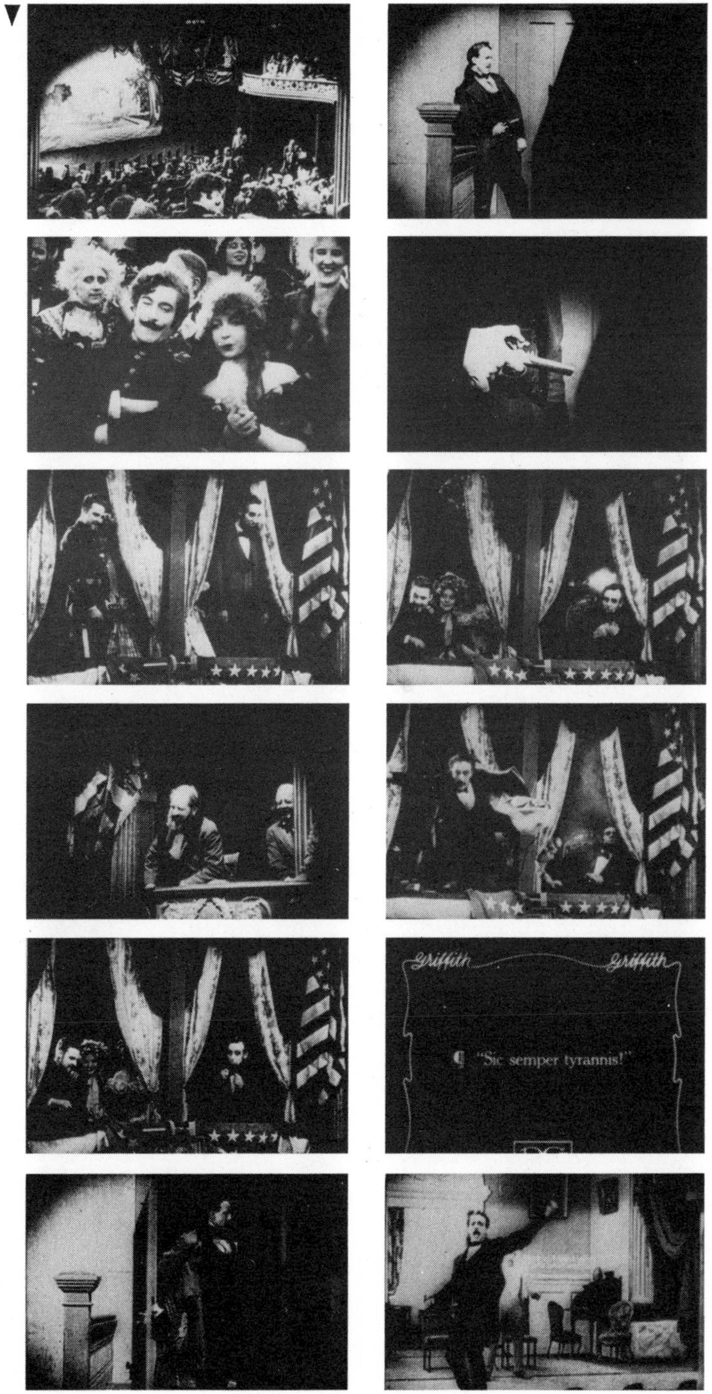

Production

Anyone who has ever observed the set of a movie production is surely aware of the enormous amounts of time, personnel and equipment that must be invested in every single shot. Lights must be moved, rigged, dimmed, reflected to capture the proper accent of brightness or shadow. The camera must be moved, set, adjusted. Slight modifications in the set may require anything from moving an ashtray to bringing in the carpenters to extend a room three feet. Microphones must be put in place and tested. Finally the actors come out and may do no more than look at one another over a table or speak a single word, though even for that the director may require several reshootings, or "takes." Then the set is disassembled, the lights unclamped, the camera moved, and the process begins again. Making film is a slow, arduous, tedious business, most of it a maneuvering and organizing of numerous people and bulky equipment, and always slowed and hindered by a fuse blowing, a cloud passing, or any of the thousandfold minute things that can go wrong, and do.

For these obvious reasons, movies are costly—certainly the costliest art invented by man. And because the stakes are so high—no investor is all *that* interested in art if his money is funding the project—movies tend to be a highly commercial art, rewarding its hacks far more extravagantly than its geniuses. The director who can bring a film in at or under budget, giving no more on the set than a slight dramatic fleshing to the script, is far more likely to succeed in the movie business than the director who takes chances, tries shooting a scene in risky ways, and is likely to go over budget or the allotted shooting time. And though it may seem obvious that the latter director is more likely to make a film of imagination and originality, he is also less likely to make another movie, unless, of course, his films make lots and lots of money, which is the major criterion in the film industry.

And film, no question, is an industry before it even has a chance of becoming an art. The money required is substantial. A feature film in color can cost anywhere from $250,000 —considered *very* low-budget—to several million dollars. The investment is made usually on the basis of "properties," a best-selling novel, a screen star who has agreed to make the picture, a proven director: in effect, on the basis of a source that has been proven, or cast or director who have been proven, or more frequently, some combination. Today such "packaging" is generally done by independent producers (quite often, actors' agents, who control those properties), who present the idea to the major studios for financing and distribution. Already one can see that the original impetus to a film is not so often a writer's or director's idea—most writers and directors are hired after the source idea has been chosen—but an idea that can be sold to a studio or distributor.

Once financing has been assured, preproduction can begin, the first of the three phases in the making of any film. The completed script is used to draft the production board, a complex chart that enables the production manager and director to best allocate their use of actors, sets and crew so that fifteen people won't show up (and be paid) for a day when they're not needed. Someone is sent to scout locations. Once found, a location must be secured, and with it nearby accommodations for cast and crew during shooting, as well as meals, sanitary facilities, etc. Meantime the director is casting actors, hiring the critical members of the crew (cameraman, lighting and sound men, art director, set designer, assistant director, script or continuity girl, and perhaps already—though their work doesn't begin till later—the composer and musicians, and the editor and sound mixer).

Indeed, it may seem to those involved in a movie that the next stage, of actual production, often kept within thirty or forty days, is, despite its appearance of chaos, more ordered and organized than preproduction. In a way,

Orson Welles on set of *Citizen Kane*, 1941

Alfred Hitchcock, Ingrid Bergman and crew on set of *Spellbound*, 1946

it has to be, since everyone now is on payroll; time equals money, and sizable amounts of money—an average *day's* shooting for a color feature costs generally between $50,000 and $65,000. There simply isn't the time to make big mistakes or, once made, to correct them. Even the time-honored system of looking at the "rushes" (the footage shot the day before) each day can help only so much; often a scene cannot be reshot with the full setting and presence of all the actors—if only because the set has been dismantled and some of the actors flown to other productions in other countries.

Movies are shot to make the most efficient use of actors and crew and locations, which means that the scenes are almost never shot in their proper sequence in the film. On its first day of shooting, a production crew might well begin with the first and last scenes of the film, if they take place at the same location. This method of shooting a film suggests how drastically film in production differs from a play, in which the dramatic momentum of each progressing act "charges" the actors and director with a growing involvement in the play itself. A film is shot in such a shredded, fragmentary manner that the actors have only their knowledge of the script, their talent, and—perhaps more important than in theater—the suggestions and demands of the director to guide them. For that matter, anyone watching the production of a film without benefit of reading a script is likely to be baffled by the seemingly unrelated actions, dialogue, and movements that are organized and repeated before the lights and cameras.

When production is completed, post-production begins, the phase that requires fewest people, and yet during which the spine of a good film can be broken (though it's less likely that one can be added that isn't already there). Most of post-production is editing and related activity: mixing sound, scoring and mixing the music, having the film laboratory technicians cut the original negative and add the final soundtrack so that prints can be struck. Editing, considered the artistic essence of film by

Shirley Temple on the set of *Our Little Girl,* 1935

many directors and theorists, becomes, for many productions, a way of salvaging weakly shot scenes. With the help of "cover shots"—footage from additional cameras that provide, say, closeups while the main camera took medium shots—the editor can invigorate a slow and thinly acted passage with quick editing between the faces of the actors. This doesn't make for a better movie but simply a jumpier and more visually blasting effect. The audience simply isn't allowed to become aware how boring the scene is. "We can save it in editing" —a phrase as old as the movies—generally means, "We can fake it in editing."

Though the picture is edited, mixed, and "in the can" ready for projection, it isn't necessarily finished. Studio executives and film bankrollers tend to be nervous people. They want their "product" tested before it's launched by expensive advertising (sometimes advertising and distribution will cost more than the initial budget of the picture). Consequently there is the "preview screening" in which director and producer and possibly writer and some of the cast and crew sit in a theater while a regular off-the-street audience comes in to watch a film they've never heard of before and, if they don't like it, may never hear of again. The effect of a preview screening can be disastrous or it can totally change a movie for the better. Frank Capra, a leading director of the thirties, tells how he sat next to Columbia Studio's mogul

Marlene Dietrich on the set of *Golden Earrings,* 1947

Harry Cohn during a preview screening of *Lost Horizon* and watched in horror as the crowd guffawed at a totally serious picture and Cohn squirmed in torment. Later, in desperation, Capra tore the first two reels off the film, added titles at the beginning of the third reel, and persuaded Cohn to try another preview screening. This time the audience marvelled, and *Lost Horizon* became a runaway success. To this day it remains one of the best romantic fantasies ever to come from Hollywood. More often, though, the effects of a badly received preview screening tend to cut a film off forever from its potential audience. An alarmingly large number of films made every year—no one seems to quite know how many—sit on the studio shelves, unreleased because executives doubt their potential, or just as often, because they're uncertain how to advertise and promote them.

Indeed, film production is but the first step on a chain, and the following steps, distribution and exhibition, often prove infuriatingly difficult, particularly to independent filmmakers. Without a distributor, a film has no way of reaching the theaters; yet most distributors — till recently controlled by the studios, though that control has gradually been eroding—tend to be wary of films that appear to lack enormous box office potential. Even after signing a contract and taking on a film, a distributor might well do nothing with it—a quiet opening in a small theater, with no trade screenings for the critics, no promotion. And when the movie understandably fails to draw an audience, the distributor says, "Aha! I thought so," and relegates the film to obscurity on a shelf. The dismal fact is that the power once in the hands of the studios has, with the decline of the studios, increasingly been assumed by the distributors.

Ultimately, good movies do get made and distributed and seen, and perhaps one might marvel that a system so calculated to rob movies of any originality or authenticity or force could work as often as it does to produce good films.

Filmmaking Is...

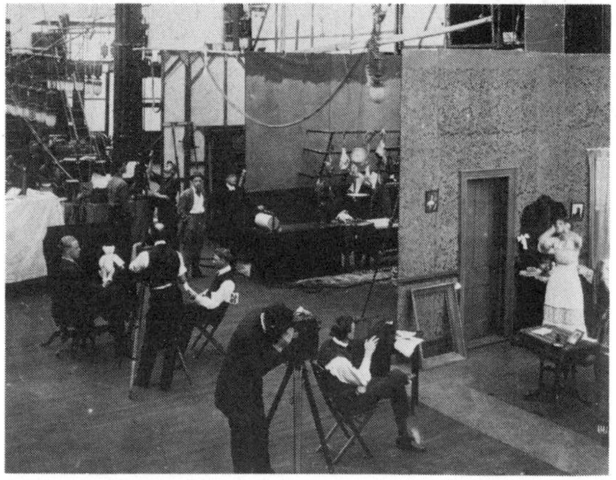

Edison Studios in 1912.

"Every book purchased for motion pictures has some individual quality, good or bad, that has made it remarkable. It is the work of a great array of highly paid and incompatible writers to distinguish this quality, separate it, and obliterate it."—Evelyn Waugh

"A director is a kind of idea and taste machine; a movie is a series of creative and technical decisions, and it's the director's job to make the right decisions as frequently as possible. Shooting a movie is the worst milieu for creative work ever devised by man. It is a noisy, physical apparatus; it is difficult to concentrate—and you have to do it from eight-thirty to six-thirty, five days a week. It's not an environment an artist would ever choose to work in."—Stanley Kubrick

"I make movies in the same way that I talk to people—whether it's a friend, a girl, a priest, or anyone: to seek some clarification. That is what neo-realism means to me in the original, pure sense."—Federico Fellini

"A few years ago, I asked the director of a sprawling, flattened-out epic what had gone wrong. He said that so many years had elapsed between his initial impulse to buy the property and the actual shooting of the picture, and there had been such a mammoth effort involved in the production—handling the huge crew and moving to locations in the snow and the heat— that by the time he was in the middle of the movie he no longer remembered why he had wanted to do it. He wasn't even sure any longer what it was about—the script had been rewritten so often—and he was so damned tired of the whole thing that it died on him, and when he and the editor finally tried to put the pieces together it just wouldn't take off."—Pauline Kael

"Whenever I am making a film, I find myself in a dream-like trance. The outside world completely disappears and the dream life of the studio fills my whole existence."—Jean Cocteau

"In exterior settings the details, the light bring essential cinematic ideas. One is in contact with life, which one is not, on the stage or studio. The people and the landscape dictate to you elements which have nothing to do with theories, be they even of Eisenstein."—Satyajit Ray

"Give me a good script and I'll be one hundred times better as a director."—George Cukor

"I am like a young man going to his girlfriend to propose. I pick up a small bouquet of flowers which I carry in my hand, and as I go over to her place I rehearse in my mind all the things I am going to say and exactly how it is going to be. But of course when I arrive there and start to talk something entirely different happens."—attributed to Jean Renoir

John Wayne, James Gleason, John Agar during the filming of *Sands of Iwo Jima.*

"For me, shooting a film represents days of inhumanly relentless work, stiffness of the joints, eyes full of dust, the odors of makeup, sweat and lamps, an indefinite series of tensions and relaxations, and uninterrupted battle between volition and duty, between vision and reality, conscience and laziness. I think of early risings, of nights without sleep, of a feeling keener than life, of a sort of fanaticism centered about a single task, by which I myself become, finally, an integral part of the film, a ridiculously tiny piece of apparatus whose only fault is requiring food and drink."—Ingmar Bergman

"In one way it's very nice . . . but you know we can't go on forever and not tell our friends and relatives how we are earning a living."—D. W. Griffith

"A film is never really good unless the camera is an eye in the head of a poet."—Orson Welles

"The director and the photographer must be one and indivisible; the camera is one of his tools, perhaps his most important one."—Joseph von Sternberg

"Just as actors have nightmares that they'll never get another part, I have a recurring fear that I'll never find another story I like well enough to film."—Stanley Kubrick

"I've never been able to make a still photograph. To make a film it is not necessary to know anything technical at all. It will come with time."—Bernardo Bertolucci

"The only technique worth having is the technique you invent for yourself."—Jean Cocteau

" 'Film-making' is for me a necessity of nature, a need comparable to hunger and thirst. For some, self-expression involves writing books, climbing mountains, beating one's children or dancing the samba. In my case, I express myself in making films."—Ingmar Bergman

"In brief, they (the movies) are idiotic because their production is mainly in the hands of idiots!—with a few cynics interspersed to watch for the times when even idiots show some sense."—H. L. Mencken

"A good director is like a good psychiatrist. He knows what conclusions he wants you to reach, but he lets you discover it for yourself. He acts as a guide rather than as a commander."—Rod Steiger

Film Size actual size

The gauge or width of the film stock used in filmmaking is determined by the kind of production and sometimes cost. Here, roughly, are some of the differences:

8mm
The old gauge of home movie film: precisely half the size of 16mm, with narrow frames. Gradually 8mm has been replaced by super 8mm.

Super 8mm
Slightly wider, higher frames, and a narrower strip for the sprocket holes. Generally a brighter, bigger image on the screen, but super 8mm is rarely used for purposes beyond making home movies.

16mm
The standard non-theatrical film gauge. Used widely in television for shooting news footage, running old movies, etc. The image quality is fine if the screen size isn't too large.

35mm
Since Edison, 35mm has been the standard size for shooting and projecting motion pictures. The image is sharp and brilliant even on an immense screen.

70mm
A recent (and costly) film gauge. 70mm gives a Cinemascope picture—note the great width of each frame—without using a transitional (anamorphic) lens, the lens used to shoot Cinemascope films in 35mm.

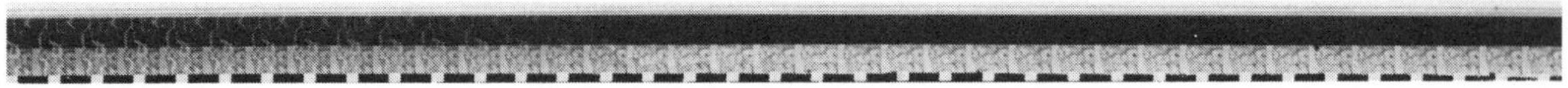
8mm

Super 8mm

16mm

35mm

70mm

Screen Size

CINEMASCOPE

When television forced the movies into retreat in the early fifties, Hollywood devised a range of schemes to lure people back to the theatres: 3-dimensional films, Cinerama, and—the only innovation of that period that lasted—Cinemascope. The Cinemascope screen is more than twice as long as it is high and requires different kinds of composition.

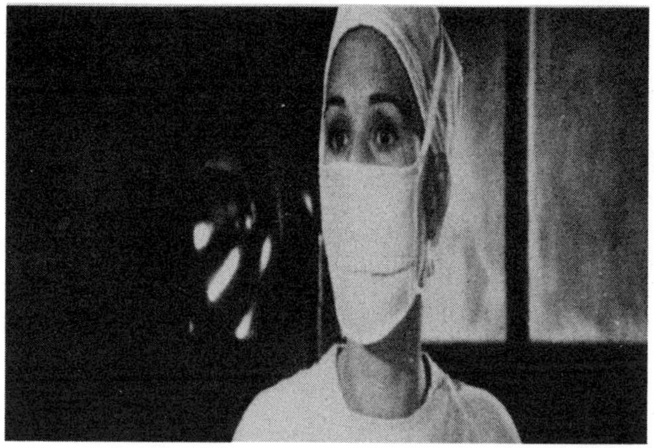

An enlarged frame from a Cinemascope film, *M*A*S*H:* these films are run through a special (anamorphic) lens to create the wide-screen effect.

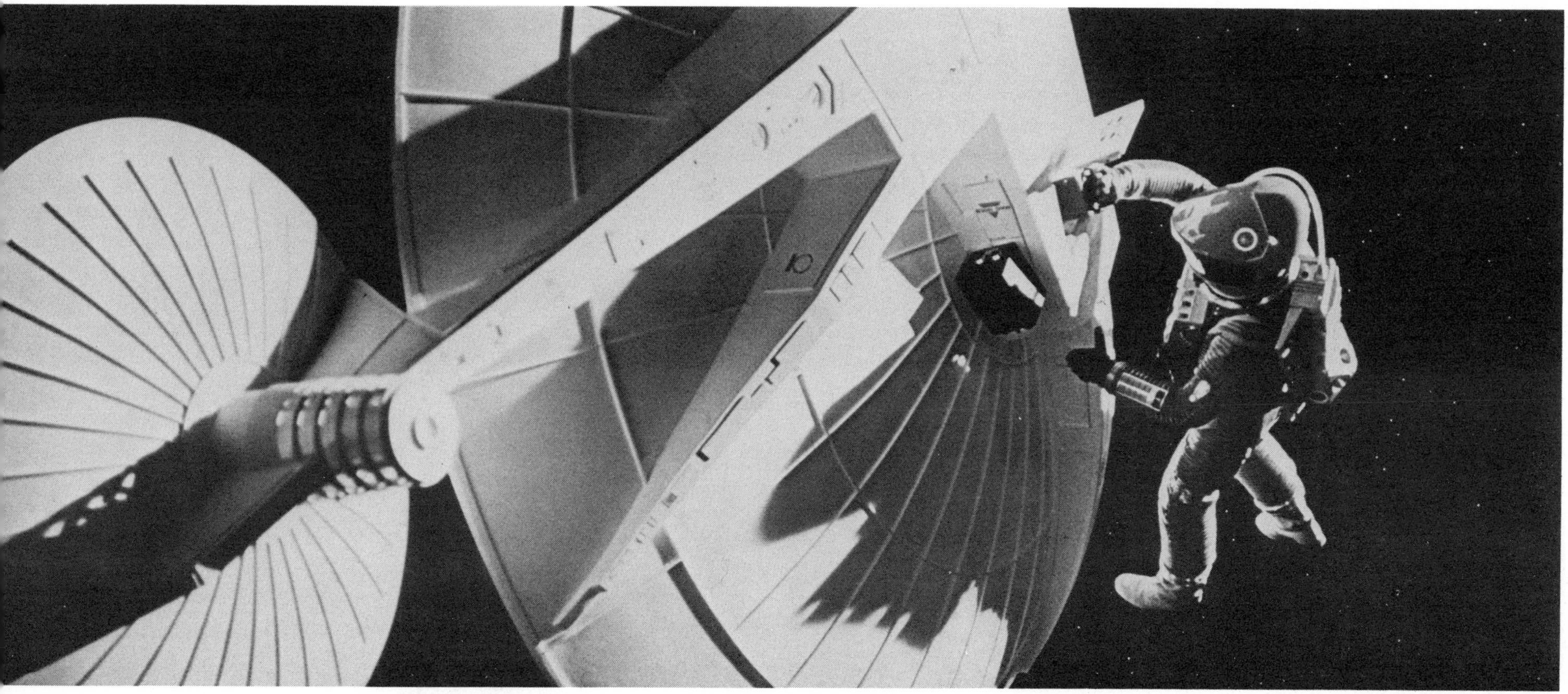

2001: A Space Odyssey: this film was shot in 70mm, providing for a Scope image without requiring the squeezed frame.

Evolution of a Script

Pretty Poison is a snappy, engaging thriller built on a fascinating premise, that Sue Ann Stepanek, a clean-cut, all-American drum majorette for the high school band (Tuesday Weld) can murder as easily and as guiltlessly as a Mafiosa hit man. Tony Perkins plays Dennis Pitt, just freed from a mental institution, who is given to impulsive fantasies. He convinces Sue Ann that he works for the CIA, is on a top-secret assignment at a local chemical plant, and—when he's fired from the plant—persuades her to help him sabotage its piping system. In the process, she murders a guard. The act excites her. She discovers that she *likes* to murder people, and it leads her to persuade Dennis to murder her mother.

Stephen Geller's novel *She Let Him Continue* is the source of *Pretty Poison*. In his novel Geller depicts Dennis as actually holding the gun, aiming at Mrs. Stepanek, and trying to shoot. Typical of a Dennis situation, the safety catch is on, the gun won't fire, and Sue Ann grabs it from him to finish the job. As the script underwent revisions (the first screenplay by the novelist, Stephen Geller; the final screenplay by Lorenzo Semple, Jr.), so did the concept and dramatic structure of the scene.

Here is a sampling of the curious ways in which scripts evolve from novels, and later scripts evolve from earlier scripts, and the final productions evolve from later scripts. Here are several versions of that scene, each one approaching what director Noel Black finally filmed, a scene in which the early emphasis on Dennis' point of view has shifted to a contrast between Dennis and Sue Ann.

-131-

SUE ANN

She's in there.

DENNIS SHAKES HIS HEAD.

SUE ANN GLARES. OPENS CLOSET DOOR.

I'll go to my room. I'll call her. You stay in the closet. Come out when you hear her coming.

DENNIS SMILES A LITTLE. ENTERS CLOSET.

CUT TO:

INTERIOR CLOSET.

WE SEE SUE ANN SHUT IT, FROM DENNIS' POV.

DENNIS LOOKS AROUND AT CLOTHES. STARTS TO GIGGLE.

SUE ANN

Mother?

DENNIS HOLDS HAND TO MOUTH TO KEEP FROM LAUGHING.

Mother?

LIGHTS APPEAR UNDER DOOR. WE HEAR FOOTSTEPS.

DENNIS OPENS CLOSET.

MRS. STEPANEK JUMPS BACK.

TURRET PAN TO SUE ANN, WHO RUSHES OUT OF HER BEDROOM.

SHE GRABS THE GUN FROM DENNIS. MOTHER RUNS BACK TO ROOM.

TRUCK WITH HER.

SUE ANN SWITCHES ON LIGHT.

MRS. STEPANEK IS LYING ACROSS THE BED, REACHING FOR PHONE. SUE ANN KICKS IT AWAY FROM HER, POINTS GUN.

-132-

IT DOESN'T SHOOT.

MRS. STEPANEK

Please...pity...stop it, Sue Ann, please, stop it...

SUE ANN ANGRILY HANDS DENNIS GUN.

HE LOOKS AT IT, REMOVES SAFETY.

MRS. STEPANEK IS SITTING UP, HYSTERICAL.

Sue Ann, God, don't...please don't...

GUN GOES OFF, A FOOT FROM MRS. STEPANEK.

DENNIS SHRUGS, FEELING SILLY. HE LOOKS HELPLESSLY AT MRS. STEPANEK, AND SUE ANN.

SUE ANN GRABS GUN.

MRS. STEPANEK RUSHES SUE ANN, WHO PUSHES HER BACK TO BED.

SHE SHOOTS.

MRS. STEPANEK ARCHES BACK, TURNS.

SUE ANN SHOOTS AGAIN, AGAIN.

MRS. STEPANEK IS SPRAWLED ALL OVER THE BED.

SUE ANN

Get out!

DENNIS LOOKS AT HER.

Go!

DENNIS LEAVES.

WE HEAR ANOTHER SHOT. DENNIS WINCES.

from Stephen Geller's first draft screenplay, *She Let Him Continue*

106.

294 CONTINUED - (2):

DENNIS
Yeah ...

Dennis takes the gun, stares down at it.

SUE ANN
It's loaded. The safety's off. She'll be in the kitchen with her back turned, it'll be a pot-shot.

Dennis nods, starts toward the door like a dreamwalker. He stops, looking at something on Sue Ann's bureau.

295 A PHOTOGRAPH ON BUREAU

Framed picture of a GRINNING YOUNG SAILOR in uniform.

DENNIS
(v.o.)
Who's that?

SUE ANN
(v.o.)
I dunno. Some sailor from New London or somwhere.

296 BACK TO SCENE

DENNIS
Did he make out with you, Sue Ann?

SUE ANN
I don't remember. Maybe.

DENNIS
But ... You said you never did, before me.

SUE ANN
So what's the difference?

A beat as Dennis stares at her. Suddenly Sue Ann turns, reacts to something. Urgent whisper:

SUE ANN
(continuing)
Listen! I think she's coming up the stairs ...

107.

HALL AND STAIRWAY

Mrs. Stepanek is starting up it, carrying a nice glass of ORANGE JUICE.

SUE ANN'S ROOM

Terrible things are going on inside Dennis. He moves to the door, turns knob, opens it a bit. He raises the gun. Suddenly Dennis's hand BEGINS TO SHAKE. He lowers the gun again, looks stupidly at Sue Ann. Exasperated, Sue Ann makes a LITTLE SOUND and grabs the gun from Dennis. Her movement accidentally knocks a SMALL TRANSISTOR RADIO off the bureau top.

THE RADIO

Impact of hitting floor TURNS IT ON. Instant LOUD MUSIC: some POP BIG BEAT COMBO screeching an inane repetitive lyric. Dennis pounces on the obscene radio, blunders and kicks it around, catches it finally. But the blow has disordered the device, it WON'T TURN OFF. Dennis pounds it, trying to kill it, bashes it, still it plays, then Dennis races with it through doorway into:

SUE ANN'S BATHROOM - DAY

Dennis hurls the radio violently INTO TOILET.

INTO TOILET

There's the radio under the water: still playing, the horrible SOUNDS weirdly AMPLIFIED AND DISTORTED. Suddenly over it: a BLASTING PISTOL SHOT, then a CRASH, then ANOTHER SHOT. Denis retches, can't vomit, flushes toilet. SWIRLING WATER, crazy vortex, then suddenly the RADIO CUTS OUT, short-circuited, drowned.

SUE ANN'S BEDROOM

It is empty. The door is open. Then Sue Ann walks back in, holding the pistol (smoking, if revolvers really do such a thing) with a lacy handkerchief around the grip. She drops the gun on the bed, dabs absently at her nose with handkerchief, then stuffs it in a pocket. Sue Ann sits on edge of the bed, then suddenly flops back supine and lies there with her eyes wide open, glittering.

from Lorenzo Semple, Jr.'s, final draft screenplay, *She Let Him Continue*

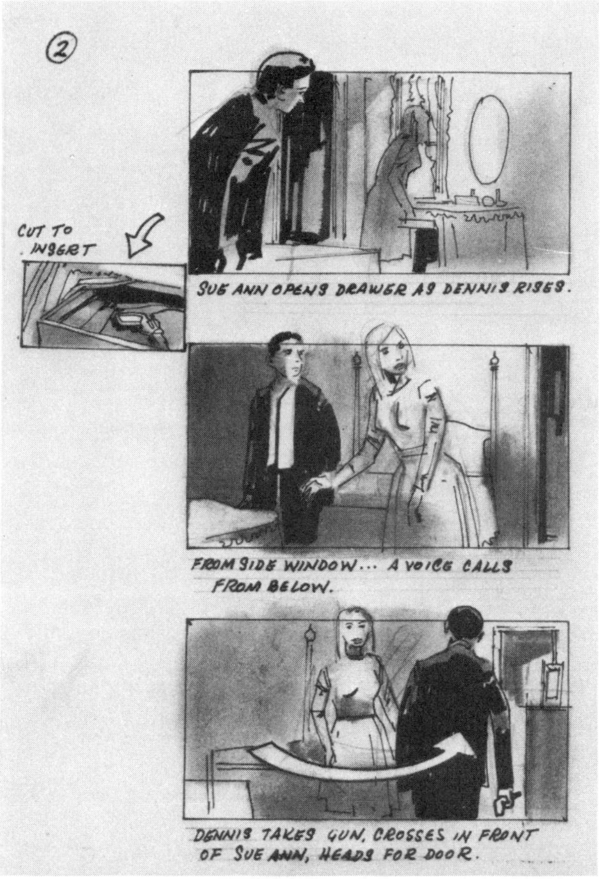

2
CUT TO INSERT
SUE ANN OPENS DRAWER AS DENNIS RISES.
FROM SIDE WINDOW... A VOICE CALLS FROM BELOW.
DENNIS TAKES GUN, CROSSES IN FRONT OF SUE ANN, HEADS FOR DOOR.

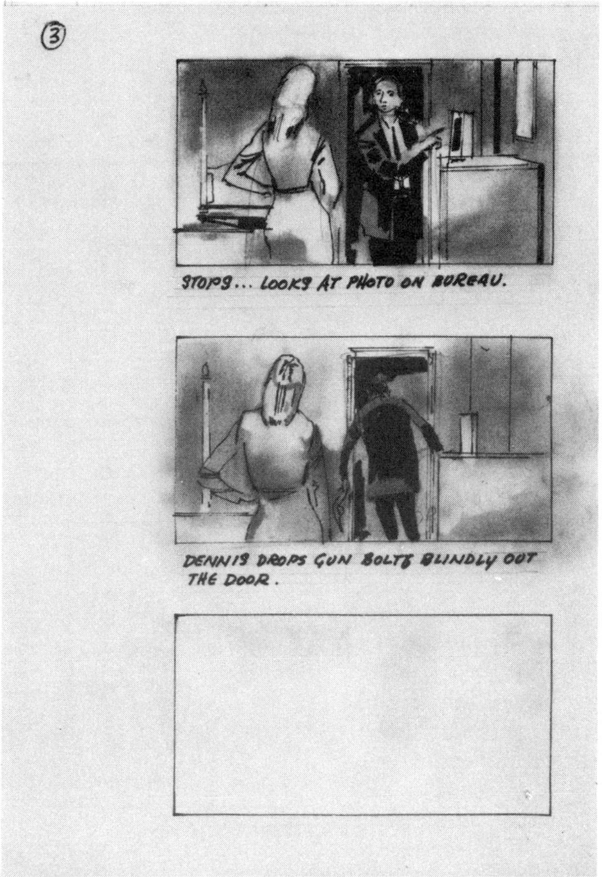

3
STOPS... LOOKS AT PHOTO ON BUREAU.
DENNIS DROPS GUN BOLTS BLINDLY OUT THE DOOR.

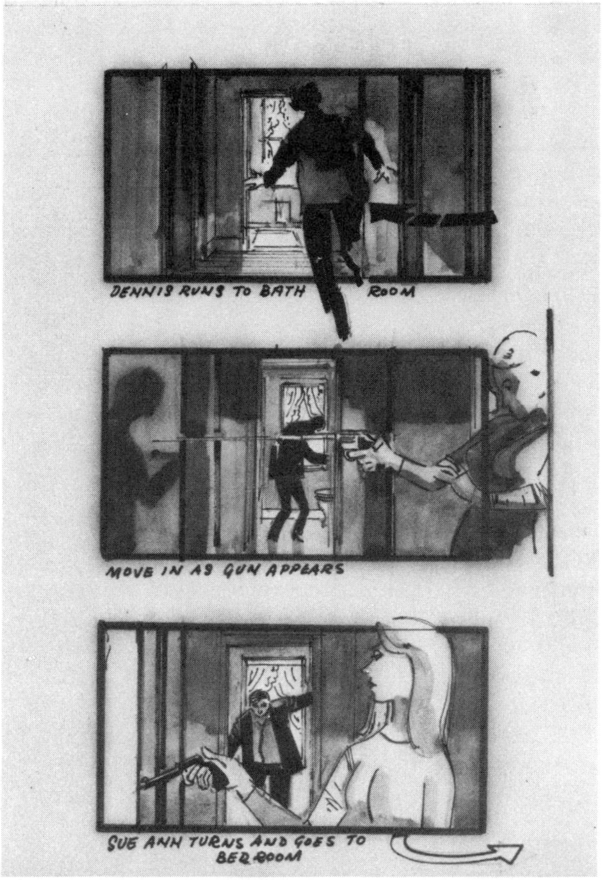

DENNIS RUNS TO BATH ROOM
MOVE IN AS GUN APPEARS
SUE ANN TURNS AND GOES TO BED ROOM

Storyboard sketches for filming the scene in which Sue Ann murders her mother, based on the final screenplay.

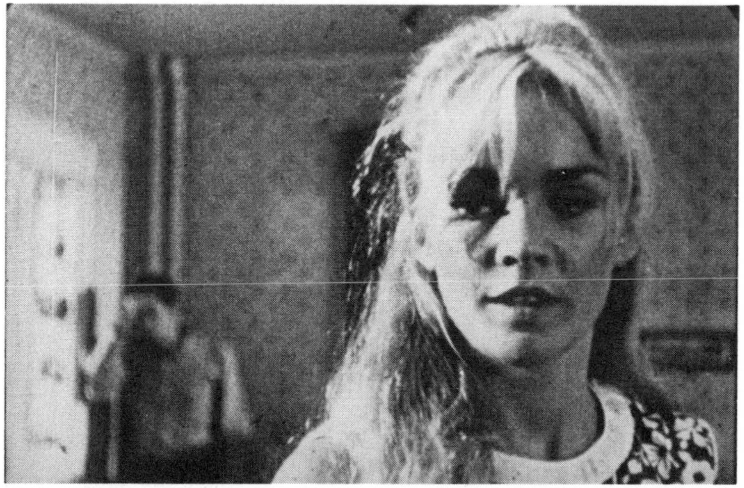

These stills realize the words of the final draft script on page 38: "HALL AND STAIRWAY Mrs. Stepanek is starting up it . . ." (left photo) and "Terrible things are going on inside Dennis." (right photo)

Like Waging a Military Campaign

The problems of film production are akin to those of managing an army on a battlefield: maneuvering supplies and equipment and men, organizing and deploying resources for full efficiency, and when the weather or the tide of battle abruptly changes, being able to shift everything on sudden notice. Thus a major share of the energies that go into film production is often not directly or even distantly artistic; it is purely organizational, and supremely necessary. The key figure here isn't the producer or director (though they're involved) but the unsung and quintessential production manager. Often he'll aid in the preparation of the budget, and he may have more to do than anyone else on the film with keeping the production under budget, for he's likely to be the one who arranges to buy supplies, provide transportation, make sure the exposed film gets to a lab for developing quickly, the kind of costs that can skyrocket if he's not careful.

One of the first jobs of the production manager is to break down the scenes in the script into a production board, a chart that relates the actors, locations, special demands and other requirements of each scene to one another. The board is invaluable for providing instant information on questions like how many days a certain actor will need to be hired for, or how many days will be required for the shooting at a location that must be rented. The production board also aids in the preparation of the shooting schedule, a breakdown of shooting days and locations matched to scenes in the script. All this before production begins; and once it's begun, the production manager's headaches truly begin, because then he's responsible for making sure everyone knows the next day's location and where it is and that they have a means of getting there. And if the lead actress's indispensable poodle gets lost in the woods, it's likely as not the production manager who has to go chasing after it. Maybe it's easier to be a director.

Starting Date August 14, 1967
Finishing Date September 25, 1967
Production Days 30 + 1 P.U. Shots + 1 Holiday (5 Day Week Basis)
FORM 450-SHEET #2

TWENTIETH CENTURY-FOX FILM CORPORATION
PRELIMINARY PRODUCTION
COST ESTIMATE

Release Season

Production No. G-36 Color Color
Producer L. Turman, M. Backlar
Director Noel Black No.
Title "SHE LET HIM CONTINUE"

DESCRIPTION	7-15-67 Accumulated Cost	BUDGET	Total	APRIL 24	
Story Rights	20,000	20,000			
Scenario	267	1,000			
Producer	4,089	216,700			
Director	3,000	20,000			
Cast	70	168,500			
ABOVE-THE-LINE	27,426		426,200		
OVERHEAD			106,550		
TOTAL ABOVE-THE-LINE			532,750		
Music		28,760		28,760	
Dance Director & Staff		---			
Extras	17	7,742		5,170	
Staff	5,206	34,461		32,174	
Art Costs	4,029	20,530		6,700	
Set Costs		25,225		5,815	
Light Platforms		---			
Set Strike Labor		500		350	
Operating Labor & Material		35,566		20,240	
Miniatures		---			
Camera	93	31,010		28,561	
Sound		13,020		10,497	
Electrical		28,840		24,675	
Mechanical Effects		4,016		6,800	
Set Dressing & Props		15,277		11,299	
Animals & Action Devices		35		35	
Women's Wardrobe		7,365		1,425	
Men's Wardrobe		1,675		4,125	
Makeup & Hairdressing		7,788		5,489	
Process		---			
Re-recording		12,938		12,938	
Special Camera Effects		3,010		500	
Production Film & Lab. Work		38,637		34,214	
Stills	19	6,340		7,000	
Opticals		---			
Titles		4,750		4,600	
Post-Prod. Film & Lab. Work		20,721		23,242	
Projectionists	1,099	4,600		3,500	
Transportation—Cars & Trucks	1,175	37,698		41,858	
Talent Tests	4,386	4,600			
Editorial		41,435		40,805	
Fringe Benefits	2,493	72,500		40,000	
Location Expense	318	94,200		101,100	
Producer's Charges		---			
Miscellaneous	4,157	24,257		19,000	
Rental Charges & Fees		2,000			
BELOW-THE-LINE	22,992		629,496	520,977	
OVERHEAD			157,354	130,244	
TOTAL BELOW-THE-LINE			786,850	651,221	
GRAND TOTALS	50,418		1,319,600		

Remarks

Date Compiled: July 21, 1967

Estimator

Correct:

Head of Estimating Dept.

34 DAYS

July 18, 1967

"SHE LET HIM CONTINUE"

WEEKLY SCHEDULE

	DAY		SCENE #'S	PGS.
Mon., Aug. 14	1	- Bridge Over Stream	9,10	5/8
	1	- Drill Field & Bridge	151-154	6/8
	1	- Hot Dog Stand - Phone	155	3-3/8
	1	- Hot Dog Stand - Phone	149	5/8
Tues., Aug. 15	2	- Hot Dog Stand & Bridge	342-344	3-2/8
Wed., Aug. 16 -1	3,4	- Hot Dog Stand	46-61	4-1/8
Thurs., Aug. 17	4	- Hot Dog Stand	90-95	1-5/8
	4	- Hot Dog Stand	138	2/8
Fri., Aug. 18	4,5	- Hot Dog Stand	169-170	1-2/8
	5	- Factory Entrance	17,18,20,22,24,26	7/8
			TOTAL	16-6/8
Mon., Aug. 21	6	- Factory Entrance & Street	126-133	4-1/8
Tues., Aug. 22	7	- INT: Factory Time Clock	27	2/8
	7,8	- INT: Factory - Dennis' Post	28-36,38-45	4-1/8
Wed., Aug. 23	8	- INT: Factory - Dennis' Post	124,125	7/8
	8	- INT: Factory - Dennis' Post	134,135,137	1-1/8
Thurs., Aug. 24	9	- INT: Guard's Room	182,184	2/8
(Night call)	9	- Bridge Over Stream	221	1/8
Fri., Aug. 25	9,10	- Factory - River & Chute	177-181, 183,185-200	5-1/8
			TOTAL	16

1A

"She Let Him Continue" 7-20-'67

EXTRAS

PROD. DAY	B.D. Pg #	SET	Local N.Y. Bits Bits	EXTRAS CARS	GEN. EXTRAS	PHOTO Dbls. + STUNTS
# 1	1	EXTERIOR HIGH SCHOOL FIELD			(Cov. by Flat Amt.)	
2	1A	EXTERIOR HIGH SCHOOL FIELD	Bits listed		"	
2	2	EXT. BRIDGE OVER STREAM	on Cast	1		
3	10	EXT. HOT DOG STAND	Page	1	14	
4	10A	EXT. HOT DOG STAND		2	4	
6	5	INT. DENNIS' ROOM				
7+8	5A	INT. DENNIS' ROOM - BATHROOM				
8	6	EXT. MOTEL + CABIN				
8	24	INT. MOTEL OFFICE				
9	9	INT. FACTORY			30	
10	9A	INT. FACTORY			30	
10	29	INT. FACTORY OFFICE			1	
10	30	INT. FACTORY OFFICE				
11	7	EXT. FACTORY			40	
12	7A	EXT. FACTORY		2	40	
12	7C	EXT. FACTORY			46	
13	7D	EXT. FACTORY				
13	22	INT. PHONE BOOTH FACTORY			10	
14+15	7B	EXT. FACTORY		1	1	
16	35	INT. POLICE OFFICE			9	
16	21	INT. AZENAUER'S OFFICE				
17+18	16	INT. CAR				1. (Stunt)
17+18	17	EXT. WOODLAND LANE				
19	17	EXT. WOODLAND LANE				
20	17A	EXT. WOODLAND LANE			1	
21+22	19	EXT. QUARRY + FOREST			1	
22	26	INT. POLICE CAR				
23	19A	EXT. FOREST		1		1 (Stunt)
24	33	EXT. HIGHWAY GAS STATION			10	
24	31	INT. ROADSIDE STORE			3	
24	32	EXT. ROADSIDE STORE PARKING LOT		4	8	
25+26	25	INT. STEPANEK LIVING ROOM				
27	23	INT. SUE ANN'S BEDROOM				
27	34	INT. STEPANEK HALL + STAIR				
28	18A	EXT. STEPANEK'S HOUSE				
29	18	EXT. STEPANEK'S HOUSE		1		
30	11	INT. MOVIE HOUSE			10	
30	13	EXT. MOVIE HOUSE		4	3	
30	14	EXT. TOWN SIDEWALK		2	6	
30	27	EXT. BEANERY			3	
30	28	EXT. CHILDREN'S PLAYGROUND				
		PICKUP SHOTS				
1	8	EXT. FACTORY			10	
1	15	EXT. HIGHWAY		4		2 (Auto Dbls) (Cov.)
1	17B	EXT. WOODLAND				
			TOTALS	23	294	4

Breakdown Page	51	52	53	170	171	252	172	294	295	296
Day or Nite	D	D	D	D	N	D	N	D	D	D
Location or Studio	L	L	L	L	L	L	L	L	L	L
Sequences										
No. of Pages	2/8	1/8	1/8	1 7/8	1/8	6 1/8	3 2/8	1 7/8	3/8	4/8
Title PRETTY POISON Director NOEL BLACK Producer M. BACHLAR N. BLACK Asst. Dir. ROGER ROTHSTEIN Script Dated 4-14-67	SUE ANN ARRIVES AT PETE'S STAND. SHE ASKS FOR CHANGE.	DENNIS STARES AT SUE ANN	DENNIS SEES SOMETHING O.S., PANICS	AT HOT DOG STAND SUE ANN TELLS DENNIS HE'LL HAVE TO VISIT HER MOTHER	INSERT: FRAMED PHOTO OF MARGARET ST. ONGE & MRS. STEPENEK	DENNIS CONFESSES TO SUE ANN HIS FANTASY. SHE PROPOSES THEY RUN AWAY.	MRS. STEPENEK QUESTIONS DENNIS. SHE & SUE ANN FIGHT. DENNIS & SUE ANN LEAVE	IN SUE ANN'S BEDROOM SHE URGES DENNIS TO SHOOT HER MOTHER	INSERT: PHOTO OF GRINNING YOUNG SAILOR	DENNIS & SUE ANN REACT TO MOTHER COMING UP STAIRS
Character / Artist / No.										
DENNIS PITT / TONY PERKINS / 1	1	1	1	1		1	1	1		1
SUE ANN STEPANEK / TUESDAY WELD / 2	2		2	2		2	2	2		2
AZENAUER / JOHN RANDOLPH / 3										
MRS STEPANEK / BEVERLY GARLAND / 4							4	4		
MRS BRONSON / CLARICE BLACKBURN / 5										
BUD MUNSCH / DICK O'NEIL / 6										
PETE / JOE BOVA / 7	7			7						
SAM JOYLES / PARKER FENNELLY / 8										
9										
10										
11										
12										
13										
14										
15										
16										
17										
18										
19										
20										

Here are some of the working records used to produce the movie on time within a budget and as planned.

PRETTY POISON

Script page	Production board strip #	Date on shooting schedule
12	51,52,53	Wed Aug. 16
63	170,171,172	Friday August 18 Thur. Sept. 21
91	252	Thurs. Aug31
106	294,295,296	Tues. Sept. 26

And Always, Difficulties...

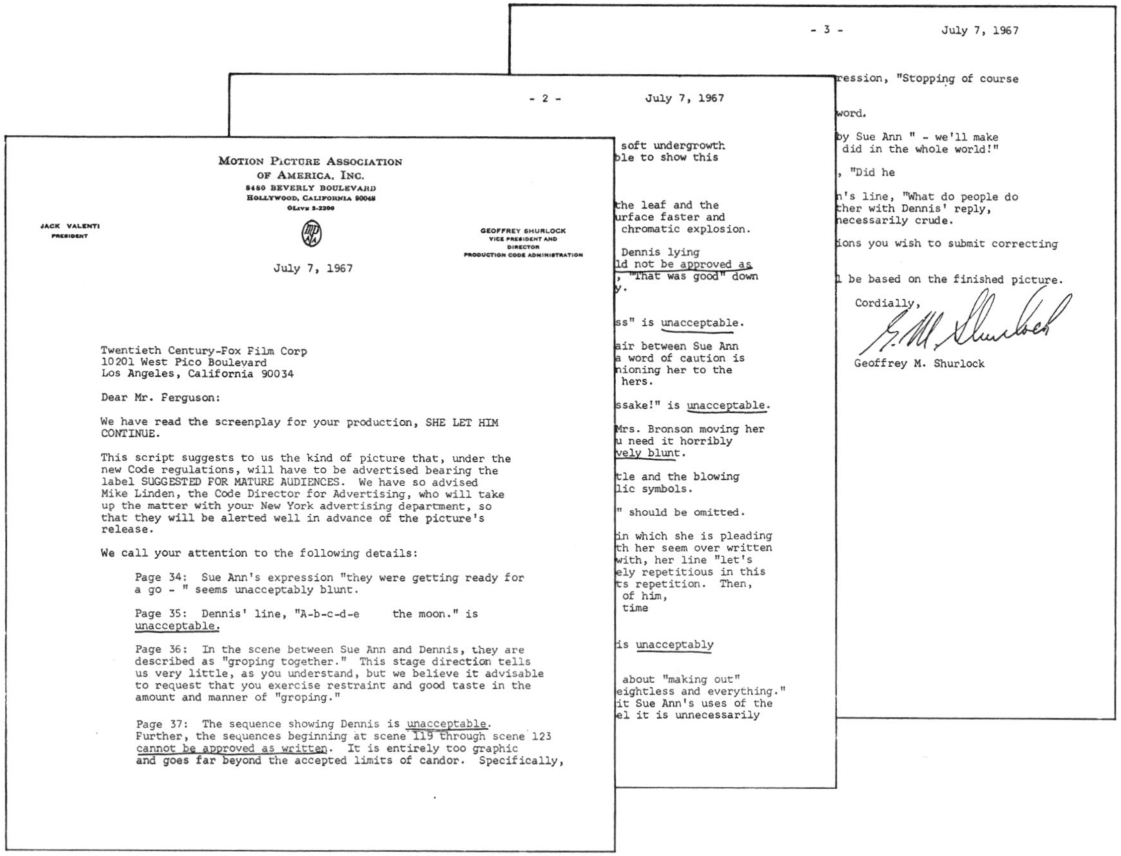

MOTION PICTURE ASSOCIATION
OF AMERICA, INC.
8480 BEVERLY BOULEVARD
HOLLYWOOD, CALIFORNIA 90048
OLIVE 3-2200

JACK VALENTI
PRESIDENT

GEOFFREY SHURLOCK
VICE PRESIDENT AND
DIRECTOR
PRODUCTION CODE ADMINISTRATION

July 7, 1967

Twentieth Century-Fox Film Corp
10201 West Pico Boulevard
Los Angeles, California 90034

Dear Mr. Ferguson:

We have read the screenplay for your production, SHE LET HIM CONTINUE.

This script suggests to us the kind of picture that, under the new Code regulations, will have to be advertised bearing the label SUGGESTED FOR MATURE AUDIENCES. We have so advised Mike Linden, the Code Director for Advertising, who will take up the matter with your New York advertising department, so that they will be alerted well in advance of the picture's release.

We call your attention to the following details:

Page 34: Sue Ann's expression "they were getting ready for a go - " seems unacceptably blunt.

Page 35: Dennis' line, "A-b-c-d-e the moon." is unacceptable.

Page 36: In the scene between Sue Ann and Dennis, they are described as "groping together." This stage direction tells us very little, as you understand, but we believe it advisable to request that you exercise restraint and good taste in the amount and manner of "groping."

Page 37: The sequence showing Dennis is unacceptable. Further, the sequences beginning at scene 119 through scene 123 cannot be approved as written. It is entirely too graphic and goes far beyond the accepted limits of candor. Specifically,

- 2 - July 7, 1967

soft undergrowth
ble to show this

the leaf and the
urface faster and
chromatic explosion.

Dennis lying
ld not be approved as
, "That was good" down
y.

ss" is unacceptable.

air between Sue Ann
a word of caution is
nioning her to the
hers.

ssake!" is unacceptable.

Mrs. Bronson moving her
u need it horribly
vely blunt.

tle and the blowing
lic symbols.

" should be omitted.

in which she is pleading
th her seem over written
with, her line "let's
ely repetitious in this
ts repetition. Then,
of him,
time

is unacceptably

about "making out"
eightless and everything."
it Sue Ann's uses of the
el it is unnecessarily

- 3 - July 7, 1967

ression, "Stopping of course

word.

by Sue Ann " - we'll make
did in the whole world!"

, "Did he

n's line, "What do people do
ther with Dennis' reply,
necessarily crude.

ions you wish to submit correcting

l be based on the finished picture.

Cordially,

Geoffrey M. Shurlock

YES YOU CAN, NO YOU CAN'T

It's been replaced now by those big circled letters, G and PG and R and X, but until 1968, the year after *Pretty Poison* was made, the Code Office (officially the Production Code Administration of the Motion Picture Association of America) overruled more scenes in more films than an historian will ever be able to count. From 1934 to 1968 the Code Office had the absolute power to do just that, and it wielded that power—as this letter shows—in a manner that verged on autocratic arrogance. The Code Office could be quite fussy about what it permitted and didn't permit. It may seem comic now—the Code Office is gone—but for over thirty years every film made by an American studio underwent precisely the same treatment.

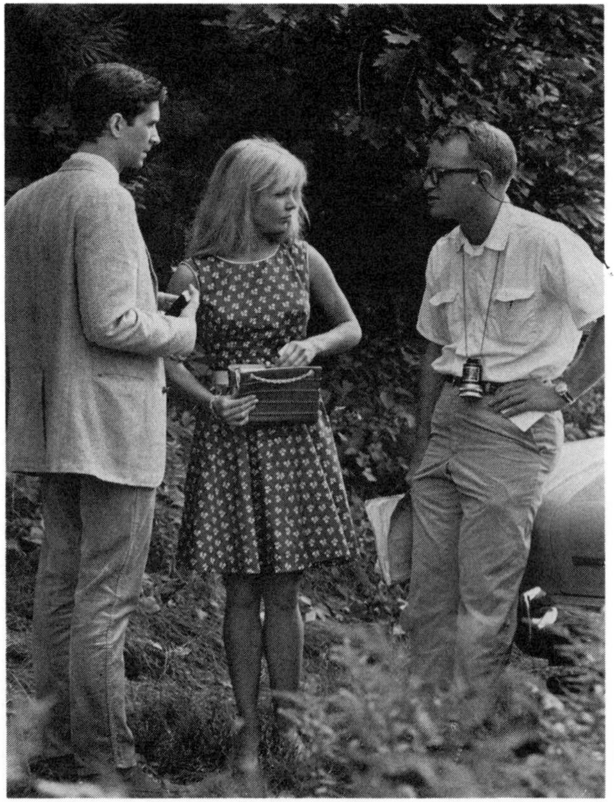

Pretty Poison is Noel Black's first feature. He became involved when the executive producer of the film, Larry Turman, who had seen Black's award-winning short *Skater Dater*, contacted Black about doing the project. *Pretty Poison* was budgeted at about $1.5 million, at the time (1967) the lowest-budgeted feature produced by the Fox studios in about four or five years.

WHY IT WASN'T CALLED, 'SHE LET HIM CONTINUE'

As you may have noticed from the previous pages, throughout the production of *Pretty Poison* the working title was *She Let Him Continue,* the title of the novel. You may have your own preference (director Noel Black and others on the film much preferred *She Let Him Continue*); but the executives at 20th Century-Fox wanted to be sure. They paid an opinion research company, Marplan of Los Angeles, to conduct a study that would interview 999 people in four parts of the U.S. Each person heard a synopsis of the film, then was asked which of the three titles was preferred—*She Let Him Continue, Sweet Poison, Pretty Poison.* The study concluded that the highest percentage of people interviewed—though by no means a convincing majority—preferred *Sweet Poison.* Subsequently, 20th Century-Fox entitled the film *Pretty Poison.* Will scripts in the future—and casts and directors—become the province of opinion surveys?

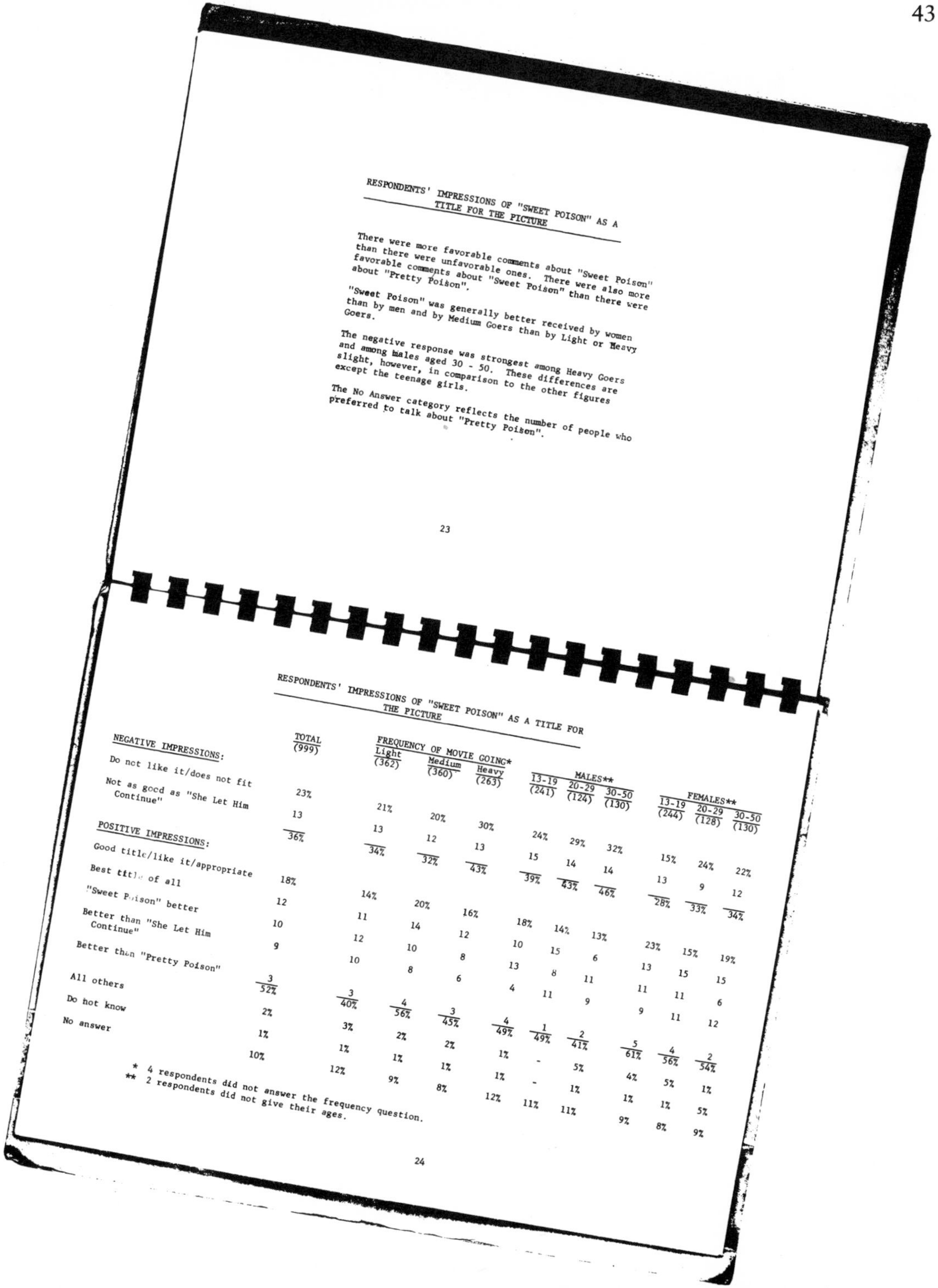

RESPONDENTS' IMPRESSIONS OF "SWEET POISON" AS A TITLE FOR THE PICTURE

There were more favorable comments about "Sweet Poison" than there were unfavorable ones. There were also more favorable comments about "Sweet Poison" than there were about "Pretty Poison".

"Sweet Poison" was generally better received by women than by men and by Medium Goers than by Light or Heavy Goers.

The negative response was strongest among Heavy Goers and among males aged 30 - 50. These differences are slight, however, in comparison to the other figures except the teenage girls.

The No Answer category reflects the number of people who preferred to talk about "Pretty Poison".

23

RESPONDENTS' IMPRESSIONS OF "SWEET POISON" AS A TITLE FOR THE PICTURE

	TOTAL	FREQUENCY OF MOVIE GOING*			MALES**			FEMALES**		
	(999)	Light (362)	Medium (360)	Heavy (263)	13-19 (241)	20-29 (124)	30-50 (130)	13-19 (244)	20-29 (128)	30-50 (130)
NEGATIVE IMPRESSIONS:										
Do not like it/does not fit	23%	21%	20%	30%	24%	29%	32%	15%	24%	22%
Not as good as "She Let Him Continue"	13	13	12	13	15	14	14	13	9	12
	36%	34%	32%	43%	39%	43%	46%	28%	33%	34%
POSITIVE IMPRESSIONS:										
Good title/like it/appropriate	18%	14%	20%	16%	18%	14%	13%	23%	15%	19%
Best title of all	12	11	14	12	10	15	6	13	15	15
"Sweet Poison" better	10	12	10	8	13	8	11	11	11	6
Better than "She Let Him Continue"	9	10	8	6	4	11	9	9	11	12
Better than "Pretty Poison"	3	3	4	3	4	1	2	5	4	2
	52%	40%	56%	45%	49%	49%	41%	61%	56%	54%
All others	2%	3%	2%	2%	1%	-	5%	4%	5%	1%
Do not know	1%	1%	1%	1%	1%	-	1%	1%	1%	5%
No answer	10%	12%	9%	8%	12%	11%	11%	9%	8%	9%

* 4 respondents did not answer the frequency question.
** 2 respondents did not give their ages.

24

The care taken to find what the public thought about the title is demonstrated by the detailed report at right.

Advertising the Movie: The Pressbook

Every movie has its "pressbook," a collection of ready-made news stories, advertisements, and other media messages—TV ads, for example—supplied free to theater operators. A sampling from the Twentieth Century-Fox Corp.'s pressbook for *Pretty Poison* includes fairly lurid ads, in a wide variety of sizes (the theater name is inserted where "sig," for signature, is shown), "live radio spots," for one-minute and half-minute use, and a synopsis for the film, which is not supplied to the public before the film showing.

PRESSBOOK

What Brought A Nice Kid Like Sue Ann To A Shocking Moment Like This?

A shook-up story of the up-tight generation.

20TH CENTURY FOX PRESENTS
A LAWRENCE TURMAN PRODUCTION
"Pretty Poison"

STARRING
ANTHONY PERKINS • TUESDAY WELD
PRODUCED BY MARSHAL BACKLAR AND NOEL BLACK DIRECTED BY NOEL BLACK SCREENPLAY BY LORENZO SEMPLE, Jr
BASED ON A NOVEL BY STEPHEN GELLER MUSIC BY JOHNNY MANDEL • COLOR BY DELUXE SUGGESTED FOR MATURE AUDIENCES

SIG

130 lines x 3 columns (390 lines)
3 columns x 9¼ inches
MAT—321

LIVE RADIO SPOTS

60-seconds

Announcer: They met on Monday...fell in love on Tuesday...were unfaithful on Wednesday...and killed a guy on Thursday. How's that for a crazy week? That's the kind of week Tony Perkins and Tuesday Weld have in the motion picture "PRETTY POISON"...He's such a nice guy, she's such a sweet girl...together...they'll scare the daylights out of you! Just wait till you see what they do to his aunt...and to the night watchman...and to her mother..."PRETTY POISON"...A shook-up story of the uptight generation. Life Magazine called "PRETTY POISON" "the most original movie of the year"..."A marvelous thriller," applauded Newsweek...And The New York Times hailed "PRETTY POISON" as "one of the ten best movies of the year." Starring Tony Perkins and Tuesday Weld -- "PRETTY POISON," from Twentieth Century-Fox, in Color. It's the motion picture Time Magazine called the "nicest, nastiest crime film to come out of Hollywood in years."

30-seconds

Announcer: They met on Monday...fell in love on Tuesday...were unfaithful on Wednesday...and killed a guy on Thursday. How's that for a crazy week? It's the kind of week Tony Perkins and Tuesday Weld have in "PRETTY POISON." But just wait till you see what they do to his aunt... and to the night watchman...and to her mother! "PRETTY POISON"...A Shook-up motion picture about the uptight generation. The New York Times hailed it as "one of the ten best pictures of the year. "PRETTY POISON"...from Twentieth Century-Fox, in Color.

What Brought A Nice Kid Like Sue Ann To A Shocking Moment Like This?

"Pretty Poison"
ANTHONY PERKINS • TUESDAY WELD
SIG
100 lines x 2 columns (200 lines)
2 columns x 7 inches
MAT 223

COMING! "Pretty Poison"
6 lines x 2 columns (12 lines) 2 col x ½ inch
MAT—226

A Shook-Up Story Of The Up-Tight Generation!
"Pretty Poison"
ANTHONY PERKINS
TUESDAY WELD
79 lines x 2 columns (158 lines)
2 columns x 5⅝ inches
MAT 224

"Pretty Poison"
28 lines x 2 columns (56 lines)
2 columns x 2 inches
MAT—222

"Pretty Poison"
14 lines x 1 column
1 col x 1 inch
MAT—121

"Pretty Poison"
1 col x ½ inch
MAT—123

"Pretty Poison"
21 lines x 1 column
1 col x 1½ inches
MAT—122

A Shook-Up Story Of The Up-Tight Generation!
"Pretty Poison"
ANTHONY PERKINS
TUESDAY WELD
70 lines x 1 column
1 col x 5 inches
MAT—125

ANTHONY PERKINS. TUESDAY WELD-2A

"Pretty Poison"
14 lines x 2 columns (28 lines) 2 col x 1 inch
MAT 221

SPECIAL AD MAT NO. 1 - Order from NSS

ANTHONY PERKINS, TUESDAY WELD STAR IN
20TH-FOX'S PORTRAIT OF YOUTH, "PRETTY POISON"

Starring Anthony Perkins and Tuesday Weld, "Pretty Poison" is set to open on ____________ at the ______________ Theatre. This Lawrence Turman production, released by 20th Century-Fox, was filmed in DeLuxe Color entirely on location in Great Barrington, Mass., where the first armed resistance to the British crown was offered in 1774 in a prelude to the Revolution.

"Pretty Poison" marks a series of "firsts" as a production. The producers, 31-year old Marshal Backlar and 30-year-old Noel Black are making their feature motion-picture debut. They had but three short films to their credit before being given the assignment by executive producer Lawrence Turman on "Pretty Poison." Black directed as well as serving as co-producer. The screenplay by Lorenzo Semple, Jr., is based on the first novel of 25-year-old Stephen Geller.

Those three short films by Backlar and Black -- which formed a trilogy on ABC-TV -- included the many honored shorts "Skaterdater" and "The River Boy."

The story of "Pretty Poison" gives a vivid and hair-raising portrait of youth in the throes of love, passion and hate tinged with the hallmarks of our times: promiscuity, pills and a disregard for life.

"The story has all the elements of a classic," says Backlar. "It's a beautiful love story between a boy and a girl. And it has what I think of as a kind of black widow element in that the girl lures the man and then destroys him."

SYNOPSIS

Pressured, and at odds with the dreary trivia surrounding his confused life, Dennis Pitt (TONY PERKINS) creates a fantasy world of being a CIA agent. It is a harmless fantasy where he imagines he is spying on the very people who make his life miserable in the chemical factory where he works.

Then Dennis encounters the lush, high school color guard member, 17-year-old Sue Ann Stepanek (TUESDAY WELD).

He immediately contrives to enlist her in his fantasy world, explaining that his job at the chemical plant in the small New England town is just a cover for his operations as a secret agent. She seemingly believes him and becomes involved in the wild romanticism of his plotting, and the equally wild sexual stimulus of pills, which Dennis refers to as A.C.T.S.

Dennis is on probation for arson in which he burned down his home, including his aunt. His probation officer, Azenauer (JOHN RANDOLPH), has tracked him down and Dennis is given notice by the factory (where he is not too well liked anyway). Sue Ann's mother (BEVERLY GARLAND) is also giving trouble about her daughter's staying out at night.

Now Dennis' fantasy world reaches its peak, for he and Sue Ann are about to indulge in a plot of counter-espionage at the water supply. They go to the plant to gimmick one of the disposal chutes but are caught in the act by a guard. To save Dennis' CIA reputation and the fate of the mission, the guard is killed by Sue Ann.

The next day Dennis is suspected of the murder and his probation officer arrives. With Sue Ann's help, Dennis goes into hiding - explaining that he is expendable and they will jail him. Sue Ann has a plan, however. They will go to Mexico in her car. Early in the morning she picks him up and they go to her home to rifle her mother's strongbox. Once again they are interrupted when mother comes home. Sue Ann uses the murdered guard's pistol to kill her.

Dennis takes the body in Sue Ann's car to dispose of it, but en route he faces reality and turns himself in. Sue Ann has no difficulty in convincing everyone of his guilt on all counts.

Sometime later, Sue Ann is back at the hot dog stand, scene of her first meeting with Dennis. A young man strikes up a conversation, and as they leave Sue Ann is telling him about her foster parents...

"Now about these people, what we've got to plan....."

A Visual Dictionary

CHAPTER THREE

A Visual Dictionary

The final result and proof of a film is the response it elicits from an audience. You needn't know the difference between a wide-angle shot and a jump cut to respond to a good film; yet some knowledge of the techniques of filmmaking—and the vocabulary of those techniques—can help you judge how a film aroused a certain response or where it failed. The massive, sometimes cumbersome technology of film has provided a substantial range of technical possibilities for the filmmakers and to become aware of these techniques is to become aware at the same time of his artistic choices.

THE SHOT

When D. W. Griffith separated a long shot (in which the camera holds at a distance from the subject) from the closeup (in which the subject is seen at very close range, as in a facial shot), he not only created types of shots, he created the shot itself. Previously, with exceptions like the work of Edwin S. Porter, movies were shot as though they were stage plays, with the camera at a fixed, immobile distance from the action. Characters entered the frame and left it as on a stage. Griffith's discovery of the dramatic potential in varying the shots themselves made the camera, and its distance from the subject (and the ways in which it used that distance), part of the basic language of film. It is not only what we see, but how we see it.

Generally, camera distance is inherently related to the nature of the action. A long shot gives us perspective, a sense of people in relation to their environment, an awareness of the relationships between opposing forces within the same frame (two gunmen approaching one another in a Western; or two armies in a war movie). The medium shot—in which we see most of a human figure, or several figures clustered together—permits us to get in closer: to see features, expressions, gestures, relationships on a smaller and more intimate scale.

At the closeup, the scale becomes even more intimate, and can carry potent dramatic force. A man's face seen in closeup can, with only the slightest hint of expression (and often with virtually *no* expression) suggest tension, emotional struggle, uncertainty, decisiveness. In the closeup, we are seeing a face or a hand or an object amplified to the size of a theater screen (sometimes a vast Cinemascope screen) and—if closeups are not used judiciously—the effect can sometimes be over-blown, operatic. Yet the best closeups can convey a sense of life seen at startling and revealingly close range. Writes the critic Béla Balázs: "Closeups are often dramatic revelations of what is really happening under the surface of appearances. You may see a medium shot of someone sitting and conducting a conversation with icy calm. The closeup will show trembling fingers nervously fumbling a small object—sign of an internal storm."

Carl Dreyer's film *The Passion of Joan of Arc* follows the events that lead to the burning of Joan of Arc at the stake, but in a manner comprised almost entirely of closeups. We grow slowly, keenly aware of a vast difference between Joan and her persecutors. Her face, even in torment, is touched with a purity and a repose that contrast vividly with the spite and vindictiveness in the globular faces of the bishops and their yes-men. As a result the film affects us with a brutal, almost numbing force, as though we had been present during the actual proceedings. Writes the French critic Moussinac about Dreyer's technique in making the film: "His refusal to use make-up gives the faces a strange and terrible force, allowing them to express internal feelings and thoughts with a singular power. All the fingerprint techniques in the world identify less from the outside than such a facial detail reveals from the interior only by means of a closeup of a mouth, an eye, or a wrinkle."

ANGLE

In the distance between camera and subject, film approximates the psychological effect of our seeing an event from a certain distance or position. The same psychological proximity is true of the angle at which the camera takes in the subject. A low angle—in which we look up at a subject—gives us the sense of being dwarfed, imposed upon by the figure. A high angle enables us to look down at someone or something. Distorted, or "dutch" angle catches the world slightly off balance, as though we were seeing it while reeling at a tilt.

The Cabinet of Dr. Caligari, a bizarre, disorienting German film made in 1919, depicts a world of twisted, angular hallways, misshapen doorways, and buildings that look as though they might have come out of a surrealist painting. To heighten this odd, expressionist effect of the sets, director Robert Wiene used camera angles to further suggest total abnormality: the camera is often tilted, so that figures seem to be walking on a sloping funhouse floor (the uneven sets provide almost no gauge by which we can tell what is level and

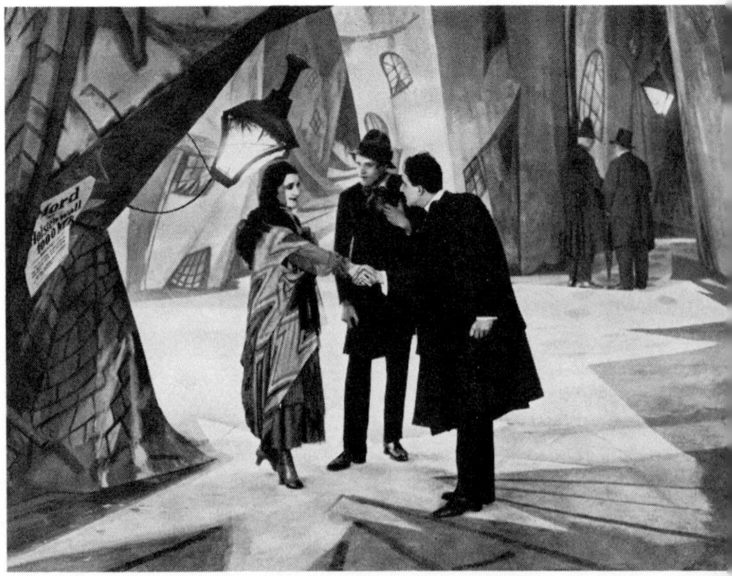

what isn't). The use of angle becomes more than simply a vehicle for conveying the point of view (which we ultimately learn is that of the demented mind of the doctor in charge of an asylum). It recreates the physical world as a virtually different place—again, how we see something can change the very nature of what we see.

Angle can suggest more than point of view. Often a carefully arranged camera angle can align characters and their environment in such a manner that we become conscious of important relationships. In *Dr. Strangelove,* one of the most hilarious and frightening characters is the bomber captain, Major "King" Kong, played with raunchy gusto by Slim Pickens. Major Kong rather *likes* the idea of dropping an H-bomb. Close to the target, he discovers something is wrong with the bomb chutes. Kong goes back to check the bombs and chutes. In a shot that depicts the long, tubular bombs with Major Kong squeezing low between them, director Stanley Kubrick suggests something of Kong's relation to the bombs: he is simply physically and morally and mentally overwhelmed by them.

Orson Welles, one of the masters of angle in film, rarely uses the straight-on angle that typifies most shots in most films. Indeed, all of Welles' films have, almost as a trademark, camera angles set low, giving everything a slightly ominous tinge. Characters interacting never simply seem to be talking with one another—they always seem to be *gathering* on one another, a convening of overbearing presences. *Touch of Evil,* in which Welles plays a desultory sheriff of a dirty Mexican border town, creates the sheriff's character as much by the use of angle as by Welles' prodigious acting. We always see the man from a low angle, often with the camera just slightly tilted, and usually with his bulk filling much of the frame. His presence—outsizing and diminishing every other character in the film—becomes virtually inseparable from Welles' performance. We come to fear and despise and yet—strangely—pity this grotesquery of a man.

LENS

The lens is the eye of the camera, and how it sees depends on which lens is chosen for any specific shot. Essentially there are three types of lenses: wide-angle, regular, and telephoto. The wide-angle lens has the advantage of taking in a wide field; depth is exaggerated, and, with a wide-enough angle lens, actual physical features can become distorted. In *Seconds,* a film about transformed personalities, cinematographer James Wong Howe used an extremely wide-angle lens in several sequences to suggest the spiritual distortion of a man about to be transformed into another personality. Facial features seem to swim across the screen; a room becomes a fluid, dreamlike chamber in which spaces are exaggerated, distorted, unbalanced.

The effects of the telephoto lens (which is capable of telescoping space and showing, say, a closeup of an event forty or fifty feet away) are precisely the opposite of those of the wide-angle lens. Depth within the shot is not exaggerated, it is compacted, creating an effect of things squeezed tightly together. In *Medium Cool,* Haskell Wexler's brilliantly photographed film about a TV news photographer, Wexler uses the telephoto lens often to create a sense of spaces being pressed together. In an empty outdoor amphitheater, a boy races between the rows of seats that seem to crowd into one another in tight lines. Another shot, of stalled traffic on a highway, creates a sense of endless ranks of cars pressed together like bodies in an elevator: examples of how the telephoto lens (used most often for the distance it can overcome) can become an expressive tool for the filmmaker.

The zoom lens isn't a single lens, as are wide-angle or regular or telephoto; but a barrel with a varying focal length, permitting the cameraman to change the lens within a single shot—moving, for example, from wide-angle to regular to telephoto. A zoom shot might begin at a distance, showing, say, a distant building with a beehive of windows. Then, as the camera "zooms in," we see the building looming closer and closer, till the frame is filled with varying windows; then, only a few windows; then only one—the one in which the next shot takes place. A zoom shot looks similar to a moving camera, or dolly shot, in which the camera *itself* moves in on (or away from) a subject, but there is a critical difference. The zoom lens makes no change in perspective whatsoever: we're seeing the subject essentially from the same vantage point, only magnified; a tracking shot changes the perspective at each moment, giving us a distinct sense of movement through real space. It's the difference between looking through a telescope at a mountain and gradually focusing on the top, and the sensation of riding the cable-car up the mountain till you've reached the top.

FOCUS AND DEEP FOCUS

An important way in which the camera and its lens differ from our eyes is the range of focus. Depending on the type of lens, a camera generally can only focus on a given area, and the closer the subject is to the lens, the narrower that area. So that (with the exception of deep focus, to be discussed soon) if several people are standing at varying spaces in a room, the camera can provide sharp focus on only some of them. This limitation of focus makes for an expressive possibility of the camera, forcing the cameraman to choose what should be in focus, and what shouldn't be in focus, and to some extent helping the viewer by separating subjects from one another or from their surroundings.

Citizen Kane marked an important revolution in filmmaking when Orson Welles' cameraman Gregg Toland devised a means for shooting "in depth": shooting so that everything in a wide area was sharply in focus. Previously, with the camera capable of capturing only a limited area, unless the camera moved through the scene there was no way of fully using the spaces for dramatic impact or as a means of clarifying relationships. The actors were "set up" for each shot, and the camera provided the audience with all the necessary information. But with deep focus, actors can move freely within a set and the camera needn't move or cut to enable us to follow them. As the critic André Bazin has argued, deep focus permits a kind of filmmaking that is closer to the real world than previous techniques of changing different shots in cutting; we see things not as the filmmaker obviously (by camera movement or cutting) sets them up to happen, but as they seem to happen normally, within relative spaces.

Perhaps the ultimate benefit of deep focus is that it requires more from the eye: you cannot sit back and have every dramatic inflection thrust at you; you are forced to watch more carefully, to assess distances and relationships and movements. In *The Manchurian Candidate*—a film that uses deep focus shooting with a superb sense of dramatic relationships—the scene in which Raymond Shaw (played by Laurence Harvey) kills his father-in-law is depicted entirely in deep focus shots, in which foreground and background interact significantly. When Raymond Shaw enters the kitchen, we see his gun in the foreground and Senator Jordan, oblivious of its presence, taking a milk carton out of the refrigerator in the background. The shot at once rouses suspense, and intimates what is to come. In a later shot, as the daughter—and Shaw's new wife—comes down the steps, she stands in the foreground while in the background Shaw stands over the Senator's body with the gun dangling from his hand. Again, a complex dramatic situation is laid out in a single shot, her horrified discovery that her husband has just killed her father; our expectant horror that he'll turn (as he does) and kill her.

TRANSITION

Dissolves, fade-ins, fade-outs, and wipes are part of the stagecraft of filmmaking, methods of making transitions in time or place with a certain fluidity and for a specific effect.

The dissolve transforms one image into another, with an overlapping superimposition of the two images for a brief time on the screen. A dissolve gently ends one scene and relates it—by the brief superimposition—to the next, suggesting some continuity between the two. Dissolves are used often in montage sequences, where a sequence of events is presented in an edited format, such as a passage or movement from one place to another: in *I Was a Fugitive from a Chain Gang,* Paul Muni's movement across the country is presented by a series of dissolves showing his feet, maps of various states, and the roadsigns he passes on the way.

Dissolves can be used for other purposes as well. In *Strike,* Eisenstein dissolves from one of the characters to a dog in such a manner that the superimposition draws our attention to some very striking similarities between the man and the dog. Perhaps one of the most artful dissolves in film history takes place at the conclusion of the magnificent diving sequence in *Olympia,* Leni Riefenstahl's documentary on the 1936 Berlin Olympics. The sequence, superbly edited slow-motion footage of divers leaping into space, gradually worked from full dives to the beginnings of dives; and finally all the dives are seen against the panoply of clouds. To end the sequence, Miss Riefenstahl holds the camera on a single diver who spins off into space; then, with the diver sweeping loftily, she dissolves to the same clouds, now without the diver, suggesting that the diver has vanished into the air—or that the diver belonged finally, ultimately, *to* the air.

Fade-out and fade-in are optical devices, like the dissolve, used to end one scene and begin another. But whereas the dissolve suggests some bridging of one scene to the next, the fade-out and fade-in suggest a gap, usually a significant break in time or space.

Wipes are optical devices—generally more obvious than dissolves or fade-ins, used for a variety of purposes. The original "iris wipe"—created by Griffith's cameraman Billy Bitzer and used by him originally to focus on a small action within a scene—darkens the edges of the frame and gradually encircles an increasingly smaller part of the frame; or moves outward from the center with a similar effect. Wipes can sweep along from left to right, or above to below; they can fragment the image; they can enclose an image or blossom out from the center in kaleidoscopic fashion. Most often wipes change one scene directly into another, but they can also darken the frame like a fade-out, preparing us for the next scene. Wipes were a staple feature of the serials of the thirties and forties, where they were sometimes used to bridge virtually every scene—giving the entire episode an extra, if artificial, visual flair.

CAMERA MOVEMENT

Early in *The Manchurian Candidate,* Frank Sinatra, just returned from a stint in the Korean War, falls asleep and has a dream. In the dream he is sitting with his platoon in a room, and the camera slowly moves to reveal a woman speaking; it is some kind of garden club, and the topic is hydrangeas. We know that something dreadful has happened to that platoon in Korea—something to do with brainwashing, but hydrangeas? The camera keeps moving, in a slow encompassing circle, across all the seated, listening ladies, and back to members of the seated platoon: a full 360° arc. Then the voice changes—no longer a woman; now a man, a bald, heavy Chinese; and in the final sweep of the camera we see that he is standing exactly where the lady had stood before, and he is speaking of brainwashing. The subtle notion that in being brainwashed, Sinatra and his buddies had been "programmed" to imagine this ladies' auxiliary meeting (rather than the actual event) is presented with impressive economy and immediacy in this single shot. But the moving camera here does more: it suggests a pure continuity between the one phase or level of Sinatra's dream and the other, a continuity impossible to achieve through editing.

In *Catch 22,* two of the characters are

walking down one of the airfield's runways, talking about something inconsequential like the price of candy bars. Overhead a plane sputters, swoops low, valiantly tries to lift, cannot, and—in full sight of the two men—smashes into the ground and billows into flames. The two men go on walking, talking about the price of candy bars. Everything was shown in a single moving camera shot: the men, the plane, the explosion, their reaction—or the absence of a reaction. Obviously it was a far more costly shot than had the director, Mike Nichols, cut from the men to the sputtering plane, back to the men, to the plane, etc. But that unbroken quality created by the single shot can be far more convincing and dramatically compelling (or in this case outrageously ironic) than the effect you might get from cutting back and forth.

The essence of the moving camera shot is unbroken space. We see things as they are connected and related in real space, and not as the camera picks and chooses them in separate shots. There are basically five types of camera movement: in the first two the camera moves only slightly—it is fixed in space, but moves on an axis: the tilt, in which the camera tilts up or down; and the pan, in which it sweeps across on a horizontal axis. In the latter three the camera *itself* moves through space. In the tracking or dolly shot the camera moves on a track or in a ground vehicle, creating a sense of forward motion in space. Such shots can go from the speed of a racing car—as in the racing sequences from *Grand Prix*—to the slow movement that might be used to suggest somebody walking through a house or yard. The "boom" or "crane" shot gives a camera even more flexibility to move in space. Mounted on a boom or crane, the camera can rise in air, descend, move right or left or forward as the crane moves.

A final type of camera movement—used increasingly in recent years for budgetary reasons and often to give films a documentary flavor—is the hand-held camera, in which the cameraman walks with the camera. With a careful and knowing cameraman like Haskell Wexler in *Medium Cool,* the effect can be vigorous and convincing. With some amateurs, the hand-held camera work is jerky, uneven, and seriously impairs the film.

Panning and tilt shots involve the least amount of real movement for the camera but can be significant nonetheless. In *Duck Soup* there is a pan—used as casually and gratuitously as a throw-away line—in which the camera sweeps along the bottom of a bed. First we see a pair of men's shoes; then a pair of women's shoes; then a pair of horseshoes. When William Powell is comforting lovely young Maureen O'Sullivan in a spare bedroom during a Christmas party, the door opens. Director Willard Van Dyke pans from Myrna Loy—Powell's wife—entering the door, across the room to Powell, who mugs teasingly at his wife.

The tracking shot creates a much more fluid and continuous sense of movement, since the camera is actually plunging forward (or backwards) in real space; as a result, one of the most striking uses of the tracking shot is to reveal, as the camera moves, spaces and depths and relationships that were not evident at the beginning of the shot. Early in the nightclub scene in the "Lullaby of Broadway" sequence of *Gold Diggers of 1935,* the camera holds on two dancers on steps illuminated by a spotlight. Then the camera begins pulling back, revealing slowly, gradually, an enormous expanse of steps; and the sheer overwhelming vastness of the dance floor. In an earlier dance sequence from the same film, "The Words Are in My Heart," a similar shot begins with a single piano, then begins pulling back, revealing another, yet another; and finally—rising on steplike plateaus—fully one hundred pianos.

THE CUT

As graceful and exquisite as the moving camera can be, it only rarely approximates the way in which our eyes see. Generally we don't sweep our head slowly from one side of the room to another; the shifting of attention tends to be more abrupt, like a cut in a film. When Porter and later Griffith discovered the principle—that you can change the focus of attention in a film simply by cutting different pieces of film and gluing them together—they created what would become the syntax of film, the underlying structure by which the pieces could be fit into a final, coherent whole.

The cut both separates and relates two shots: separates them by the simple jump from one shot to the next; connects them because the previous shot and its dramatic momentum linger into the next shot. Sergei Eisenstein, the great Russian director who in both his films and his theoretical writings took editing to extraordinary heights, always claimed that the fundamental principle of film is juxtaposition, one image following another image, creating yet a third, separate effect in the mind of the viewer. In his film, *October,* for instance, he cut from the puppet leader Kerensky to a strutting peacock, intimating that Kerensky is no more *than* a strutting peacock. Such conceptual editing has proven, since Eisenstein, to be problematic for audiences; but there is much to Eisenstein's contention that the interaction of shots within a film is what creates much of the total effect for audiences.

To return to Porter and Griffith, the first use of the cut was to vary the perspective and *size* of the shot, to move from say a long shot, for example, to a medium shot to a closeup, depending on the dramatic emphasis required for each shot. Indeed, by the time he made *The Birth of a Nation,* Griffith had learned that one can create a powerful dramatic rhythm by intercutting between long shots and closeups, a technique which Eisenstein and later directors would develop to even more sophisticated extremes.

The cut can change not only our physical relationship to the subject, but our point of view toward the subject. In *The Wind,* when Lillian Gish looks out the window toward the barren sand heap where she had only a brief while ago buried a man, she sees the man's face partially exposed. The film cuts back to her horrified face. This interaction of seeing her face, then taking her perspective, seeing what she sees, then cutting back to her face, suggests how cutting can create a complex, fluid shifting of the point of view within a very brief segment of a film. In *The Wild Bunch,* when the aging outlaw gang takes over a government train, there is a marvelous brief vignette in which we see a rifle slowly rising above some boxes; gradually a head appears; then a cut to the soldiers, suddenly aware of the presence; then Ernest Borgnine, grinning triumphantly from behind the gun. Again, note the simplicity of the three shots and yet the complex shifting in point of view that they represent: an indication of how much can be done in cutting with a minimum of shots and intercutting. When Laurence Harvey in *The Manchurian Candidate* is taken to a hospital, he is put into a hypnotic trance and watches lethargically as two agents argue over whether he should be sent out to kill someone for a test, and if so, whom. The cutting structurally maintains his point of view, but since we know that he's oblivious of the real meaning of the conversation, that point of view becomes itself ironic; we are doubly amazed at the extremity of the brainwashing, that he can watch this conversation as though it were a Ping-Pong game.

Often the cut itself can convey a theme, or make a transition to a new scene in a distinctive and striking way. In *Citizen Kane,* when boss Gettys has threatened Kane with exposing his mistress before the election, the final shot in the scene hovers at the doorway as Gettys and Kane's wife depart; the camera tilts up, holding on the doorway; a dissolve cuts from the real doorway to a photograph in a newspaper, and backs away, showing the headlines in the paper: "Candidate Kane Caught in Love Nest with 'Singer'." A fluid, and brilliantly economical transition. In *I Am a Fugitive From a Chain Gang,* Paul Muni is in court; the judge is about to announce the verdict and pounds down the gavel; the gavel never hits, but instead the action is completed by a hammer pounding together the chains between Muni's legs. A similar cut takes place in *Pretty Poison.* Tony Perkins' boss, angry at him, slams down his fist—the action is completed by a hamburger being slapped onto a griddle, the next scene in the film.

With a cut, a film can race through time and space, flashing into the future or the past or revealing a state of mind or an image in a character's imagination. Again, in *Pretty Poison,* when Perkins' parole officer makes mention of a misdeed from years ago, the film cuts instantly to a burning house, an indication that Perkins had once been an arsonist. *An Occurrence at Owl Creek Bridge,* a taut, engaging thriller about a man being hanged, is structured largely around flashbacks and flashforwards. When the man stands in the final minutes awaiting the hanging, for example, the film cuts to his wife on a broad plantation lawn, an image from his mind, but as vivid and convincing for us as it is for him.

Some of the terms associated with the cut suggest its basic varied uses within the structure of a film. The cut-in, for example, is used whenever the filmmaker cuts from a larger action to some smaller area within that action to draw our attention to a specific detail. In *Ben Hur,* when the two chariots draw close together and the wheel axles grind into one another, an insert or cut-in shows that smaller but more dramatic action. The cut-away is precisely the opposite: cutting from one field of action to something else, though usually related. In *Hollywood: The Dream Factory* there is a cut-away that can bring tears to your eyes. An excerpt from *The Wizard of Oz* shows Dorothy receiving the brilliant red magical shoes from the Good Witch and the beginning of the dance down the Yellow Brick Road—cut from a closeup of the shoes to a man holding the same shoes at an MGM auction, and announcing: "Sold: $15,000." Often cut-in and cut-away can be combined to increase the dramatic tension. When Walter Pidgeon squints into the viewfinder of a high-powered rifle in *Man Hunt* from a ledge overlooking Hitler's summer home, the film cuts in to a closeup of his finger at the trigger; then cuts away to what he sees through the viewfinder: Hitler, pinned in the crosshairs. That precise combination—a cut-in of his finger on the trigger, a cut-away of the target—creates a moment of tension and ambiguity (when he pulls the trigger, the gun isn't loaded) that will run through the entire movie.

There are other familiar terms related to the cut. Matching action describes a cut which begins in the middle of one action—say, a man opening a door—and concludes, in the next shot, with the completion of that same action—coming into the next room, with the door open exactly as much as it had been at the end of the previous shot. When James Cagney pitches peanuts into a dish in *White Heat,* the cut between Cagney and the dish makes it seem that the peanut were somehow caught in mid-air. The precise opposite of matching action might be the jump cut: a jerky jump from one action to what would seem to be a slightly later part of the same action—as though the film were choppy. The jump cut used to be considered a simple error, created by changing shots without moving the camera far enough away or closer in, but lately it has come into vogue almost as a style—like the handheld camera. In *Take the Money and Run,* Woody Allen spoofs that style in a quaint love scene on the beach. One moment he and the girl are approaching one another—click, the next moment they're in each other's arms.

Intercutting—and more will be said of it in the chapter on editing—is the rhythmic combination of shots within a sequence to create a definite flow; usually with the camera returning to the same subjects at an increasing pace. At the opening of *Grand Prix,* there are several minutes before the race starts when director John Frankenheimer intercuts the drivers, the cars, the spectators, the managers and officials, in a growing momentum that puts increasing emphasis on closeups. Then, suddenly, the beginning of the race.

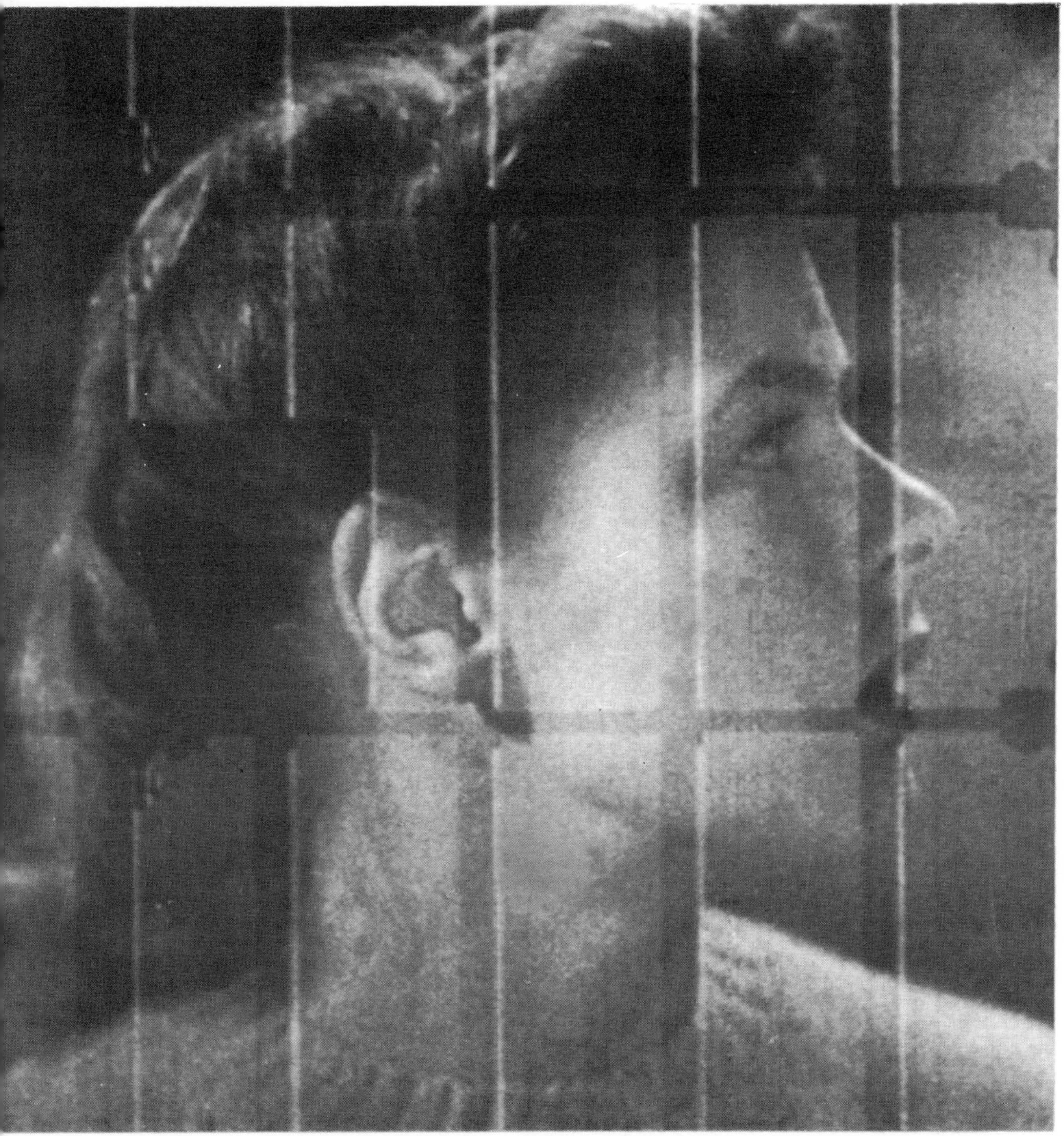

OTHER TERMS

When a film has been shot, the soundtrack prepared, there is still an optical "finish" required: the addition, for example, of titles, dissolves, fades, and similar optical transitions.

Titles are perhaps the most familiar of all optical devices: during the silent era, they were used for dialogue and explanations of the story—sometimes even commentary; today, they are used only rarely, perhaps as an indication of a lapse in time or a change of place. Subtitles, which appear at the bottom of the picture, are used most often for translating films in a foreign language—considered by many to be preferable to dubbing, in which the voices of other actors are used against different lip motions of the original actors.

Superimposition is an optical technique used to lay one picture over another: often in a montage the images will be superimposed to create a sense of burgeoning activity, of things happening all at once; in *The Magnificent Ambersons,* Orson Welles used superimposition several times to create a pastiche of characters seen against the town. In *The Crowd,* director King Vidor experimented with superimposition to suggest what was happening in the mind of his central character by superimposing at first the numbers (that the character, an accountant, is working with) then, daydreams of his children, over the man's forehead. Such uses of superimposition tend to be a bit corny and aren't used so much as full superimpositions of one full-frame image over another, as in Hitchcock's *Spellbound,* when Ingrid Bergman—anticipating prison for the man she loves—is seen against a superimposition of jail bars.

The terms of filmmaking can help one recognize and assess various techniques, but it would be a mistake to look at a film just to be able to spot and call out, "Closeup!" "Dissolve"—for in any but the most appalling films, the story, characters, and theme will transcend technique, indeed, in all but a few cases render it invisible.

The Shot

The shot is the basic unit of film: it begins when the camera switches on, ends when the camera switches off. Within a single shot the camera can move in any direction, can alter its perspective, its angle, its lens.

The most frequently used terms referring to shots relate to the *distance* in a shot: long, medium, closeup—how far the camera is from the subject. Different distances create different effects: in a long shot, we see a figure or group in large perspective; in an extreme closeup, the tightening of a cheek muscle can convey powerful dramatic suggestion.

An establishing shot introduces a scene, usually by showing us the place in long shot, as in the military intelligence room in *The Manchurian Candidate.*

One-shot, two-shot, and three-shot refer simply to the number of people in the shot.

ESTABLISHING SHOT

The Manchurian Candidate

ONE-SHOT

TWO-SHOT

THREE-SHOT

All the King's Men

LONG SHOT

MEDIUM SHOT

MEDIUM CLOSEUP

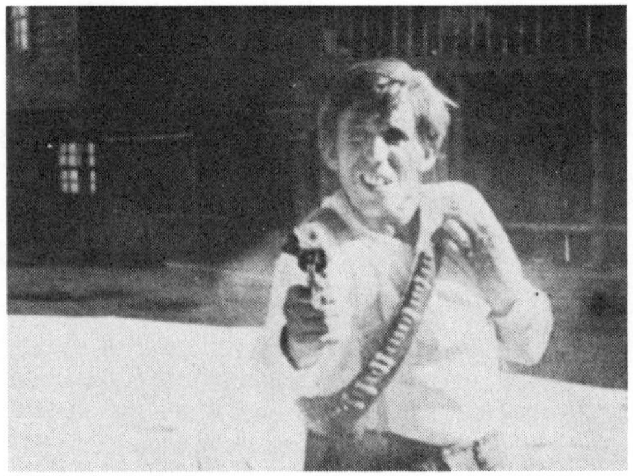

CLOSEUP

For a Few Dollars More

The Closeup

The closeup gives film much of its uniqueness, its power, and its expressiveness. On a stage an actor's face can be seen only at a distance: he must depend on gestures, or exaggerated facial expression. The closeup changes that: the slightest nuance of expression in an actor's face—a hint of a smile, a tautening of the lips—is magnified by the closeup, and can become immensely significant. In *Seconds,* Arthur Hamilton, whose identity will soon be changed by a bizarre organization, falls asleep and has a dream that anticipates what will happen. The closeups—combined with distorting lenses—give the scene a sense of vigor and immediacy. In *Greed,* director Erich von Stroheim used growing closeups of McTeague the dentist as he bends over the anaesthetized Trina in the dentist chair to kiss her. Frank Sinatra's reaction when he sees Henry Silva at an army buddy's apartment is going to be violent; the tight, cropped closeup of Sinatra's face tells us as much (from *The Manchurian Candidate).*

"Our 'closeups,' or 'inserts,' as I call them, are sometimes cumbersome and disconcerting. I invented them, but I have tried not to overuse them, as many have done. It is a mechanical trick, and is of little credit to anyone."
—D. W. Griffith

EXTREME CLOSEUP

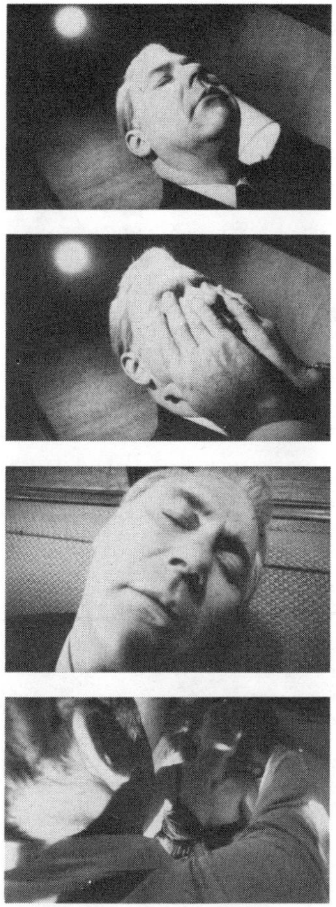

Seconds

Greed

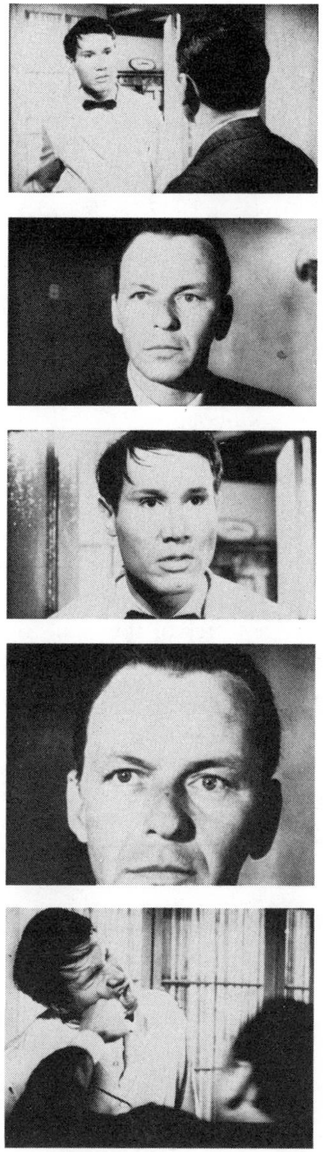

The Manchurian Candidate

Angle

Angle is the direction of camera placement: the way in which figures appear on the screen. If the camera has been placed low, the figures will seem to tower on the screen. Indeed, much of the way we feel toward the characters or toward a situation can be created by camera placement. In the "Lullaby of Broadway" sequence from *Gold Diggers of 1935,* almost every shot is taken at a slightly distorted angle; we get the feeling of a world slightly at a tilt, of things not quite what they seem to be. This angular distortion (combined with other techniques, like a blurred screen and dizzying transitions) gives the entire "Lullaby of Broadway" sequence a tone of perversity—as though the marvelous night life depicted in the sequence were really a kind of dark ritual.

Angle can heighten a mood, clarify and intensify a point of view, suggest dramatic relationships or provide fresh perspectives. In *Youngblood Hawke,* the low angle that takes in James Franciscus against the skyscraper tends to transfer much of the imposing strength and solidity of the building to Franciscus, further sharpening the effect.

LOW ANGLE

In low angle a figure is seen as if from below; the effect is often one of a towering presence, a sense of hulking, overriding power—often associated with a sense of threat. In this low-angle shot from Fritz Lang's *M,* a shorter man is being interrogated by a taller man: Lang uses the camera to evoke the shorter man's sense of being overwhelmed.

HIGH ANGLE

High angle looks down on the subject, reversing the psychological effect of low angle. Again from *M,* the smaller man being interrogated: only now as he is seen by the larger man.

DISTORTED ANGLE

Distorted or "dutch" angle conveys a sense of the world being slightly tilted, off balance. In *The Manchurian Candidate,* Frank Sinatra learns that his army buddy has killed his wife and her father. It was something he could have prevented, and the news makes him nauseous. His feeling is conveyed by the distorted angle as he enters the apartment.

Point of View

North by Northwest: an ominous tinge to the high-angle shot.

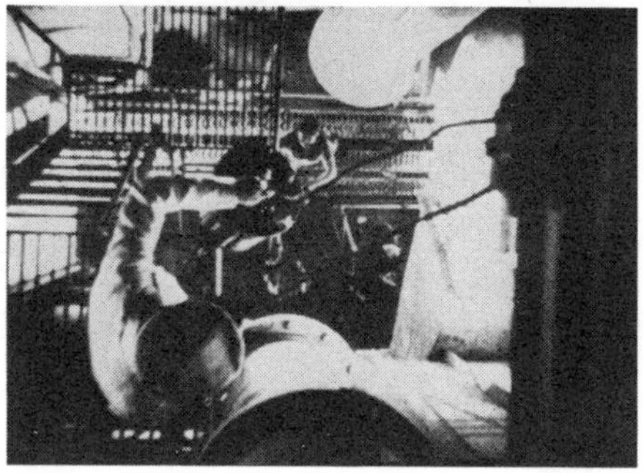

Dante's Inferno: the ship captain as seen from below, while he descends; and looking down.

Greed: Mac bites Trina's fingers—his point of view; hers.

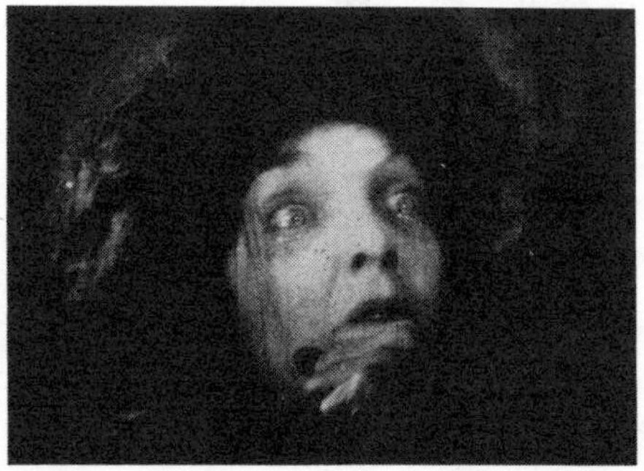

State of Mind

"Lullaby of Broadway" sequence of *Gold Diggers of 1935:* note how even commonplace things like a pencil sharpener become strange, slightly unreal.

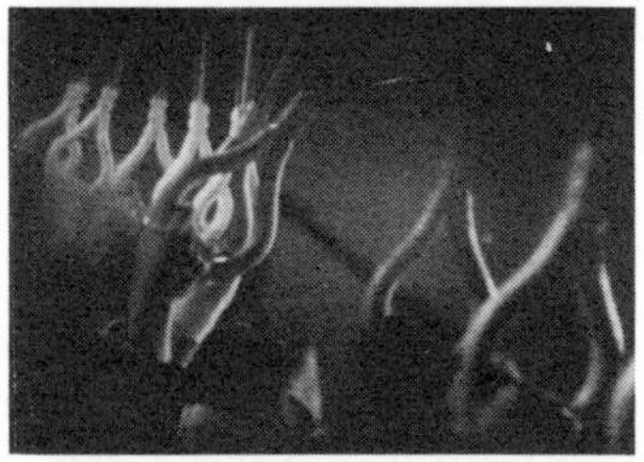

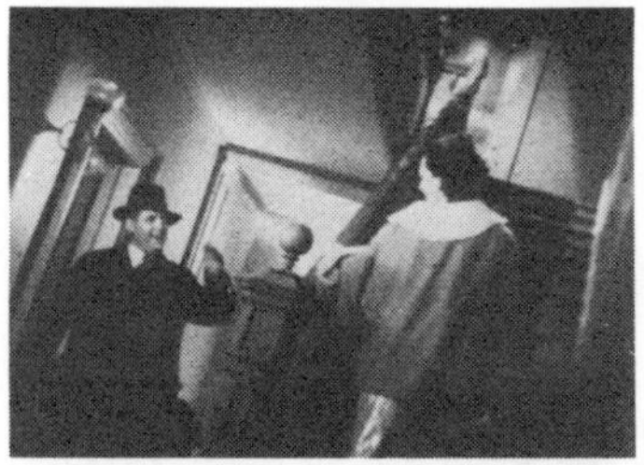

Dramatic Effect Through Angle

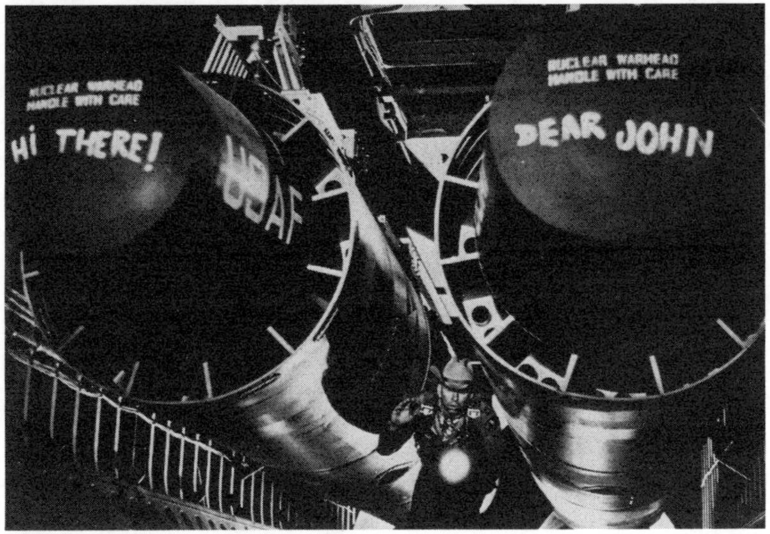

RELATIONSHIP

In *Dr. Strangelove,* Stanley Kubrick's bleak, perverse comedy of nuclear mishap, the bomber captain (played by Slim Pickens) goes back to check out the two H-bombs: the angle conveys their immensity, dwarfing him. He'll soon be riding one of them down as though it were an airborne bronco.

PERSPECTIVE

In *White Heat* James Cagney is a prisoner, working in the machine shop, where another prisoner is preparing to kill him. We watch as an overhead hoist rolls to a point above Cagney's head. The angle conveys their relationship, anticipates the "accident."

DRAMATIC INTENSITY

Orson Welles' *Touch of Evil* centers on a seedy border-town sheriff, played by Welles, whose figure seems always hulking, immense, imperturbable, like some vast heap of clay. The camera angle by which we often see Welles adds to this effect: not only set low, as in this shot, but at such an angle as to emphasize his girth and sheer density.

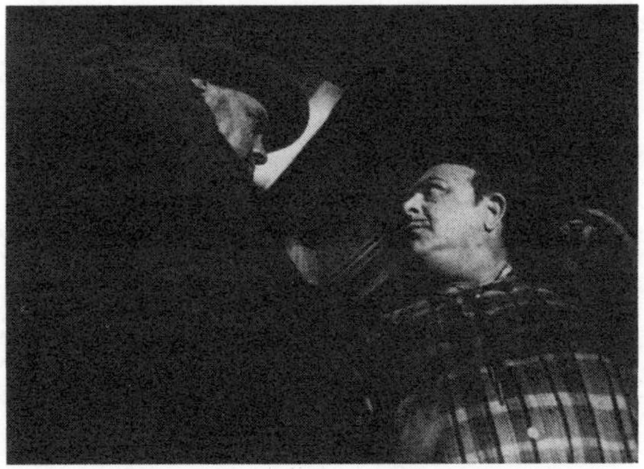

SYMPATHY THROUGH ANGLE

Johnny Belinda, the court scene: note how the camera presents prosecutor, judge, jury: all from an angle that heightens their might; and Belinda, the deaf girl on trial, is seen as dwarfed and vulnerable, trapped in the witness box.

The Lens

WIDE-ANGLE

Two uses of the wide-angle lens: from *Seconds,* in which the face becomes distorted by the severely angular emphasis of the lens; and *Spellbound,* the dream sequence.

ZOOM

The choice of a lens can provide a specific visual effect on the screen. Essentially there are three types of lens, or sizes of lens:

wide-angle, which takes in a wide perspective and exaggerates distances;

normal, which recreates space much as the human eye sees it; and

telephoto, which compresses spaces, creating a tight, squeezed effect.

The *zoom lens* combines all three, and is capable of "zooming" in or out, moving from close to distant as in these frames from *An Occurrence at Owl Creek Bridge.*

In *The Crowd,* director King Vidor used the wide-angle lens to accentuate a powerful scene in which a child forces his way up the stairs of his apartment building to learn that his father is ill. Note how the tiny figure is dwarfed by the blank, exaggerated spaces of the hallway, and how only gradually he separates himself from the crowd below. Film critic Rudolf Arnheim says of this scene: "Nothing is more commonplace than that a staircase gets larger with decreasing distance; but the trite fact, used in this manner, results in a deep, compelling symbolism such as is found in good folk songs."

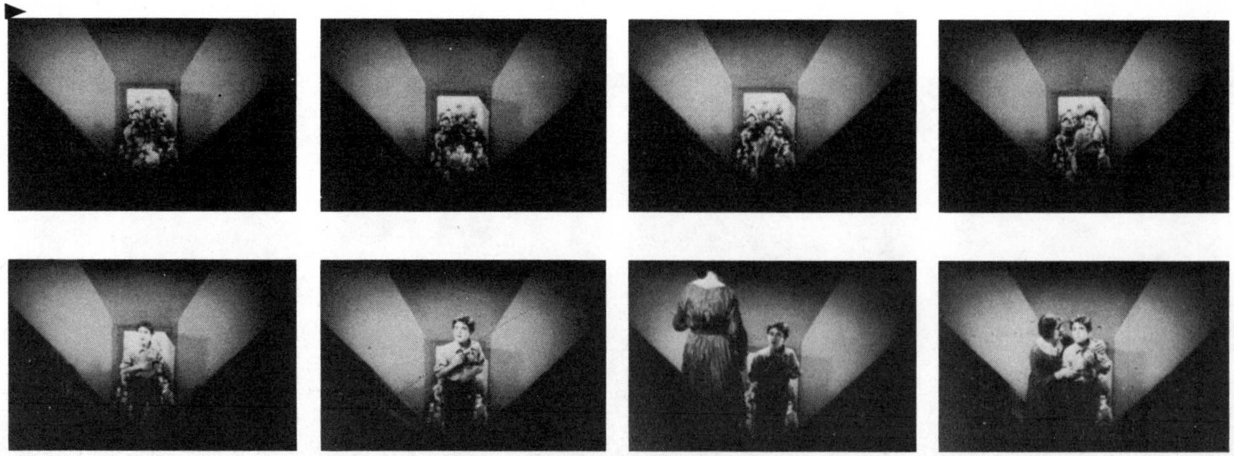

Yul Brynner in *The Madwoman of Chaillot,* an extreme wide-angle shot.

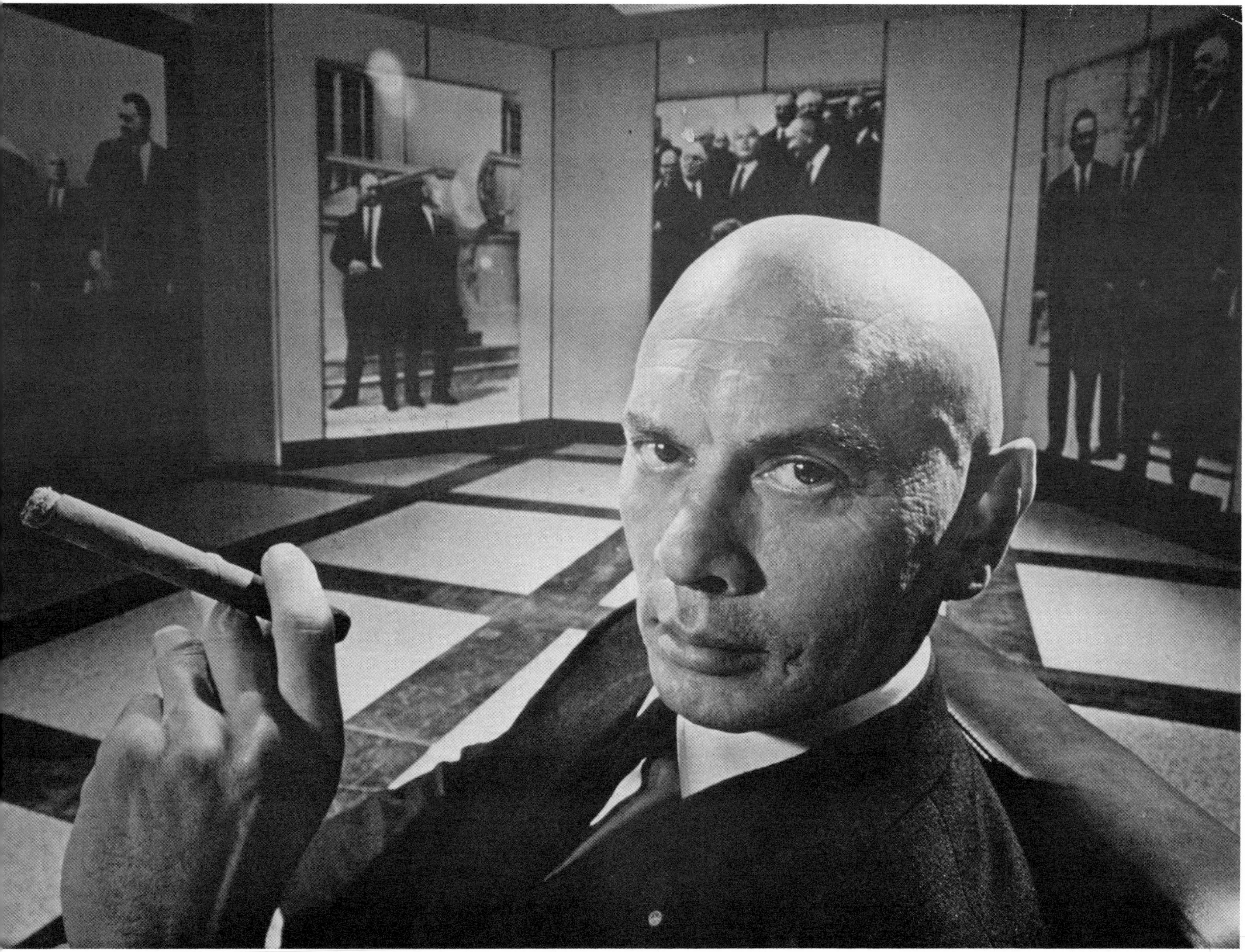

Focus

The manner of focus itself—how sharply we see the image—can become an important element in filmmaking. Normal focus presents images with the clarity of form our eyes see. Soft focus, used quite often in silent and early sound films, presents a "softened" image—the features not so sharp. The effect is of seeing something through a slight glaze.

I Am a Fugitive From a Chain Gang.

NORMAL FOCUS

SOFT FOCUS

RACK FOCUS

▼

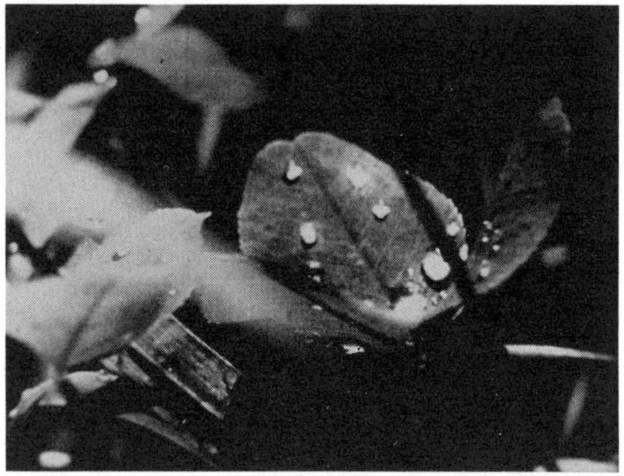

Rack focus is a movement of the lens, in which the focus changes from one area to another. In these frames from *An Occurrence at Owl Creek Bridge,* you can see how the focus on the leaf changes to a focus on a blade of grass.

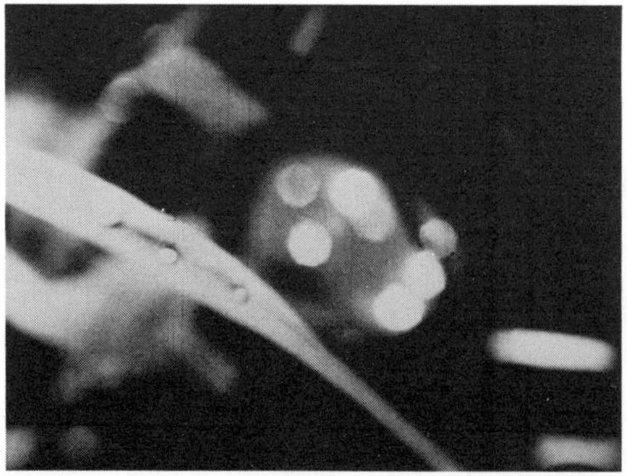

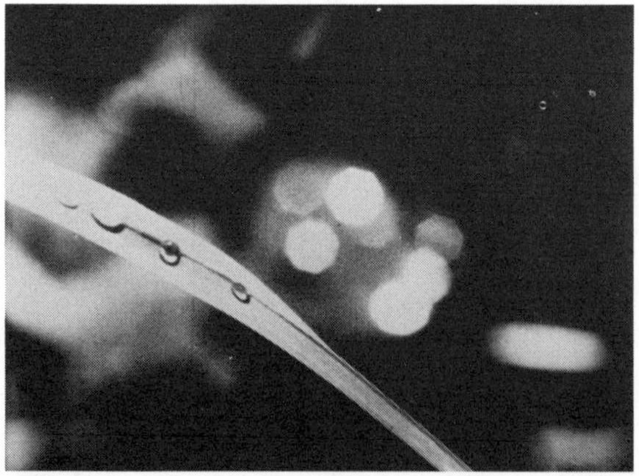

Deep Focus

"The more I learn about my trade the more I incline to direction in depth relative to the screen. The better it works, the less I use the kind of set-up that shows two actors facing the camera, like two well-behaved subjects posing for a still portrait." —Jean Renoir

WHEN FOREGROUND
EXPLAINS BACKGROUND

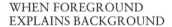

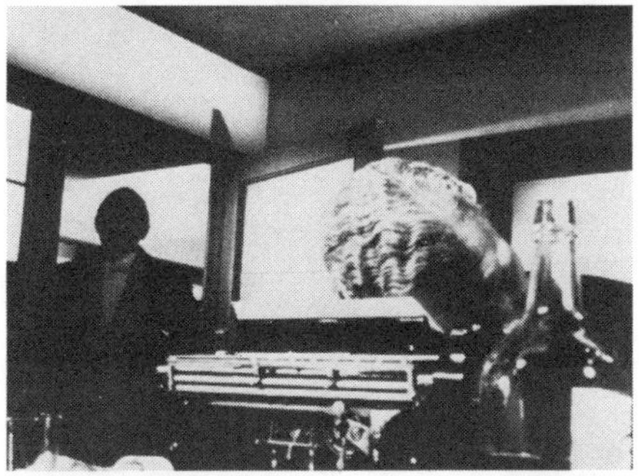

Three images with a similar theme: the upper two from *Citizen Kane*, the lowest from *Dr. Glas*. In the best composed of deep-focus shots, a dramatic relationship is created between foreground and background, and the space within the screen is charged with a dynamic tension.

►

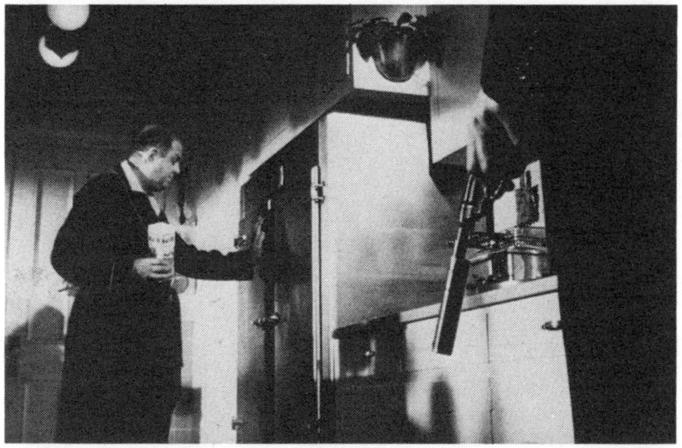

In the sequence where Raymond Shaw kills Senator Jordan, his father-in-law in *The Manchurian Candidate*, director John Frankenheimer uses depth within the shots to give the scene an added dramatic quality. Note, in the final two frames, how the foreground images—the gun, Shaw's wife—transform the significance of the background images.

Transition

Dissolves, fades and wipes are the most common means of making the transition from one scene to another in a film while at the same time suggesting something about that transition.

The *dissolve* superimposes the fresh image over the old one, creating, for a moment, a sense of continuity between the old and the new, often (as with the dissolve from *Strike*) creating a graphic effect with the superimposition.

The *fade-in* and *fade-out* suggest a lapse of time or a shift in the story: in a fade-out, the screen darkens; in a fade-in it goes from darkness to an image. The *blur-in* and *blur-out* are like fades, in that the screen image hazes in or out; usually blurring effects are used (as here) to suggest a point of view.

Wipes come in a variety of types, though the most common is the iris wipe, in which a circle widens or narrows to encompass the screen. The iris wipe, like the other techniques, were originally done in cameras; now are added to the film later by optical processing.

DISSOLVE

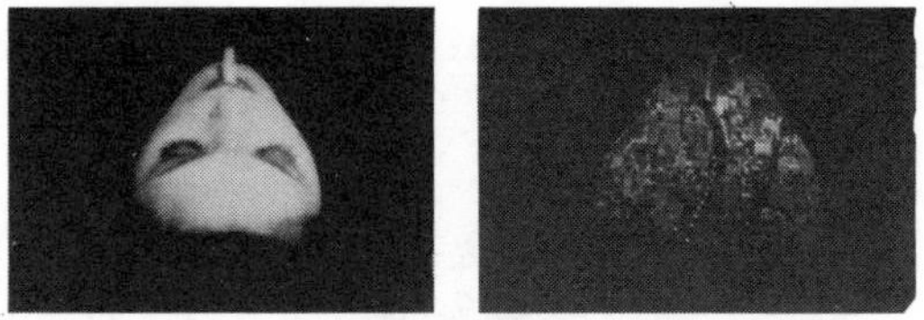

The famous dissolve that opens Busby Berkeley's "Lullaby of Broadway" sequence in *Gold Diggers of 1935*.

In *Johnny Belinda,* the dissolve becomes a way of showing the medical examination of the girl Belinda in shorthand.

In *Strike,* Eisenstein comments on the man by this dissolve to the dog: which looks more like a dog?

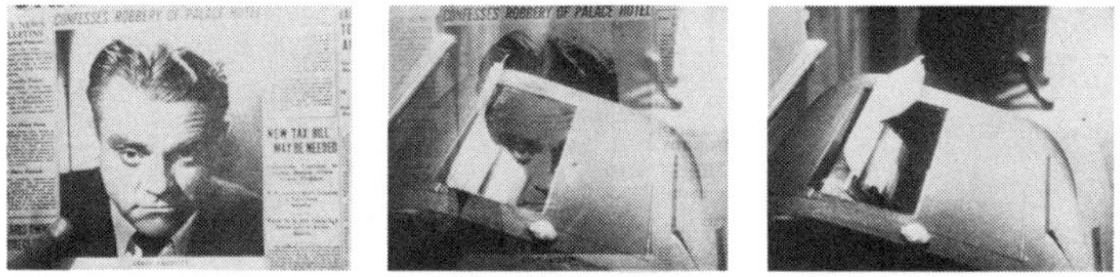

A dissolve from *White Heat:* the newspaper account to a teletype machine.

From the titles of *I Am a Fugitive from a Chain Gang:* look carefully.

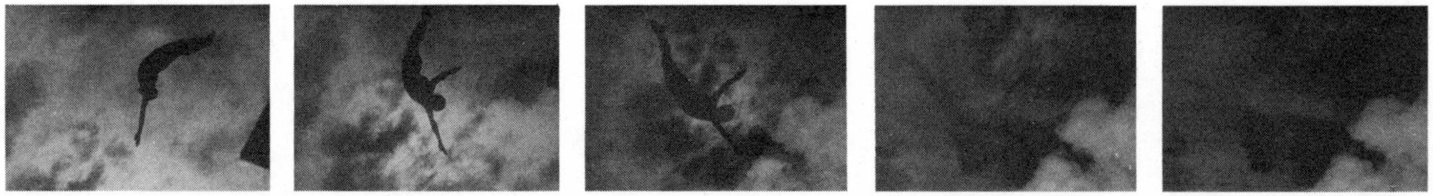

The magnificent diving sequence in *Olympia* concludes in a dissolve of a diver into the sky—an intimation that the divers may belong as much to the gods as to us.

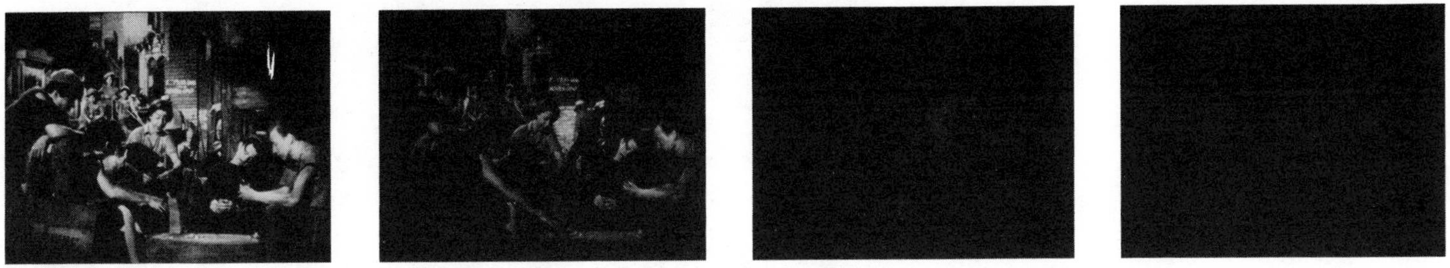

FADE-OUT

FADE-IN

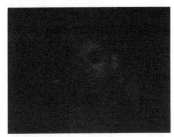

Dead End: fading out on the gang, fading back in on the face of the sympathetic gang member.

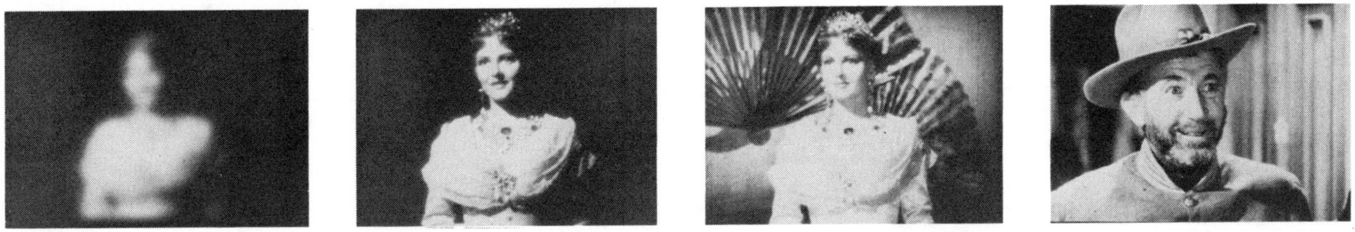

BLUR-IN

Walter Brennan seeing the woman over whom he'd fantasized for a lifetime: from *The Westerner.*

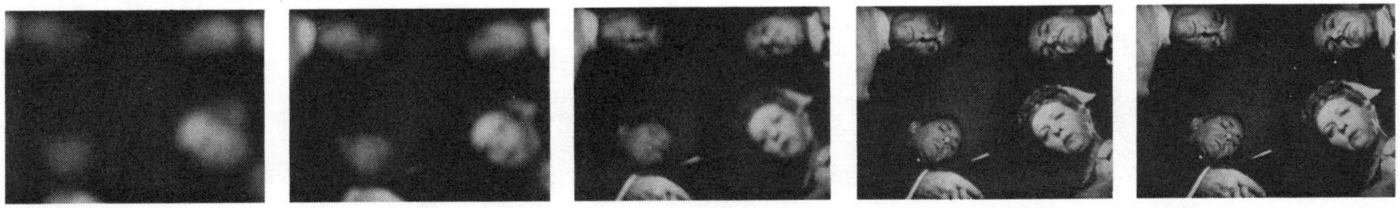

Dead Reckoning: Bogart's point of view as he becomes conscious, amid doctors, nurse and priest.

Camera Movement

"The moving camera is especially useful when the scene of action is not an immobile setting, in which the actors come and go, but the actors are, as it were, the constant setting while the surroundings vary."—Rudolf Arnheim

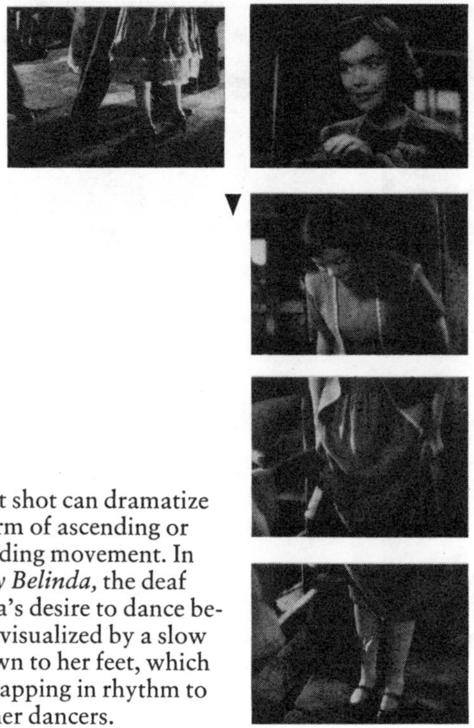

TILT

The tilt shot can dramatize any form of ascending or descending movement. In *Johnny Belinda,* the deaf Belinda's desire to dance becomes visualized by a slow tilt down to her feet, which begin tapping in rhythm to the other dancers.

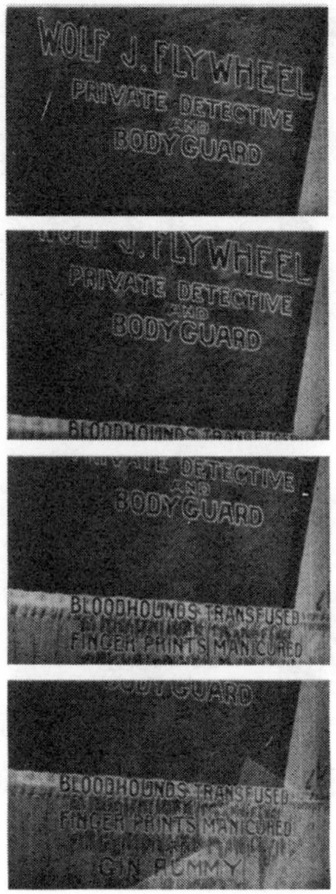

The Big Store: Groucho's office; the camera moves down the door.

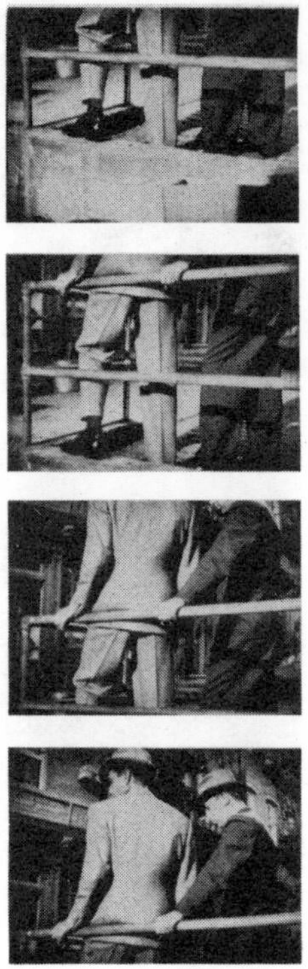

A tilt shot: our first introduction to Bogart, the gangster come home, in *Dead End.*

PAN

Duck Soup: camera moves left to right.

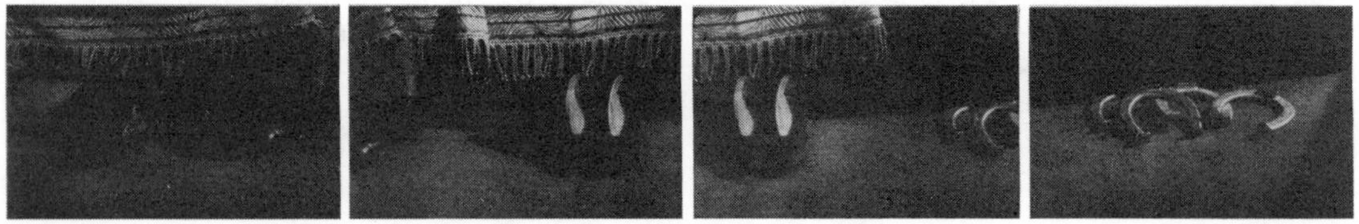

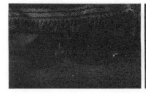

In *The Thin Man,* William Powell is comforting a young lady when his wife enters—a panning shot tells us the rest.

THE WIPE

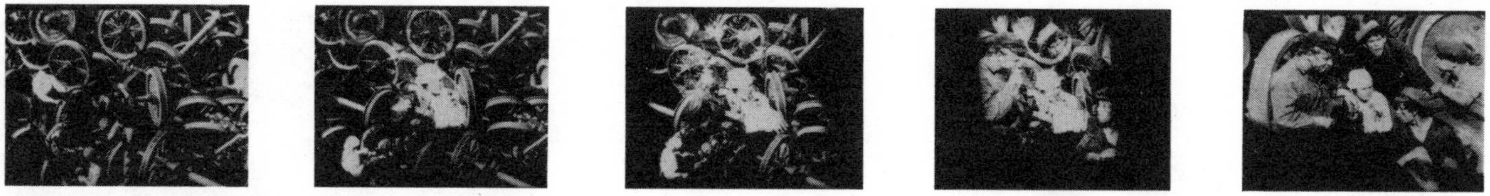

Strike: note that Eisenstein is combining a wipe with a dissolve.

A wipe that segments the spaces within the frame: from *Hollywood: The Dream Factory*.

An iris wipe that moves out from screen center: from *Hollywood: The Dream Factory*.

A vertical wipe from *Greed:* but one that opens as the streetcar moves.

An iris wipe from *Greed*. Note how it closes in, concentrating our focus on the accordion.

Crane/Track/Dolly

Shots in which the *camera itself* moves through space are referred to variably as tracking or dolly or crane shots, depending on the type of vehicle used; everything from helicopters to wheelchairs can be used to give the moving camera a fluidity in space.

In *The African Queen,* Bogart and Katharine Hepburn get stuck in the low swamp waters while attempting to reach a lake. Director John Huston uses a high, craning shot to pull away from the exhausted pair in the boat and to let the audience "discover" how close to their goal they lie. The arrangements of the frames here attempt to convey the short distance from boat to lake (far left) and the leisurely pace of the camera (left) as it moves to the lake.

A famous shot from King Vidor's *The Crowd,* in which the camera rises up the face of a building, then subtly cuts inside: note the similarity of forms in the shots.

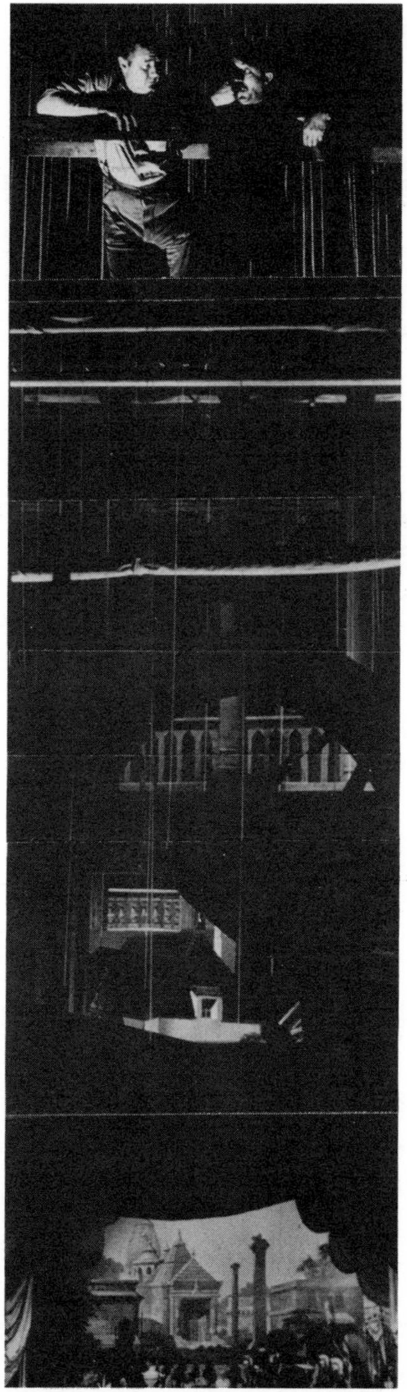

The boom shot is a vertical movement of the camera up or down in space on a crane or "boom." Perhaps the most famous boom shot in film history in this one from *Citizen Kane* in which Kane's wife Susan makes her disastrous opera debut. A booing audience of thousands could never have conveyed the wit or pungency of this single upward shot to the stagehands, one of whom is "commenting" on the performance by holding his nose. Ironically, this isn't a true boom shot but a fake: the interim ropes and stage deckings are miniatures, optically fixed to mix with the real scenes at the beginning and end of the shot.

TRACKING SHOT VS. ZOOM

In a tracking shot, perspective is always changing. You have the sense of being in a different place at each moment. A zoom lens makes no change in perspective. It only telescopes a distant object and makes it seem closer or more distant. Examples of each, from *An Occurrence at Owl Creek Bridge*.

Through Fluid Space

CAMERA MOVEMENT VS. EDITING

In Sinatra's dream early in *The Manchurian Candidate,* he and his platoon are present at a ladies' auxiliary meeting. The camera tracks round the meeting, and eventually holds on a Chinese doctor who is lecturing. Again, the platoon is present, but the setting has changed, and, obviously, the meaning. What has *actually* happened is that Sinatra's mind has pierced a level of brainwashing—he was "programmed" to imagine the ladies' club; instead, he remembers what really happened. The fluid, almost 360° camera movement in this shot creates a sense of continuity between the two settings with far greater force than the later editing (below) of separate audiences and settings juxtaposed does.

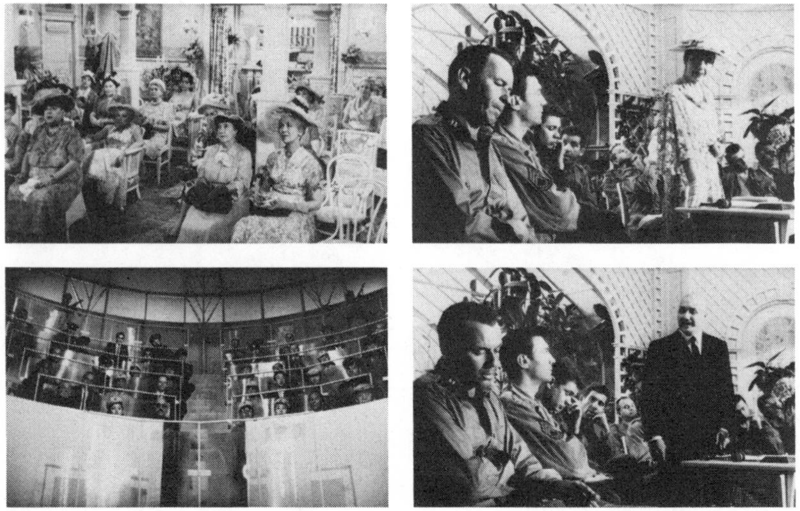

Camera movement can create a vital sense of continuity: our impressions of something's size, or a relationship, or an ironic undercurrent tend to be much stronger if created within a single shot. The elaborate scale of this dinner table in *Wild Orchids* (1929), a Garbo silent film, becomes doubly impressive in the long, backtracking shot that seems to pull away endlessly.

"The camera can advance and retreat and encircle with or against the action it encounters. It can produce a fluid composition, related to the sum of all its shifting images and make every movement part of the entire conception."—Joseph von Sternberg

A tracking shot from *Psycho* that reveals and relates two objects: an envelope filled with money and a prepared suitcase; the camera's movement (right to left) is enough to inform us of Marion Crane's intentions.

At the close of the shower killing sequence in *Psycho*, Hitchcock focuses on the drain as bloody water runs into it. A subtle dissolve transforms the drain into the open eye of the dead Marion Crane; then slowly, Hitchcock draws the camera back to reveal her face, stiff, lying flat on the bathroom floor. The transition, combined with the camera movement, intensifies our awareness of her death.

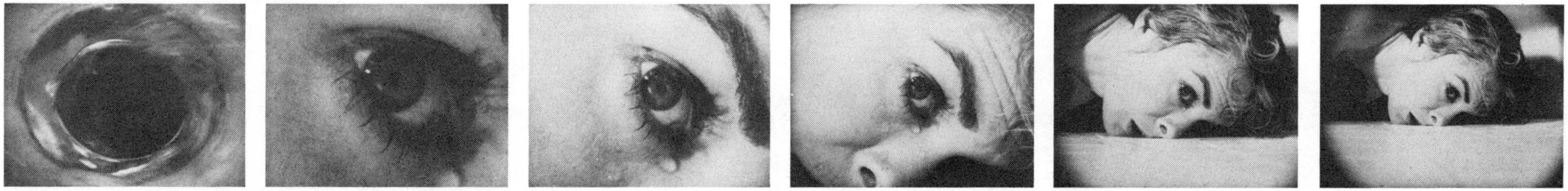

Purposes of the Cut

CHANGING THE SHOT FOR DRAMATIC EMPHASIS

The Westerner: Gary Cooper and Walter Brennan. The two shots provide two separate perspectives.

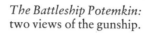

The Battleship Potemkin: two views of the gunship.

INTERACTION AND REACTION

In *The Wind,* the sands shift.

Ernest Borgnine in *The Wild Bunch.*

The Manchurian Candidate.

VISUAL CONTINUITY

Citizen Kane: tilting up, the transition. ▲

A cut breaks our attention from one shot, drawing it to another. Early in *Johnny Belinda,* we are introduced to the village men in a slow panning shot. To establish the man who will later be the rapist, the director cuts, thus separating him in our mind from the other villagers.

POINT OF VIEW

Tomorrow, two points of view, emphasizing the man's.

THEMATIC CUTTING

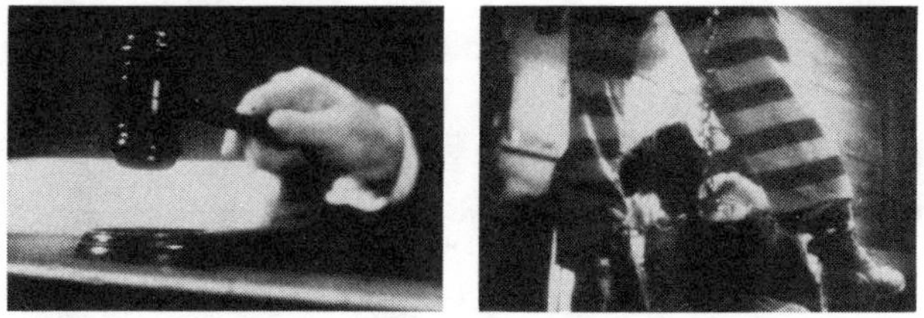

In *I Am a Fugitive from a Chain Gang,* the judge bangs his gavel down, it becomes a hammer.

THE FLASHBACK

As he waits for hanging, the prisoner in *An Occurrence at Owl Creek Bridge* recalls his wife.

Pretty Poison: a remark by his parole officer stimulates this memory of Tony Perkins'.

The Cut: Terms

CUT-IN

A cut-in changes the shot from a larger area to some critical smaller field in the same scene, as in this cut-in from the original (1926) *Ben-Hur*.

CUT-AWAY

The cut-away goes *from* one scene to another: Dorothy and her shoes in *Oz,* a cut to the same shoes being auctioned—*Hollywood: The Dream Factory*.

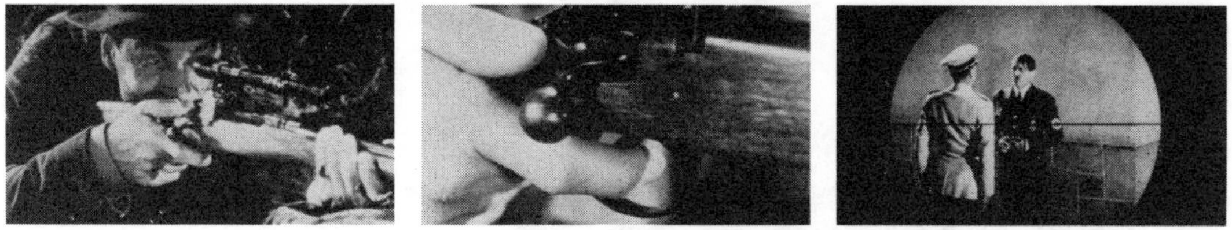

CUT-IN AND CUT-AWAY

Man Hunt, Walter Pidgeon focuses on his quarry—with an unloaded gun.

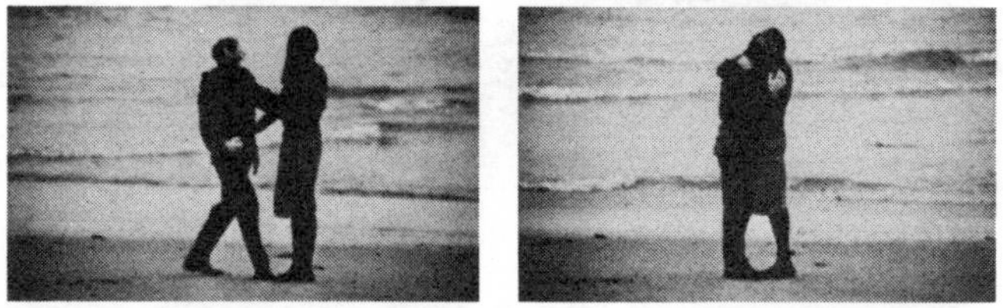

JUMP CUT

Take the Money and Run, the saga of a nebbish gangster: a jump cut looks as though the film were slightly chopped, missing part of the movement; once considered a gaffe, now popular.

INTERCUTTING

Grand Prix: a shifting of focus from one action to another.

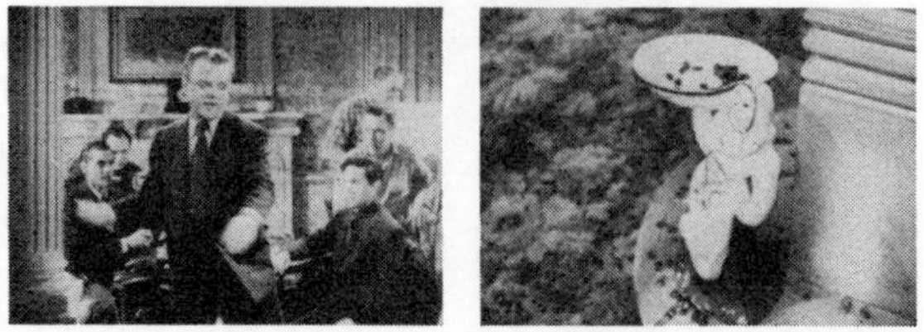

MATCHING ACTION

Cagney tossing peanuts into a dish in *White Heat:* matching action means that an action begun in one shot is continued fluidly in the next.

Other Terms:

TITLES

Titles—used as gags in *Start the Revolution Without Me.*

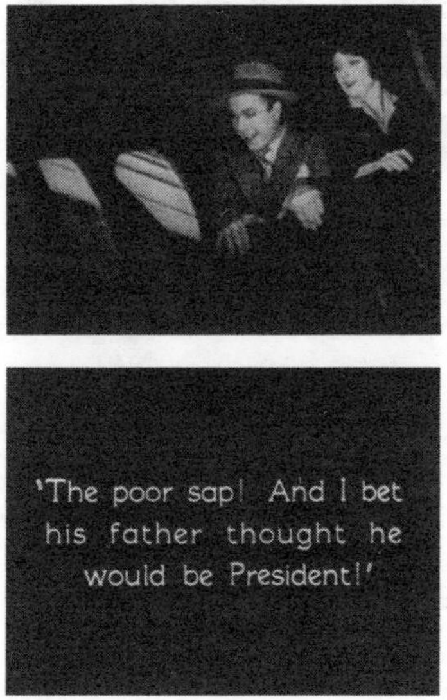

Titles were used in silent films for dialogue: from *The Crowd.*

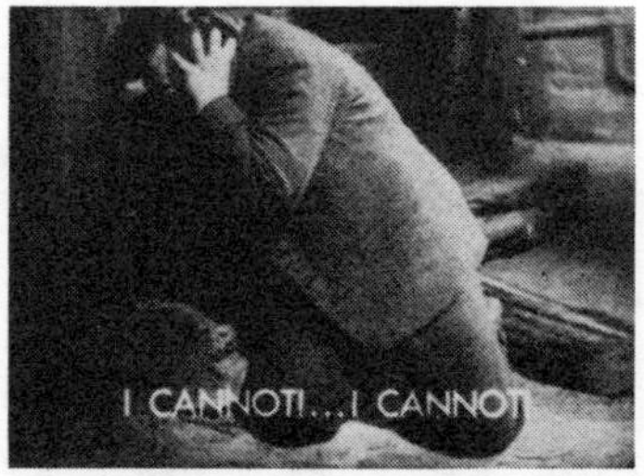

Subtitles—used often for translating dialogue: from *M.*

SPLIT SCREEN

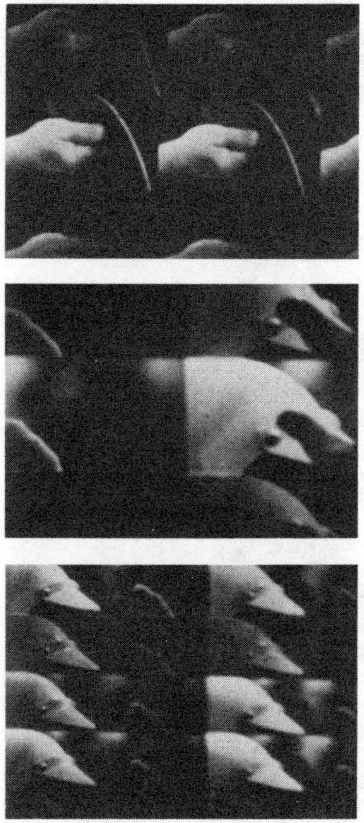

Optical processes can repeat an image, or set one against another: from *Grand Prix.*

SUPERIMPOSITION

In *The Crowd,* director King Vidor superimposes images of numbers, an automobile, a little girl over the head of the man at the office to suggest the tension between his work and his daydreaming.

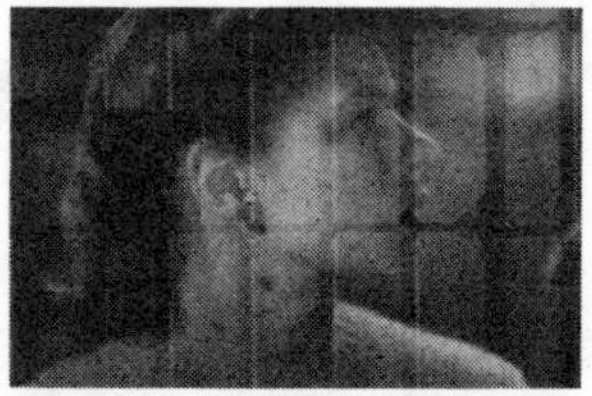

Hitchcock's *Spellbound:* Ingrid Bergman and a sense of imprisonment.

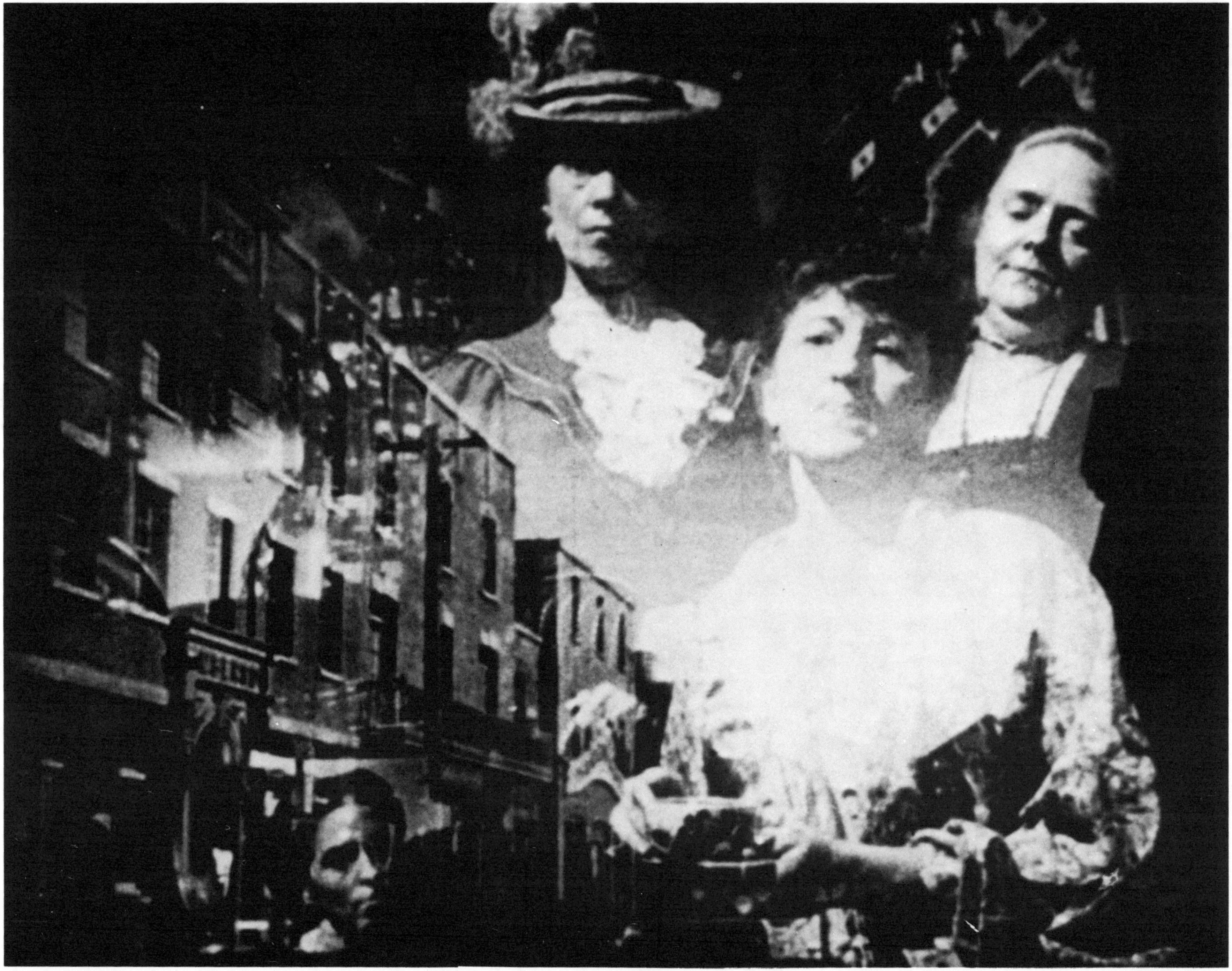

Superimposition lays one image over another: from Orson Welles' *The Magnificent Ambersons*.

CHAPTER FOUR

The Image

The Image

"Film," said the French director Jean-Luc Godard, "is reality at twenty-four frames a second." The image we see on the screen can reflect an outrageous fantasy; it can record an actual event or conversation; it can fix on a single immobile figure, inviting our bewilderment or apprehension or boredom; but at any given moment that image is the dominant reality of the film, and by the quality of its images we may assume much about the overall quality of a film.

The image in a film—even if it is not moving—is never fully static: always it draws from the momentum of what has gone before, and from our expectations for what is to come. Indeed, the central difference between an image from a film and a photograph—no matter how superbly composed, organized, lit, and arranged each one may be—is that in film the image always belongs to a larger, progressing whole; it may be exquisitely beautiful of its own right, but it doesn't exist of its own right—it belongs to what has preceded it and to what will follow, much as the stroke of a painting belongs to the figures it serves to create.

Yet the filmmaker has at his command all the techniques and possibilities available to the still photographer in creating each image. He, like the photographer, creates forms and spaces and relationships with light; he is capable of evoking textures, colors, moods from a setting; if he is good enough, he can transform a mundane situation into a landscape of feeling by the softest touches of arrangement, composition, lighting, and camera placement.

COMPOSITION

As Rudolf Arnheim has shown in his studies of visual thinking, even the most primitive drawings of children reveal a complex and satisfying sense of composition. A child's drawing of his family at a table might include the table, both parents, and in the middle the child, all elements balanced harmoniously, and the relationships—with the horizontal frame of the table dominating the drawing and the parents providing the strong vertical upthrust—made vividly clear. Composition is perhaps more a spontaneous visual intuition than anything that can be explained or scientifically analyzed.

Composition is primarily balance: an ability to structure the elements within the frame so they form a coherent, satisfying whole. Most often a well-composed image requires within itself some tension between graphic elements. A naked seascape—spread, horizontal shore—is not as visually interesting as a seascape with a single vertical figure in the foreground, perhaps to the side of the frame. The superb outdoor photography in John Ford's Westerns often owe much to Monument Valley, where high, stolid mesas jut upwards, breaking the desultory horizontal emphasis of the desert.

In *Tomorrow*, a black-and-white film based on a Faulkner short story, the shots are as softly and deliberately and carefully arranged and presented as though the film had been made by a superb still photographer: the film is steeped in the classic qualities of composition. Much of the story takes place in and around a backwoods Mississippi cabin, and the cinematographer shoots with such a sensitivity to naturally lit textures that by the simple qualities of lighting on the scoured wood and the parched trees you are always conscious of the time and the mood of the day. Much of the film is composed in depth, requiring little cutting, but providing within each scene a totally natural and yet fully visually realized tableau of relationships and events. The camera itself rarely forces its presence into the world of the characters: things are often seen at a slight distance, with a side of a cabin, a pile of logs, a skein of trees offsetting and balancing the characters—we are kept conscious, at every moment in *Tomorrow*, of the world these people inhabit and from which they have sprung. In *Tomorrow* these qualities of composition don't exist for their own sake; they are intimately, profoundly part of the story, the texture and quality of the film.

Indeed, each film—by its structure, its story, its setting, and factors such as whether it is in black and white or color, and screen size—creates its own requirements for composition. Ingmar Bergman's morose, brooding style that captures a chilling world of bleak settings and wintry textures would be a laughable anomaly if used for a musical. Composition is ultimately evocative; it creates an emotional bond between the audience and the inner world of a film—and the way in which this is done will vary necessarily from film to film.

Consider a visual motif: the isolated human being—and how a variety of films convey this isolation with a variety of qualities and emphases. In *Dead End,* director William Wyler sets Bogart's leaning, brooding figure in the foreground, slightly to the right as his former girlfriend (whom he's just discovered to be a hooker) walks off, lit by the arc of a streetlamp. Bogart's dark figure merges with the blocks of shadow, both further isolating him and touching off a sense of emptiness. In *The Informer,* Victor McLaglen as the toady who has just informed on an old friend sits in a police station as he waits for the reward money. Against the background, vertical activity of the cops, McLaglen's figure is squeezed, cramped in on himself: an isolation doubly effective from the foreground-background separation and from the graphic differences. In *Tomorrow,* the woman played by Olga Bellin sits alone at a table. A barren window to her right and a shaft of naked light on the bleak table are the only lit surfaces beside her face. Their emptiness further suggests an emptiness in her. *The Trial,* by Orson Welles, is a metaphysical fable told in images, and perhaps the most common image is that of a man surrounded by hostile spaces, often seen in long shot, with shattering light and bleak shadows that press around it. The figure of Anthony Perkins on a broad empty street at night suggests, as does much of the rest of the film, an isolation so complete that we (and Perkins) have come to take it for granted. Depth within the frame can underscore the motif of isolation; Tony Richardson's *The Loneliness of the Long Distance Runner* depicts Tom Courtenay in one shot seen against a receding, empty street, on one side the monotonous grillwork of a braided steel fence. His expression is dismal; so, as well, is the world against which we see him. The structure of this shot—with Courtenay to the right (visually surrounded by the fence), and the empty street to the middle and left—evokes a moody, foreboding atmosphere, a sense of being lost in a familiar place. *Point Blank* stars Lee Marvin as an old-styled gangster who sets himself against a corporation—like syndicate; thematically, Marvin's separation from the modern urban world is underscored by fixing him against every mode of contemporary architecture: elevators, high-rise buildings, parking lots. In one striking shot, he sinks into the corner of an empty apartment, and the camera settles over him: he might as well be in a jail cell. The hard lines of the floor that meet at the corner seem to fix him graphically in a locked space—expressing potently his mood and condition.

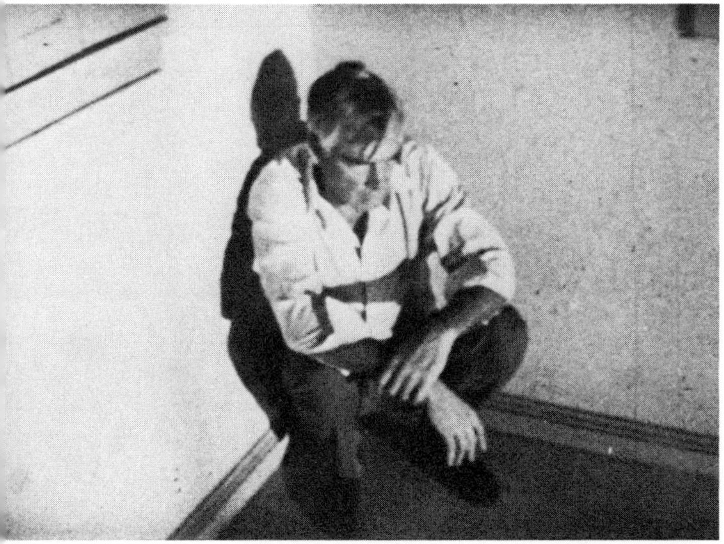

THE SET-UP

"Angle and set-up lend the pictures in a film pathos or charm, cold objectivity or fantastic romantic qualities. The art of angle and set-up are to the director and cameraman what style is to the narrator and it is here that the personality of the creative artist is the most immediately reflected,"—Béla Balázs

For the director and cameraman as they are making a film, each fresh shot presents the problem of set-up: where to set the camera, at what angle and distance; how to arrange the figures in relation to one another; and how to light the ensemble for the best effect. This combination of elements, sometimes called by the French *mise en scène,* is one of the most important—and relentlessly demanding—creative choices the filmmaker can make. For it is in the set-up that we see things in a film as they relate to one another; characters as they impinge on one another and on their environment; the setting as it affects the characters. And if the director and cameraman are good and shrewd and careful enough, they can invest in each separate set-up a distinctive emotional quality, so that the actors and the setting evoke more than what the lines or actions obviously state.

It was the Russians of the twenties—Eisenstein and Pudovkin and Dovzhenko—who first revealed the full potential of set-up. Obviously, earlier filmmakers had worked out problems of set-up, but never with the audacity and intense emotional qualities of the Russians. The low, uptilted angle shots in *Earth* with which Dovzhenko depicted blossoming flowers aside blossoming peasant women; the angular emphasis in the battle footage from Pudovkin's *Storm over Asia*—but it was Sergei Eisenstein who explored most fully the potential of set-up, using carefully elaborated set-ups in a rhythmic edited flow to create a visual movement of stunning emotional impact. In *October,* a film he made to commemorate and depict the 1917 revolution, Eisenstein used as a key motif the statue of the Czar: its awesome, weighty presence; then its disruption and collapse as the storming crowds tear it down. To further emphasize and virtually animate the statue, Eisenstein used low, portentous lighting that fixed its expression in a kind of gloomily hostile mood. He intercut from parts of the statue—its weighty hand, its bulky torso, its feet, its head. The statue came to *mean* more than simply a symbol of Czarist rule. We can *feel* its overpowering girth, its massiveness, its imposing presence and its arrogant indifference. A symbol, yes, but a symbol given supreme emotional weight by the trenchant use of set-up.

Later in the same film, when the soldiers storm the palace, Eisenstein used a low, barely tilted angle and rear lighting that depicts the oncoming soldiers in silhouette: the effect is stunning. The set-up enables us to feel the pressing, weighted charge of the soldiers in a manner that is unforgettable. The density of light and the blocks of shadow; the enormity of the great cannon wheel: all serve to rouse a vivid sense of the soldiers' feelings, and the demanding physical ordeal of the movement forward.

Eisenstein used set-up often for less auspicious themes, sometimes with a sardonic, satiric touch. In *Strike,* he depicts an industrialist smoking a cigar. By the simple glowering bulk of the man, and the almost obscene movement forward as he spews smoke from a cigar like a spouting chimney, we come invariably to despise the man: Eisenstein's intention, precisely.

Much of the expressive power of a set-up comes from the relation of characters in space —a relationship conveyed not only by their postures and movements, but as well by the nature and qualities of the space that separates and relates them. In *An Occurrence at Owl Creek Bridge,* the bridge itself serves to make the movement of the soldiers before the hanging even more foreboding. Their movement along the bridge conveys the effect of visual echoes. In *One-Eyed Jacks,* Marlon Brando, almost bushwhacked by a man he had just beaten up, turns to shoot; the depth within the frame creates a strong sense of the sudden tension. In *Odd Man Out,* James Mason looms in the foreground, half hidden in shadow—he is a man being hunted; the woman in the background, seen against the lighted street, sets off his figure effectively.

FRAMING

The set-up can include parts of the environment—or the bodies of the characters—to further focus our attention on the action by framing it. Framing is a visual device that localizes part of the image and—in well-framed shots—uses the framing device to suggest something about that which we see in the background. In *The Graduate,* for example, when Dustin Hoffman gets to the wedding of the girl he wants to marry, he reaches up a hand, almost instinctively, to stop the proceedings below. We see the altar, supposed bridegroom and bride framed between his raised hand and his head. In *Walkabout,* the aborigine youth who has saved a middle-class Australian girl and her little brother in the bush country is shown in one shot against the corrugated sides of an old farm building; he is blocked in shadows, and the double framing—the vertical sides of the building, the thick tilted shadows—serves both to isolate him within the frame and to distinguish his presence.

Solo, a striking film about a mountain climber, frames one shot of the climber tugging his way up a vertical slope on a rope, through a crevice in the rocks, doubly accenting the vertical ascent by the strong dark emphasis of the straight black rocks.

Background can be used for framing as well as foreground. In *The Trial,* when Tony Perkins stands before a lit, naked screen in a darkened world, he is isolated by the sharply rectangular effect of the screen, and in fact framed by it.

Framing can be a method of emphasizing and clarifying a mood or condition. In *The Secret of Santa Vittoria,* when Anthony Quinn waltzes tipsily through a wine cellar, he is framed in endless racks and bottles of wine, underscoring his tipsiness. A similar use of framing is apparent in one of the later sequences of *Citizen Kane.* Susan leaves Kane, walking through a battery of doorways in the vast Xanadu. Kane watches in the foreground, his figure a bleak shadow, itself part of the framing of the shot. The consecutive series of doorways creates an echo-like visual effect of the desolation and bitterness Kane feels at that moment.

Shots can be framed from within, organized in such a way that the internal graphic structure gives us an immediate, distinct idea of the drama. In *The Battleship Potemkin,* one of our earliest introductions to the sailors aboard the soon-to-be mutinized battleship depicts them in their sleeping quarters, where they lie in crowded hammocks that intersect at bizarre, tight angles with one another, like the spiderweb lines in broken glass. Immediately we have a dark knowledge of the sailors' condition: the crowding, the disorder, the hint of an underlying ever-threatening tension.

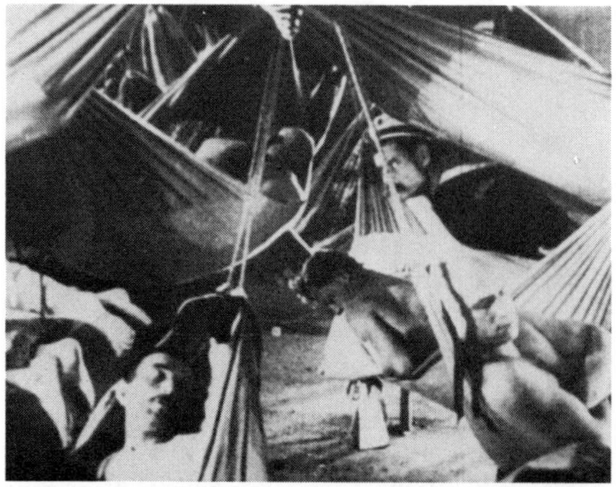

LIGHTING

When film runs through a camera it is capturing light. Colors, textures, forms, movements—all are no more than implications of the manner in which light affects the sensitive grain on a strip of celluloid. And though we are generally probably less conscious of lighting than of just about any other expressive aspect of the image, the style of lighting can profoundly affect the style of the image. The same face, lit in a variety of manners, can become in turn cheerful, morose, somber, impervious. By lighting we not only see the image, we are led to feel something about it as well.

The basic types of lighting are considered in terms of the relationship between the source of light and the subject: low lighting, rear lighting, side lighting, front lighting, top lighting, etc. But beyond this the cameraman can haze the light (usually by hazing the lens) to create a washed, hazy effect; he can break light and shadow over the subject in a manner that illuminates only part of the subject—sometimes called keyhole lighting. He can go even further and shatter the light into fragments of light and shadow, a technique used quite often in Welles' *The Trial.*

But the source of light is less important, finally, than the effects of any given use of lighting; and the possibilities of light as it is used to give emotional inflection to a subject or a set-up are endless.

In *Point Blank,* when Lee Marvin is escaping after being left for dead at the deserted island prison Alcatraz, director John Boorman presents several images in which the broken pattern of lighting over Marvin's figure suggests a barred, enclosed motif. In *The Sea of Grass* a woman in white stands against a darkening, dusky sky and a bleak, dark plain. The contrast summons a brooding, moody atmosphere.

Arranged with care, lighting can give fresh life to surfaces and textures, so that we become fully conscious of the inner life of an image from the sensation that we can reach out and touch the subject. Satyajit Ray's *Pather Panchali,* a tender, lyrical work focusing on a family in an Indian village, has a slow, meditative quality; Ray's camera dwells on the characters and the village at length, and under the softly tinged light the faces of villagers become etched as exquisitely as the faces in a Rembrandt painting. *Dante's Inferno,* a silent film from which footage was used ten years later for a Spencer Tracy version, contains powerful images of figures in a seething world of tormenting forces: the writhing damned of these sequences seem amazingly real, unforgettable, from the tones of light that merge their bodies with the oppressive world around them.

SHADOW

In the long history of moving images, it is probably not far wrong to suggest that the very first moving images were shadows thrown upon the walls of caves by our distant ancestors who, for amusement, fluttered their hands before a fire to imitate animals they hunted. Our fascination with moving shadows is at root inseparable from our fascination with movies, themselves but highly sophisticated forms of moving shadows.

The expressive advantages of shadows within filmmaking are considerable. A shadow can anticipate a moving figure, or an action; its size can far outscale the size of normal figures, enabling a shadow to tower over its source figure, thus suggesting some unique mood or relationship or coming dramatic moment; the movement of a man parallelled by his shadow can give added emphasis to his condition or feeling, underscoring it by amplifying the movements.

Essentially, though, shadows work on our imagination: they enable us to create in our own mind an unseen image, giving it an added power and intensity. When Walter Pidgeon is captured in *Man Hunt* after being found with a loaded rifle which he was pointing at Hitler, the S.S. chief, played by George Sanders, tries to extract his signature to a document claiming he had been sent by the British government to assassinate the Fuhrer. Pidgeon refuses and Sanders sends him out to be tortured. We don't see Pidgeon when he returns, only his shadow, at first dragging from the arms of two S.S. guards, then bent forward weakly in a chair. Director Fritz Lang composes the scene so that graphically Sanders seems to be talking to the shadow. The scene is powerful, largely for the effect of seeing Pidgeon not as he looks after the torture but, far more effective, as we imagine he looks.

In *Johnny Belinda,* shadows delineate and suggest the rape of a deaf mute girl who is visited by the village rake. Belinda, working in the barn at night, sees him enter; her figure and his are lit, with the background fully in shadow. He takes out a violin—he had noticed

at a dance the week before that she enjoyed touching the violin of a player—and proceeds to play. But the notes are screechy, out of control; and Belinda knows this. She looks up at him uncertainly; he begins to touch her; she backs away; and as she backs into a corner of the barn her face slowly melts into the shadows, till in one last closeup, we see the expression of terror in her eyes. Here the sensation of being enveloped by shadows becomes a sensitive way of treating the rape scene.

Like shadows, silhouettes can suggest figures without fully delineating them. In Howard Hawks' *Red River,* there is a superb sequence in which we see the wagons and horsemen as dark livid forms against the expansive dusk: the effect is strikingly beautiful, and conveys the rich feeling of plains, of flung spaces, of men in harmony with the natural elements. Eisenstein uses the silhouette of a pipe-smoking figure in *Strike* to play graphic elements against one another and suggest something of the man's character. In *The Crowd,* the hero and his girl (later his wife) are seen at almost all times as ciphers in the vast urban turmoil of crowds. When in one sequence they get into the countryside and climb a hill beside a waterfall, director King Vidor uses silhouettes to further emphasize their privacy and solitude.

REFLECTION

One of the truly great sequences in Marx Brothers movies—and in all comedy—takes place in *Duck Soup,* when Harpo, in search of Freedonia's war plans, dresses up as Groucho: mustache, glasses, nightcap, nightshirt and all. Running through the house, he slips in his socks and smashes through a full-length mirror, shattering it to the floor. There happens to be a room behind the mirror, and Harpo is standing there, at the entrance to the room, when Groucho comes along.

From the first, Groucho suspects it isn't *quite* his reflection, but Harpo, skilled at anticipating Groucho's every move, poses as the reflection and goes through all the inane gestures, movements and tests that Groucho concocts to find out. When Groucho comes out dancing on one foot, Harpo comes out dancing on one foot. When Groucho turns away, then suddenly whirls and turns to check, Harpo anticipates and follows suit. As Allan Eyles writes, "Now the obvious solution would be (for Groucho) to feel and see if the mirror was there; but Groucho knows the rules. He has to play and outwit Harpo legitimately." The play goes on in a rising crescendo of comic inventiveness. They circle round the mirror, trading sides. Harpo drops a hat and Groucho graciously picks it up and returns it to him. Only when Chico appears—himself dressed as Groucho—and tries to join the game does Groucho get wise and grab at Chico's nightshirt. Harpo, sensibly, escapes.

The gag is uproariously funny because for much of the sequence it *could* be a reflection; and only what we know—and the small, beautifully timed mistakes—give away fully that it isn't reflection, but a delightful play on a character standing and mugging before a mirror.

In reflection a figure can come to mean something slightly more or different than when seen normally. When Joe Buck (John Voight) in *Midnight Cowboy* mugs before a mirror alongside a movie poster of Paul Newman, we're highly conscious of a man's need to parade his masculinity before himself. In *The Manchurian Candidate,* before one of his innumerable speeches, Senator Iselin sits in a make-up chair while his wife tells him what to say. A small magnifying mirror he holds below his chin gives us—as his turned-away profile doesn't—his expression: flatulent, subservient. We know immediately that his wife in the background is the one with the authority, the assurance. In Jean Cocteau's *Blood of a Poet,* the poet in a dreamlike dance virtually massages a mirror with his body before it envelops him, permitting him entry into another world. Here reflection becomes metaphorical as well as a potently visual suggestion of the poet's narcissistic obsession.

In Fritz Lang's *M,* we discover the full

Blood of a Poet

psychopathic dimension of the child murderer, played by Peter Lorre, partly through a judicious and telling use of reflection. Lorre is a sad, estranged, pathetic creature who for amusement seems to be able to do nothing more enlivening than mugging to himself in a mirror. Standing before an array of guns and shells in a store, Lang plays the reflections against Lorre, hinting at some similarity in the explosiveness of the harmless looking shells and the harmless looking Lorre. And when Lorre has been spotted and identified as the

child murderer by the underworld, and the back of his coat marked in chalk with the insignia "M" (for *mörder,* or murderer), he sees the damning insignia in a reflection. What makes these and other uses of reflection in *M* so telling is that we are constantly seeing Lorre split on the frame; the psychotic split between this gentle-seeming, harmless-looking man and the child murderer takes on a direct visual expression in that split that the reflections create and further suggest.

PERSPECTIVE AND POINT OF VIEW

The flexibility of the camera permits the filmmaker to structure a film not (as usually a writer is obligated to do) from a single fixed point of view, but from a variety of perspectives, shifting point of view fluidly from shot to shot. The very mobility of the shots, once organized in cutting, creates a changing, flexing point of view, enabling us to identify with one character one moment, another the next.

To some extent point of view controls the image: the filmmaker can choose what point of view will best bring out the dramatic momentum of a particular shot, and arrange his camera accordingly. The basic options of first person, second person, third person are as much available to the filmmaker as the writer, only the filmmaker is capable of moving between them fluidly.

But what makes point of view a significant factor of the image in filmmaking is the ability of film to involve the audience in a variety of subtle ways. In *The Crowd,* the man and his wife are riding through the tunnel of love. We watch as he eyes her, she eyes him, and they kiss: cut to outside, where a sign announces, "Do they neck? Watch"—and a group of spectators are lined up to do just that. The curtain suddenly lifts on the car, and instantly our point of view has changed from one of intimacy with the couple to voyeurs, like the other spectators.

Dead End has a sequence in which the street gang finally manages to convince a pansy rich boy to join them in the cellar of a nearby building. Till now the film has intercut between the street gang's world and the rich boy's: while they swim in the river and roast wieners over a fire, he takes French lessons from a private tutor. The set-up is obvious, and our sympathies do tend to align with the street kids who we know are about to smash the daylights out of the rich boy. But after they've escorted him into the basement and the door closes, the camera pulls back to reveal Bogart—once a street kid himself, now a wanted gangster—as he leans against a wall and watches the closed doorway with full knowledge of what is happening. Suddenly our point of view has changed, and the entire incident takes on a more glowering air because we have been made conscious of the injustice in what is happening.

One of the most common uses of point of view in filmmaking is to create a strong bond of identification between the audience and a major character. Hitchcock is a master at establishing this identification, and in *Psycho* there is a scene where Marion Crane is leaving town with $40,000 that she has stolen from her boss. She had asked for the afternoon off, and as she drives out of town with the money, she pauses at a stoplight. Hitchcock holds on her face as she waits for the light to change, then cuts to a first-person shot of her boss walking across the street. He happens to glance toward her. Cut to her reaction, stiffening behind the wheel. Cut to the boss, now *his* reaction, a kind of uncertain puzzlement. Cut again to Marion Crane as she grips the wheel, anxious to drive off. In five brief shots we've been brought fully into her predicament, given a full dose of her tension and uneasiness.

Robert Enrico's *An Occurrence at Owl Creek Bridge* centers on a man about to be hanged. Everything is amplified, modified to suggest the man's experience as he awaits the rope: sounds seem slowed, almost distorted; the movements of the soldiers on the bridge and in a camp above appear to us—as they appear to him—to take an intolerably long time.

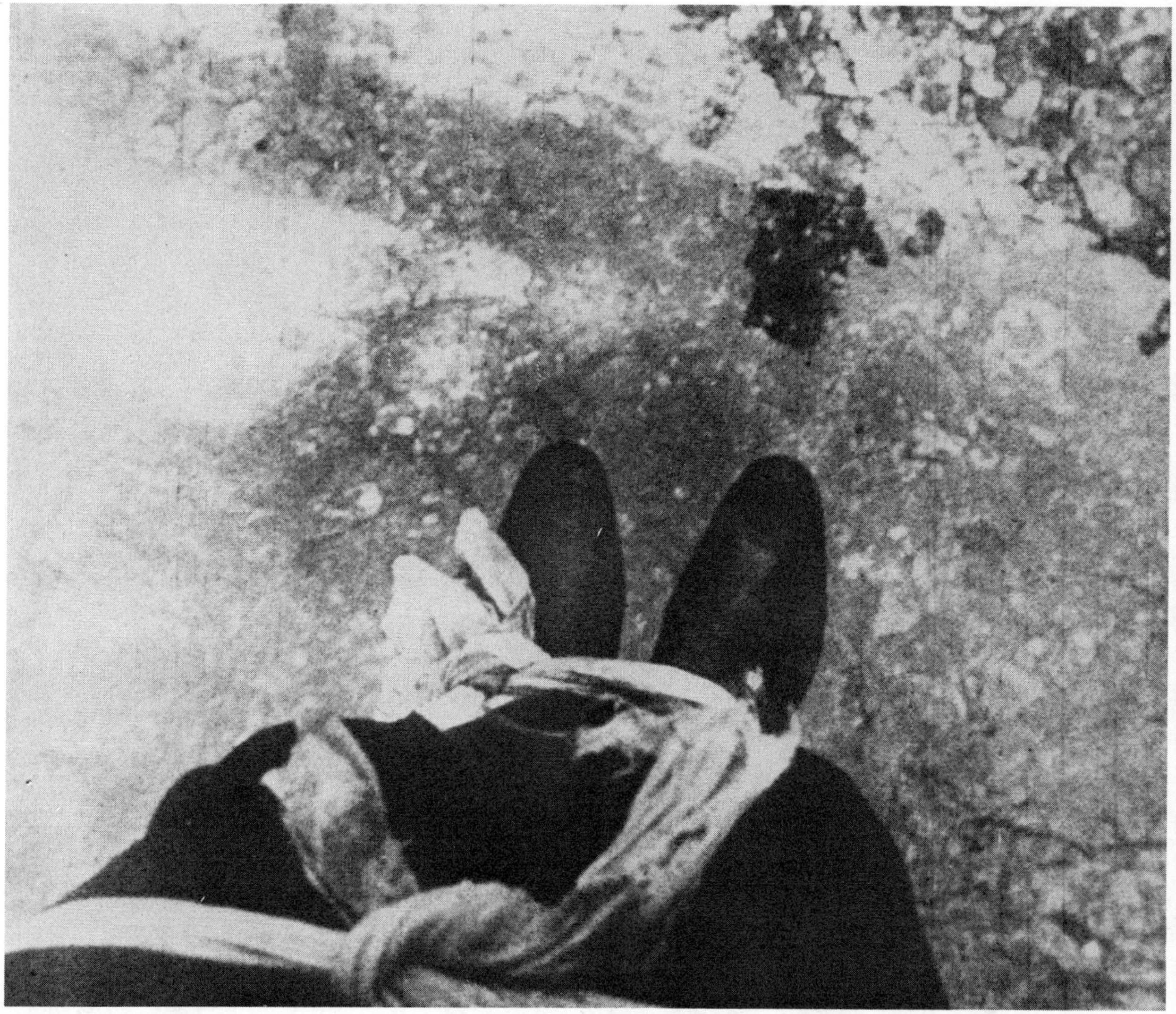

By the moment of the hanging, we already identify strongly with the man. But when the hanging finally takes place, when the soldier steps off the plank and the man falls straight down, toward the water, there is a critical and powerful first-person shot looking down, as his body and roped legs knife toward the river. Cut to the shot, underwater now, of the man at the end of a broken rope. This judicious use of a first-person shot gives us much the same relief and snapped tension as the man feels. (*An Occurrence at Owl Creek Bridge* uses point of view brilliantly throughout; only at the last moment—as the man approaches his wife, his head jerks back, and the film cuts to the man breaking his neck on the rope—do we learn that all the ensuing events were racing thoughts in his mind; and only then is the point of view switched from him to a more distant, third-person approach.)

Composition

Three frames from *Tomorrow,* a film rich in the classic values of composition: texture, arrangement, light and shadow, a sense of balanced spaces. Note the depth created by the foreground logs in the one frame; the boards of the building offsetting the woman's presence in another—and the relationship between the two men, one crouched, one standing, in the lower frame.

CINEMASCOPE COMPOSITION

The wide screen, introduced in the fifties, required a new approach to the composition of the screen: one that took advantage of the strong horizontal bias of the long, wide screen. Below: a shot from *Giant*, with James Dean.

Isolation

THE EMOTIONAL FORCE OF COMPOSITION

Humphrey Bogart in *Dead End*: he has just learned that his old love is now a hooker; as she walks away his figure, half in shadow, becomes doubly forlorn.

Orson Welles' *The Trial* is shaggily replete in images of a man lost in overpowering spaces; here the man (Tony Perkins) is seen as a tiny figure in a vast, spotlighted street.

Gypo (Victor McLaglen) has just informed on Frankie McPhillip in John Ford's *The Informer*: set in the foreground of the police station he bends down, separating himself even further from the standing figures behind him.

Tom Courtenay in *The Loneliness of The Long Distance Runner*: the tapering distance of the street and fence act as a visual counterpoint to Courtenay's face.

Tomorrow: the isolation of the woman (Olga Bellin) is emphasized by the barren lighting and the depth within the frame.

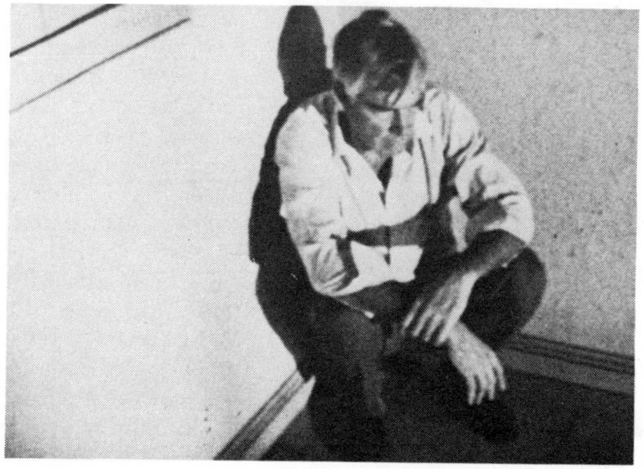

In *Point Blank,* Lee Marvin sinks into a corner, and the camera hovers over him: a statement of mood created more by the camera than by Lee Marvin's acting.

Set-Up

"Set-up and angle can make things hateful, lovable, terrifying or ridiculous at will."
—Béla Balázs

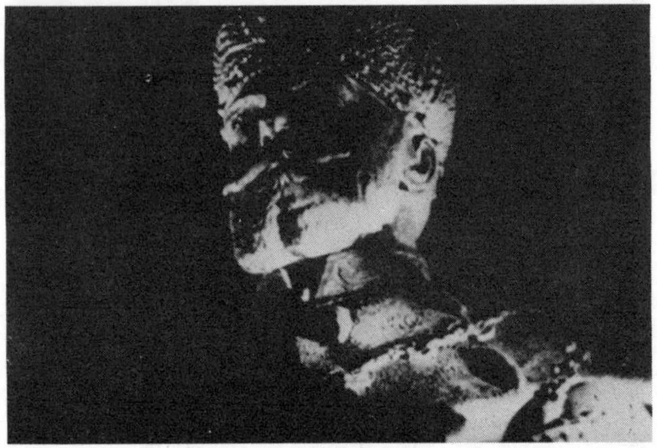

October

The Trial

Welles' *Macbeth*

The Crowd

"What gives the impression of large crowds is not the actual numerical multitude. In the perspective of an endless desert even a hundred thousand men can appear a mere handful. It is the business of perspective and set-up to produce the illusion required."—Béla Balázs

EISENSTEIN, GENIUS OF THE SET-UP

Sergei Eisenstein, the Russian filmmaker who revolutionized film technique with his powerful rhythmic editing, was the first director to explore the full potential of camera set-up. The statue of the Czar in *October* takes on portentous somber authority by the low angle and splayed, low lighting. In the charge against the palace from the same film, we *feel* the weight of the cannon and the pressing urgency of the soldiers, simply from a shrewd use of angle, lighting, set-up.

DEPTH WITHIN THE FRAME

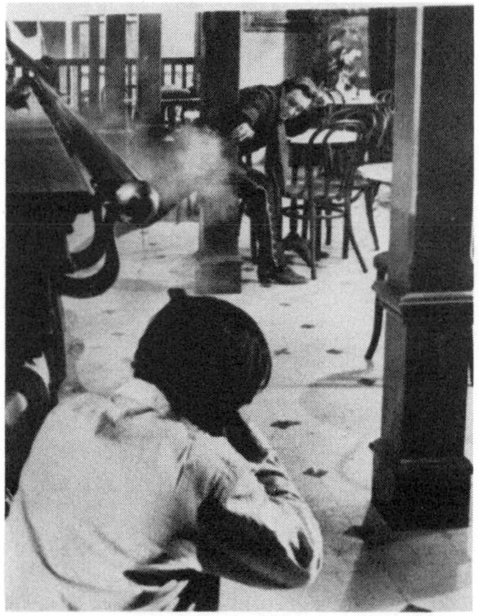

Three images in which the use of depth within the frame connotes a mood, a manner of action, or a point of view: from *An Occurrence at Owl Creek Bridge; One-Eyed Jacks; Odd Man Out.* Note the structural similarities between the latter two frames.

WHAT A SET-UP CAN REVEAL

The Manchurian Candidate: note how director Frankenheimer uses the TV screen as a way of clarifying relationships basic to the film: with James Gregory as the McCarthy-like Senator Iselin seen on-screen and in the background; and his wife, the real force, Angela Lansbury in the foreground. Also note the bust of Lincoln in the foreground, later.

PHYSICAL DETAIL

In *Strike,* Eisenstein presents a cigar-smoking industrialist in varying poses as he bends forward. In each case we're reminded of his immense girth, his bland, balloon face, and the smoke that spews out of his mouth as though from a smokestack.

FOREGROUND VS. BACKGROUND

Four studies in the tensions created by setting foreground action against background action: from *Greed; The Mask of Dimitrios; Citizen Kane; The Manchurian Candidate.* Why do our sympathies tend to go with the foreground figure?

Framing

Every image on a film, by the simple fact of the limits of the screen, is already "framed" —whether well or badly. But even within the image, framing—the use of some foreground device that organizes the central action for our eyes—can become a potent way of forecasting a mood, anticipating or commenting on the story. In *The Graduate,* the scene when Ben arrives at the wedding to stop it and take the girl off himself is realized fully by framing the wedding with his upraised hand. Foreground and background interact in a way that explains and dramatizes what is happening.

WALKABOUT

There are three characters in *Walkabout*: a teenage girl lost in the Australian bush; her little brother, along with her; and a tribal youth, about her age, alone on his ritual "walkabout," a survival test to prove his manhood. The primitive befriends and saves the girl and her brother, and in a haunting sequence at a deserted farm, director Nicholas Roeg uses framing devices to characterize deep differences between the native and the girl. Note how she sits in an almost somnolent repose; he is standing, always with a certain alertness.

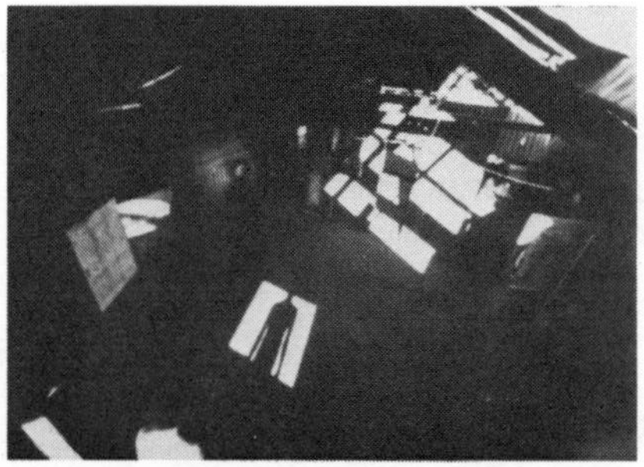

TO ISOLATE . . .

Johnny Belinda and Orson Welles' *The Trial.* The human figure as separated and cut off from others, a common framing device.

TO ANTICIPATE . . .

The Third Man and *Man Hunt*: images of men being pursued, their fate hinted in the manner of framing: a guillotine-like form, a tunnel of foreground darkness.

TO UNDERSCORE ACTION . . .

I Am A Fugitive From A Chain Gang: Muni escaping in the truck. Both the dark tunnel and the bright bridge frame the oncoming vehicle.

TO AMPLIFY A MOOD . . .

Anthony Quinn wanders tipsily in *The Secret of Santa Vittoria* and Kane watching as Susan leaves Xanadu in *Citizen Kane*.

Solo

Broken Image

One technique of framing uses part of the foreground of the set to *break up* the action in the background—in effect, multiplying the images we see on the screen. This technique can give us an immediate visual idea of the action within a scene.

In *White Heat,* two detectives prepare for a gunfight with the gangster Cody. Note the use of repetition in the image. The two detectives seem totally alike, in stance, in the style of their hats, hinting that they are indistinguishable from each other. Only the gangsters seem to have individualized characters.

During a scene late in Orson Welles' *The Trial,* while the main character Tony Perkins is being interrogated, a little girl looks in. The shot is framed so that we only see her eyes, emphasizing not her face or her reaction, but simply her presence as an observer.

In *The Battleship Potemkin,* Eisenstein shows the sailors sleeping in hammocks aboard the ship. The shattered lines and the crowded angular effect gives us a potent sense of the oppressive mood and the pinched, cluttered world of the sailors, who are soon to rise up in mutiny.

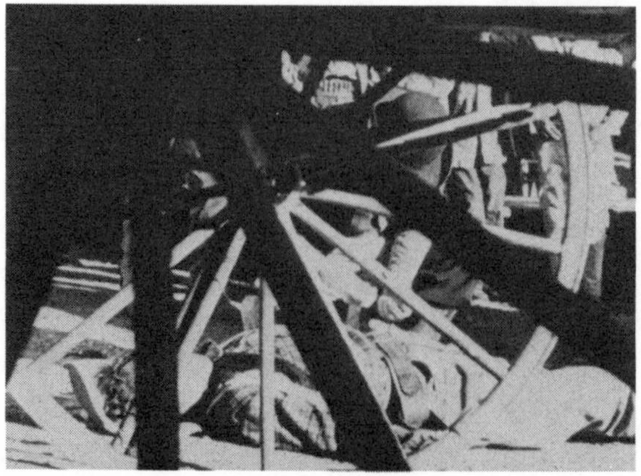

In *The Westerner*, at the end of a gunfight, we see the fallen gunman framed behind the spokes of a wagon wheel—creating a splintered visual effect.

Lighting

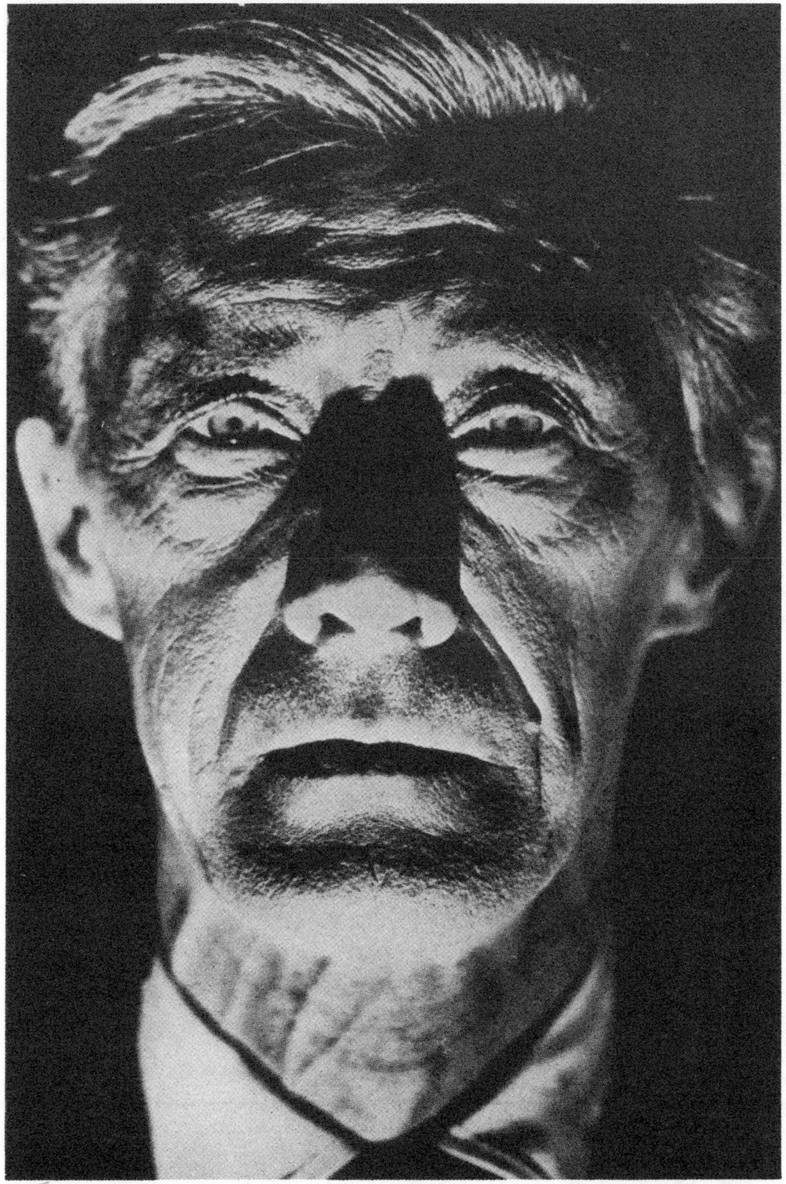

LOW LIGHTING
John Carradine in *The Invisible Invaders*

REAR LIGHTING
Citizen Kane

HIGH-CONTRAST LIGHTING
Citizen Kane

SIDE LIGHTING
Johnny Belinda

KEYHOLE LIGHTING
Citizen Kane

HAZED LIGHTING
Greed

SHATTERED LIGHTING
The Trial

Lighting For...

CONTRAST

The white of the woman's dress against a darkening dusky sky creates a foreboding, almost eerie sense of contrast: from *The Sea of Grass*.

MOTIF

Point Blank: Lee Marvin at Alcatraz: an imprisonment doubly suggested by the barred lighting of his figure, as seen from above and below.

TEXTURE

Precise lighting effects can create a textural quality that is almost tactile in its appearance: from *Pather Panchali* and *Dante's Inferno*. Note how skin texture is exactly rendered in both these frames.

MOOD

In *The Manchurian Candidate* Angela Lansbury's outraged face is accentuated and amplified by strong side lighting.

The statue of the Czar, from Eisenstein's *October*.

Smoke, Rain, Fog and Dust

JOSEPH VON STERNBERG:

"Above all, the greatest art in motion picture photography is to be able to give life to the dead space that exists between the lens and the subject before it. Smoke, rain, fog, dust and steam can emotionalize empty space, and so can the movement of the camera."

THE INFORMER

John Ford's film focuses on Gypo, a sullen, barren-souled man who turns in a friend for reward money during the Irish Revolution. Throughout the film Ford uses a dense, ubiquitous fog that comes to suggest the state of Gypo's clouded conscience. Not only does the fog give the film a textural and visual richness; in some subtle way it brings us closer to Gypo, enabling us to inhabit the same mental world.

CITIZEN KANE

The smoky screening room where "News on the March" reporters discuss Kane and Rosebud. Light is splayed, has a texture of its own.

THE WIND

Swedish director Victor Sjöström makes the dusty Texas wind the central character and the major force in this epic study of a young woman's reaction to an alien physical and psychological terrain. Images of the wind abound in the film: always gusting, howling, sweeping through crevices and doorways; the tactile quality is so strong that, seeing the film, you can almost taste the gritty texture of the blown sand in your teeth.

Shadow

THE POWER OF THE IMAGINATION . . .

In Fritz Lang's *Man Hunt,* Walter Pidgeon, captured by the German SS near Hitler's lair, is tortured; we don't see him after the torture, only his shadow, but the effect is all the stronger. No amount of bruises or welts could make Pidgeon's beating seem as dreadful as his shadow.

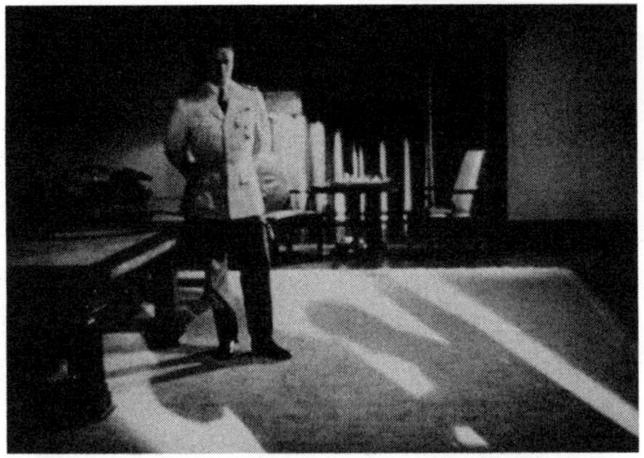

TO AMPLIFY . . .

The shadows of two men against walls, in each case amplifying the emotional quality of their movement: Charlton Heston in *Touch of Evil,* walking with a hasty urgency; and Robert Ryan in *The Set-Up,* after he has been beaten for failing to go down in the ring as his manager promised.

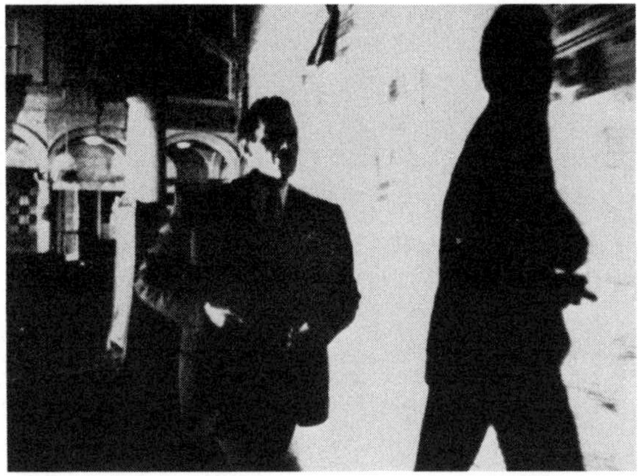

"No horror can be so horrible, no beauty so enchanting, if really seen, than the horror or enchantment suggested by its shadow."
—Béla Balázs

TO ANTICIPATE . . .

A shadow of an emerging figure flung into an open space accentuates the figure, doubly anticipates his entry: left to right, *The Trial; Gold Diggers of 1935; The Trial.*

DRIVEN INTO SHADOWS: ►

The rape sequence from *Johnny Belinda*: how shadows can be used with subtle dramatic force.

SHADOW PLAY

In a sequence spoofing chain gang movies from Woody Allen's *Take the Money and Run,* Woody, a chain gang prisoner, is forced to watch a whipping which we—and he—had seen previously only in shadow. When Woody gets there, the guard is reprimanded for whipping not the man, but his shadow.

▼

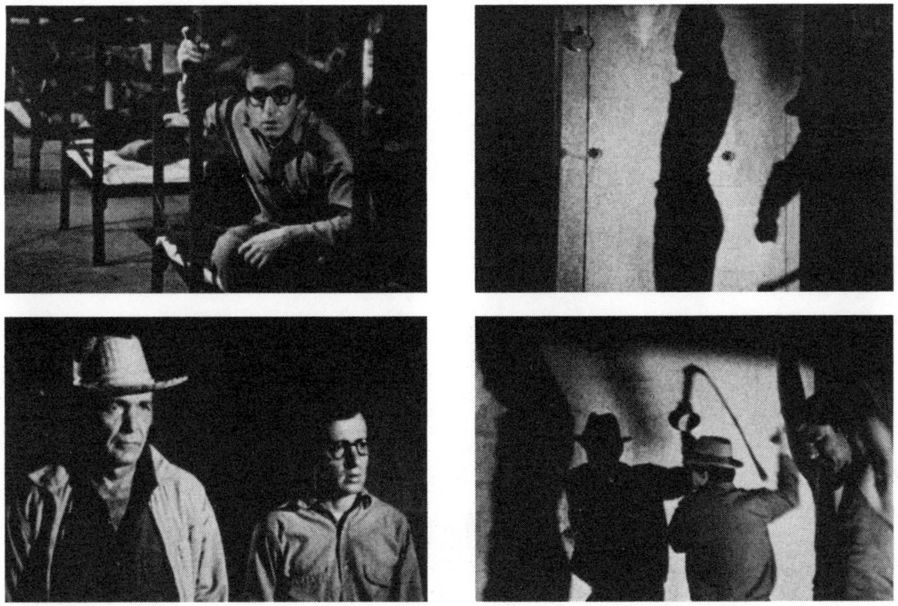

SILHOUETTE

For romantic effect: from *Red River*.

To dramatize a character: from *Strike*.

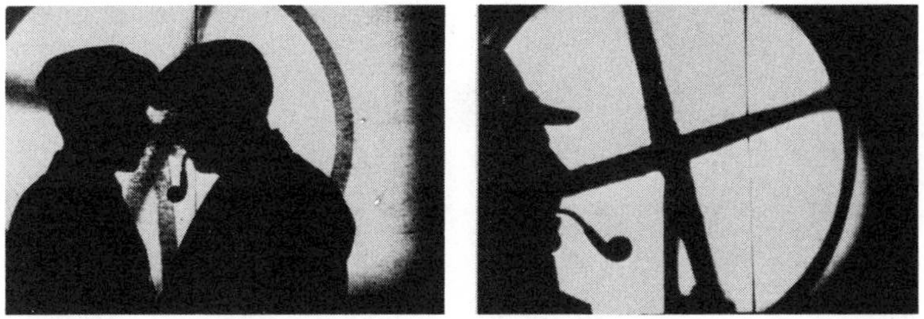

To emphasize landscape: from *The Crowd*.

Reflection

Mirrors, glass, water: any surface that can capture the elusive qualities of light, or repeat a figure for us within the frame, provides a natural source of play for the filmmaker's image. Reflection can give added movement and life to a shot, suggesting the mood of light; it can become part of the set-up, offsetting or duplicating a character so that we see him from two separate and revealing angles; it can catch with subtle ease a psychological truth, a relationship, a significant play of movement in the frame.

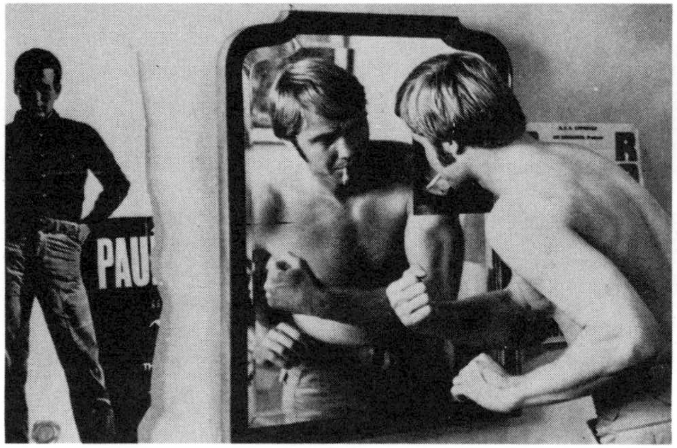

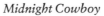

Midnight Cowboy

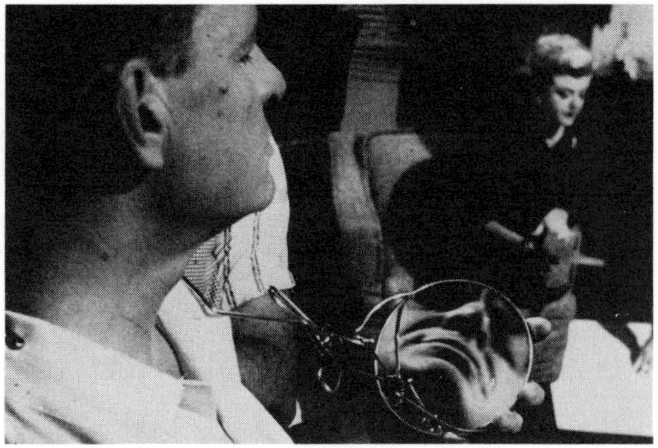

The Manchurian Candidate

PORTRAIT OF A PSYCHOPATH: REFLECTIONS IN *M*

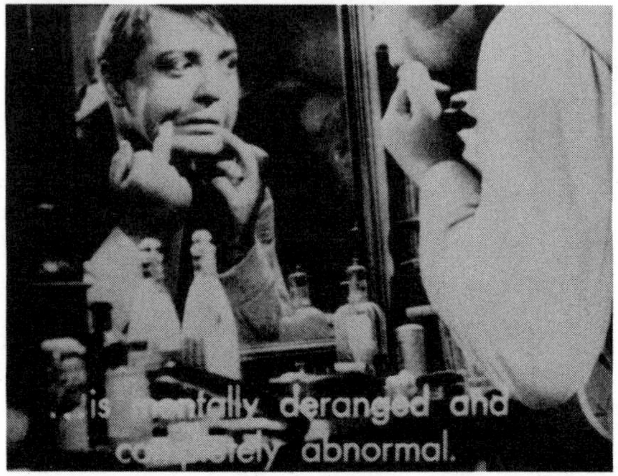

A SPLINTERED PERSONALITY

In *M*, the extraordinary study of a child murderer, director Fritz Lang uses reflection as a recurrent visual motif to suggest the splintered mind of the psychopath played by Peter Lorre. Here reflection serves not only the camera, but the deepest intricacies of character as well.

MIRRORING A MOTIF

The Informer

The Crowd

ACTIVE SURFACES

Grand Prix

Johnny Belinda

Reflection as Gag

Duck Soup

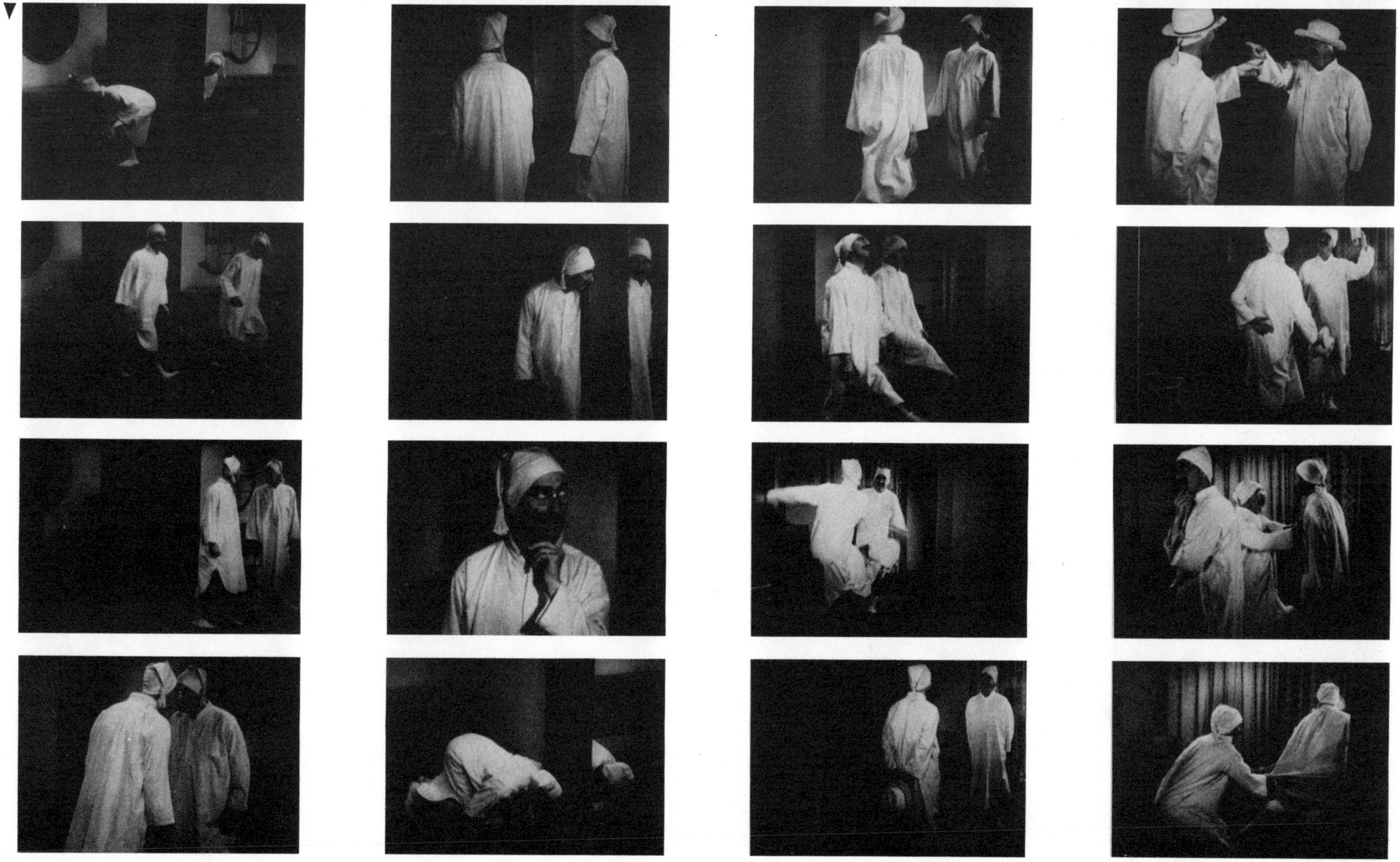

Perspective and Point of View

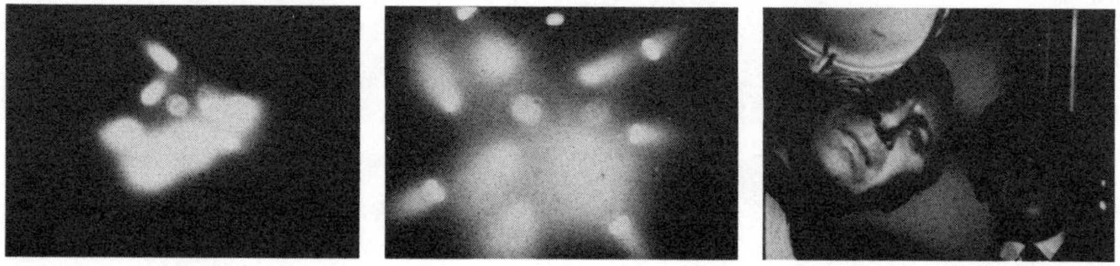

FIRST PERSON

Dead Reckoning: Bogart on the operating table.

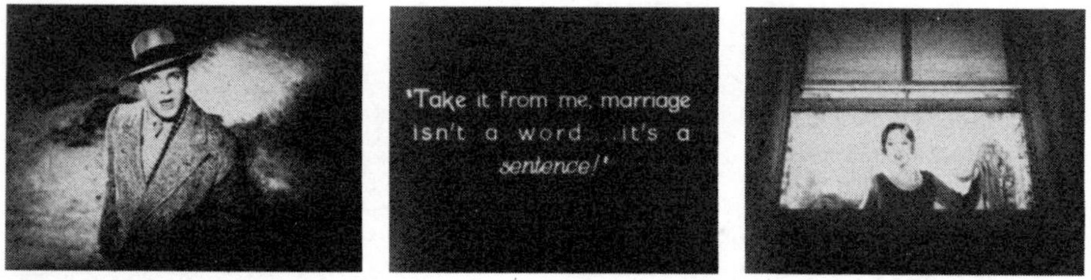
"Take it from me, marriage
isn't a word ... it's a
sentence!"

SECOND PERSON

Two points of view, alternating—from *The Crowd*.

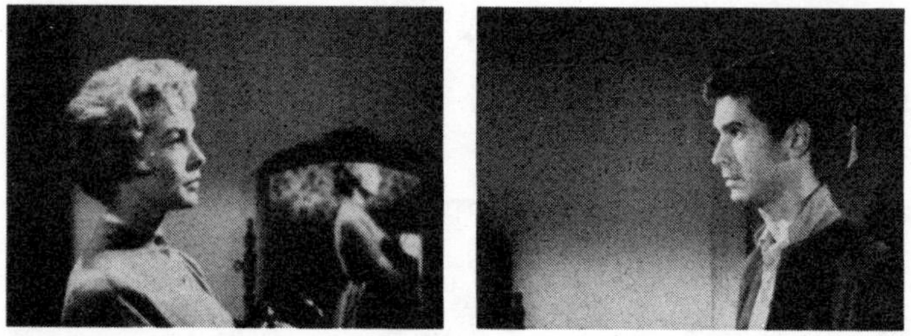

THIRD PERSON

The camera almost as a disinterested observer; from *Psycho*.

Herve Villechaize as Beppo the Dwarf in *The Gang That Couldn't Shoot Straight*.

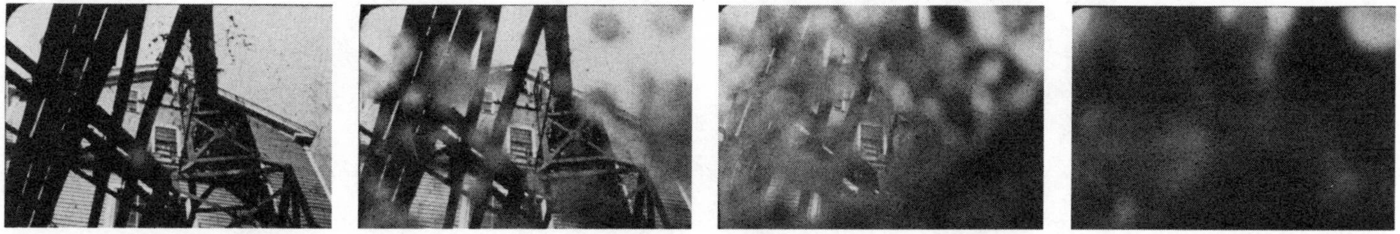

NO LONGER A SPECTATOR

Pretty Poison: the chute collapses, the pipe breaks open and the noxious wastes —a major theme of the film— come pouring out; director Noel Black lets the chemicals totally obscure the lens to dramatize the spillage.

In *An Occurrence at Owl Creek Bridge*, our identification with the man to be hanged is brought off by a crucial first-person shot: as he falls down into the water.

Psycho: Marion spots her boss, and we feel her anxiety.

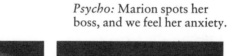

A DIFFERENT KIND OF SPECTATOR

Two subtle uses of point of view in which our loyalties and feelings are shifted: from *Dead End,* the street kids invite a rich kid into a cellar where we *know* he's going to be stomped; cut to Bogart, the gangster, who looks on with bemused interest—inviting us to do the same. In *The Crowd,* man and wife kiss in the tunnel of love until the camera cuts and we see the kiss from an altogether different and unexpected perspective.

The Dramatic Image

ORSON WELLES' *LADY FROM SHANGHAI*

Despite his failure to find sufficient financial backing for his films after *Citizen Kane,* Orson Welles has remained nonetheless the single true genius of American filmmaking. In *The Lady from Shanghai* (1948) he created a four-minute sequence which remains among the most visually intriguing and memorable in the history of film.

The "Hall of Mirrors" sequence begins when Welles, stunned by a blow, enters a funhouse which is at once real and illusionary: indeed, the sequence plays with reality and illusion as though the two were simply different images on the distorting funhouse mirrors. He wanders through a room reminiscent of the sets in *The Cabinet of Dr. Caligari,* falls down a serpentine slide, and enters the hall of mirrors.

All the dramatic tensions that have been building up in the film explode in the hall of mirrors, and in a way that reflects the shattered personalities and relationships of the film. An astounding sequence, a tour de force of pure filmmaking, and proof that Welles is among the greatest of living filmmakers.

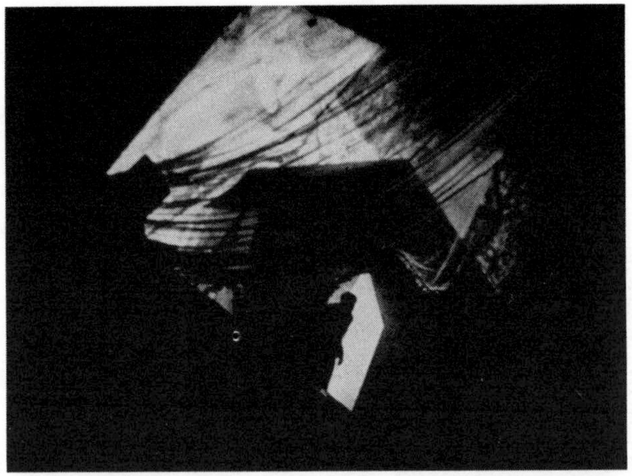

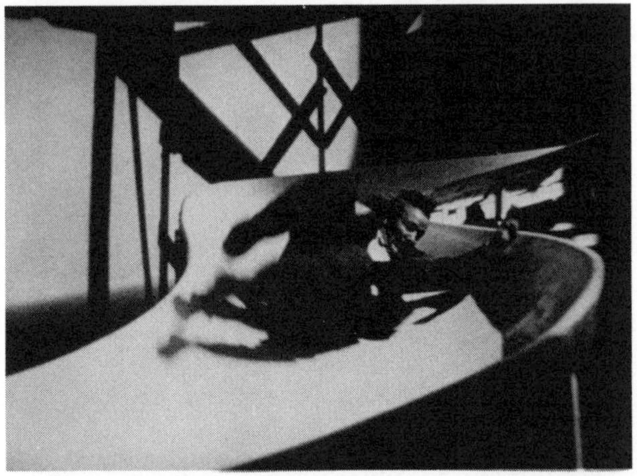

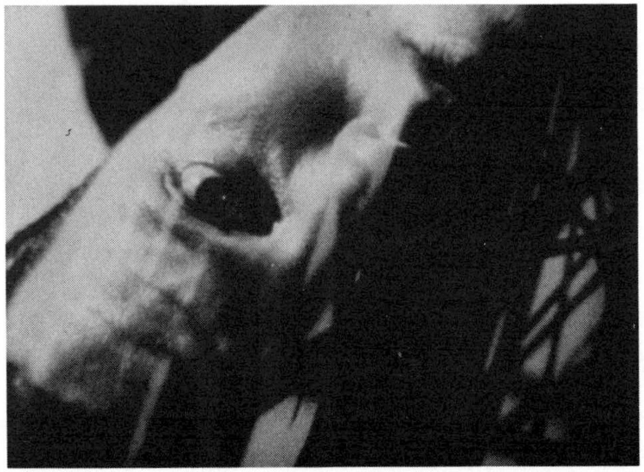

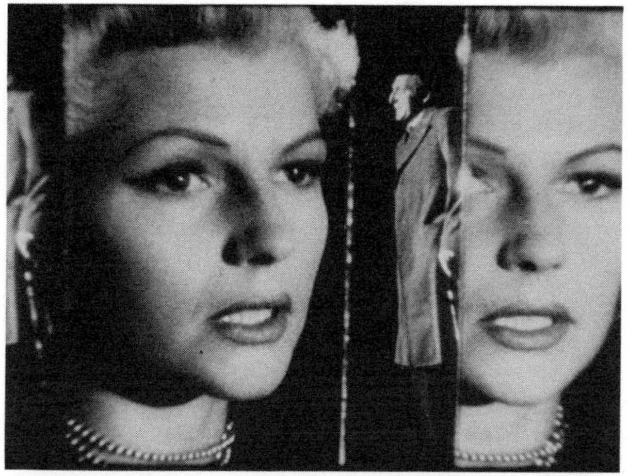
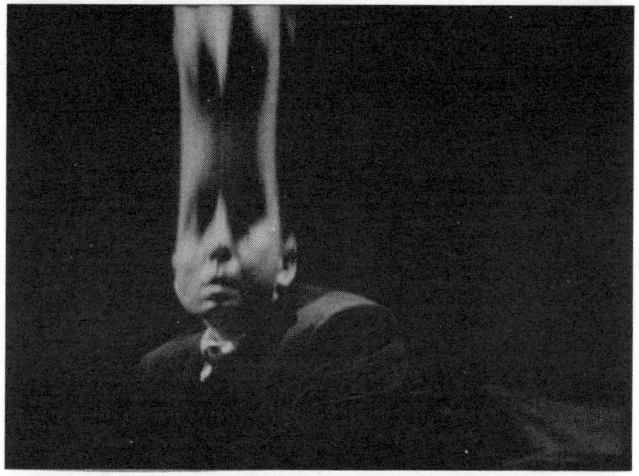

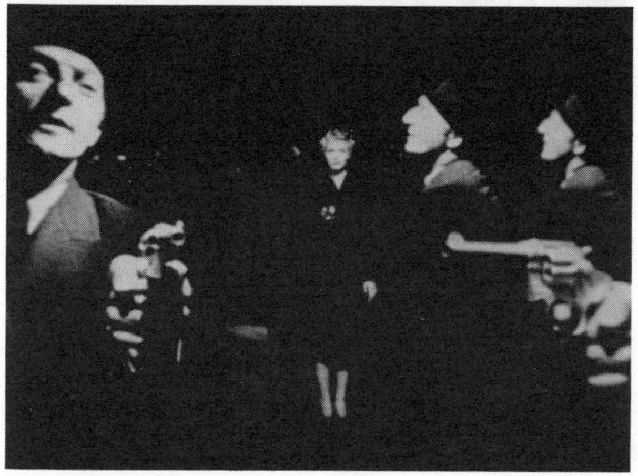

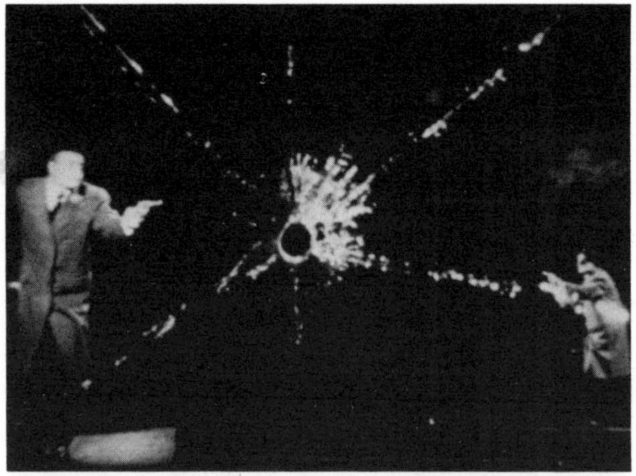

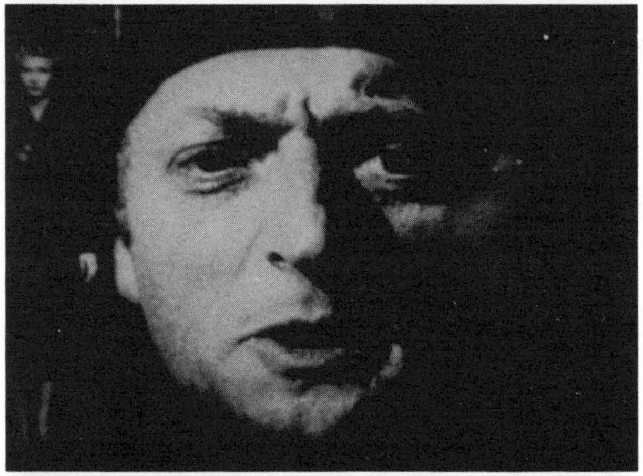

CHAPTER FIVE

Image of the World

Image of the World

Each artistic medium has its limits, just as each medium has its unique expressive possibilities. Film cannot depict with the depth of a novelist the turmoil of a confused mind. It cannot lodge permanently, clearly behind a single man's eyes as can the novelist. Yet what it can do—capture the human face and figure in motion; depict action and man's relationship to the world around him with a vivid immediacy; charge objects and surroundings with emotional qualities—film can do better and more forcefully than any artistic medium known to man.

In effect, the unique possibilities of film tend to give us a distinct image of the world. The medium, as Marshall McLuhan might say, shapes the nature of its message.

Film is photography and captures strictly the surfaces of things. It can show a bitterly smiling face, leading us to surmise what tensions and disturbances lie beneath it. It can create with dramatic gusto a conflict between two men, as long as that conflict is expressed in action or gesture. But it is at the surfaces that film must show us enough to suggest the further depths and complexities. You might say that film is a medium of appearances, and in order to overcome this bias of the camera, the filmmaker's responsibility lies mainly either in using appearances to explore further meanings, or in charging the film with the deceptions that undermine those appearances. In *Greed,* the film that critic James Agee called the Magna Carta of American movies, director Erich von Stroheim used a brutal naturalism to empower the faces and movements of his character with a life that glowers on the screen. Mac and Trina, the doomed couple around whom the film centers, are shown with a savage, uncompromising directness. We see Mac bend over an anaesthetized Trina in his dentist chair to kiss her while she is helpless to stop him. We see Trina counting and clutching her little hoard of gold, and how that very greed gradually ravages her face and mind. We see the rising, growling tension between Mac and Trina, culminating once in a fit where Mac bites off Trina's finger, and later when he murders her. Every character and object in *Greed* is empowered with a life of its own, but that life never varies from what we see in the images. *Greed's* awesome power lies precisely in the brutally telling force of its appearances.

But film can as well—and almost as powerfully—create its effect by undermining appearances. In Hitchcock's *Vertigo,* James Stewart plays a private detective hired to follow a man's wife, a woman obsessed with the life of another woman who had died close to a hundred years ago. Stewart follows her from a museum with a painting of the dead woman to a hotel where the dead woman had lived to a graveyard where she is buried: the wife seems to believe that she is, in fact, this woman. Stewart falls in love with the wife, and when she kills herself—so it appears—her death plunges Stewart into a moody depression that lasts for months. Only when he happens upon a woman one day in the streets who reminds him of his lost love—and makes her up to look like the woman who had died—does he discover the enormity of the deception of which he is the victim. He had never known the wife, only an actress made up to look like the wife; and he had been used, quite effectively, to set up a brilliant murder scheme to do away with the wife.

Like its title, *Vertigo* is dizzying in its theme of appearances hiding and belying the truth: the wife and her obsession with the past —a world of appearances that summons a sense of the dead, and yet which engrosses Stewart to a point of infatuation—is it a living or a dead woman that Stewart loves? Ultimately it is an appearance, a role, a pretense; and we are drawn as inexorably as Stewart into this affair with a reality that exists only in its alluring appearances.

Whether a film progresses in terms of its appearances or by playing those appearances against one another or—as is most frequent—by some combination of the two, it is with appearances, faces, textures, surfaces that a film must deal. That surface life—and what it can reveal of the human world—is the true matter of film.

THE HUMAN FACE

In *Bananas,* Woody Allen is invited to have dinner with the president of a tiny banana republic in Latin America. He arrives nervously, and as he sits down to dinner is invited to join a toast. He lifts his glass and, trembling, gives a magnificently fake grin, chuckles at himself, takes the glass to his lips and—anxious to the point now of mindlessness—chomps on the glass, chews feverishly, and proceeds to consume the glass like candy. The gag is funny enough in itself, if a bit contrived; but Woody makes it memorable by his face. For beneath the anxiety and nervousness there is a palpable effort to be cordial, a good guest; and there is also—once he has begun chewing on the glass and sickeningly realizes it *is* a glass—Woody's determination to see it through to the end, to finish off what he has begun. It is brilliant mime, but more. Woody's face, in those shimmering few seconds of the scene, comes to reveal a rushing complexity of reactions, bewilderment, terror, anxiety, and fake pleasantries. Through his face we see a transformation of moods as tenuous and freely changing as shadows on moving water.

When Griffith invented the closeup, he was primarily looking for a means with which to focus on smaller dramatic actions and give them immediate, vital significance. But the closeup soon came to be a means (for the most part, not always) of enlarging on the actor's manner of expression, transforming the bold, exaggerated gestures of the theatre into the subtle, evanescent language of the smallest inflections in the human face.

Nowhere in film do we look for or expect to find emotional meaning as in the human face. In its subtlety, its moodiness, its capacity for evoking virtually every emotion, the human face brings us intimately into the life of screen characters. The distance that has always separated the stage actor from his audience—and required dialogue primarily and gesture secondarily—no longer exists in film. We can be brought so close that a blink or a barely discernible sagging of the mouth expresses fully and without doubt an inner feeling.

The expressive life of the human face can conflict with the words that a character speaks, creating a volatile tension between what we see and what we hear. In *The Night of the Hunter,* Robert Mitchum plays an itinerant preacher with the word LOVE tattooed across the fingers of one hand, and the word HATE tattooed across the fingers of his other hand. (His favorite sermon involves a grappling between his hands and a commentary on the forces of love and hate battling one another.) When Mitchum learns that the children of a man who has been sentenced to death know the location of the money he stole, he marries the mother and gradually tries to coerce the information out of the children. In one scene he speaks to them in gentle words about their father and what he might have said to them before the police arrived; but in his face there is a fixed and hostile expression of pure contempt. Only the boy can recognize this discrepancy, and back away. His little sister is taken in by the preacher, and she eventually, unwittingly, reveals the whereabouts of the money.

Even—indeed, quite often—in an absence of expression the actor's face can come to signify much. The classic experiment by the Russian teacher Kuleshov indicates the extent to which we tend to read emotion and expression into an actor's face. Kuleshov took from a film an impassive closeup of the actor Mosjukhin, then intercut the closeup with several other shots: first a plate of soup on a table; next a woman's body lying in a coffin; next a small girl with a teddy bear. In *Film Technique* Pudovkin writes about the experiment:

When we showed the three combinations to an audience which had not been let into the secret the result was terrific. The public raved about the acting of the artist. They pointed out the heavy pensiveness of his mood over the forgotten soup, were touched and moved by the deep sorrow with which he looked on the dead woman, and admired the light, happy smile with which he surveyed the girl at play. But we knew that in all three cases the face was exactly the same.

This experiment points out not only the suggestive power of editing, but as well the importance of *limiting* the expressiveness of a face seen in closeup. Splayed out on a large screen, the face in closeup can easily become overwhelming and its effect verge on bathos if its expressions are not extremely controlled. Much for this reason, stage actors with a penchant for forceful, exaggerated expressions proper to the stage seem sometimes in film to be overblown, since the closeup captures every inflection.

Not only overwhelming expression, but a sheer volume of closeups can hurt a film. Television, with its almost instinctive reliance on closeups—particularly for reaction shots—has used the human face most often not for uncovering emotional wealth, but for sheer economy: it's easier, and less costly, to cut from face to face than to work out with precision a set-up that enables us to dwell at length on characters as they move and relate in space with one another.

Despite its abuses, the face remains, as Ingmar Bergman has said, "the starting point for our work." Of all subjects for the camera, the face is at once the most familiar and inexplicable, the most poignant and elusive.

LANGUAGE OF THE BODY

Early in *Bonnie and Clyde,* when Clyde Barrow and Bonnie Parker meet for the first time, they seem to circle one another, pacing back and forward and around in a kind of slow, carefully elaborated mating dance. Bonnie, bored and restless, is electrically, sexually conscious of Clyde. Clyde, with a kind of dumb Huck Finn innocence, can't help showing off to Bonnie. He looks around, sees no one else, and slides a fat revolver out of his belt to show Bonnie. The dialogue is brief, sporadic, only barely revealing. ("What's it like?" "Prison?" "No, armed robbery." "It's . . . I don't know . . . It isn't like anything.") But within those first few moments Bonnie and Clyde become etched indelibly in our minds. Bonnie drawn in toward Clyde, with a surface haughtiness that barely masks her fascination and heightening sensual awareness, Clyde, playing a matchstick between his teeth in an almost adolescent manner of cocky diffidence. It is not by their words so much as the evocative expressions of their bodies and faces. These two people come alive, become fully real for us, in a revelation of gesture and physical movement.

When *Bonnie and Clyde* shortly becomes violent—and the violence is abrupt, bloody, and unflagging—that very violence is localized, and felt, in the same characters we have known throughout; Bonnie, plunging through a creek with Clyde and C. W. Moss, screaming in pain from a bullet wound; Clyde fighting off a store manager who had attacked him with a meat cleaver, forced to smash the man with his gun ("He was trying to kill me!" says Clyde, incredulously); and, in the final massacre, both Bonnie's and Clyde's bodies dancing in a spastic surrender to a shower of bullets.

In film, most often the features and physical movements that create convincing characterization appear purely natural, almost spontaneous. In *Greed,* Trina's cousin Marcus sits with her outside Mac's dental office where she meets him for the first time. Director von Stroheim holds the camera on the impatient Marcus, who cannot keep his hands away from his face. He is forever scratching, cleaning out his ear, testing a sore tooth. These uninhibited, compulsive movements give us a brief and brilliantly succinct idea of Marcus.

The filmmaker can use a single part of the body to focus on a character's intention or disposition or mood. In *The Wind,* Lillian Gish as an Eastern girl out West hesitantly marries a cowboy. On their wedding night she stands uncertainly while he approaches her. The director, Victor Sjöström, shows only the feet at the crucial meeting, first his, walking across the wooden floor, then hers; then his as he reaches her. The rigid stance of her two feet, moving neither forward nor backward, tells us much about her near-paralyzing terror. In *Greed,* when Mac's temper flares at Trina—who will not give him even enough money for a few beers—we see his hand rising in the air, and, in near anguish, the fingers curling into a fist. The movement of his hand expresses his heightening torment with potent economy.

In previous arts the movement of the human body was the domain of dance and the related world of sport. The finest movement of a dancer or runner or vaulter or diver has a symmetry and precision that require an exceptional camera eye to be captured fully on film. In the bountifully rich short *Nine Variations on a Dance Theme,* dancer Bettie de Jong wends through nine versions of a dance motif, rising first from the floor, then spreading her body into rhythmic arcs in space, gradually enclosing the spaces around her in a growing crescendo of movement, and finally retreating back to the floor. The cinematographer and director Hilary Harris focuses on her movements from a rousing variety of perspectives, holding now on an arm, then a leg, then a sweep of hair and torso, and editing all into a smooth, extraordinary flow of pure supple movement—itself a ballet of camera and cutting. The movement of the camera and of the cutting become counterpoints to the movement of the dancer, suggesting the variety of ways in which the human figure in motion can be realized on film.

Even more visually seductive, and among the most marvelous moments of the human figure in motion on film, is the diving sequence from Leni Riefenstahl's *Olympia,* her chronicle of the 1936 Berlin Olympics. Riefenstahl set the cameras at a variety of places, catching the divers from below, above, at the side. Edited in a series of increasingly short vignettes, the divers become lucid with motion: their figures jut, arc, rise, sweep into the air, and we can only marvel at the balance and pure flow of their movements and their taut, seemingly easy twists in mid-air. The sequence moves progressively from showing entire dives—from the movement on the board to the diver's entry into the water—toward the most breathtaking part of the dive, the vault off the board. The bodies of the divers become almost abstractions, figures that belong seemingly to some purer and less clumsy species than ours—part, certainly, of the hail-Nazi intentions that lurked somewhat behind the making of the film.

OBJECTS

One of the fundamental and unique features of film is the adaptability of its scale. Mount Everest can appear in a satellite shot as a flyspeck in the vast wild stubble of the Himalayas; a drop of water, magnified enough, becomes a world unto itself, a great bilious sac reflecting even greater and stranger worlds. Most films at most times are scaled to human proportions, but even within this scale the camera can focus on smaller dramatic moments and draw from them a strength and even poignancy. It is within this scale that objects can become highly significant dramatic characters.

Consider two scenes in Fritz Lang's *M,* about a child murderer. In one scene the mother of a little girl who has disappeared combs the building to look for her. We see her walk through empty rooms, stare into empty corridors, look forlornly down a naked stairwell. But to further emphasize the girl's absence, Lang proceeds to show her table setting, untouched, and her ball in the play yard, unmoving. The implication is bitterly evident and poignantly felt. In another scene, the murderer, played by Peter Lorre, takes out his knife to peel an apple. When a young girl with whom he has spoken before appears, he nervously drops the knife. She picks it up and hands it to him. This focus on the knife provides a shrewd way of accenting Lorre's character as a psychopath, at once dangerous and pathetic.

In the proper context, the slightest object and the slightest movement of that object can become immensely significant. Lionel Barrymore plays the aging father of a stern, uncompromising army commander during World War I in *The Road to Glory.* Barrymore wants desperately to go to the front lines for battle; his son, the commander, played by Fredric March, adamantly opposes it. When a slip of paper arrives ordering the old man elsewhere, Barrymore is anguished by the fact and stares at the sheet of paper helplessly. Someone enters the room, the draft blows the paper to the floor, and Barrymore slowly realizes how vulnerable that little sheet of paper is. With another man's help, he kneels to puff and whisk it toward the fire, an effort that finally results in success.

Objects needn't be in direct interaction with people to take on and develop their dramatic tensions. Toward the end of *Sahara,* Bogart, who is defending an oasis outpost against encircling Germans during World War II, sends a man out to contact the army and bring help. The man walks for miles, gradually runs out of water, and staggers in the broiling sun. He drops his gun, his canteen, his supplies and can move only falteringly through the hot sands. All this isn't seen. It is suggested by images of objects—the supplies, the rifle, the canteen, naked objects in the sand while footprints stretch away from them.

ENVIRONMENT AS CHARACTER

Just as objects can add to the dramatic quality, virtually providing "characters" who, though not human, interact significantly with the human characters in the story, so environments can become a vital part of the film's visual and moral structure—only more so.

In a film no environment is neutral. The quality and evocative associations of the surroundings—the kind of furniture in a room, the spaces that surround the characters, the mood of weather or the scale of the walls—create a mood that can heighten the emotional feeling of a scene, or provide a counterpoint to it, or underscore it with an ironic touch. In film, where the environments are as visible, as tangible as the characters and where we see characters moving in space within these environments, the set is often more than simple setting.

The Cabinet of Dr. Caligari, an early German film in which walls and corridors and doorways twist and intersect in perverse, angular distortion, was one of the first films to use the sets in a manner fully conscious of the shaping power of environments. The people and the circumstances are abnormal enough; but they seem ordinary, even typical when set within these grotesque, disfigured spaces. We learn through the film that this is an asylum, and at the end we learn that we have seen everything as an inmate of the asylum—himself a madman—sees it; and to some extent this "explains" the use of such bizarre sets. But the sets give *Caligari* an impressive visual power. They evoke the sense of a world gone berserk, of ordinary places that have ceased to be ordinary, become indeed hostile and debilitating, so that the characters within them cannot help but become themselves grotesques and monstrosities.

In *The Crowd,* director King Vidor uses settings like traps. The film's theme—that the modern urban man is an alienated cipher in a vast, swirling crowd—is evoked, suggested, brought home by the use of sets throughout the film. The architecture of skyscrapers, with its flat, endless surfaces and its innumerable same-looking windows; the hospital, in which director King Vidor used a trapezoidal set to create a vivid impression of endless rows of beds and patients; even the funhouse sequence, with its playful games that spin and wind the same for everyone: throughout, the film repeats its theme forcefully by its locales and sets.

The Trial, Orson Welles' mordant, architecturally rich adaptation of the Kafka classic, has a similar theme. But instead of using crowds, Welles uses naked buildings, vast haunted interiors, and places where harsh lights mingle with black shadows to evoke a sense of unnatural contrast. The story and dramatic structure of *The Trial* are confusing, at times inexplicable, yet the film projects a powerful feeling of being lost, of a single man imperiled in an almost metaphysical way by hostile, overwhelming environments.

Architecture can become immensely significant even within more traditional types of films. The classic gangster films, for example, seem to be characterized by their scenes of dark nighttime streets; of black looming buildings and the halo wash of an infrequent street lamp. In Lang's *M,* itself a superlative gangster film, the damp, fetid streets of Berlin take on an ominous, portentous air because we know that the psychopathic killer walks them. When he is trapped by the organized criminals, it is in an empty building, and the dark enclosed spaces of the building give the sequence a taut, dramatic edge. Compare this to a much later gangster classic, *Point Blank,* in which the modern architecture of Los Angeles is depicted in shattering sunlight, a different world, and for the old-style gangster loner played by Lee Marvin, a world that he must battle on his terms. In both cases the moral struggle of the film is reflected—indeed, one suspects partly created—by the architecture.

Often an environment becomes most potent when it manages to project the interior life of the characters. At the end of *Greed,* when Mac has killed Trina and fled with her money, he is pursued by her cousin Marcus, and the two men meet in the center of Death Valley. Surrounded by the parched, cracking dirt, the two men fight over money that we suspect neither of them will ever escape from Death Valley to be able to spend. When a stray bullet hits the canteen, wasting the minute remainder of the water, we're aware that Mac's and Marcus's greed has led them to a condition which is palpably visible in the parched desert around them.

Writes Lewis Mumford: "Though it has been so stupidly misused, the motion picture nevertheless itself announces itself as a major art of the (modern age). Through the machine, we have new possibilities of understanding the world we have helped to create." That film enables us to see ourselves in a complex relationship to a new technological world we have created since movies began is perhaps one of the ultimate benefits of the movies, for film, like any art at its height, belongs ultimately to its time, and rises from the profoundly felt needs of the time.

SCREEN ACTING

Anyone who looks at the early melodramas of the silent era becomes immediately aware of a difference in the actors. They tend usually (not always) to be grandiose in their expressions, "theatrical," flamboyant. They were, in effect, merely imitating the style of acting then popular on the stage. The best directors of the time, D. W. Griffith and Rex Ingram, and gradually directors like Ford and Chaplin and von Stroheim, came to realize that screen acting required a totally different approach, and for a variety of peculiar reasons.

On the stage, an actor stands before hundreds, some of whom can see only his most exaggerated gestures. If he were to tug slightly at an earlobe, it might go unnoticed by two-thirds of the audience. So the stage actor tends to invest his energy and talent in his lines, the inflection and gusto he brings to them, the inner life they must convey. On the stage, acting is largely speech and delivery, often carried with an emphasis and forcefulness that are exaggerated for the benefit of again, that two-thirds of the audience that isn't sitting nearby.

By the mobility of its perspective, film can assume everyone is sitting up close, and the slightest tug of an earlobe can be immensely significant. The screen actor will speak lines, true; but the full power of his presence on the screen and his dramatic relationship to the story is brought across less by dialogue than by the way in which he is present in the image—his posture, his dress, and manner and movement. Marlon Brando speaks in stumbling, half-heard phrases in *On the Waterfront*. Sometimes we can't even quite make out exactly what he's saying. But that the nervous puzzlement he conveys, and the slumped, in-puckered manner in which he walks tells us far more about his character than what he says, just as his dialogue is more significant for its stumbling manner than its content.

Screen acting poses peculiar difficulties for the actor, which helps explain why many actors prefer the theater. On a movie set, the actor has no real audience, only a director, some crewhands, and the glazed unnatural eye of the camera. There is no one whose attention can be riveted by the startling phrasing of a line, no crowd whose very breathing can be played by the measured utterance of his words. And, perhaps more critically, movies are shot in tiny bits and pieces. An actor might step before the camera to do nothing more than make a frightened look. Within a play, that same frightened look might come at the high point of the drama, a point at which the actor would be emotionally keyed to fix his face in a manner that's unforgettable. On the set, he's sitting with a cup of coffee, is called by the director, and is expected to make a look that will send shivers down the spines of audiences around the world.

Moreover, film acting requires far more constraint of an actor. It is generally better, at least safer, to underact in film than to overact. In the baleful gaze of a closeup, the actor's slightest inflections are magnified hundreds of times over for the big screen. His actions must appear at once believable, convincing and natural. Indeed, a natural quality of movement, gesture, inflection, speech is inescapable for screen acting. Movies show us so much that we recognize as real, that if a performance—and indeed, the entire story—is to be convincing, we must recognize it as real, believe it to be natural.

There is another distinct problem posed by screen acting, perhaps not implicit in the nature of film itself, but developed over the years as a fundamental part of the movie system. As early as 1914, when Theda Bara played a glowering vamp in *A Fool There Was,* the producers and promoters of movies worked to build certain actors into popular figures, whom audiences would look forward to seeing in the next movie. Theda Bara wasn't much of an actress (she looked splendidly seductive on publicity posters, though) and she set an important precedent for many movie stars to follow. Acting talent is not necessarily a prerequisite for a star. But even those stars who could act became aware of a critical limitation. They were expected to play the same role—or some variation on that same role, which was their public image—in every film. When a Bogart acted magnificently as a collapsing personality in *The Treasure of the Sierra Madre,* Bogart audiences (who could usually be expected to make sure any Bogart film made money) suddenly weren't interested.

The screenwriter Dudley Nichols has argued that the essence of screen acting is not acting as such, but *reacting,* that a film is structured in such a way that an actor's basic job is to react to a situation, to be, as Nichols says, "acted upon." The intercutting of brief shots —none of which truly permits a full expression of complex emotions—would seem to bear this out. But in effect Nichols is not so much explaining the nature of screen acting as justifying a certain limited kind of screen reacting. The full potential of screen acting lies not so much in cutting back and forth from one reaction to another, but in permitting a strong actor with good lines some degree of expression before the camera. There is an explicit danger in reaction shots, in that they tend to simplify what could otherwise be more entangled and engaging emotional experiences.

IMAGERY, SYMBOLS AND MEANING

In *Winter Light,* Ingmar Bergman's harsh, ascetic tale of the lonely anguish of a country priest, there is a single image, running through much of the film, that haunts the mind afterwards: a naked light bulb hanging from the ceiling, casting a pale, almost cold light over the priest's impoverished empty room. That light bulb, one realizes, is much like the priest, spare, unaided, without a single warm receptive surface to reflect onto, and necessary. It is hardly an obtrusive symbol; it may not be, in the manner of literary or mythical symbols, a symbol at all. But it is an inescapable part of the world we see on the screen, and imparts to us some of the raw, scoured quality of that world.

Because of its inherent naturalism, film is uneasy with intentional symbols that might be set there as "guideposts" to some separate, elusive meaning. The most effective symbols in film are those that appear a natural, even inevitable part of the surroundings and the drama. Only on reflection do we become aware of their subtler meanings. In *The Wild Bunch,* a film that follows the last days of an aging outlaw gang in the early years of the new century, one of the first images we see is a group of Mexican children crowded over a savage little spectacle: a scorpion in an anthill, struggling under a seething blanket of ants. It is not an explicit or obvious symbol, and, indeed, it works less by a direct analogy to the action than by the patent force of what we see. It's a grisly sight, but a consequence of the violent struggle in nature—and the Mexican children, like us, the audience, like to watch a violent struggle.

John Ford's film *The Informer* uses symbolic images in a more telling, one might say almost literary manner. The theme of the film is the slow birth of conscience in a man's fogged mind. Set during the Irish Rebellion, it centers on Gypo, who is seduced by reward posters and a travel poster into turning in Frankie McPhillip, a leader of the Rebellion and in some way a friend of Gypo. Ford uses a number of visual devices to suggest what is happening inside Gypo's mind. When Gypo passes a cafe and sees Frankie seated inside, a poster reflects off the glass just below Frankie, transforming what Gypo (and the audience) sees into a poster, and its promise. When Gypo walks down the street after tearing a poster off the wall, the poster follows him, gusted by winds, and slaps into the back of his legs—a direct suggestion of the way in which the reward money haunts and follows Gypo everywhere. And, in a poignant scene with a blind man, Gypo bumps into the man and only discovers slowly that he is blind, a realization that disturbs Gypo, for he thought the man was following him. Throughout such scenes, Ford uses a minimum of dialogue and conveys the rising tension (a difficult tension for a film to express, since it's strictly within a single man's mind) by means of such visual metaphors.

Greed, discussed already for the powerful and direct naturalism of its imagery, shows the range of screen imagery and the fundamental difference between the direct and the indirect use of imagery. In the wedding sequence there is a banquet, at which the wedding crowd feasts on the food, and the audience feasts on the grotesquerie of the wedding crowd. These people—including a man so fat he dwarfs the chair he's sitting in—don't simply eat, they attack the food, stuffing and wedging it into themselves compulsively. The scene is overdone, but its force is direct, vivid, inescapable. Contrast such a scene with the use of two canaries to symbolize the marriage and mutual destinies of the main characters in *Greed,* Mac and Trina. When Mac first meets Trina in his dentist's office, he cannot resist an impulse to kiss her (while she's under anaesthetic), and, at the same time, a cat attacks the canaries. On their wedding night, as Mac and Trina kiss, the canaries chirp happily. When they fight, the canaries screech, and so on. The symbolic structure here, though not obstrusive, is certainly less direct and immediate than the wedding dinner.

The Manchurian Candidate, a thriller and a satire on the McCarthy paranoia that passed itself off as super-patriotism, is rich in images that ironically suggest how real patriotism has gone mad. The key figures, Senator John Iselin as the McCarthy-type Senator and his domineering wife (played ferociously by Angela Lansbury), are seen often against such things as busts and paintings of Lincoln, images associated with the glories of American history. One shot particularly, the opening of a grotesque costume ball, shows in closeup a bright large American flag. Suddenly a hand with a scoop sweeps down, shovels into the center of the flag, and scoops out a spatter of caviar. The camera backs away to show that it's Senator Iselin, dressed (how else?) as Lincoln, and the irony becomes fiercely sarcastic.

Imagery can give film a resonance and an inner structure that balances the dramatic structure, but the best images and symbols rarely are evident as images and symbols while we're seeing the film. They should appear so natural and commonplace within the story that they seem almost basic fixtures of the characters and plot and setting.

A WORLD DISTORTED

If a writer—say, a William Burroughs or a James Joyce—wants to give a distorted, off-balance view of the world, from whiskey or drugs or whatever, his style will adapt to create the distorted effect. In film, such distortion can become immediately and vividly apparent by the very expressive means within the image, the use of the camera, lens, setting.

In *The Last Laugh,* F. W. Murnau's masterpiece about a pathetic doorman sliding to the bottom of the social heap, Murnau uses distorted lenses in a few of the sequences to capture the faces of the women in the man's life. Their features swim on the screen, barely recognizable as faces, suggesting forcefully the man's inward terror of them, and how unreal and mocking their presence has become.

Hitchcock's *Spellbound,* a thriller with the theme of psychiatry, contains a remarkable dream sequence in which the sets (designed partly by the surrealist painter Salvador Dali) present weird events—a game of cards at an enormous table, a man cutting through the painted eyes on a vast curtain behind it; a man pushing a twisted bicycle wheel across a house rooftop in a perversely strange landscape, and the sets are such that space itself seems bent out of shape, like the bicycle tire.

Seconds, John Frankenheimer's film about a man who undergoes the ultimate plastic surgery—he is transformed, literally, into Rock Hudson—anticipates the operation in a dream sequence in which the man imagines himself walking through a corridor, then entering his wife's room. His face, drastically foreshortened by an extreme wide-angle lens, seems sickeningly unreal, and the room in which his wife sleeps, seen from her point of view, becomes a bizarre place of liquid walls and cavernous spaces, distortions so immediate and thorough that the sequence conveys a rare disturbing quality.

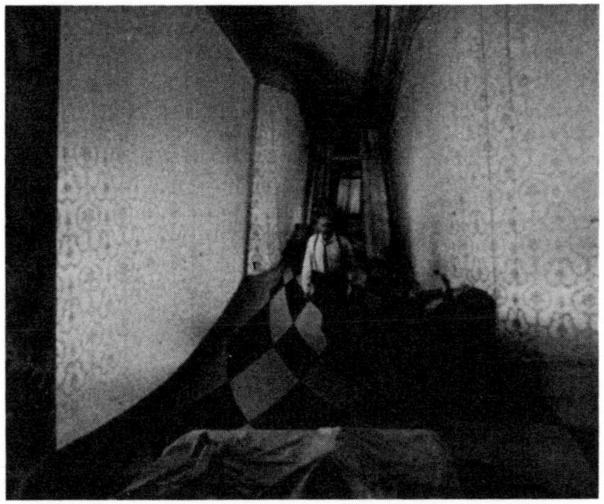

The Human Face

It has long been the ambition of artists and sculptors to capture in their material the emotions, stresses, and subtler inflections of the human face. Filmmakers, armed with the technology to capture the human face in all its expressive range, have at their command not the one expression which a painter must fix, but the capability of showing how expressions—and the moods and urges that give rise to them—flex and merge, rise and erupt.

For the filmmaker, a face can undergo several transformations in a moment. Greta Garbo became the greatest screen star largely because her face was forever haunted by a flight of moods: in one moment she seemed eager, gay; the next, torn and indecisive; the next, trembling and guilt-ridden.

Even in the sound film, the face can express far more than the dialogue. A woman proclaiming her love can become, given a fine enough actress, a woman whose words belie what her face tells the audience. Indeed, much of the best tension in films rises from the discrepancy between what the words tell us and what the face tells us.

In *The Manchurian Candidate,* Angela Lansbury plays the dominating mother of a returning war hero. In a scene aboard a plane early in the film, she establishes immediately the forcefulness, the brash insistence, and the sputtering violence of the mother's character. The dialogue suggests some of this, but the energy, the vehemence, and the arrogance are far more evident in her face.

Woody Allen chewing glass in *Bananas.*

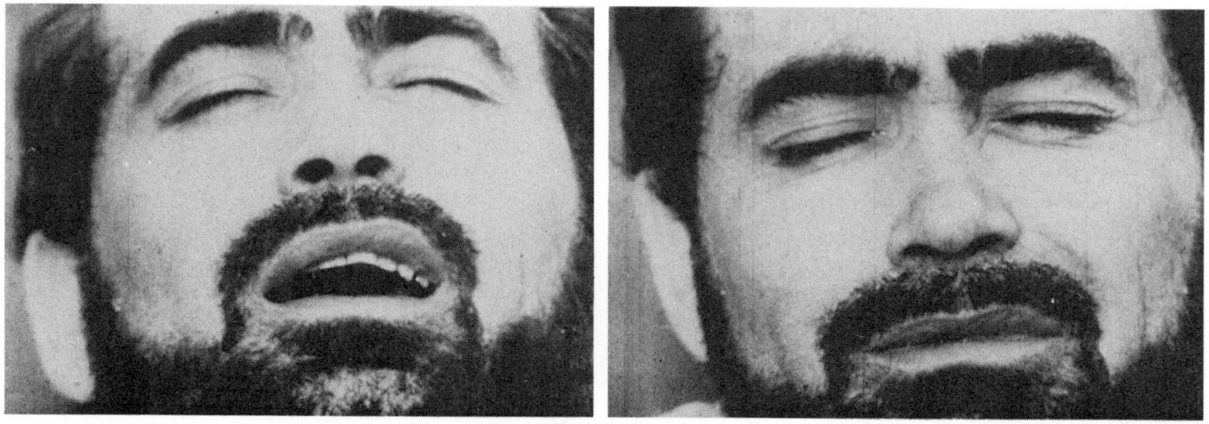

Roger Jacquet in *An Occurrence at Owl Creek Bridge.*

A Thousand Faces in One

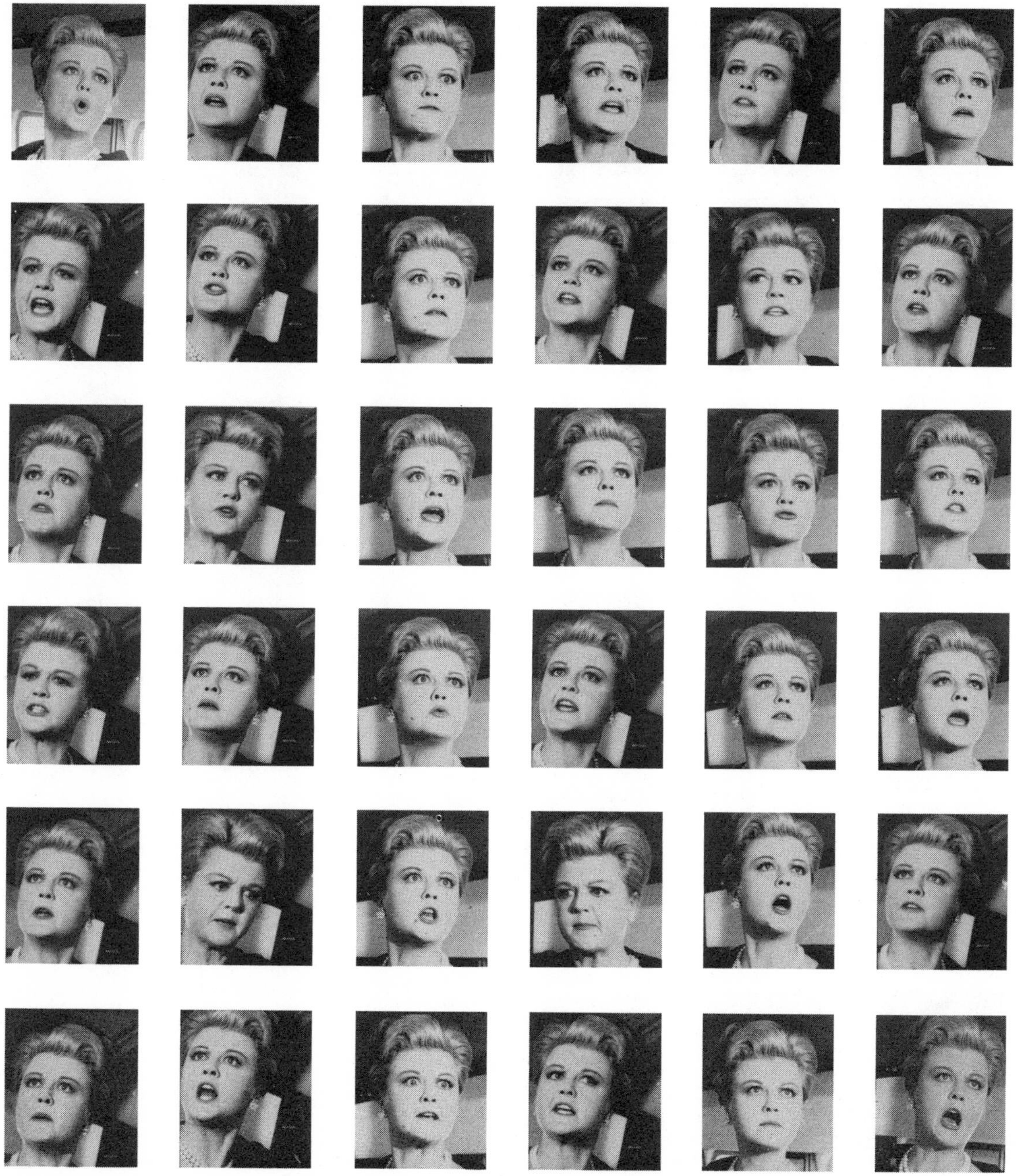

"Monstrously enlarged as it is on the screen, the human face should be treated like a landscape. It is to be viewed as if the eyes were lakes, the nose a hill, the cheeks broad meadows, the mouth a flower patch, the forehead sky, and the hair clouds."—Joseph von Sternberg

"It may be reasonable to assert that an actor can never achieve the same depth of artistry in a silent film as on the stage for the material at his disposal—the mere expression of face and gesture without the interpretation of spoken words—is too primitive."—Rudolf Arnheim

"The human face is the starting point for our work. The camera must take part only like a totally objective observer. The actor's most beautiful means of expression is his look. Simplicity, concentration, an awareness of details, these must be the constant factors in each scene and each ensemble."—Ingmar Bergman

"Not only can facial expression itself tell us things for which we have no words—the rhythm and tempo of changes in facial expression can also indicate the oscillation of moods which cannot be put into words. A single twitch of a facial muscle may express a passion for the expression of which a long sentence would be needed . . . The most rapid tempo of speech lags behind the flow and throb of emotions; but facial expression can always keep up with them, providing a faithful and intelligible expression for them all."—Béla Balázs

Angela Lansbury in *The Manchurian Candidate*

Language of the Body

THE TELLING GESTURE:

Gestures, particularly those which appear natural rather than theatrical, can be a potent way of revealing character, emotion, attitude in film. Above, from *Greed*: Trina's cousin Marcus waits with her outside McTeague's dental office. What is your impression of this man?

Bonnie and Clyde reveals director Arthur Penn's talent for a vivid sense of characters heightened and brought off by their physical actions: gesture, the nuances and inflections of face and body, in brief a manner of style, so authentic that the violence seems merely to extend it.

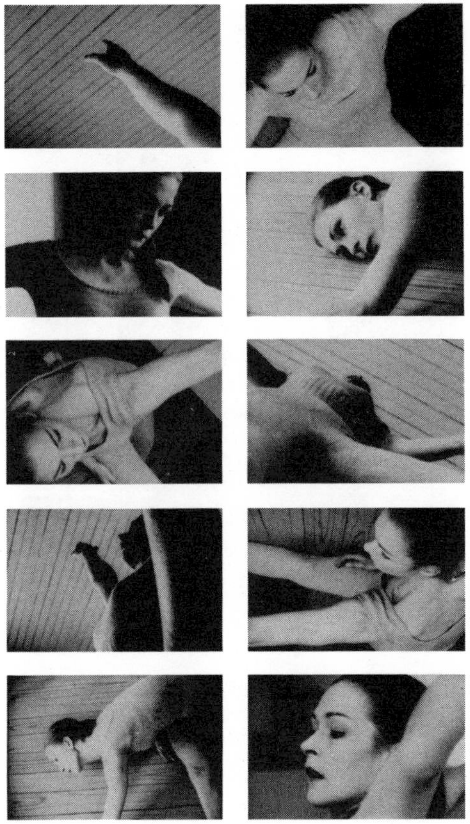

THE BODY IN MOTION

Nine Variations on a Dance Theme is a superbly edited study of a dancer and camera in simultaneous movement: the jutting flow is remarkable; even more so is the sense of movements gradually erupting, as though, in seeing the film, we were experiencing the vitality of movement from within the dancer's psyche.

MICROCOSM OF THE BODY

Part of the body can be as telling as the entire body.

The Wind: Lillian Gish and her first night with her husband.

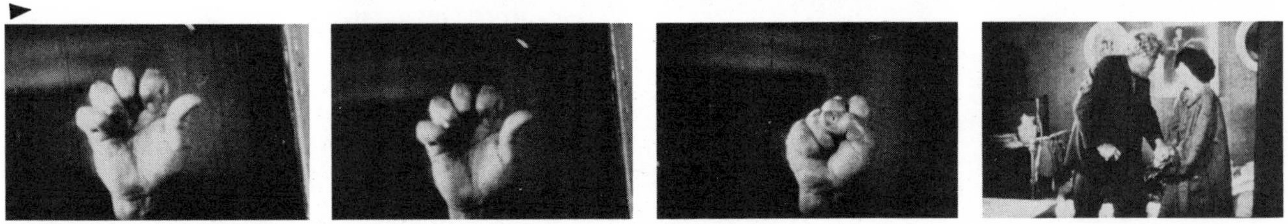

Mac's anger at Trina, *Greed*.

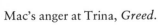

Objects

"What interests me now is to place the character in contact with things, for it is things, objects and materials that have weight today."—Michelangelo Antonioni

Film, which captures whatever surfaces appear before the camera, makes no distinction between human or inhuman, animate or inanimate. Thus objects and settings can take on enormous significance given a sufficient dramatic context.

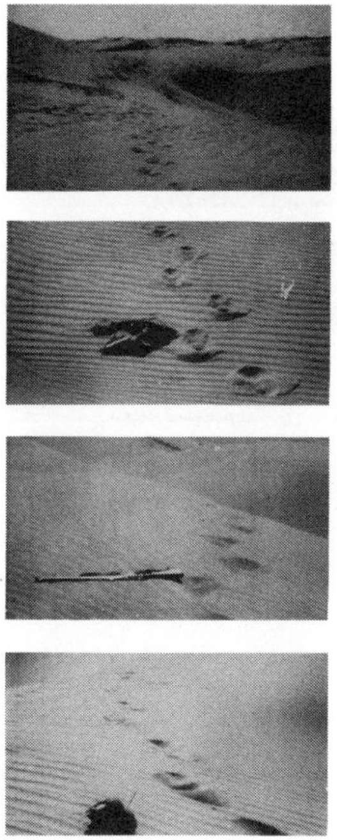

A SENSE OF THE FORLORN

M: the disappearance of a girl is echoed in the emptiness of the staircase, but even more forcefully in her untouched plate and ball. Above: from *Sahara,* could a stretched skeleton suggest more?

HINGES OF FATE

An empty barrel in *Wild Boys of the Road* becomes more than an empty barrel when we know that the boy running from the cops is hiding there. A familiar gag when used earlier in numerous slapstick comedies, here the empty barrel gimmick conveys dramatic tension with the simple question: Will they look?

ODYSSEY OF A PURSE

A sequence in the strange musical, *Hallelujah, I'm a Bum!* depicts the journey of a purse laden with a thousand-dollar bill. Left at the table in a restaurant, it is swept up with the tablecloth; thrown into the trash, but falls loose outside where the tramp leader (Al Jolson) tosses a newspaper unnoticingly over it—again destined for the trash. Jolson, looking for a fresh newspaper, spots it, retrieves it, and discovers, of course, the thousand dollars. Much of the delight in this sequence comes from the persistent inability of anyone to spot the purse.

▼

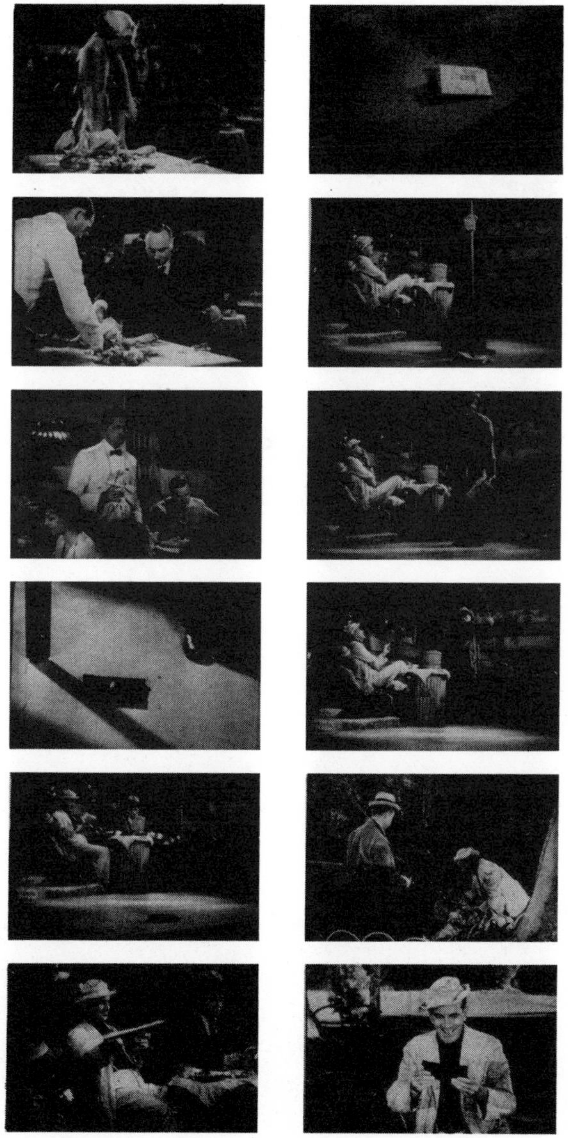

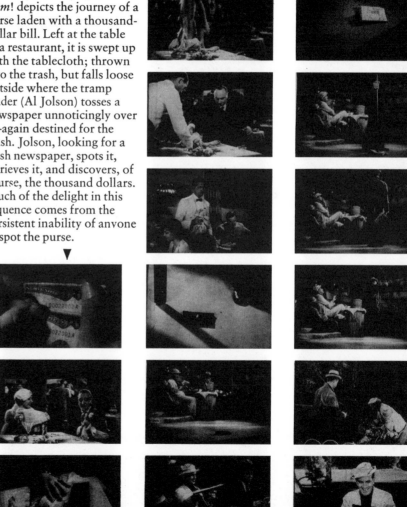

Environment as Character

THE CABINET OF DR. CALIGARI

The first major film seriously to use sets as considerably more than settings, *The Cabinet of Dr. Caligari* (Germany, 1919), centers around a doctor and his somnambulistic servant-slave who rises at night to murder or kidnap. The incidents and plot constitute one of the finest horror films ever made, but throughout the film it is the sets that often captivate and unsettle us. Walls are distorted, twisted; floors slope; the world seems to have been evoked (which it was) from a series of cubist paintings. *Caligari* is the most stunning of the early German "expressionist" films and shows to what extent environments and settings can create the psychological milieu in a film.

"The things surrounding men do not merely act upon them—men react on their surroundings too and while they allow things to change them, they in return change things. The clothes and household goods of a man permit a sure conclusion to be drawn as to his character. Nature forms man and man forms nature and this, too, is a natural process . . . Man set down in the middle of an immense world cuts himself a little world out of it and hangs it full of his own images."—Wolfgang Goethe

"I am very susceptible to landscape. When I am shooting a film, I always try to establish a rapport between characters and landscape."
—Michelangelo Antonioni

"The mood of a landscape, or of a room, prepares us for the scene to be enacted in it."
—Béla Balázs

When a boy struggles through a bundle of ropes in Eisenstein's *Strike,* the ropes themselves seem alive.

The wretched end of *Greed,* in the middle of Death Valley: Mac and Trina's cousin Marcus fighting over the money when the canteen is almost dry.

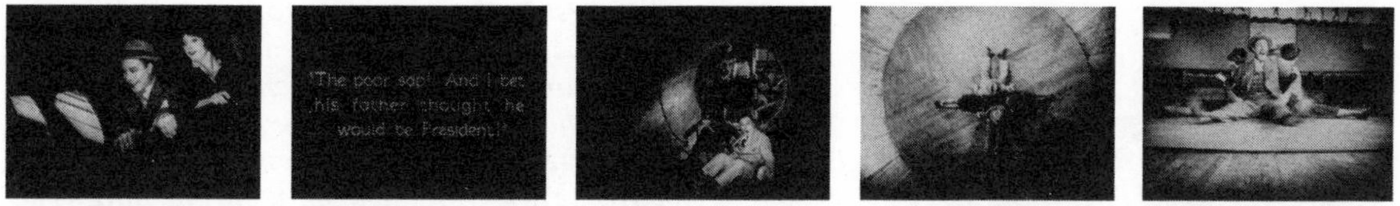

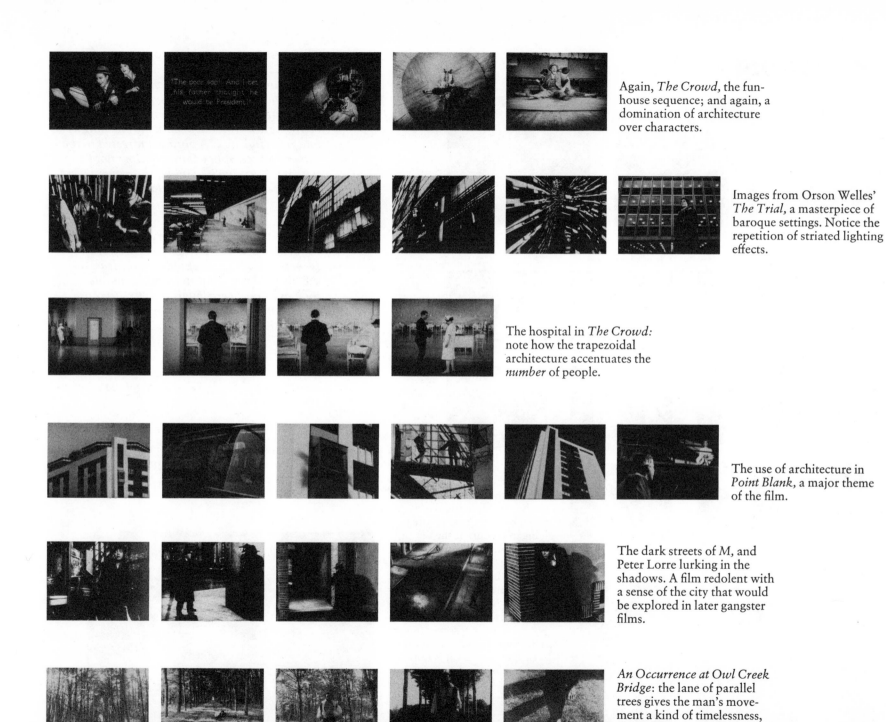

Again, *The Crowd,* the fun-house sequence; and again, a domination of architecture over characters.

Images from Orson Welles' *The Trial,* a masterpiece of baroque settings. Notice the repetition of striated lighting effects.

The hospital in *The Crowd:* note how the trapezoidal architecture accentuates the *number* of people.

The use of architecture in *Point Blank,* a major theme of the film.

The dark streets of *M,* and Peter Lorre lurking in the shadows. A film redolent with a sense of the city that would be explored in later gangster films.

An Occurrence at Owl Creek Bridge: the lane of parallel trees gives the man's movement a kind of timelessness, appropriate for the dream in which he is running.

Screen Acting

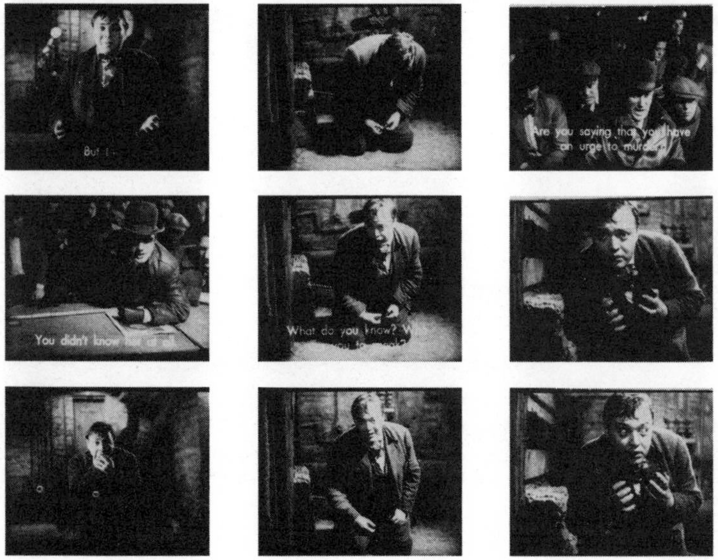

Peter Lorre projects something both pitiable and chilling in *M*, particularly when he is dragged before a kangaroo court of the Berlin underworld. We come to sympathize with him even as we draw back in horror from his admitted need to murder. Some of this response comes from Fritz Lang's restrained, potent directing; some from Thea von Harbou's trenchant script; but mainly it is Lorre's performance—a staggering creation of a psychopathic personality that rings with a fierceness and a depth rarely achieved by any actor on the screen.

"The first quality of a director is to see. This quality is also valuable in dealing with actors. The actor is one of the elements of the image. A modification of his pose or gestures modifies the image itself. A line spoken by an actor in profile does not have the same meaning as one given full-face. A phrase addressed to the camera placed above the actor does not have the same meaning it would if the camera were placed below him."—Michelangelo Antonioni

"The 'natural acting' of everyday life is curious . . . A man's facial expression often does not seem to the average beholder in the least indicative of his mental state. Some people look as if they were laughing when they are crying, and some people's smiles are very acid."—Rudolf Arnheim

"Acting has nothing to do with (the net construction of a film); it can only get in the way."
—Robert Bresson

"The great actors work with very slight expenditure of muscular energy, they achieve a substantial effect by their very presence."
—Rudolf Arnheim

...Or Reacting ?

"Unthinking people speak of the motion picture as the medium of 'action'; the truth is that the stage is the medium of action while the screen is the medium of reaction. It is through identification with the person acted upon *on the screen and not with the person acting, that the film builds up its oscillating power with the audience."—Dudley Nichols*

The church sequence in *Johnny Belinda* is a virtual orchestration of reactions, those of the townspeople as Belinda and her father enter; then of Belinda and the doctor as Belinda spots the man who raped her.

The calamity of a car accident (in *The Crowd*) expressed potently in the reactions of the parents as they watch horrified. Note that we don't actually see the truck strike the child, but we feel it through the parents' faces.

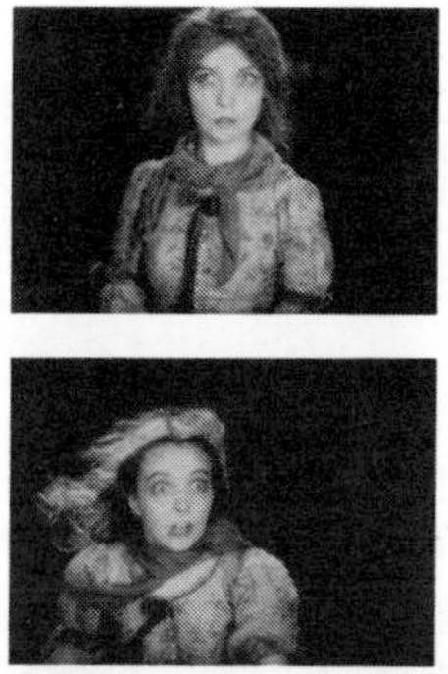

In *The Wind*, Lillian Gish plays an Eastern girl who goes to Texas and marries a cowhand; her unfamiliarity with this new world and her rising horror at her husband, the wind, and a man she is forced to kill (then see unearthed by the wind) is expressed always in reaction shots, yet always convincing reaction shots.

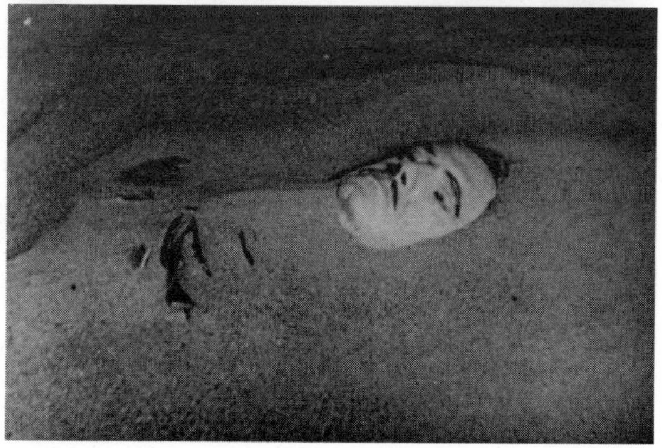

A World Distorted

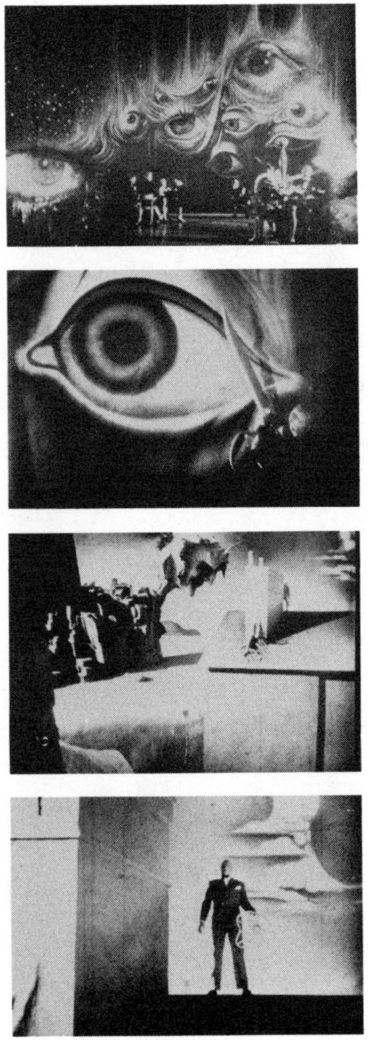

The dream sequence in Hitchcock's *Spellbound.* Salvador Dali helped design the sequence; note the distorted quality of space itself.

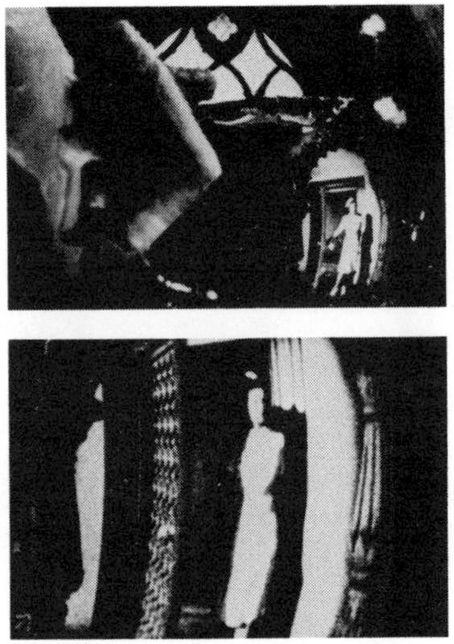

From *Citizen Kane*: the death sequence at the beginning; the approaching nurse seen through the glass ball.

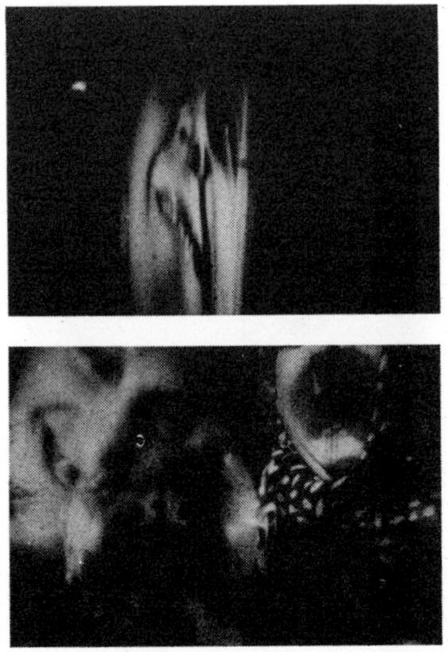

In F. W. Murnau's *The Last Laugh,* a pitiable doorman sees the women around him through the distortion of his own disturbed mind.

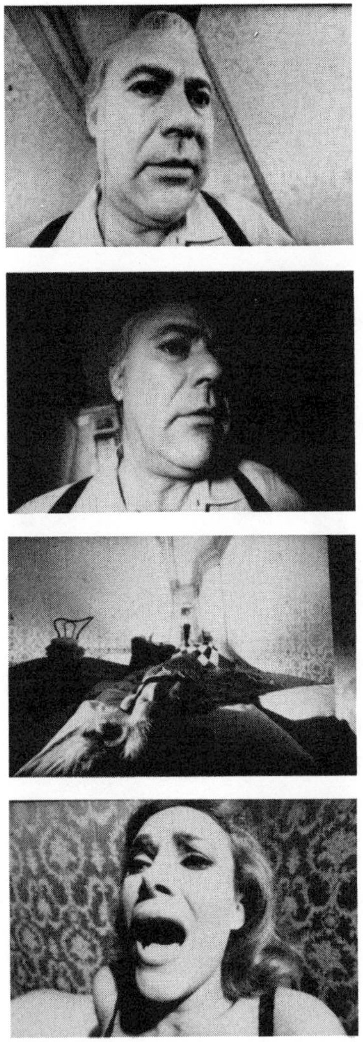

Images from *Seconds,* a study of identity transformation, made in this wide-angular, distorted style.

A montage sequence in Raoul Walsh's *The Roaring Twenties* presents in a single image —this abstract, burgeoning stock market ticker—the dizzy economic swell of the twenties.

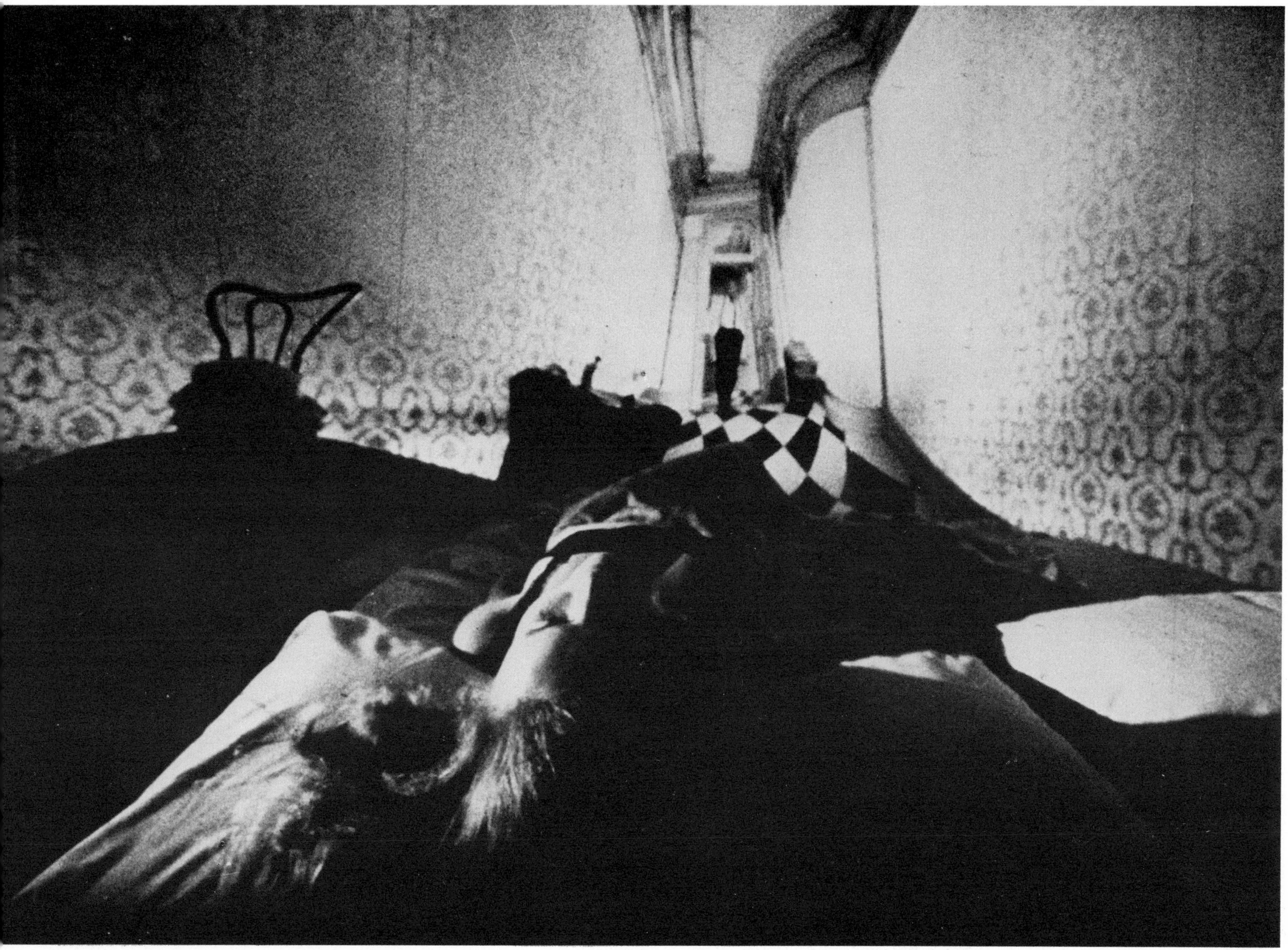

Seconds

Imagery, Symbols and Meaning

PATRIOTISM GONE AWRY:

The Manchurian Candidate is about—among other things—the McCarthy era in American politics and the caustic dangers of misplaced patriotism. The film is redolent in images of just such patriotic mishmash, as when a costume party opens on a caviar American flag; Senator Iselin, a whiskey-soused, Communist-taunting buffoon, is seen reflected ironically against a portrait of Lincoln; indeed, the use of such juxtapositions throughout the film serves as a reminder—like the newspapers in *Kane*—of a kind of social context.

THE CHARGED IMAGE:

The Queen of Diamonds

It begins as the "code" that unlocks the controlling mechanisms of Raymond Shaw's brainwashed mind, but gradually through the film the card, which we see in newer and more astounding contexts (as when his girlfriend, Josie, wears it as a costume) takes on increasing meaning: as Raymond's brutal mother; as a reminder of his condition; as, hopefully, an antidote to that condition.

THE INFORMER

Reflections of a haunted conscience: in *The Informer,* Gypo tears down a poster announcing the reward for a man he is thinking of turning in; the wind blows the loose poster against his legs. With a blind man he is startled, only slowly discovering the man is blind. And when he sees the wanted man in a window, the words are reflected in glass; the image becomes the poster.

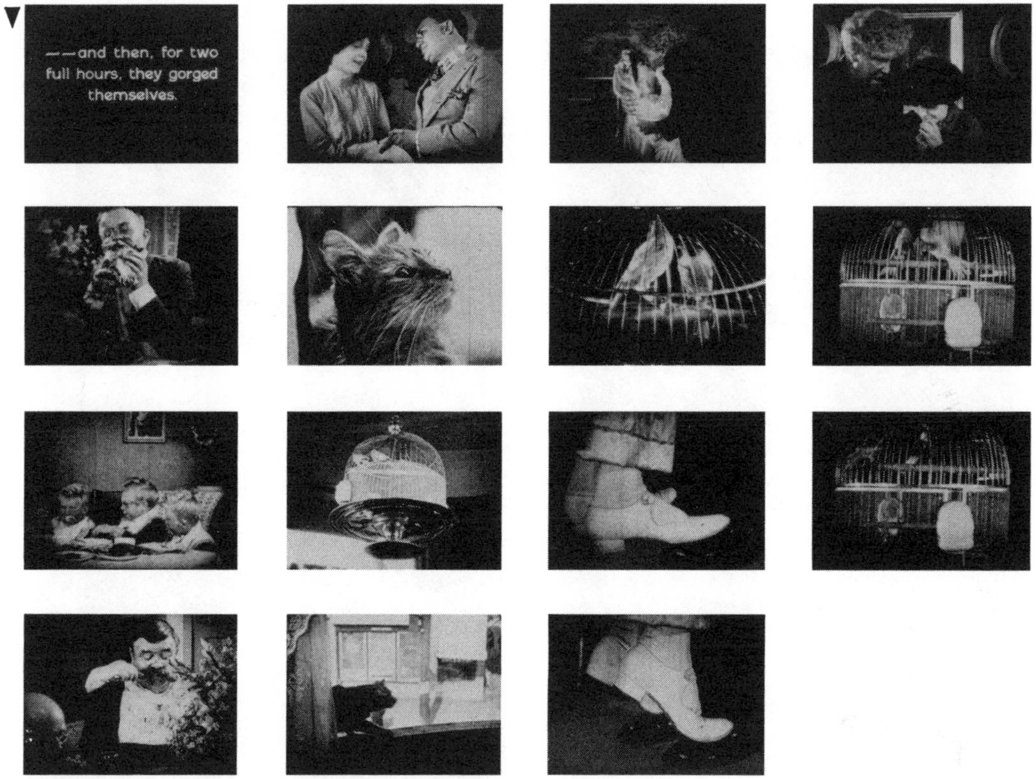

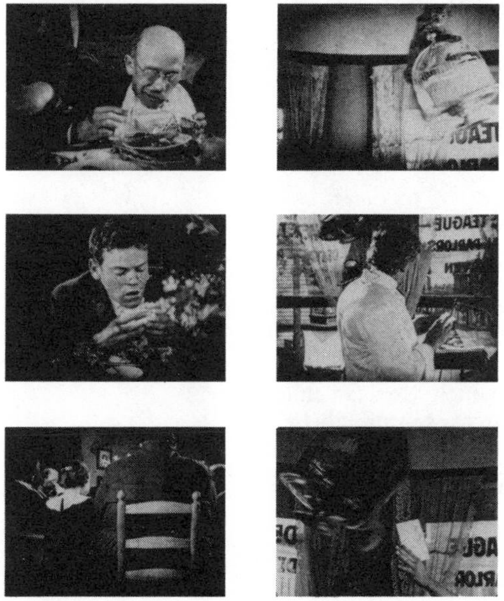

GREED

Two kinds of imagery from *Greed*: the direct and somewhat overdone wedding dinner—a montage of human rapacity; and the two birds that come throughout the film to reflect the state of Mac and Trina's marriage: cooing on the wedding night; attacked by a cat when Mac first meets (and kisses) Trina; screeching violently when Mac and Trina fight. At the end of the film, when Mac has fled with Trina's money after killing her, he is alone in a desert with another man and now a single sparrow; he releases it, but the sparrow will not fly away.

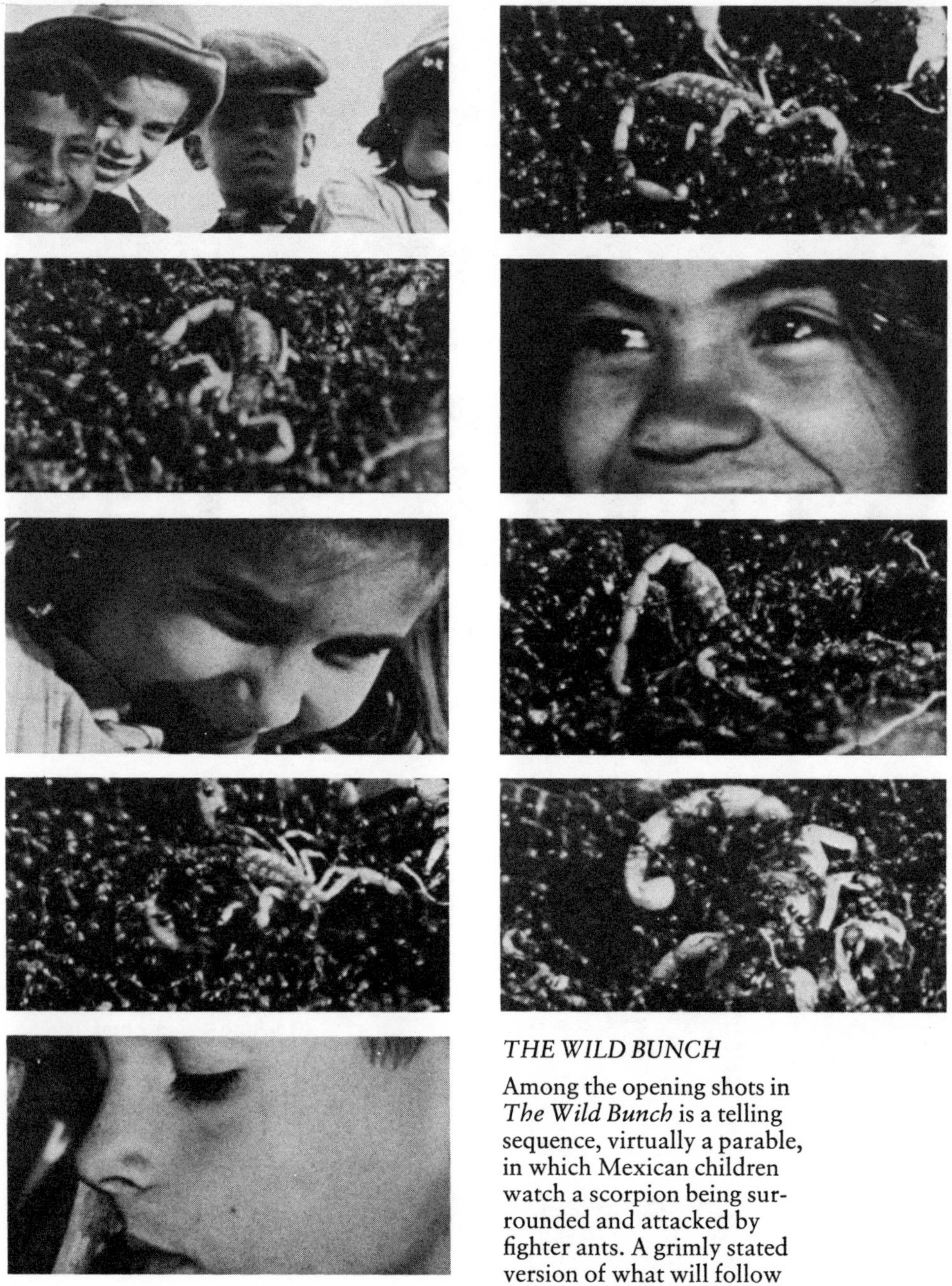

THE WILD BUNCH

Among the opening shots in *The Wild Bunch* is a telling sequence, virtually a parable, in which Mexican children watch a scorpion being surrounded and attacked by fighter ants. A grimly stated version of what will follow in the film.

CHAPTER SIX

Editing

Editing

If film is reduced to its essential components—movement, image, language, music, editing—it is clearer that all these elements are present in some way in the older arts: movement in ballet and drama; image and imagery in painting, sculpture, photography; language in drama and the novel; only one—editing—represents a drastic new form of expression, a technique belonging to film alone.

Editing is the culmination and architecture of film. Mechanically, it is the final phase of filmmaking, the point at which a huge, multi-million-dollar production will narrow to a single man in a small room, studying and cutting pieces of film and fitting them into place to create the final whole. But editing belongs to the beginning of a film as much as the end. Any script will have as a basic part of its construction a breakdown of scenes and sequences (if not specific shots) that present to the director and cameraman the arrangement of the parts and how they will fit together into the final film. True, the rhythm of editing and perhaps distinctive touches might be made by the director during shooting and later in the cutting room, but rarely does a well-edited film emerge from a script that does not contain much of the editing in it.

Of all the aspects of a film, editing is the most plastic. By altering the succession of shots, a director or editor can transform the meaning of a sequence. One of the most famous examples of this is shown in what a Scandinavian censor wanted to do with Eisenstein's classic, *The Battleship Potemkin.* Disturbed by the revolutionary tenor of the film, he asked Eisenstein if he could change a few sequences, promising not to leave a single shot out of the film; he wanted only to replace the order. In the film as Eisenstein made it, the mutiny on board the *Potemkin* is foreshadowed by several incidents, the first of them being a demonstration by the crew of the maggots crawling through the meat supplies, the final—and most important—being an execution called by the captain, in which the sailors refuse to fire on their fellows. The censor wanted to lift this execution sequence from the beginning, and place it at the end of the film, when the *Potemkin* draws other near vessels that threaten to fire upon it for mutiny, but finally do not (the other sailors sympathize with the mutiny and the *Potemkin* is allowed to steam off freely). Obviously, the replacement of the execution would have given the film an entirely different significance: the sailors would have mutinied apparently for the simple reason of maggots in their food; and their action would have been reprimanded by an execution at the end.

Mainly because it is so malleable an element, editing is often used to "save" a weak film. "We can save it in editing," is the long-echoed phrase of directors and producers. In the silent era, directors like Griffith could indeed "save" a film in the editing room, but as the camera grew more mobile and particularly after sound, the use of editing to cover mistakes and weaknesses in the shots tended to make a film choppy, rather than rhythmic, imparting a sense of incompleteness. Writes Pauline Kael: "Fast editing *can* be done for aesthetic purposes, but too much of it is done these days to cover up bad staging and shooting, and the effect is jerky and confusing." The best uses of editing in film—and one can see and feel it on the screen—tend to work from the strength, rather than the weaknesses of shots.

2 + 2 = 5

Eisenstein and Pudovkin—the leading Russian film directors and theorists of the twenties—both believed that editing is the aesthetic of film: that, in effect, all the other elements—the shot, set-up, lighting, movement—serve only as the raw material to be constructed by editing into the final film. Their films, particularly Eisenstein's, reflected this belief. In *The Battleship Potemkin* and *October* and *The General Line,* Eisenstein takes editing to extremes of rhythmic and visually awesome power never equalled before or since. True, not all filmmakers and critics agree with the Russians about the supremacy of editing; the eminent French critic and theorist André Bazin would later argue that editing breaks the flow of reality, and forces the viewer through an artificially constructed sequence of images, which does not respect the activity of the viewer's eyes or the nature of real time and shape. Yet Pudovkin and particularly Eisenstein have shown, in their writings and more emphatically in their films, the extent to which editing as an art can be used to create films of extraordinary power and dynamic inner movement.

It is not so much a matter of whether the Russians are right or Bazin is right. The films that Bazin extols—such as Welles' *Citizen Kane,* or William Wyler's *The Westerner*—are superb films for their own reasons, a depth of inner spaces within the frame that permits our eyes to linger and follow movement as though we were watching a canvas with a life inside it. Yet even Bazin cannot refute the original power and raw rhythmic force of the Odessa Steps sequence in *The Battleship Potemkin,* or that this sequence represents a supreme achievement of film *as* film—in no other medium could the rising crescendo of emotional turmoil and rage be possible.

The essence of editing, Eisenstein argued, is that two plus two equals five. One shot, connected to another shot, creates inevitably in the minds of an audience, a third, separate, distinct impression; and editing is largely the art of summoning and guiding those impressions. In *The Battleship Potemkin,* Eisenstein depicts a priest on board the battleship; our first impression of him, seen in medium shot, is that he is a formidable but perhaps gentle man, large, bearded, carrying a cross-shaped sceptre in his hands. But in a closeup Eisenstein reveals something to alter our impression considerably: his hand clenches round that cross in an iron fist; the cross might as well be a sword or a club. It isn't simply the second shot that gives us our full impression of the priest; it is the precise combination of both shots, as well as their succession in time. Our lingering impression of the priest seen in medium shot combines with the more forceful, direct insert of his hands, and that juxtaposition is what makes us thoroughly aware of the priest's antagonism toward the mutiny, and how he wields the power of the church as the Czar wields the power of the state.

This example of the priest in *The Battleship Potemkin* is the oldest and most basic technique of editing: to cut from a medium shot to a closeup, in which the field of action is re-created on a greater scale, permitting us to see as the entire action something that had been a small part of the earlier action. Of course there are variations on this. In the battle scenes of *The Birth of a Nation,* Griffith intercut between extreme long shots of the battle and closeups of the soldiers in hand-to-hand combat. The effect of jutting from long shot to closeup can be jarring and compelling. Not only does our perspective change drastically, but we are subtly aware of the relationship between the immensity of battle and the human terrors of two people brandishing bayonets at one another in a tiny corner of the battlefield.

With a single cut, time or space can be transformed instantly. In *The Big House* a spacious prison cafeteria is shown empty, all geometric rows of naked seats and tables. Suddenly in a cut the cafeteria is full, a jump in time that takes place within a fraction of a second. The same is true of place and time. In *Point Blank,* Lee Marvin escapes at the beginning from the deserted island prison Alcatraz, and we see him staggering wearily into the cold choppy waters of San Francisco Bay. A woman's voice-over comments on the island, and the bay; cut to Marvin, now dressed in a business suit and standing on a tourist boat, dourly observing the island he had earlier escaped. The cut is sudden, with no more overlap than the voice of the girl on the boat, but it establishes immediately the transition in time and space.

Sometimes a transition can be handled with extreme fluidity, so that we are not aware of a cut at all until the end of the second shot. At the conclusion of *North by Northwest,* Cary Grant and Eva Marie Saint are dangling from the stone faces of Mount Rushmore; he tugs her up. There is strain on his face, terror on hers; cut back to Grant and the final sweep in which he pulls her up—though now, we realize, they're in a Pullman sleeping car on a train; a moment of tension transformed by a continuous action cut into a happy-ever-after ending.

The cut can be used to associate internal or external relationships. When James Cagney, in a prison shop in *White Heat,* suddenly undergoes one of his chronic mental fits, director Raoul Walsh cuts to the grinding, whirring action of lathes and other shop machines to suggest graphically the rasping turmoil of Cagney's fit. In *Pretty Poison,* Tuesday Weld mentions to Tony Perkins that they should run away to Mexico. At the moment they are standing in a forest, and Perkins glances at the trees; director Noel Black cuts to a shot of beach and palm trees, stating visually what Perkins sees at that moment . . . not the forest, but a vision of a longed-for Mexico.

Associations can be external as well. During one of the numbers in the musical *Hallelujah, I'm a Bum!* the film cuts from the faces of the singing tramps to a row of crows, arranged in exactly the same graphic formation on the screen—intimating not only a similarity (and quite a strong one) between the tramps and the crows, but that the crows are singing along as well.

The soundtrack can both bridge a cut (as in the example from *Point Blank* of the overlapping soundtrack) and give a cut its significance. *The Manchurian Candidate* depicts James Gregory as Senator John Iselin, a tipsy, swaggering boor who rushes before the TV cameras each day to proclaim a new number of card-carrying Communists in the State Department. When he complains to his wife that the number keeps changing—she seemingly has engineered his demagoguery—she smiles acidly and holds up a paper and says, "Are they asking whether there are Communists in the State Department? No, they're asking how many." Nevertheless he pleads, and as he thwaps the (Heinz) ketchup bottle over his meat, she appears to give in. Cut to Iselin in the Senate chamber, announcing there are 57 card-carrying Communists in the State Department.

TIME, PLACE AND STATES OF MIND

"Parallel to the invention of perspective in painting," writes the critic Gilbert Seldes, "the invention of cutting in the movies is a landmark in the history of art. For cutting is the essential element in creating a second time-span for the spectator: he lives in his own sense of duration, knowing that sixty minutes and no less makes an hour, and at the same time he lives by the durations of the movie, in which it may take half an hour to show the events of ten minutes or a lifetime may be condensed into three hours."

In the movies, space is totally fluid and mobile as a result of the camera's ability to perceive the action from a infinite variety of shifting perspectives; in that sense, the camera (and the intercutting of different types of shots or camera movement) obliterates real space and creates instead its own kind of space. The same is true of time. In a film, time can be condensed, expanded, tricked, reversed, slowed down or speeded up. There is no real time within film, only that mode of time created by the filmmaker.

One of the most graphic sequences in Eisenstein's *Ten Days That Shook the World* depicts the raising of a bridge. A horse is crossing the bridge, several people are on the bridge, and though the actual bridge-raising might take only a few moments in reality, Eisenstein draws out the action, extends it in time by elaborate intercutting of the mechanisms that move the bridge, the slow growth of the cleavage between the two halves of the bridge, the horrors that happen to the people (and, most grotesque among them, the horse that dangles helplessly over the edge) on the bridge. Time is expanded, giving the sequence an even more explosive and compelling power.

Time can as well be condensed. The "News on the March" newsreel in *Citizen Kane* depicts a man's lifetime in fewer than eight minutes. In the opening scenes of *An Occurrence at Owl Creek Bridge,* we and the man about to be hanged anticipate his hanging with growing anxiety because every movement and sound seems drawn out in time; then, when the rope snaps, and he escapes, an entire sequence of actions—his flight downriver, his exultation that he's alive, his escape from the guns of the soldiers, his race back to his plantation, his near-reunion with his wife—take place that are shown, in the last terrible image of the film as his neck snaps—to have lasted only a fragment of a moment, seen from within his mind. Here time is both expanded and condensed, a balance that gives the film much of its extraordinary impact.

With the control of time editing can take on a perhaps even more flexible form of expression, one might say the control of consciousness. Obviously, flashbacks and flashforwards, when they result from a character's state of mind, represent this sort of control, but developed with enough subtlety and agility, sequences and entire films can probe a condition of mind much as a novelist might, but using images instead of words.

Anthony Perkins plays a chronic daydreamer in *Pretty Poison,* and his job at a chemical factory seems suited to nothing so much as daydreams. He must sit behind a special filter and watch as red bottles click past on an assembly line, to identify in them chemicals imperfections that would show up in the filter. Not long after sitting down and staring at the bottles, an image flashes through his mind and over the screen: a row of marching high school majorettes, seen the day before, flashing past with their red uniforms and moving at the same speed, in the same graphic direction, with the same color as the bottles. The daydream picks up: lithe legs, Tuesday Weld's striking face, drums, cymbals—the march of the bottles becomes the march of the band, until Perkins, grinning lecherously through the distorting glass, misses a tipped bottle that smashes in the machinery. Not only does this sequence show how well and how convincingly careful editing can reflect a state of mind; the rhythmic interflow of bottles and marching girls keeps a graphic, mobile continuity running over the screen so that we're aware how the one summons and reflects for Perkins the other.

In *Time Piece,* a shrewd short film of split-second shots and a jazzy, vivid editing tempo, a man and his wife sit down to dinner and the camera cuts between them in a lively montage. With each succeeding shot, they eat with a growing fury—at first sucking hungrily at the soup, then, in 17th-century costume, gnawing rapaciously at turkey legs; finally, as cavemen, tearing into raw meat. The sequence—a kind of spoof on civilization—projects this regression from mannered eating habits to primitive bestiality by intercutting, at a growing clip, between the man and the woman as they face each other.

Its unique ability to play with time itself gives film a capacity to examine time, perhaps in a way unavailable to any other medium. An exquisite and moving and memorable film that combines a terrifying science fiction fable with a poignant love story, Chris Marker's *La Jetée* uses the edited structure of his film—as well as its narrative structure—to examine the nature of time, and implicitly, time within film. The story takes place after World War III, when the central character, now living with other survivors in catacombs below Paris, is brought as a subject into a strange but critical experiment. Using his mind as a bridge, the scientists want to reach into the past or the future, whence they can draw the necessary fuels and foodstuffs to keep themselves alive. The man has long been haunted by an image from his youth: Sunday afternoon at Paris's Orly airport, before the all-destroying war, and a beautiful woman stunned, with a look of shock. Propelled by this image, the man gradually steps into that other world of the past, meets the woman and falls in love with her. The affair is beautiful, touching; but it leaves the scientists dissatisfied. The man has still not been able to provide the food and fuel they need. When visitors from the future appear to the man—they, it appears, have long been able to travel through time—he begs to enter their world. This they refuse, but they do give him energy and food sources; and—as an alternative to execution, since his usefulness has ended—offer to set him into that past world he has so often visited. There he stands on the jetée once more, only to discover that the image that had haunted him so long was his own death, foreshadowed in the girl's horror as she watches him being killed by an emissary from the catacombs.

To describe *La Jetée* so briefly is to rob it of its poignancy and stunning impact, yet the narrative is interwoven so thoroughly with the film's unique construction and editing that the two become inseparable. For apart from one slight exquisite exception, there is no movement within the frames of *La Jetée.* All images are frozen, halted in time, still photographs (actually, enlargements of frames from earlier footage that Marker had shot). In effect, each moment of the film—a fixed image that will soon dissolve into another fixed image—is much like the image of the woman on the jetée that haunts the man within the film. He can travel through time, but within these locked, frozen images. It is as though, in escaping the confines of the ruinous present, he (and by extension ourselves) were able to enter another zone of time, but even that new zone locks us within the barrier of those frozen moments. As film can shuttle between past and future and present (though on film there is finally only one tense, the present), the man in *La Jetée* moves increasingly between the present and the past, only to discover at the end that all this movement could in no way breach that final crunching pall of time, the inevitability of his own death. Thus filmic time and the

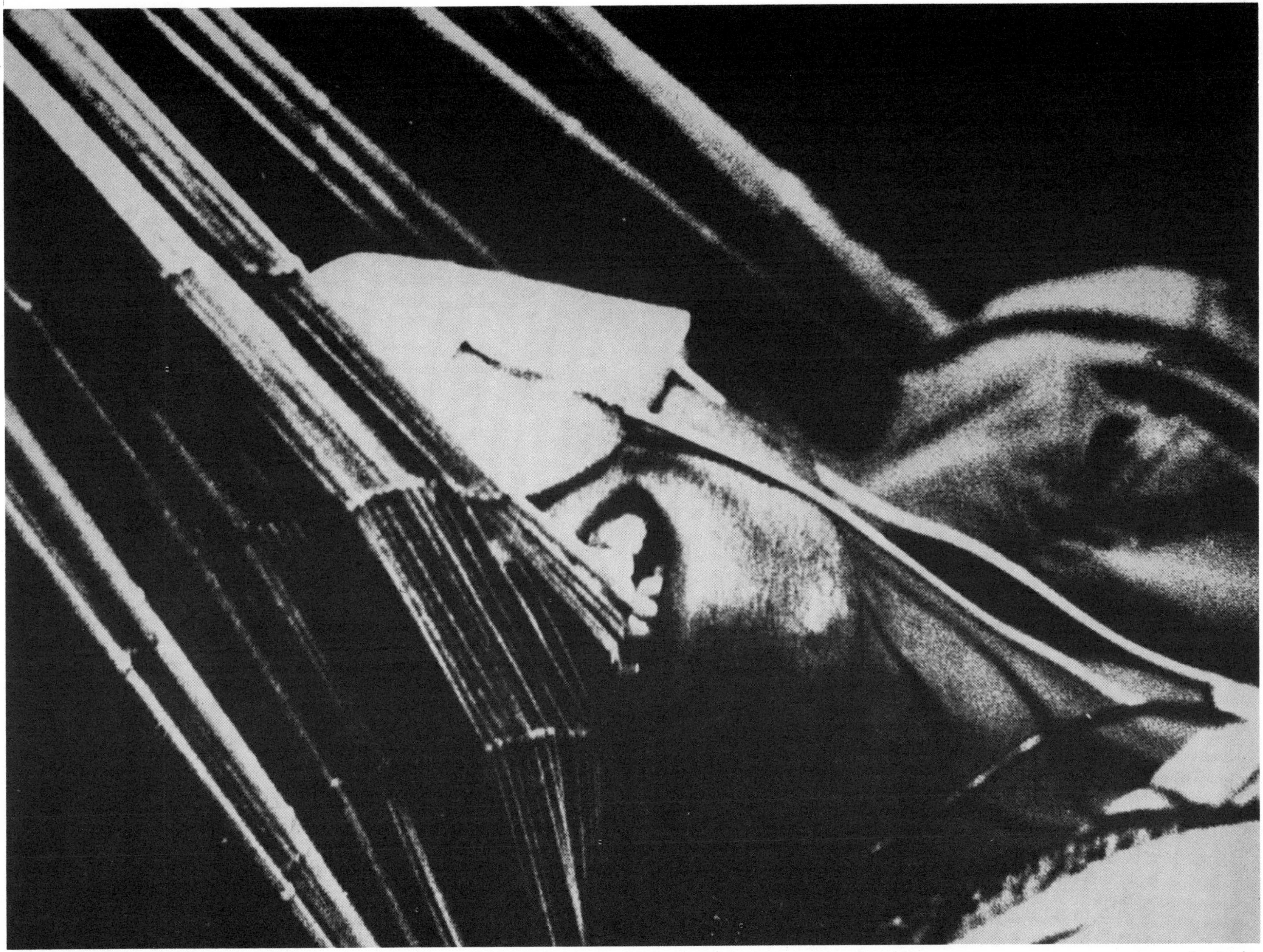

La Jetée

use of time as a structured part of the narrative become one and the same. Chris Marker's fable extends, almost effortlessly, to the reasons we look at movies and the way in which time within the movies becomes for us the same delightful but ultimately deceptive escape it was for the man in *La Jetée.*

ODESSA: THE GENIUS OF EDITING

If one sequence from one film were to be used to show the possibilities of editing at its summit, probably most critics and film historians would agree on Eisenstein's Odessa Steps sequence from *The Battleship Potemkin.* Triumphant in its pacing, its rhythm, its bold juxtapositions and its use of graphics and motion to create intersecting and conflicting movements, this stormy and ferocious sequence is as tightly constructed as the movement of a Beethoven symphony.

The sequence takes place when the *Potemkin* docks at Odessa and the people of Odessa come to greet it and wave sympathetically to the rebellious sailors. Indeed, the sequence opens on a pleasant, convivial note. The waving handkerchiefs of the Sunday strollers from along the high, broad steps, and the sailors waving back. Suddenly Cossack troops —most feared and hostile of the Czar's forces —appear at the top of the steps, and begin marching down them, shooting the people of Odessa as they march. Eisenstein intercuts, at an increasingly rapid tempo, to characterize the cloddish Cossacks and the sheer brutality of their slaughter: indifferent boots stomping the bodies of the victims; men and women rushing to escape the guns; in a deep, horizontal formation, the rifles lifting, steady, shooting; a young man watching the massacre, his face breaking out in horror, seen increasingly in tighter closeups. The focus subtly shifts from the downward movement of the Cossacks to the effects of the invasion on the people massed along the steps: a mother carrying her dead son grimly up the steps, toward the troops—she is shot unhesitatingly; a woman with a baby stroller, shot, and the stroller bumps unchecked down the long steps; a woman screaming in outrage, then shot in the eye—details on a human scale set against the vast moving force of the marching troops, intercut with one another, offsetting and explicating one another.

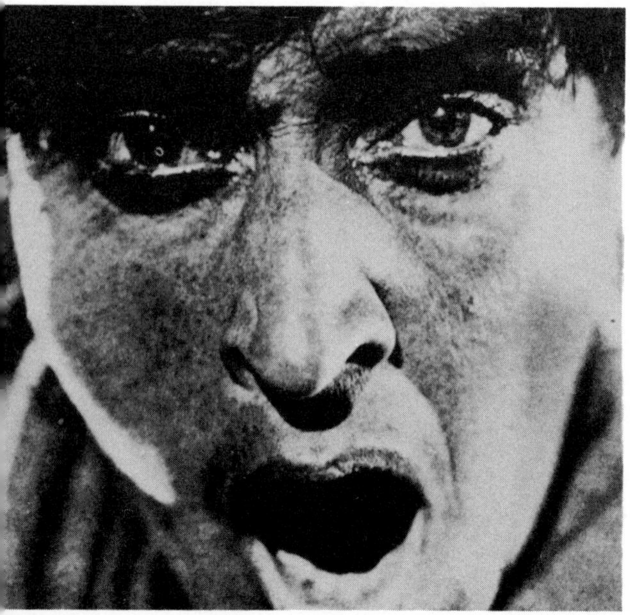

The sequence is unforgettable for anyone who has seen *The Battleship Potemkin*: emotions rise and crowd one another out as you are caught, almost unbelieving, in the rising crescendo of the massacre: horror gives way to outrage, which gives way to further horror—and the almost documentary style in which Eisenstein filmed the sequence makes every shot seem to have come from a newsreel camera. But above all, what makes the sequence so powerfully affecting is Eisenstein's sheer genius in editing; the human vignettes—the mother walking up the steps, the baby carriage on its fatal, unheeded roll—are intercut with the always mechanical movement of the soldiers in rising tempo. The graphic forces conflict: the direction of the movement, and the way these directions flow against one another on the screen. And the nature of the different movements—the bestial, steady thudding of the Cossacks' feet against the panicky, horrified reactions of the townspeople—interact as opposites, doubling the force and the tension. Hundreds of small, separate shots, yet wielded and ordered into the whole sequence, becoming one of the most staggering depictions ever created of a theme as old as art.

DRAMATIC EDITING

The Odessa Steps sequence is constructed with an almost architectural sense of the interaction of opposing forces (Eisenstein, no coincidence, was trained as an engineer): but such structural exactitude is not always necessary for an editing sequence to take on a momentous dramatic impact. Indeed, the style of editing is dictated to some extent by the narrative considerations: the mood to which a sequence should contribute; the intensity of action (or inaction) it should suggest; the pacing and tempo and relationships that best bring out the hidden forces in the story.

In *Sahara,* Bogart is defending a desert oasis against the Germans with the help of a handful of soldiers. He sends one soldier on foot across the desert to try and reach the Allied headquarters and return with more troops. For a while we follow the soldier, but then, instead of showing his slow collapse in the broiling sands, director Zoltan Korda intimates what is happening to him by showing only isolated objects . . . his back-pack, with footprints dragging away; his canteen, empty, and more trailing footprints; his rifle. Finally, when the camera does show the man, he is barely moving, trying to reach the knoll of a dune. In closeups, we see the sand trickling down under his fingers, suggesting his futility and desolation.

In *North by Northwest,* Cary Grant has narrowly escaped several attacks by a crop duster airplane in the middle of an isolated cornfield. In the distance he sees a truck approaching, and he races out to flag down the truck. Oblivious of the danger, he stands directly in the middle of the highway, waving his hands wildly. Hitchcock intercuts between Grant, seen at the same relative distance on the screen, and the truck, seen as it comes closer and closer. The emphasis makes us see the events—the truck as it virtually plows him down—from Grant's viewpoint, heightening the dramatic effect of the scene.

Such a use of changing spaces as a means of heightening the dramatic momentum is used in *An Occurrence at Owl Creek Bridge,* but to extract an added—and somewhat dreamlike—tension, director Robert Enrico stretches out space, and time. The prisoner, having escaped the hanging, has raced back to his plantation. He stands at the open gate, breathing heavily, marvelling that he has arrived. In the distance he sees his wife. He begins racing to her. She smiles, anticipating him, opening her arm in a slow half-wave. He races harder. The space as we saw it in long shot hardly seems that long, but despite all his running, he doesn't seem to be able to close the distance. When finally he does get to her and she reaches out to hold him, his neck jerks back, and Enrico cuts suddenly to the man hanging from the end of a rope—all that went before was imagined in that fraction of a second before he died.

Bonnie and Clyde is a film replete with killings of all kinds. To give the final massacre of Bonnie Parker and Clyde Barrow an effect more shattering than any of the graphic killings that preceded it, director Arthur Penn structures the sequence at first with slow, extended deliberation, then into a montage that is at once graceful and jerkily spastic. When Bonnie and Clyde are driving back to the house of C. W. Moss's papa, they see him at the side of the road, beside his stopped truck, waving his arms. They pull aside, Clyde gets out, and the film begins cutting in quick immobile shots among Clyde, the papa, and Bonnie. In none of the shots is there movement of the figures—rather, a growing tensing of face and body. Birds flutter, the bushes rustle, increasingly the faces of Bonnie and Clyde appear expectant, poised, sharply aware. In the last moment before the gunfire begins, Penn intercuts swiftly between Clyde, bending into a crouch, and increasingly tight closeups of Bonnie's face. When the gunfire does start—machine guns from everywhere around the clearing, in a merciless spatter of untold bullets—Bonnie jerks back, Clyde rolls; movements seem at one moment slow, fluid, dancelike, and jerkily swift. Penn shot the sequence with cameras at different speeds, variants of slow and fast motion, and intercuts the slow and speeded movements to suggest what he calls the "spasm of death"—an effect both fluid and abrupt. Critics at the time charged that Penn was glorifying violence, making it attractive to watch. He was —but with the critical difference that he was undercutting that very attractiveness with the brutal assault of fast-motion shots and the bullet-riddled bodies of the two people we had come to know through the film. Throughout *Bonnie and Clyde* the blood and violence come to have an appeal of their own, but whatever we might savor in the gunfire and brutality works against us in this final sequence. Rarely has a gangster film ever suggested with such force and poignancy that those who live by the code of violence are doomed by it as well.

NO LONGER SPACE OR TIME: LENI RIEFENSTAHL'S 'OLYMPIA'

The 1936 Olympics in Berlin provided the content—if not exactly the subject—for perhaps the most remarkable sports film ever made: Leni Riefenstahl's majestic, four-hour-long *Olympia.* Structured in two parts, *Olympia* treats the sports events and the athletes in a manner similar to the way Riefenstahl had earlier treated a massive Nazi rally in her film *Triumph of the Will*: with a powerfully Nordic, almost Wagnerian surge of mythic force. The athletes in *Olympia* become something other than mere mortals dashing the hundred yards or flinging the discus. Shot often in slow-motion, from low angles and edited to emphasize pure physical prowess and an almost statuesque sense of the human body, the athletes become godlike, idealized, representing a pure essence of form and movement rather than men and women contesting in an athletic event.

In few sequences is this idealized quality so evident—or Leni Riefenstahl's genius for filmmaking so conspicuous—as in the acclaimed diving sequence, which takes place during the second film, *Olympia II.* Riefenstahl herself has described her approach as taking "the same style as the high jumps"—and, indeed, the sequence rushes before the eyes in a spilling, fluid cascade of sky and water and crowds as these must appear to the high diver. But her editing creates an even further, more exalting fluidity: there seem to be no breaks, barely any separation between one diver and the next, and each dive has its own breathless continuity—created either by superb overlapping editing or, as often, amazing camera movement.

Says one of her cameramen, Jaworsky: "She had a special camera for diving that went down on rails so you could shoot the diver in mid-air coming down and it went under water with the diver and automatically changed the exposure under water." Such techniques enabled Leni Riefenstahl to evoke from the divers' sequence a sense of pure and exultant movement, of the human body in flight.

Indeed, the structure she gives the sequence by her editing suggests nothing so much as the triumph of the divers over space. At the beginning we see the bodies as they enter the water; and gradually, as the sequence progresses, we no longer see the water or the masses of spectators, only the divers set against a broken clouded sky, bouncing from the board and flinging themselves into the sky as though the sky—and not the water below—were their destination. A varied use of slow motion gives the entire sequence a sense of suspension and purity of movement. And toward the end of the sequence, when she pairs divers in the same frame and matches their forms as though in a *pas de deux,* we are no longer watching divers performing in an Olympic game but some triumphant ritual of the body in space—a point underscored by the final shot, in which a diver, seen against the sky, dissolves into the clouds.

The exquisite overlapping editing of the diving sequence in *Olympia* shows to what extent well edited film can triumph over the most basic problems of time and space. True, the sequence would have been impossible without the superb slow-motion footage of the divers that Riefenstahl had to work with. Nonetheless, she transformed that footage into a spectacle of pure form, a conquest of the divers over space, and a conquest of the film over time.

INTERCUTTING

Rarely is the naked emotional power of editing so conspicuous as in action films in which climactic events are depicted with deft intercutting. A novelist or a dramatist is generally limited to focusing on one action at any given moment, but the filmmaker can intercut within fractions of a second from one action to another to another; and when the actions are related, indeed, when they impinge on one another dramatically, the over-all sequence can become immeasurably powerful with audiences. That basic premise of any cut—that the audience will search out a relationship between the two shots—is here extended to an elaborate framework of actions constructed around some basic dramatic tension. Done well, such sequences represent what film perhaps can do best; involve us in complex actions with a direct and visceral force unknown to any other art.

The chase—as old as *The Great Train Robbery,* and the most enduring staple of the action film—provides perhaps the most familiar structure for tense intercutting. In *The French Connection,* director William Friedkin added a new twist to the urban chase by having the film's central character, a slouch-faced and brutal detective named Popeye, tear after an elevated train from below in an automobile. The sequence seen on the screen is literally dizzying in its impact and unabated movement; the speed of the runaway elevated train—the gun-wielding sniper has ordered the engineer to drive it at full throttle—becomes matched in its straight, whizzing motion against the frantic, zigzag high-speed driving of Popeye in a car below. And within this basic chase there are innumerable details that intensify the dramatic power of the chase itself. The sniper (who had tried to kill Popeye and is racing to escape Popeye) boards the train while Popeye watches from across the tracks; once on the train, he discovers Popeye is chasing him, goes to the engineer and forces him not to stop at the next station. This attracts a conductor, whom the sniper shoots, as well as the engineer, creating panic on the train. Intercut with this drama is Popeye's harrowing drive below: missing a truck, piling up other cars in accidents that he rushes away from; and one genuinely frightening moment—Popeye heading straight toward a woman pushing a baby carriage; she sees him, screams; he screeches at her, twists the wheel, and narrowly avoids her but smashes into a fruit stand instead. When the train finally crashes into an immobile train in front of it, and the sniper, dazed, forces his way from the car, Popeye meets him at the bottom of the station steps.

The rising tempo of intercutting and the parallel, disjointed motions of the elevated train and Popeye's car keep the sequence in constant and always faster movement, like an orchestra that builds into an ever-accelerating pitch of rising notes. The inner dramatic details balance the sheer speed, and give us a heightened sense of things totally out of control. What began as an angry chase becomes, in effect, total assault on pedestrians, traffic, and the helpless riders on the elevated train. Popeye, on reflection, emerges as no hero. His enraged, relentless pursuit of the sniper results in two otherwise unnecessary murders and who knows how many injuries, pointing out that the chase, while dramatically enthralling, is morally no simple matter of a good guy going after a bad guy. It's a deadly war played out in the midst of a city of bystanders.

The chase at the conclusion of *The Manchurian Candidate* is of a totally different nature, and involves us in a less directly visceral but more complex manner. Laurence Harvey, the brainwashed victim who has been programmed to assassinate the presidential candidate in the midst of his acceptance speech at the convention, stands in a tiny booth in a far corner of Madison Square Garden, unpacking his rifle and setting the telescopic sight. Frank Sinatra arrives at the Garden, knowing that Harvey will be there, and determined to stop him. Senator John Iselin, the whiskey-primed demagogue who, as the plans have it, is to lift up the body of the presidential candidate and make a rousing, impassioned speech, sits beside his wife, Harvey's mother, who has not only helped engineer the entire thing, but is the Communist agent controlling Harvey's mechanized mind. With the consideration that nothing in American politics is truly improbable, the set-up has superb dramatic possibilities, and director John Frankenheimer, in an extended elaborated sequence, takes full advantage of them. With rising momentum, a dovetailing of political ritual with the inexorable movement of events, and its use of parallel cutting, the sequence builds to a staggering finale. Sinatra has just located and barely reached Harvey's booth. Harvey swerves his aim from the presidential candidate and shoots not the candidate but his own mother and Senator Iselin. Sinatra steps inside the booth, and Harvey—pausing to don his Medal of Honor—tells Sinatra that no one else could have stopped them, then shoots himself.

The sequence is structured in a classic manner, jumping from Sinatra, weaving through the crowds, to Harvey, assembling the rifle in the booth, to Iselin and his wife, seen mostly in slightly low-angle, side shots that suggest a rigidity and controlled impatience. During the singing of the National Anthem, Sinatra glances nervously around the stadium, till he notices the single shaft of light coming from a

distant room high in the dark stadium. As Sinatra races toward the room, the editing tempo gradually builds—shots are briefer, closeups tighter; Sinatra's race is seen often in long-shot, with the camera at a distorting tilt, giving his race against time a sense of being somehow the only unpredictable element in a scenario we already know full well. The use of the soundtrack gives an even further dimension to the sequence. We know with what phrase of the candidate's speech Harvey is supposed to shoot the candidate; we know what words precede the phrase, and as the candidate speaks and we recognize his words, the tension is even further heightened.

Partly because it uses its setting so well—all that triumphant pageantry and hoopla of political conventions that both mask and vividly amplify the coming assassination—and because Frankenheimer cuts so tersely and so well between the principals, the sequence accumulates increasing tension with each moment. We're held spellbound, less because of what we don't know, but because of how much we do know, a tactic no doubt partly drawn from the master himself, Alfred Hitchcock.

HITCHCOCK'S DIAGONAL EDITING

Critic Andrew Sarris has said that Hitchcock is the only major American director who has mastered the German school of camera movement and the Russian school of editing. And indeed, Hitchcock's best sequences are often edited with a remarkable precision and an ability to extract astounding tension. In his 1956 remake of *The Man Who Knew Too Much,* he culminates the film in a manner quite similar to the climax of *The Manchurian Candidate* (and which well may have influenced the climax to *The Manchurian Candidate*). An assassin is supposed to shoot a diplomat at the clashing of the cymbals in an orchestral symphony. Doris Day, who knows it's coming, and when, stands helplessly inside the symphony hall, looking around for the spy, while Hitchcock deftly intercuts among the spy, Doris Day, the diplomat, and especially the orchestra: closeups of the snare drum, of a page of the musical score, of the cymbalist as he steps forward, holds the cymbals and lifts and separates them. The rising crescendo of the sequence succeeds largely because it is matched, both in emotional strength and in its relation to the plot, by the symphony that we know is to provide the cue and the cover for the assassination.

One of the best-edited sequences in Hitchcock's work—and possibly in the history of American film—is the shower murder in *Psycho.* The remainder of the film was shot in just over three weeks, but Hitchcock spent a painstaking seven days on this scene that barely occupies two minutes in the film. The sudden driving violence of the scene—it is certainly one of the most violent scenes ever filmed—acts not only as a potent shock to audiences who had been identifying with Marion Crane (Janet Leigh) to the point of the shower scene; its battering impact remains with an audience throughout the film, giving *Psycho* much of its harrowing sense of unbridled terror.

The scene is structured and edited to bring out the full shock of the suddenness and brutality of the killing. Marion Crane, who has paused at a motel en route to her fiancé with $40,000 in stolen money, talks with Norman Bates (Anthony Perkins), the hotel's reclusive manager, then retreats to her room to take a shower and go to bed. When she enters the shower, Hitchcock makes the action seem refreshing, sensuous—he might be making a TV commercial for a shampoo. She steps into the stall, turns on the water, and looks up. A first-person shot shows the arched needles of spray shooting down from the nozzle. She stands beneath the water, letting it roll over her face; then Hitchcock cuts to the door and we can see a tall figure entering, with a knife poised and raised, and immediately the tempo picks up: the knife in closeup; Marion Crane's face in tightening closeups, till it's only her mouth, in an open scream; the knife against her body; her face; the figure raising the knife; then a few medium shots—the figure leaving the bathroom; Marion Crane as seen from above, grasping hold of the shower curtain for support; then, in a series of memorable closeup vignettes, Marion sinking against the tiled wall; her hand slipping slowly down against the wet wall; another hand upraised, grabbing at the shower curtain, and the holes at the top of the curtain popping out of the brackets, one by one; then finally naked immobile feet and a slow movement of the camera to the drain where the dark water swirls. The camera closes on the drain in a tightening, moving closeup, until the drain fills the frames, then a slow dissolve and the camera backs away again, this time from the dead, fishlike eye of the woman lying on the cold, naked floor.

The events themselves are startling, graphic, disturbing, but the way in which Hitchcock shot and structured them heightens the impact considerably. The entire sequence, for example, is framed by the shower water. The sequence opens with that magnificent shot of the nozzle splaying water, and closes with the drain that collects the water, now mingled with blood. Both shots feature a rounded figure, both shots suggest that the shower itself is no incidental aspect of the murder, it is somehow an integral part of what happens to Marion Crane.

The shots of the moving knife against Marion Crane's body are often in slow motion, giving the movements within the scene a jerky, irregular rhythm. We never actually see the knife touch the body; it isn't necessary—what we do see, a montage of face and knife and shadowed figure, is more effective and more involving, for it enables us to see the killing, not from some third point of view, but precisely from the perspectives of (primarily) Marion Crane, and the killer.

Moreover, Hitchcock structures the sequence with distinct and unique graphic ingenuity. The actions in the sequence are played on intersecting diagonals. The shower water comes down from the upper left hand corner of the frame, toward the lower right hand corner. The knife juts almost always in the opposite diagonal: from the upper right hand corner to the lower left hand corner. This basic intersecting of the two primal movements in the sequence works much like the interweaving of two dissonant melodic sources in a modern musical composition. The friction between the two heightens our awareness of the separate and opposing quality of each one.

Consider another Hitchcock sequence in which conflicting diagonals are likewise used to heighten the tension: the crop duster scene in *North by Northwest*. Cary Grant has been set up to be murdered in a flat, desolate Illinois cornfield. He arrives by bus and stands in the middle of a totally horizontal nowhere. In every direction the land is level, there is only the road, a ditch, and the outflung empty spaces. He is waiting to meet the man for whom he has been mistaken, George Kaplan, whom we know to be nonexistent. In most intercut sequences that build to a heightened tempo, the tendency is toward abbreviated shots and tighter and tighter closeups. In this sequence Hitchcock uses almost the reverse, lengthy shots (some of them almost a minute), taken from long distances. Indeed, the first half of the sequence (and it is a long sequence), is simple sheer waiting on Cary Grant's part, and we're forced to wait with him. Slight things happen. Cars pass. Any one could carry Kaplan, and Grant watches expectantly for one to slow and stop. None does. A car comes by and a man gets out, a farmer; he stands across the road from Grant, and they stare at one another for a while in an almost comic manner, till Grant crosses the road to ask if the man is Kaplan. He isn't, of course; but he does notice a distant plane, and the first rumbling intimations of coming disaster can be heard in his line, "Funny, that plane's dusting crops where there ain't no crops." A bus comes by, stops, the farmer gets on, and Grant is once again alone.

It is mainly the waiting that creates much of the effect of the sequence. Cary Grant (and, by extension, ourselves) feeling isolated and somewhat foolish in the middle of this shrubbed naked farmland, a feeling caught not so much by any distinct actions or reactions on Grant's part as by the shots—more than half of them from Grant's point of view—of the receding highway, the empty surroundings, the slow approach of a truck or bus. Hitchcock shrewdly shot and edited this part of the sequence in real time: we're aware of everything, the approach and the whizzing away of every car and truck and bus, not only prolonging the build-up, but strengthening our identification with Cary Grant.

And when the crop duster airplane does approach, we see it coming from Grant's point of view. He dives, it flies overhead, and turns to bank. At this point the editing tempo begins to build, the shots are briefer, they hold on Grant more tightly, and as Grant races from the plane, the camera moves in front of him, framing the running Grant and the pursuing plane within the same shot. After such a long wait and the static immobility of Grant on the roadside, the movement of Grant and the plane becomes all the more dramatic and feverish. The tempo of editing and movement builds to Grant's final desperate effort to flag down the oncoming oil truck, where the shots jut back and forth between Grant's anguished face and the hulking face of the closing truck. There is a brief moment of relief when Grant goes down, and we know he can crawl out; and a more satisfying, even comic, relief when he takes off in the truck containing an upright refrigerator and a bow-legged farmer chases him down the road.

The editing of the sequence has furious pacing and intercutting between related actions, but the pacing never does become dizzy, and the events are quite simple. What is unique is how Hitchcock uses Grant's point of view and the flattened landscape to heighten our expectations to a rare pitch, then the drama of the buzzing, shooting plane to satisfy those expectations completely.

Visually the sequence is superb. Hitchcock's compositional sense—filling and balancing the frame always in a visually intriguing manner—makes us look down the road or across the cornfields with the careful, expectant gaze of Grant himself. The spaces are empty, but since we're looking for something—we're

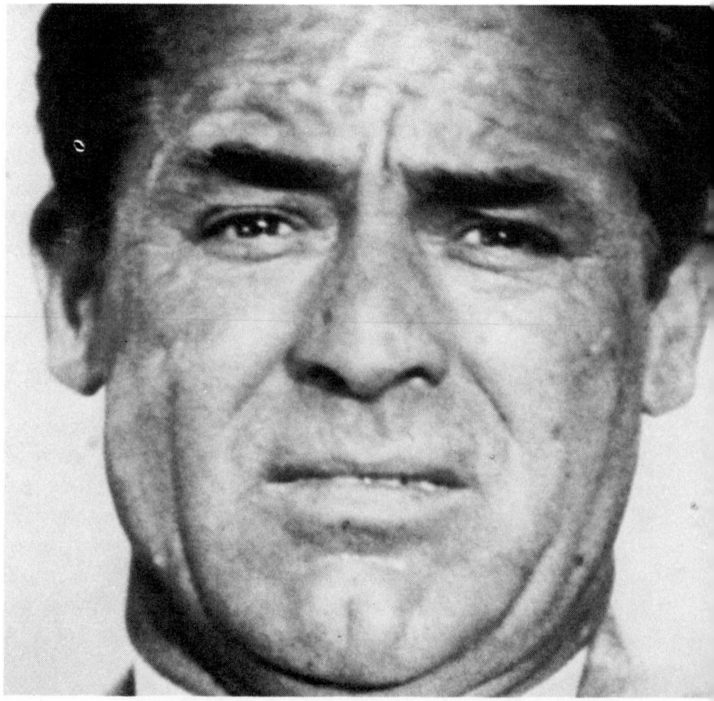

not even sure what—their emptiness becomes dramatically significant. For the same reason, the long, long wait is never boring; never for us, never for Grant.

Graphically, Hitchcock uses the naked landscape as more than a setting. With the exception of Grant's immobile standing figure (and, when he appears, the farmer's), the lines are predominantly horizontal. The blue empty sky is apparent in every frame (until Grant seeks refuge in the cornfield), and the span of empty space and sky within the shots keeps us highly conscious of place and time—just as the constantly spouting water from the shower kept us highly conscious of the setting in the murder sequence in *Psycho*.

The sequence succeeds brilliantly—it is one of the most memorable moments in Hitchcock's film, pure Hitchcockian—largely because it works against the conventional motif of a man facing a terrible threat. Usually the man is trapped in a tight space and it's night. Here it's broad daylight and the man is "trapped" in expansive, open space. Hitchcock uses that space well, and he makes us feel it with an amazing clarity. Our identification with Grant is never so strongly welded throughout *North by Northwest* as in this sequence.

THE FORCE OF REACTION

The Set-Up is a late '40s low-budget film about an over-the-hill fighter (Robert Ryan) who needs to prove to himself that he can still win despite his manager's set-up for him to go down in a fight.

Director Robert Wise focuses our attention on Ryan, but uses that focus to examine and denounce the bloodthirsty nature of the boxing world. This approach has a contradiction almost implicit within it. By encouraging us to sympathize with Ryan, Wise makes us cheer for him during the fight, which is depicted virtually in real time, all six rounds. Yet the point that Wise is trying to underscore is that the people who make boxing such a disreputable sport are precisely the spectators. Perhaps partly as a means of separating us from the spectators within the film he depicts them as howling, gruesome deformities. One suspects that Christians thrown to the lions in the Roman days never had an audience so eager to watch them devoured. A fat man gobbles popcorn and hot dogs with a face that intimates that the boxing heightens his sensual pleasure in eating; a woman screams so ferociously she might be receiving the blows; a blind man hollers, "Go for his eyes!" Nothing within or around the ring—not even the Judas action of Ryan's manager—quite equals the squalid and contemptible faces of those spectators.

The spectators in *The Set-Up* are exaggerated figures, but the sheer force and volubility of their reactions give the film much of its inner tension and transforms our own reaction to the fight. Without these spectators, the fight would become a contest between Ryan and his opponent, and, on a deeper level, between Ryan's determination to win and the temptation to sell out. But by intercutting—often quite skillfully—the fight with its howling audience, Wise (who edited *Citizen Kane)* makes us feel uncomfortable in cheering Ryan: we become uneasily aware of the similarities between ourselves and the spectators in the film.

Intercutting with reaction shots can change not only our reaction, but our comprehension of an event itself. In Robert Rossen's *All the King's Men,* among the best political films ever made in America, the candidate Willie Stark (later to become an omnipotent and demagogic governor) makes a sudden transformation from a man who reads glossed speeches in a tone of sullen boredom to a man who can galvanize a rural audience with phrases that ring of thunder and passion. Such a momentous transformation is difficult to convey without straining credibility, and Rossen wisely uses the changing reactions of Willie's audience to convince us of the full thrust of Willie's change. At first the audience seems barely expectant, gathered there because it *is* a political picnic and they have nothing better to do at the moment. Willie casts away the written speech he's prepared and tells, in colorful rural language, how he'd been conned by the political machine to run for governor and conveniently split the ticket so their candidate would win. It's a good, vital, rousing speech; but it doesn't convince us of the transformation in Willie Stark nearly so much as do the reaction shots that Rossen gives of the assembled crowd. He shoots from low angles, giving the farmers and children a gentle dignity and a kind of breathless awe. It is these shots—stilling, admirably composed, portraitlike—that convey the full meaning of Willie Stark's speech. By intercutting them with Willie and with long shots that encompass Willie and his audience, Rossen tells us immediately and convincingly that Willie's future in politics is absolutely assured.

Reaction shots can likewise be used to amplify our own reaction to a momentous event, often felt more brutally through the reactions of others than were the event seen directly by us. In *Wild Boys of the Road,* a deeply felt and often disturbing narrative of the plight of wandering, homeless youths during the Depression, a crucial sequence takes place in a railroad yard as a train carrying dozens of the youths pulls in. The kids spot an assembly of officials prepared to corral them as they arrive and begin jumping from the train. One of the boys whom we've followed from the beginning of the film jumps and races alongside the train, but smashes into an unseen signpost, falling unconscious over a track. A train is approaching, of which the boy at first is unaware; he glances up, sees the train, and the film cuts to the reactions of his friends—too distant to reach him, helpless and petrified. The intercutting rises in a steady crescendo: the boy, slowly, barely moving himself from the tracks; the oncoming train, looming larger and closer; and—most critical because it's most telling—the reactions of the other kids, going from paralysis to wild screams and finally, as the train plows over the boy's leg, holding in petrified horror. The shock and brute terror of the event is felt strongly because of the way in which we see it —reflected on the faces of his watching friends.

2+2=5

Editing is cumulative. We see one image, then another image, and the mind rushes to conceive a relationship between the two. The fact that the audience's minds will do much of the work of editing provides wide ambits for filmmakers, and a range of ways in which images can be juxtaposed and interrelated with one another.

"Two film pieces of any kind, placed together, inevitably combine into a new concept, a new quality, arising out of that juxtaposition."
—Sergei Eisenstein

THE BIG HOUSE

A cut from the empty prison cafeteria to the same cafeteria, full. The effect is not at all the same with, say, a room and a few people; there it looks like some kind of gimmickry. Why?

PRETTY POISON

Like flashback—flash forward; here Tuesday Weld has just suggested to Tony Perkins that they flee to Mexico; Perkins sees a forest, where he's standing—but suddenly it becomes a shimmering beach, as he imagines Mexico.

THE MANCHURIAN CANDIDATE

Using the soundtrack to make a telling cut; Iselin has been complaining to his wife as he pours ketchup on his dinner that he hasn't been able to fix the number of Communists in the State Department; cut to Iselin in the Senate Hearing Room, announcing 57 Communists in the State Dept.

WHITE HEAT

Cagney's mental fit, suggested by a montage of machines, lathes and drills; the grinding, screeching movement of the machines gives us a potent idea of Cagney's mental state.

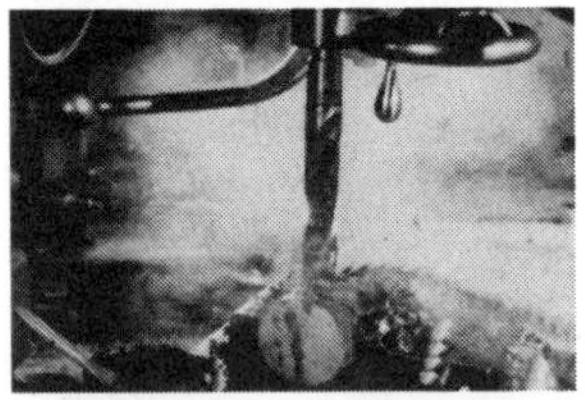

NORTH BY NORTHWEST

Matching the action from one setting to another. On Mt. Rushmore, Cary Grant tugs Eva Marie Saint up the cliff; Hitchcock cuts subtly to the same movement in a Pullman car on the way home.

THE BATTLESHIP POTEMKIN

One of the oldest and most basic functions of the cut—from medium shot to closeup, or the cut-in. More than dramatic emphasis, the cut-in re-creates the fields of action.

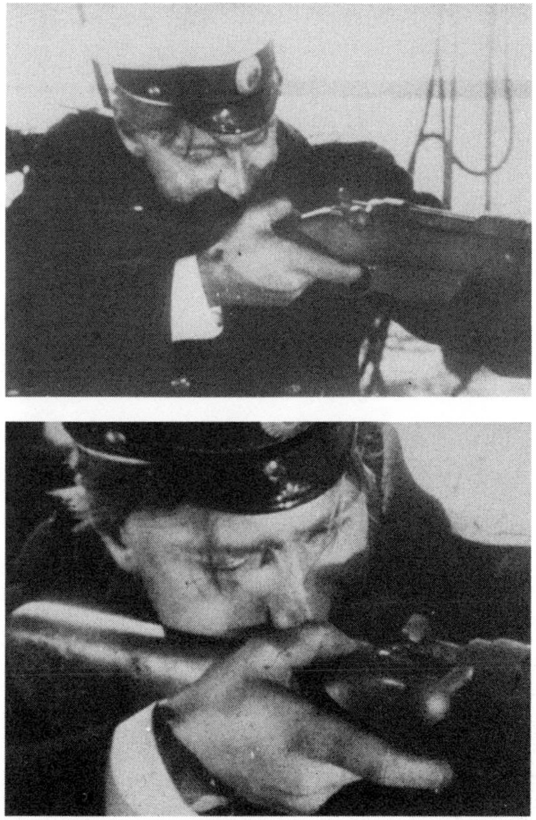

HALLELUJAH, I'M A BUM!

A visual parallel between the singing tramps and a row of singing crows, suggesting both that the men are like the crows and that the crows are joining in the song.

Time, Space and States of Mind

PRETTY POISON: THE HAZARDS OF DAYDREAMING

In *Pretty Poison,* Anthony Perkins plays a young man just released from a detention home whose job in a chemical plant involves watching red bottles pass behind a detection screen. Perkins has recently watched a high school band, with Tuesday Weld as the majorette, and her face haunts his mind. Given to fantasizing at the best of times, Perkins watches the bottles ride past, and—at the same rhythm, with the same graphic direction across the screen—the marching band sweeps past intercut with the bottles, building in tempo till Perkins is enjoying himself considerably; and a bottle breaks. Director Noel Black maintains an ingenious, rising rhythm through this sequence, matching movement, direction, and even color—the red bottles and the red costumes of the marching band.

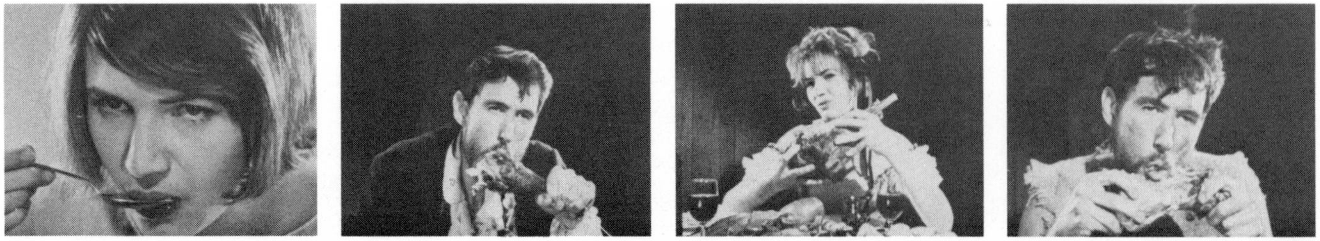

TIME PIECE: THE RHYTHM OF REVERSION

Time Piece is a brief, striking short with lively sequences created through quick cutting from one level of fantasy to another, always following a principle of reversion—from the modern businessman to a kind of primitive, engaged in some similar or related activity. The dinner sequence, reminiscent of the seductive meal in *Tom Jones,* intercuts between man and wife as they regress from contemporary to primeval, all suggested by the growing speed and ferocity with which they eat.

Frozen Time

Chris Marker's *La Jetée* is an extraordinary film, one that explores in both its story and its technique the nature of time and memory. The film begins with World War III, following which a few survivors huddle in catacombs below the city. Short on food and energy reserves, they attempt to break through time. The future seems closed, so they attempt the past, using drugs and other techniques to burrow into one character's vivid memory of a day on the Paris airport jetty before the war, and of a girl he saw there. Gradually the man steps into that memory; he meets the girl, falls in love with her—though always being returned to the dark catacombs, the looming face of the doctor. When finally the man has broken through time, he is visited by emissaries of the future, who refuse to take in these ancestors, but who do provide food, energy sources. The man is allowed finally to return to the past: but only to experience that fateful moment he saw on the jetty—his own death.

What is most remarkable about *La Jetée*, though, is its technique. With one slight exception, *there is not a moving image in the film.* Images are frozen, fixed on the screen as though retrieved from memory. Somehow this technique makes the science fiction more harrowing, the romance more acutely felt, the theme riveted deeper in our minds.

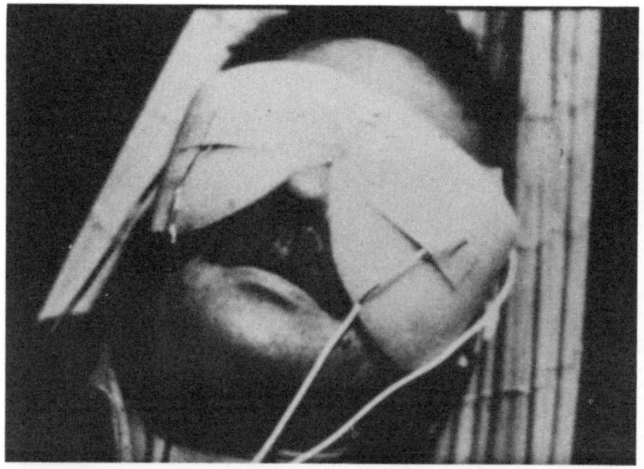

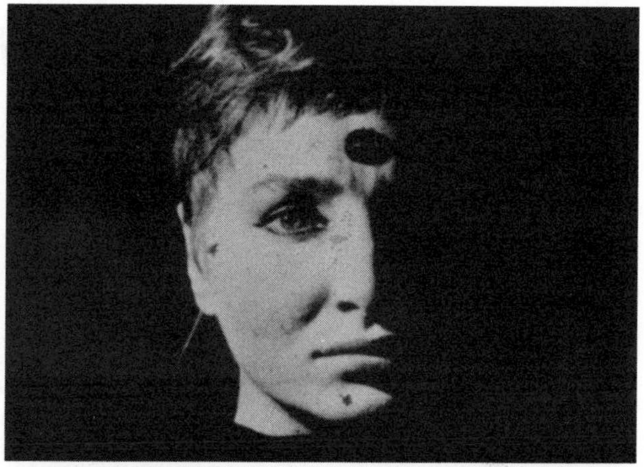

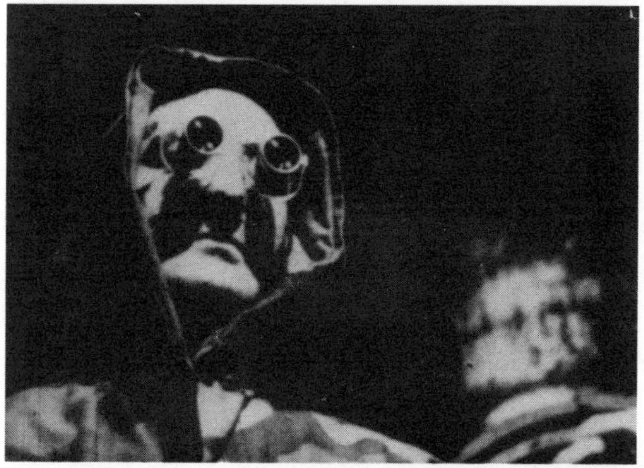

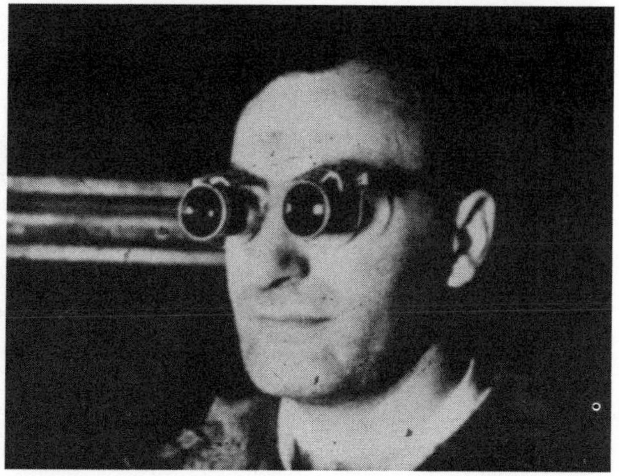

Odessa: A Commentary by Eisenstein

Sergei Eisenstein comments on the Odessa steps sequence from *The Battleship Potemkin:*

How are the events arranged and presented in this scene?

Leaving aside the frenzied state of the characters and masses in the scene, let us see how one of the structural and compositional means—*movement*—is used to express mounting emotional intensity.

First, there are *closeups* of human figures rushing chaotically. Then, *long-shots* of the same scene. The *chaotic movement* is next superseded by shots showing the feet of soldiers as they march *rhythmically* down the steps.

Tempo increases. Rhythm accelerates.

And then, as the *downward* movement reaches its culmination, the movement is suddenly reversed: instead of the headlong rush of the *crowd* down the steps we see the *solitary* figure of a mother carrying her dead son, *slowly* and *solemnly going up* the steps.

Mass. Headlong rush. *Downward.* And all of a sudden—

A *solitary* figure. Slow and solemn. *Going up.* But only for a moment. Then again a *leap in the reverse direction. Downward* movement.

Rhythm accelerates. Tempo increases.

The shot of the rushing crowd is suddenly followed by one showing a perambulator

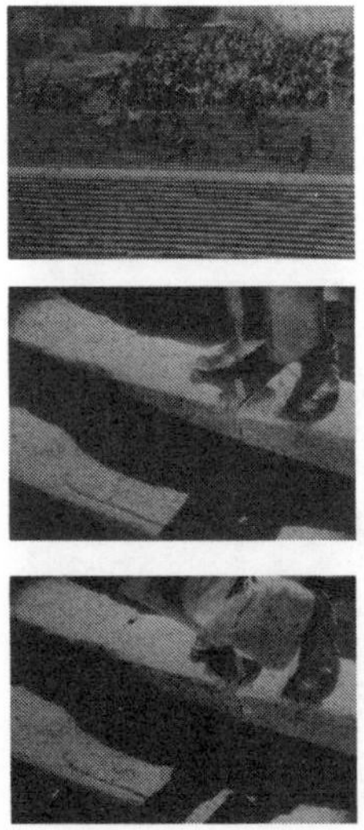

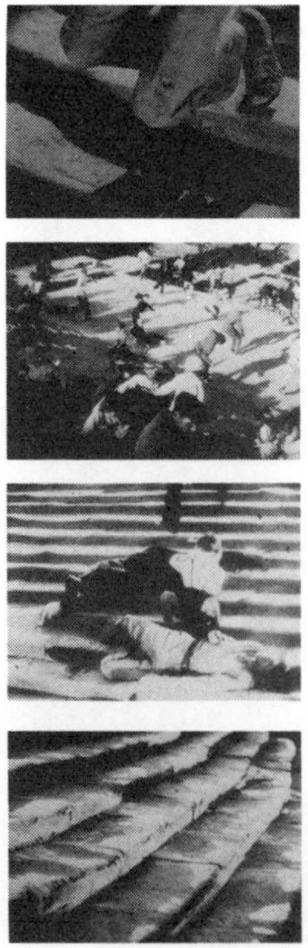

hurtling down the steps. This is more than just different tempos. This is a *leap in the method of representation*—from the abstract to the physical. This gives one more aspect of downward movement.

Closeups, accordingly, give place to *long shots.* The *chaotic* rush (of a mass) is succeeded by the *rhythmic* march of the soldiers. One aspect of movement (people running, falling, tumbling down the steps) gives way to another (rolling perambulator). *Descent* gives place to *ascent. Many* volleys of *many* rifles give place to *one* shot from *one* of the battleship's guns.

At each step there is a leap from one dimension to another, from one quality to another, until, finally, the change affects not one individual episode (the perambulator) but the whole of the method: the risen lions mark the point where the *narrative* turns into *a presentation through images.*

The visible steps of the stairs marking the downward progress of action correspond to steps marking qualitative leaps but proceeding in the opposite direction of mounting intensity.

Thus, the dramatic theme, unfolding impetuously in the scene of shooting on the steps, is at the same time the structural leit-motif, determining the plastic and rhythmical arrangement of the events.

—Sergei Eisenstein

(translated by X. Danko)

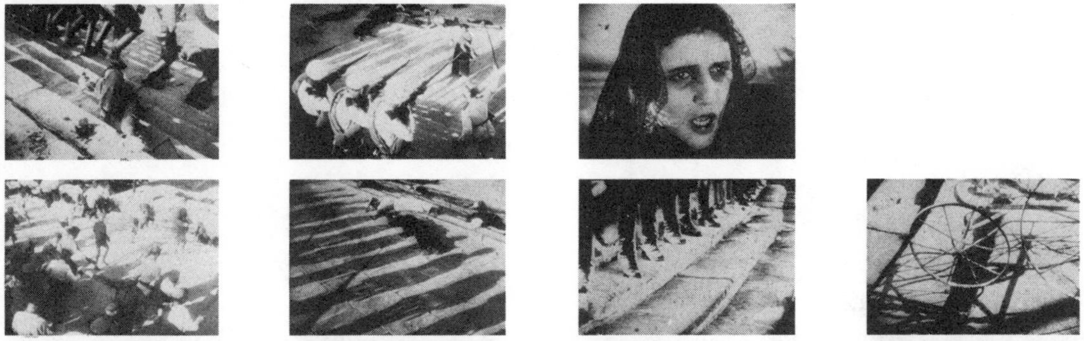

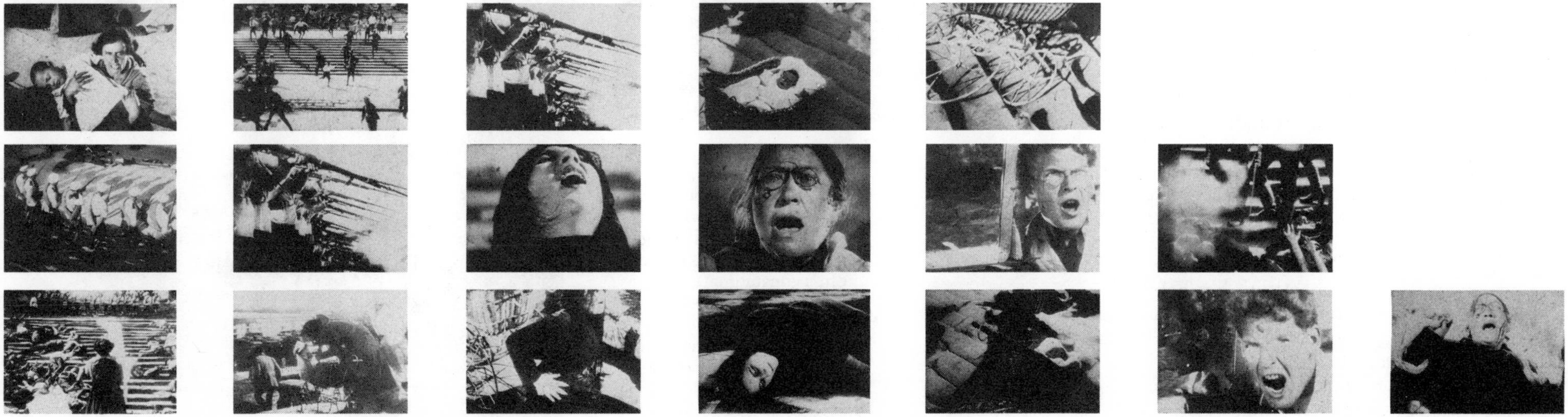

'The very stones roar.'-Eisenstein

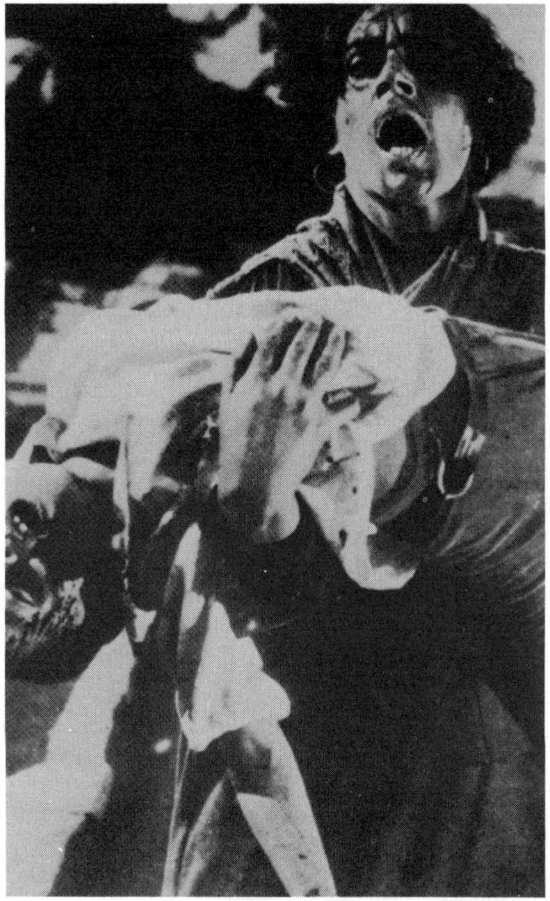

When Eisenstein's *The Battleship Potemkin* was released throughout Europe in 1926, it was banned in Germany and other countries —largely, no doubt, for the awesome power of the Odessa Steps sequence.

The Battleship Potemkin depicts an uprising aboard a naval battleship in 1905; Eisenstein was commissioned to make the film as part of the 20-year anniversary of the original revolution.

He originally had other intentions for the Steps sequence, but when he saw the actual steps—their heroic size, their cascading rows—he got excited, went back to rewrite the sequence, building into it an extraordinary structure of cross-moving editing, of dramatically rising events, and of profoundly felt human feeling.

Much of the impact of this sequence rises from Eisenstein's trenchant use of human details: the boots of the soldiers clomping over dead bodies; the mother who ascends the steps with her dead son in her arms, her face twisted with anguish; the woman with her baby carriage—she is shot, and there is a long, terrifying roll of the carriage down the steps. The details are so alive, so real that in the context of Eisenstein's furious cross-editing they become even more charged, more disturbing.

This brief sequence, shown at the conclusion of the Odessa Steps montage, cuts from a sleeping, to an awakening, to a thoroughly roused stone lion; a consummate metaphor, the three lions evoke a sense of volcanic energies let loose—a brilliant way of suggesting the reaction of the Russian people to the carnage of Odessa.

Montage

The word *montage,* adapted from the French term *monter* (to mount or assemble), has had different meanings for different generations. To Eisenstein and the Russian filmmakers of the twenties, montage was *the* creative process in film, the manner by which separate pieces of film were joined, creating a new, emotionally charged whole. More recently, in Europe and America, the term has come to refer to certain *kinds* of edited sequences: notably those in which quick cutting, superimpositions, and a repetition of basic actions are used to create a specific effect—often as a device for providing a general idea about something relative to the film story. In *Red River,* Howard Hawks quick cuts among the cheering, waving cowhands at the beginning of a cattle drive, creating a rousing sense of the drive. *Grand Prix* opens with a series of shots of spectators and closeups just before the race begins. In *Roaring Twenties* a brief montage sequence explains Prohibition, who drinks the bootleg liquor, who makes it.

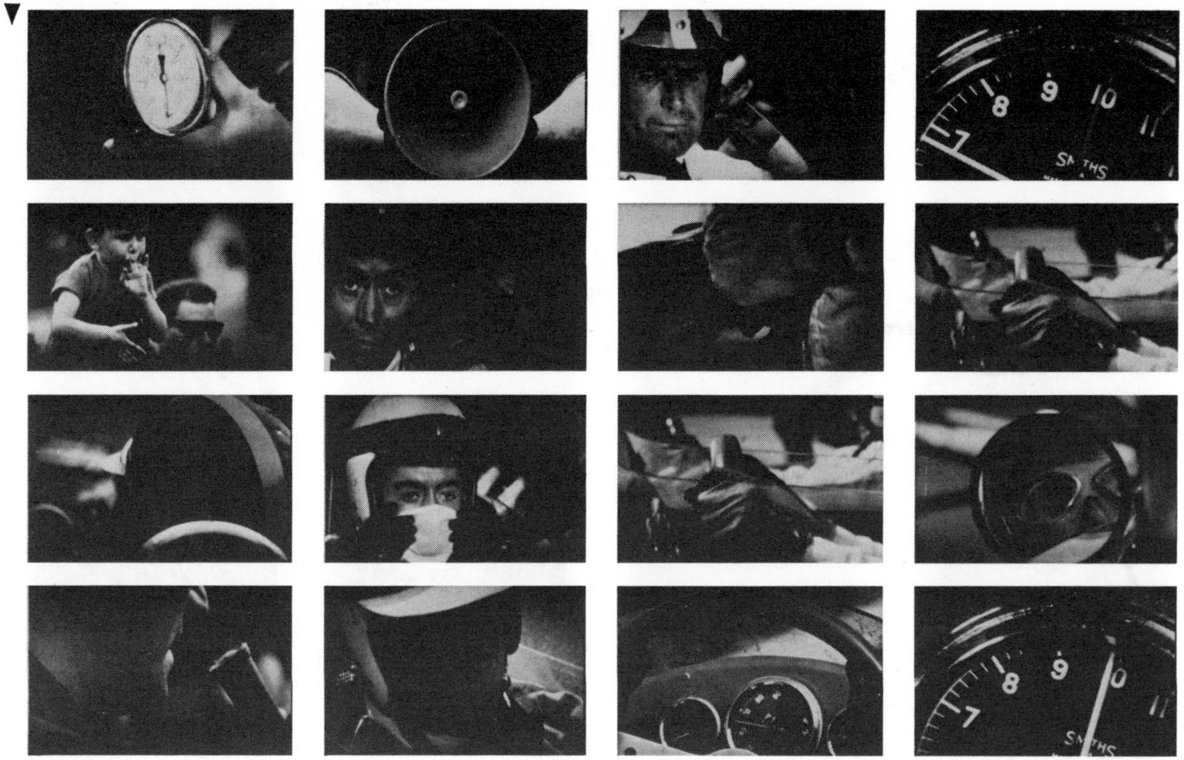

Beginning of the race; from *Grand Prix.*

Beginning of the cattle drive; from *Red River*

The Prohibition Montage; from *The Roaring Twenties.*

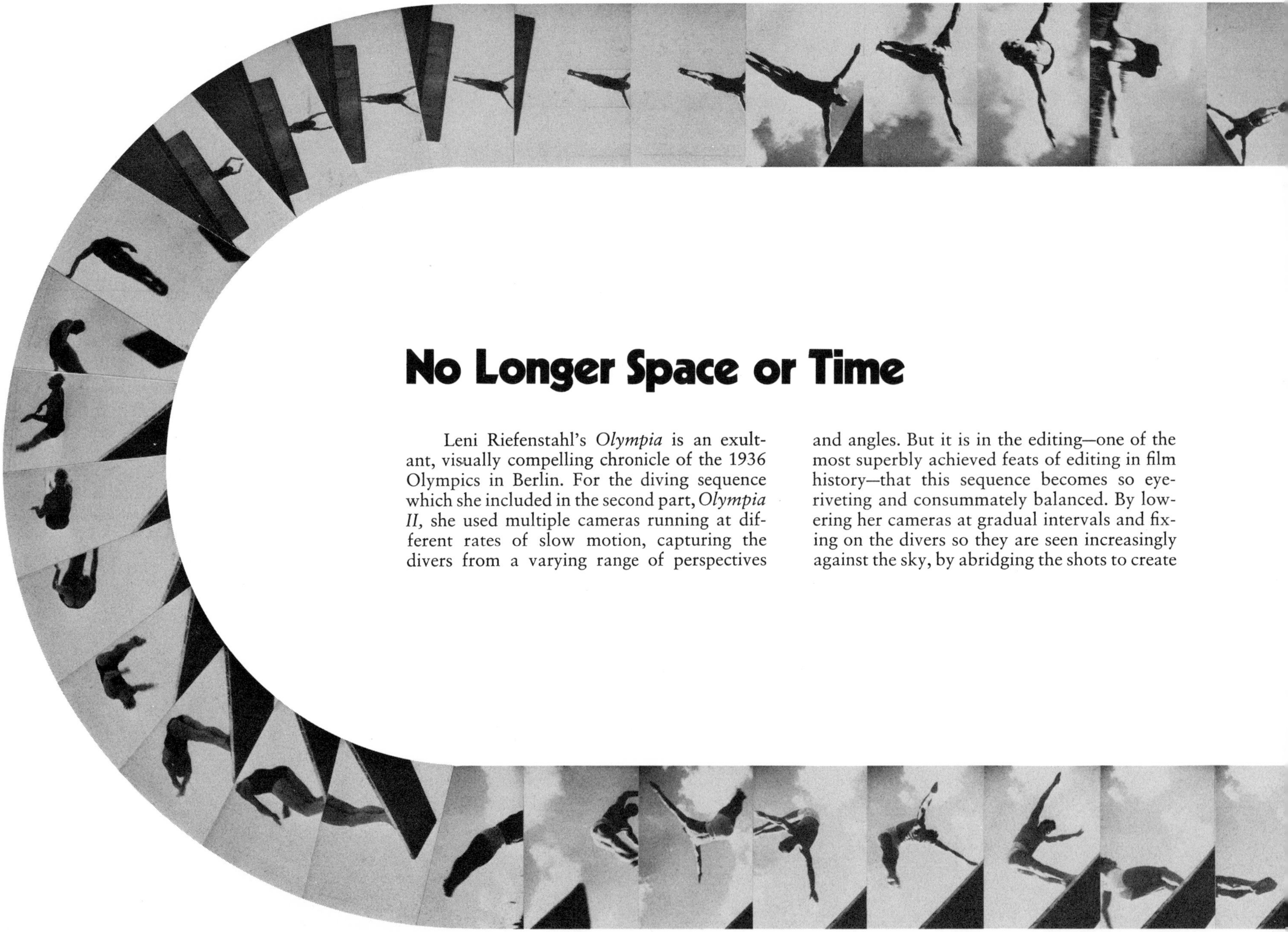

No Longer Space or Time

Leni Riefenstahl's *Olympia* is an exultant, visually compelling chronicle of the 1936 Olympics in Berlin. For the diving sequence which she included in the second part, *Olympia II,* she used multiple cameras running at different rates of slow motion, capturing the divers from a varying range of perspectives and angles. But it is in the editing—one of the most superbly achieved feats of editing in film history—that this sequence becomes so eye-riveting and consummately balanced. By lowering her cameras at gradual intervals and fixing on the divers so they are seen increasingly against the sky, by abridging the shots to create

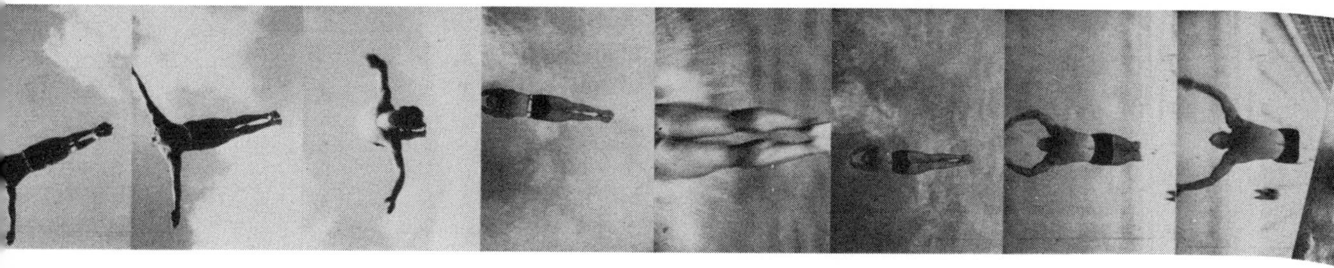

an effect of momentum toward the pure flight of a dive, by matching the movements so that the juxtaposition of separate divers takes on a fluid, continuous motion, Riefenstahl transformed a series of well-photographed dives into a few minutes of pure film spectacle. The sweep, the grace, the splendor of the dives have been captured and framed and structured so that in a rare and unforgettable manner, we cease watching people dive, we behold the purest expression of the dive, the human form in flight, in a manner no longer bound to the compression of time, or the localized limits of space.

Dramatic Editing

NORTH BY NORTHWEST ▼

To escape from an airplane that has been attacking him, Cary Grant races onto the highway and waves wildly as he stands in the path of an oncoming oil truck. Hitchcock intercuts the truck and Grant at increasingly tighter distances, to create a jarring effect of the truck about to plow Grant over—which it just barely does. Cut to Grant under the wheels, looking up to see the plane coming straight at the oil truck; then, from a distance, the explosion. The truck driver shouts for Grant to run—the tanks will blow at any moment; and Grant races from the holocaust. The editing here is precise, economical, and by emphasizing Grant's point of view manages to highlight every stage of action.

▼

SAHARA

The man whom Bogart sends for reinforcements walks through the searing desert, dropping canteen, rifle, supplies behind him. First seen against an enormous backdrop of desert he is small, a tiny figure in an expanse of blinding sand. Then, as the camera comes up close, we see his struggle to mount a hill; the camera cuts between his efforts and the sliding sand, as though to suggest the futility of movement, the impossibility of getting out.

AN OCCURRENCE AT OWL CREEK BRIDGE

Having escaped from a hanging and his pursuers, the prisoner races back to his plantation where his wife sees him, runs to him. Director Robert Enrico intercuts the two figures running toward one another for an interminably long time; finally they meet, she reaches to touch him . . .

BONNIE AND CLYDE

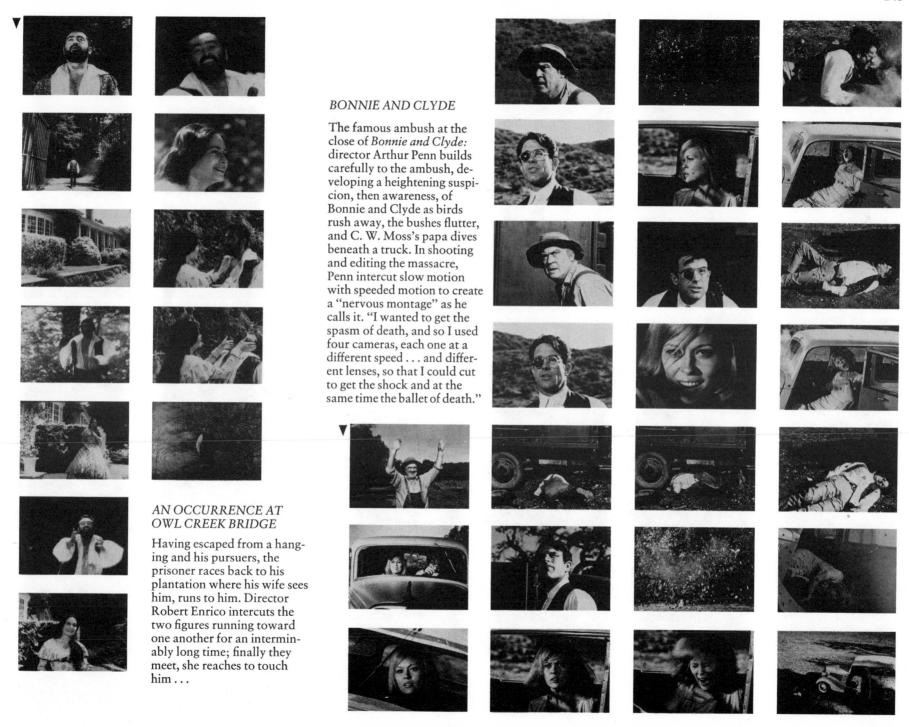

The famous ambush at the close of *Bonnie and Clyde:* director Arthur Penn builds carefully to the ambush, developing a heightening suspicion, then awareness, of Bonnie and Clyde as birds rush away, the bushes flutter, and C. W. Moss's papa dives beneath a truck. In shooting and editing the massacre, Penn intercut slow motion with speeded motion to create a "nervous montage" as he calls it. "I wanted to get the spasm of death, and so I used four cameras, each one at a different speed . . . and different lenses, so that I could cut to get the shock and at the same time the ballet of death."

Intercutting

THE FRENCH CONNECTION

The staggering car-and-elevated train chase in *The French Connection:* a terrifying, roller coaster ride of a sequence, made effective not only by the speed of the train and Popeye's careening car, but by an energetic use of detailed actions and gripping vignettes within the over-all chase. Popeye, the crass, dogged police detective (played by Gene Hackman) is shot at by a sniper; he charges to the roof and sees the sniper escaping below; he follows him to an elevated train where the sniper makes it on but Popeye doesn't. Popeye commandeers a car, chases the train from below, while above the sniper takes over the train with a gun, forcing the engineer not to stop at the next station. The editing tempo and the charge of events build steadily—the sniper killing the engineer and a conductor; Popeye almost killing pedestrians; until the train smashes into another train and Popeye spots and shoots the fleeing sniper. The sequence is jarring in its heightening speed and tempo; and the intercutting between Popeye and the sniper tightens the suspense to a point near unbearable. Note in these frames the emphasis on long shots cutting to closeups, a technique common to the best of intercut sequences since Griffith.

THE MANCHURIAN CANDIDATE

The concluding, powerful sequence at the presidential convention where Sinatra tries to find Laurence Harvey before he commits the assassination for which he had been brainwashed and programmed. Director John Frankenheimer uses a classic technique of intercutting—going back to the same focal points in a rising, spiraling rhythm of faster cutting—to charge the sequence with tautening suspense and a heightening sense of impending disaster. We learned earlier in the film that Harvey is supposed to kill the presidential candidate at a certain phrase in his speech, and we know the words that precede that phrase; after the national anthem, as Sinatra—who has spotted a lone lighted room in the distant heights of the stadium—races to the room, we hear the beginning of the nominee's speech, and the sound track becomes as vividly a part of the build-up as would a ticking bomb that we know is about to explode. Note the use of slightly distorted angles in Sinatra's race, and the growing insistence of closeups of both Harvey and Angela Lansbury and the Senator as the sequence reaches its climax.

Hitchcock's Diagonal Editing

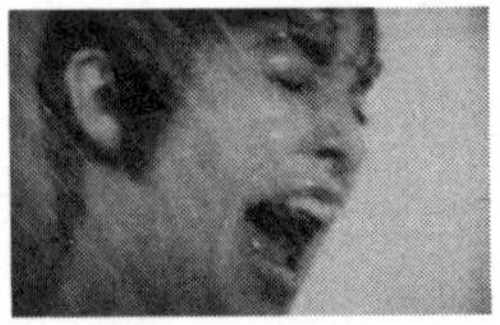

PSYCHO

The shower sequence in *Psycho* is remembered by anyone who has seen the film as one of the most terrifying moments in any film. The abrupt, paralyzing shock of this sequence comes largely from the elaborately crafted feelings we have toward Marion Crane from the beginning of the film, and partly from the place where the brutal killing happens—in the aseptic bathroom of a roadside motel. But much of the power in this scene comes from Hitchcock's superb editing. By intercutting footage in slow motion and at regular speed, he gives the sequence a brutal, irregular rhythm. Moreover, the shots give the sequence a diagonal structure: note the direction of the shower spray in the early shots; then the direction of the knife, and the thrust of action during the stabbing; then, at the end, as Marion's body slumps to the floor, the diagonal shower spray is still evident—a graphic way of framing the violence in the scene.

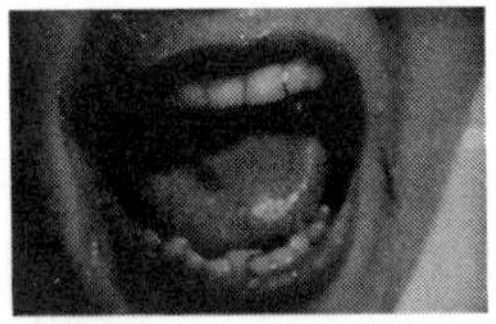
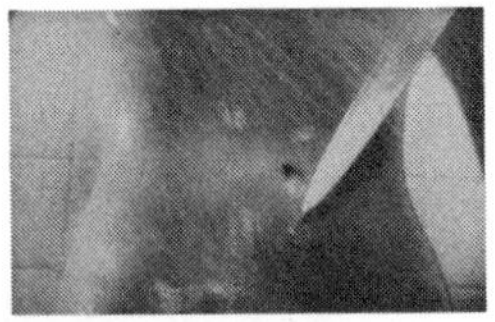

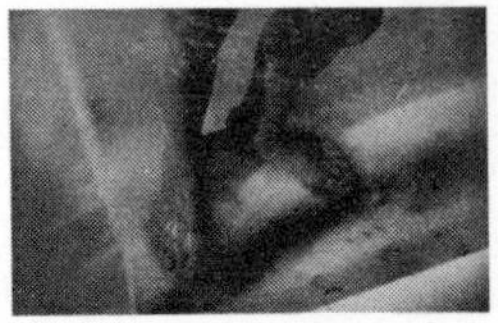

Janet Leigh in *Psycho*.

Horizontal vs Vertical

NORTH BY NORTHWEST

One of the most powerful and purely Hitchcockian sequences from Hitchcock's films is Cary Grant's race from a bullet-spouting airplane amidst flat cornfields in *North by Northwest*. The context is significant: here is a man about to be murdered, not in a dark alley late at night, but in broad daylight, amidst open spaces. In structuring and editing the sequence Hitchcock relies on the graphic contrasts between the flat horizon and Grant's vertical figure. Indeed, from the beginning of the sequence this contrast helps build the slow tension.

The Force of Reaction

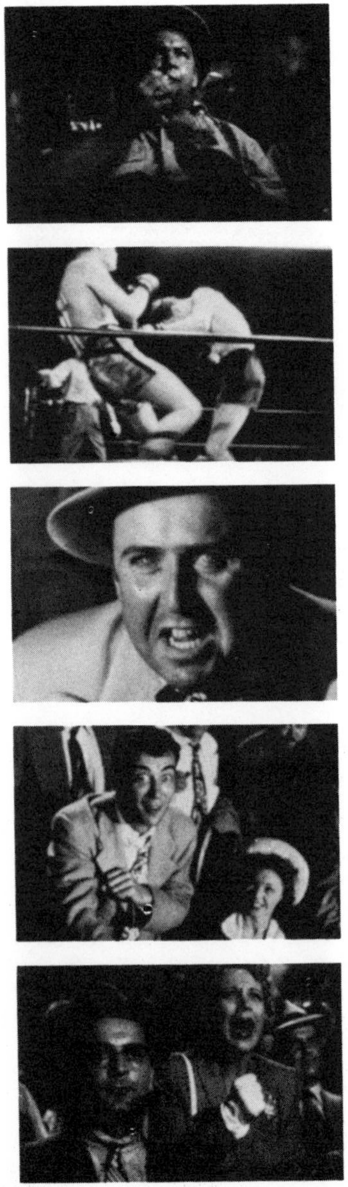

REACTION AS INDICTMENT

In *The Set-Up,* a film that goes almost overboard in proclaiming how brutal prizefighting really is, reactions are used forcefully, if in some ways ambiguously. The screaming lady seen in growing closeup becomes genuinely ugly; the blind man (third frame) keeps shouting, "Go for his eyes!" Yet most of the film is the fight itself, which we are invited to watch with much the same reactions.

VICARIOUS TERROR

A major theme of *Wild Boys of the Road* is the solidarity of the kids. This solidarity makes the train accident—in which one of the boys loses his leg in the railway yard—all the more potent and deeply felt. We don't see the train hit the boy; but we see the rising horror on the faces of the other kids, which express fully the force and terror.

BIRTH OF A POLITICIAN

Willie Stark, the rising politician in *All The King's Men,* begins his real rise to fame at a rally the night after he's learned that he's been set up by party bosses to split the ticket. His speech is good, but it's the reactions to his speech that convince us how good.

CHAPTER SEVEN

Sound

Sound

"It is the business of the sound film to reveal for us our acoustic environment, the acoustic landscape in which we live, the speech of things and the intimate whisperings of nature; all that has speech beyond human speech, and speaks to us with the vast conversational powers of life . . . from the mutterings of the sea to the din of a great city."—Béla Balázs

In Woody Allen's *Bananas,* Woody has come to a Latin American country of week-end revolutions and settled into a seedy hotel. There is a knock on the door, and a messenger hands him a letter. It's from the President: an invitation for Woody to dine with him that evening. Woody, who had come to the country as a prospective revolutionary, is so overwhelmed that he settles back on his bed, his face glazed with a dreamily intoxicated expression, and gentle harp music starts to play. *He's going to have a dream,* we think; and so does Woody, until he starts looking around, wondering where the harp music is coming from. He opens the closet door and inexplicably, a man is sitting there, playing a harp.

The gag is reminiscent of Keaton: it undercuts our expectations from the screen by revealing a layer of the fakery that goes into the screen—after all, we always assume that the musical track is to be heard by us, not the characters in the movie. But the harp gag also reminds us just how conventional film music generally is: we hear a note, an instrument, a riff, and invariably, we're conscious of the mood it's supposed to arouse—so much so that the music often works much like dialogue or sound effects in synchronizing with the screen action precisely, rather than rubbing against it or falling out of step with it.

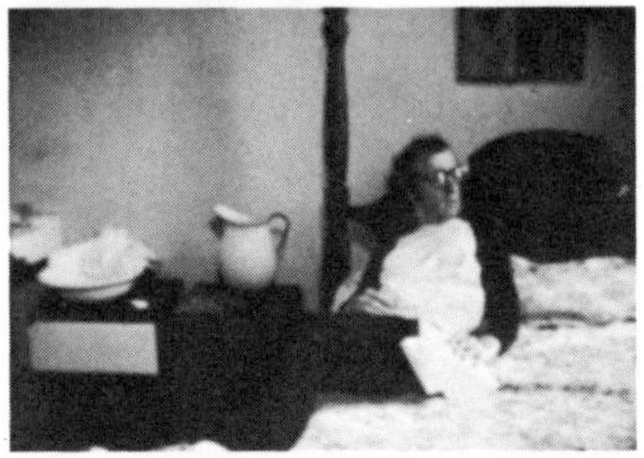

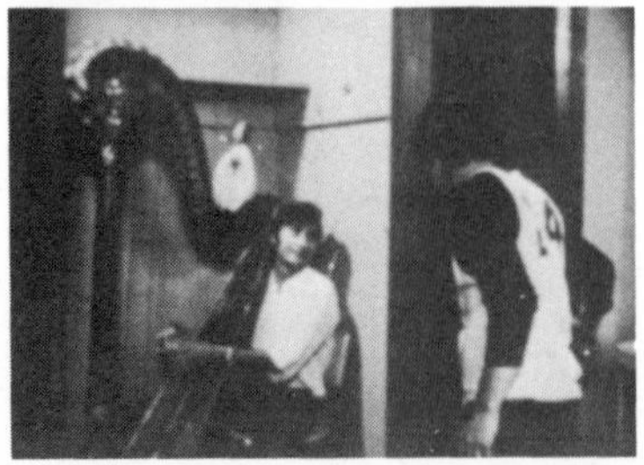

Yet often the most creative and striking uses of sound take place when the soundtrack is set *against* the visual action on the screen, so that one plays against the other, charging the movie with a lively kind of friction. In Jacques Tati's *Mon Oncle,* a middle-class French family lives in a house that is controlled entirely by gadgets. Everything from the toaster to the front gate is wired, automatic, lifeless. One of the most hideous concoctions in this robot playland is a kind of fountain, a huge garish fish that rises from the middle of a scrubbed grassless courtyard. The amount of water the fish spits out can be controlled from inside the house, and we learn that the height of the spray is really a barometer of the social standing of whoever enters the courtyard. And so when a salesman comes to the door, the woman runs inside and turns the fountain on so there's barely a trickle; when the gangling posh lady from next door arrives, the fish bursts with water. A great enough gag as it stands, but by modulating his soundtrack Tati does extraordinary things with it. For it's not just the size of the water column that interests us; it's the noise it makes. The fish sputters, chokes, gasps, squeals, screeches—even when it's working right. And when the innocent Hulot—Tati, as the film's one character who hasn't been seized by the spirit of gadgetry—jabs a stake into the ground, he somehow severs the connecting pipe; in the middle of a garden party the fish makes grotesque dying sounds and spouts a torrent of black gook. The soundtrack not only heightens the absurdity of this status fountain; it makes the fountain more convincing, and therefore more appalling—and certainly funnier. It is as though the fountain, in its own mechanical lifeless way, were protesting this insane garden party—an effect perhaps not possible through images, but brought off superbly on Tati's unique soundtrack.

The soundtrack came to the movies late, but not sound. Even the so-called "silent" films were seen with some kind of musical accompaniment, if only one man banging away at a piano in the front of the theater. Irving Thalberg, the young production head at MGM in the late twenties and the thirties, has said:

There was never a silent *film. We'd finish a picture, show it in one of our projection rooms, and come out shattered. It would be awful. We'd have high hopes for the picture, work our heads off on it, and the result was always the same. Then we'd show it in a theater, with a girl down in the pit pounding away on the piano, and there would be all the difference in the world. Without that music, there wouldn't have been a movie industry at all.*

A critical hint can be found in these remarks about the nature of sound—perhaps the psychology of sound—within a movie. Movies were *never* absolutely visual, without a soundtrack; always, from the beginning, they involved the ear as well as the eyes; and always audiences expected them to. It well may be in the nature of movies—the most realistic and immediate and convincing of the arts—to require the dimension of sound to be present in some way: we see a man move through a dismal, empty corridor, and we hear nothing. It's not all there, something is missing, though what we hear doesn't necessarily have to be his footsteps or the creaking floorboards. Sound gives film an important dimension of believability, of resonance, of the real world echoed in a myriad of ways. But sound can be even more. Again, Balázs, writing (quite optimistically) at the beginning of the sound era in films:

The vocation of the sound film is to redeem us from the chaos of shapeless noise by accepting it as expression, as significance, as meaning.

Jeanette MacDonald during production of *Monte Carlo* listening to a playback of herself singing.

Music

Pather Panchali

Anthony Quinn as Zampanò and Giulietta Masina as Gelsomina in *La Strada*

In Satyajit Ray's Indian film, *Pather Panchali,* there is a luminous sequence that suggests how profound are the links between music and film. The camera focuses on the face of a pool, capturing the skittering, lazy movement of waterbugs along the surface. It is a beautiful, lyrical moment, the tiny bugs skipping, darting from flower to leaf, mirrored in the tranquil water. But what makes the sequence unforgettable is the soundtrack, the gentle, trickling strings of a sitar, matched so precisely, so gracefully to the movement in the film that you feel Ray had somehow managed to evoke from that image some nascent, hidden music already present there. The sequence barely lasts a few minutes, but it holds us so enraptured, we are no longer aware of watching a film. The scene draws sight and sound together into a single spellbinding whole, the two senses have ceased to exist separately.

Only rarely can music so infuse the images on the screen with life that the two become totally interdependent. Bernard Herrman's electronic, whirring score during the shower killing and the murder of the detective Arbogast in Hitchcock's *Psycho;* the way Kubrick used Strauss waltzes—particularly the Blue Danube Waltz—to transform the spaceship dockings in *2001* into a cosmic ballet; the sad, evocative tune in Fellini's *La Strada,* that picks up increasingly evocative power each time we hear it—so that by the last time, when we and the brutish Zampano overhear a laundress humming the tune, we know that the girl who sang it for so long in an earlier time is dead, the tune has become a poignant, stirring elegy. Examples such as these show that music can become inseparable from a film: not simply a kind of last-minute addition heaped onto the film from a pile of "canned" recordings.

Often music can be used within a story as a form of comment or an amplifying device. In *Bonnie and Clyde,* following a successful bank robbery, Bonnie and Clyde and C. W. Moss enter a darkened theater where a Busby Berkeley musical is playing; the number? "We're In The Money." The film cuts to Bonnie humming the tune later as she fixes her hair in the mirror. The song "As Time Goes By" is the emotional center of *Casablanca.* The way the song haunts Bogart fixes his character in our minds in a combination of toughness and nostalgic yearnings.

Music can act as a counterpoint to the images in a film, an idea much relished by Eisenstein in his essays on sound. One of the most bizarre and yet strangely compelling examples takes place at the end of *Dr. Strangelove.* The nuclear bomb that detonates the "doomsday device" has been dropped; the entire world is about to go up in holocaust. A burst of light; a mushroom cloud; then a succession of mushroom clouds—and all against the soundtrack, a woman doing a nightclub rendition of "We'll Meet Again." The sequence borders on that spectral region between high tragedy and farce, yet in some perhaps demented way it works; we tend to laugh and choke at the same time—terror and a kind of vulgar joke brought off by a peculiar association of imagery and music.

Dialogue

William Powell is hosting a Christmas eve party in *The Thin Man,* and a guest has just noticed him speaking to the very enticing Maureen O'Sullivan: "Who is she?" the guest asks. "I used to bounce her on my knee," Powell says. "Which knee? Can I touch it?"

If we've forgotten how good dialogue can be in the movies, it's no doubt because it hasn't been nearly that good for some time—not since the thirties, when Hollywood was populated by some of the best writers in the country: William Faulkner, Dorothy Parker, Lillian Hellman, F. Scott Fitzgerald, George S. Kaufman, Herman J. Mankiewicz, Preston Sturges, to mention a few. They were the halcyon days of movie dialogue, a flush of ripe talent and uncommon energies creating scripts that were often far superior to the talents that played in and directed them.

It is often argued that movies are—or should be—a great distance from plays; that the fundamental expression should be visual, not dialogue; yet the evidence of so many of the better movies suggests that dialogue—when it's good enough, snappy and sprightly enough—can carry a movie, especially light comedy, the genre that seems most dependent on rich dialogue, and the genre at which the studios once excelled.

THE POWER OF DIALOGUE: BOGART AND MARJORIE MAIN IN *DEAD END* (1937)
►

Bogart, playing Baby Face Martin, a notorious gangster, has returned to the neighborhood where he grew up; he sees his mother enter the tenement and follows her in:

Baby Face: Mom! Mom! It's me. It's me. I only had my face lifted.

Mother: You little tramp.

Baby Face: Mom, aren't you glad to see me?

(She slaps him)

Mother: That's how glad I am. You dog. You dirty old dog you.

Baby Face: Mom, what kind of talk is that?

Mother: Don't call me mom. You ain't no son of mine. What do you want from me now?

Then get out of here, before I crack your face again. Get out of here.

Baby Face: I killed a guy for looking at me the way you are now.

Mother: Yeah, you're a killer all right. A murderer. You're a butcher, sure. Why don't you let me forget you? You've got troubles enough with the cops, the newspapers bothering me . . . Just leave us alone, you've never brought us nothin but trouble, just stay away and leave us alone, leave us alone. . . .

Written by Lillian Hellman, adapted from the play by Sidney Kingsley; © 1937 by Samuel Goldwyn.

Great Lines

First . . . chance had brought them face to face; now . . . mysterious instincts, as ungovernable as the winds of the heavens, were knitting their lives together.

Greed

'Oh, bury me not on the lone prai-rie,
Where the wild coyotes will howl over me!'

The Wind

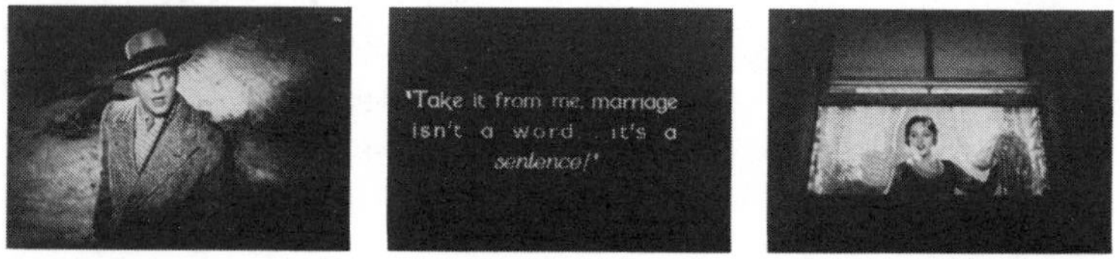

'Take it from me, marriage isn't a word . . . it's a sentence!'

The Crowd

"Friends for life——"
"——or . . . death!"

Greed

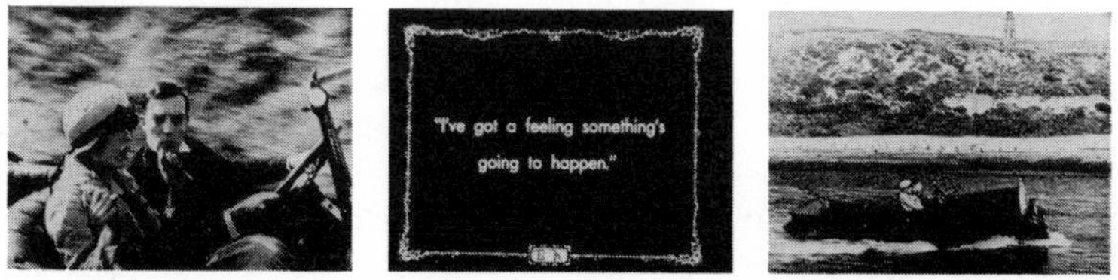

"I've got a feeling something's going to happen."

Keaton's *Sherlock Jr.*

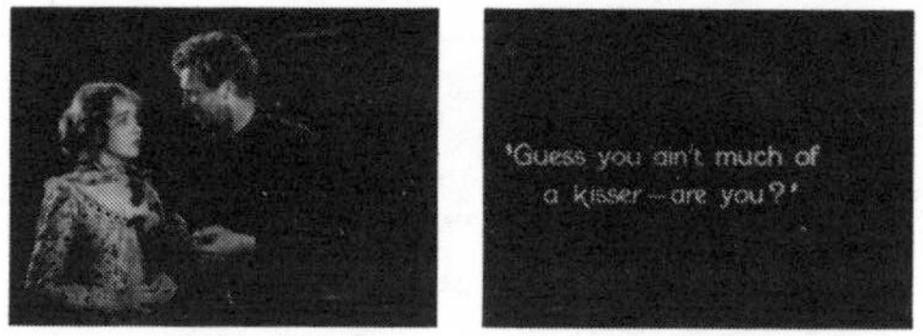

'Guess you ain't much of a kisser—are you?'

The Wind

"Let's go over and sit on the sewer."

Greed

The Wind

"I liked best . . . the fellow who played 'Nearer My God to Thee' . . . on the beer bottles."

'Your ship? A worm must be towing it down from the North Pole!'

The Crowd

Before and

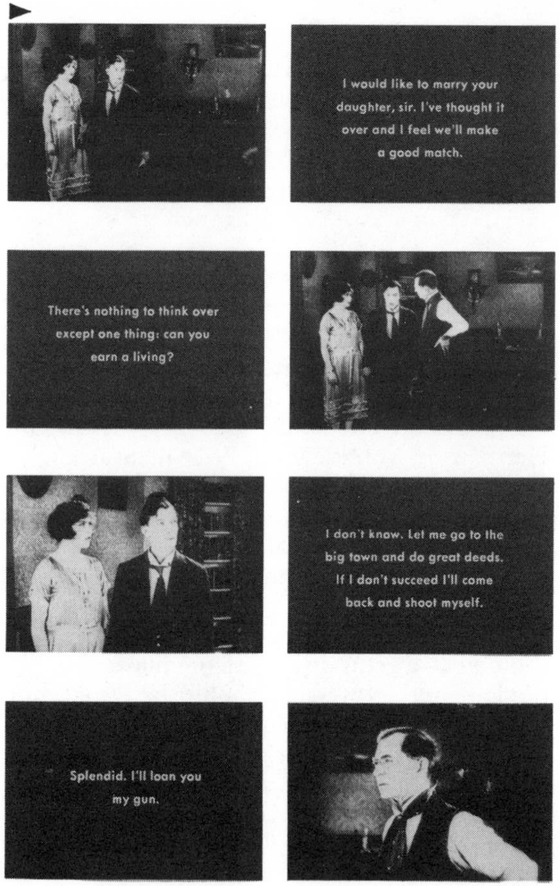

I would like to marry your daughter, sir. I've thought it over and I feel we'll make a good match.
There's nothing to think over except one thing: can you earn a living?
I don't know. Let me go to the big town and do great deeds. If I don't succeed I'll come back and shoot myself.
Splendid. I'll loan you my gun.

Keaton's *Daydreams*

"——if I'd a' kept Trina, I'd a' had . . five thousand bucks!"
"I want that five thousand!"

Greed

After the Talkies

Spencer Tracy:
"You know I wouldn't hurt anyone else. I wouldn't hurt a fly. (Then to himself:) Unless I caught him eating some of my cake."
—Dante's Inferno

"You can shake the sawdust out of your hair, but you can't shake it out of your hearts."
—The Big Top

"I'm not one of those 'eye for an eye' men. No, I always take two eyes."—Luther Adler to John Wayne in Wake of the Red Witch

Barmaid: "What about you, Jonny, what kind of trouble are you looking for?"
Brando: "Whaddaya got?"—The Wild One

"I told you to keep away from that radio. If the battery is dead, it'll have company."
—Cagney in White Heat

Drunk to William Powell: "Those were the good old days."
Powell: "Don't kid yourself. These are the good old days."—The Thin Man

"The prison has not been built that can hold me. I'll get out of this one if it means spending my entire life here."—Woody Allen, Take the Money And Run

"Ya know. . . . There's only two things finer than a good gun: a Swiss watch and a woman from anywhere."—Red River

Reporter: "Cut it out, Tatum. We're old friends, we're all in the same boat."
Kirk Douglas: "I'm in the boat. You're in the water."—Ace in the Hole

Banker to Joel McCrea: "I must say, Mr. Judd, I expected a much younger man."
McCrea: "Well, I used to be."—Ride The High Country

"People here are funny. . . . They work so hard at living they forget how to live."—Gary Cooper, as Deeds in New York: Mr. Deeds Goes To Town

Wyatt Earp: Mac, you ever been in love?
Mac: No, I've been a bartender all my life.
—Henry Fonda as Wyatt Earp in My Darling Clementine

Walter Brennan: "Don't you trust me, Cole?"
Gary Cooper: "When I was a kid I had a pet rattlesnake. I'd play with it, but I wouldn't turn my back on it."—The Westerner

"Remember, you're fighting for this woman's honor, which is probably more than she ever did."—Groucho Marx, Duck Soup

Marlene Dietrich to Orson Welles: "You're a mess, honey. You've been eating too much candy."—Touch of Evil

"I want to walk barefoot through your hair."
—Clark Gable to Jeanette MacDonald, in San Francisco

Bogart: "What you being so mean for, miss? A man takes a drop once in a while, it's only human nature."

K. Hepburn: "Nature, Mr. Allnut, is what we are put in this world to rise above."—The African Queen

"Toto, I have a feeling, we're not in Kansas anymore."—Judy Garland, The Wizard of Oz

Joan Crawford: "What do you want to hear?"
Sterling Hayden: "Lie to me—tell me all these years you've waited."—Johnny Guitar (1954)

"I never thought I could sink so low as to become an actor."—John Barrymore, The Twentieth Century

Hedda Hopper to Mae West: "How is it that you know so much about men?"
Mae West: "Baby, I went to night school."

The Sound of Sound...and Silence

In Alfred Hitchcock's *The Birds,* Melanie and Mitch's family are trapped in Mitch's house while outside the birds—uncounted, unseen hordes of them—have been gathering for hours. When the attack does come, Hitchcock handles it with his characteristic touch of subtle perversity. For a long while we don't see a single bird. But the sequence is terrifying nonetheless: for we hear the birds, hear them as we've never heard birds before; and hear them in a way that threatens forever to undermine our delight in the simple trill of a skylark. The sounds are ferocious, jarring, deafening: screeches and shattering near-screams; smashes of birds into wood; grotesque caws and rasps, and brutish, amplified pecking; and above and throughout it all, a wind tunnel of thwapping wings. On the screen we see Melanie and the others cringing in dim light; a sense of helplessness hinted by the low angle and lighting, but conveyed finally by the powerful soundtrack.

Jessica Tandy, Tippi Hedren, and Rod Taylor in *The Birds.*

It was an adage of radio that the most frightening or beautiful or awesome experiences can best be summoned by the imagination; and the same is true to some extent of film. Often what we don't see, but hear (and therefore imagine) acts upon us in a more disturbing and vivid way than what we see. In *The Haunting,* there is a frightening scene in which the two women are in the bedroom at night and a knocking begins at the door. The pounding grows, becoming louder and louder, till it is nearly deafening; the camera cuts between the door and the terrified faces of the two women. The sounds—and whatever is making them—become as grim and ominous to us as it is to them.

The sounds of things can amplify what we see, charging them with fresh and larger meanings and implications. In Fritz Lang's *M,* the child murderer played by Peter Lorre walks the dark streets of Berlin while the city is locked behind closed doors in terror. Lorre's character is a dumpy, pathetic creature who, once we see him, can't really frighten *us.* He's simply a sad little nonentity who whistles and likes to play with his face in the mirror. Yet as he walks the streets of Berlin, his footsteps ring with pale echoes, and he whistles, creating an ironic tension between what we know of the man and what we know he has done to the city. Sounds such as echoes and whistling here create the effect of a grotesque shadow cast by a seemingly harmless child, though a child we know secretly to be a murderer.

In *An Occurrence at Owl Creek Bridge,* echoes are used in a quite different manner: as a means of stretching and expanding time. A man is about to be hanged, and the director, Robert Enrico, uses images—but especially the soundtrack—to suggest his point of view. He waits for dawn on a wooden bridge while soldiers march up and down, clicking their feet in long, loud echoes. The echoes seem to freeze time; sounds are not real, but mirrored; and the wait—a short wait in real time, a long wait for the condemned prisoner and for us—becomes doubly tense.

An Occurrence at Owl Creek Bridge uses another sound technique to create the effect of time stretching and expanding in the mind: *slowing* the soundtrack, so that normal sounds are heard in a prolonged, lingering manner, as though a record were being played on a phonograph at a slower speed. When the prisoner is hanged, the rope breaks and he plunges into the water; sputtering to the surface, he can hear the sounds of the soldiers in the distance—not normal voices, but voices distorted, heard in the unreal, faster-moving time of his own tensed psyche.

An Occurrence at Owl Creek Bridge

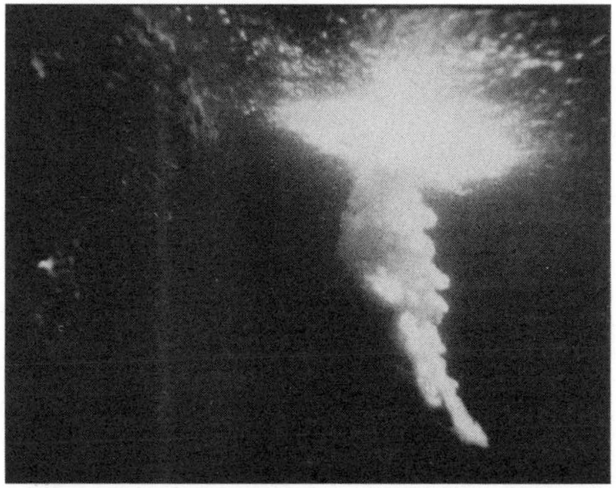

A similar—and thoroughly chilling—version of this same technique is used in Kubrick's *2001: A Space Odyssey,* when the spaceship's computer HAL runs amok and kills all the men aboard except Bowman. In self-defense Bowman climbs into the vast horizontal chamber that holds the circuitry of HAL's brain and slowly, methodically unscrews the gleaming terminals. HAL protests, but as his "memory banks" gradually fade, the vast computer character is reduced to what he first learned: a song, "Daisy, Daisy," which grows slower and slower as Bowman feverishly unscrews more and more terminals. The effect is eerie, and genuinely disturbing. HAL's voice—which had communicated more character and held more interest for us than any of the human characters in the film, now becomes a fading, ground-out series of laborious sounds, a lively voice sputters and diffuses into silence.

Perhaps the most potent of all sounds—as any musician knows—is silence. Not naked silence (there may not be such a thing), but silence charged with the barest hint of sound: the fading echo of an earlier scream; a low, barely audible rumble, or the sound we hear in our ears as we expect a certain sound.

Hitchcock has used silence supremely well in various moments as a way of heightening the suspense in a scene. In *Frenzy,* the man we know to be a strangler takes a woman into a building where she has a room. Hitchcock doesn't follow them in; rather, he holds on the barren brick wall of the building and we wait, interminably, it seems; wait for the scream that's inevitable. When, after moments pass and nothing happens, two secretaries on their lunch hour walk past, talking, we're so pent up that we listen carefully to their patter—simply because it's *a* sound. *Then* comes the scream; but what interests us now are the reactions of the secretaries; they look at one another, look around, and go on walking, and talking—the long silent build-up was Hitchcock's preface to a grisly little joke about bystanders.

At the conclusion of *The Birds,* Mitch steps outside the door to see spread before him

a world teeming with birds. They sit everywhere . . . on lawn, fences, roads: but they are silent, or almost silent. "I wanted an electronic silence," says Hitchcock, "a sort of monotonous low hum that might suggest the sound of the sea in the distance. It was a strange, artificial sound, which in the language of the birds might be saying, '. . . We're like an engine that's purring and we may start off at any moment'."

There is another moment in *The Birds* when silence creates an effect more acute than sound would: Jessica Tandy, as Mitch's mother, discovers the body of a farmer; she opens her mouth to scream—but no sound; only when she races into a truck and the truck backfires do we feel a relief, as though she finally *had* screamed.

The Birds

Sound and Image

In *Medium Cool,* Haskell Wexler's sleekly photographed account of a TV cameraman during the Chicago convention in 1968, there is a sequence that takes place in a roller derby, the kind of roller derby that's all elbows, knees, and violent jostling. The journalist has taken a girlfriend there, but Wexler's real purpose in the sequence seems to be a comment on the brute, insensitive violence of spectator sports, and, by extension, of society. The images themselves are disturbing enough, but matched to the soundtrack—Wild Man Fisher's rollicking, crude, caustic "Merry Go Round"—the sequence becomes nearly surreal. Wild Man Fisher belts out the lines, it seems, almost between hiccoughs; like the people in the roller derby, the song threatens at every moment to go totally out of control, out of the range of feeling or comprehension, driven by some mad primal impulse. It is an exquisite, stunning match of image and soundtrack, each shading and affecting the other, the lunatic wildness of the song underscoring the idiocy of the roller derby, and the violence of the derby giving a sharper edge to the song, and both moving in a shaggy, circling rhythm of mounting energy.

Like two pieces of film in the editing process, image and soundtrack when combined can create a third, unique and separate impression, another instance of 2 plus 2 equalling 5. The precise ways in which image and soundtrack can be matched vary considerably. Consider, for example, one of the earliest creative uses of sound in the movies—the Walt Disney Mickey Mouse cartoons of the late twenties and early thirties, in which Disney was among the first to use sound imaginatively in film. In *Steamboat Willie,* the first sound cartoon, just about the entire cartoon is made up of musical stanzas matched to the action of Mickey Mouse as he "plays" various animals and gadgets as though they were musical instruments, a goat's tail, the teeth of a hippo, the tails of suckling piglets, the duck—every animal yields its own sound, matched exactly to the instruments on the soundtrack.

Sometimes image and soundtrack can reinforce one another, intensifying and even clarifying the impression that each one creates. Orson Welles and his cameraman Gregg Toland shot the Xanadu scene in *Citizen Kane* in a block lit, vast-scaled gothic style, creating a feeling of immense empty spaces and the hulking, dead presence of statues and stone. The interiors suggest a vast mausoleum. Moreover, there are considerable mirror and reflection shots, so that we see Kane's presence exaggerated by such repetition. The soundtrack is all echoes: haunting, distant sounds that keep repeating one another like the images, heightening and sharpening the tomblike feeling that Xanadu projects. The visual and acoustic suggestion of Xanadu as a vast echo chamber becomes overpowering.

Sound vs Image

Hallelujah, I'm a Bum! is a curious, engaging musical made at the height of the Depression, in 1933. Al Jolson plays a character named Bumper, a self-proclaimed "Mayor" of all the tramps in Central Park. The film's message—and it comes through strong—is that if you don't have money, take advantage of the situation and enjoy it anyway, a kind of unmilitant Marxism. But perhaps most striking about the film are its musical numbers—a world apart from Busby Berkeley's grandiose finales, or the suave, peppery Fred Astaire films. The tramps sing numbers like, "What Do You Want With Money?"—and the songs are lively, spunky, even catchy; but they're underscored by the tramps we *see* singing the songs; very convincing tramps indeed, unshaven, tinged with a hint of hostility. From the images alone one might conclude that they're gathering into an angry mob. This discrepancy gives the film much of its curious flavor, and catches—perhaps quite accurately—the desperation of a time when you could secretly wish to go out and blithely sing, "What Do You Want With Money?"

As Eisenstein pointed out at the beginning of the sound era, sound becomes most interesting when it acts as a counterpoint to the images in a film. The effect can be ironic, as in *Hallelujah, I'm a Bum!*—or much stronger, as in the famous "Singin' in the Rain" sequence in Stanley Kubrick's *A Clockwork Orange*. The Droogs—a kind of teenage gang of the future—invade a man's home, stomp him near to death and hold him to watch as they rape his wife, all the time to the beat and rhythm of their vibrant rendition of "Singin' in the Rain." Violence of this sort—meshed with the song—takes on a particularly grotesque, almost apocalyptic character; bad taste aside, the combination appalls and appeals to us at the same time; we feel almost like humming along, and kicking along with Alex and his Droogs—as though the music could somehow break down our abhorrence of the brutish invasion and beating and rape.

Contrast such a sequence with the scene in *The Loneliness of the Long Distance Runner,* where another beating is juxtaposed ironically to a song, but with a totally different point of view and a considerably different effect. A boy who has tried to escape from the borstal house—a British reform school—has been caught, and returned, and flung into a cell. While the rest of the boys in chapel sing the stirring spiritual "Jerusalem," a guard mercilessly beats the boy in his cell, bludgeoning him nearly to death as the high, rousing notes in the song peal out. Fiercer than irony, the juxtaposition of the spiritual and the beating rouses our contempt for the guard—and the whole borstal system—in a manner far stronger than the simple beating ever could.

The "What Do You Want With Money?" number from *Hallelujah, I'm a Bum!*
▼

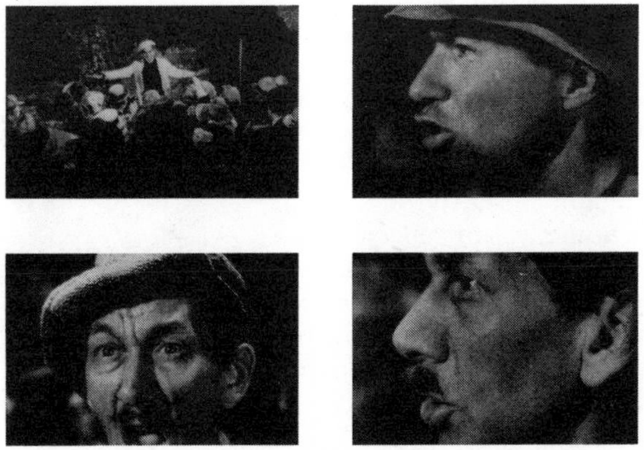

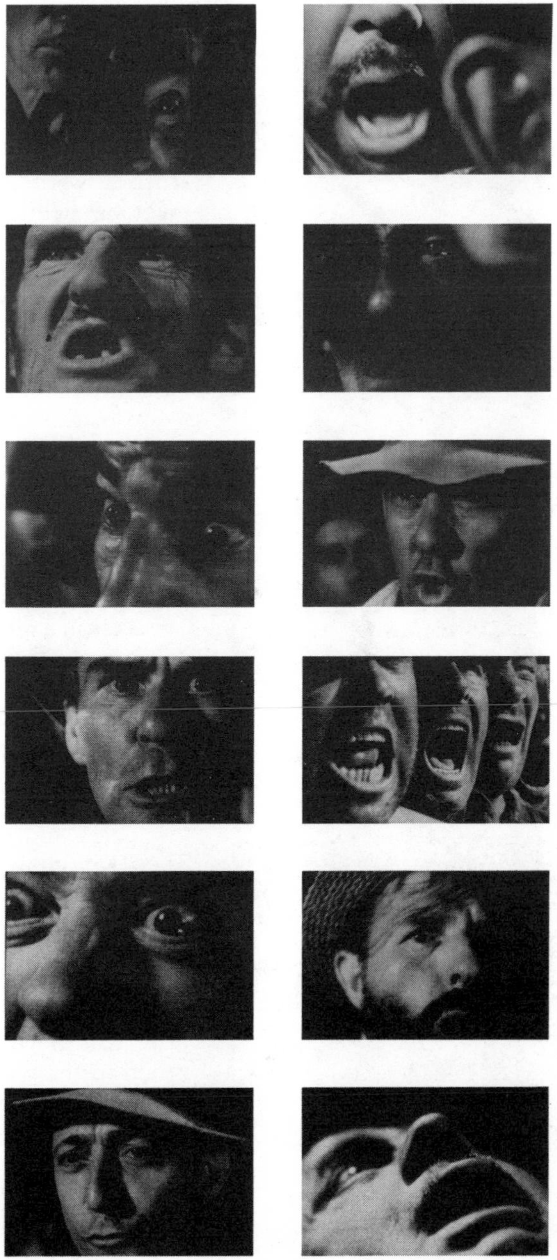

Editing and the Sound Track

At the end of *The Manchurian Candidate,* Frank Sinatra arrives at the tiny booth in the convention center where Laurence Harvey has just killed his dangerous mother and stepfather with a high-powered rifle. Sinatra watches helplessly as Harvey slips his Congressional Medal of Honor over his neck and turns the rifle on himself. The camera holds on Sinatra's stunned face, and there is a brief dissolve as we hear the gunshot; lightning crackles, Sinatra is standing at a window, looking into the rain, and the gunshot has become a clap of thunder. He speaks of Harvey's heroism, reads accounts of other Medal of Honor winners; but the mood is considerably heightened by the dissolve—both visual and aural—from the gunshot to the thunderclap.

Sound offers a range of opportunities for bridging, exaggerating, unifying the editing process in a film. Since the soundtrack can exist separately from the images, its own progression and rhythm can differ considerably from the images, providing a wide range of creative possibilities. *Point Blank,* a film shaggily rich in its uses of sound and editing, offers two impressive sequences in which the soundtrack anticipates and echoes later action. In the first, Lee Marvin is walking down a long blank corridor in a modern building, with his footsteps clicking loudly in a ringing succession. Cut flittingly to his wife (it's she he's walking toward)—in a beauty parlor, reflected in a succession of mirrors; still the echoing of heels on tile. Cut to Marvin again, closer to the camera; then to the wife, at home, again reflected in a mirror; back to Marvin. Such deft intercutting at once establishes Marvin's movement and motive, and the imagery of the wife—reflected in the different mirrors—provides a visual equivalent to the echoes on the soundtrack.

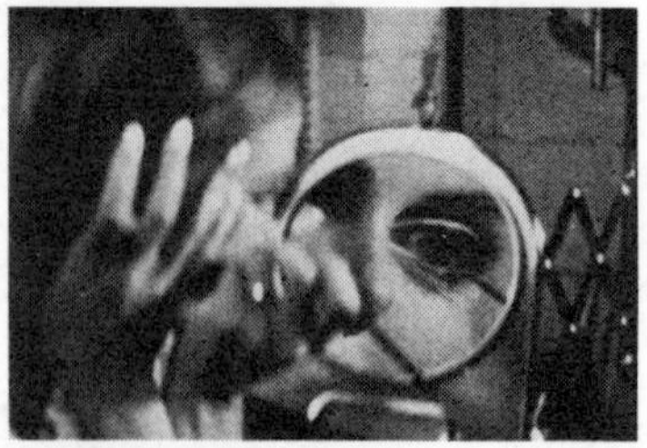

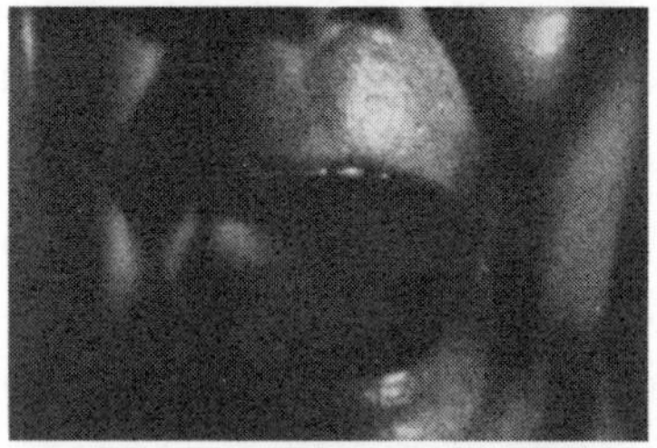

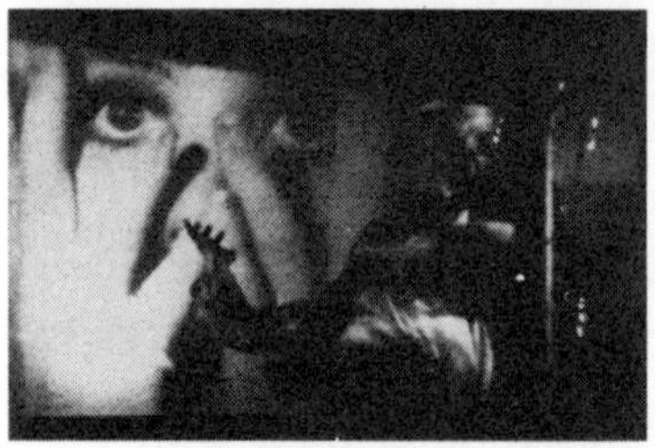

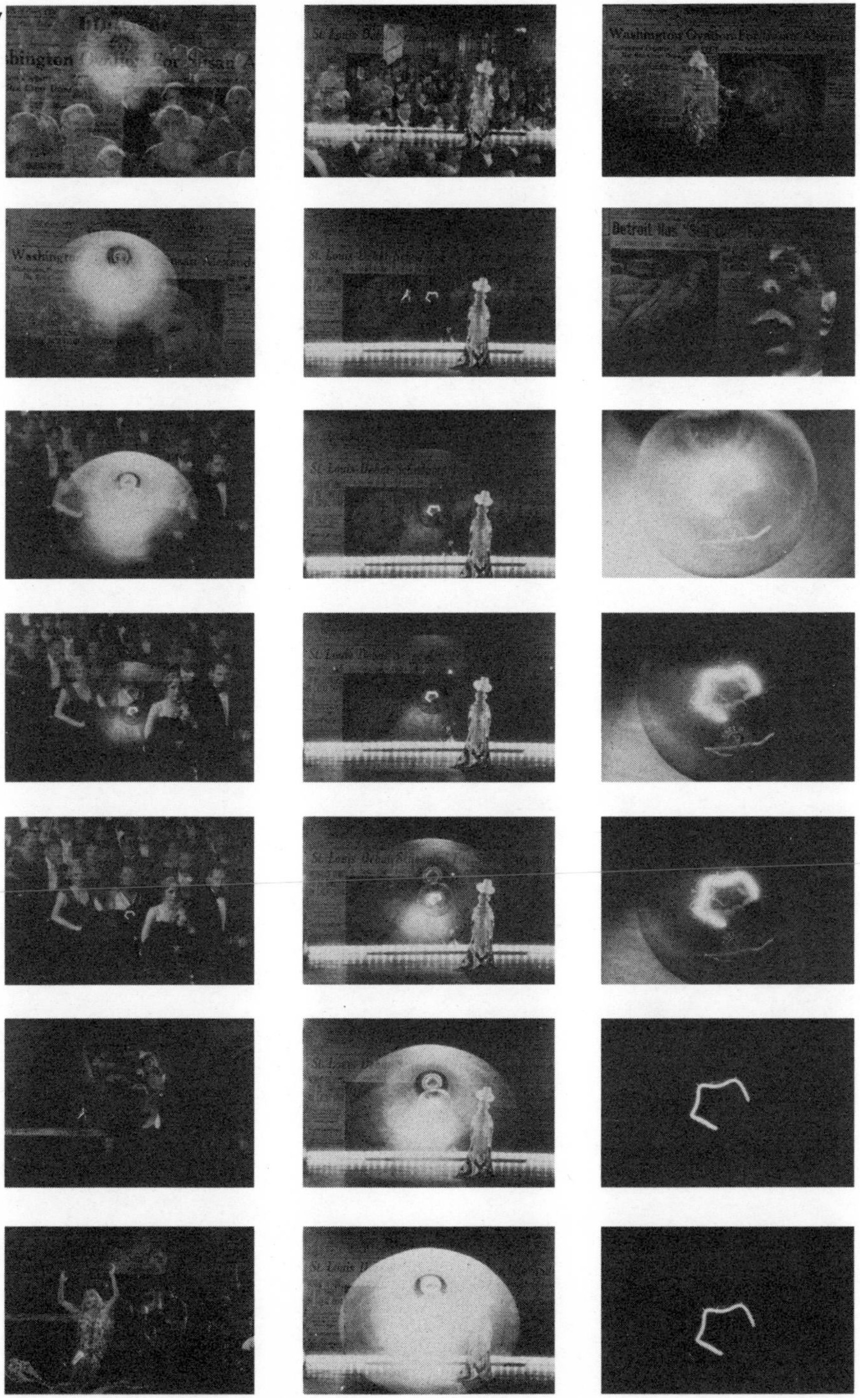

In a later sequence, Marvin stomps two Mob thugs in the back room of a discotheque. The rock singers are blasting out amplified grunts and screams that convey powerfully the impact of the dimly seen fight. Director John Boorman cuts between the fight and the band in a manner that suggests the men are beating one another to the rhythm of the brutal music, a kind of fisticuff ballet.

Montage sequences offer unique opportunities for fresh soundtrack ideas, if only because the normal dramatic rules need not apply. When Susan Alexander Kane recounts the rise and collapse of her singing career, it is depicted as a montage sequence of superimpositions: opera stages, Susan singing, audiences, the opera coach's frustrated expressions, all over a score of (Kane's) newspaper headlines and, running like a visual motif through it all, the bright glare of a spotlight. On the soundtrack we hear snatches from the operas, bits of bombastic music; then the image becomes solely the spotlight, and the soundtrack begins to thin—till the music dies like a slowed phonograph, and the spotlight fades to a single dimming filament; a brilliant shorthand way of conveying Susan's abrupt, disastrous singing career.

A montage sequence in *The Roaring Twenties* begins with a subtle series of cuts from James Cagney and friend making bathtub booze to the bottles they're using to the same labelled bottle, now in a different room, with a different man lifting a glass, taking a sip, and proclaiming, "You can't fool me—that's the real stuff." A superb shorthand expression of how the bootleggers did it.

CHAPTER EIGHT

The Director

The Director

"It is wrong to liken a director to an author. He is more like an architect, if he is creative. An architect conceives his plans from given premises—the purposes of the building, its size, its terrain. If he is clever, he can do something within these limitations."—John Ford

In the fifties and early sixties, growing ranks of movie-goers began to hear the names of new "stars": Bergman, Fellini, Truffaut, Ray, Antonioni, Kurosawa, Resnais. Not stars who could galvanize audiences by the way they lit a cigarette onscreen; these stars never appeared on the screen. But they were stars nonetheless. These were the European and Japanese and English directors whose films reflected a more trenchant and honest universe than the diminishing products of the faltering Hollywood studios. The ripening awareness of film artists who shape their own work has led, since then, to an overdue (if often overpaid) estimate of the director as the most critical shaping force behind the production of a movie.

Generally speaking, the director is the most important figure in the production of a film. Even under the old Hollywood system a director might oversee every step of a film from the script-writing to the final stages of editing and sound mixing. But with the few exceptions of supremely established directors like Stanley Kubrick or Alfred Hitchcock, the Hollywood director has never had ultimate and total control of his film, meaning, he could never be absolutely certain that his completed film would be released by the studio completely intact. Moreover, the Hollywood director always worked under the studio's aegis. He had to satisfy and please producers and the front office, and usually, to some extent, he shaped his work accordingly.

This raises the problem, when you compare American and European directors, of some directors being freer to shape their own work than others. For example, it is a traditional freedom among French and Italian and Swedish directors to be able to write their own scripts; some don't, but it's easier to do there than in Hollywood. In effect, one must be hesitant to ascribe to a director, particularly an American director, the role of an "author" when more often he is a hired craftsman, given the authority and responsibility to guide a production to its conclusion in the stipulated time and without going over budget.

Indeed, there is much that limits a director—in Hollywood as well as in Europe. Like water that cannot rise above its own level, a movie can almost never become any better than its script. "A good director," writes the critic Pauline Kael, "can attempt to camouflage poor writing with craftsmanship and style, but ultimately no amount of a director's skill can conceal a writer's failure; a poor script, even well directed, results in a stupid movie—as, unfortunately, does a good script poorly directed." Deficiencies in script—and the same is true of actors and the technical crew—can flatten or smother an otherwise good movie, despite all the efforts of a fine director.

Yet apart from rare performers like Garbo or Chaplin or Brando, there is no question that the great artists of film have been directors, and the great achievements of film art like *The Battleship Potemkin, Greed, The Grand Illusion* have been the creations of directors. Indeed, with the best of directors it is possible and helpful to look at the whole of their work as though it were a single, large opus, to follow the development of a theme, a style, a heightening sensibility, though such a study becomes of questionable value with minor directors.

The focus in this chapter will be on four directors, all of whose films are represented to some degree throughout this book: briefly on Eisenstein and Welles and John Ford; and more thoroughly on Alfred Hitchcock. Each man has made a substantial contribution to film. For Eisenstein, it's perhaps incalculable—if we've ever had a true genius working on film, it was Eisenstein; Orson Welles was turned away from the studios after *Citizen Kane* but has gone on independently to make flawed and muted masterpieces; and John Ford has created in his films a near-mythical history of America. His films have a simplicity and a classical style that no other director has been able to capture or even imitate. As for Hitchcock, the renowned "master of suspense" is perhaps the shrewdest storyteller ever to use film as his vehicle. A master technician, Hitchcock has created films of enormous visual vitality, films in which the audience's response is governed by the subtlest and most striking uses of camera movement, editing and locale.

Orson Welles framing a shot.

Orson Welles (1915-)

He came upon the movies with an almost mythical fury, creating, at age 25, one of the most vigorous, ingenious and unprecedented movies ever made: *Citizen Kane*. The industry that had beckoned him, given him carte blanche on his very first film, soon came to shut him out, forcing him to make his films on puny budgets between the hectic acting roles that provided those budgets. Yet Orson Welles has given the movies that rare, incandescent touch of genius. "One can question his talent," the French director François Truffaut has remarked of him, "but never his genius."

There is no mistaking an Orson Welles film. The depth of focus that he and cinematographer Gregg Toland created and explored is vivid, structuring every shot. Sharp, sometimes glaring lighting mixes with thick, black shadows. And always the angular, baroque, "here-I-am" presence of the camera. Welles, who from the age of sixteen was a prodigy in theater and radio, brought with him the techniques of theater and radio, as well as his Mercury Theatre cronies, to the making of *Citizen Kane*. The soundtrack, so maligned and ignored and misused before Welles, became a separate, active organizing element in a Welles film: natural sounds are amplified and sometimes distorted; dialogue overlaps; musical scores skip from scene to scene like impetuous children. Welles has taken motion picture technique to new, sometimes startling extremes—and always with his erratic, baroque, even bizarre touch of wit and theatricality.

His films, particularly those after *Kane*, are drastically uneven, a visual magnificence often set against an appalling soundtrack; or the heightened use of his baroque style to hide face so we can't tell that the (later dubbed) voices aren't synchronized to the soundtrack. One dreams (no doubt in vain) of a time when he will be able to make a movie with the solid backing and the studio professionals he had

Welles, in *Catch 22*.

available when making *Kane*. *The Magnificent Ambersons,* which he made for RKO in 1942, was re-edited before its release; and his third project for RKO, *Journey into Fear,* was taken from him and turned over to another director. After the war he made *Lady from Shanghai* (1947), thinly scripted, but majestically brought off, and, his reputation with the studios by now depleted, he moved to Europe.

Except for the dour, grime-textured thriller *Touch of Evil* (1957), Welles has made his later films in Europe, and under varying kinds of control, and with varying degrees of technical finesse. *Macbeth* (1948), for example, an ambitious adaptation of Shakespeare, is heavily marred by a clumsy and often unsynchronized soundtrack. Yet Welles has shown no willingness to stop making movies because of the cost; he is almost fanatical about making movies, driving himself, his crew, his actors, to the necessary extremes. "I don't like films except when I'm shooting," he says. "You have to know how not to be timid with the camera, how to do it violence, drive it to its ultimate limits, for it is a base mechanism. Poetry is what counts."

Critics have claimed that Welles' films are too theatrical, too self-conscious, too evasive, and finally, hollow. Yet film, like any other art, can only take the directions ultimately provided by its most astute artists, and Welles has proven himself—in *Kane* and after *Kane*—as a master of cinema on a par with any other living director. If Welles is excessive (and Welles can be inordinately excessive), it is usually the excess of genius: ideas that flow so quickly that they cannot be stanched. Indeed, it is true of most Welles films that the parts are considerably more impressive than the whole. One suspects he steps onto the shooting set every day with a fresh, burgeoning batch of new ideas, sometimes totally different from the ones he was working at the day before.

Welles himself can be as enigmatic and confusing as his films. "I don't think I will be remembered someday," he has observed, with a modesty that verges on cunning. "I find it as vulgar to work for posterity as for money."

"Stars no longer exist because the director no longer exists in a supporting capacity; he has himself become the star, his style unmistakable and his performers interchangeable, as likely as not green unknowns."—Hildegard Knef

Sergei Eisenstein (1898-1948)

Sergei Eisenstein is the one true titan of the movies. A genius, impassioned and aflame with the possibilities of the new, struggling art, he imparted to film capabilities and powers it had not possessed before him or achieved since him. He shattered conventions, outraged audiences, and took the fledgling technique of editing to a point of sheer syncopated mastery. For Eisenstein the single images in a film were like single notes in a composition. It was the flow, the organization, the consummate architecture of those shots that created the symphonic whole.

Till Eisenstein the important progress in editing had resulted from Griffith's structuring of a scene for dramatic effect. The intercutting of close-up, medium shot and long shot provided a means of dramatizing a sequence by focusing on single high points. Eisenstein paid tribute to Griffith—"He was the father of us all"—but went further. By using more abbreviated shots, by building central motifs and returning to them with rising emphasis, and by structuring his sequences by contrasting modes of graphic emphasis, Eisenstein used editing with fury and an incredible momentum.

As a student, Eisenstein studied architecture and engineering, though once out of school he entered the theater, first as a stage designer and later as a director. His first film, *Strike* (1924), already reflects his fascination with editing and his ability to depict a mass of people as the film's "hero." *The Battleship Potemkin* (1925) made him world-famous at the age of 27. *October* (retitled *Ten Days That Shook The World)* was something of an experiment, an attempt to take some of his theories of editing to their ultimate conclusion. *The General Line* (1929) is a lyrical, sumptuously edited statement of the age of the machines and the co-op coming upon rural Russia. In the early thirties Eisenstein went to Hollywood at the invitation of Paramount, which turned down his proposals for several films. Instead he initiated a project with Upton Sinclair which would undoubtedly have been his masterpiece: a triumphant visualization of Mexican life, entitled *Que Viva Mexico!* Financial disputes with Sinclair disrupted the project. Eisenstein returned to Russia, unable to claim and edit the hundreds of thousands of feet of film he had shot. This tragedy, combined with difficulties in Russia, left him isolated, depressed, and embittered. There were later films, majestic in their own right, yet somehow without the lustre and energy of his early work. Eisenstein accomplished much, but one suspects his best years were wasted. The movies, it seems, are too perilously financial a venture to leave in the hands of geniuses.

The rising, phenomenal power of Eisenstein's editing: a cream separator is introduced to a rural village that has formed a co-op in *The General Line,* and the skeptical villagers watch as it performs for the first time. Eisenstein used a principle of "pyramid editing," returning to basic images and motifs at an accelerated rate, building the architecture of shots as though in pyramid fashion. The closeups on the spout of the machine, intercut with the faces of the villagers, give the sequence a wild momentum.

Eisenstein editing *October,* 1928.

Eisenstein at his ease as he directs production of *The General Line (Old and New)*, 1929.

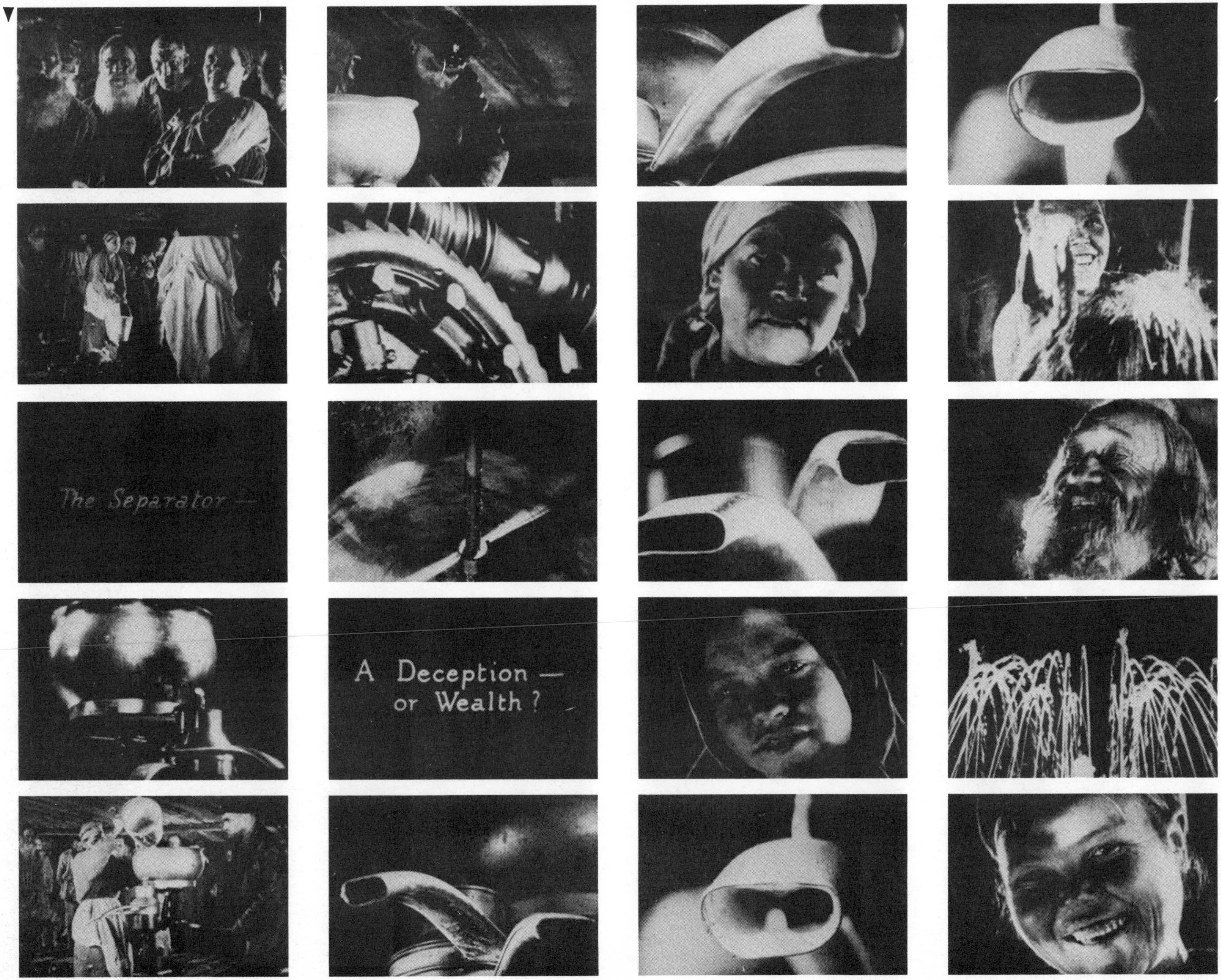

The cream separator sequence from Eisenstein's *General Line*

John Ford (1895-1973)

When asked which filmmakers he admired most, Orson Welles replied, "The old masters, by which I mean, John Ford, John Ford, and John Ford."

There is a fundamental decency and a breadth of human feeling that runs like a current through the work of John Ford. His films evoke the sense of a lost past, of values that we'd still like to believe in, of an America that grew out of courage and a communal struggle to transform the continent. And Ford's visual style—superbly composed cinematography, a feeling of deep, monumental expanse in his exteriors—intensifies and in a way verifies the americana that forms the thematic touchstones of his films. John Ford is the truest and most American of American directors.

Born Sean O'Fearna, the son of Irish immigrants, he began working in the studios in

John Wayne watches John Ford on the set of *The Long Gray Line*.

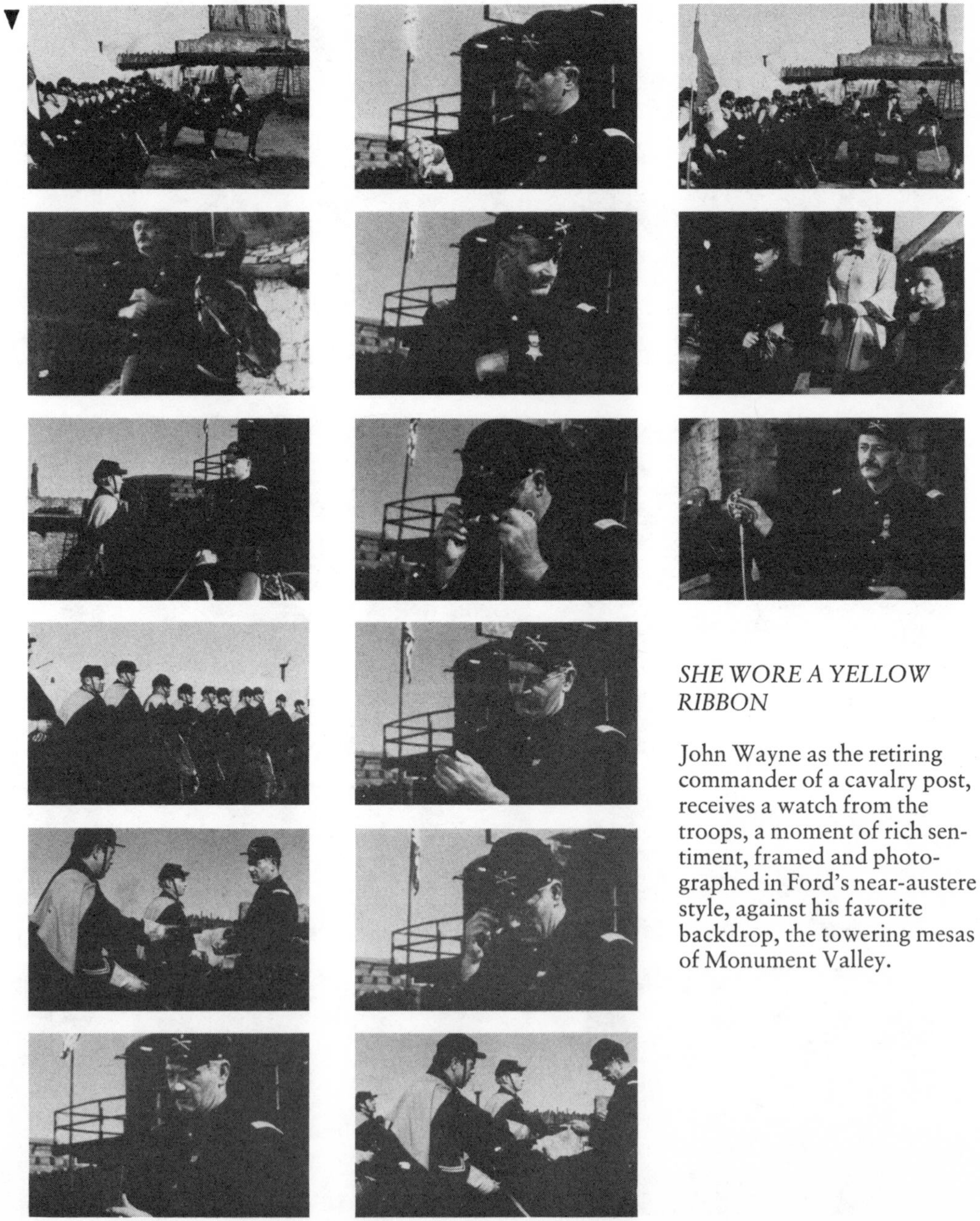

SHE WORE A YELLOW RIBBON

John Wayne as the retiring commander of a cavalry post, receives a watch from the troops, a moment of rich sentiment, framed and photographed in Ford's near-austere style, against his favorite backdrop, the towering mesas of Monument Valley.

1913 as an assistant to his brother Francis. By 1917 he was writing and directing features, mostly Westerns, mostly starring Harry Carey, at the rate of five or six a year. By the late thirties Ford had proven himself *the* master of Westerns (with exquisite films like *The Iron Horse,* 1924, and *Stagecoach,* 1939) and one of the masters of film in Hollywood. Sergei Eisenstein has said of Ford's *Young Mr. Lincoln* (1939) that it's "the film I wish I had made."

The seeming simplicity of Ford's films tends to hide the subtlety and clarity and shrewdness with which they are constructed. Ford is one of the most economic and least insistent of filmmakers, permitting a soft touch to suffice where another director might bombard the screen with emphatic closeups. In a profoundly touching sequence from *The Grapes of Wrath,* Ford conveys the emotional eruption of the Joad family leaving its homestead by focusing on the mother, as she scours through the relics of the past in a last glimpse of the life they're leaving behind. Pale mementos—a newspaper clipping, a postcard, a china souvenir, earrings—but as the mother (Jane Darwell) sorts through them, Ford tacitly evokes a rich sense of the Joads' history, and suggests the haunting loss that the Joads' exodus from the homestead represents.

This is perhaps the final marvel of Ford's films: how, in single scenes, he can summon history, delineate character, and suggest touches of chivalry or nobility or sentiment, never threatening that delicate balance, never overwhelming the audience with a frantic emphasis on any one element.

There is a rich, rare sense of community—of men and women facing and overcoming hardships together—that rings through Ford's films; as he told an interviewer, "I would think that it is for me a means of confronting individuals. The moment of tragedy allows them to define themselves, to take stock of who they are, to shake off their indifferences, inertia, conventions . . . To find the unusual in the commonplace, the heroic in the everyday, is a dramatic device that suits me."

The films of John Ford span over 50 years of film history; yet the subjects and themes span an even greater period, framing and summoning all of American history. Ford's films will last, if only because they are touchstones of a people, a cultural heritage as basic as the novels of Mark Twain, the music of Stephen Foster.

The Grapes of Wrath

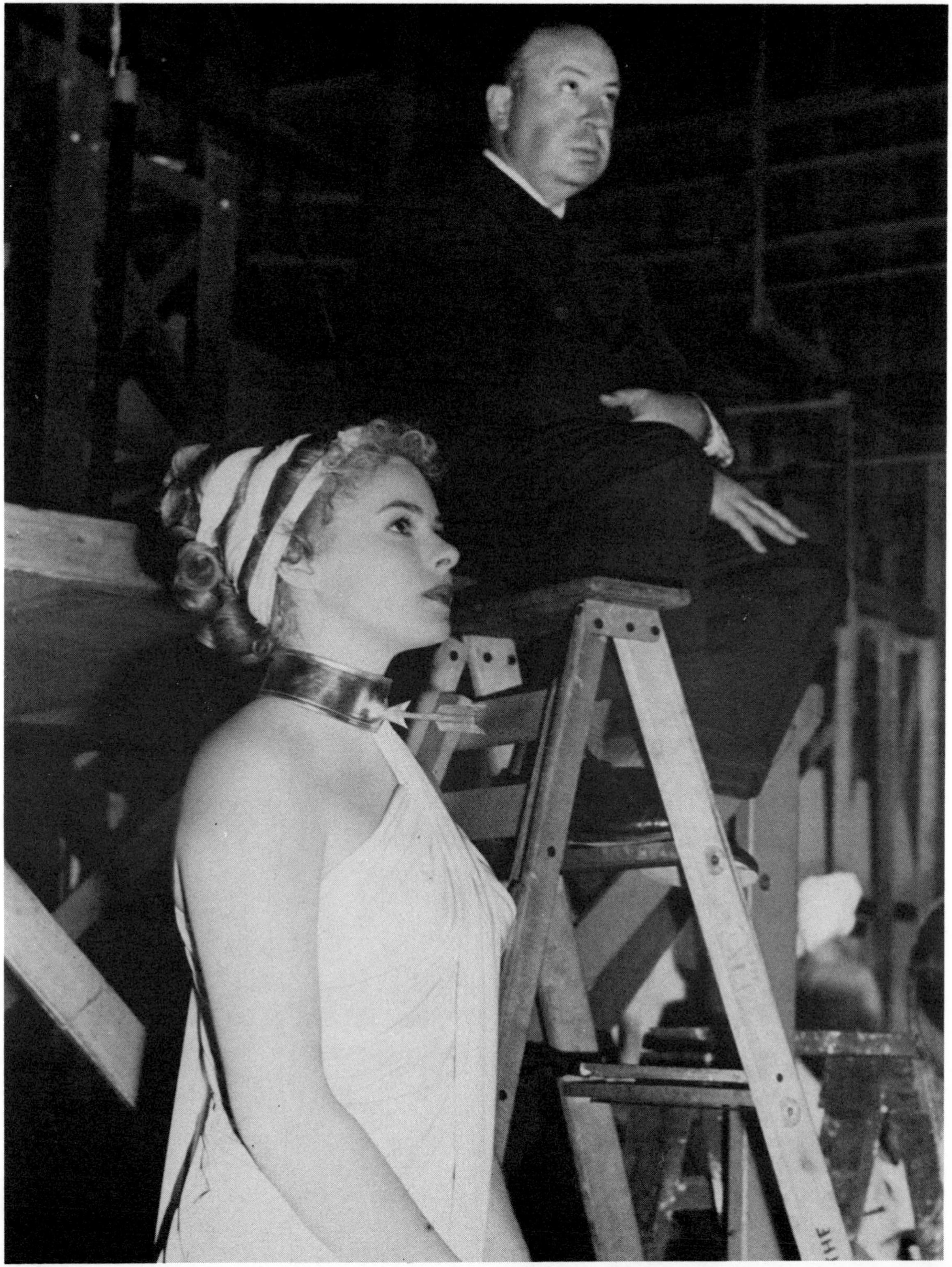

A Deeper Look:

"Hitchcock is one of the greatest inventors of form in the history of cinema. Perhaps the only other filmmakers who can be compared with him in this respect are Murnau and Eisenstein . . . Here, form does not merely embellish content, but actually creates it."—Eric Rohmer and Claude Chabrol, Hitchcock

"If, in the era of Ingmar Bergman, one accepts the premise that cinema is an art form, on a par with literature, I suggest that Hitchcock belongs . . . among such artists of anxiety as Kafka, Dostoevsky, and Poe—François Truffaut, Truffaut/Hitchcock

"If I made Cinderella, *they would be content only if I put a corpse in the coach. The audience screams and cannot bear the agony in some of my films. That gives me great pleasure; I am interested less in stories than in the manner of telling them."—Alfred Hitchcock*

He is known to audiences throughout the world as a master of suspense; and within the industry as the supreme technician of filmmaking, capable of going to any extreme to create an effect that's exactly right. Yet only in recent years, and by way of the French critics like Rohmer and Chabrol and Truffaut (now themselves all major established directors) has Hitchcock received the attention and critical analysis that have long been his due as one of the most imaginative, original and uniquely cinematic of film artists.

His career has spanned almost fifty full years and more than fifty feature films. An Englishman, he began directing there in the twenties and after building a reputation for slick, toughly paced suspense films like *The 39 Steps* and *The Man Who Knew Too Much,*

Hitchcock on the set of *Spellbound,* with Ingrid Bergman.

Alfred Hitchcock (1899-)

came to Hollywood, where with a few exceptions, he has worked since. His films—almost all within the suspense genre—show an amazing diversity and range, from the moodily elegant and time-haunted *Vertigo,* to the cryptic humor of *The Trouble with Harry,* to the tongue-in-cheek escapades of *North by Northwest,* to the apocalyptic sense of doom that underscores *The Birds.* Yet throughout his films a viewer never has any doubt that he is watching a *Hitchcock* movie, and the strains that might run through his films are numerous and present on a variety of levels: the splendid technical exactness of his shots and his editing; the sure, clean sense of composition; the deftly structured plots, that begin so normally and move inexorably toward and into the abnormal; the frequent themes of displaced guilt and of teeming anxiety below the tenuous fabric of "civilization." And always, beneath it all, like a resounding echo, is the humor, the feeling that for Hitchcock—no matter how terrifying the film—it's only a joke played on the audience after all.

At the heart of Hitchcock's best films is a rigorous morality, which indicts both the characters in the film and us, the audience who have identified with the characters. Few Hitchcock heroes (and never his best heroes) are lily-white: James Stewart in *Rear Window* is a genuine snooper, a true voyeur; Cary Grant in *Notorious* treats Ingrid Bergman so shabbily that we're surprised she remains a spy for him; Tippi Hedron in *The Birds* is shallow, a bored rich girl; even Farley Granger as Guy in *Strangers on a Train* seems a mite cocky and aloof. But the one overriding characteristic of the Hitchcock hero (and by extension, of the audience) is a bland complacency, a feeling that the world is as secure and as pleasant as we'd all like to think it is. It's this complacency that Hitchcock goes after, with a vengeance.

Consider the structure of *North by Northwest* (analyzed brilliantly by Robin Wood in his study *Hitchcock's Films*) as an indication of the way Hitchcock attacks and undermines such complacency. Cary Grant plays Roger Thornhill, a wisecracking, reasonably well off Manhattan adman who supports, as he puts it, several ex-wives and at least one bartender. At a luncheon he is abducted by two gunmen who take him to a mansion on Long Island. There he is addressed as George Kaplan, soused down with bourbon, and put into a car at cliff's edge, a murder attempt he barely escapes. When he takes the cops back to the mansion, it turns out the owner is to address the General Assembly of the United Nations that afternoon. Thornhill goes to the U.N. building, meets the owner just as the man is stabbed in the back, with Thornhill reaching for the knife in surprise. Now wanted as a murderer, he flees on a train to Chicago, where he meets Eve Kendall (Eva Marie Saint), who agrees to help him find Kaplan. A meeting place is arranged—a naked stretch of highway in flat cornfields north of Chicago—and in one of Hitchcock's most brilliant sequences he is attacked by a crop-duster plane. He returns and is shaken to learn that Eve Kendall is the mistress of Van Damm, the master spy. Almost trapped in an auction where Van Damm and Eve meet, he narrowly escapes, and finally learns that George Kaplan does not exist, was in fact "created" by the American operatives to avert suspicion from their own agent, Eve Kendall.

Thornhill, now in love with the girl, is able to save her in a last-minute, bravado sequence atop the faces of Mount Rushmore; the enemy spies are stopped; and Thornhill returns to New York aboard the same train with the new Mrs. Thornhill.

North by Northwest seems shaggy, wildly loose in its construction: events spill into other events with such rapidity and such shifting locales that we're left breathless. Yet a closer look suggests how carefully Hitchcock has structured the film, and how each stage of the film takes Thornhill—and us—deeper into chaos, further from the clear, complacent world in which we began.

Wood points out that there are three stages in the film: in New York; on the train, Chicago, and the cornfield; and later, at Mount Rushmore. At each stage we see a deepening of Thornhill's character: from his mock-toned, cocky manner at the beginning, to a growing resolve, and finally to a clear commitment when he risks his life to save Eve from Van Damm. At the center of this progression is the superb crop-duster sequence in the cornfields. Writes Wood: "Thornhill has always been *inside:* inside cities, buildings, vehicles: and we know him as a man at home in the complacency-encouraging security of office and cocktail-bar. Now, suddenly, he is in open country . . . a flat landscape, treeless, houseless, shelterless, parched . . . In the midst of this he stands, an isolated speck with the whole world against him, absolutely exposed and vulnerable: modern man deprived of all his amenities and artificial resources . . . It is a marvelous conception, central to the film in more ways than position."

In *North by Northwest,* as in other Hitchcock films, the supports that separate our organized, civilized world from teeming chaos below are flimsy and insecure. A single false step, and one can be plunged into the chaos, only to be saved by one's own actions and wits.

Hitchcock's favorite theme—of displaced or transferred guilt—further heightens the effect of shattering our complacency and reminding us of how fragile the seemingly normal order really is. Guilt, depicted in a myriad of ways, is almost a preoccupation with Hitchcock: the "traded" guilt between Bruno and Guy in *Strangers on a Train;* the implicit guilt of the voyeur, Jefferies, in *Rear Window;* the assumption of guilt in *I Confess;* mistaken guilt in *The Wrong Man* and chase films like *The 39 Steps, Saboteur* and *North by Northwest;* Scottie's self-lacerating sense of guilt in *Vertigo;* and the subtler uses of guilt—almost as red herrings—in *Psycho* and *The Birds.* The notion of guilt is central to Hitchcock's films, and particularly for the responses he draws from his audiences.

For the audience is invariably invited to share in the hero's guilt: to think, at a critical scene, "Go ahead, do it!" and by that very process to become quiet accomplices, implicated in the same furtive or illegal or questionable act of the hero. Hitchcock has pointed out that if a villain is rummaging through someone's apartment, and we hear footsteps below, we'll tend to side with the villain: hurry up, find it, get out. It's in the nature of such a set-up for our sympathies to side with the burglar. This principle guides much of Hitchcock's filmmaking, so that in effect we become guilty parties, and the nerve-racking suspense we undergo has to some extent been deserved, merited by our own feelings.

Hitchcock has been criticized for engineering such responses, in effect, for controlling his audience's reaction to such an extent that we're never free to choose our own response. The criticism is a valid comment on Hitchcock's filmmaking; he does guide and control every quiver of apprehension, every anxious laugh; yet it's of questionable value as criticism. Hitchcock intends exactly such iron control, he prides himself on it. And that control provides much of what is most original, technically superb, and revealing in Hitchcock's art.

In *Strangers on a Train,* there is a tennis game between the hero Guy and an opponent. In the stands is Bruno, who has killed Guy's wife and expects in return that Guy kill his father. Bruno sits among many other spectators, who watch the game with that necessary movement that causes what the British call "Wimbledon neck," a bobbing back and forth. Only Bruno doesn't move; he is staring straight at Guy, unrelenting. So the image depicts dozens of spectators, their heads turning left, right, left, right, and Bruno, immobile, among them. A marvelous image. We laugh, but apprehensively. Our response has been engineered with cunning exactness; yet the film medium is used with brilliant flair and style.

Hitchcock is as exacting in his methods of production. In his conversations with Hitchcock, Truffaut remarks that Hitchcock is known as "undoubtedly the director who gets the least surprises when he looks at the rushes." Hitchcock prepares everything ahead of time. Camera movements are sketched out, worked into an intricate choreography; the nuance of an actor's expression, the relationships between objects on a set, the finest detail of a cut: with Hitchcock nothing is left to chance. Though he admits (almost guiltily), to improvising a few times, Hitchcock prefers to do all the work before he enters the studio. What happens there is simply the virtual acting out of already schematized plans.

This rigorous care—and his use of the broadest range of cinematic techniques—has proven Hitchcock a master technician. But he's clearly more than that. As critic Andrew Sarris comments, "His is the only contemporary style that unites the divergent classical traditions of Murnau (camera movement) and Eisenstein (montage)." Hitchcock has shown an equal—and in both cases superlative—flair for camera movement and editing, and has experimented significantly, widely with both.

In *Rope,* made in 1948, Hitchcock attempted an audacious and perhaps foolhardy experiment, a film made in real time, with almost no cutting—the entire progression, movement and balance of the film would depend on camera movement. Says Hitchcock: "The mobility of the camera and the movement of the players closely followed my usual cutting practices. In other words, I maintained the rule of varying the size of the image in relation to its emotional importance within a given episode." *Rope* is not a strong Hitchcock film, but the unbroken camera movement and, indeed, the nature of the experiment, suggest how strongly Hitchcock feels about the possibilities of keeping a continuous dramatic flux through the mobile camera.

Hitchcock is as well a master of montage. No living American director has used editing with such rhythmic strength or such a deft touch at creating a rising crescendo of graphically opposed forces. The crop duster sequence in *North by Northwest* and the shower stabbing in *Psycho* have a measured control rare in any montage since Eisenstein. The intercutting in the remake of *The Man Who Knew Too Much*—where Doris Day in a symphony hall tries to spot and avert an assassination that we know will take place when the cymbalist strikes his two cymbals—moves with a rousing, rising power that matches exactly the music and doubly intensifies the climax. In *Rear Window,* the editing is more subtle, but just as effective. James Stewart peers through his telephoto lens into the windows across his courtyard, and Hitchcock keeps cutting back to Stewart's face. The expression hasn't changed, but our assessment of the expression changes with each vignette we see in the windows.

His talent for editing—indeed, his broad facility for every kind of cinematic technique—gives Hitchcock a kind of freedom in developing his pictures that few directors—most very hidebound to conventional techniques—have shown. He mentions to Truffaut, for example, his idea of filming a story entirely in a telephone booth, a cramping of space that would be anathema to just about any other director.

"Let's imagine there's a couple in that booth. Their hands are touching, their lips meet, and accidentally one of them leans against the receiver, knocking it off the hook. Now, while they're unaware of it, the phone operator can listen in on their intimate conversation. The drama has taken a step forward. For the audience, looking at the images, it should be the same as reading the opening paragraphs of a novel . . . You might say that a filmmaker can use a telephone booth pretty much in the same way a novelist uses a blank sheet of paper."

In Hitchcock's films there is an abundance of visual hints, suggestions, intimations, often as objects or settings. Remarks Sarris on Hitchcock's use of objects (such as the cigarette lighter in *Strangers on a Train* and the ominous glass of milk in *Suspicion*): "Hitchcock's objects are never mere props of a basically theatrical mise en scene, but rather the very substance of his cinema. These objects embody the feelings and fears of characters as objects and characters interact with each other in dramas within dramas." Objects and places take on emotional force in Hitchcock's films; as Hitchcock remarks about the lovebirds in *The Birds:* "With a little effort, even the word 'love' can be made to sound ominous."

With Sylvia Sidney on the set of *Sabotage,* 1936.

As taut and spellbinding as Hitchcock's films can be, few of them fail to disclose at some point the ripe, and perhaps distinctly British sense of humor of the man who made them. Alfred Hitchcock *enjoys* scaring people. He said of *Psycho,* that it was "made with quite a sense of amusement on my part." Sometimes that humor is hidden, barely suggested, as in *Psycho* (though one line from Norman Bates does hint at it: "My mother, she's not . . . how do you say it? . . . quite herself today."). But often the humor is distinctly obvious, as in *North by Northwest,* which may well be Hitchcock's funniest movie, alongside *Frenzy.* Says Hitchcock of a scene he had wanted to do in *North by Northwest:* "When Cary Grant was on Mount Rushmore, I would have liked to put him inside Lincoln's nostril and let him have a sneezing fit."

The humor that accompanies and underscores Hitchcock's films—from the murder mystery fan in *Shadow of a Doubt* to the what-do-we-do-with-the-body games played in *The Trouble with Harry* to the inspector and his wife's experimental cooking in *Frenzy*—indicates that Hitchcock is perhaps above all a practical joker, using the screen as a way of teasing and pulling pranks on an unwary audience. Not that there isn't a deeper, more serious intent (Hitchcock privately considers himself a serious artist—as he certainly is)—yet his art is finally what he can do with film; and the stories, the suspense the route he has chosen to take.

Hitchcock Filmography

1922: *Number Thirteen, Woman to Woman*
1923: *The White Shadow*
1924: *The Passionate Adventure*
1925: *Pleasure Garden*
1926: *The Mountain Eagle, The Lodger*
1927: *Downhill, Easy Virtue, The Ring*
1928: *The Farmer's Wife, Champagne*
1929: *Harmony Heaven, The Manxman*
Blackmail
1930: *Elstree Calling*
Juno and the Paycock, Murder
1931: *The Skin Game*
1932: *Rich and Strange, Number Seventeen*
1933: *Waltzes from Vienna*
1934: *The Man Who Knew Too Much*
1935: *The Thirty-Nine Steps*
1936: *The Secret Agent, Sabotage*
1937: *Young and Innocent*
1938: *The Lady Vanishes*
1939: *Jamaica Inn*
1940: *Rebecca, Foreign Correspondent*
1941: *Mr. & Mrs. Smith, Suspicion*
1942: *Saboteur*
1943: *Shadow of a Doubt, Lifeboat*
1944: *Bon Voyage, Adventure Malgache*
1945: *Spellbound*
1946: *Notorious*
1947: *The Paradine Case*
1948: *Rope*
1949: *Under Capricorn*
1950: *Stage Fright*
1951: *Strangers on a Train*
1952: *I Confess*
1954: *Dial M for Murder, Rear Window*
1955: *To Catch a Thief*
1956: *The Trouble with Harry,*
The Man Who Knew Too Much (remake)
1957: *The Wrong Man*
1958: *Vertigo*
1959: *North by Northwest*
1960: *Psycho*
1963: *The Birds*
1964: *Marnie*
1966: *Torn Curtain*
1969: *Topaz*
1972: *Frenzy*

A Visual Touch

One of the criticisms brought against Hitchcock is the patent "unreality" of his movies—not the implausibility of the stories, but his sets, his staging, his use of visual detail to offset a scene. Few movies look as much unlike documentaries as Hitchcock's.

A failure, perhaps, in terms of the most stalwart realism. But Hitchcock isn't after realism; indeed, his best films suggest the moods and spiralling terrors of a dream. In *Vertigo* James Stewart falls helplessly in love with a woman who seems possessed by someone out of the distant past. The film is set almost entirely in places that summon this sense of the past—in a cemetery, among the vast, ancient Sequoias, in a museum, at a deserted mission. The places to which Stewart follows the woman (Kim Novak) become themselves the most potent expression of what's happening to him—a dizzying infatuation with the past, a doomed love for someone long dead.

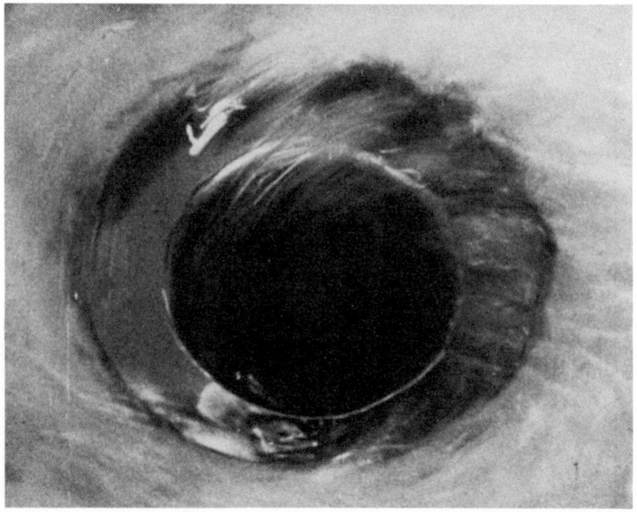

In *Strangers on a Train,* Hitchcock sets up a classic suspense situation and presses it to a gripping extremity. Guy, a pleasant tennis player, meets Bruno—a wary, dark-minded psychopath—on a train; Guy admits that he's caught in a paralyzing marriage, and Bruno detests his father and wants him killed. It's Bruno's idea to "trade" murders, though Guy finds the notion revolting. This doesn't stop Bruno, who goes on to murder Guy's wife at an amusement park. Guy, horrified by the murder, is shadowed for days by Bruno, who hounds him to kill his father. When Guy won't, Bruno returns to the amusement park to plant Guy's lighter there as evidence against him. In one of the most brilliantly cross-edited sequences in Hitchcock's films, he cuts between Guy's furious tennis game—played out in the open, amidst a cheering crowd—and Bruno, bent over a sidewalk grate, scraping his fingers against the bottom in a frantic effort to retrieve the dropped lighter. The use of light and dark, of Guy's body dashing across the court to return a ball against Bruno, cramped down over the grate, creates a remarkable tension. We tend, nevertheless, to root for Bruno as much as for Guy (in some ways, more so—the tennis match isn't nearly as compelling).

Hitchcock's films are rich in this kind of visual tension. In *To Catch a Thief* one scene depicts Jesse Royce Landis at breakfast. As an indication of her character (and because Hitchcock has a long professed hatred of eggs) she stubs out her cigarette in an egg yolk.

FRAMING THE SHOWER MURDER IN *PSYCHO:* VISUAL IRONY

The opening shot in the famed shower sequence in *Psycho* is the nozzle of a shower, spraying water in a rounded, umbrella-like form. Hitchcock concludes the sequence on a tight closeup of the drain, where blood mixed with water swirls down: a dissolve transforms the drain into an eye, and the camera backs away to reveal the dead stare of Marion Crane. Note the continuity—both graphic and from water's source to end—with which the sequence is framed.

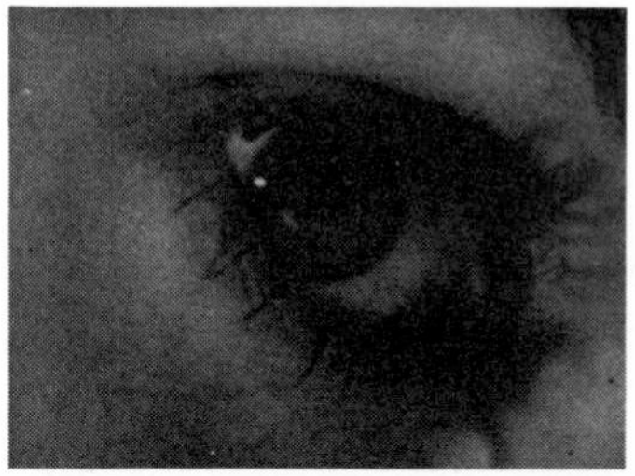

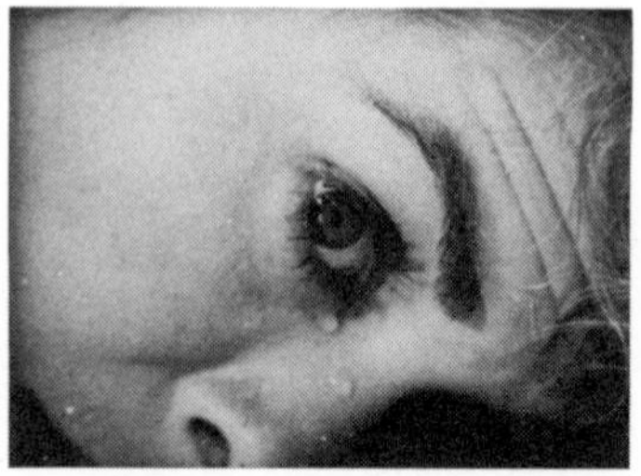

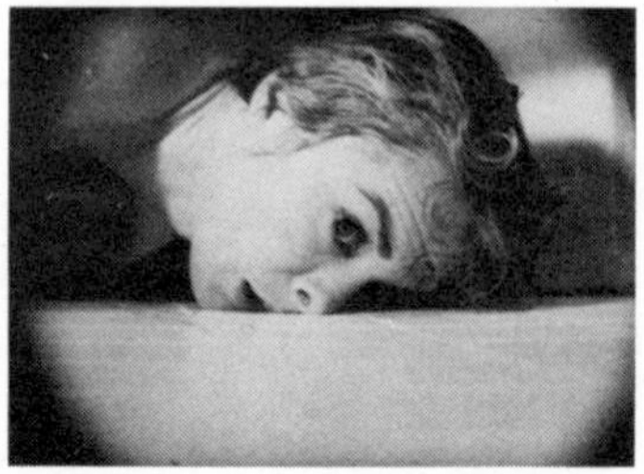

Visual Irony

An image tends to be more than simply an image in a Hitchcock film: the airplane in *North by Northwest,* the lovebirds in *The Birds*. Hitchcock plays with images, sets them in odd contexts, gives them ominous new meanings.

"The placing of the images on the screen, in terms of what you're expressing should never be dealt with in a factual manner. Never! You can get anything you want through the proper use of cinematic techniques, which enable you to work out any image you need."—Alfred Hitchcock.

In *The Birds,* Melanie admires two birds in a birdcage at the beginning. Later, when the town is besieged by birds, she takes refuge in a telephone booth, which becomes her cage. Hitchcock calls it "a reversal of the age-old conflict between men and birds." A sly joke, nonetheless.

In *Foreign Correspondent* the critical clue to a spy hideaway is among the windmills in Holland. The blades of one windmill spin *against* the wind.

An assassination (actually, a pseudo-assassination) in *Foreign Correspondent* takes place on a rainy day in Holland. The assassin escapes through a crowd of people holding black umbrellas. The effect is like seeing ripples in a stream covered with flowers.

The act of sabotage in *Saboteur* suggested vividly and simply by a growing swarm of black smoke against the door of an airplane plant.

Cary Grant plays a martini-loving advertising man in *North by Northwest*. When the spies plan to do him in, they load him down with liquor first, a hint that with Hitchcock, punishment should fit.

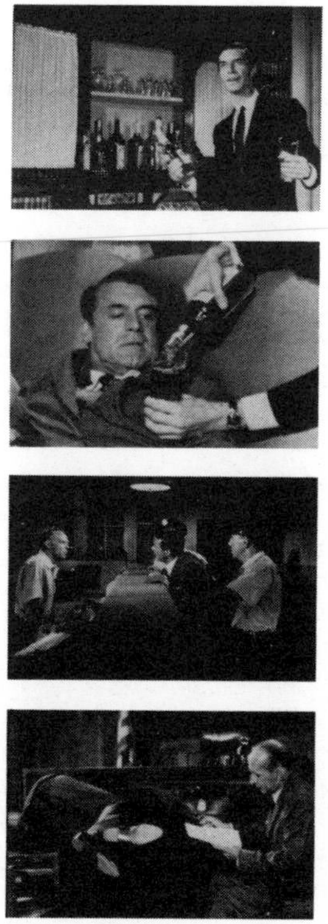

Hitchcockian Suspense

When the detective Arbogast (played by Martin Balsam) in *Psycho* goes into the old house behind the motel to visit Norman's mother, we are already apprehensive. He isn't. Already we've seen Marion Crane killed (we think) by that same mother. The set-up couldn't be more gripping: a superb example of Hitchcockian tension. *We* know that something's going to happen; Arbogast doesn't. The way in which Hitchcock shot the sequence shows that it was worthy of his build-up. Arbogast enters, and Hitchcock intercuts between him, the rising stairs as *he* sees them, and—as he rises —the view down the stairs as someone from the landing might see. This shifting point of view, emphasizing especially the detective as seen from the landing, prompts a rising sense of anticipation. Then, suddenly, Hitchcock cuts to a high overhead shot. A volatile, whirring electronic score comes on the soundtrack, and the door we'd seen open just a crack is wide open now; a figure comes out with a knife and the camera cuts back to Arbogast, in closeup now, as he tumbles backwards down the stairs, a terrifying, unbalanced fall that amplifies the effect of his murder.

Suspense is anticipation touched with dread. We know that something can happen, a bomb in the closet might explode; a prowler

Arbogast's fatal journey up the steps in *Psycho*.

"I aim to provide the public with beneficial shocks. Civilization has become so protective that we're no longer able to get our goose bumps instinctively. The only way to remove the numbness and revive our moral equilibrium is to use artificial means to bring about the shock. The best way to achieve that, it seems to me, is through a movie."—Alfred Hitchcock

downstairs may be climbing the steps with a loaded shotgun, and that knowledge heightens our anxiety, involves us emotionally, scratches our nerve endings. Hitchcock likes to distinguish between suspense and mystery, the latter being essentially a puzzle to be solved, the former a gripping emotional condition.

Hitchcock's trademark is suspense. He dominates the genre as almost no other directors have dominated any other genre, and yet Hitchcock's *mode* of suspense is unique, his own, inimitable. For most directors a suspense film might be considered successful if it holds an audience fixed to their chairs. Yet Hitchcock in his best films goes after something more, a manner of identification with a character that forces the viewer to make moral judgments, if only in his imagination, yet judgments which condemn him as much as the character on the film. In *Psycho* we cheer Marion Crane on with her stolen money. The shower killing is doubly shocking because of the painstaking identification Hitchcock had set up between her and us. We shared her guilt, and to that extent we undergo her murder. In *Strangers on a Train,* Bruno has murdered Guy's wife, and he expects Guy to repay him in kind by murdering his father. One night Guy goes to Bruno's house, armed with a gun. He meets a hostile dog that he manages to quiet, and he begins rising the stairs. We think he's on his way to kill the father, and the way Hitchcock has set things up we just about *want* him to kill the father, a superb example of Hitchcockian suspense at work, for the dilemma isn't simply one of mounting tension, it's aggravated by our complicity.

Hitchcock's ability to make *us* guilty along with the character in the film (or, as in *Stranger on a Train, more* guilty—when the father isn't there we learn Guy had no intention of killing him) suggests that for him suspense isn't simply a means of holding an audience in terror; it is a means of getting to that audience in deeper, even more disturbing and unnerving ways. Hitchcock may finally be more of a moralist than a "master of suspense."

The first attack on Melanie (Tippi Hedren) by a gull, in *The Birds*.

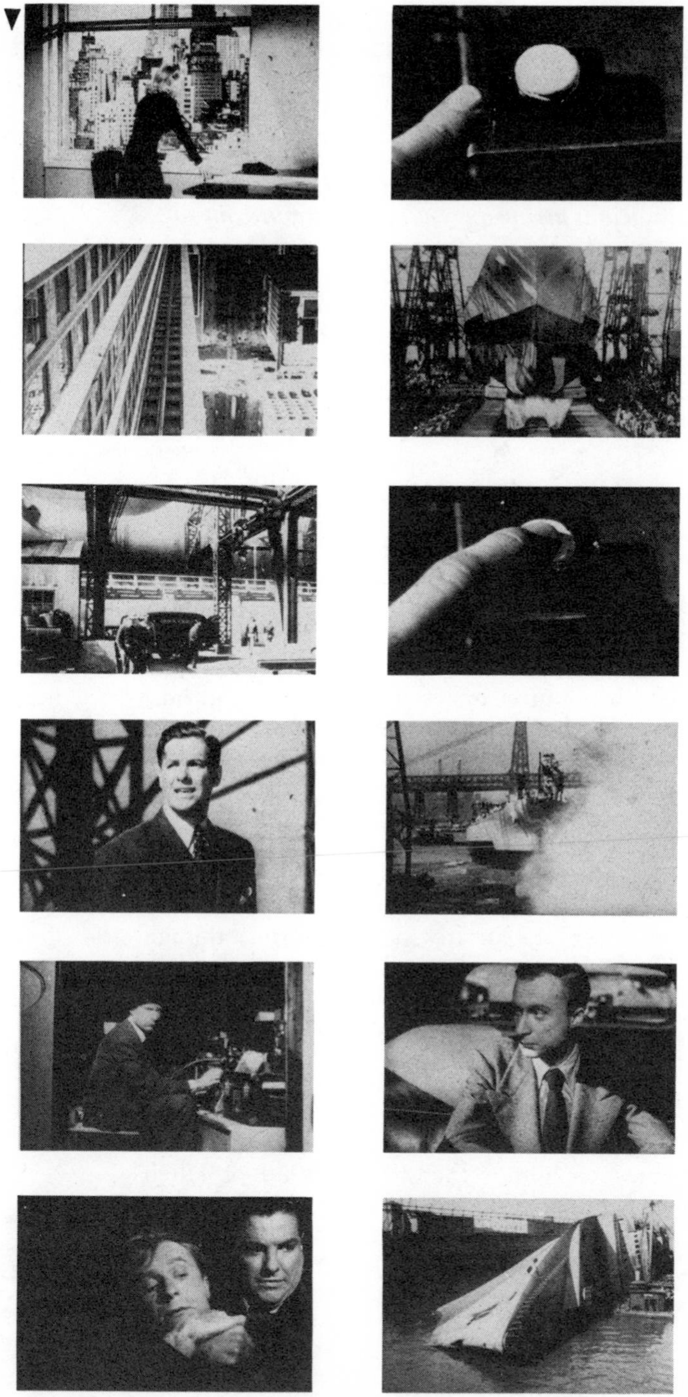

The intercutting of the sequence in *Saboteur* where Robert Cummings tries to stop the sabotage of a naval ship about to be launched, as Priscilla Lane makes her escape from an office building.

The MacGuffin

". . . It's the device, the gimmick, if you will, or the papers the spies are after. . . . The logicians are wrong in trying to figure out the truth of a MacGuffin, since it's beside the point. The only thing that really matters is that in the picture the plans, documents or secrets must be of vital importance to the characters. To me, the narrator, they're of no importance whatsoever."—Alfred Hitchcock

Hitchcock is rather modest when he discusses the MacGuffin, his own term referring to what motivates the characters in their chases and flights. The MacGuffin figures significantly in the way we, the audience, are prompted to react.

In *Psycho,* Marion Crane's theft of $40,000 becomes our strongest tie with her, and once she's fled Phoenix with that money, we're aware of the danger she's in. So when she falls asleep in her car off the side of the road, and is awakened next morning by a dour-looking highway cop, the scene takes on a mounting, disturbing tension, especially when the cop follows her to a used car lot where she buys another car. Strictly a MacGuffin, though. Hitchcock is quietly building to the shocking murder in the shower, and the money means nothing after that point. In effect, the MacGuffin becomes here a tactic by which Hitchcock keeps us in suspense—albeit a fake suspense, meaning nothing—till he pulls the real stunner.

The MacGuffin suggests as well the mischievous humor that underlies all of Hitchcock's films. (He said of *Psycho,* shortly after making it, that it is "a film made with quite a sense of amusement on my part. To me it's a *fun* picture. The processes through which we take the audience, you see, it's rather like taking them through the haunted house at the fairgrounds.")

Mort Mills, Janet Leigh in *Psycho.*

North by Northwest begins with Cary Grant plunged into a world of spies chasing spies, and the more he tries to escape, or vindicate himself, the more immersed he becomes, as in his trip to the United Nations to speak to the man whose home he had been dragged to when kidnapped. The man is murdered as Grant speaks to him, and Grant is assumed to be the murderer. The movie focuses so deftly on Grant that the reasons behind all the antics become nearly irrelevant. Yet there is a MacGuffin, indeed the one Hitchcock considers his "best"—"and by that I mean the emptiest, the most nonexistent, and the most absurd." The man Cary Grant is continuously mistaken for does not, finally, exist. "Here, you see," says Hitchcock, "the MacGuffin has been boiled down to its purest expression: nothing at all!"

Cary Grant in *North by Northwest.*

Playing the Audience

"Psycho *has a very interesting construction and that game with the audience was fascinating. I was directing the viewers. You might say I was playing them, like an organ.*"—*Alfred Hitchcock*

WHAT WE KNOW THAT THEY DON'T KNOW

One of Hitchcock's favorite techniques with an audience (and he isn't the only one to do it, he simply seems to do it *better* than anyone else) is to let us in on something that one of the characters doesn't know. It's the equivalent of watching a man in a movie receive and begin to unwrap a package. We know there's a bomb in the package, he doesn't, and of course there's no way we can tell him.

In *Spellbound,* Gregory Peck plays a disturbed man haunted by memories and dreams. We know there is a killer loose, and we are led to suspect that it's Peck. When he comes downstairs to speak to the old doctor whose house he's staying in, he carries a straight razor. Hitchcock's camera focuses on the razor, suggesting of course that he's about to kill the doctor. (He doesn't, because he's Gregory Peck and therefore can't be the murderer.)

A more impressive and effective use of the same technique takes place in *The Birds* when Melanie sits outside the school, waiting for class to let out. Behind her is a jungle gym, at first with only a couple of birds, but, as Hitchcock intercuts, the birds begin to cluster in greater and greater numbers, until there are hundreds, an ominous foreboding. Through this, we're shown the birds against Melanie's lassitude as she waits, making the simple presence of the growing flock considerably more disturbing.

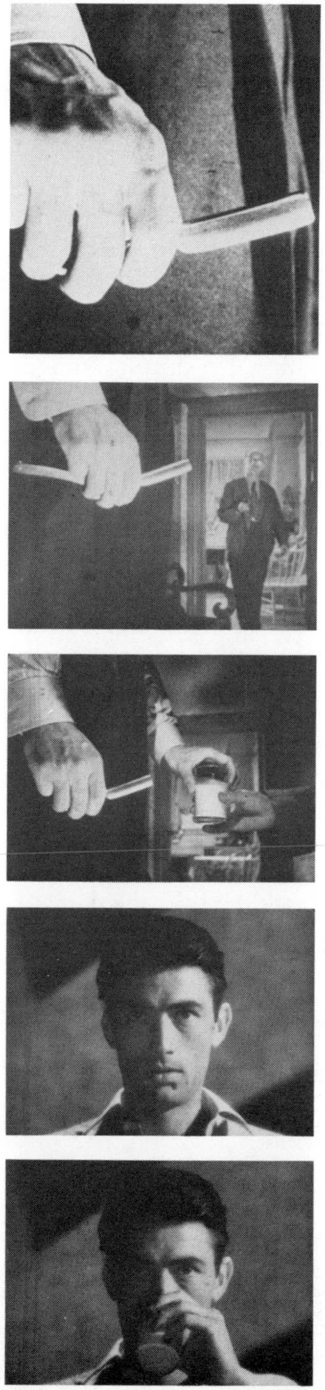

Spellbound

The Birds

Point of View

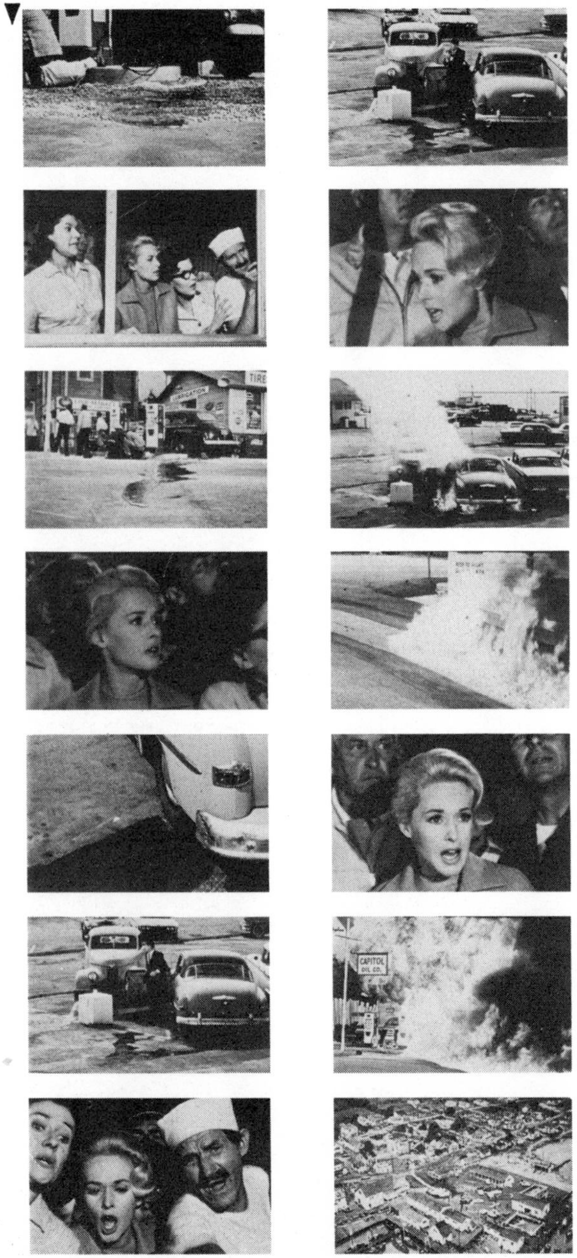

In *The Birds,* the first attack of the birds on the village has abated, but one result was a filling station attendant hurt, maybe killed, by an attacking bird. He had dropped the gas hose, and some oblivious character waiting for gas lights a cigarette. The situation is a ripe one, and Hitchcock extracts a lot from it, mainly by shifting and flexing the point of view. His central focus remains Melanie, trapped now in the diner with others, and Hitchcock uses their reactions to amplify the mounting sense of danger from the spilled gasoline and man lighting his cigarette. We see most of the events at the filling station from a distance—assumedly the distance to the diner—and in a heightening tempo of intercutting between gas station and diner window. When the fire has started and spreads to the gas tanks, suddenly Hitchcock cuts to a different vantage point altogether: a high aerial shot looking down on the town, with gulls flitting over the scene. The fire, a moment before so dreaded and terrible, is now barely visible. And the presence of the birds gives it an added, eerie significance, as though the gulls were quietly chuckling over the damage they had wrought, preparing for the next attack and yet more damage.

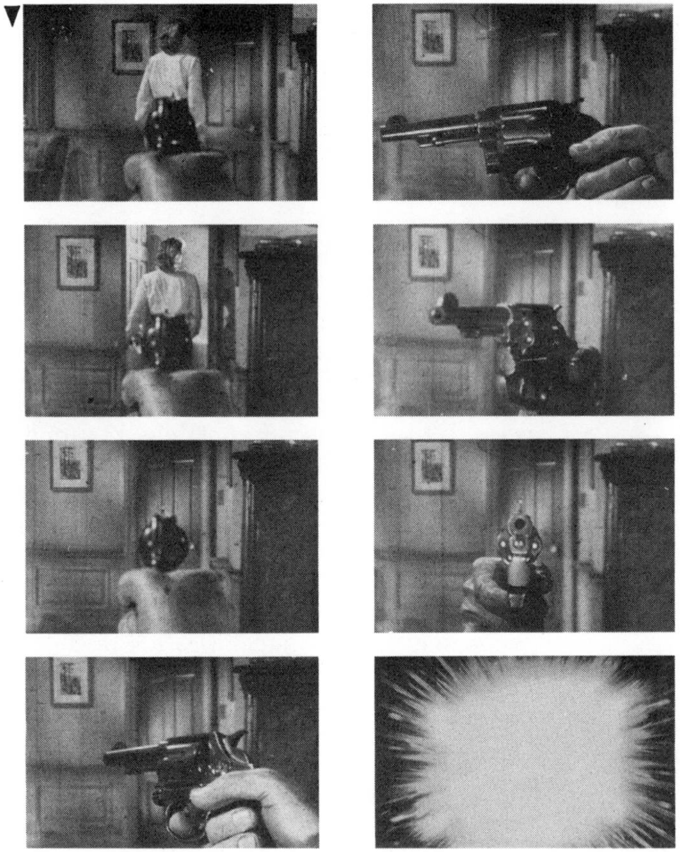

Spellbound

Sometimes Hitchcock can use point of view almost as a trick on the audience, as in the conclusion of *Spellbound,* when Ingrid Bergman confronts the director of the hospital with her knowledge that he is a murderer. Using his point of view, Hitchcock depicts Ingrid Bergman leaving, with a gun pointed directly at her. She escapes through the door safely, the gun turns in a slow arc and explodes—as if to chastise us for enjoying that feeling of having someone at gunpoint.

The Audience as Voyeur

"[A critic] made some comment to the effect that *Rear Window* was a horrible film because the hero spent all of his time peeping out of the window. What's so horrible about that? Sure, he's a snooper, but aren't we all?"—Alfred Hitchcock

Rear Window, among Hitchcock's own favorite films and among his best, stars James Stewart as a photographer immobilized for several weeks with a broken leg. Bored, he amuses himself by watching through the windows of the apartments across the courtyard. Each apartment contains its own vignette: newlyweds who now and then come up for air; a couple that lavishes inordinate affection on their dog; a fumbling, frustrated songwriter; and a man whose wife is gone, and whom Stewart increasingly suspects of being a murderer. The film is amazingly confined. Only once does Hitchcock take us out of Stewart's apartment without Stewart; yet the suspense builds powerfully, and the film succeeds brilliantly. Part of the reason is the technique of showing an apartment window and cutting back to Stewart's face, a technique that provided Hitchcock with what he calls "a purely cinematic film." Stewart's expression remains the same, but in light of what we've just seen (along with him), we read different reactions into it— a principle discovered by the Russian film teacher Kuleshov in the twenties. But *Rear Window* succeeds for yet another reason. It involves us as voyeurs. We're peeping in those windows right along with Stewart, enjoying it as much, and we're as unconcerned about consequences and (until the consequences begin) as oblivious of our guilt in peeking. Hitchcock, who plays on just such weaknesses in his audience, would have it that we're all voyeurs at heart. Perhaps the act of watching a movie itself is a kind of subtle voyeurism, and satisfies that same impulse.

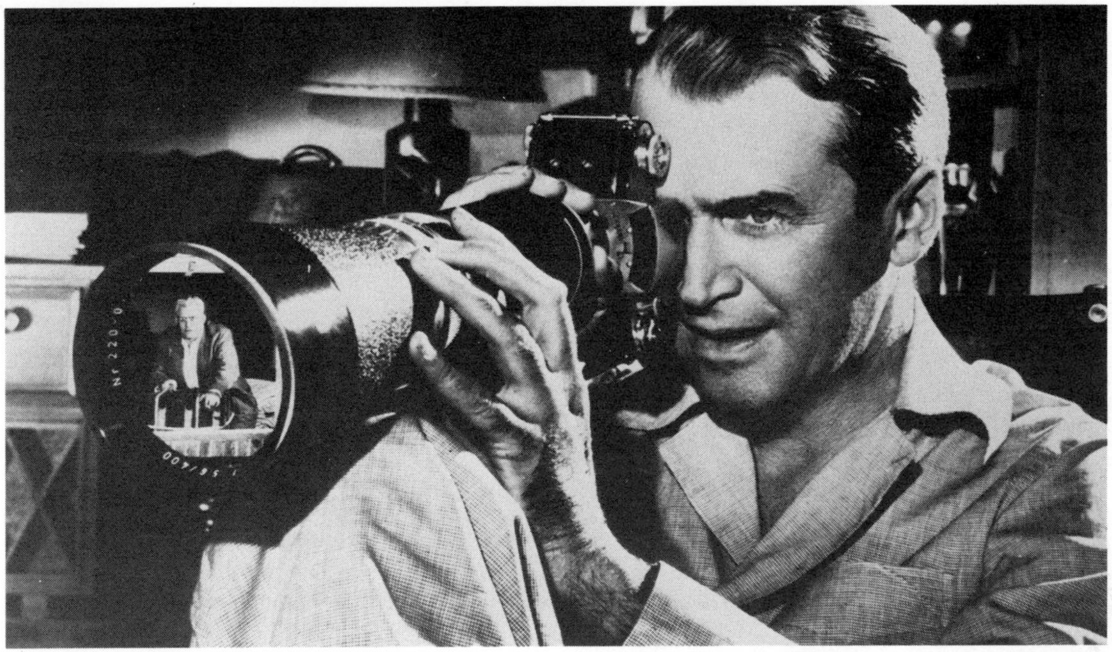

Rear Window

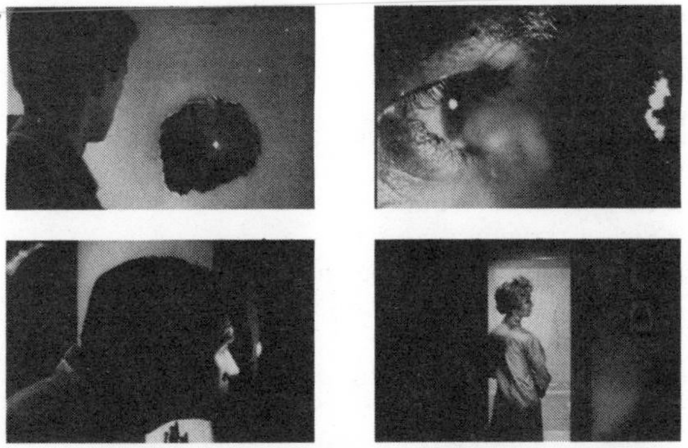

PSYCHO: WATCHING WITH NORMAN BATES

When Norman Bates spies on Marion Crane at the motel in *Psycho,* Hitchcock perversely lets us peek in with him. Later, when Norman cleans up the bathroom after the brutal killing, we're forced to watch the slow labor—a kind of subtle penalty?

A Sense of Time...and Place

"I'm very concerned about the authenticity of settings and furnishings. When we can't shoot in the actual settings, I'm for taking research photographs of everything."—Alfred Hitchcock

When one thinks back over his favorite moments of Hitchcock movies, he is not so likely to remember scenes that were touching (Hitchcock's characters are too cynical for that), and sometimes not even the most terrifying, but rather scenes in which the action and the locale somehow work together so beautifully, so perfectly, that they become part of our highest regard for Hitchcock's films: the crowded chamberpot chimneys after the kidnapping in the remake of *The Man Who Knew Too Much;* the United Nations building and the bleak cornfields in *North by Northwest*—the setting for one murder and for an attempted murder; the ancient Sequoias and mission in *Vertigo* (where place functions more than dialogue in developing story and creating an exquisite mood). In effect, Hitchcock uses settings and all the slight delineations of setting with a striking precision of effect, staging his action against an unlikely setting for contrast or irony, sometimes framing his action within a specific setting as a way of amplifying and adding resonance to the action. Place is never neutral in a Hitchcock movie.

Nor is time. When the murder attempt on Cary Grant was to take place in *North by Northwest,* Hitchcock comments: "Now, how is this usually done? A dark night at a narrow intersection of the city. The waiting victim standing in a pool of light under the street lamp. The cobbles are 'washed with the recent rains.' . . . Now, what was the antithesis of a scene like this? No darkness, no pool of light, no mysterious figure in windows. Just nothing. Just bright sunshine and a blank, open countryside with barely a house or tree in which any lurking menaces could hide."

The favorite Hitchcock device of countering a darkly foreboding action (say, the discovery that a man is surrounded by the enemy) within a bright, unalarming context of time and place (say a society ball, or an auction) not only gives an ironic twist to such scenes, but reveals something of the nature of Hitchcock's humor, for invariably the trapped hero is forced to subvert the social function or setting, the urgency of his desperation supplanting and belying the social amenities of the situation. Hitchcock treats such moments almost tongue-in-cheek. We're invited to laugh, but the laughter comes through the tension only uneasily, a comic touch at the gallows.

SETTING AS IMPLICATION

Norman and Marion Crane in the motel den in *Psycho;* a slow scene, but in setting Norman against the stuffed birds, Hitchcock is suggesting Norman's character, his stiffness, his immunity to time, his active roaming eyes.

ESTABLISHING TIME AND PLACE

The beginning of *Psycho,* focusing first on a city, giving a date; then on a building, giving a time: implying that it's arbitrary, it could be any city, any building, any couple inside . . . an effort from the very beginning to encourage identification with Marion Crane. Titles by Saul Bass

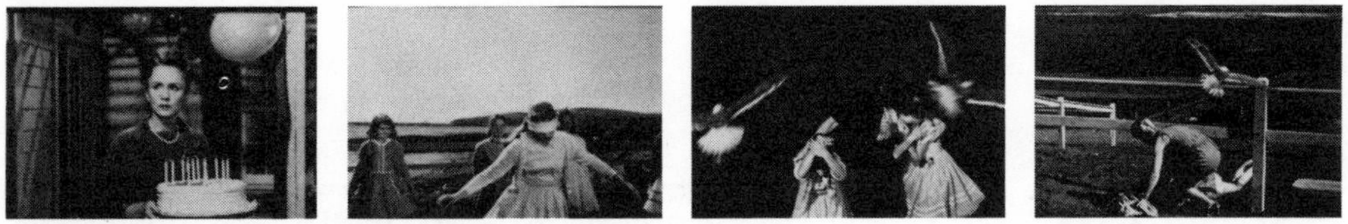

SETTING AS COUNTERPOINT

In *The Birds* the first big attack comes at a bright afternoon birthday party for a little girl, a context that sets off, by contrast, the brutality of the attack.

THE TRAPPED MAN MOTIF

Two versions of essentially the same idea: a man at a highly constrained social function discovering that he's trapped, and working against the social function to escape. In *Saboteur,* Robert Cummings find himself trapped in a society matron's ball; to escape, he announces brazenly to the gathered socialites that the hostess has volunteered to auction off her necklace. In *North by Northwest,* made almost twenty years later, Cary Grant, similarly trapped—now *at* an auction—makes ridiculous bids and a sore nuisance out of himself, till finally cops come to drag him away. Says Hitchcock: "Anyone in the situation would go up to someone and say, 'Look, I'm a prisoner here.' And the answer would be: 'You must be crazy.' " Making the situation even more frustrating.

GAG ON AN ELEVATOR

Jesse Royce Landis, as Cary Grant's mother in *North by Northwest,* sweetly asks the two spies on an elevator, "You gentlemen aren't *really* trying to kill my son, are you?" Everyone cracks up: spies, the mother, the other people on the elevator, except Grant, of course.

A Master Storyteller

"Making a film means, first of all, to tell a story. That story can be an improbable one, but it should never be banal. It must be dramatic and human. What is drama, after all, but life with the dull bits cut out."—Alfred Hitchcock

In a century or two, when today's movies are being screened with something like that mixture of impatience and surprise with which we look at the earliest of silent movies, the best of Hitchcock's films may well find true audiences—as they have in our time. For Hitchcock's "art"—however his disciples laud it or his critics deride it—is the art of a unique and masterful storyteller, with roots that stretch beyond the history of movies, to Dickens, Shakespeare, Aesop. When D. W. Griffith "invented" the closeup and techniques of intercutting, they were for him simple expediencies enabling him to better tell and dramatize a story. Hitchcock's cinema, in all its richness of technique, inflection, and invention is organized solely around a single purpose: to keep you so rooted to your seat that you don't get up for another box of popcorn. The storyteller's art may well be the oldest art there is, and Hitchcock's genius may well one day be seen as a genius for assimilating into this relatively new medium the oldest crafts of the cagiest fireside tale-spinner, fixing in the minds and imaginations of an audience a world that terrifies and fixes and enthralls them. In Hitchcock's films everything is expressive, laden with meaning: an egg, a glass of milk, a windmill. The world turns mysterious and sinister at the master's touch. Things are never quite what they normally seem to be. And our perceptions are heightened, our nerve endings electrified. We're suddenly thrown into a condition of anxiety, unease, which—the eternal paradox of good storytelling—we relish, even regret when it's ended. Few directors in the history of movies have done this so well or so often as Hitchcock; and very possibly, few will again. His knack for exacting touches, for impeccable timing, for characters that force us to breathe with them is rare in storytellers, rarer in film directors. Hitchcock may well be a superlative "engineer" of a filmgoer's reactions, as his critics say; but that may be the highest compliment one can pay to a storyteller. And Hitchcock, if nothing else, has elevated movies to a new plateau of storytelling.

THE HITCHCOCK SIGNATURE

Like Picasso's familiar scrawl, Hitchcock leaves an unmistakable signature on each movie he's made since *The Lodger* in 1926. For a brief moment he appears in the movie, usually as part of some street or crowd scene, often with an amusing twist, as when he misses a bus at the beginning of *North by Northwest.*

▼

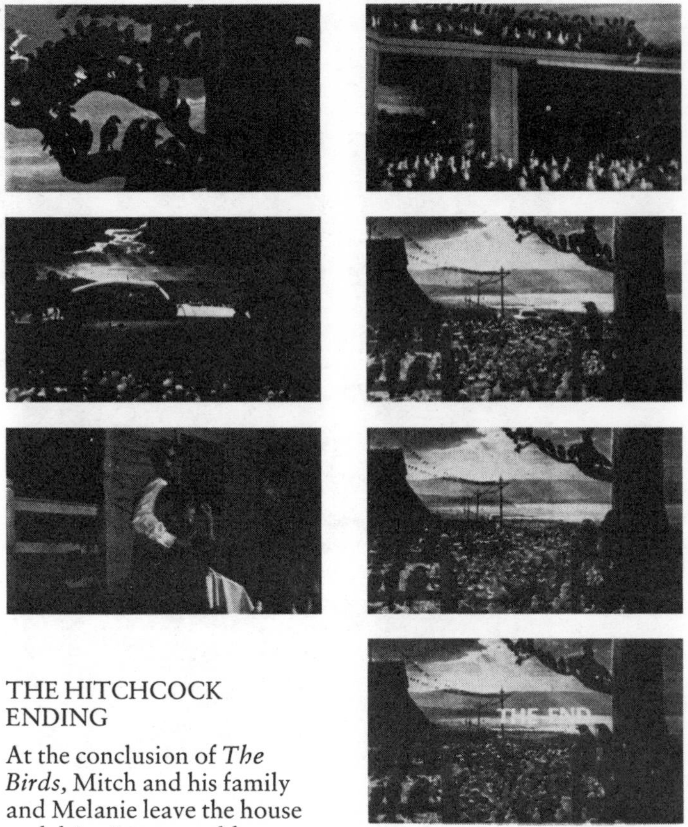

THE HITCHCOCK ENDING

At the conclusion of *The Birds,* Mitch and his family and Melanie leave the house and drive into a world teeming with silent, perched, countless birds, an ending which leaves us with an ominous sensation of doom rather than any cheering feeling that things are all right after all. Known as a "Hitchcock ending," it's a taste of Hitchcock's macabre wit and his ability to ride a dramatic premise to the very end.

"The fact is, I practice absurdity quite religiously."—Alfred Hitchcock

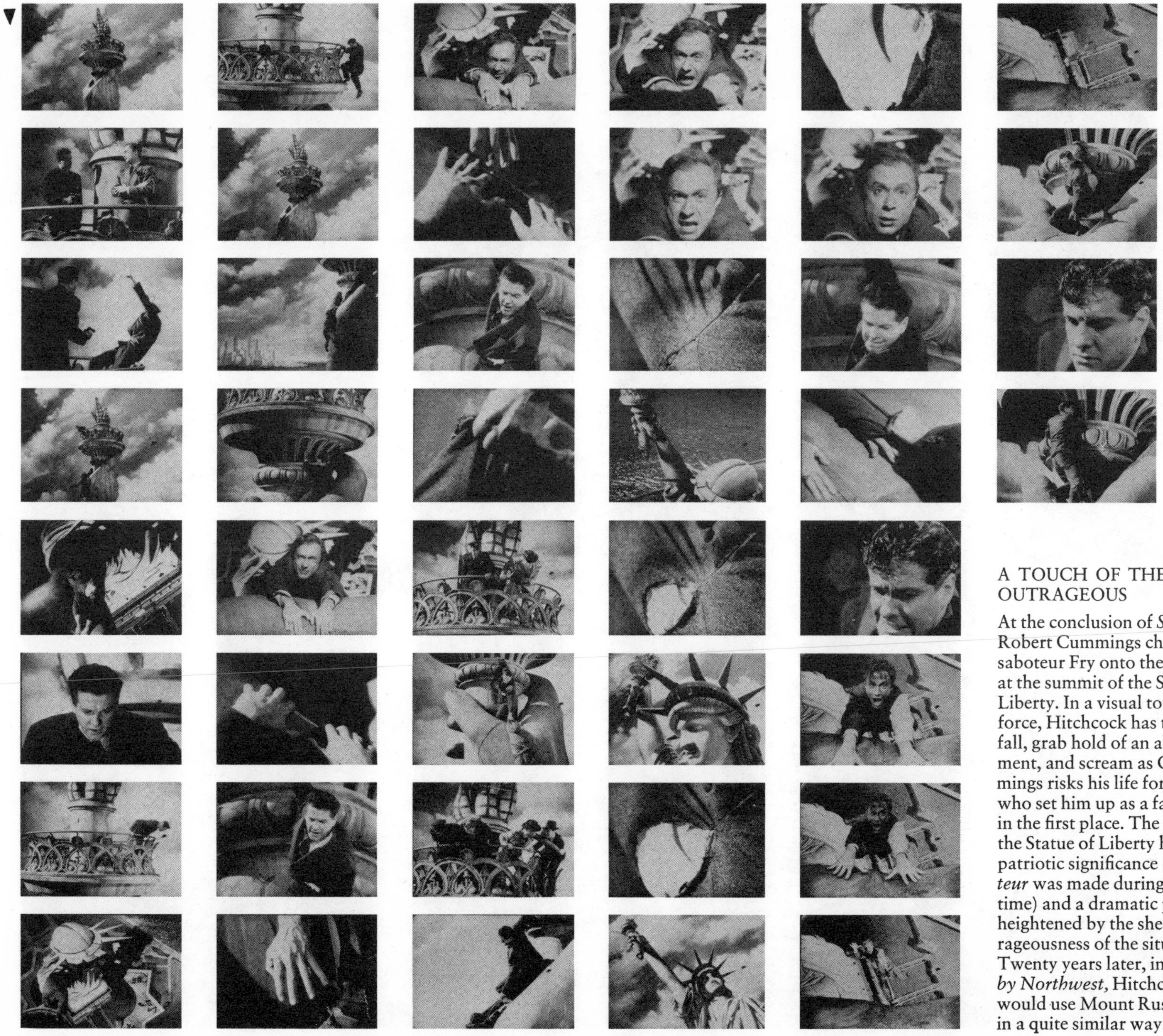

A TOUCH OF THE OUTRAGEOUS

At the conclusion of *Saboteur,* Robert Cummings chases the saboteur Fry onto the parapet at the summit of the Statue of Liberty. In a visual tour de force, Hitchcock has the spy fall, grab hold of an abutment, and scream as Cummings risks his life for the man who set him up as a fall guy in the first place. The use of the Statue of Liberty had both patriotic significance (*Saboteur* was made during wartime) and a dramatic power heightened by the sheer outrageousness of the situation. Twenty years later, in *North by Northwest,* Hitchcock would use Mount Rushmore in a quite similar way.

The famous *Psycho* house crouches on its furry hill, waiting for its master to fill its halls with eerie monologue.

CHAPTER NINE

Animation

Animation

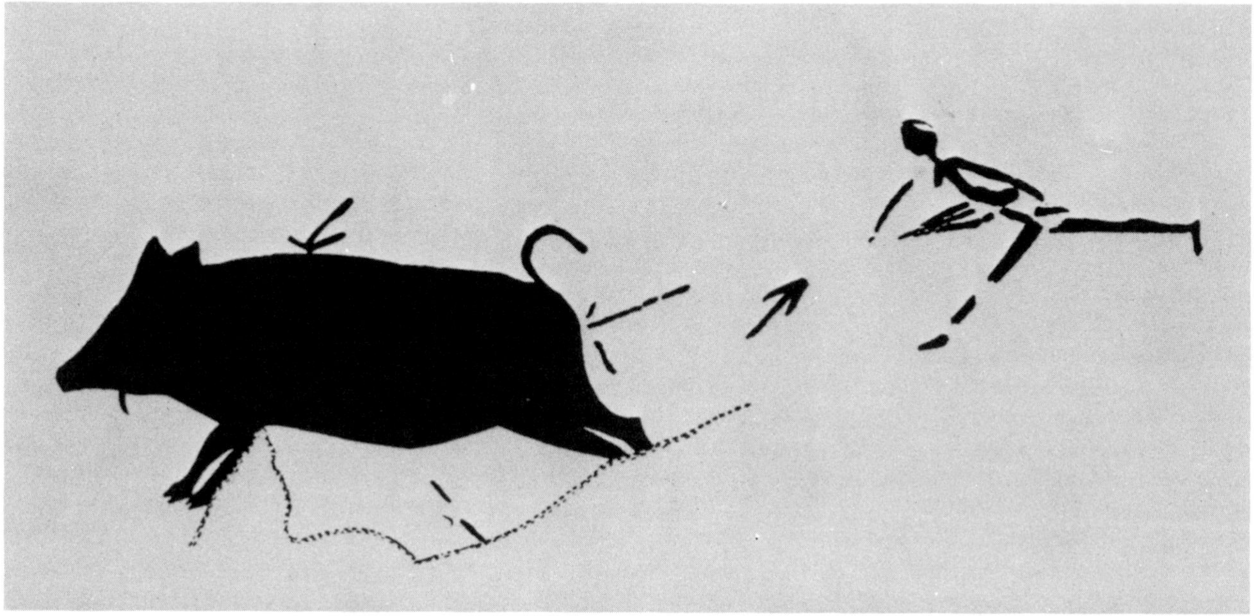

Cave drawings dating from paleolithic times show that man's fascination with movement is no modern phenomenon.

"To animate: to give life and soul to a design, not through the copying, but through the transformation of reality."—Collective statement of Zagreb animators, Zagreb Studio, Yugoslavia.

At the Annecy Film Festival in 1962, a film was shown which had a jarring effect on many of the viewers. Though extremely rough-hewn and primitive in style, it showed a buffalo running, then stumbling, then pitching forward into a pit, unable to get out, while men surrounded the pit. What made the film so extraordinary is that the drawings had been photographed off cave walls—drawings made by an unknown artist some 20,000 years ago.

The urge to animate, to give life to a succession of images, is as deeply rooted as a child's delight in playing his hands before a light to make shadows into favorite animals. There are striking evidences throughout the history of art—Egyptian tableaus of developing actions, Greek vases with figures in movement, books and cathedral murals from the Middle Ages—that depict processes, movements, actions in sequential progression. One can only suspect the nascent discontent of many an artist for whom the very essence of what he wanted to express—motion—was impossible, except by this indirect means. For it is in motion that the world is often most expressive, most eye-catching, and the manners of movement—the supple flexing of a muscle, the rippling of a field, the dart of a frog's tongue—have never been, till recently, a true province of the artist.

The motion picture camera changed that. Indeed, one of the often overlooked benefits of the movies is that they have given the artist a means of creating real movement in time, and to that extent, of widening the possibilities of art itself. True, when we think of animation, we rarely think of art. Animation is mostly cartoons, and cartoons are mostly conventional gag farces like Tom and Jerry, Bugs Bunny, Roadrunner, or worse, the spastic jerkings of Saturday morning television. But over the years, and increasingly in the present, serious and talented artists have turned to animation as a way of capturing more thoroughly the evanescent beauties and the longings and anxieties of our century. One can approach a history of animation as the commercial development of successful cartoon series and a handful of features, but one can also approach it as an art.

A few words, briefly, about the *process* of

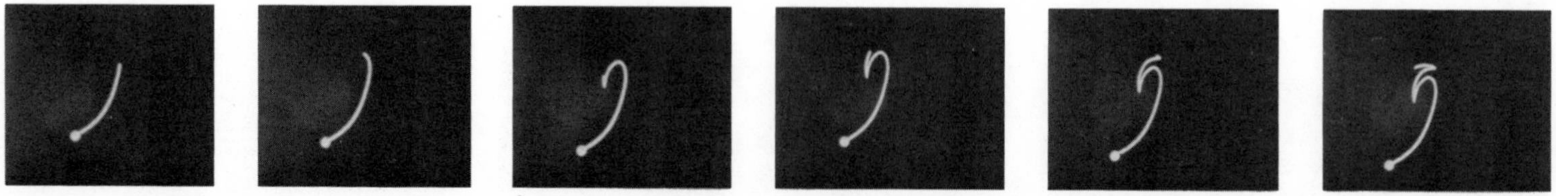

A demonstration of the basic principle of animation: movement controlled frame by frame. Norman McLaren, from *The Eye Hears, The Ear Sees.*

animation, for the animated film is created by a method far more time-consuming and rigorous than normal film. On a strip of 16mm or 35mm, there are 24 frames per second, or 1,440 frames per minute. The animator generally must create a fresh drawing for every two frames—meaning 720 *different drawings* for one minute of film. Or 7,200 drawings for a ten-minute film. Moreover, to create fluid and convincing movement, these drawings must be carefully calibrated in the slightest shift from one drawing to another: if the gap between say, a figure's raised arm in one frame and his lowered arm in the next is too wide, the arm will seem to 'jump'—giving the movement a jerky, skittish quality. The filming process itself is almost sheer mechanics—once the drawings are completed, they're placed on an animating stand, usually locked into place so each "cel" (a drawing on transparent acetate) is perfectly aligned, and shot with a single-frame camera. Even if one is dealing with very simple figures, little or no color, and makes only a two-minute film, that's still a considerable amount of work. And the kind of work that animation involves—sitting at a board and drawing the same figure for maybe weeks at a time—has neither the glamor nor excitement of "real" filmmaking, which is far more corporate and energetic.

Another difficulty of animation, particularly since television, is that it has a diminishing market. Theaters rarely rent animated shorts to precede the movies anymore (they can get "sponsored" travel or sport featurettes for nothing), and the animation that television buys and uses, with a few exceptions, is made by a method so streamlined—some studios simply program a computer to match a hundred or so basic modes of movement—that the central delight of animation, movement, becomes its least interesting aspect. Consequently, a serious animator must either work in total solitude, with his own capital and little hope of regaining it, or find an umbrella studio to support him (such as Zagreb in Yugoslavia or the National Film Board of Canada—there is none in the U.S.), or do animation for commercial purposes—as animators like John and Faith Hubley and Fred Wolf and Jimmy Murakami have been doing.

Yet despite all these limitations and discouragements, animation artists have emerged and make films of stunning force, bizarre humor, delightful whimsy. Indeed, in the past fifteen years the best work in animation worldwide has shown that artists of the first rank—artists who might well have made formidable reputations working on canvas or in traditional forms—have chosen animation, and those same artists have redefined and given a new meaning to the word "animation." Anyone who has seen Jimmy Murakami's *Breath*, or Ryan Larkin's *Street Musique* or Jan Lenica's *Labyrinth* or the best work of Zagreb Studio in Yugoslavia, or of Norman McLaren or Wolfgang Urchs or John Hubley or Walerian Borowczyk can never again think of animated film as "cartoon." Such men have destroyed forever that equation, and proven that animation can be a serious art, the equal of any other art in its range of expressive capabilities and imaginative resources.

There is such a remarkable diversity and imagination and range to the best work in animation that one hesitates to make any generalizations about what animation is and can be; surely someone will emerge to prove those generalizations wrong. In terms of something as basic as movement, styles can vary widely. The films of Poland's Jan Lenica, for example, with their bizarre Victorian ornamentation and their subdued tonal colors, use movement only sporadically—and often in strobic or juttingly quick ways. The sardonic Japanese animator Yoji Kuri will repeat a movement or hold on a static shot for what seems an interminable time, but always to contribute to a jarring shock effect. In *La Vita* the droll Italian animator Bruno Bozzetto creates a violent contrast, using movement, color, pace, and a squeezed frame, between a man's everyday boxed-in life and his glorious moments of love or fantasy. In *Sirene*, the Belgian Raoul Servais dissolves immobile images into one another, often in such fluid harmony that the result is much like movement—a technique used similarly in Ryan Larkin's *Syrinx*.

To trace the origins of this recent flowering in animation, one need look at a few key figures, pioneers whose animation helped inspire and prompt later artists. Max Fleischer is best known for adapting Popeye to cartoons, but in his earlier animation work (notably the Koko the Clown and Betty Boop series which he developed over the later twenties and early thirties, and even in some of the early Popeye shorts), Fleischer revealed an inventiveness and capability for abrupt shifts in mood, concept and the shapes of figures (a man can become an automobile with fluid grace in a Fleischer short) that was more ingenious than, though not as comically effective as, the work of Disney during the same period.

Disney himself, of course—the empire builder of animation—has exerted a profound influence on future animation, though often in an inverse manner. Disney's work of the thirties—his acute and evocative use of color, his brilliantly timed and quite funny gags, his extraordinary ability to match his animation to a musical counterpoint—has probably in some manner influenced every major animator since. But *the* direction in which Disney took animation was toward an extreme naturalism. His artists were taught muscular anatomy to enable them to draw figures in convincing three-dimensional movement. He had an animation stand built for his films that enabled his artists to create backgrounds in real depth—sometimes upwards of seven or eight cels, just for foreground and background; and the precision of detail in Disney's animation is a marvel to see—the shading of separate leaves on a tree, the separate rivulets of water as it courses past pebbles in a stream. Disney took animation to the extremity of realistic detail to which the Dutch painters had taken painting in the 17th century. Contemporary animators (some of whom, like John Hubley, once worked at Disney's studio) argue that such realistic detail is both too expensive (it's outrageously expensive—enough so that there will probably never be another animator working on Disney's scale again) and works against the nature of animation, in which the artist is ultimately free to paint the world as he sees it, not as though it had been photographed. Indeed, there is often a starkness, a kind of two-dimensional comic strip simplicity, to the best work of a Yoji Kuri or a Bruno Bozzetto or a Jimmy Murakami. Movement and concept and life are at the heart of an animation work, not detailed sets and figures.

The Canadian Norman McLaren (born in Scotland) never worked for a major studio, nor did he make any cartoon series that we have come to recognize. McLaren's work has been of a more experimental, tentative nature, but with a few other experimentalists, such as Hans Richter and Len Lye, McLaren has made a profound impact upon contemporary animation, both in the techniques he pioneered and in the mood of playful serendipity that his work projects. McLaren was among the first to experiment with animation that's drawn directly *onto* the film frame; he developed a technique for actually drawing an optical soundtrack, able to match a certain pen stroke to a distinct kind of sound. He was among the first to "animate" live actors, a process known as pixillation, in which man can be made to to hop on one leg across a yard by shooting his movement in single frames. With his recent *Pas de deux* he has used optical strobe techniques to create a semi-animated effect with live actors.

Barely recognized in his own day, but now heralded as the pioneer of an entirely new form of film—one often requiring computers and only tangentially related to animation—is the German Oskar Fischinger, who came to the U.S. shortly before World War II and worked for a time with Disney. Fischinger's animation is abstract, shapes and forms and interlaced colors dancing through space is synchronization to the music. Indeed, what fascinated Fischinger was the possibility of using the moving image as a visual corollary to a musical score. In *An American March* he matches the notes of a trombone to roundish forms, while drums evoke cubic forms; the forms appear, dance on the screen to the presence of each note, then disappear to be replaced with new forms, new notes. The effect is like *seeing* sound, a dazzling and vivid impressionistic glimpse of music as a graphic phenomenon. Fischinger, along with pioneers like Hans Richter and Mary Ellen Bute, has created the groundwork for recent motion graphics films of artists like John and James Whitney, Jordan Belson and John Stehura. Their films, which display abstract forms in motion, often with an eerie sense of depth and a beguiling use of color and movement, promise a form of film which is neither animation (for the method of creating movement may vary from frame-by-frame work to the filming of carefully devised optical movements) nor "real" film, but rather a drastically new form with its own future and possibilities.

The future of animation perhaps looks better now than it has at any time in the past. The "cartoon" as we knew it has been mostly relegated to television; the animation studios at Warner Brothers and MGM and UPA have long been closed, and animation today lies increasingly in the hands of independents or creative studios like Zagreb in Yugoslavia, probably the foremost animation school and studio in the world. It will require a new generation seeking quality animation, and no doubt a distribution system that can reach that generation (most likely not so much through the theaters as though some manner of selective television) before the animators who are doing such exceptional work now will be fully seen and recognized and rewarded.

'Gertie' Takes a Bough

The first true animated film is credited to a cartoonist working for the *New York Herald,* Winsor McCay. Appearing about 1909, *Gertie the Dinosaur* is at once an explanation of how a cartoon is made and a demonstration of what the cartoon can do. The film begins with McCay himself explaining the technique to some friends, then standing before a drawn image of a cave. He backs away, and a rather pleasant-looking brontosaurus comes bouncing out, munches on a rock that rolls down its throat like an adam's apple, and takes on a whole tree, bite by bite. The principle in *Gertie* was simple enough: to give a drawn figure movement that is at once convincing and yet impossible, a premise that would guide the cartoon through Disney and Bugs Bunny and beyond.

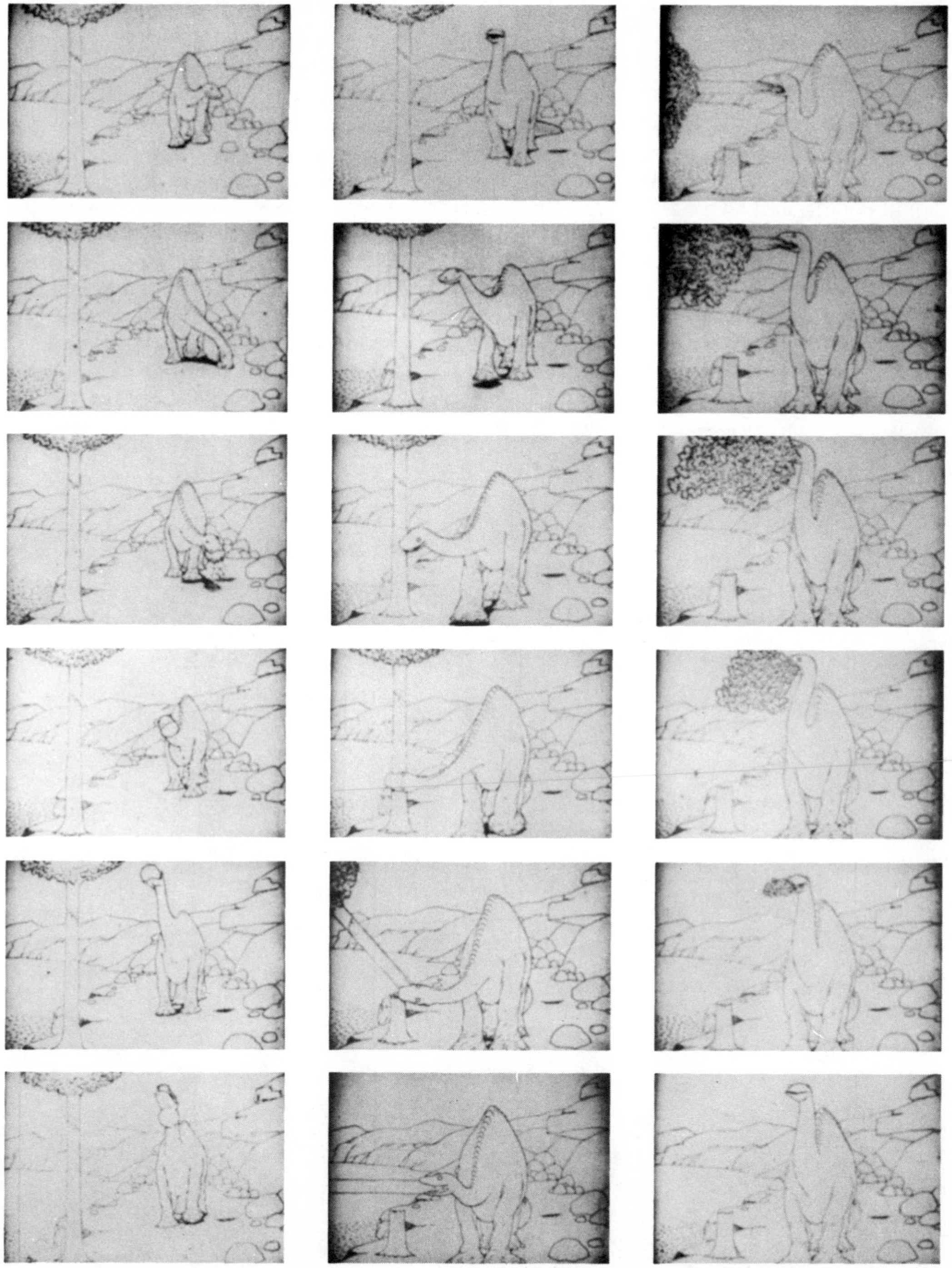

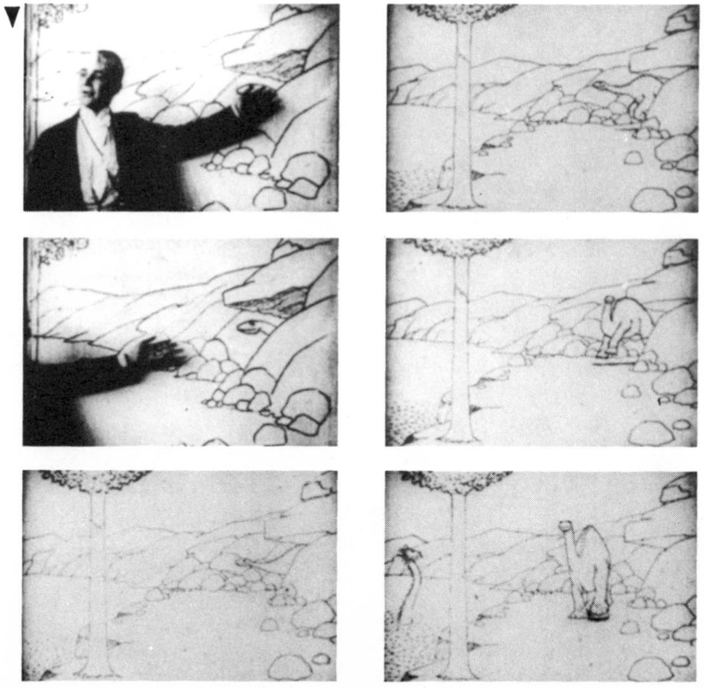

Gertie the Dinosaur

Disney

Disney bestrides the world of animation like a colossus. With his genius for intuiting public taste, his shrewd and canny organizational talents, and an ambition that would settle for nothing less than empire, Disney took animation to a stage of exhaustive blueprintings and exquisite detail. His most developed animation, particularly the features, are built with the care and complexity—and the vast array of personnel—that one would expect of an Apollo rocket.

Indeed, Disney solved problems that most animators have never had to face: convincing three-dimensional movement (part of his studio was an art school and laboratory); characterization of animals in a naturalistic style (he kept a zoo at the studio and later hired nature photographers); the uses of sound and color. He leapt at new technical advances and would often throw out immense amounts of completed work to have his artists redo it in the new technique (this happened to *Snow White and the Seven Dwarfs* when color became available). Perhaps above all, he came to think and got his artists to think in terms of the animated image. Disney on the reasons animation favors animals over people as its subject:

Walt Disney

". . . there's the matter of plastic masses . . . masses of face, or torso, and so on. Animation needs these masses. They're things that can be exaggerated a little and whirled about in such a way as to contribute the illusion of movement, you see, like a bloodhound's droopy ears and floppy gums or the puffy little cheeks and fat little torsos of chipmunks and squirrels . . . For contrast, think of the human being as the animator sees him. It takes the devotion of a whole boyhood to learn to wiggle an ear as much as three-sixteenths of an inch, which isn't much. The typical man of today has a slim face, torso and legs. No scope for animation, too stiff, too limited."

Bashful, one of the dwarfs in *Snow White*, takes shape on an artist's sketch pad.

Disney made his name virtually synonymous with animation in the public mind and even though generations are growing up without seeing a single Mickey Mouse or Donald Duck cartoon, the identification holds for them as well. Disney made animation into something that was at once exuberant, comic, richly detailed and nostalgic. It's a combination that will never be equalled again.

Flowers and Trees, 1933 (right), a Silly Symphony, was the first film in full Technicolor.

The success of Mickey Mouse, which began with *Steamboat Willie* (below) made possible the first full length cartoon, *Snow White and the Seven Dwarfs,* 1937 (right, below), and the ones that would follow.

The Old Gag

Perhaps because of its origins in the newspaper cartoon, perhaps because it lends itself to the sudden visual coup, animated films have by and large been built around the gag, enough so that we generally expect a cartoon to be funny. The earlier cartoons, like Felix the Cat, Mutt 'n Jeff, and Betty Boop, often used unpredictable transformations as the source of gags. In *Felix Makes Whoopee,* a silent cartoon, the intoxicated Felix watches, astounded, as a bottle becomes an automobile. Later cartoons—particularly after Mickey Mouse and Popeye—resorted increasingly to direct confrontations between characters and a kind of violent gag, seen vividly enough in Tom and Jerry, and Bugs Bunny, yet reaching a kind of abstract, surreal pitch in Chuck Jones' Roadrunner series, where the gags are treated as formulas freeing the cartoons to take on fresh graphic emphasis; playing with spaces, gravity, and the mutability of physical laws.

Snow White

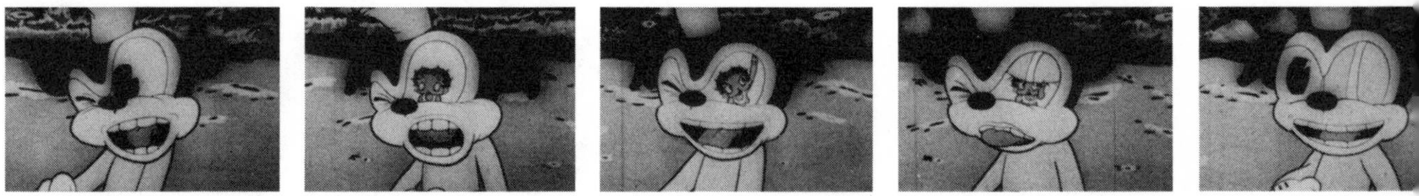

Betty Boop's Desert Isle

Roadrunner: from *There They Go-Go*

Felix Makes Whoopee

The New Gag

If the gags of American studio cartoons tended to be abrupt, violent, and almost always touched with a ring of vengeance, the gags of the newer, independent animators tend instead toward the allegorical, the satiric, the surreal. In *The Wall,* made at Zagreb Studio in Yugoslavia, a small man in a bowler hat sits beside a brick wall as a naked fanatical character tries to climb, blast, penetrate the wall. When he does, and dies in the process, the other man walks through the hole and waits at another wall. *K-9000, A Space Oddity,* by the American Haboush Studio, is a spoof of Kubrick's *2001.* A dog is sent into space, where he encounters stupefying wonders: a floating cow, a battery of mammoth ink pens, twinkling stars from a salt shaker; there is a sequence in which he enters a vast phonograph and sees swirling, ebbing colors (a direct play on the Stargate Corridor sequence of *2001*) ending in the dog's transformation into an older dog, then a pup.

Raoul Servais' *Goldframe* satirizes the archetypal movie mogul, in its characterization of a pompous, abrasive magnate who gets his kicks after work by sitting against a blank wall of the studio before a spotlight and trying to outspeed his shadow. "I must be first," he keeps muttering; and his violent efforts to outwit his shadow lead from a nervous dance to Goldframe flying. Finally he *does* outspeed his shadow, and the film's abrupt conclusion, a brilliant surreal touch, depicts the shadow pounding down an enormous fist on the tiny Goldframe.

Goldframe is an astute satire that illustrates the potential of the gag beyond a diverting round of punch and punch back. In less than five minutes, Servais creates a vivid character, mocks him and the movies in general (the shadow play is a brilliant touch)—and caps it off with a gag ending both brutal and surreal, and right.

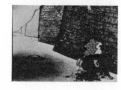

The Wall

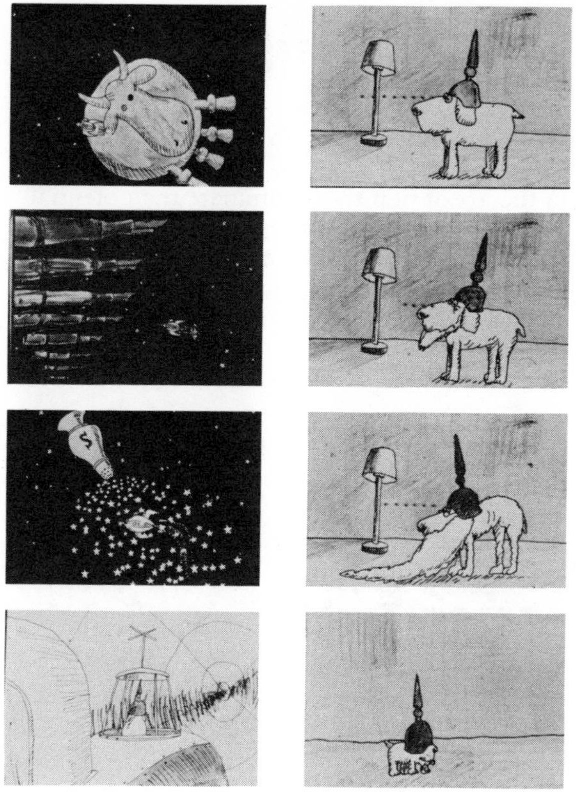

K-9000, A Space Oddity

Goldframe

Graphic Ingenuity

Chromophobia is an animated film. Like *Citizen Kane,* it is one of those rare moments in the art of film that illuminate the potential of the medium. *Chromophobia* is incredibly rich in all manner of invention. Its use of graphic movement, transformations, visual similes and color is constantly fresh, constantly original.

Raoul Servais, a Belgian animator, made *Chromophobia* in 1967. The basic metaphor of the film—regrettably it can't be reproduced here—is color. To begin, there is the lovely village in every hue, and there are the black goons, who shoot down every sign of color they see.

Chromophobia is not, perhaps, the most trenchant or sophisticated work of animation in recent years, but it is surely one of the most imaginative, inventive, and resourceful.

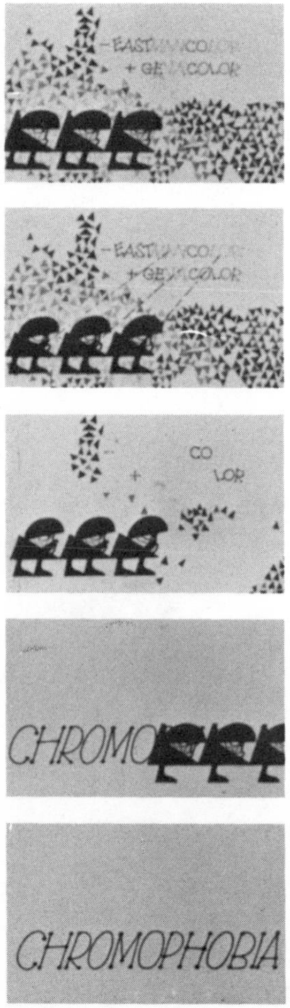

Even in the credits the color phobia of the goons is apparent. They shoot down letters from the titles, and decimate a pattern reminiscent of a map of Europe. (Throughout, there are many visual references to World War II and especially the concentration camps.)

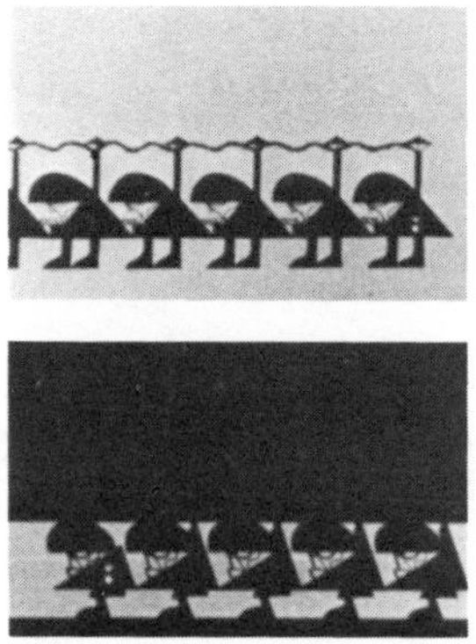

The goons always march in a kind of geometric precision. All are totally alike, and Servais gives them a blockish stolidity which is a marvelous example of the animator's art of characterization.

When commanded, they repeat the same activity. Note the way their backs become barred TV sets. These are genuinely stupid men. On order they become tanks, and set forth to overpower the village.

In one inventive episode, a recalcitrant painter sees the goons coming and hides behind his canvas, pulling a cord and switching it off like a light. When he peeks again to see whether the goons have gone, he clicks on the light, and bars appear in the canvas. Trying to escape, he is grabbed. There is no escaping the goons.

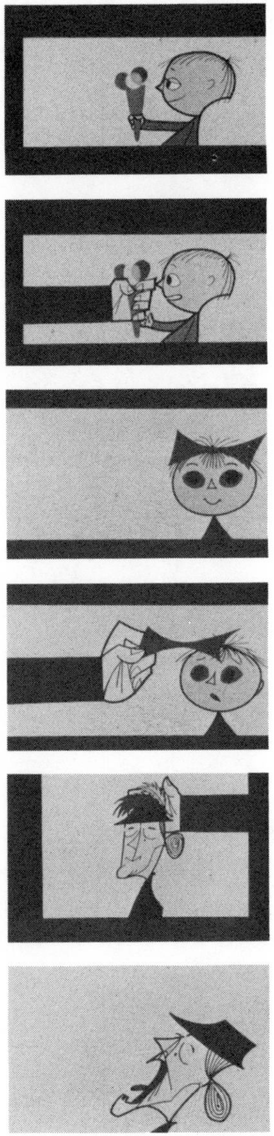

Servais also uses masking techniques, emphasizing the gruesome actions of the goons by framing them in close-up. The woman's final scream is more than good graphics; it reminds one of the screaming horse in Picasso's "Guernica."

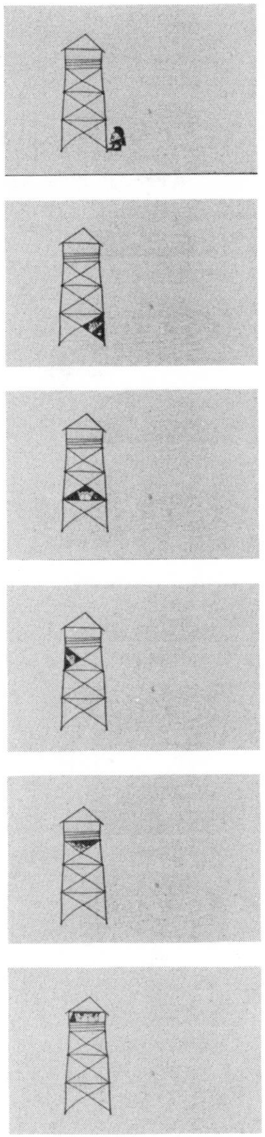

Servais characterizes the goons by using geometric shapes. When a goon climbs his watchtower, his form becomes one of the triangles, which flits upward to the top of the tower.

Once atop the tower the goon reveals his true character. A mechanical owl pops out of his head, terrifying a real owl. A brief but marvelous image.

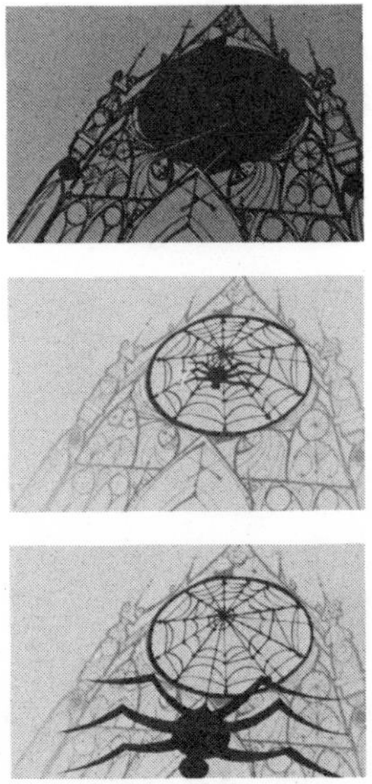

Servais depicts their conquest of the village in several ways, all of which are indirect and graphically ingenious. The high round window of a cathedral becomes a big spider that lunges downward, a potent symbol of the take-over by the goons.

The rescuer is a jester. He emerges from a flower, and by sprinkling the petals of another flower over the heads of the prisoners, he turns them into more jesters.

The jesters treat the goons playfully, which is the last thing the goons are capable of appreciating. In one delightful gag, a goon smashes the paint tube of the artist. A jester plays on his flute, making the squirming paint become a living line that segments and disrupts the goon; the power of cubist art?

Cartoon Serendipity

Ryan Larkin's *Street Musique* is a beguiling and sumptuous film, and a celebration of the purest possibilities of animation. The figures elide through swift metamorphoses, following a course as winsome and spontaneous as the spry music, played by a street band that opens and closes the film. Larkin gives his figures strong angular emphasis and fluid rhythmic movements, and our impressions are sharp, if kaleidoscopic. His mutations invariably involve total forms, which he plays adroitly and mischievously: a great-beaked bird sitting in a hat becomes a man stooped over, who rises. There are color sequences with almost iridescent richness of hue and texture, as radiant as the most exquisitely crafted works of stained glass. *Street Musique* conveys a mood of exuberant play, and whimsical associations; and the ineffable, perhaps sad beauty of those things that can be conjured only on the animator's moving sketchpad.

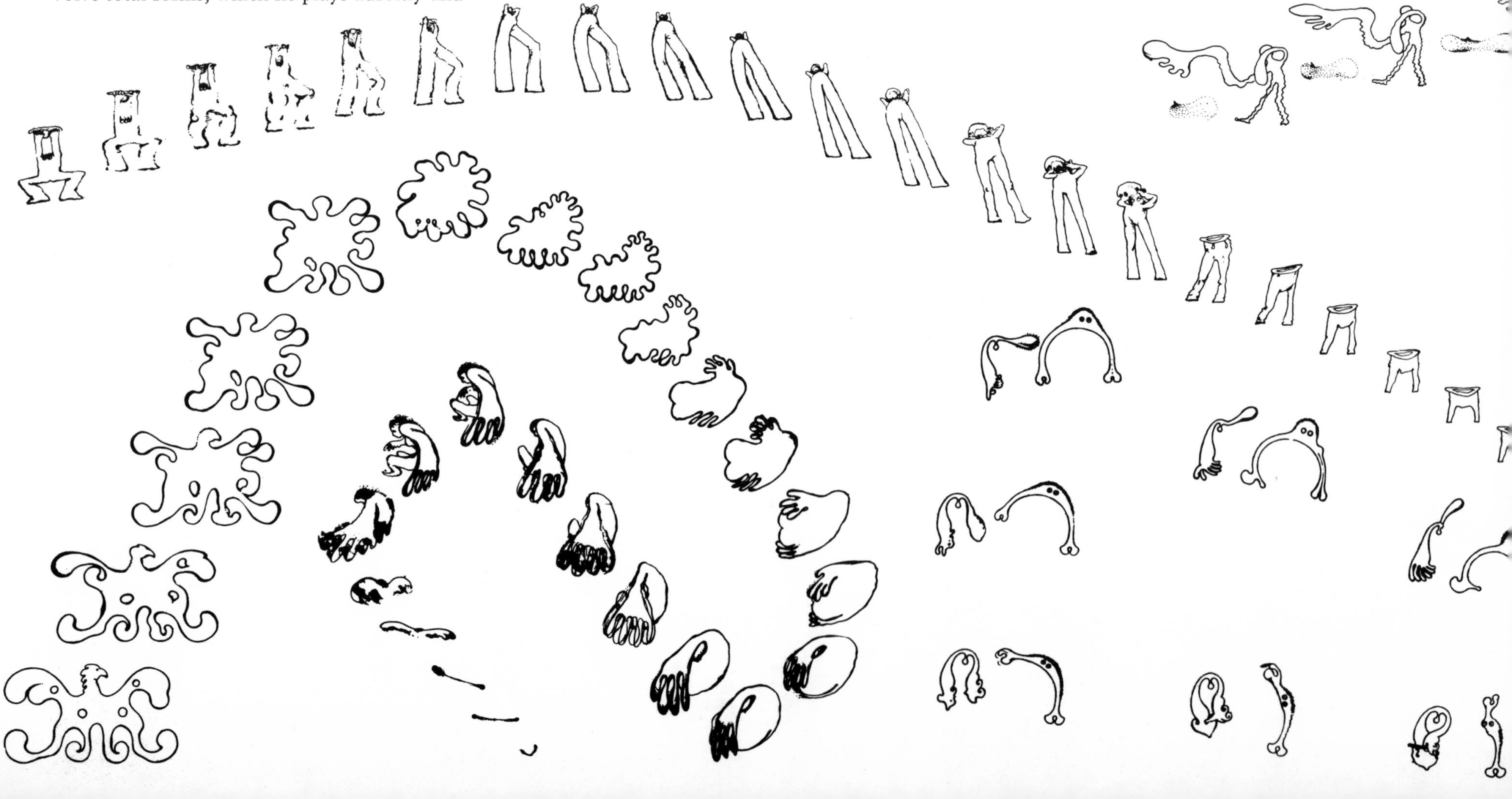

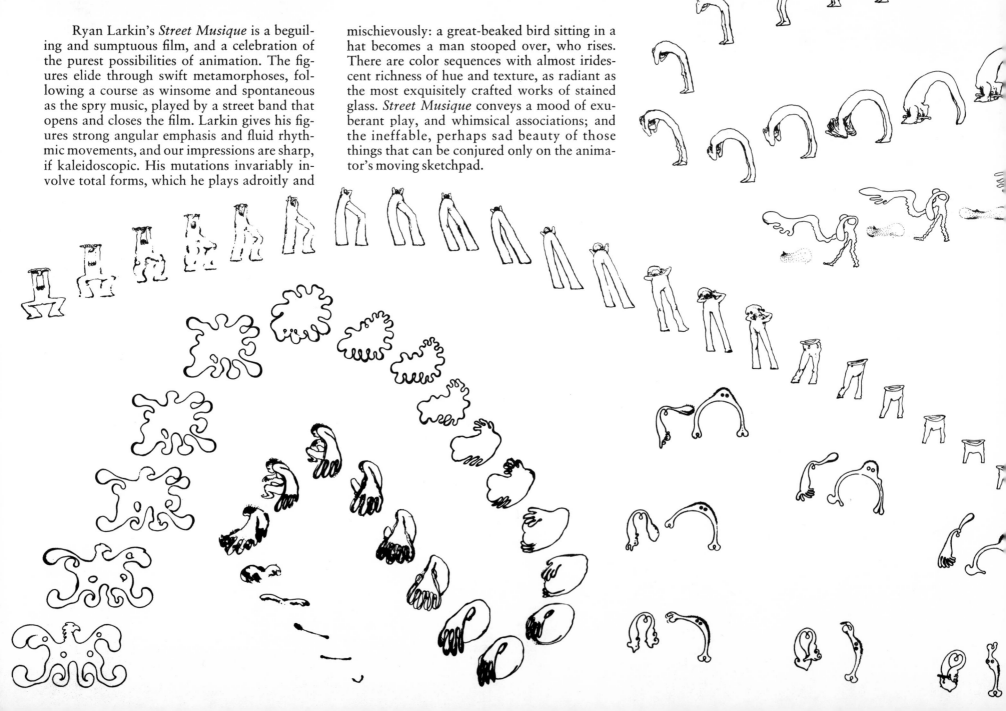

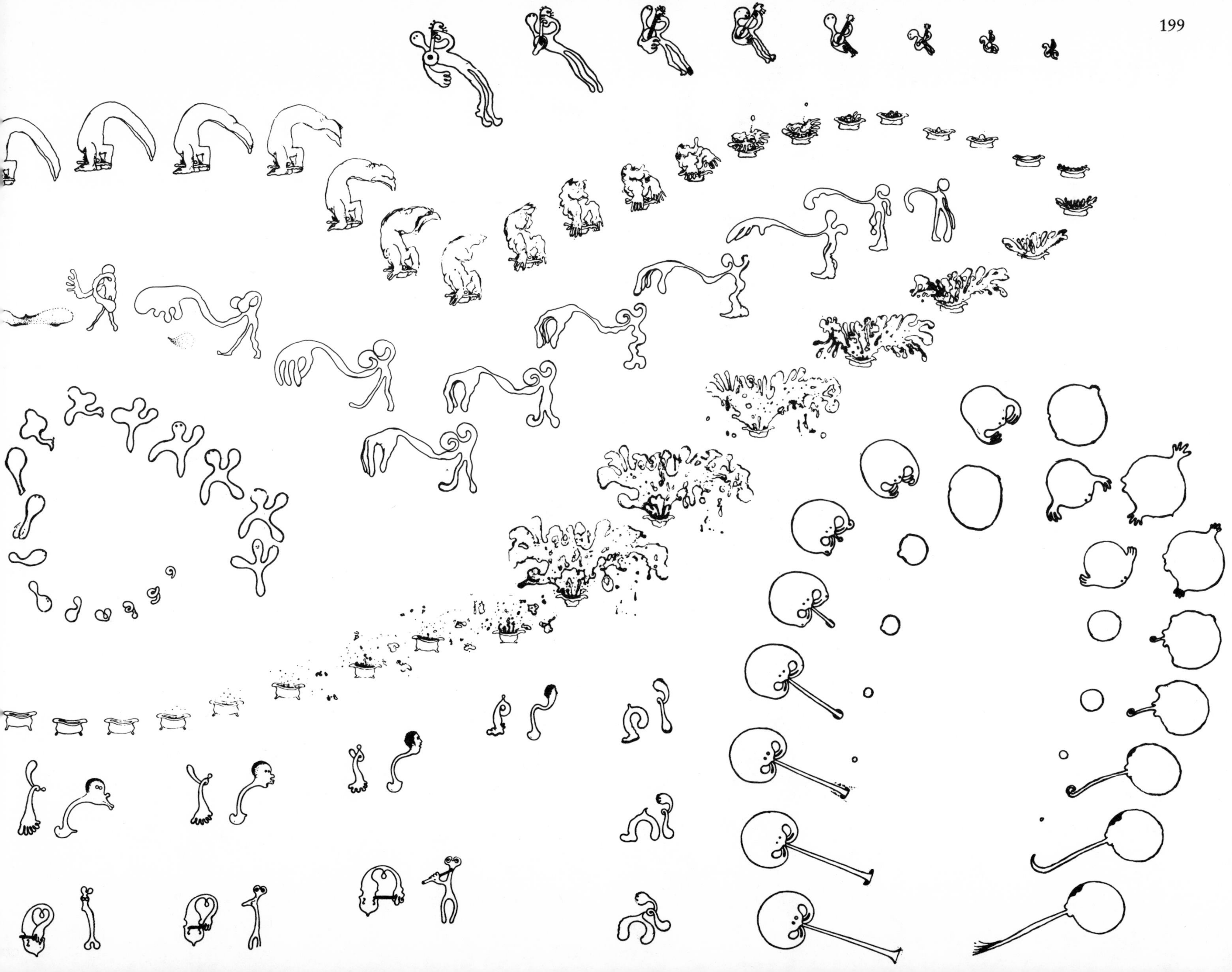

Transformation

No technique belongs so purely to the animator and the animator alone as transformation. By the slightest inflections of line, a drawing can go from one thing into another thing, and then yet another, all capable of providing, in the transitions, elaborations of story, or gags, or touches that range from whimsical to surreal. Indeed, one might say that transformation is close to the center of the animator's art, and the abundance of ways in which it can be handled suggests much about the range and possibilities of animated art.

In *Frame by Frame,* a short film about animation technique, two brief exercises suggest two of the basic possibilities of transformation. When a television set (right) reaches out its antennae to ensnarl and capture and finally swallow its victim, the basic transformation of an object into an animated character (the oldest and most basic use of transformation in cartoons) is apparent. When a girl's tongue becomes a snake that proceeds to engulf her, the transformation is more abstract, surreal, unexpected.

This latter type of transformation can be seen in sequences from three separate cartoons, in the ingenious masterpiece by Max Fleischer, *Snow White,* the witch transforms Betty Boop's companion Koko by hooping her mirror over him. As Cab Calloway sings "The St. James Infirmary Blues" to the dancing figure, his legs twist, transforming him into a watchchain. Later there is a marvelous sequence in which his head becomes a bottle, from which he pours a drink for himself.

In *Felix Makes Whoopee,* the soused Felix falls into a river, where he is swallowed by a fish, that hiccoughs him up even as it becomes a tuba, then a trombone, transitions so fluid and quickly paced they tend to dizzy the eyes. *Pulse,* an unusual, abstract film by Peter

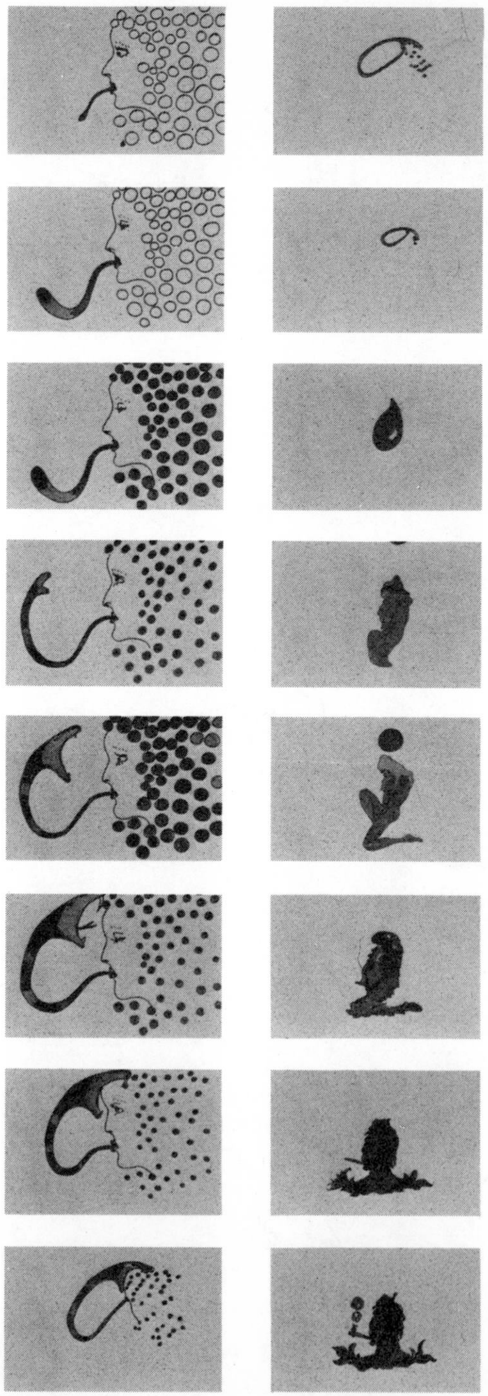

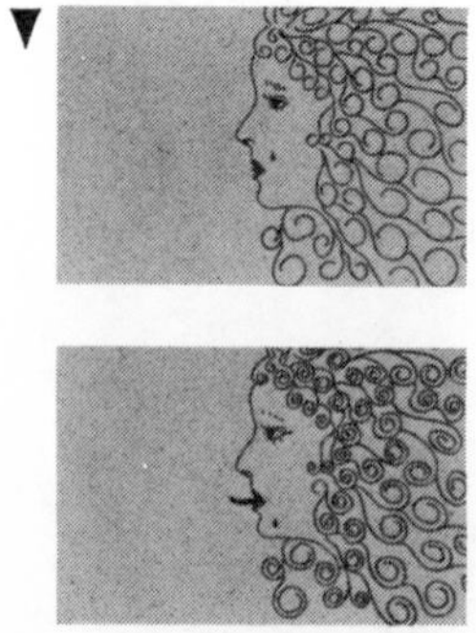

Sequences from
Frame by Frame.

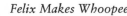

Spoecker, fills the entire frame with designs that mutate and shift with impressive speed and fluidity. Such transformation of the entire frame is rare in animation because of the enormous work required.

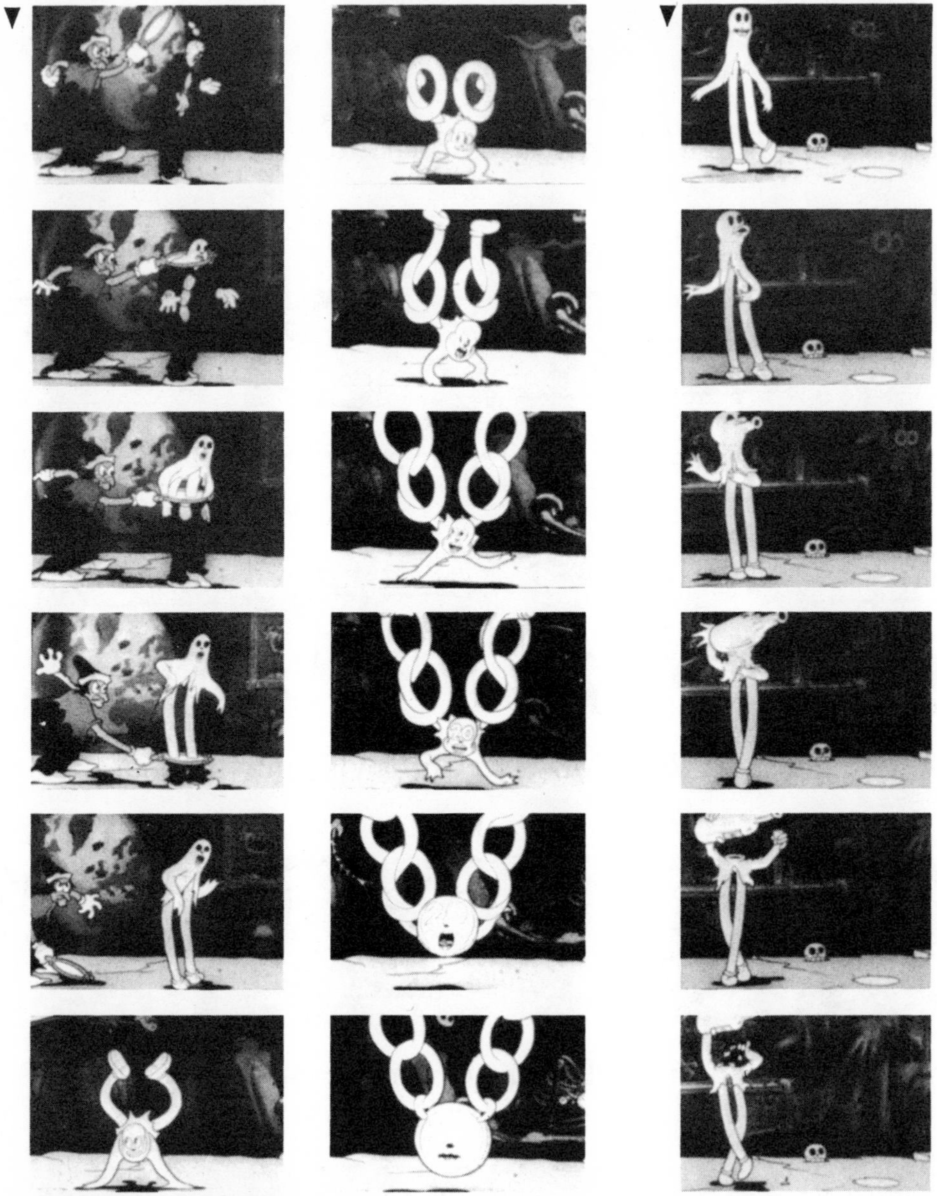

Max Fleischer's *Snow White*, a Betty Boop cartoon

Felix Makes Whoopee

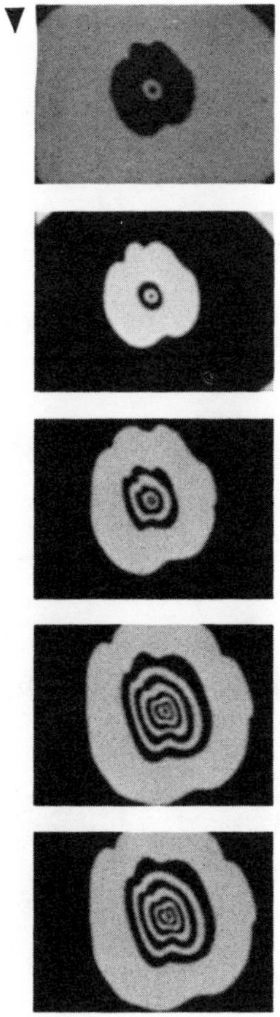

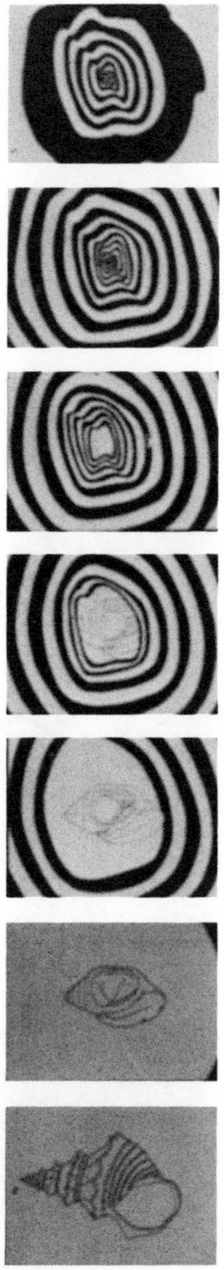

Pulse

Allegorical

Machine: An animated short film of dark intimations about technology

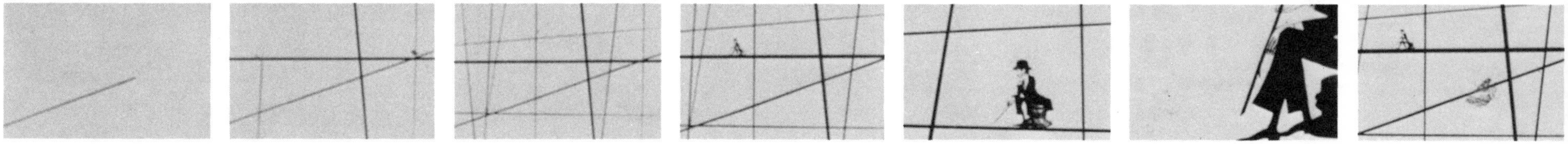

beginning with a natural order, symbolized by a pattern of lines; and an inventor, visited by a bright angel who

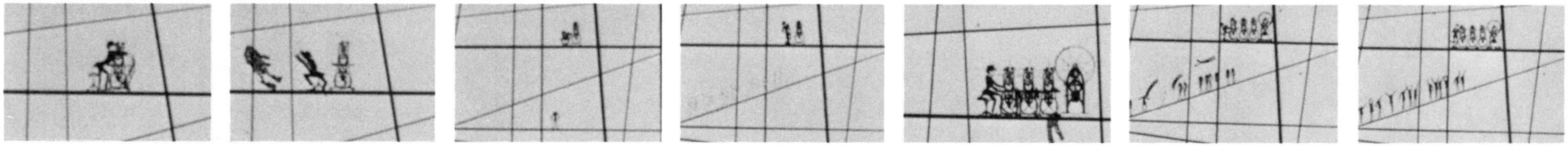

for one man below; but others clamor, encouraging more machines, more clothes, and a visit now from a

any competition. With a big enough machine, no point in competition; the Machine can make baby rockers,

over which they fight — requiring the Machine to grow beyond size, or limits; all to provide cannons for the

inspires the inventor to build the first machine, albeit a modest machine. It turns out a simple suit of clothing

sinister angel who inspires a machine that shatters the natural boundaries, and that can be made to discourage

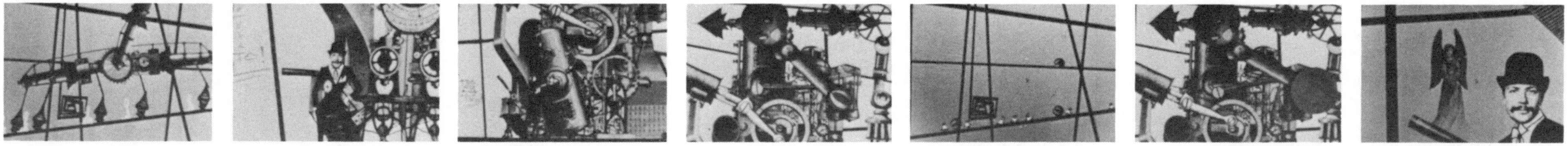

it can rock them for the mothers; no limits to what it can do, how big it can grow. Beach balls for the infants,

men below and toll their deaths; and as coffins roll below they adore the Machine — a god now, even to itself.

Cartoon Surrealism

In Max Fleischer's *Snow White* there is an amazing transition that illustrates a nascent kinship between animation and surrealism. The Queen/Witch glares down at Betty, and as a way of emphasizing her glaring eyes, Fleischer transforms her face into two fried eggs sitting in a frying pan. The transformation is so abrupt, so unexpected, that its displacing shock is stronger than its comic effect. We laugh, but warily.

The Fly, by Aleksander Marks and Vladimir Jutrisa of Zagreb Studio, has not the slightest comic touch. It is a mounting horror story, a nightmare that begins when a dull-faced man steps on a fly and the fly grows to a mammoth size, reversing the scale of fly to man. The huge fly smashes the world around the man, till he begins falling into blank, empty space. When he lands, it is to embrace the fly in an eerie marriage where both are the same size.

No doubt the most consciously surreal animator of recent times is Jan Lenica, a Polish artist whose masterpiece *Labyrinth* depicts a world haunted with empty spaces and replicas of a dead past. It is a disturbing film, of grotesques and of incidents that border on some mad dream. A dinosaur skeleton bays with a chilling hollow sound on an empty street. A flood of flies wisps into an empty refrigerator, which closes. Clocks turn backwards. A man in a bowler hat turns into a monster. He is set before a machine that burrows into his head, in some uncanny mockery of mind control. When he escapes at the end on wings he is attacked in the sky by batlike creatures with faces, and the final image shows him falling with skeletal wings. A somber film that leaves you disturbed, as if from a nightmare.

Snow White

Labyrinth

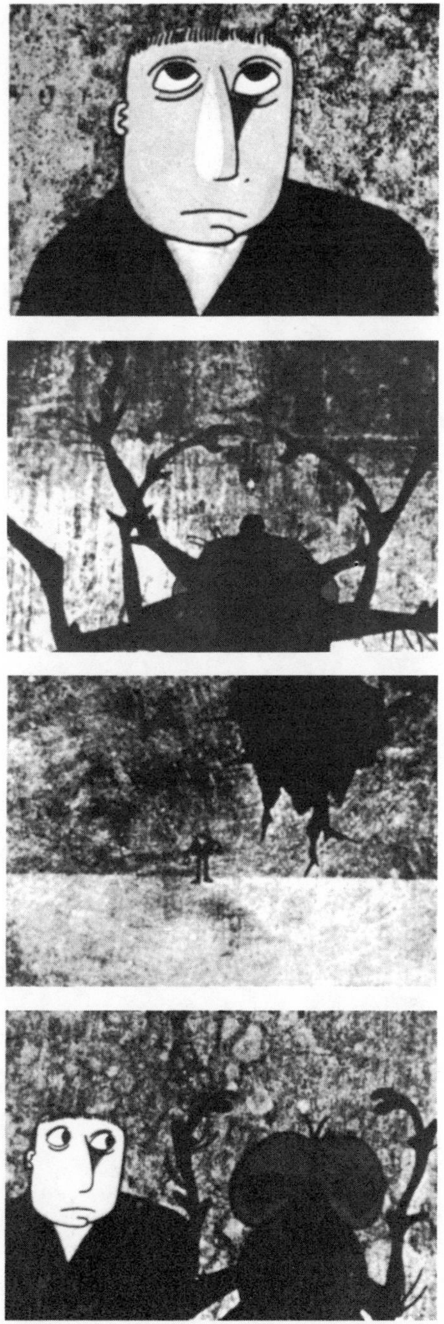

The Fly

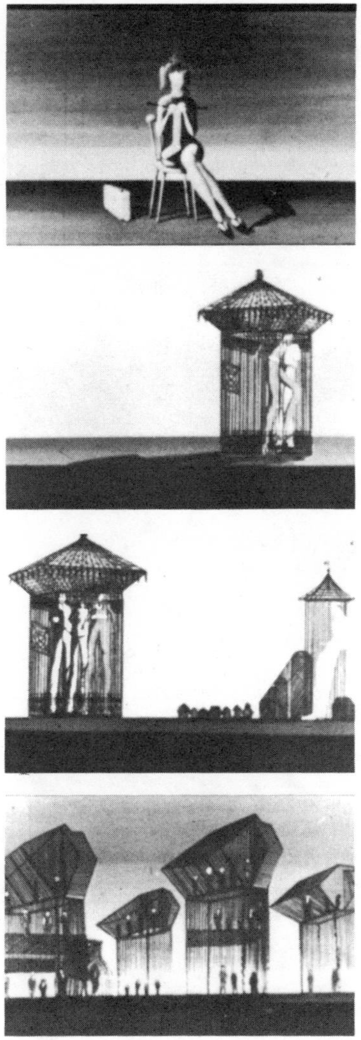

HOBBY

A woman sits knitting and occasionally snatches men from the air, from cars. She keeps them in a city of cages from which finally she releases them. Mordant, haunting. Featurette Studio, Poland.

TAMER OF WILD HORSES

A dour allegory about a horse trainer who meets a gigantic horse that becomes in turn a vast machine and a flying, mystical figure. Pungent, puzzling. Zagreb.

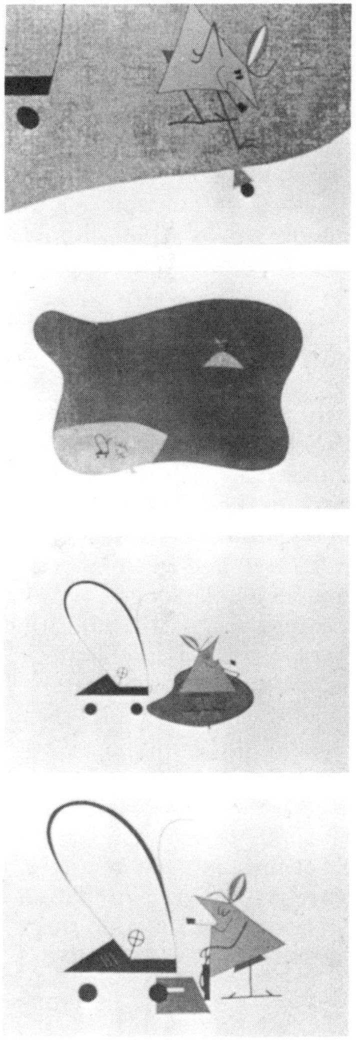

ERSATZ

A witty fable of a world in which everything, even its characters, can be inflated—and deflated. Leaving a scene, the character can deflate the world and inflate a new highway. Zagreb.

Live Animation

Norman McLaren has been for over thirty years one of the great innovators in animated filmmaking. He was one of the first to do direct painting on film stock—a technique now commonly practiced in schools all over the country. He pioneered the art of drawing the optical track, thereby creating types of totally unique sounds.

One of McLaren's most recent areas of experimentation lies in combining live film with animation techniques, in effect, creating from the raw stuff of the real world something other than realistic footage, frame by frame.

In *Pas de Deux* two exquisite dancers move through a ballet, but it is as though McLaren and his camera and his optical techniques are dancing as well, for by using stroboscopic effects and duplicating and overlapping the images, McLaren creates a sense of liquid motion. The dancers move, but their movements follow them, in a way that is vibrating, scintillating, rippling. Only when they pause do their repeated figures gradually subside, an effect that entices and delights the eye.

Pas de Deux enlivens the dance it records, broadens it, heightens our response to it, a masterful use of animation techniques to recreate the real world afresh.

Pas de Deux

The Graphics Film

As early as the mid-thirties, Oskar Fischinger (who proposed the idea of the film *Fantasia* to Disney and who, before leaving the project, designed one of its best sequences) was making films in which geometric forms moved smoothly through three-dimensional space. Fischinger was especially interested in the counterplay between moving images and music, how the images could come to interpret the soundtrack. His early experiments like "Composition in Blue," "Motion Painting #1" and "An American March" remain as fresh today as they were when he created them.

Fischinger's technique was animation. He painted the images on cels, then moved them subtly or repainted them, a staggering amount of work for a man to do alone, without studio facilities and crew. More recent graphics films rarely require this direct animation technique. Indeed, two modern masters of the graphics film, John Whitney and Jordan Belson, have developed their own techniques. Whitney has programmed an analog computer. Belson uses a variety of optical techniques and effects.

John Whitney, along with his brother James, has pioneered new possibilities of film art using the computer. "My computer program," he says, "is like a piano. I could continue to use it creatively all my life. The process which Whitney goes through in preparing one of his films is as arduous in its way as animation. Once a program is prepared for the computer, he must make fresh adjustments on the computer for every slight movement in the image—which is created electronically, on a cathode tube, like a TV set. The films are shot off the cathode tube, one frame at a time. Color is added later.

Yet Whitney's figures hardly suggest the laborious effort that goes into them. They move fluidly, vibrantly in space. Colors shift and change. Often, particularly in films like

Allures by Jordan Belson

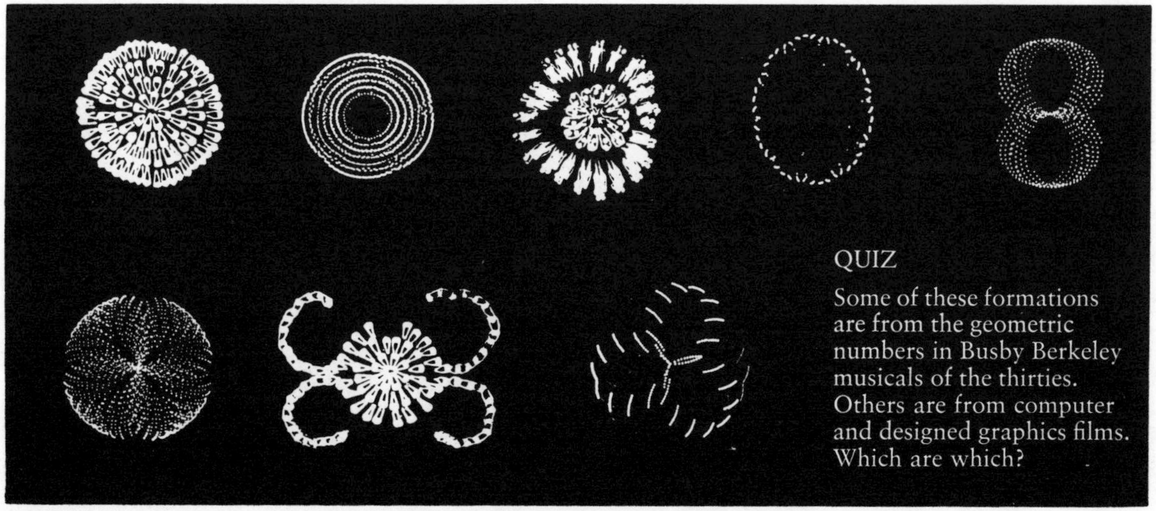

QUIZ

Some of these formations are from the geometric numbers in Busby Berkeley musicals of the thirties. Others are from computer and designed graphics films. Which are which?

Allures, Jordan Belson
Catalog, John Whitney
Experiments in Motion Graphics, John Whitney

Catalog and *Permutations,* the figures seem almost organic—living, pulsing creatures, perhaps from a distant galaxy. Whitney himself has often compared his work with music: "People talk about abstraction in graphics as being cold or inhuman. I just don't see that at all. What is a musical note? It's totally abstract . . . The essential problem with my kind of graphics must resemble the creative problem of melody writing."

Jordan Belson's films depend more on a variety of optical techniques than on a computer. And though they are as fluid and as three-dimensional as the films of Whitney, they are also more mysterious, hesitant, withdrawn. In *Allures,* Belson's masterpiece, the screen is black through most of the film. Figures emerge from the darkness, pressing toward the front of the screen, then gradually dissolve back into the darkness—like living things, with only the briefest of lifespans.

Belson, like Whitney, is particularly concerned about the integration of image and sound. His soundtracks seem at once harsh and eerie, distant and compelling. So well combined is the total effect of image and sound that Belson has said, "You don't know whether you're seeing or hearing it." In *Allures,* for example, a tiny rod of light wanders in circles round the center of the darkened frame while on the soundtrack there is a reverberating gonglike echo.

There is little question but that Fischinger, the Whitneys, and Belson have opened up a vast and promising new area of filmmaking, though one even more dependent on complex technologies than those of the past.

John Whitney at work on the pendulums which create synthetic sound for *Five Film Exercises.*

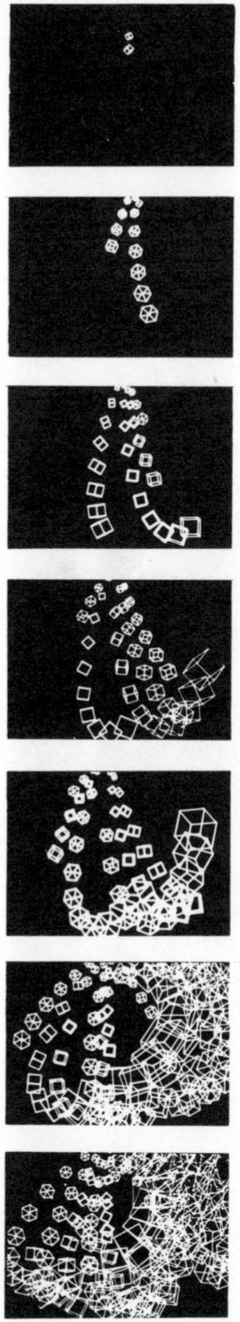

Whitney's *Matrix.*

CHAPTER TEN

Criticism

Criticism

The function of a good critic has little to do with persuading us to see or not to see a movie: that role is played (and overplayed) by the movie columnists of virtually every magazine and newspaper. A clue: it's almost never the serious critics whose names you'll find attached to quoted excerpts in the movie ads. Another clue: a good critic is better read *after* you've seen the movie, a columnist before. Ultimately the difference is a level of perceptiveness and intelligence that the best critics possess and which separates them unmistakably from the columnists.

Good film criticism is shrewd. If you're reading about a movie you've seen, a superb critic can make you suspect it's a movie you haven't quite seen. The references may point to scenes you'll recall, performances still etched in your mind. But what the critic makes of these scenes and performances won't be precisely what you made of them. The critic will either draw out inferences or relationships or qualities that you missed, or tug at something you barely noticed till he reveals a shabbiness or fakery that, under the spell of the movie, you were conned into accepting. With a good critic it's always a little more than his taste versus yours. He is able to draw your attention to qualities in the film that can be discerned, argued, interpreted separately from whether you simply liked them or didn't. Indeed, with the very best of film critics—say a Manny Farber or an André Bazin—you're sometimes left wondering whether in fact the critic did or didn't *like* the movie; but you're never left wondering about the nature and sources of its strengths and weaknesses.

Ultimately the best film criticism can teach us how to open ourselves to what's new and vital and strong in films, and how to overcome the treacheries of prejudice or boredom. Something in the antennae of a strong critic can get close to and under the surface of a movie and feel around inside that movie with an assurance matched perhaps only by director and writer. When a film expresses a unique sensibility, or when it attempts a daring use of technique that we've never encountered before, we're often put off. It's something we don't recognize, and therefore can't easily adjust to. The critic adjusts faster, and knows, by honed perception and seasoned judgment, when it's demeaning to adjust, when, in fact, the film is a very deceptive and engaging fluke.

The following are six samples of what this writer considers intelligent and acute film criticism. They have been chosen partly to introduce the reader to these critics, partly to show the differences—in personality, perspective, and logic—among possible approaches. Extremities are touched here: Manny Farber's brazen, gut-level style is a world away from André Bazin's subtle and carefully etched arguments. James Agee's essay on *The Treasure of the Sierra Madre* is as much tribute as criticism, but tribute of a high order. Compare it with Pauline Kael's shrewd and illuminating commentary on *The Godfather,* in which she admits the film's success on its own terms, but then probes deeper to get at some truth about those terms. Andrew Sarris' essay on *The Man Who Shot Liberty Valance,* by John Ford, reflects both the strengths and the limitations of the auteur theory (in which the director is considered total "author" of a film). Gerald Mast's piece on the Howard Hawks comedy *Bringing Up Baby* is a rich example of analytical criticism. In comparing it with *What's Up, Doc?* he showcases the robust comic vigor of the Hawks original, and the crutch-supported infirmities of Bogdanovich's remake.

JAMES AGEE

When James Agee died in 1955, America lost not only its most articulate and passionate film critic, but a major literary talent whose only two completed works (Let Us Now Praise Famous Men *and* A Death in the Family) *remain high proof of his genius for moving, sensitive prose. Agee brought that genius to the film criticism he wrote for* The Nation *and later, for* Time, *but he also brought the finally decisive credential of a first-rank film critic—an impassioned, unmitigated love affair with the movies. Agee could find something positive to say about every movie he reviewed, though he could as well rouse a metaphor to dispel any doubts about a film he deplored. Of a best-forgotten 1948 potboiler, he says a couple of moderately nice things, then comments, "Otherwise the picture deserves, like four or five other movies, to walk alone, tinkle a bell, and cry, 'Unclean, unclean.' "*

A rarity among critics, Agee was often at his consummate best in seeking out the strength of movies he admired, rather than excoriating the weaknesses of films he didn't. His essays on "The Golden Age of Comedy" and "The Undirectable Director" (John Huston) are classics, and indeed, his collected film reviews, Agee On Film, *deserves to be read for the breadth and clarity of his perceptions—above and beyond the movies (most of them forgotten) that he writes about. The following is his review of John Huston's* The Treasure of the Sierra Madre.

THE TREASURE OF THE SIERRA MADRE
by James Agee (1948)

Several of the best people in Hollywood grew, noticeably, during their years away at war; the man who grew most impressively, I thought, as an artist, as a man, in intelligence, in intransigence, and in an ability to put through fine work against difficult odds, was John Huston, whose *San Pietro* and *Let There Be Light* were full of evidence of this many-sided growth. I therefore looked forward with the greatest eagerness to the work he would do after the war.

His first movie since the war has been a long time coming, but it was certainly worth waiting for. *The Treasure of the Sierra Madre* is Huston's adaptation of B. Traven's novel of the same title. It is not quite a completely satisfying picture, but on the strength of it I have no doubt at all that Huston, next only to Chaplin, is the most talented man working in American pictures, and that this is one of the movie talents in the world which is most excitingly capable of still further growth. *The Treasure* is one of very few movies made since 1927 which I am sure will stand up in the memory and esteem of qualified people alongside the best of the silent movies. And yet I doubt that many people will fully realize, right away, what a sensational achievement, or plexus of achievement, it is. You will seldom see a good artist insist less on his artistry; Huston merely tells his story so straight and so well that one tends to become absorbed purely in that; and the story itself—a beauty—is not a kind which most educated people value nearly enough, today.

This story and Huston's whole handling of it are about as near to folk art as a highly conscious artist can get; both also approach the global appeal, to the most and least sophisticated members of an audience, which the best poetic drama and nearly all the best movies have in common. Nominally an adventure story, this is really an exploration of character as revealed in vivid action; and character and action yield revelations of their own, political, metaphysical, moral, above all, poetic. The story unfolds so pleasurably on the screen that I will tell as little as possible of it here. Three American bums of the early 1920s (Walter Huston, Humphrey Bogart, Tim Holt) run into lottery luck in Tampico and strike into the godforsaken mountains of Mexico in search of gold. The rest of the story merely demonstrates the development of their characters in relation to hardship and hard work, to the deeply primitive world these modern primitives are set against, to the gold they find, and to each other. It is basically a tragic story and at times a sickeningly harsh one; most of it is told as cheerfully brutal sardonic comedy.

This may be enough to suggest how rich the story is in themes, semi-symbols, possible implications, and potentialities as a movie. Huston's most wonderful single achievement is that he focuses all these elements as simply as rays in a burning-glass: all you see, unless you look sharp, is a story told so truly and masterfully that I suspect the picture's best audience is the kind of men the picture is about, who will see it only by chance.

But this single achievement breaks down into many. I doubt we shall ever see a film more masculine in style; or a truer movie understanding of character and of men; or as good a job on bumming, a bum's life, a city as a bum sees it; or a more beautiful job on a city; or a finer portrait of Mexico and Mexicans (compare it with all the previous fancy-filter stuff for a definitive distinction between poetry and poeticism); or a crueler communication of absolute desolateness in nature and its effect on men (except perhaps in *Greed);* or a much more vivid communication of hardship, labor, and exhaustion (though I wish these had been brutally and meticulously presented rather than skillfully sketched); or more intelligent handling of amateurs and semi-professionals (notably the amazing character who plays Gold-Hat, the bandit leader); or a finer selective eye for location or a richer understanding of how to use it; or scenes of violence or building toward violence more deeply authentic and communicative (above all in Huston's terrific use of listlessness); or smarter casting than that of Tim Holt as the youngest bum and that of Bruce Bennett as an intrusive Texan; or better acting than Walter Huston's beautiful performance; or subtler and more skillful collusions and variation of tempo (two hours have certainly never been better used in a movie); or a finer balance, in Ted McCord's perfect camera work, in every camera set-up, in every bit of editing, of unaffectedness, and sensitiveness. (As one fine example of that blend I recommend watching for the shot of Gold-Hat reflected in muddy water, which is so subtly photographed that in this noncolor film the hat seems to shed golden light.) There is not a shot-for-shot's sake in the picture, or one too prepared-looking, or dwelt on too long. The camera is always where it ought to be, never imposes on or exploits or over-dramatizes its subject, never for an instant shoves beauty or special meaning at you. This is one of the most visually alive and beautiful movies I have ever seen; there is a wonderful flow of fresh air, light, vigor, and liberty through every shot, and a fine athlete's litheness and absolute control and flexibility in every succession and series of shots. Huston shows that he is already capable of literally anything in movies except the profoundest kind of movie inventiveness, the most extreme kind of poetic concentration, artiness, soft or apathetic or sloppy or tasteless or excessive work, and rhetoric whether good or bad. His style is practically invisible as well as practically universal in its possible good uses; it is the most virile movie style I know of; and is the purest style in contemporary movies, here or abroad.

I want to say a little more about Walter Huston; a few thousand words would suit me better. Rightly or wrongly, one thing that adds to my confidence that the son, so accomplished already, will get better and better, is the fact that the father has done that, year after year. I can think of nothing more moving or happier than every instance in which an old man keeps right on learning and working, and improving, as naturally and eagerly as a child learns the fundamentals of walking, talking, and everything else in sight until his parents and teachers destroy his appetite for learning. Huston has for a long time been one of the best actors in the world and he is easily the most likable; on both counts this performance crowns a lifetime. It is an all but incredible submergence in a role, and transformation; this man who has credibly played Lincoln looks small and stocky here, and is as gaily vivacious as a water bug. The character is beautifully conceived and written, but I think it is chiefly Walter Huston who gives it its almost Shakespearean wonderfulness, charm, and wisdom. In spite of the enormous amount of other talent at large in the picture, Huston carries the whole show as deftly and easily as he handles his comedy lines.

There are a few weaknesses in the picture, most of which concern me so little I won't even bother to mention them. Traven's Teutonic or Melvillean excitability as a poet and metaphysician sometimes, I think, misleads him—and John Huston; magnificently as Walter Huston does it, and deeply as he anchors it in flesh and blood, the Vast Gale of Purifying Laughter with which he ends the picture strikes me as unreal, stuck-onto-the-character, close to arty; yet I feel tender toward this kind of cliché, if I'm right that it is one. One thing I do furiously resent is the intrusion of background-music. There is relatively little of it and some of it is better than average, but there shouldn't be any, and I only hope and assume that Huston fought the use of it. The only weakness which strikes me as fundamental, however, is deep in the story itself: it is the whole character of the man played by Bogart. This is, after all, about gold and its effects on those who seek it, and so it is also a fable about all human life in this world and about much of the essence of good and evil. Many of the possibilities implicit in this fable are finely worked out. But some of the most searching implications are missed. For the Bogart character is so fantastically undisciplined and troublesome that it is impossible to demonstrate or even to hint at the real depth of the problem, with him on hand. It is too easy to feel that if only a reasonably restrained and unsuspicious man were in his place, everything would be all right; we wouldn't even have wars. But virtually every human being carries sufficient of that character within him to cause a great deal of trouble, and the demonstration of that fact, and its effects, could have made a much greater tragicomedy—much more difficult, I must admit, to dramatize. Bogart does a wonderful job with this character as written (and on its own merits it is quite a character), miles ahead of the very good work he has done before. The only trouble is that one cannot quite forget that this is Bogart putting on an unbelievably good act. In all but a few movies one would thank God for that large favor. In this one it stands out, harmfully to some extent, for everything else about the picture is selfless.

It seems worth mentioning that the only thing which holds this movie short of unarguable greatness is the failure of the story to develop some of the most important potentialities of the theme. In other words, "Hollywood," for once, is accountable only for some minor flaws. This is what it was possible to do in Hollywood, if you were talented enough, had standing enough, and were a good enough fighter, during the very hopeful period before the November Freeze. God knows what can be done now. But if anybody can hope to do anything, I count on Huston, who made *San Pietro* and *Let There Be Light* as an army officer and *The Treasure of the Sierra Madre* as a Hollywood writer-director.

—(From *Agee on Film*, 1969, Grosset & Dunlap, reprinted with permission)

ANDRÉ BAZIN

Only recently, with the publication of his essays in English (What Is Cinema? *volumes I and II), has the late French critic André Bazin become well known in America. As a teacher and mentor, he guided the young men—Alain Resnais and François Truffaut and Jean-Luc Godard—who were to become the innovative directors of the sixties, transforming forever the face of movies in France. Bazin writes of film with a critical acuity and a fascination with aesthetic problems that draws you into some very basic issues about the nature of movie reality, the structure of the frame, the impositions of editing. He championed the "deep focus" approach to cinematography developed by Gregg Toland in* Citizen Kane *as the most momentous breakthrough in film-making since Griffith. His writings are trenchant, scrupulous, concise, and always guided by a shrewd use of argument. Writes Pauline Kael: "Bazin must be read for the beauty of his argument. He has a genius for argument. His great gift is that the argument does not stay on the page; the reader fights back, sometimes finding that Bazin has anticipated his objections and covered them in the next paragraph. He gets involved in a running battle that is an extraordinary, elating experience." The following is Bazin's essay on "The Evolution of the Western," drawn from* What is Cinema? Vol. II, *translated by Hugh Gray.*

THE EVOLUTION OF THE WESTERN
by André Bazin (circa 1955)

By the eve of the war the western had reached a definitive stage of perfection. The year 1940 marks a point beyond which some new development seemed inevitable, a development that the four years of war delayed, then modified, though without controlling it. *Stagecoach* (1939) is the ideal example of the maturity of a style brought to classic perfection. John Ford struck the ideal balance between social myth, historical reconstruction, psychological truth, and the traditional theme of the western *mise en scène*. None of these elements dominated any other. *Stagecoach* is like a wheel, so perfectly made that it remains in equilibrium on its axis in any position. Let us list some names and titles for 1939-1940: King Vidor: *Northwest Passage* (1940), Michael Curtiz: *The Sante Fe Trail* (1940), *Virginia City* (1940); Fritz Lang: *The Return of Frank James* (1940), *Western Union*, (1940); John Ford: *Drums Along the Mohawk* (1939); William Wyler: *The Westerner* (1940); George Marshall, *Destry Rides Again*, with Marlene Dietrich (1939).

This list is significant. It shows that the established directors, having perhaps begun their careers twenty years before with serial westerns made almost anonymously, turn (or return) to the western at the peak of their careers—even Wyler whose gift seemed to be for anything but this genre. This phenomenon can be explained by the widespread publicity given westerns between 1937 and 1940. Perhaps the sense of national awareness which preceded the war in the Roosevelt era contributed to this. We are disposed to think so, insofar as the western is rooted in the history of the American nation which it exalts directly or indirectly.

In any case, this period supports J.-L. Rieupeyrout's argument for the historical realism of the western.

But by a paradox more apparent than real, the war years, properly so-called, almost removed the western from Hollywood's repertoire. On reflection this is not surprising. For the same reason that the westerns were multiplied and admired at the expense of other adventure films, the war film was to exclude them, at least provisionally, from the market.

As soon as the war seemed virtually won and even before peace was definitely established, the western reappeared and was again made in large numbers, but this new phase of its history deserves a closer look.

The perfection, or the classic stage, which the genre had reached implied that it had to justify its survival by introducing new elements. I do not pretend to explain everything by the famous law of successive aesthetic periods but there is no rule against bringing it into play here. Take the new films of John Ford. *My Darling Clementine* (1946) and *Fort Apache* (1948) could well be examples of baroque embellishment of the classicism of *Stagecoach*. All the same, although this concept of the baroque may account for a certain technical formalism, or for the relative preciousness of this or that scenario, I do not feel that it can justify any further complex evolution. This evolution must be explained doubtless in relation to the level of perfection reached in 1940 but also in terms of the events of 1941 to 1945.

Let us call the ensemble of forms adopted by the postwar western the "superwestern." For the purposes of our exposé this word will bring together phenomena that are not always comparable. It can certainly be justified on negative grounds, in contrast to the classicism of the forties and to the tradition of which it is the outcome. The superwestern is a western that would be ashamed to be just itself, and looks for some additional interest to justify its existence—an aesthetic, sociological, moral, psychological, political, or erotic interest, in short some quality extrinsic to the genre and which is supposed to enrich it. We will come back later to these adjectives. But first we should indicate the influence of the war on the evolution of the western after 1944. The phenomenon of the superwestern would probably have emerged anyway, but its content would have been different. The real influence of the war made itself deeply felt when it was over. The major films inspired by it come, naturally, after 1945. But the world conflict not only provided Hollywood with spectacular scenes, it also provided and, indeed, forced upon it, some subjects to reflect upon, at least for a few years. History, which was formally only the material of the western, will often become its subject: this is particularly true of *Fort Apache* in which we see the beginning of political rehabilitation of the Indian, which was followed up by numerous westerns up to *Bronco Apache* and exemplified particularly in *Broken Arrow* by Delmer Daves (1950). But the profounder influence of the war is undoubtedly more indirect and one must look to find it wherever the film substitutes a social or moral theme for the traditional one. The origin of this goes back to 1943 with William Wellman's *Oxbow Incident,* of which *High Noon* is the distant relation. (However, in Zinnemann's film it is also a rampant McCarthyism that is under scrutiny.)

Eroticism also may be seen to be at least an indirect consequence of the war, so far as it derives from the triumph of the pin-up girl. This is true perhaps of Howard Hughes' *The Outlaw* (1943). Love is to all intents and purposes foreign to the western. *(Shane* will rightly exploit this conflict.) And eroticism all the more so, its appearance as a dramatic springboard implying that henceforth the genre is just being used as a foil the better to set off the sex appeal of the heroine. There is no doubt about what is intended in *Duel in the Sun* (King Vidor, 1946) whose spectacular luxury provides a further reason, albeit on formal grounds, to classify it as a superwestern.

Yet *High Noon* and *Shane* remain the two films that best illustrate the mutation in the western genre as an effect of the awareness it has gained of itself and its limits. In the former, Fred Zinnemann combines the effect of moral drama with the aestheticism of his framing. I am not one of those who turn up their noses at *High Noon.* I consider it a fine film and prefer it to Stevens' film. But the great skill exemplified in Foreman's adaptation was his ability to combine a story that might well have been developed in another genre with a traditional western theme. In other words, he treated the western as a form in need of content. As for *Shane* this is the ultimate in "superwesternization." In fact, with it, George Stevens set out to justify the western—by the western. The others do their ingenious best to extract explicit themes from implied myths but the theme of *Shane* is the myth. In it Stevens combines two or three basic western themes, the chief being the knight errant in search of his grail, and so that no one will miss the point, Stevens dresses him in white. White clothes and a white horse are taken for granted in the Manichean world of the western, but it is clear that the costume of Alan Ladd carries with it all the weighty significance of a symbol, while on Tom Mix it was simply the uniform of goodness and daring. So we have come full circle. The earth is round. The superwestern has gone so far beyond itself as to find itself back in the Rocky Mountains.

If the western were about to disappear, the superwestern would be the perfect expression of its decadence, of its final collapse. But the western is definitely made of quite other stuff than the American comedy or the crime film. Its ups and downs do not affect its existence very much. Its roots continue to spread under the Hollywood humus and one is amazed to see green and robust suckers spring up in the midst of the seductive but sterile hybrids that some would replace them by.

To begin with, the appearance of the superwestern has only affected the more out-of-the-ordinary productions: those of the A-film and of the superproduction. These surface tremors have not disturbed the commercial nucleus, the central block of the ultracommercial westerns, horseback or musical, which may even have found a second youth on television. (The success of Hopalong Cassidy is a witness to this and proves likewise the vitality of the myth even in its most elementary form). Their acceptance by the new generation guarantees them several more cycles of years to come. But low-budget westerns never came to France and we have to be satisfied with an assurance of their survival from the personnel of American distribution companies. If their aesthetic interest, individually, is limited, their existence on the other hand is probably decisive for the general health of the genre. It is in these "lower" layers whose economic fertility has not diminished that the traditional western has continued to take root. Superwestern or no superwestern, we are never without the B-western that does not attempt to find refuge in intellectual or aesthetic alibis. Indeed, maybe the notion of the B-film is open to dispute since everything depends on how far up the scale you put the letter A. The productions I am talking about are frankly commercial, probably fairly costly, relying for their acceptance only on the reputation of their leading man and a solid story without any intellectual ambitions. *The Gunfighter,* directed by Henry King (1950) and starring Gregory Peck, is a splendid example of this attractive type of production, in which the classic theme of the killer, sick of being on the run and yet forced to kill again, is handled within a dramatic framework with great restraint. We might mention too *Across the Wide Missouri,* directed by William Wellman (1951), starring Clark Gable, and particularly *Westward the Women* (1951) by the same director.

In *Rio Grande* (1951), John Ford himself has clearly returned to the semiserial format, or at any rate to the commercial tradition—romance and all. So it is no surprise to find on this list an elderly survivor from the pioneer days of old, Allan Dwan, who for his part has never forsaken the old Triangle style, even when the liquidation of McCarthyism gave him the chance to broaden the scope of the old-time themes *(Silver Lode,* 1954).

I have still a few more points to make. The classification I have followed up to now will turn out to be inadequate and I must no longer explain the evolution of the western genre by the western genre itself. Instead I must take the authors into greater account as a determining factor. It will doubtless have been observed that the list of relatively traditional productions that have been little influenced by the superwestern includes only names of established directors who even before the war specialized in fast-moving adventure films. It should come as no surprise that their work affirms the durability of the western and its laws. Howard Hawks, indeed, at the height of the vogue of the superwestern should be credited with having demonstrated that it had always been possible to turn out a genuine western based on the old dramatic and spectacle themes, without distracting our attention with some social thesis, or, what would amount to the same thing, by the form given the production. *Red River* (1948) and *The Big Sky* (1952) are western masterpieces but there is nothing baroque or decadent about them. The understanding and awareness of the means matches perfectly the sincerity of the story.

The same goes for Raoul Walsh, all due allowances being made, whose film *Saskatchewan* (1954) is a classical example of a borrowing from American history. But his other films provide me—and I am sorry if it is a little contrived—with the transition I was looking for: *Colorado Territory* (1949), *Pursued* (1947) and *Along the Great Divide* (1951) are, in a sense, perfect examples of westerns just above the B-level, made in a pleasantly traditional dramatic vein. Certainly there is no trace of a thesis. We are interested in the characters because of what happens to them and nothing happens that is not in perfect accord with the western theme. But there is something about them that, if we had no information about their date, would make us place them at once among more recent productions.

I have hesitated a great deal over what adjective best applies to these westerns of the fifties. At first I thought I ought to turn to words like "feeling," "sensibility," "lyricism." In any case I think that these words must not be dismissed and that they describe pretty well the character of the modern western as compared with the superwestern, which is almost always intellectual at least to the degree that it requires the spectator to reflect before he can admire. All the titles I am about to list belong to films that are, if not less intelligent than *High Noon* at least without *arrière-pensée,* and in which talent is always a servant of history and not of the meaning behind history. There is another word, maybe more suitable than those I have suggested or which provides a useful complement—the word "sincerity." I mean by this that the directors play fair with the genre even when they are conscious of "making a western." At the stage to which we have come in the history of the cinema naïveté is hardly conceivable, but although the superwestern replaces naïveté by preciousness or cynicism, we have proof that it is still possible to be sincere. Nicholas Ray, shooting *Johnny Guitar* (1954) to the undying fame of Joan Crawford, obviously knows what he is about. He is no less aware of the rhetoric of the genre than the George Stevens of *Shane,* and furthermore the script and the director are not without their humor; but not once does Ray adopt a condescending or paternalist attitude toward his film. He may have fun with it but he is not making fun of it. He does not feel restricted in what he has to say by the limits of the western even if what he has to say is decidedly more personal and more subtle than its unchanging mythology.

It is with an eye on the style of the narrative, rather than on the subjective attitude of the director to the genre, that I will finally choose my epithet. I say freely of the westerns I have yet to name—the best in my view—that they are "novelistic." By this I mean that without departing from the traditional themes they enrich them from within by the originality of their characters, their psychological flavor, an engaging individuality, which is what we expect from the hero of a novel. Clearly when one talks about the psychological richness of *Stagecoach,* one is talking about the way it is used and not about any particular character. For the latter we remain within the established casting categories of the western: the banker, the narrow-minded woman, the prostitute with a heart of gold, the elegant gambler, and so on. In *Run for Cover* (1955) it is something else again. The situation and characters are still just variations on the tradition, but what attracts our interest is their uniqueness rather than their generosity. We know also that Nicholas Ray always treats his pet subject, namely the violence and mystery of adolescence. The best example of this "novelization" of the western from within is provided by Edward Dmytryk in *Broken Lance* (1954), which we know is only a western remake of Mankiewicz's *House of Strangers.* For the uninformed, *Broken Lance* is simply a western that is subtler than the others with more individualized characters and more complex relationships but which stays no less rigidly within the limits of two or three classic themes. In point of fact, Elia Kazan has treated a psychologically somewhat similar subject with great simplicity in his *Sea of Grass (1947),* also with Spencer Tracy. We can imagine many intermediate grades between the most dutiful B-western and the novelistic western, and my classification is inevitably arbitrary.

Nevertheless I offer the following idea. Just as Walsh is the most remarkable of the traditional veterans, Anthony Mann could be considered the most classical of the young novelistic directors. We owe the most beautifully true western of recent years to him. Indeed, the author of *The Naked Spur* is probably the one postwar American director who seems to have specialized in a field into which others have made only sporadic incursions. In any case, each of Mann's films reveals a touching frankness of attitude toward the western, an effortless sincerity to get inside its themes and there bring to life appealing characters and to invent captivating situations. Anyone who wants to know what a real western is, and the qualities it presupposes in a director, has to have seen *Devil's Doorway* (1950) with Robert Taylor, *Bend of the River* (1952) and *The Far Country* (1954) with James Stewart. Even if he does not know these three films, he simply has to know the finest of all, *The Naked Spur* (1953). Let us hope that CinemaScope will not rob Anthony Mann of his natural gift for direct and discreet use of the lyrical and above all his infallible sureness of touch in bringing together man and nature, that feeling of the open air, which in his films seems to be the very soul of the western and as a result of which he has recaptured—but at the level of the hero of the novel and no longer of the hero of the myth—the great lost secret of the Triangle days.

The above examples show that a new style and a new generation have come into existence simultaneously. It would be both going too far and naïve to pretend that the novelistic western is just something created by young men who came to filmmaking after the war. You could rightly refute this by pointing out that this quality is evident in *The Westerner,* for example, and there is something of it in *Red River* and *The Big Sky.* People assure me, although I am personally not aware of it, that there is much of it in Fritz Lang's *Rancho Notorious* (1952). At all events it is certain that King Vidor's excellent *Man Without a Star* (1954) is to be placed in the same perspective, somewhere between Nicholas Ray and Anthony Mann. But we can certainly find three or four films made by the veterans to place alongside those that the younger men have made. In spite of everything, it is chiefly the newcomers who delight in the western that is both classic and novelistic: Robert Aldrich is the most recent and brilliant example of this with his *Apache* (1954) and especially his *Vera Cruz* (1954).

There remains now the problem of CinemaScope. This process was used for *Broken Lance, Garden of Evil* (1954) by Henry Hathaway (a good script at once classic and novelistic but treated without great inventiveness), and *The Kentuckian* (1955) with Burt Lancaster which bored the Venice Festival to tears. I only know one film in CinemaScope that added anything of importance to the *mise en scène,* namely Otto Preminger's *River of No Return* (1954), photographed by Joseph LaShelle. Yet how often have we not read or have even ourselves written that while enlarging of the screen is not called for elsewhere, the new format will renew the westerns whose wide-open spaces and hard riding call out for wide horizons. This deduction is too pat and likely sounding to be true. The most convincing examples of the use of CinemaScope have been in psychological films such as *East of Eden.* I would not go so far as to say that paradoxically the wide screen is unsuitable for westerns or that it adds nothing to them, but it seems to me already an accepted fact that CinemaScope will add nothing decisive to this field.

The western, whether in its standard proportions, in Vistavision, or on a super-wide screen, will remain the western we hope our grandchildren will still be allowed to know.

—(From *What Is Cinema?,* vol. 2, 1971, University of California Press, reprinted with permission)

MANNY FARBER

Manny Farber has been writing film criticism since the early forties. His style is adroit, spare, and—like the American action movies he likes best and can treat better than any critic alive—he's tough-edged and totally unsentimental. Dwight MacDonald calls him "an im-

possibly eccentric movie critic whose salvoes have a disturbing tendency to land on target." Beneath the hectic surfaces of Farber's prose there are perceptions so acute they can transform what you see on the screen. For example, he's profoundly conscious of the nature of space created by and within the frame. The book of his collected criticism is entitled Negative Space. *From its introduction: "Bresson deals in shallow composition as predictable as a monk's tonsure whereas Godard is a stunning de Stijlis using cutout figures of American flag colors asymmetrically placed against a flat white background. The frame of* The Wild Bunch *is a window into deep, wide, rolling Baroque space; almost every shot is a long horizontal crowded with garrulous animality."*

His sensitivity to the uses of space reveals some startling insights, but so does his recognition of implicit driving tendencies within the films of an era, and his razor-honed ability to discern whatever is rigged, forced, unfelt in a film. The following essay, "The Gimp," was written in 1952 and analyzes some trends in the postwar film with a prescience that makes many of his points in the essay remarkably valid for films being made today. Note his comments, toward the conclusion, on Citizen Kane. *They comprise one of the most maddeningly outrageous but eerily convincing commentaries on* Kane *ever written.*

THE GIMP
by Manny Farber (1952)

Somebody once told me, no doubt inaccurately, that lady golfers in the Victorian era used a certain gimmick that went by the name of "Gimp." It was a cord running from hem of skirt to waistband; when preparing to hit the ball, you flicked it with your little finger and up came the hem. Thus suddenly, for a brief instant, it revealed Kro-Flite, high-button shoes, and greensward, but left everything else carefully concealed behind yards of eyeleted cambric. Something like this device has now been developed in Hollywood. Whenever the modern film-maker feels that his movie has taken too conventional a direction and is neglecting "art," he need only jerk the Gimp-string, and—behold!—curious and exotic but "psychic" images are flashed before the audience, pepping things up at the crucial moment, making you think such thoughts as "The Hero has a mother complex," or "He slapped that girl out of ambivalent rage at his father image, which, he says, he carries around in his stomach," or "He chomps angrily on unlit cigarettes to show he comes from a Puritan environment and has a will of iron."

Over the past couple of years, one movie after another has been filled with low-key photography, shallow perspectives, screwy pantomime, ominously timed action, hollow-sounding voices. All this pseudo-undershot stuff, swiped from any and every "highbrow" work of films, painting, literature, has gone into ultraserious movies that express enough discontent with capitalist society to please any progressive. In these beautifully controlled Freud-Marx epics, the only things that really move are the tricks and symbols designed to make you think, "God, this is sensitive!"

Somehow the nature of this new mannerist flicker has been misinterpreted by critics, by the good ones as well as the merely earnest publicists. With their preconceptions, their ennui, and their formularized responses to stimuli, the critics go their complacent (or disgruntled) ways, finding movies better (or worse) than ever, but never noticing that movies *aren't* movies any more. Not so long ago, the movies, whatever their oversimplifications and distortions, still rested on the assumption that their function was to present some intelligible, structured image of reality—on the simplest level, to tell a story and to entertain, but, more generally, to extend the spectator's meaningful experience, to offer him a window on the real world. What are they now?

Well, icebergs of a sort, one-tenth image, action, plot, nine-tenths submerged popular "insights" *à la* Freud or Jung, Marx or Lerner, Sartre or Saroyan, Frost, Dewey, Auden, Mann, or whomever else the producer's been reading; or they are Dali painting, surrealist fun-houses with endless doors leading the spectator to inward "awareness" and self-consciousness, and far away from a simple ninety-cent seat in a simple mansion of leisure-time art and entertainment, or they are expressionistic shotguns peppering the brain of that deplored "escapist" with millions of equally important yet completely unrelated pellets of message—messages about the human personality and its relations to politics, anthropology, furniture, success, Mom, etc., etc. The trick consist in taking things that don't belong together, charging them up with hidden meanings, and then uniting them in an uneasy juxtaposition that is bound to shock the spectator into a lubricated state of mind where he is forced to think seriously about the phony implications of what he is seeing.

Most readers will remember the calculated moment in *Sunset Boulevard*—the kept man in the fashionable men's shop, ashamed of buying the vicuña coat with the ex-star's money. Up to a certain point, this scene was unfolded in a straight narrative line, and then Director Billy Wilder pulled his Gimp-string. The camera moved in for a very close close-up, the atmosphere became molecular and as though diseased—and there was a sleek clerk whispering to the slightly ill gigolo: "After all, if the lady is paying . . . ." Thus Wilder registered spiritual sickness and business-world corruption in an ad-libbed shot that had all the freshness of an old tire-patch, consisting as it did, under the circumstances, of naïve moral gibberish that no adult in his right mind would mouth. This indirect shot, with its leaden over-pantomiming going back to and beyond Theda Bara, offers a classic example of what the Gimp can do for a director, helping him avoid monotony (by switching from storytelling to symbolic "pseudoaction"), explaining hidden content, and ensuring his position in movies as a brave, intransigent artist.

One of the most confusing films of all time, *People Will Talk,* dealt with an unflaggingly urbane gynecologist, a liberal-minded doctor, who cured patients with friendliness, played with electric trains, scoffed at ration programs and packaged food, and generally behaved like a Lubitsch portrait of an enlightened college professor. One scene showed him making vague epigrams and looking down his nose at overconscientious notetakers in an anatomy class. Obviously all this suavity needed some excitement, and so Director Mankiewicz jerked his string and provided the well-analyzed doctor with a weird trick that you'll never see again in a movie. The doctor undrapes the corpse on the slab before him, and—surprise!—you are looking at a naked brunette, not only the most ravishing person in the movie but the whitest and least dead-looking. While the doctor talks on about heartless people and gracefully does things with the corpse's Godivalike tresses, the audience is so shocked by the beauty and lifelikeness of the corpse that it starts thinking all sorts of things about how society nags the individual, even unto death. (Visually, in the best Gimp tradition, this scene was bewitching for its pure unusualness; Cary Grant's classy erotic playing with the dead girl evokes a compound of evil, new kinds of sex, and terrific grace.)

The Gimp is the technique, in effect, of enhancing the ordinary with a different dimension, sensational and yet seemingly credible. Camera set-ups, bits of business, lines ("They don't make faces like that any more") are contrived into saying too much. Every moment of a movie is provided with comment about American society. "Original" characters are sought, the amount of illogical and implausible material is increased, to such a point that movies which try to be semidocumentary actually seem stranger than the Tarzan-Dracula-King Kong fantasy.

We are getting such characters as the abortionist in *Detective Story,* a close-mouthed Dutchman dressed like a low-paid respectable clerk from an early Sinclair Lewis story about department-store life in the Midwest. To make him look as though he has emerged from the bowels of common life in America, he is given a pinched, deathly pallor and a sickly personality that hardly allows him to breathe, much less talk. The apparent intention was to set up a significantly ordinary, true-to-life, entirely evil, grass-roots American; the result was a surrealistic creature who seemed ready at any moment to throw up. Thanks to the canny acting of George Macready, possibly Hollywood's most impressive character actor, this sour figure provided the film with its only good moments.

Two recent pictures have made especially adroit and unrelenting use of the Gimp. In *A Place in the Sun,* Director George Stevens, not content with letting a climax of violence follow naturally upon an inevitable train of events, treats us constantly to macabre darkenings of the landscape, metronome-timed hootings of a loon, and about six other sensational effects reeking with recondite significance. The story is about a not-quite-bright social climber, and Stevens so buries him in symbols of money, dominance, and sex that every last member of the audience must become involved with the vague meanings of the boy's daydreams. Wherever he walks, there is sex or wealth—usually both together—written out so big that no one can miss it: billboards that out-Petty Petty, languid and sophisticated aristocrats, a Gus Kahn love lyric coming from a midget radio. And of course his dingy furnished room in a depressed urban area must have a window facing on a huge neon factory sign standing for wealth and achievement.

In one protracted example of contrivance, a luscious babe in a Cadillac flashes by the boy as he hitchhikes on some spacious highway, and then comes a broken-down truck chugging straight out of *The Grapes of Wrath* to pick up the disappointed hiker. Immediately, the audience was saying to itself one or all of these things: "This is about the unfair distribution of wealth in the United States," or "His spirit is crying out for joy, ease, and love," or "He has a complex about being raised in a poor, harsh, confined neighborhood." Whenever any particularly delectable symbol crossed the boy's line of vision, he would freeze up with yearning, refusing to act, not answering questions for minutes on end, his wispy shoulders almost but not quite jerking, and occasionally one dead word straying out of his twisted mouth. There were eccentric scenes in which the boy met up with a deputy cop and a suspicious boatman, who—with the help of acting that was probably coached by Emily Brontë, and camera angles that gave the actors height and took away width—looked like ominous scoundrels from the Dark Ages and showed you Society intimidating the Outcast, American Justice breaking the Common Man on the wheel.

Symbols are a dime a dozen in Hollywood's storehouse, and Stevens bought up the stock: police sirens, train whistles, double shots of a boy's face and a remembered kiss, the lame leg of the sadistic district attorney (which makes him more formidable), a shadow going over a face to indicate an evil thought. Such things may seem to come from real life, but actually they are the products of medieval imaginations capable of grasping glaring features of contemporary life only in cliché terms. These creators have entrenched themselves within a vicious circle of decay: having helped to create and foster the world of lurid wealth, romantic love, and Big City glamour, they now express despair and chaos by exaggerating the same corny symbols they originally invented.

It has always been obvious that the movie camera not only reflects reality but interprets it. This fact used to imply the deepening and enrichment of an intelligible structure of plot and character. What is happening now is the complete disappearance of reality in the fog of interpretation: the underground "meaning" of every shot displaces the actual content, and the moviegoer is confronted with a whole crowd of undefined symbolic "meanings" floating entirely free. Shove the camera up against the pimple on an actor's face, and you automatically produce an image of immense importance: it will mean *something*—no matter if you don't know exactly what, and no matter if you have made it impossible to tell your story. Just as comedians now manufacture their humor out of immense card indexes of gags, so directors dip into their mental gag file of disconnected bits of social significance, amateur psychiatry, and visual shock effects.

In *A Streetcar Named Desire,* Elia Kazan pulls the Gimp-string so mercilessly that you never have one plain character or situation, but vast bundles of the most complicated sociological phenomena. For example, the hero, a sharp-witted Polish mechanic, conveys heavy passion by stuttering the first syllables of his sentences and mumbling the rest as though through a mouthful of mashed potatoes, a device that naturally forces the spectator to sociological speculation; disgusted with the fact that the hero has apparently been raised in a pigpen, the spectator is impelled to think about the relation of environment to individual development. Tennessee Williams' hero is getting ahead in his work, is a loving husband, makes "those colored lights" with his sexual genius, and is possessed of a delicate moral sensitivity. But all these bourgeois attributes have to be matched with their opposites for the sake of excitement, and so Kazan pulls his string and you see the Polack slobbering, licking his paws, howling like a troglodyte, hitting his wife so hard that he sends her to the maternity hospital, playing poker like an apeman, exuding an atmosphere of wild screams, rape, crashing china, and drunkenness. And to make sure every two-year-old will understand how bad life is in this Grimm's fairytale hovel, Kazan hammers his point home with continual sinister lights, dancing shadows, gaseous oozings.

With its freakish acting, nightmare sets, and dreamy pace, *Streetcar* may seem like traditional, Hollywood poeticism, but looked at more closely, it becomes very different from movies of the past, and in the same odd, calculated way as *A Place in the Sun, People Will Talk,* etc. For one thing, the drama is played completely in the foreground. There is nothing new about shallow perspectives, figures gazing into mirrors with the camera smack up against the surface, or low intimate views that expand facial features and pry into skin-pores, weaves of cloth, and sweaty undershirts. But there is something new in having the whole movie thrown at you in shallow dimension. Under this arrangement, with the actor and spectator practically nose to nose, any extreme movement in space would lead to utter visual chaos, so the characters, camera, and story are kept at a standstill, with the action affecting only minor details, e.g., Stanley's back-scratching or his wife's lusty projection with eye and lips. On the screen, these grimly controlled gestures appear huge, florid, eccentric, and somewhat sinister. Again, there is nothing new about shooting into incandescent lights and nebulous darks, but there is something new in having every shot snotted up with silvery foam, black smoke, and flaky patterns to convey decay and squalor. Never before has there been such a use of darkness in masses as we find in the new films (at least not since the Russians, who probably didn't have any lights). All this to jazz up a pseudodrama in which nothing really happens on the screen except dialogue in which you see two faces talking, then a close-up of the right speaker asking, then a close-up of the left speaker answering, then back to the two, etc. The spectator is aware that a story is being told, but mostly he feels caught in the middle of a psychological wrestling match.

Though there has never been so massive a concentration on technique, the fact is these films actually fail to exploit the resources of the medium in any real sense. Kazan, Stevens, and their colleagues have been shrinking films down to an almost babyish level in situation and grouping. With slumbrous camera movement, slow choreographies of action, sustained close-ups of enigmatic faces surrounded by areas of gloom, and drifting dialogue that seemed to come out of the walls, Stevens in *A Place in the Sun* had time only to unreel in grandiose terms a kiss, a seduction, and a drowning that would have taken him all of five minutes to examine with the straight storytelling technique he used in *Penny Serenade* and *Alice Adams,* both of which he made in the 1930's. *Streetcar,* for dramatic action, shows one big character—a neurotic Southern girl on the last lap to the mental ward—in one main situation: talk, talk, talk with an uninhibited couple in a two-room apartment. *The African Queen* was shot entirely in the Belgian Congo, but the characters do almost nothing that couldn't have been done on one studio set with the aid of some library shots.

Movies have seldom, if ever, been so physically overbearing in their effect. The scenarios are set up so that the story can be told with a small cast, little movement, and few settings. The camera fastens itself on the actors with such obsessive closeness that every moment becomes of overwhelming importance and threatens to disclose some terrifying psychic or emotional fact. The effect becomes even stronger and more curious when the actors occasionally move across the room and this all-revealing eye just barely moves to keep them in focus—as in *Something to Live For,* when a worried advertising ace paces his office, while the camera seems to move back and forth no more than a fraction of an inch. One has the feeling that nothing is any longer of importance except a magnification of face, gesture, and dress, and that these can tell you all you need to know about life in our time.

All this seems to have started in an exciting, if hammy, 1941 picture called *Citizen Kane.* This grim mixture of suspense thriller and tabloid obituary, in which most of the surface facts paralleled events in the career of William Randolph Hearst, combined the thunderous theatrical trickery of Orson Welles with a reckless use of darkish photography and funny angles by a top cameraman named Gregg Toland. Toland threw into the film every device ever written into the accomplished cameraman's handbook—everything from undercranking (to make the people in "newsreel" clips jerk and scuttle) to crane-shots, two-shots, floor-shots, and his favorite perspective shot in which figures widely spaced and moving far off down long rooms were kept as clearly in focus as the figure closest to the audience. This stuff helped make an exciting film, though marred by obvious items of shopworn inspiration: camera angles that had been thoroughly exploited by experimental films, and the platitudinous characterization of Kane as a lonely man who wanted love from the world but didn't get it because he had no love of his own to give. This unpeeling of a tycoon was clearly the most iconoclastic stroke in major studio production since the days when D. W. Griffith and his cameraman, Billy Bitzer, were freeing movies from imitation of the stage. Orson Welles' bold jumbling of techniques from theater, radio, and film led inevitably to a shock-happy work that anticipated everything that has become fashionable in American films.

Oddly enough, this film, which had the biggest cultural build-up before release since Eisenstein's Mexican film, made little impression at the time on Hollywood's veterans. Only in the 1950's did the ghost of *Citizen Kane* start haunting every A picture out of Hollywood. Before the advent of Orson Welles, the most important thing in motion-picture technique had been the story, the devising, spacing, and arranging of shots into a plot line that moved easily from one thing to another. Welles, more concerned with exhibiting his impudent showmanship and his deep thought about graft, trusts, yellow journalism, love, hate, and the like, fractured his story all along the line, until his film became an endless chain of stop effects. At every instant, the customer was encouraged to pause over some Kubla Khan setting, some portentously lit floor-shot of an actor, or some symbol (the falling-snow toy, the bird screaming in escape), and think in the terms of what it had to tell about a publisher's immoral pursuit of love-power-respect. The plot was simple enough: a famous man said something ("Rosebud") just before dying in his castle on a mountain, and "March of Time" sent out an inquiring reporter to make a story out of it. Eventually we did get the answer, not through the flashbacked memories of those interviewed —Kane's oldest friend, his newspaper manager, the girl, the butler in the castle—but in a final nerve-tingling shot, privy to the director and audience, of the "Rosebud" sled of Kane's lost, barren childhood. The story was presented in such complicated ways and made so portentous with the shadows of meaning cast off by a hundred symbols that you could read almost anything into it, including what Welles had put there. There were certain dramatic high points like the rough-cut in the "March of Time" projection room, the kid outside the window in the legacy scene, and the lurid presentation of an electioneering stage. But in between these was a great deal of talk, much less action, and almost no story.

Welles bequeathed to Hollywood, which had grown fat and famous on hurtling action films, a movie that broke up into a succession of fragments, each one popping with aggressive technique and loud, biased slanting of the materials of actual life. He told his story backward —which was nothing new—and slowed it even more by breaking it into four situations that didn't flow together but settled stiffly and ambiguously into a sort of parallel construction. He also complicated and immobilized each shot with mismated shock effects that had never been seen before in Hollywood. For example, the ominous figure of Kane was shown in the dark alongside a clearly lit pseudo-Grecian statue and a vast undone jigsaw puzzle that the cameraman had cleverly shot so that it seemed strewn over a marble floor. The spectator had trouble arranging these disparate items into a convincing visual whole, but his brain was mobilized into all sorts of ruminations about avarice, monomania, and other compulsions. Even the devices for moving the story along were complicating and interrupting: again and again, you went from the first part of a sentence spoken at one time and place to the last part of the same sentence spoken years later; this made one less conscious of time passing than of a director stopping time to play a trick on reality.

Welles also showed the Hollywood craftsmen how to inject trite philosophy, "liberalism," psychoanalysis, etc., into the very mechanics of moviemaking, so that what the spectator saw on the screen was not only a fat, contrived actor screaming down a staircase, but also some exotically rendered editorializing contributed by everyone from the actor to the set designer. The movie opened and closed on the iron fence around Kane's castle. In between this repetition, which spelled out the loneliness and baronial character of a tycoon, were similarly meaningful images: Kane in his castle among the boxed accumulations of his collecting; hopeful and innocent Kane gesticulating in front of a huge electioneering poster that showed him as a sinister demagogue. And always, practically on top of the cameraman, his unreal figure suggesting a blown-up cue ball adorned with the facial features of Fu Manchu, with nothing inside him but a Freudian memory giggling around in the fumes cast off by Welles' ideas about how an American big shot goes wrong.

The hidden meanings and the segmented narration were the two most obvious innovations of this film. Toland's camera provided the third, and it was anything but what you'd expect from a film that was advertised as using an unbound camera. Toland's chief contribution was a shallow concept of movie space. His camera loved crane-shots and floor-shots, but contracted the three dimensional aspect by making distant figures as clear to the spectator as those in the foreground. To accomplish this, Toland had to arrange his actors in widely spaced, parallel arrays across the screen. He also had to immobilize them and cut them off from the natural obscurations of scenery and atmosphere. His powerful lens did the rest. The spectator was faced with an image that exaggerated the importance of the figures it showed to a point where the deep space between them seemed to have been negated. The chief visual effect was the microscopically viewed countenance, one into which you could read almost anything. Almost as important was the static grouping of figures, amounting to a reversal of everything Hollywood had previously perfected in the creation of fluid groupings in unbounded space.

Citizen Kane and its Gimp-effects were generally laughed off by high-brows in Hollywood and elsewhere. Their opinion of the film was that it was too obviously theatrical and exhibitionistic to be linked to the main journalistic path of cinema. But one had the feeling, during the war years, that, as Hollywood turned out dozens of progressively more realistic action films—Western, war, detective—it was more than a little concerned with what Welles had done in the symbolic enriching of a movie through florid mannerisms. For Hollywood directors and actors couldn't forget that *Citizen Kane* was crazily three-dimensional in the manner of a psychoanalytic hour and that it did start you thinking at every moment of ambiguous drives hidden inside each character. *Citizen Kane* seems to have festered in Hollywood's unconscious until after the Wylers and Hustons returned from their government film chores; then it broke out in full force.

In the acclaimed films of the early postwar years (*The Lost Weekend, The Best Years of Our Lives, The Treasure of the Sierra Madre, Champion),* one began to see Welles' theatrical innovations effectively incorporated into certain films that otherwise tried to look like untouched records of reality. There still had to be a long training in what is known as "semi-documentary" technique (movies shot in real streets with nonstudio make-up, natural lighting, spontaneous pantomine) before Hollywood could link Welles' florid symbolism with enough of the appearance or actuality to make it appear moderately reasonable. But by now the lesson has been learned, and the ghost of *Citizen Kane* stalks a monstrous-looking screen. The entire physical structure of movies has been slowed down and simplified and brought closer to the front plane of the screen so that eccentric effects can be deeply felt. Hollywood has in effect developed a new medium which plays odd tricks with space and human behavior in order to project a content of popular "insights" beneath a meager surface.

Thus has a revolution taken place in Hollywood, probably unbeknownst to the very men—directors, actors, and critics—who have led it. If the significance of the New Movie is understood, it may well be that Hollywood will never be able to go home again. Any attempt to resurrect the old flowing naturalistic film that unfolds logically and takes place in "reasonable" space seems doomed to look as old-fashioned as the hoop skirt. For better or worse, we seem stuck with an absurdly controlled, highly mannered, overambitious creation that feeds on everything in modern art and swallows it so that what you see is not actually on the screen but is partly in your own mind, partly on the screen, and partly behind it. You have to read these pictures in a completely different way from the one you've been accustomed to. They are no longer literally stories or motion pictures, but a succession of static hieroglyphs in which overtones of meaning have replaced, in interest as well as in intent, the old concern with narrative, character, and action for their own sakes. These films must be seen, not literally, but as X-rays of the pluralistic modern mind. But the popular ideas deliberately half-buried in them have the hard, crude ring of Stone Age tools, though most of them come out of psychoanalysis and the Popular Front morality plays of the depression. The most ambitious of the current film-makers got their higher, and highest, education in the New York of the latter 1930's and have never lost the obsessive need to "improve" the world through art. They are by now too sophisticated and weary really to believe that this will work, but the hangover of conscience, regret, guilt, and frustration still produces in their movies the new Worried Look. They have lost the spirit and convictions of the radical 1930's, but the characteristic feelings of these years remain expressed vaguely in a bleak, humorless, free-floating, and essentially pointless misanthropy —social significance gone sour. They may be nothing wrong with misanthropy as a working viewpoint, but when, as in *A Place in the Sun,* it takes its conception of workers, tycoons, and debutantes from a world of ideas fantastically unrelated to current American experience, it is merely a negative sentimentality. The emotional impact of a technique committed to elegant, controlled, mismated power effects is as modern as ammoniated toothpaste; but the popular ideas to which this technique is wedded seem almost as dated and provincial as those in *Damaged Goods* or *A Fool There Was.*

—(From *Negative Space: Manny Farber on the Movies,* 1971, Praeger, reprinted with permission)

PAULINE KAEL

She can be adamant, abrasive, acute. No working critic can relegate a film to its deserved oblivion with quite the insouciance and wit of Pauline Kael. In the fifties she ran one of the first retrospective film theaters (in Berkeley), and in the early sixties began writing serious criticism. Her first book, I Lost It At The Movies, *immediately established her as one of the top-flight critics in America. Since, there have been several other collections:* Kiss Kiss Bang Bang, Going Steady, *and* Deeper Into Movies, *as well as a superbly researched and vigorous essay on the making of* Citizen Kane, *published along with Herman J. Mankiewicz' screenplay, in* The Citizen Kane Book. *Pauline Kael is extremely conscious of the audience as part of the entire film experience. She can describe the reactions of a lady sitting behind her with a novelist's shrewdly caught detail, and she can attack sham and pretension and affectation in films with such pungency and gusto that one suspects she may enjoy "getting even" with movies she doesn't like. Her appetite for movies seems inexhaustible. What she has seen colors the films she writes about. Kael can give historical resonance to an actress' inflections or a director's use of a baroque set in ways that make us itchy to see the earlier movies as well.*

No other critic seems to have been reared so completely, or so intelligently, on the movies. Kael is acutely conscious of fresh talent and accomplishment. She has championed such directors as Robert Altman, not simply because she's excited about their work, but partly as a conscious means of overcoming box-office and studio neglect. Her writing is boisterous, keen, polemical and observant; she can enter the life inside a movie with extraordinary sensitivity, as though it were no longer a movie; if a Balzac had written film criticism it might not be so different from Kael's. Miss Kael reviews films for The New Yorker. *Following is her essay on* The Godfather, *reprinted from* Deeper Into Movies.

ALCHEMY
by Pauline Kael (1972)

If ever there was a great example of how the best popular movies come out of a merger of commerce and art, *The Godfather* is it. The movie starts from a trash novel that is generally considered gripping and compulsively readable, though (maybe because movies more than satisfy my appetite for trash) I found it unreadable. You're told who and what the characters are in a few pungent, punchy sentences, and that's all they are. You're briefed on their backgrounds and sex lives in a flashy anecdote or two, and the author moves on, from nugget to nugget. Mario Puzo has a reputation as a good writer, so his potboiler was treated as if it were special, and not in the Irving Wallace-Harold Robbins class, to which, by its itch and hype and juicy *roman-à-clef* treatment, it plainly belongs. What would this school of fiction do without Porfirio Rubirosa, Judy Garland, James Aubrey, Howard Hughes, and Frank Sinatra? The novel *The Godfather,* financed by Paramount during its writing, features a Sinatra stereotype, and sex and slaughter, and little gobbets of trouble and heartbreak. It's gripping, maybe, in the same sense that Spiro Agnew's speeches were a few years back. Francis Ford Coppola, who directed the film, and wrote the script with Puzo, has stayed very close to the book's greased-lightning sensationalism and yet has made a movie with the spaciousness and strength that popular novels such as Dickens' used to have. With the slop and sex reduced and the whoremongering guess-who material minimized ("Nino," who sings with a highball in his hand, has been weeded out), the movie bears little relationship to other adaptations of books of this kind, such as *The Carpetbaggers* and *The Adventurers.* Puzo provided what Coppola needed: a storyteller's outpouring of incidents and details to choose from, the folklore behind the headlines, heat and immediacy, the richly familiar. And Puzo's shameless turn-on probably left Coppola looser than if he had been dealing with a better book; he could not have been cramped by worries about how best to convey its style. Puzo, who admits he was out to make money, wrote "below my gifts," as he puts it, and one must agree. Coppola uses his gifts to reverse the process—to give the public the best a movie-maker can do with this very raw material. Coppola, a young director who has never had a big hit, may have done the movie for money, as *he* claims—in order to make the pictures he really wants to make, he says—but this picture was made at peak capacity. He has salvaged Puzo's energy and lent the narrative dignity. Given the circumstances and the rush to complete the film and bring it to market, Coppola has not only done his best but pushed himself farther than he may realize. The movie is on the heroic scale of earlier pictures on broad themes, such as *On the Waterfront, From Here to Eternity,* and *The Nun's Story.* It offers a wide, startlingly vivid view of a Mafia dynasty. The abundance is from the book; the quality of feeling is Coppola's.

The beginning is set late in the summer of 1945; the film's roots, however, are in the gangster films of the early thirties. The plot is still about rival gangs murdering each other, but now we see the system of patronage and terror, in which killing is a way of dealing with the competition. We see how the racketeering tribes encroach on each other and why this form of illegal business inevitably erupts in violence. We see the ethnic sub-culture, based on a split between the men's conception of their responsibilities—all that they keep dark—and the sunny false Eden in which they try to shelter the women and children. The thirties films indicated some of this, but *The Godfather* gets into it at the primary level; the willingness to be basic and the attempt to understand the basic, to look at it without the usual preconceptions, are what give this picture its epic strength.

The visual scheme is based on the most obvious life-and-death contrasts; the men meet and conduct their business in deep-toned, shuttered rooms, lighted by lamps even in the daytime, and the story moves back and forth between this hidden, nocturnal world and the sunshine that they share with the women and children. The tension is in the meetings in the underworld darkness; one gets the sense that this secret life has its own poetry of fear, more real to the men (and perhaps to the excluded women also) than the sunlight world outside. The dark-and-light contrast is so operatic and so openly symbolic that it perfectly expresses the basic nature of the material. The contrast is integral to the Catholic background of the characters: innocence versus knowledge—knowledge in this sense being the same as guilt. It works as a visual style, because the Goyaesque shadings of dark brown into black in the interiors suggest (no matter how irrationally) an earlier period of history, while the sunny, soft-edge garden scenes have their own calendar-pretty pastness. Nino Rota's score uses old popular songs to cue the varying moods, and at one climactic point swells in a crescendo that is both Italian opera and pure-forties movie music. There are rash, foolish acts in the movie but no acts of individual bravery. The killing, connived at in the darkness, is the secret horror, and it surfaces in one bloody outburst after another. It surfaces so often that after a while it doesn't surprise us, and the recognition that the killing is an integral part of business policy takes us a long way from the fantasy outlaws of old movies. These gangsters don't satisfy our adventurous fantasies of disobeying the law; they're not defiant, they're furtive and submissive. They are required to be more obedient than we are; they live by taking orders. There is no one on the screen we can identify with—unless we take a fancy to the pearly teeth of one shark in a pool of sharks.

Even when the plot strands go slack about two-thirds of the way through, and the passage of a few years leaves us in doubt whether certain actions have been concluded or postponed, the picture doesn't become softheaded. The direction is tenaciously intelligent. Coppola holds on and pulls it all together. The trash novel is there underneath, but he attempts to draw the patterns out of the particulars. It's amazing how encompassing the view seems to be—what a sense you get of a broad historical perspective, considering that the span is only from 1945 to the mid-fifties, at which time the Corleone family, already forced by competitive pressures into dealing in narcotics, is moving its base of operations to Las Vegas.

The enormous cast is headed by Marlon Brando as Don Vito Corleone, the "godfather" of a powerful Sicilian-American clan, with James Caan as his hothead son, Sonny, and Al Pacino as the thoughtful, educated son, Michael. Is Brando marvellous? Yes, he is, but then he often is; he was marvellous a few years ago in *Reflections in a Golden Eye,* and he's shockingly effective as a working-class sadist in a current film, *The Nightcomers,* though the film itself isn't worth seeing. The role of Don Vito—a patriarch in his early sixties—allows him to release more of the gentleness that was so seductive and unsettling in his braggart roles. Don Vito could be played as a magnificent old warrior, a noble killer, a handsome bull-patriarch, but Brando manages to debanalize him. It's typical of Brando's daring that he doesn't capitalize on his broken-prow profile and the massive, sculptural head that has become the head of Rodin's Balzac—he doesn't play for statuesque nobility. The light, cracked voice comes out of a twisted mouth and clenched teeth; he has the battered face of a devious, combative old man, and a pugnacious thrust to his jaw. The rasp in his voice is particularly effective after Don Vito has been wounded; one almost feels that the bullets cracked it, and wishes it hadn't been cracked before. Brando interiorizes Don Vito's power, makes him less physically threatening and *deeper,* hidden within himself.

Brando's acting has mellowed in recent years; it is less immediately exciting than it used to be, because there's not the sudden, violent discharge of emotion. His effects are subtler, less showy, and he gives himself over to the material. He appears to have worked his way beyond the self-parody that was turning him into a comic, and that sometimes left the other performers dangling and laid bare the script. He has not acquired the polish of most famous actors; just the opposite—less mannered as he grows older, he seems to draw directly from life, and from himself. His Don is a primitive sacred monster, and the more powerful because he suggests not the strapping sacred monsters of movies (like Anthony Quinn) but actual ones—those old men who carry never-ending grudges and ancient hatreds inside a frail frame, those monsters who remember minute details of old business deals when they can no longer tie their shoelaces. No one has aged better on camera than Brando; he gradually takes Don Vito to the close of his life, when he moves into the sunshine world, a sleepy monster, near to innocence again. The character is all echoes and shadings, and no noise; his strength is in that armor of quiet. Brando has lent Don Vito some of his own mysterious, courtly reserve: the character is not explained; we simply assent to him and believe that, yes, he could become a king of the underworld. Brando doesn't dominate the movie, yet he gives the story the legendary presence needed to raise it above gang warfare to archetypal tribal warfare.

Brando isn't the whole show; James Caan is very fine, and so are Robert Duvall and many others in lesser roles. Don Vito's sons suggest different aspects of Brando—Caan's Sonny looks like the muscular young Brando but without the redeeming intuitiveness, while as the heir, Michael, Al Pacino comes to resemble him in manner and voice. Pacino creates a quiet, ominous space around himself; his performance—which is marvellous, too, big yet without ostentation—complements Brando's. Like Brando in this film, Pacino is simple; you don't catch him acting, yet he manages to change from a small, fresh-faced, darkly handsome college boy into an underworld lord, becoming more intense, smaller, and more isolated at every step. Coppola doesn't stress the father-and-son links; they are simply there for us to notice when we will. Michael becomes like his father mostly from the inside, but we also get to see how his father's face was formed (Michael's mouth gets crooked and his cheeks jowly, like his father's, after his jaw has been smashed). Pacino has an unusual gift for conveying the divided spirit of a man whose calculations often go against his inclinations. When Michael, warned that at a certain point he must come out shooting, delays, we are left to sense his mixed feelings. As his calculations will always win out, we can see that he will never be at peace. The director levels with almost everybody in the movie. The women's complicity in their husband's activities is kept ambiguous, but it's naggingly there—you can't quite ignore it. And Coppola doesn't make the subsidiary characters lovable; we look at Clemenza (Richard Castellano) as objectively when he is cooking spaghetti as we do when he is garrotting a former associate. Many of the actors (and the incidents) carry the resonances of earlier gangster pictures, so that we almost unconsciously place them in the prehistory of this movie. Castellano, with his resemblance to Al Capone and Edward G. Robinson (plus a vagrant streak of Oscar Levant), belongs in this atmosphere; so does Richard Conte (as Barzini), who appeared in many of the predecessors of this movie, including *House of Strangers,* though perhaps Al Lettieri (as Sollozzo) acts too much like a B-picture hood. And perhaps the director goes off key when Sonny is blasted and blood-splattered at a toll booth; the effect is too garish.

The people dress in character and live in character—with just the gewgaws that seem right for them. The period details are there—a satin pillow, a modernistic apartment-house lobby, a child's pasted-together greeting to Grandpa—but Coppola doesn't turn the viewer into a guided tourist, told what to see. Nor does he go in for a lot of closeups, which are the simplest tool for fixing a director's attitude. Diane Keaton (who plays Michael's girl friend) is seen casually; her attractiveness isn't labored. The only character who is held in frame for us to see exactly as the character looking at her sees her is Apollonia (played by Simonetta Stefanelli), whom Michael falls in love with in Sicily. She is fixed by the camera as a ripe erotic image, because that is what she means to him, and Coppola, not having wasted his resources, can do it in a few frames. In general, he tries not to fix the images. In *Sunday Bloody Sunday,* John Schlesinger showed a messy knocked-over ashtray being picked up in closeup, so that there was nothing to perceive in the shot but the significance of the messiness. Coppola, I think, would have kept the camera on the room in which the woman bent over to retrieve the ashtray, and the messiness would have been just one element among many to be observed—perhaps the curve of her body could have told us much more than the actual picking-up motion. *The Godfather* keeps so much in front of us all the time that we're never bored (though the picture runs just two minutes short of three hours)—we keep taking things in. This is a heritage from Jean Renoir—this uncoercive, "open" approach to the movie frame. Like Renoir, Coppola lets the spectator roam around in the images, lets a movie breathe, and this is extremely difficult in a period film, in which every detail must be carefully planted. But the details never look planted: you're a few minutes into the movie before you're fully conscious that it's set in the past.

When one considers the different rates at which people read, it's miraculous that films can ever solve the problem of a pace at which audiences can "read" a film together. A hack director solves the problem of pacing by making only a few points and making those so emphatically that the audience can hardly help getting them (this is why many of the movies from the studio-system days are unspeakably insulting); the tendency of a clever, careless director is to go too fast, assuming that he's made everything clear when he hasn't, and leaving the audience behind. When a film has as much novelistic detail as this one, the problem might seem to be almost insuperable. Yet, full as it is, *The Godfather* goes by evenly, so we don't feel rushed, or restless, either; there's classic grandeur to the narrative flow. But Coppola's attitudes are specifically modern—more so than in many films with a more jagged surface. Renoir's openness is an expression of an almost pagan love of people and landscape; his style is an embrace. Coppola's openness is a reflection of an exploratory sense of complexity; he doesn't feel the need to comment on what he shows us, and he doesn't want to reduce the meanings in a shot by pushing us this way or that. The assumption behind this film is that complexity will engage the audience.

These gangsters *like* their life style, while we—seeing it from the outside—are appalled. If the movie gangster once did represent, as Robert Warshow suggested in the late forties, "what we want to be and what we are afraid we may become," if he expressed "that part of the American psyche which rejects the qualities and the demands of modern life, which rejects 'Americanism' itself," that was the attitude of another era. In *The Godfather* we see organized crime as an obscene symbolic extension of free enterprise and government policy, an extension of the worst in America—its feudal ruthlessness. Organized crime is not a rejection of Americanism, it's what we fear Americanism to be. It's our nightmare of the American system. When "Americanism" was a form of cheerful, bland official optimism, the gangster used to be destroyed at the end of the movie and our feelings resolved. Now the mood of the whole country has darkened, guiltily; nothing is resolved at the end of *The Godfather,* because the family business goes on. Terry Malloy didn't clean up the docks at the end of *On the Waterfront;* that was a lie. *The Godfather* is popular melodrama, but it expresses a new tragic realism.

—(From *Deeper Into Movies,* 1973, Atlantic Monthly Press, reprinted with permission)

ANDREW SARRIS

Andrew Sarris has had inestimable influence in America, less as a critic specifically than for the cause his criticism has come to champion: the auteur *theory, an approach to film criticism and film scholarship that focuses on directors as the major creative forces behind movies, and in which movies are analyzed, interpreted, examined for what they reveal of the director's personality or style or outlook. To quote Sarris himself from his manifesto on* auteurism, *the Introduction to* The American Cinema: *"Ultimately the auteur theory is not so much a theory as an attitude, a table of values that converts film history into directorial autobiography. The auteur critic is obsessed with the wholeness of art and the artist. He looks at a film as a whole, a director as a whole. The parts, however entertaining individually, must cohere meaningfully."*

There are advantages (the most striking being an awareness of the continuities that run through a strong director's work) and disadvantages (the elevation of consistent hacks to artistic stature while talented men with a zest for new directions go ignored) to the auteur approach to film criticism. In Sarris's review of The Man Who Shot Liberty Valance *one can see how auteurism can work both ways for a critic as natively good as Sarris. In extolling the film, he leans over backwards to extol it in terms that relate to the rest of Ford's work. There are some striking insights, and some overreached conclusions. Mr. Sarris, who teaches at Columbia University, has published two books of criticism.* Confessions of a Cultist, *and* The Primal Screen *(from which the following review has been taken).*

THE MAN WHO SHOT LIBERTY VALANCE
by Andrew Sarris (1962)

The Man Who Shot Liberty Valance is a political western, a psychological mystery and John Ford's confrontation of the past—personal, professional and historical. The title itself suggests a multiplicity of functions. "The man who" marks the traditional peroration of American nominating conventions and has been used in the titles of more than fifty American films. In addition to evoking past time, "shot" may imply a duel, a murder or an assassination. "Liberty Valance" suggests an element of symbolic ambiguity. This is all *a priori*. After the film has unfolded, the title is reconstituted as bitter irony. The man who apparently shot Liberty Valance is not the man who really shot Liberty Valance. Appearance and reality? Legend and fact? There is that and more although it takes at least two viewings of the film to confirm Ford's intentions and at least a minimal awareness of a career ranging over 122 films in nearly half a century to detect the reverberations of his personality.

The opening sequences are edited with the familiar incisiveness of a director who cuts in the camera and hence in the mind. James Stewart and Vera Miles descend from a train which has barely puffed its way into the twentieth century. Their powdered make-up suggests that all the meaningful action of their lives is past. The town is too placid, the flow of movement too stately and the sunlight bleaches the screen with an intimation of impending nostalgia. An incredibly aged Andy Devine is framed against a slightly tilted building which is too high and too fully constructed to accommodate the violent expectations of the genre. The remarkable austerity of the production is immediately evident. The absence of extras and the lack of a persuasive atmosphere forces the spectator to concentrate on the archetypes of the characters. Ford is well past the stage of the reconstructed documentaries *(My Darling Clementine)* and the visually expressive epics *(She Wore a Yellow Ribbon)*. His poetry has been stripped of the poetic touches which once fluttered across the meanings and feelings of his art. Discarding all the artifices of surface realism, Ford has attained the abstract purity of a Renoir. James Stewart and Vera Miles are more than a Western Senator and his lady returning to the West. Ford's brush strokes of characterization seem broader than ever. Stewart's garrulous pomposity as the successful politician intensifies his wife's moody silence. She greets Andy Devine with a mournful intensity which introduces the psychological mystery of the film. Devine, Ford's broad-beamed Falstaff, must stand extra guard duty for the late Ward Bond and Victor McLaglen. Ford, the strategist of retreats and last stands, has outlived the regulars of his grand army.

Stewart seizes the opportunity to be interviewed by the local editor and his staff and entrusts his wife to Devine, who takes her in a buckboard to the ruins of a house in the desert. They sit in quiet, mysterious rapport until Devine descends to pick a wild cactus rose. Stewart is concluding his interview in the newspaper office when, through the window, the buckboard enters the frame of the film. We have returned to the classic economy of Stroheim's silent cinema where the action invaded the rigid frame and detail montage took it from there. However, Ford reverses the lateral direction of the film up to this point to lead his characters into an undertaker's shop, where they are reunited with Woody Strode, also artificially aged.

A man is lying in a coffin. We never see him, but we learn that his boots have been removed, that he is being buried without his gun belt and that, in fact, he has not worn his gun belt in years. Although we never see the corpse, we feel the presence of the man. The mood of irrevocable loss and stilled life becomes so oppressive that the editor (and the audience) demand an explanation. At a nod from his wife, Stewart walks into the next room away from the mourners, away from the present into the past. Just as Vera Miles begins to open her hat box, there is a cut to Stewart introducing the flashback by placing his hand on a historical prop, a dismantled, dust-ridden stagecoach. From the cut from the hat box to that climactic moment nearly two hours later when we see a cactus rose on the coffin, the cinema of John Ford intersects the cinema of Orson Welles. As Hitchcock and Hawks are directors of space, Ford and Welles are directors of time, the here and there, as it were, opposed to the then and now.

It is hardly surprising that the plot essence of the flashback is less important than the evocations of its characters. Whatever one thinks of the *auteur* theory, the individual films of John Ford are inextricably linked in an awesome network of meanings and associations. When we realize that the man in the coffin is John Wayne, the John Wayne of *Stagecoach, The Long Voyage Home, They Were Expendable, Fort Apache, She Wore a Yellow Ribbon, Rio Grande, Three Godfathers, The Quiet Man, The Searchers* and *Wings of Eagles*, the one-film-at-a-time reviewer's contention that Wayne is a bit old for an action plot becomes absurdly superficial. *The Man Who Shot Liberty Valance* can never be fully appreciated except as a memory film, the last of its kind, perhaps, from one of the screen's old masters.

The first sequence of the flashback is photographed against a studio-enclosed skyscape far from the scenic temptations of the great outdoors. A stagecoach is held up almost entirely in close-up. Again this is not a stagecoach but *the* stagecoach. James Stewart, an idealistic dude lawyer from the East, gallantly defends Anna Lee, a Fordian lady since *How Green Was My Valley*, and is brutally flogged for his trouble by Liberty Valance, a hireling of the cattle interests. Indeed, Lee Marvin and his equally psychotic henchmen convey an image of evil so intense that the unwary spectator may feel that the film is drifting into the Manichean conventions of horse opera. Unlike Welles and Hitchcock, Ford has never exploited Murnau's expressive camera movements which are capable of reversing moral relationships. Liberty Valance will be as much of a mad dog at the end as he is at the beginning. Every entrance he will make will be outrageous, but whip, gun and all, he represents something more than the pure villainy of the whining killers in *Wagonmaster*. As a political instrument of reactionary interests, Liberty Valance represents the intransigent individualism which Stewart is dedicated to destroy. However, Marvin and Wayne are opposite sides of the same coin, and when Wayne kills Marvin to save Stewart for Vera Miles, he destroys himself. Burning down the house in the desert he had built for his bride, he is washed away by the stream of history. Wayne is seen for the last time walking away from a tumultuous convention about to nominate Stewart as the man who shot Liberty Valance.

Ford's geography is etched in as abstractly as his politics. We are told that the cattle interests operate north of the picket line, but we never see the picket line, and we never have a clear concept of the points of the compass. We are treated to a territorial convention without any explicit designation of the territory seeking statehood. (One may deduce one of the territories in the Southwest, Arizona or New Mexico, from the sympathetic presence of a Spanish-American contingent.) The alignment of farmers, merchants and townspeople against the ranchers is represented by scattered Ford types—Edmond O'Brien with the drunken eloquence of a newspaper editor sent west by Horace Greeley, John Qualen with the dogged tenacity of a Swedish immigrant, Ken Murray with the harsh fatalism of a frontier doctor. Even lower on the credit roster one sees the familiar Ford gallery of scrambling humanity. There is still the same proportion of low humor, still disconcerting to some, derived from gluttony, drunkenness, cowardice and vainglory. Through the entire flashback Andy Devine fulfills his duties as town marshal by cowering behind doorways to avoid Liberty Valance. Yet, Devine's mere participation in the fierce nobility of the past magnifies his character in retrospect. For Ford, there is some glory in just growing old and remembering through the thick haze of illusion.

Godard's neo-classical political collage in *Le Petit Soldat* is matched by Ford in a schoolroom scene where Stewart is framed against a picture of Washington and Woody Strode against a picture of Lincoln. Ford's obviousness transcends the obvious in the context of his career. For a director who began his career the year after Arizona and New Mexico were admitted to the Union, the parallel ambiguities of personal and social history project meanings and feelings beyond the immediate association of images. No American director has ranged so far across the landscape of the American past, the worlds of Lincoln, Lee, Twain, O'Neill, the three great wars, the western and transatlantic migrations, the horseless Indians of the Mohawk Valley and the Sioux and Comanche cavalries of the West, the Irish and Spanish incursions and the delicately balanced politics of polyglot cities and border states.

In accepting the inevitability of the present while mourning the past, Ford is a conservative rather than a reactionary. What he wishes to conserve are the memories of old values even if they have to be magnified into legends. The legends with which Ford is most deeply involved, however, are the legends of honorable failure, of otherwise forgotten men and women who rode away from glory toward self-sacrifice. In what is perhaps the last political assemblage Ford will record, John Carradine, the vintage ham of the Ford gallery, matches his elocutionary talents on behalf of the cattle interests against Edmond O'Brien's more perceptive expression of a new civilization. When Carradine has concluded, a cowboy rides up the aisle and onto the speaker's rostrum to lasso the rancher's candidate. This inspired bit of literal horseplay suggests a twinge of regret in the director's last hurrah for a lost cause. Shortly thereafter, Wayne strides out of the film past a forlorn campaign poster opposing statehood.

The shooting of Liberty Valance is shown twice from two different points of view. Even Kurosawa can be superficially clever with this sort of subjective maneuver. Ford's juxtaposition of an action and its consequences from two different points of view is far more profound when the psychological chronology is properly assembled in the spectator's mind. The heroic postures of Wayne, Stewart and Marvin form a triangle in time. The conflicting angles, the contrasting plays of light and shadow, the unified rituals of gestures and movements and, above all, Ford's gift of sustained contemplation produce intellectual repercussions backward and forward in filmic time until, on a second viewing, the entire film, the entire world of John Ford, in fact, is concentrated into the first anguished expression of Vera Miles as she steps off the train at the begining of the film, and everything that Ford has ever thought or felt is compressed into one shot of a cactus rose on a coffin photographed, needless to say, from the only possible angle.

Although *The Man Who Shot Liberty Valance* achieves greatness as a unified work of art with the emotional and intellectual resonance of a personal testament, there are enough shoulder-nudging "beauties" in the direction to impress the most fastidious seekers of "mere" technique. There is one sequence, for example, in which Edmond O'Brien addresses his own shadow, repeating Horace Greeley's injunction to go west, which might serve as a model of how the cinema can be imaginatively expressive without lapsing into impersonal expressionism. The vital thrust of Ford's actors within the classic frames of his functional montage suggests that life need not be devoid of form and that form need not be gained at the expense of spontaneity. *The Man Who Shot Liberty Valance* must be ranked along with *Lola Montès* and *Citizen Kane* as one of the enduring masterpieces of that cinema which has chosen to focus on the mystical processes of time.

—(From *The Primal Screen,* 1973, Simon & Schuster, reprinted with permission)

ANALYTICAL CRITICISM: GERALD MAST

Like Robin Wood's Hitchcock's Films *or Leo Brady's* Jean Renoir, The Comic Mind *by Gerald Mast is a book that can enrich our understanding of the movies by its careful and revealing analyses of specific films. Such a manner of film criticism is similar to good literary criticism in its scrupulous attention to style and structure. Written usually in the larger framework of a full-length study, it has advantages of dealing with films that have been around for some time, and of comparing them to other films within the author's framework. In this excerpt from his chapter on Howard Hawks in* The Comic Mind, *Mast parallels Hawks'* Bringing Up Baby *with the Peter Bogdanovich imitation,* What's Up, Doc? *The contrasts and parallels prove extremely revealing—of both Hawks' superb talent for inventive comic interplay (and the source of that interplay in the characters) and of the mirror-like failures of Bogdanovich's remake.*

HOWARD HAWKS
by Gerald Mast (1972)

Although he is not predominantly a director of comedies, no Hollywood director made better comedies than Howard Hawks. Like his non-comic films, Hawks' comedies refuse to sentimentalize or moralize. They show bizarre, lunatic people doing "screwball" things without ever explicitly telling us why they do them and without every saying (or even implying) that underneath the surface lunacy they are just plain folks. Hawks never apologizes for his comic characters and never strips away the veneer to let them bare their souls. They remain unswervingly true to their bizarre schemes, hopes, and interests. In a Hawks comedy the characters do not play at being silly; they are so consistently, believably, devotedly silly that their silliness itself becomes a serious, believable, consistent way of life.

The dominant psychological trait in Hawks' comedies (as in his non-comedies) is ego. If his characters seem loony, it is simply because they are wrapped up in their own heads. They can't see beyond their own intentions—and they don't want to. This selfishness is a striking psychological characteristic in an era when the conventional protagonist was distinguished by his selfless concern for people and principles outside himself. The supremely ironic twist in Hawks' comedies of ego, however, is that they are also comedies of love. That seeming contradiction is precisely the starting point of a comic Hawks plot.

The problem for a Hawks character is to let his egoistic guard down enough to see that he loves someone else and to let that someone else see she is loved. And vice versa—for Hawks doesn't sentimentalize the women in the comedies either. Like Lubitsch, Hawks doesn't put his women on pedestals but shows them to be at least as aggressive and conniving as his men. And unlike Frank Capra, Hawks does not solve the romantic conflict by revealing the cynical girl's soft heart beneath the layers of toughness.

For Hawks, as for Lubitsch, the human moral center is the brain. (For Capra it is the heart.) Hawks resolves sexual conflicts without betraying his characters' intelligence or competitiveness. Though his lovers perceive their need for each other by the end of the film, they do not make any conversions as a result of that perception. The endings of the films imply that the future union of the central couple will be as antagonistic and competitive as their strange courtship. The literary ancestors of Hawks' sexual attraction-antagonism are Shakespeare's Beatrice and Benedick and Shaw's Jack Tanner and Ann Whitefield, two pairs of intellectual opponents who also happen to love each other desperately. The cinematic ancestors of Hawks' egoistic lovers are perhaps Monescu and Lily of Lubitsch's *Trouble in Paradise,* who can't help competing as thieves despite their union (both sexual and vocational).

The Hawks characters love each other precisely because of their strong-willed, independent minds. They do not fall for sexual clichés on the one hand or romantic clichés on the other. One strong mind feels attraction to the strength and integrity of another. For Hawks to change either or both of these minds in his sexual resolution would rob the couple of the very basis of their relationship. As a result, Hawks' lovers fight more than they love; but without the underlying attraction and mutual respect, they wouldn't bother to fight at all. Their feelings are almost never verbalized; the lovers are rarely nice to each other. In *I Was a Male War Bride,* Ann Sheridan commands Cary Grant, "Get out of here, Henri, or say something nice." Grant stumblingly replies, "Well, I don't know, Catherine . . ." "That was nice, Henri," she sincerely answers. That inarticulate mumbling is as nice as Hawks comedies get.

Hawks' *Bringing Up Baby* (1938) . . . begins with an anti-sentimental premise. Although the title seems to promise some nice domestic comedy (along with its evocations of the comic strip, "Bringing Up Father"), the "Baby" in this script by Dudley Nichols and Hagar Wilde is no human infant but a tame leopard which responds with special affection every time he hears his favorite song, presumably because he hears his name in its first line, "I Can't Give You Anything but Love, Baby." In the course of the film, Baby wanders off and must be caught. Unfortunately, Baby gets confused with another leopard, an escaped mad killer, who does not think much of "I Can't Give You Anything but Love" or any other human song. In addition to chasing leopards, the characters also chase after dead animals, for the film is about a zoologist who is assembling the skeleton of a brontosaurus. One crucial bone, the intercostal clavicle, has disappeared. It has disappeared because George, an anti-social terrier, has sniffed it, taken to it, and buried it.

Apparently a mad chase after leopards and bones, the film is really Katharine Hepburn's hunt for her man, the scientist, played by Cary Grant. Katharine is far more predatory than Baby. The reason for *this* chase is that Cary Grant doesn't want to be caught—for two reasons. First, he is nearsighted, figuratively and literally, and doesn't see that he is Katharine's prey. Second, Cary is engaged to marry a dry, sexless, stiff woman who would seem a more appropriate mate for a dry, stiff scientist than the bubbling, bizarre, unconventional Katharine. So all the fighting, chasing, and lunacy in *Bringing Up Baby* are merely a surface deception for the film's real action—Katharine's efforts to put Cary, not a leopard, in a "cage." The film literally does cage him, for in the course of the chase Cary ends up in jail. But Katharine also wants to free him: she succeeds in springing him not only from jail but also from the emotional prison that has enveloped him.

As is typical in a Hawks' comedy, the tension between surface madness and underlying feeling is implied but never stated. Katharine never verbalizes her feelings or her intentions, but Hawks conveys them in a brilliantly cinematic way. One sequence of *Bringing Up Baby* reveals Hawks' command of cinematic distance and composition. Hepburn's first closeup in the film comes almost 30 minutes into it—at the moment when she first learns that Cary is engaged to be married. As she hears this news, Hawks cuts to an unexpected close shot of her face, and the action and dialogue suddenly pause. After a few vague flickers of conflicting feeling on her face, the fast-paced talk and action resume in a longer shot. Hawks' usual reliance on fast pace and the middle-distance shot gives great power to those special moments when the pace slows and the camera leaps very close.

The comic power of *Bringing Up Baby* emerges by comparison. Leo McCarey's *The Awful Truth* is also a comic contrast of surface and depths, of apparent battle and underlying love. But McCarey's film is a softer, sweeter, less funny, and slower-paced treatment of the contrast. The couple is, first of all, a married couple seeking divorce—so we know (according to Hollywood definitions) that they really love each other. The animal in the film is not a music-loving leopard, dinosaur, or mischievous terrier, but a cute, sentimental terrier named Mr. Smith which brought the couple together originally. And the potential lovers that the squabbling couple dig up—a dumb, vulgar Southern belle for Cary Grant; a plodding, stupid Oklahoma millionaire for Irene Dunne —cannot be seen as serious, credible threats to their relationship. When these sentimentalities and implausibilities in the script that McCarey and Viña Delmar wrote are wedded to McCarey's slow pacing of the dialogue and unrhythmic cutting, the result is a film that looks more like fooling around (often quite enjoyable fooling) and less like life than *Bringing Up Baby*. Hawks reveals that the comic spark of life can only emerge from the creation of a consistent, credible world in a film, not a world in which the characters seem to know that they are making a comic movie.

The comic perfection of *Bringing Up Baby* becomes clearer from yet another comparison, with a much later film that attempts to duplicate the Hawks style and method, Peter Bogdanovich's *What's Up, Doc?* (1972). Several essential differences between *Bringing Up Baby* and *What's Up, Doc?* account for the comic life of the earlier film as opposed to the sputtering, occasionally funny comic business of the later one. First, pace. The Hawks comedy moves with breathless rapidity; the Bogdanovich film constantly slows down to provide the stars with glamorous close-ups or to emphasize human and comic details that don't require emphasis. The Hawks film never stops moving; the audience picks out the relevant details for itself as the story whirs dizzily by. As early as Mack Sennett (and, of course, such classic stage farces as Feydeau's) it was clear that a furious pace is one way to confer the breath of comic life on a sequence of events that is incongruous and improbable.

Second, the Hawks tension between surface and depths, a tension that is the real human material of *Bringing Up Baby*, does not exist in *What's Up, Doc?* What is not voiced in the Hawks film—that Katharine wants Cary—is one of the first sentiments to leap out of Barbra Streisand's mouth, followed by long, obvious close-ups that reveal (and reveal and reveal) everything about the direction of her affections. Where *Bringing Up Baby* is apparently a chase after a comic object (the leopard) but is really a woman's chase after her man, *What's Up, Doc?* is apparently a woman's chase after her man but is really a chase after a comic object (suitcases). Despite *Bringing Up Baby's* surface absurdities, it is a film about an internal emotional process; despite *What's Up, Doc?'s* explicit emotional statements, it merely manipulates comic gimmicks and superficial absurdities.

Third, lacking this tension between surface and depths, the Bogdanovich film also lacks the egoistic tension between male and female, between two strong minds. Grant's intellectual drive and Hepburn's romantic drive, which communicate themselves in the driving hardness and crispness of their talk and movements, are replaced by the softness and warmth of Barbra Streisand and Ryan O'Neal. If one can speak of the unanimity of director and writer in the dialogue tradition, *Bringing Up Baby* is a reminder that the stars must be added to this synthesis. The surface coldness and crackle of the Hepburn-Grant style is completely suited to the story's dizzy pace, its contrast of cold surfaces and warm depths, and its battle between two strong minds. Both Hepburn and Grant are "intellectual" actors who successfully convey the impression that their heads, like their mouths, are not stuffed with cotton. But the warmth and obvious vulnerability of Streisand and O'Neal—qualities that make them stars of the 1970s—make them completely unsuited to "screwball" comedy, which must race along a cold, slick surface if it is to live at all. Further, although it is possible to accept the premise of Barbra's blatant sexual attraction to Ryan, it is not possible to accept the premise that Ryan O'Neal (*a*) is an intellectual; (*b*) if he were an intellectual, could acquire a Eunice for a fiancée; and (*c*) knows anything at all about igneous rocks except how to pronounce the word. Cary Grant may not be very credible as a zoologist, but the sheer speed of his performance diverts us from considering this potential incredibility.

Finally, the collapse of dramatic and comic tension between the central pair of *What's Up, Doc?* leads Bogdanovich to shift his comic focus from the stars to the supporting players and to impersonal cinematic gimmicks (the comic chase echoing Mack Sennett, *Bullitt,* and *The General,* among others). Where character players like Charles Ruggles were delightful and yet obviously subordinate in *Bringing Up Baby,* the comic doings of minor figures overshadow the central pair in *What's Up, Doc?* The spiteful machinations of Ryan O'Neal's musical rival, the pseudo-hip pretentiousness of the head of the Arts Foundation, the hypochondriac sadist who serves as judge of the night court, and especially the sexless, nasal, sanctimonious, bitchy, henpecking Eunice become the film's major comic interests. The sexless fiancée rarely appeared on screen in *Bringing Up Baby,* a strategy that did much for that film's credibility, since we never had to wonder why our hero was attached to such a woman. But Eunice is funnier and more interesting than anything else in the film.

Hawks' film owes its success not just to comic devices, but to his ability to find and develop the human source of gravity that pulls comic incidents and business together to form a complete comic world.

—(From *The Comic Mind,* 1973, Bobbs-Merrill, reprinted with permission)

CHAPTER ELEVEN

Genre

Genre

The famed French psychotherapist and hypnotist Jean Charcot often said, "We see only what we are ready to see." This holds as true for the movies as it does for psychotherapy. Indeed, the fact that movies are a popular art and that a movie must draw a sizable box office return simply to pay off its investment has meant—throughout the history of movies—that an audience knows to some extent what it's going to see before it enters the theater. There is a subtle psychology at work here, a desire for something fresh that's based largely on expectations for conflicts and characters that we already know. What is it that draws us to look at a John Wayne Western when we know exactly the character Wayne will play, the moral structure of the conflict, and the fact that Wayne will win out in the end?

But that's exactly what appeals to us in any genre. In a sense it's a matter of knowing the rules. We know in a science fiction film, for example, that some threat to the world is going to appear, and grow more threatening over time; and that knowledge does nothing to detract from our enjoyment of the movie. Indeed, the fact that we already know the structure can help lure us further into the movie, enable us to focus on the way in which characters and action support and develop the structure. Genre needn't at all be a limit to artistic freedom. Many of the masterpieces of 15th-century Italian art are madonnas, a genre as rigid and conventional for its time as westerns have become for ours. A good filmmaker, like a Renaissance artist, simply approaches the conventions of a western or musical or gangster film as a given, and works from there.

Precisely in this sense a genre can help a film, by providing recognizable basic elements —its setting, its structure, the moral differentiation between the good and bad guys. It can free a filmmaker to concentrate on style and elaboration and gesture and inflection. One of the marvels of Ford's Westerns is that we take for granted as much as he does; we assume certain things about the West, and the men and women who inhabit it, and these assumptions become an unspoken link between us and the action on the screen. Such assumptions, or conventions, are basic to any genre: the trigger-edge of violence among the gangsters; the very fact that people can suddenly break out in song and dance in musicals; the belief that flying saucers do exist in science fiction films.

Genres are largely composites of their conventions. Consider the gangster film. What is it, precisely, that we expect? A certain tragic quality to the gangster, for one—a sense that this man—inevitably he's violent, sometimes obsessively so—is doomed, and that before the movie ends he'll die, and that death itself will be violent. We expect the gangster's world to reflect him just as much as it entraps him, and it is almost invariably the city, a place of stark shadows and desolate streets and grubby back rooms. We expect competition fiercer than mere rivalry, ambitions that are rarely fully satiated, conflicts that can be resolved only by further violence. In effect, the gangster genre summons a world, a personality type, a private morality, a physical setting that embodies and defines that world.

If genres were only this—the structures that films can build from—they would probably cease to be interesting after we'd seen so many. But precisely for the reason that genres like the Western or the gangster film continue to thrive, we're led to suspect something else about genre, namely, that genres contain the myths and hopes and anxieties of their audiences.

By now it is a truism that what we relish about the Western is what, in an overly organized and technological society, we have lost. Think of the Western hero: he's a loner, a man who will uphold his honor at the cost of his life, and he lives in a society where honor counts highly, and where there are opportunities for maintaining it. Romantic wish-fulfillment? Of course, but maybe more. The Westerner is never defined by anybody else's rules. He may follow the law, he may not, but he makes the choice of his own volition, on the basis of his own code. This code may vary from movie to movie, but not by much. There's a taut line that stretches from the silent two-reeler of William S. Hart to the veteran robbers of *The Wild Bunch*. Though Western heroes may grow less law-abiding and even—yes—neurotic, they remain in some nascent, inexplicable way admirable. They are, finally, men, and perhaps that's why we still find their presence on the screen attractive. Manhood isn't something they're selling in a cologne commercial. It's a way of life that, however treacherous and debauched, could never do ultimate damage to a man's private image of himself.

It may be that we *need* genres like the Western, that movies, beyond being an art or an entertainment, are perhaps primarily an exorcism of inner doubts and terrors, a way of believing briefly that there is some order and coherence and meaning to a world that makes too little sense outside the movie theater. Genres give us myths and reasons for believing in those myths; and though outside the theater we may consider those myths foolish and romantic and unrealistic, we do go back to the theater, don't we?

GENRES

Gary Cooper in *High Noon:* WESTERN
Edward G. Robinson in *Little Caesar:* GANGSTER
2001: A Space Odyssey: SCIENCE FICTION
Boris Karloff in *Son of Frankenstein:* HORROR
Barbra Streisand in *Hello, Dolly!:* MUSICAL
Charlie Chaplin in *The Circus:* COMEDY

'The Western does not age.' —André Bazin

The Great Train Robbery 1903

The Wild Bunch 1967

It is the oldest and most durable of all movie genres—partly no doubt because it stresses conventions that are supremely fitted to the camera: great expanses of space, physical movement (the first chase was in a Western—*The Great Train Robbery),* and conflict always expressed physically, in a brawl, or more critically, that classic motif of the Western, the gunfight.

Yet there are unquestionably other and subtler and deeper reasons the Western has drawn audiences throughout the history of movies, reasons perhaps closer to myth and a sense of historic identity than to the action on the screen. The critic André Bazin suggested that it is the epic nature of the movie screen to create bold, historic myths. "There are legends," he writes, "that come into being almost instantaneously, that half a generation suffices to ripen into an epic . . . Without the cinema the conquest of the West would have left behind, in the shape of the western story, only a minor literature."

And on reflection, what do we expect from a Western? The action, surely, but always action within a context: a hero who is striking not only for his prowess with a gun, but for a kind of rugged nobility of character (indeed, there's always the assumption present that he's good with a gun *because* he's more noble, more moral than the bad guy). As the critic Robert Warshow put it, "The Westerner is the last gentleman, and the movies which over and over again tell his story are probably the last art form in which the concept of honor retains its strength."

"The best of women is not worth a good horse."—The Outlaw

Prelude to the Gunfight

"Lawyer, ah? Well, I'll teach you the law . . . Western law."—The Man Who Shot Liberty Valance

A gunfight is to a Western as a kiss is to a romance; we know what's coming, we know what the result will be, and so what matters is the preparation—what precedes it, and how striking and convincing the style of the prelude is. Indeed, we remember gunfights best from the moments that lead up to them: the long, agonizing morning in *High Noon;* the growling sense of impatience that rises in our reaction to Gregory Peck in *The Gunfighter;* the marching temperance league and the quick intercutting of armed men in *The Wild Bunch.* There is an almost ritual structure to what happens before the gunfight, an isolation of the gunfighters against empty streets; *the walk*—as the gunfighters move stolidly toward one another and, implicitly, their fate; and—inevitably—some moment of truth before the first gun is drawn: a hint not only about who will win, but who *should* win.

FOR A FEW DOLLARS MORE

Sergio Leone's Italian Westerns seem stripped to a kind of nostalgic essence. His gunfights (and the films are crowded with them) invariably require a good five minutes of build-up, with the music rising to a grandiose pitch, and a quickening tempo of tighter and tighter closeups, a cinematic style verging on opera, yet compensating for meandering plots and flat barren characters.

MY DARLING CLEMENTINE

The famous battle of the O.K. Corral, in which Wyatt Earp (Henry Fonda) and Doc Holliday (Victor Mature) meet the Clantons in a final, deadly showdown, remembered as history, elevated as myth. John Ford treats the build-up in classical style, cutting between Earp and the Clantons in low, ominous angles, and treating the event with a certain dramatic authenticity, as though highly conscious that he was revisiting history. When Earp pauses to inform the Clantons that they are under arrest and can turn themselves in, there is a sense of proven honor; the stage is set for Earp to win.

The Gunfight

"A tenth of a second, one way or the other," Paladin once said. "It's a curious thing for a man to devote his life to." Yet the Westerner is of necessity a gunfighter, not because he likes to kill, but because the gunfight is the arena where he must prove his honor and where his manhood—and for the audience, his morality—are tested. The gunfight does represent a bold, violent solution to conflict, but as Warshow points out, "Really, it is not violence at all which is the 'point' of the Western movie, but a certain image of man, a style, which expresses itself most clearly in violence." When the hero walks onto the street, gun strapped to his thigh, townspeople backing into doorways, we know from his style—his presence, his manner, a sense of obligation that gives him almost a serenity—that, whether he wins or not, he deserves to win. Indeed, there is something basic and appealing about the gunfight, where conflicts can be settled cleanly, immediately, and on the single (if dubiously valid) merit of the draw. Law, civilization, the order of society itself, these are the consequences and outcome—and not the arbiter—of the direct conflict expressed in the gunfight.

A gunfight from *For a Few Dollars More*

The Life and Times of Judge Roy Bean

Of Honor and Manhood

To a technologically driven and overcivilized culture, the appeal of the Western hero is almost naked in its simplicity, a world in which order must be settled by an act that requires courage and a faster gunhand, in effect, a world where it's still possible to prove one's manhood in terms that are universally acknowledged.

The notions of manhood and honor are the moral core of the Western. It's not simply the *West*—those broad, shimmering spaces—or the fury and movement of horses, posses, Indians; it's the simplicity of a world in which one's manhood can be tested in clear, decisive ways, in which we can separate the good guy from the bad guy not on the basis of his adherence to a distantly established code, but on the basis of style, presence, a clarity of posture. "A hero," says Warshow, "is one who looks like a hero."

In John Ford's commentary on the decline of the Western, *The Man Who Shot Liberty Valance,* James Stewart plays a lawyer who rises to political eminence partly because at one point he had supposedly killed the notorious outlaw, Liberty Valance. He hadn't—John Wayne did, surreptitiously—but because the railway has come in, because the territory has become a state, and because Stewart shrewdly parlays the heightening sense of civilization into building his own political future, he survives and triumphs. John Wayne dies virtually unknown. Ford structures the film around Wayne's scantly attended funeral and burial, and a significant visit from Stewart. In playing past against present, Ford is quietly suggesting the real hero of the movie: not Stewart, who belongs ultimately to the East—and who represents the final conquest of the West—but Wayne, the rough-edged gunfighter who *is* the true Westerner, the man who relies not on his knowledge of lawbooks, but his wits, his instincts, his draw.

In *The Westerner,* Gary Cooper is to be hanged in the morning, a verdict assured by Walter Brennan (as Judge Roy Bean). Nonetheless the two men hit it off well, well enough for Brennan to offer Cooper a drink, though it really amounts to a contest. Brennan finishes his big glass of whiskey in one chug. He seems the winner, but next morning as Brennan sleeps off a hangover, Cooper escapes.

Gangster

"The gangster is the 'no' to that great American 'yes' which is stamped so big over our official culture and yet has so little to do with the way we really feel about our lives."—Robert Warshow, "The Gangster as Tragic Hero"

The gangster film gives us Hollywood's darkest vision of America. At the end of *Public Enemy,* James Cagney's mother has heard that her son is coming home and eagerly makes his bed, humming and buzzing with the good news. Downstairs, Cagney's brother hears a knock at the door and goes to open it. The gang leader Cagney is a stiff, upright, dead body, wrapped in bandages. His empty face stares for a grim moment at the brother, then the body collapses forward into the hallway. It is one of the most potent endings in all of Hollywood movies, and a thwacking reminder that "Crime Does Not Pay."

The gangster is depicted as a man governed as much by the American success ethos as any of us, but he is likewise driven by it, and trapped in it. In most gangster movies, particularly the early ones, he never seems to *choose* to live outside the law, he simply inhabits a world in which the Law is something to avoid, like smallpox. His ruthlessness and cunning and violence are necessary for simple survival. In *The Line-Up,* Dancer says, "Ordinary people of your class—you don't understand the criminal's need for violence."

In Arthur Penn's *Bonnie and Clyde,* which is almost a lyric elegy to gangster movies, Bonnie and Clyde rob banks "for fun." Yet Penn carefully establishes the Depression era, the starving people of the South and Southwest, where only the bankers are fat, in such a way that we can understand how Bonnie and Clyde came to be folk heroes. The great gangster films (*Public Enemy, Little Caesar, Scarface, Dead End, Angels With Dirty Faces*) came out of the Depression, when audiences felt a distinct ambivalence toward the gangsters or bank robbers they read about in the papers. The movies came to reflect and perhaps extend that ambivalence, at least till the crunching effects of the Production Code forced the studios to depict their gangsters in a more judgmental tone. Yet in the earliest and best of the gangster movies our sympathies do lean toward the gangster, even though we know he must die in the end, not simply because if you break the law you must pay for it, but from a more basic code: those who live by violence must die by violence.

In the superb *Scarface,* a fictional account of Al Capone, the dying Scarface lies beside a window through which a neon sign proclaims, "The World Is Yours." More than a fine ironic touch, this juxtaposition suggests that in America—certainly in American gangster movies—success can finally breed only mistrust, isolation, and death.

Bonnie and Clyde

A LANGUAGE OF THEIR OWN

"Mother of God, is this the end of Rico?" —Edward G. Robinson, Little Caesar

"Whoooeeeee! We'll have ourselves a time! . . . What we gonna do?"—Gene Hackman, Bonnie and Clyde

"Don't bone me."—Sterling Hayden, The Asphalt Jungle

"If you want fresh air, don't look for it in this town."—Anthony Caruso, The Asphalt Jungle

Two bootleggers:

"Is this the real stuff, Danny?"

"I don't know, but it'll get into much better homes than we ever will."—The Roaring Twenties

The City

"The gangster is the man of the city, with the city's language and knowledge, with its queer and dishonest skills and its terrible daring, carrying his life in his hand like a placard, like a club."—Robert Warshow, "The Gangster as Tragic Hero"

We always identify a genre with a specific landscape: the Western, with wide, expansive spaces; the musical, with brilliantly colored sets; the horror film, with musty graveyards and gaunt, gloomy castles. But perhaps in no other genre is the hero connected so viscerally to his environment as the gangster.

It is no coincidence that the first films to depict the city as a dangerous, violent place were early gangster films like *Underworld* and *Public Enemy*. The titles alone suggest how the gangster films considered the city: *Asphalt Jungle, City of Fear, City That Never Sleeps, Concrete Jungle, The Frightened City*.

The gangster inhabited the city in a way that made him master of its secrets: its blunt, furtive language, its wary streets, its hunger for violence. The gangster ruled the city; he alone understood the city—and in the Bogart and Cagney and Robinson films of the thirties and forties, America came to see its cities stripped of romantic pretensions. A darkened street has perhaps never meant quite the same thing again.

Emmerich's wife: "Oh honey, when I think of all those people you come in contact with, downright *criminals, I get scared."*

Emmerich: "Don't worry dear. Crime is only a form of lefthanded endeavor."—The Asphalt Jungle.

Little Caesar

Cagney

Even more than Bogart, Cagney was the consummate gangster. His baby face and short stature served to mask a quicksilver temper that could flare into drastic violence and subside as quickly. Cagney could kill without the slightest hesitation, without a hint of moral qualm. For him the act of killing was as natural and inexorable as a sneeze. Indeed, it was his hair-trigger penchant for violence that gave Cagney a kind of natural supremacy in the gangster films that featured him. Cagney represented a kind of quintessential street fighter risen to the heights of the underworld: tough, feisty, incorrigible, and within his world, nearly invincible.

A CAGNEY RETORT

In *The Public Enemy* it's a grapefruit in the face; in *The Roaring Twenties,* it's a cigar.

A LUNCHTIME KILLING

In *White Heat* Cagney pauses between bites to shoot a hostage in a car trunk: a murder shocking not for its blood, but for Cagney's indifference.

THROUGH A DOOR

Director Raoul Walsh probably understood Cagney and Cagney's screen presence better than any other director. In *White Heat* and *The Roaring Twenties* Cagney wins a battle by shooting his victim not only in the back, as he is running, but through a door. No code of honor, only expediency.

End of the Gangster?

"In a sickening way the human body is used as a material to wrinkle the surface of the screen. Usually the body is in zigzags, being flung, scraped over concrete, half buried under tire wheels, but it is always sort of cramped, unlikely, out of its owner's control."— Manny Farber, on Point Blank

In *Point Blank,* which is possibly the best gangster movie of the sixties, Lee Marvin is a tough loner who has been shot by his old partner on a big heist and left for dead. He returns years later to locate the partner and collect the $93,000.

But the partner has by now become part of the fabric of a corporation-type Syndicate: and the explosive, aggressive Marvin must smash, beat and kill his way up the syndicate ladder to get his money. The violence takes on an added quality: as when Marvin goes for a drive with one of the syndicate flunkies, the owner of a car lot, and forces him to talk by smashing the car between the immense cement posts under a highway bridge.

The early gangster films existed in a haunted city of dark alleyways, dim shadowy streets, and smoky backrooms. In *Point Blank* the city is transformed to modern Los Angeles: shattering sunlight, highrise apartments and skyscrapers, elevators and swimming pools. This chrome and vinyl world, like the Syndicate, bewilders Marvin; and we see that his real enemy isn't the Syndicate (and certainly not the Law), but the modern city, which has turned on an out-of-date gangster like Lee Marvin in an elemental way.

Point Blank is a comment on why the gangster film is mostly gone. Modern technology and the modern city are no longer a fit habitat for the man of violence.

DEMOLISHING A LIFE STYLE

One of the most vivid—and most telling—sequences in *Point Blank* begins at "Big John's" used car lot, when Marvin takes Big John—a flunky in the mob that Marvin's after—for a spin in one of his cars. When Marvin fastens his seat belt, Big John jokes about it—till Marvin plows the car between two bridge posts—an act of violence that not only gets Big John to talk, but that suggests Marvin's final and ultimate enemy, technology, and his manner of treating that enemy.

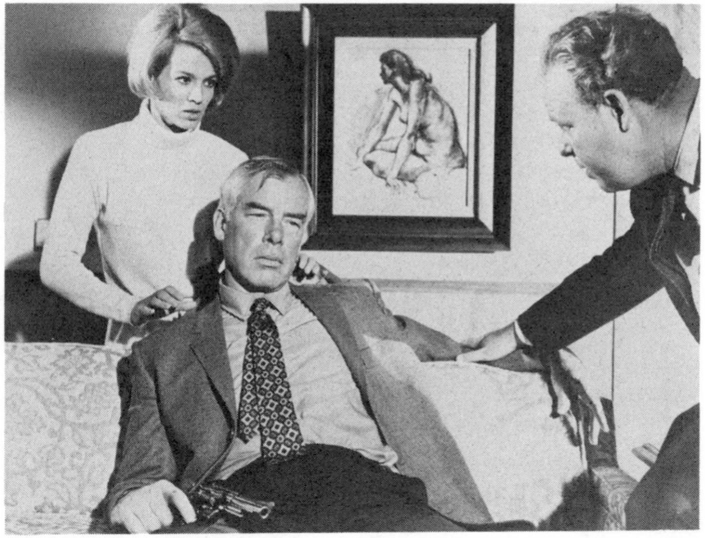

Angie Dickinson, Lee Marvin and Carroll O'Connor in *Point Blank*

▼

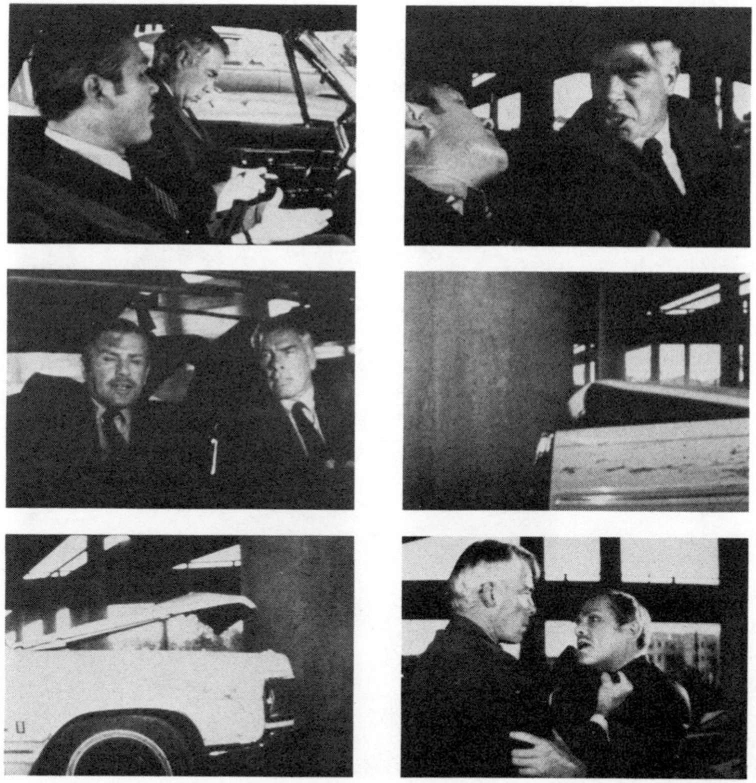

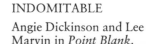

INDOMITABLE

Angie Dickinson and Lee Marvin in *Point Blank.*

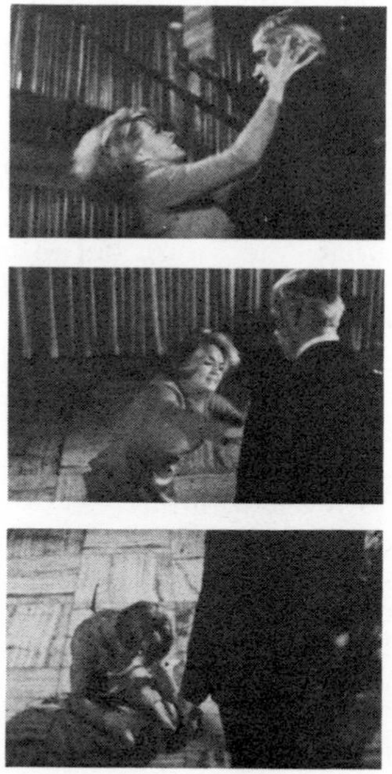

Science Fiction

"The science fiction film . . . is concerned with the aesthetics of destruction, with the peculiar beauty to be found in wreaking havoc, making a mess."—Susan Sontag, "The Imagination of Disaster"

Though the science fiction is as old as film itself—Méliès was making films like *A Trip to the Moon* as early as 1902—*the* epoch of the science fiction film was the fifties, when the threat of nuclear holocaust fixed the public imagination on the future in a newly anxious way. Despite such astute special effects as in *Forbidden Planet,* or the dramatic success of a movie like *The Thing,* essentially the fifties' science fiction movies *were* about disaster: the world coming to an end—or coming to the brink of coming to its end—as a result of a thousand different menaces, all terrifying in their immensity and immunity to man's weapons. More than anything else, science fiction movies remind us of anxieties and terrors that we live with daily but seldom consider on a global scale.

At the opening of *Them!* a terrified child rushes from the desert. She is numbed with shock and can utter only one word: "Them!" What "they" turn out to be are monstrously enlarged ants, whose size has increased as a result of recent nearby nuclear testing. Eventually some of these ants leave their mother nest in the desert and fly west, to breed in the drainage pipes deep below the city of Los Angeles. A government agent (James Arness), however, with the help of the esteemed scientist (Edmund Gwenn) and of course the scientist's daughter (Joan Weldon), is able to stop the ants before they reproduce and overwhelm Los Angeles, not to mention the rest of the world.

Them! is both typical of science fiction in its greatest era, the fifties, and a fine example of how engrossing and yet near-comical these movies could be. Most science fiction movies of the fifties, and since, haven't been concerned with the possibilities of the future save one: the way it all might end. A dreadful visitation from outer space, or some inadvertent scientific side effect quietly appears, becoming a deadlier and deadlier menace, and finally a threat to the entire planet. Ants, plants, bees, spiders, a fly: often the most effectively frightening threats seem deceptively familiar . . . until the scientist figures out the scale of the menace, and "what might happen . . ."

We tend to think of such films as "fun." Even in the fifties they were a kind of foreshadowing of camp, yet their continued popularity, using a standardized and even rigid

A Trip To The Moon, 1902

The Thing From Another World, 1952

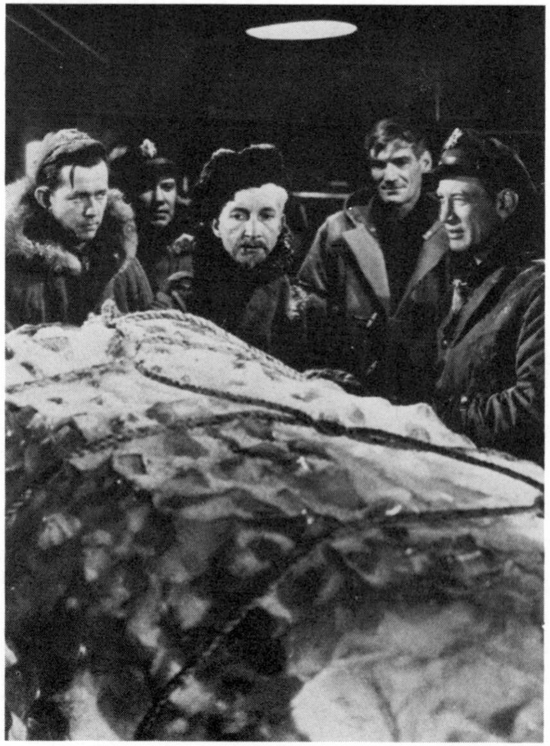

Them!, 1954

The energy monster from *Forbidden Planet*

tropolis

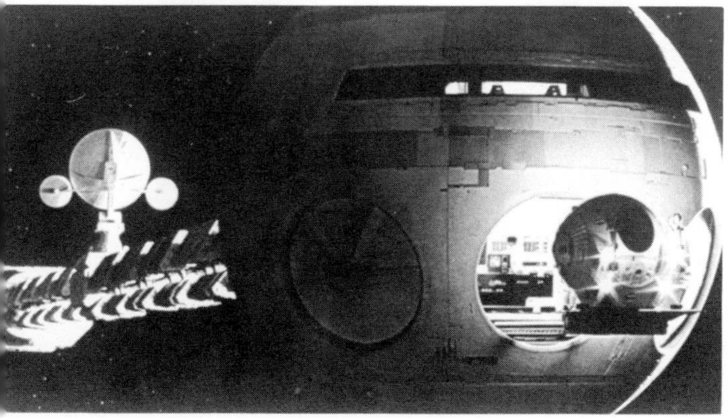

2001: A Space Odyssey

plotline, suggests that these films of near-global disaster responded to some widespread common fear. It's no coincidence that the fifties was the first era in which man had to live with the threat of nuclear annihilation, and to some extent the science fiction films helped absolve that fear. Indeed, such themes as the scientist's responsibility or ecology were first dealt with seriously in science fiction.

When science fiction films have attempted to deal more openly and speculatively about the future, they have often created some spectacular and mind-turning effects, though not as often equally impressive ideas. Fritz Lang's *Metropolis* (1927) follows a maudlin and sometimes silly storyline, yet some of the settings, and particularly the choreography of vast numbers of people working dronelike in these settings, have a strangely powerful effect. *Things to Come* (1936) seems almost a catalog of future fantastic inventions, including a boring machine that can make great tunnels in minutes. *Forbidden Planet* (1956) uses extraordinary special effects to take us inside the unbelievable Altair IV, a planet left behind by a race capable of "spiritualizing" itself. Some of the effects here—such as a great "energy" monster, seen only when it lunges into the forcefield erected around the spaceship—have a frightening, powerful authenticity.

It was with Stanley Kubrick's *2001: A Space Odyssey*, however, that science fiction showed the capability of taking the film medium itself forward into the future. *2001* is a magnificently ambitious feat, to suggest nothing less than what movies will be like at the turn of the next century. Special effects become more than scary, weird new landscapes or marvelous inventions. Kubrick depicts the docking of spacecrafts as ballet; the drama between man and computer as a cosmic chess game of minds; and man's ambiguous destiny—of venturing into deep space—as a means of somehow hurling evolution into its next stage. *2001* begins with science fiction but ends somewhere in a future that we begin to accept is going to be out there—somewhere.

The Beast From 20,000 Fathoms, 1953

IMAGES OF THE FUTURE
. . . AND LINES FROM THE PAST

"If we do not end war, war will end us."—Raymond Massey, Things To Come

"No more love, no more beauty, no more pain."—converted earthling, boasting in Invasion of the Body Snatchers

"We have made machines out of men, and now we will make men out of machines!" —Rudolf Rogge, Metropolis

"An intellectual carrot? The mind boggles." —Douglas Spencer, The Thing

"Dave, stop. Stop. Stop, Dave. Will you stop, Dave. Stop, Dave, I'm afraid. I'm afraid, Dave. Dave. My mind is going. I can feel it. My mind is going. There is no question about it. I can feel it. I can feel it. I can feel it. I'm afraid."— HAL, 2001: A Space Odyssey

Horror

As old and as basic as a child's terror of what lies behind the closet door is the root emotion and impulse of the horror film. We fear the unknown, certainly, because it is unknown. As long as that shapeless shadow does not become too clear, or until we see exactly what form creates it, our fears are at their sharpest. Horror films fom the first *Frankenstein* (1910) to the dread-rousing *Night of the Living Dead* (1969) have exploited these terrors, and in doing so have perhaps helped to exorcise them from other regions of our experience. Possibly what superstitions and forms of magic were to earlier generations, the horror film is to our century: a means of summoning, of dramatizing, of invoking the unknown, and of feeling with some satisfaction that it has been placed again, at least for now, under control.

Martha O'Driscoll: "Try to see the moon as something beautiful."

Lon Chaney, Jr.: "Until the full moon turns it into something of ugliness and horror."
—The Wolf Man

"I tell you, we haven't begun to discover what science can do to the body and mind of man!"
—Dr. Jekyll and Mr. Hyde, *1920*

"We belong dead."
—Boris Karloff, Bride of Frankenstein

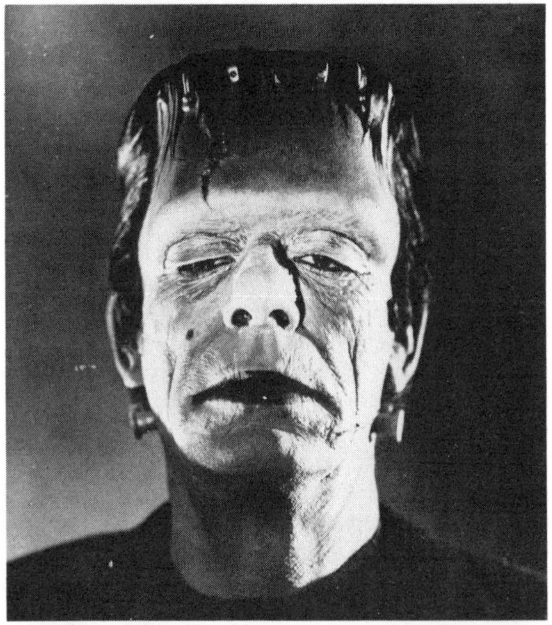

FRANKENSTEIN LIVES

Charles Ogle (top) in 1910, Boris Karloff (center) in 1931, and Christopher Lee in 1956 offered distinct interpretations of this monster of many parts.

THE ORIGINAL DRACULA

. . . was *not* Bela Lugosi, but—according to scholars Raymond T. McNally and Radu Florescu—an obscure Romanian prince of the 15th century. Bram Stoker, who wrote the original novel *Dracula* in 1897, had researched and drawn on the life of this strange, gruesome figure known as Vlad Tepes, The Impaler, a nickname derived from his famous, favorite technique of punishing his enemies. Prince Dracula was born about 1431 in Transylvania (though his castle and dominion were in the nearby Wallachia). He was a fierce and demented ruler who once frightened away an oncoming Turkish army by ordering that 30,000 prisoners be impaled and left to rot on the trees in the surrounding forest. He killed—often devising unique methods of torture—at whim. Once during a party he had the guests surrounded and most of them impaled, simply because he knew a few to be political enemies. Dracula's cruelty and bloodthirsty measures did not impede his folk reputation as a local hero of sorts. Even today he is remembered by some as a great warrior prince. Today there is a special excursion flight, sponsored by an airline, to Transylvania and Dracula's castle.

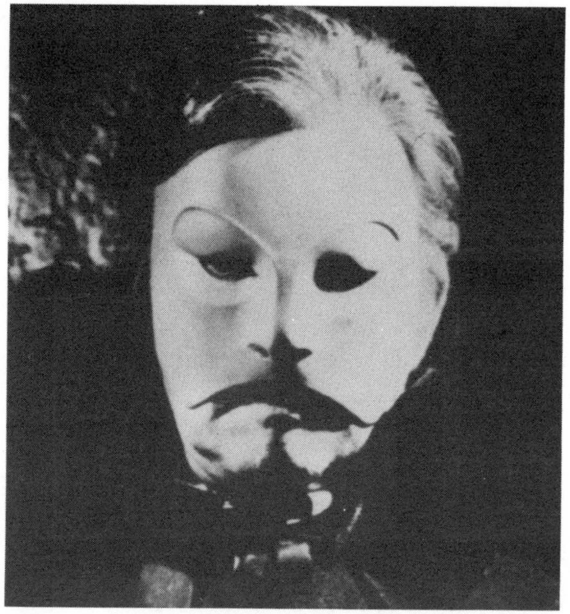

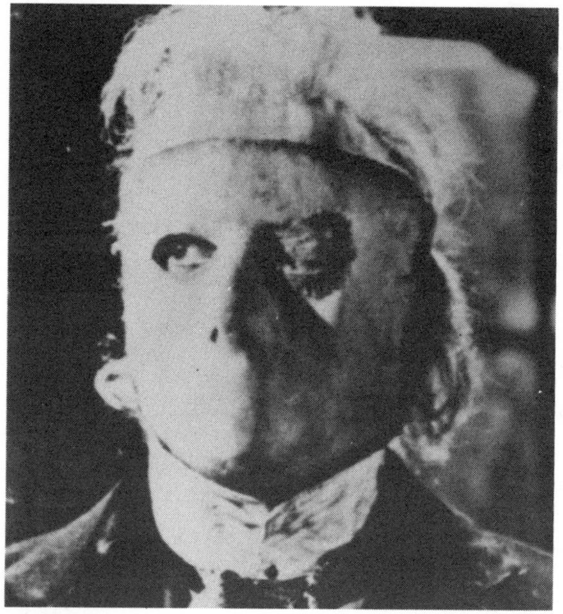

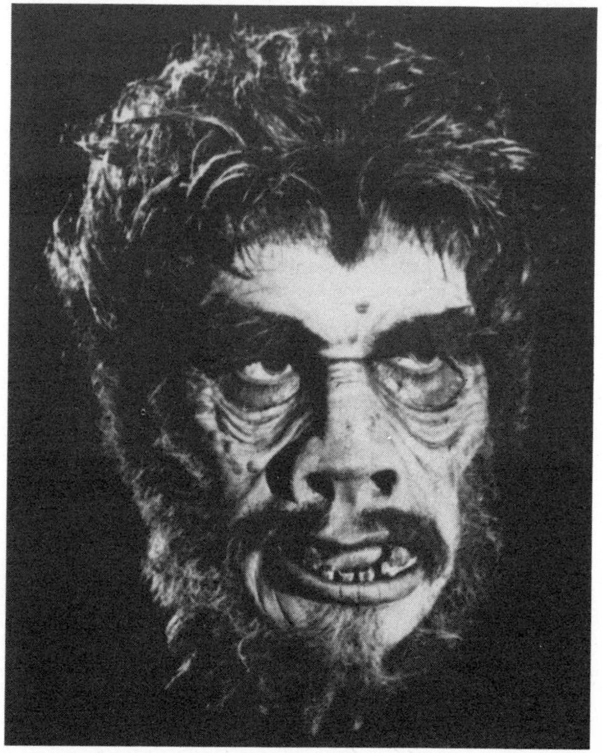

PHANTOMS OF THE OPERA

True monsters never perish, but are reborn . . .

Lon Chaney, *Phantom of the Opera,* 1925 (top left).

Claude Rains, *Phantom of the Opera,* 1943 (top center).

Herbert Lom, *Phantom of the Opera,* 1962 (above).

At far left is Lon Chaney as *The Hunchback of Notre Dame,* 1923. At left is Boris Karloff as Mr. Hyde in *Abbott and Costello Meet Dr. Jekyll and Mr. Hyde,* 1953

Musical

It is the most flamboyant of genres, the most colorful and visually seductive. It was born of the New York musical theater, with roots in vaudeville and the dance hall. By the early thirties the movies had transformed musical shows to the point where they could claim them as truly their own, in the escalating scale of the outrageous and dazzling Busby Berkeley numbers (as, here, from *Gold Diggers of 1935)* or the brisk elegance of the Fred Astaire-Ginger Rogers films.

We love musicals for their high spirits and purity and whimsy. Anything is possible in a musical: dancers tapping on huge typewriter keys (Ruby Keeler and Lee Dixon in *Ready, Willing and Able*), Fred Astaire dancing on walls and a ceiling *(Royal Wedding)*, or Judy Garland stepping into the brilliant and exuberant land of Oz *(The Wizard of Oz)*. Musicals are important not for their stories, or their conflicts, or even their stars sometimes. They are the closest the movies have come to a fairyland version of life.

In the thirties each studio had its own teams of musical stars: Nelson Eddy and Jeannette MacDonald at MGM; Fred Astaire and Ginger Rogers at RKO; Ernst Lubitsch directing smoothly sophisticated musicals at Paramount. But perhaps the most memorable today are the musicals of Busby Berkeley, particularly the extraordinary, pyrotechnical displays of his musical numbers. Hundreds of

"A great part of my work has not been the work of a choreographer strictly speaking, because for me . . . it is the camera that must dance."—Busby Berkeley

The Gold Diggers of 1935

Fred Astaire and Ginger Rogers in *Carefree,* 1938

Gene Kelly in *An American in Paris,* 1951

Donald O'Connor and Gene Kelly in *Singin' in the Rain,* 1952

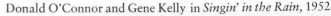

A Day at the Races, 1937

girls swim in kaleidoscope patterns in the "By a Waterfall" number of *Footlight Parade,* and "Lullabye of Broadway" in *The Gold Diggers of 1935* is a weirdly nightmarish, surrealistic montage number on Manhattan night life, a powerful depiction of both its allure and its destructive energy.

Some of the most memorable musicals were made in the era after World War II. Flamboyant in their dances, their sets and their colors, such films as *Anchors Aweigh,* or *An American in Paris,* or *Singin' in the Rain* were both spirited and polished. Gene Kelly's dance through a rainy street at night while a cop watches without amusement in *Singin' in the Rain* remains perhaps one of the best-known moments of the musicals and helps suggest why—at least till the inroads of television—they have been so popular. Without making you feel anxious or nervous or anything else, musicals can make you feel very good.

Fiddler on the Roof, 1971

Hello, Dolly!, 1968

Kathryn Grayson, Frank Sinatra and Gene Kelly in *Anchors Aweigh,* 1945

Comedy

It would seem, from the outset, that film comedy has an advantage available to no other genre or form of film: you know when it works, because it provokes laughter or it doesn't. Indeed, critic James Agee built a theory of sorts around the four kinds of laughter that comedy can arouse: the titter, the yowl, the bellylaugh and the boffo. The best of comedy, he asserted, rose from one level of laughter to the next—like climbing a ladder. "An ideally good gag, perfectly constructed and played, would bring the victim up this ladder of laughs by cruelly controlled degrees to the top rung, and would then proceed to wobble, shake, wave and brandish the ladder until he groaned for mercy."

It's a splendid analogy, and perfectly true of the silent comedy that Agee was discussing. But it's questionable whether it holds true of modern comedy, and for reasons that may have something to do with the rarity of genuine comic talents in movies over the past twenty years. Masters of comedy seem to come in generations: Chaplin, Keaton, Lloyd, Sennett, Langdon and the movies' richest period of comedy, ended for the most part, with the oncome of sound. The Marx brothers, Fields, directors like Frank Capra and Leo McCarey and Ernst Lubitsch worked in the thirties (and in France, Jean Renoir and René Clair); in the forties, Howard Hawks or Preston Sturges or Billy Wilder—but since . . . ? A few notable exceptions, like Jacques Tati in France or Woody Allen. But perhaps television (where major comic talents *do* thrive) has leached from the movies their capacity for drawing us to the theater to laugh; or perhaps our age has made the comedy a new and acute problem.

Consider one of the most original and vital comedies of the past fifteen years: *Dr. Strangelove*. The opening shot depicts an Air Force plane refueling in flight in a kind of aer-

Charlie Chaplin in *The Circus,* 1928

Eve Arden with Groucho and Chico Marx in *At the Circus,* 1939

Harold Lloyd's World of Comedy

Oliver Hardy and Stan Laurel

ial coupling, to the musical tune of "Try a Little Tenderness." One of the first characters we meet is General Buck Turgidson, a feisty, chest-thumping military type (played by George C. Scott) who is summoned to an urgent meeting at the War Room. Turgidson is a bold caricature of the military mind as an exploding peanut shell. He rages on about how easily the American bombers could pulverize Russia. "I'm not saying we wouldn't get our hair mussed. I am saying only ten to twenty million people killed, tops, depending on the breaks." His reactions to the President's efforts to stop and forestall bombers sent to Russia are themselves perversely funny. He'll lean back, his mouth cocked half open, and stare at the President without moving, in a frozen pantomime of stunned disbelief.

Sterling Hayden plays General Jack D. Ripper, the commander of an Air Force base who has gone berserk and ordered the pilots on their mad mission. General Ripper is another extremity of the military personality. He's convinced of a "Commie" plot to infiltrate our "precious bodily fluids," fluoridating the water supply, and the recent discovery that he's impotent has only confirmed his worst suspicions. Leaning back in his chair with a bravura cigar wedged in his mouth, he seems invincible, and when British aide Mandrake (Peter Sellers) tries to convince him to recall the bombers, he argues that it's necessary, a military decision too important to leave to civilians. When the army rings the base and takes it over, Ripper grieves over his "lost children" and shoots himself.

The lunacy in *Dr. Strangelove* spirals without letup. But stressing realism with the grotesquerie of his characters, director Kubrick manages to keep this madness always within a range of believability, so that the wild comic touches are always part of the central dramatic question: Will the bombers get to Russia? When the President (also played by Sellers) calls the Soviet Premier on the hot line to inform him that the bombers are coming, the dialogue brings out just that terse balance of realism and madness:

"... Hello, Dmitri. Listen I can't hear too well, do you suppose you could turn the music down, just a little? Ah, ahh, that's much better. Yes, uh, yes, fine. I can hear you now, Dmitri, clear and plain and coming through ... fine, I'm coming through fine too, eh? Good, then ... well, then as you say, we're both coming through fine. And I'm fine. I agree with you, it's great to be fine. Now then, Dmitri, you know how we've always talked about the possibility of something going wrong with the bomb ... The Bomb, Dmitri. The Hydrogen Bomb ... Well, now, what happened is that one of our base commanders, he had a sort of, well, he went a little funny in the head. You know, just a little funny. And he went and did a silly thing. Well, I'll tell you what he did. He ordered his planes to attack your country ... Well, let me finish, Dmitri ... let me finish ... well, listen, how do you think I feel about it? Can you imagine how I feel about it, Dmitri?

*M*A*S*H,* 1969

George C. Scott in *Dr. Strangelove,* 1964

It's comedy, bizarre, hilariously funny. But it's comedy mingled with a subtle dread, our knowledge, all through the film, that the B-52s are wending toward Russia with bombs that will trigger nuclear holocaust.

The success of *Dr. Strangelove* points up, ironically, a central difficulty of modern comedy; that to be effective, the comic thrust must be set against an ordered world, and when the world itself seems disordered, this natural imbalance between the comic and a normal surrounding is torn askew. In *Dr. Strangelove,* Kubrick ingeniously used this disorder to advantage, but there haven't been many *Dr. Strangeloves* since, and one wonders.

Yet a glance backwards affirms the range and richness of comic inventiveness in the movies. There have been more than a few touches of genius in film comedy. Indeed, there is perhaps something about the screen itself and the enclosed, captive audience of a theater that has engendered and nurtured comic talent more than the novel or the stage.

Slapstick: Escalating The Gag

Pie-throwing is the emblem and best-known motif of slapstick; and the best pie-throwing sequences always have a way of getting wildly out of hand, as in this exultant exhibition from Laurel and Hardy's *The Battle of the Century* (1927), in which—ever characteristic of Laurel and Hardy—innocent bystanders aren't permitted to stay innocent or bystanders very long. Note the rapid escalation from revenge to exorbitant chaos.

The Golden Age of Comedy, a classic gag set-up, and an example of how one gag wends into another. Timing is everything.

Twists on a Gag

The persistent insanity of W. C. Fields' film *Never Give a Sucker an Even Break* culminates in the car sequence in which Fields is supposedly taking Margaret Dumont to the hospital, an explosive madness involving cops, one-way streets, tunnels, and finally the ladder to a fire-truck which Fields engages, and then is engaged by. He's muttering all the while.

FARCE

When Harpo Marx is chastised by a cop in *Big Store* for parking astride a fire hydrant, he promptly runs out and dumps the hydrant into the backseat of the car, the kind of nimble-witted exchange we expect of Harpo, the gag taken to an almost surreal conclusion.

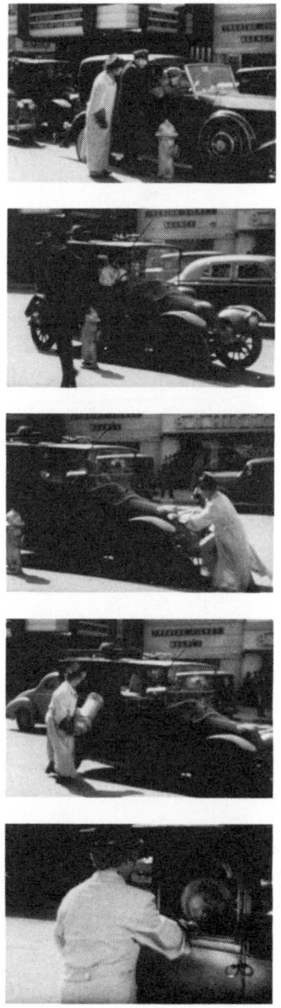

Wacky Comedy

There was a breed of comedy in the thirties and forties that has virtually died out since, a kind of spiralling calamity, invariably involving a shy, maybe scholarly man and a madcap woman. Howard Hawks directed the best of the wacky comedies: *Ball of Fire, Monkey Business, His Girl Friday* and *Bringing Up Baby*. Here, in a sequence from *Bringing Up Baby,* Cary Grant as a museum scientist is resurrecting the skeleton of a dinosaur, bone by bone, an effort that's taken him seven years. When Katharine Hepburn shows—she's already taken him through a whirlwind of frenetic chases and other madness—she climbs the ladder and teeters delightedly when Grant admits that he did have a good time. The teetering gets out of control (like everything else in the film), and the dinosaur tumbles. Hepburn doesn't.

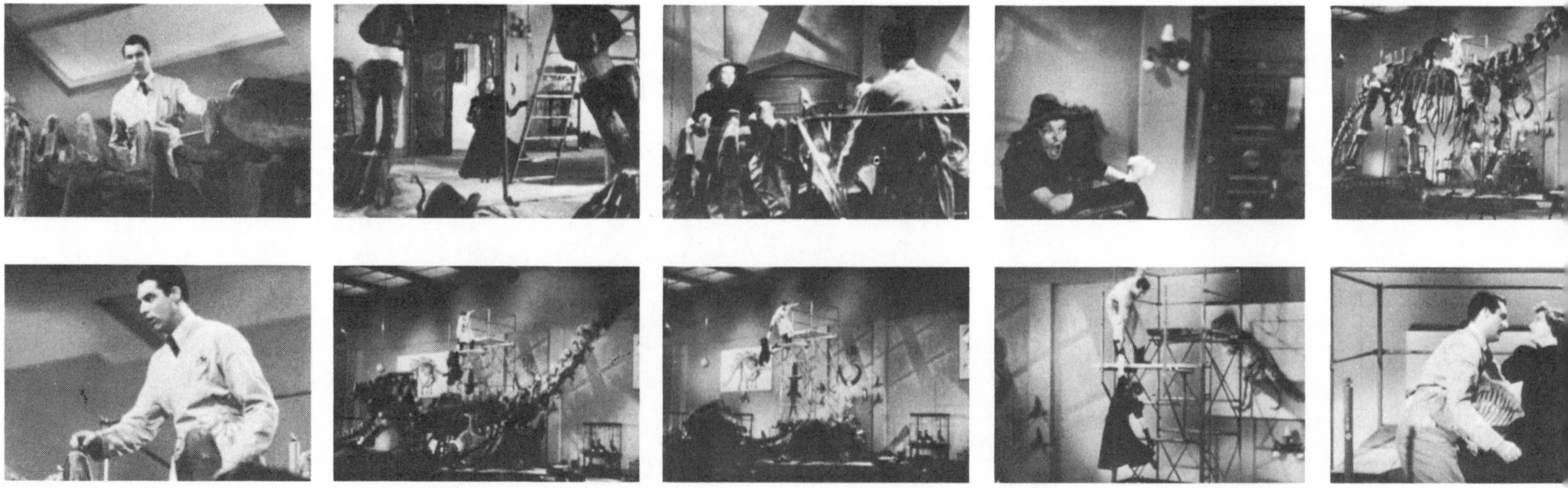

The Joys of Self-Destruction

BUSTER KEATON

Keaton's films reflect the achievement of endurance. Not only are they incredibly acrobatic, touched with danger—and always funny—but Keaton, who seems able to wander into the most implausible and dangerous situations, manages to survive these continuing disasters totally unperturbed, as though in some subtle way he rather *liked* being caught in a boat's paddle, or being fished up by a fisherman. Keaton is perhaps the most physical of comedians, yet the most unaffected.

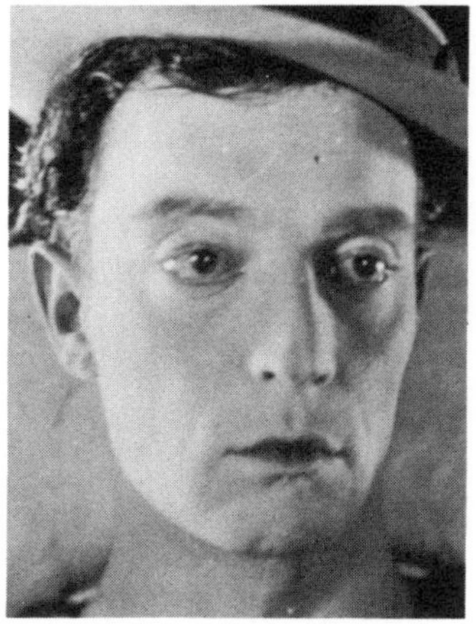

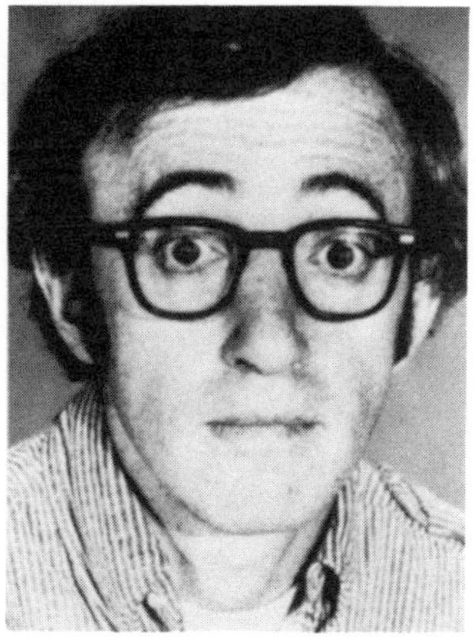

WOODY ALLEN

Woody Allen, the best of contemporary comics, has fashioned a film persona that ranks with Keaton and the Marx Brothers. In films like *Bananas* and *Take the Money and Run,* Allen has emerged as a shy, recalcitrant nebbish, a man who fails so often at so much that we're amazed he can still be surprised by yet another personally wrought catastrophe. Woody Allen's comedy is astute, classical, surprisingly unself-conscious, and contagiously funny.

Daydreams.

Bananas.

The Marxist Theory of the World: Tear It Up!

A Subverted Puppet Show: in *Monkey Business*, Harpo—racing from the officials on a ship—becomes the newest character in a puppet show; to the great delight of his audience; shortly after, when they discover he's inside the booth, they start pulling his (?) leg, and he offers to help.

Harpo is always taking something preposterous out of his pocket; in lieu of a match to light a cigar, for example, a blowtorch. From *Duck Soup*.

Harpo and the vendor in *Duck Soup:* a classic sequence of outrageous escalation, beginning with Harpo's scissors . . . but soon getting happily out of control.

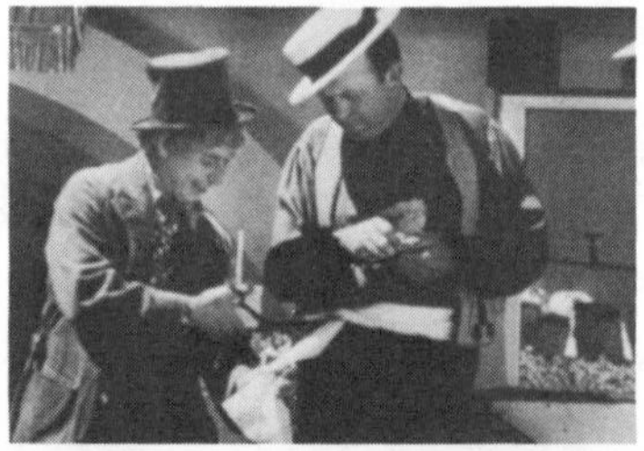

SIGHT GAG

From *Duck Soup*.

Harpo's tattoos, from *Duck Soup:* the lady wiggles; Harpo's grin widens—but the supreme touch is the doghouse, from which peeps the head of an actual dog.

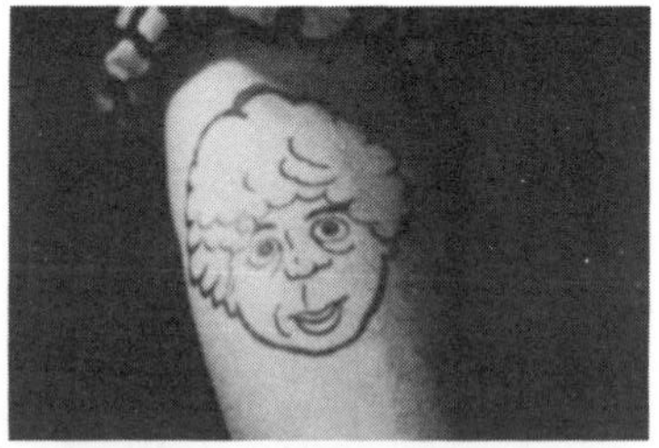

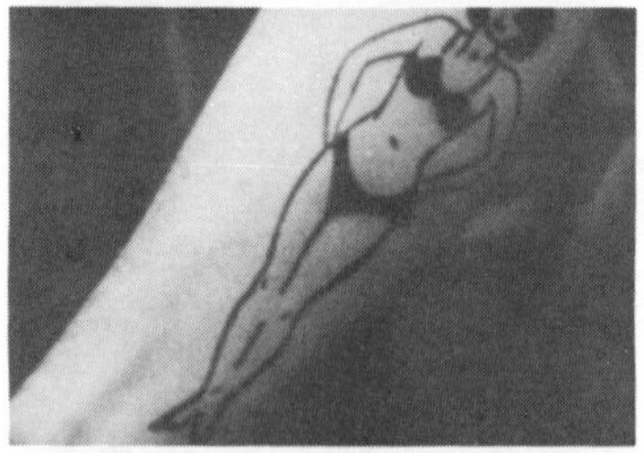

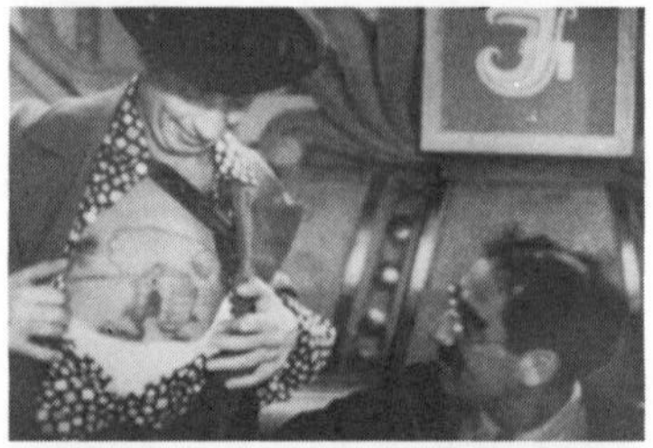

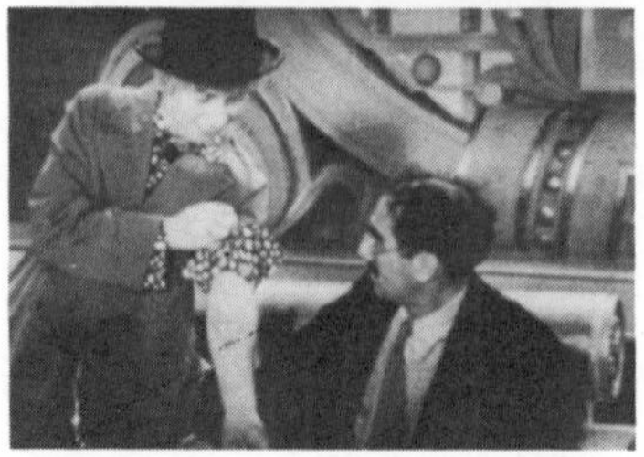

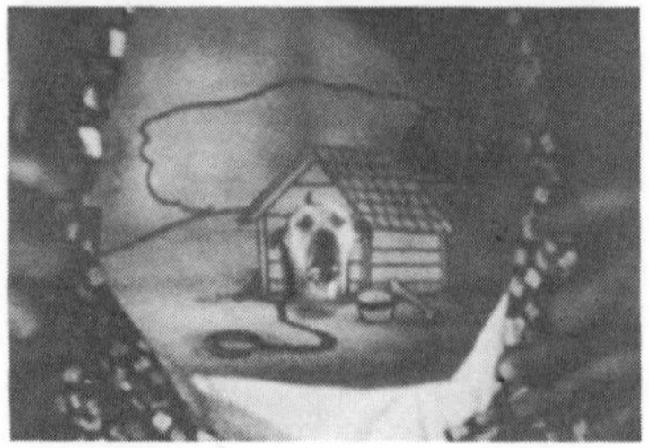

Hollywood: An Epilogue

CHAPTER TWELVE

Hollywood: an Epilogue

In the early part of the century, as a new popular diversion began to attract more and more people on Saturday nights, a handful of shrewd businessmen—largely from the hectic garment and fashion industry—began to step in and reorganize the way movies were produced and promoted. Men like William Fox (who trimmed suit linings), Adolphe Zukor (a furrier), Carl Laemmle and Samuel Goldwyn—who, by virtue of their background in the fashion industry, had developed a shrewd sense of changing taste—became the first real generation of movie producers, organizing and fitting and promoting their products with much the same tact that they might use to announce the new spring wardrobe. They created the star system, because they knew the public would adulate and daydream of faces on that big, glittering screen; they centered the movie stories on innocence and dark villains and the triumph of virtue because they knew that people wanted to see things they believed in, while at the same time sniffing a whiff or two of sin; and, as copyright conflicts and bankruptcies and the difficulties of returning borrowed equipment mounted, they fled to the ripe sunlight of Southern California, where the varied terrain and the proximity of the Mexican border offered both a way of making movies and a quick escape from the creditors when the money ran out.

Hollywood was born.

It rose within a single decade to a glittering opulence unknown in the history of man. Nothing in the Roman's day could match Marion Davies' 14-carat gold ceiling or Gloria Swanson's solid gold bathtub, accouterments considered in Hollywood's raging twenties as proper for a star, one who is, after all, closer to the gods than to the rest of us mortals.

"The cynics are always with us—those who say Hollywood cannot face reality, that everything must be glossed over and made unreal. What the cynics do not realize is that dreams are often more real than reality. There is a reality beyond that which we see and touch and feel. There exists within man a groping toward an idealistic extension of himself: an undefeatable belief that life can be pleasanter than it may be at the moment, a staunch conviction that there are possibilities beyond his own narrow horizons. The movie with the fairytale, Cinderella, happy-ending plots bring joy because it also brings hope."
—Mervyn LeRoy, "What Makes a Good Screen Story?"

It revolved around fewer than a dozen "major" studios, which were feifdom empires of their own. The power that men like Samuel Goldwyn at MGM or Harry Cohn at Columbia wielded was limitless within the studio. Directors and stars were completely at the mercy of the studios, which is to say usually at the mercy of their most recent boxoffice record. Yet the studios, for all their control over the people who worked in them, had as well the advantage of their own autonomy. They created worlds that had never existed before.

Hollywood didn't attempt to tell us about the world; it attempted to give us the world recreated by its carpenters and set designers and special effects wizards. The sets in Hollywood movies from the twenties through the fifties never look quite "real" to us; but they are all the more engaging, and fantasy-rousing for that. From the magnificent palaces in Douglas Fairbanks' *Thief of Baghdad* (1924) to the meticulous decor of a musical like *Singin' in the Rain* (1952), Hollywood movies have always depicted a world less scarred, less dirty, less everyday than the one we know. There is a fairyland, anything-is-possible ambience about virtually all these movies. Hollywood has been called a "dream factory," and it was,

The Birth of a Nation, 1915

King Kong, 1933

Gold Diggers of 1935

Gone with the Wind, 1939

but it created splendidly fabricated and highly polished dreams.

Hollywood was capable of doing anything; and the extravagant costs of some of its productions were matched only by the extravagant expectations (often met) of its producers. There is an anecdote, probably true many times over, of Cecil B. DeMille standing before a replicated version of the entire Roman army, calling through a megaphone, "Move those thirty thousand horses a foot and a half to the left."

Its strengths were its weaknesses. Even as the studios turned out hundreds of completed productions a year, they did it often at great cost to individual creative artists, and, by extension, to the public. The fact that *Greed* (1924) was released by MGM in a mutilated, shortened version is a comprehensible but sad example of Hollywood pressure on film artists. Von Stroheim's *Greed* is one of the great masterpieces of film history, and we have only the mutilated version—the rest has been lost—as a memorial of the original film.

Hollywood achieved what it did without looking back at what it had lost. It is a place without memory. The great French director Jean Renoir tells the disturbing story of a dinner given by the producers and moguls of Hollywood for the man who had literally invented their profession, D. W. Griffith. It was to celebrate Griffith, yet there was a jarring discrepancy: the sponsors were the men who had turned Griffith out, who wouldn't give Griffith work, and at the time Griffith was barely subsisting, living in a barren hotel room, and he hadn't done a movie for over ten years. After the speeches and the clapping, Mr. Griffith (who had to borrow a suit for the occasion) stepped before the audience and stated everything in one pungent question: "Can anyone here lend me five dollars?"

Hollywood is still there; and the splendid homes in Beverly Hills still have lawns shaved to the trim of a putting green. But it's not the same. MGM, once the most towering of the studios, has been bought, disbanded, and its remnants are most visible, in, of all places, a hotel in Las Vegas. Today if you walk through a studio like Universal or Paramount, most of the films you're likely to see in production are for television, and they're made on an even more slickly oiled assembly line basis than any of the earlier studio films. The studios have gradually been selling off their real estate and their costumes and props and sets, and the men running the studios now tend to be corporation heads, men appointed by the conglomerates and industries that now own the studios. There's no longer the belief among filmgoers that Hollywood is some kind of a magic place where fantasies can run rampant on and off the set. The halcyon world of Hollywood is preserved today only in its movies. Like all empires, it rose and flourished and has left only monuments—though one suspects those monuments will keep its memory alive forever.

"The movies are one of the bad habits that corrupted our century . . . For forty years the movies have drummed away on the American character. They have fed it naiveté and buncombe in doses never before administered to any people. They have slapped into the American mind more human misinformation in one evening than the Dark Ages could muster in a decade."—Ben Hecht, A Child of the Century

"Virginia Woolf wrote that the cinema was a case of the savages beginning not with two bars of iron and working up to Mozart but with grand pianos and nothing to play."—Pauline Kael, Deeper Into Movies

The Wizard of Oz, 1939

To Have and Have Not, 1942

Singin' in the Rain, 1952

Easy Rider, 1969

Hollywood Is...

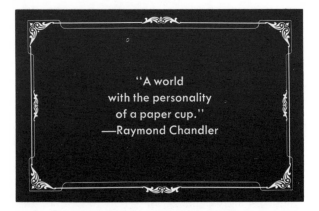

"A world
with the personality
of a paper cup."
—Raymond Chandler

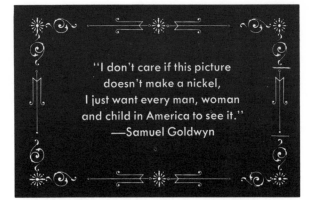

"I don't care if this picture
doesn't make a nickel,
I just want every man, woman
and child in America to see it."
—Samuel Goldwyn

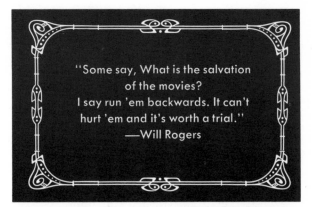

"Some say, What is the salvation
of the movies?
I say run 'em backwards. It can't
hurt 'em and it's worth a trial."
—Will Rogers

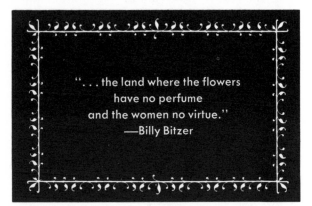

". . . the land where the flowers
have no perfume
and the women no virtue."
—Billy Bitzer

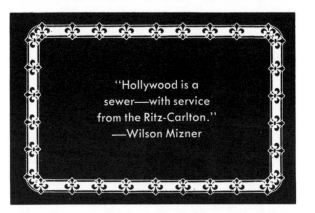

"Hollywood is a
sewer—with service
from the Ritz-Carlton."
—Wilson Mizner

"Movie stars are not usually,
or necessarily, actors; they are . . .
movie stars. The two occupations
are entirely different, although
they are sometimes compatible."
—Richard Schickel, *The Stars*

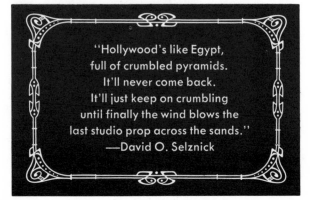

"Hollywood's like Egypt,
full of crumbled pyramids.
It'll never come back.
It'll just keep on crumbling
until finally the wind blows the
last studio prop across the sands."
—David O. Selznick

"Hollywood is a golden suburb,
perfect for golfers, gardeners,
mediocre men
and complacent starlets."
—Orson Welles

"Hollywood is a carnival
where there are no concessions."
—Wilson Mizner

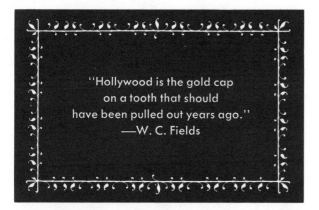

"Hollywood is the gold cap
on a tooth that should
have been pulled out years ago."
—W. C. Fields

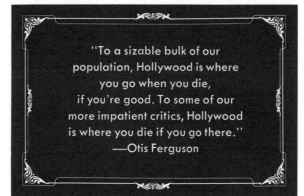

"To a sizable bulk of our
population, Hollywood is where
you go when you die,
if you're good. To some of our
more impatient critics, Hollywood
is where you die if you go there."
—Otis Ferguson

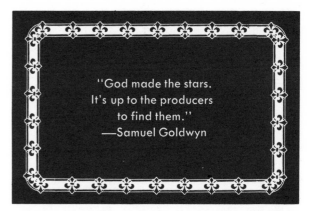

"God made the stars.
It's up to the producers
to find them."
—Samuel Goldwyn

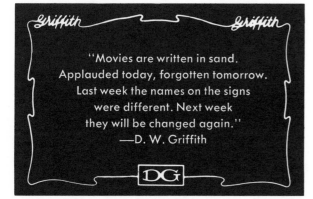

"Movies are written in sand.
Applauded today, forgotten tomorrow.
Last week the names on the signs
were different. Next week
they will be changed again."
—D. W. Griffith

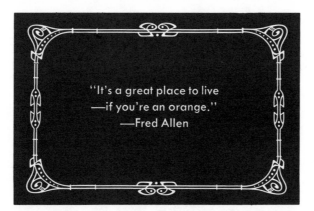

"It's a great place to live
—if you're an orange."
—Fred Allen

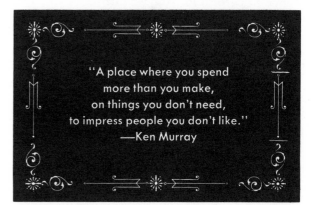

"A place where you spend
more than you make,
on things you don't need,
to impress people you don't like."
—Ken Murray

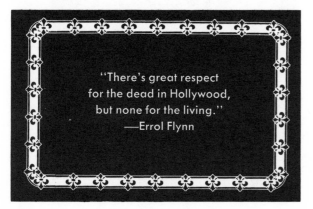

"There's great respect
for the dead in Hollywood,
but none for the living."
—Errol Flynn

"Hollywood impresses me as being
ten millon dollars' worth of
intricate and highly ingenious machinery
functioning elaborately
to put skin on baloney."
—George Jean Nathan

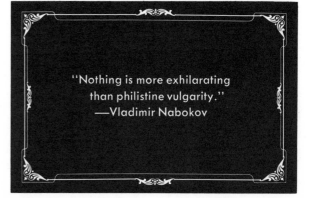

"Nothing is more exhilarating
than philistine vulgarity."
—Vladimir Nabokov

Stars

In *Dead Reckoning,* a sallow, B gangster picture made after WWII, there is a sequence between Humphrey Bogart and Lizabeth Scott in which he tells her that he's not going to run off with her after all, he's going to turn her in for Murder One. She begs him to forgive, to put it all behind them, to forget. Bogart replies:

"The trouble is, I can't forget that I might die tomorrow. Suppose you got sore at me some morning for leaving the top off the toothpaste tube. Then there's Johnny. A guy's pal is killed, he ought to do something about it."

Scott replies by pulling a gun on him, and Bogie shakes his head just slightly enough to make the cigarette between his lips waver: "It's a blue sick world for you, isn't it?"

The dialogue, the plot, the style in *Dead Reckoning* are dramatically flimsy; yet the scene is galvanizing. We cling to every word Bogart speaks, and every word seems incredibly right. What would otherwise be a pale, hollow movie becomes luminous, adroit, enthralling. And why? Bogart.

Bogart, with his waxy toughness, his wry grin that always hinted at a crack in that toughness, and his ability to glance at a camera as if it were an enemy he was threatening, has perhaps justified more bad movies than any actor in Hollywood. Bogart's presence on the screen had a separate existence and validity of its own, separate from story, dialogue, direction. In the best of his movies, when he acted serious roles (such as *The Maltese Falcon, The African Queen, The Treasure of the Sierra Madre*) he could be remarkably convincing, ranging over an emotional landscape with the dexterity of a jazz soloist wending through a dozen chords. But we know and remember him best from movies where he wasn't an actor, but simply Bogie. As Kenneth Tynan said of him, "We trusted him because he was a wary loner who belonged to nobody, had personal honor . . . and would therefore survive. Compared with many of his Hollywood colleagues, he seemed

Bogart, in (beginning top) *Dead End, Dead Reckoning, The African Queen.*

an island of integrity, not perhaps very lovable but at least unbought."

Bogart was one of a very few stars who, though big in their own time, seem even bigger today. Seeing their movies again, we're amazed at how galvanizing, how moving, how luminous they could be—a Chaplin, a Garbo, a Marilyn Monroe—men and women who seemed to make the screen bigger by their very presence, and whose faces seem to carry within them the very hopes and dreads and turmoil of their generations.

The chemistry of a movie star has been as long-sought by Hollywood producers as was the magical formula for making gold by medieval alchemists, and the effort equally futile. Bogart was doing B gangster movies for twelve years before Warners realized they owned one of the hottest stars in Hollywood. Almost as though stars don't belong to Hollywood but to the movie public, and materialize in fashions that the producers never quite predict, the stars remain somewhat separate, perhaps in a way above the industry that created them. And perhaps as well, with Hollywood no longer the true home of movies, the stars have been eclipsed and we're not likely to see the future equivalent of a Bogart or a Garbo. Hopefully we will; but in the meantime, we have the movies to see again and again, and the moments of sheer transcendent glory to marvel at.

Greta Garbo with John Barrymore in *Grand Hotel;* the famous scene in which she utters the line that epitomizes her furtive moods onscreen, her life offscreen: "I vant to be alone." Garbo, ineluctably beautiful and, even in a leading man's arms, somehow inaccessible, could transform the slightest tinge of expression into a language of mood and passion. Béla Belázs said of her, "Garbo's beauty is a beauty of suffering; she suffers life and all the surrounding world. And this sadness, this sorrow is a very definite one: the sadness of loneliness, of an estrangement which feels no common tie with other human beings."

Birthday Party

Louis B. Mayer poses with his stars on MGM's 20th anniversary in 1943. The phenomenal popular appeal represented in the names and faces of the performers shown here is rendered even more impressive by the list of those who were *absent* (see below).

1 Captain James Stewart (on leave)
2 Margaret Sullavan
3 Lucille Ball
4 Hedy Lamarr
5 Katharine Hepburn
6 Louis B. Mayer
7 Greer Garson
8 Irene Dunne
9 Susan Peters
10 Ginny Simms
11 Lionel Barrymore
12 Harry James
13 Brian Donlevy
14 Red Skelton
15 Mickey Rooney
16 William Powell
17 Wallace Beery
18 Spencer Tracy
19 Walter Pidgeon (With beard for *Madame Curie* role)
20 Robert Taylor (With G.I. haircut for real-life Navy role)
21 Pierre Aumont
22 Lewis Stone
23 Gene Kelly
24 Jackie Jenkins
25 Tommy Dorsey
26 George Murphy
27 Jean Rogers
28 James Craig
29 Donna Reed
30 Van Johnson
31 Fay Bainter
32 Marsha Hunt
33 Ruth Hussey
34 Marjorie Main
35 Robert Benchley
36 Dame May Whitty
37 Reginald Owen
38 Keenan Wynn
39 Diana Lewis (William Powell's wife)
40 Marilyn Maxwell
41 Esther Williams
42 Ann Richards
43 Marta Linden
44 Lee Bowman
45 Richard Carlson
46 Mary Astor
47 Blanche Ring
48 Sara Haden
49 Fay Holden
50 Bert Lahr
51 Frances Gifford
52 June Allyson
53 Richard Whorf
54 Frances Rafferty
55 Spring Byington
56 Connie Gilchrist
57 Gladys Cooper
58 Ben Blue
59 Chill Wills (In uniform for *See Here, Private Hargrove*)
60 Keye Luke
61 Barry Nelson
62 Pfc. Desi Arnaz
63 Henry O'Neill
64 Bob Crosby
65 Rags Ragland

Absent from this gilded gathering were
Lana Turner
Judy Garland
Charles Laughton
Laraine Day
Robert Young
Ann Sothern
Margaret O'Brien
Herbert Marshall
Robert Walker

In the armed forces were
Clark Gable
Robert Montgomery
Melvyn Douglas
Lew Ayres

Toward a Psychology of the Movies:

THE SUBTLETIES OF MOVIE ILLUSION

In Buster Keaton's *Sherlock Jr.* he plays a bored projectionist in a movie theater who falls asleep during one of the reels. A ghostlike, daydream self emerges from the sleeping figure and walks through the theater, up to the screen, unseen by that audience, seen by us. Eventually he steps *inside* the screen, walks up a set of steps and knocks at the door. Nobody answers. He begins walking down when suddenly the screen changes, and he's still walking, still in the same movement, only now falls over a pedestal. The progressions continue: Keaton's movements remain continuous. but the background and thus Keaton's physical environment keep shifting at an alarming rate. It is a staggering feat, a moment that captures the ultimate paradox of movies: how they can be at once so real and believable, and yet so fantastic, so profoundly illusionary? Keaton plays

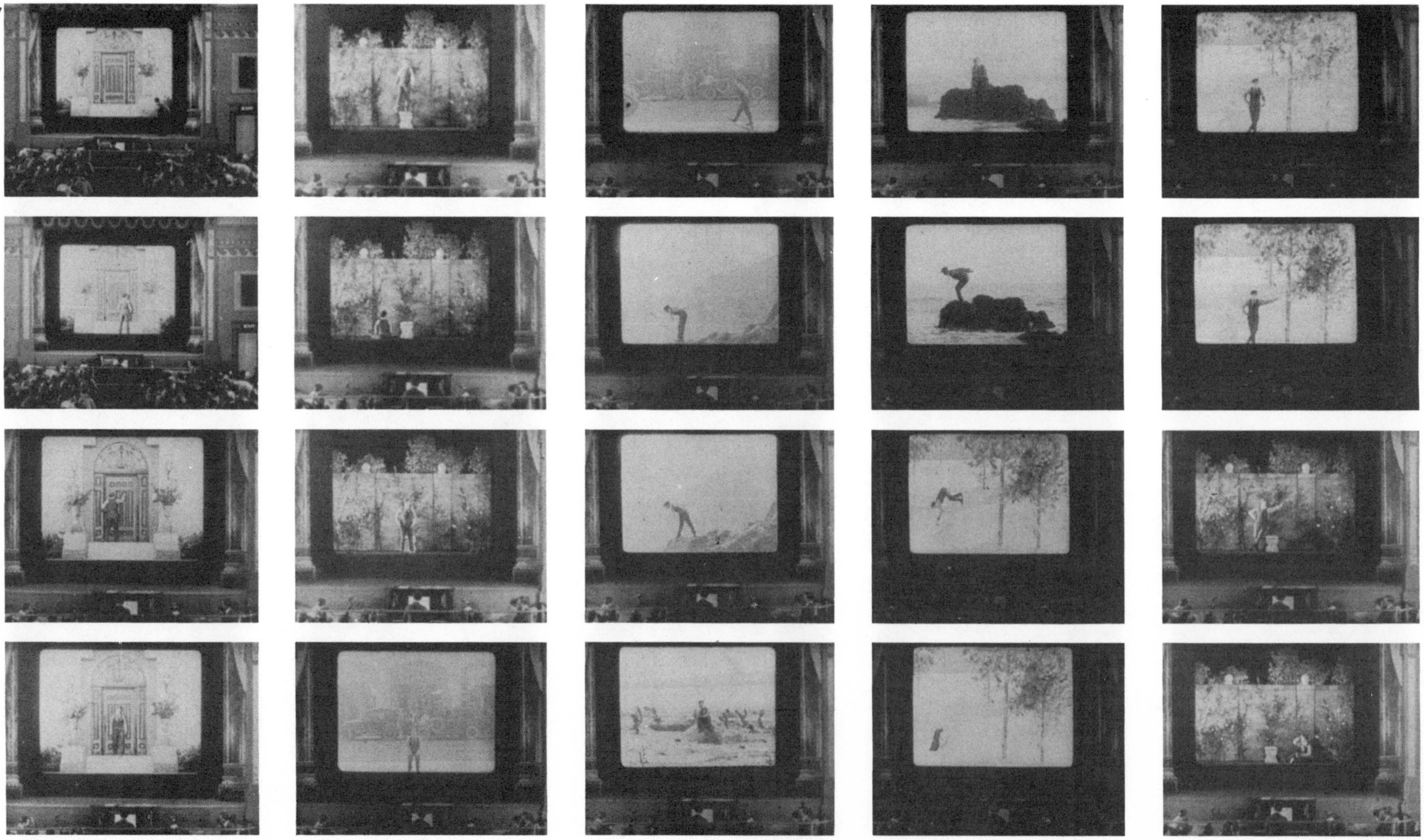

A Commentary by Buster Keaton

out this metaphysical balance as a brilliant gag, but it's likewise a trenchant comment on the nature of the movies themselves, how the changing and unchanging intersect, how illusions can be repeated and interlaced, but also how these illusions can create physical dangers.

Keaton, living in this sequence (as many a star and movie buff do) in the twilight interim between movie illusion and the real world, has made of the gag a comment on the pratfalls of movies, the nature of this most convincing of illusions.

WHERE WE LEARN IT ALL . . . ALMOST

Sherlock Jr.: Keaton meets his girlfriend in the projection booth. He's shy, there's a helpful movie playing, and the combination makes for one of the most illuminating comments in movies on what we learn and draw from the screen.

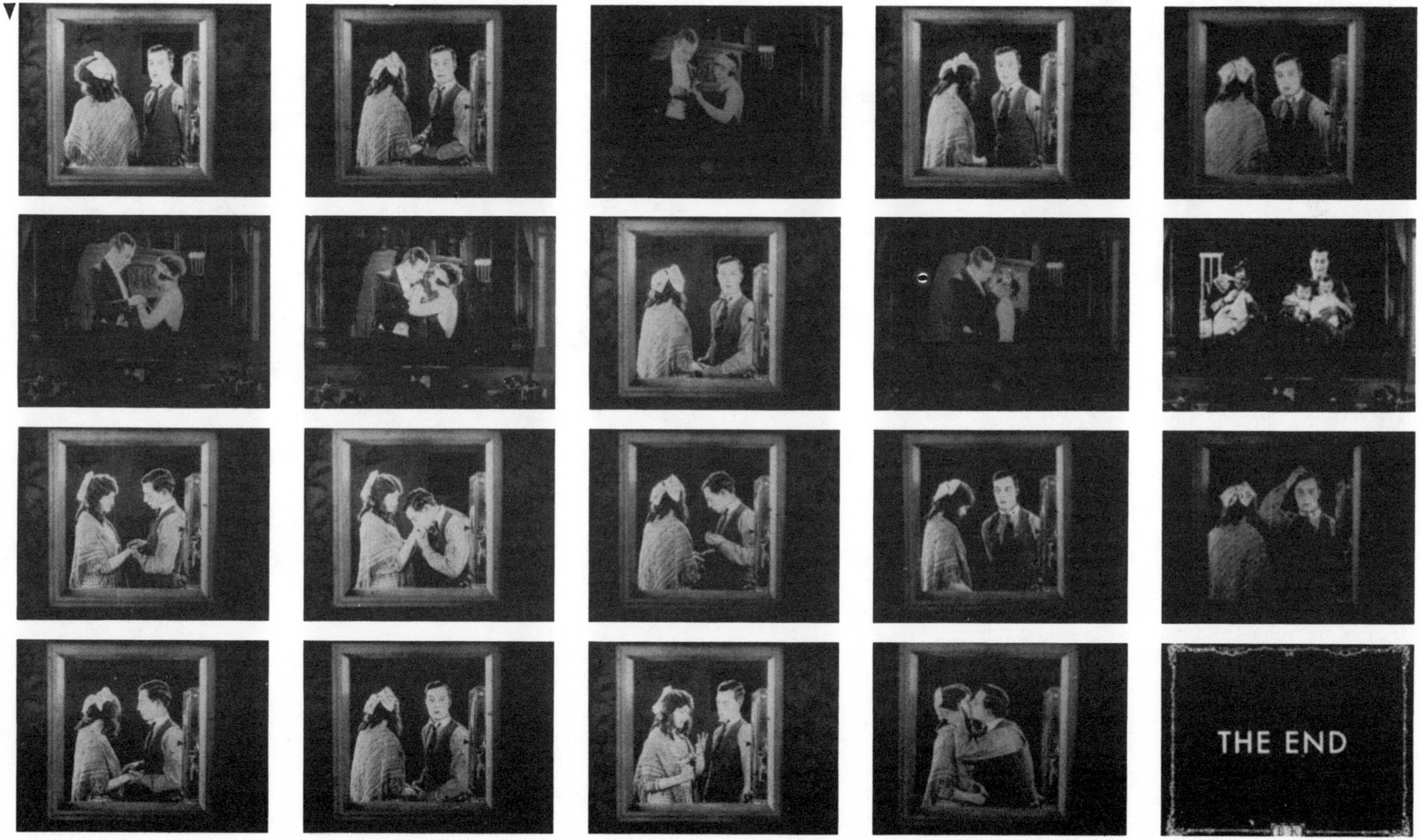

A Magic of the Camera

MARILYN

Her story has become our most familiar and disturbing legend of Hollywood, as though the weight of stardom she carried in her life has become the weight of our censure against Hollywood's crass and exploitative ways that now she must bear in her death. When she reigned in the fifties, she was the screen's most volatile expression of human sexuality. The camera loved her: before it she was incandescent, tremulous and innocent one moment, intoxicated with feeling the next; her sexuality could rage in a fury of expression, or lodge serenely, promisingly, within a demure smile. Marilyn Monroe was the last great star, and her sad death closed forever an old contract between Hollywood and its audiences, a contract that will probably never again be renewed.

"Movie glamour bears witness to the presence of the ideal at the heart of the real . . . the archetypal beauty of the star acquires the quality of the mask . . . the star's ideal beauty reveals an ideal soul."—Edgar Morin, The Stars

Bus Stop: singing "Black Magic"

Film Notes

Film Notes

What follows are notes on the films most prominently discussed or presented in this book. I've written them as a compensation. For a reader fascinated by several sequences of a film but with no idea how they might relate to one another within the film, these comments might be of some help. In most cases they reflect my own enthusiastic or ambivalent or unsatisfied feelings about a film, though almost all of them are certainly films to see. I've included the name of the distributor of each film and, at the end, a list of distributors' addresses.

All films used in school settings should be previewed.

— W.K.

THE AFRICAN QUEEN

Written by James Agee and John Huston Directed by John Huston 106 minutes color United Artists 1951 With Humphrey Bogart, Katharine Hepburn, Robert Morley, Peter Bull

A spinster and her missionary brother in a remote African outpost watch in horror as World War I and a German massacre of their village devastate their mission and their lives. The pastor (in his mind he'd never really left England) collapses from the strain; and the sister (Hepburn) can only bury him — her grief faintly tinged with relief. And then comes Bogart. It is perhaps his most brilliantly achieved role — a cockney river loner named Allnut who treks back and forth on his beat-up hulk, a man at once uncomfortable with the upper classes (which Hepburn represents) and always with the appearance of having bathed in grease. When the missionary's sister, Rosie, learns that it's possible, just barely, to take Bogart's junk down-river and use some explosives to detonate a German warship, she persuades him — he rightly finds the idea fanatical — to try it. The romance that blossoms between them and the adventure story that frames and heightens the romance are developed with a sophistication and clarity of character matched only by the illuminating performances of Bogart and Hepburn. *The African Queen* makes you wish that Agee had written more screenplays and that Huston had directed them. Based on the C. S. Forester novel. Distributed by Twyman Films, Inc.

ALL THE KING'S MEN

Written and directed by Robert Rossen 109 minutes b/w Columbia 1949 With Broderick Crawford, Joanne Dru, John Ireland, Mercedes McCambridge

Robert Rossen's screen style and his use of actors in *All the King's Men* could almost be considered a kind of demagoguery of its own: his tilted camera, his shorthand montage, and his dramatic use of space make this one of the most powerfully vivid films to follow *Citizen Kane* — and Rossen is following the example and the style of *Kane* in more ways than one. Yet *All the King's Men*, the story of the rise of Willie Stark, a demagogic politician, is considerably distinct from *Kane* in both its surfaces and its deeper, troubling questions. We start out liking Willie Stark (portrayed masterfully by Broderick Crawford). In a machine-run state, he emerges as an honest, forthright man with a deep, almost stirring sense of the people and the people's will. Used as a lever to split the vote and guarantee the reelection of the present governor, Willie is outraged and discovers that secret trick of anger and inflammatory rhetoric that can weld a listening crowd into a phalanx of support. Next time around Willie wins, becomes governor and goes about improving the state — and his political reputation — sometimes employing quite shabby means. Rossen gives Willie a near-mythic presence in this film; and as Willie's power mounts, so do the blinders that cut him off from fundamental morality. Hollywood's most notable anticipation of Watergate. From the Robert Penn Warren novel (itself based loosely on the career of Louisiana's Huey P. Long). Distributed by Twyman Films, Inc.

ALLURES

By Jordan Belson 8 minutes color/ motion graphics U.S.A. 1964

Jordan Belson's work has a gentle, almost Eastern rhythmic quality that contrasts strikingly with the battering lightshow pace of most graphics films. On a dark screen a tiny sliver of light may emerge, enlarge, and wend in liquid three-dimensional space; then mutate in color and form and begin rotating in yet another kind of space — an odyssey of form, space, color, in which the eye is beguiled and compelled.

Allures is among the best of Belson's films. The figures are sharply defined — not the muted haziness of his later work. Often they seem almost recognizable: a network of firing ruby-white darts of light along intersecting planes (atomic matter? cosmic forces?); deep, gathering lines, like a massive suspension bridge swaying before the eyes; a dancing, kaleidoscopic ring of lights, like some phenomenal fireworks display seen in slow motion. The light figures swim in and out of the darkened frame, existing, like the smallest kinds of life itself, for only a bright instant, then dissolving back into the blackness. The sound track is an electronic fugue of sorts: eerie resonant hollows and pitches that hold the ear hypnotically, as the fading figures hold our eyes. A meditation more than a lightshow; a film of the severest discipline and of the most awesome, stilling beauty. Distributed by Pyramid Films.

THE ASPHALT JUNGLE

Written by Ben Maddow and John Huston Directed by John Huston 112 minutes b/w M-G-M 1950 With Sterling Hayden, Marilyn Monroe, Louis Calhern, Jean Hagen, James Whitmore

Manny Farber likens *The Asphalt Jungle* to France's thirties films "like *Port of Shadows*, with their operatic underworld portraits getting lost in the gray trashiness of back rooms" — a superb description of the tarnished, gritty surfaces that dominate *The Asphalt Jungle* and the inner life of its characters. With the possible exception of Sterling Hayden's Dix, there isn't anyone approaching an admirable character in this film: gangsters and police alike are doomed by their own shabby dreams. No simple crime-does-not-pay B-melodrama, *The Asphalt Jungle* is Huston's autopsy on the genre itself. The focus of the story is a jewel heist, which Huston delineates with almost clinical absorption: the safecracker's delicate handling of a nitro bottle; the elaborate techniques of overcoming the alarm system. It is largely this attention to mechanics that brings us closer to the gangsters than we can remember in crime movies. A dirty light bathes the characters in a dreary, lingering gray, and we seem always to be seeing them in environments from which they're inseparable. So much so that the final scene — in which the bleeding Dix stumbles from his car and out to a horse in a Kentucky pasture to die and be nuzzled by the horse — seems doubly contrived; suddenly we seem to be in another movie. Recent gangster films and TV shows built on heist mechanics have made *The Asphalt Jungle* seem slow, old-fashioned. It isn't — it's that Huston builds his story by observation and inflection. The drama isn't thrust at you; it's there for you to find. Distributed by Films Inc.

BANANAS

Written and directed by Woody Allen 82 minutes color United Artists 1971 With Woody Allen, Louise Lasser, Carlos Montalban, Natividad Abascal, Jacabo Morales

Bananas is two movies. In the first one we're treated to Woody Allen at his most splendidly neurotic extreme — flailing through a romance with a radical girl who leaves him because he's not enough like Che Guevara; testing athletic devices that go berserk: backing away from a subway mugging and completely falling apart when the muggers turn to him (in the crushing world of New York City, nobody can seem quite as crushed as Woody Allen).

The second movie begins at the tiny banana republic where Woody goes first as a tourist, then as a budding revolutionary, and finally as the new dictator after the coup. The problem with this second movie is that fantasy overtakes calamity; if only publicly, Woody becomes a hero — and Woody isn't the stuff of heroes. There are some marvelous moments in that second half: Woody ordering a thousand grilled cheese sandwiches from a local diner; Woody chomping on his glass at the President's dinner. But they're moments that might have belonged to another comic. At his best Woody Allen is one of the few thoroughly original comic characters since Keaton. Allen is the strutting nebbish so thoroughly drawn to failure that stratagem becomes an act of self-destruction. Distributed by UA 16 (United Artists 16).

THE BATTLESHIP POTEMKIN

Written by Sergei Eisenstein and Nina Agadzhanova-Shutko Directed by Sergei Eisenstein 65 minutes b/w Produced by Goskino 1925

At the age of 27, Sergei Eisenstein — who had made only one previous film, *Strike* — was commissioned to make a film celebrating the 20th anniversary of the 1905 revolution in Russia. Originally he planned to make a film covering the entire year of tumult and repression, but after visiting the steps at Odessa he decided to focus on a single incident, the mutiny of sailors aboard a ship in the Odessa harbor, and the fate of the local townspeople who came one Monday afternoon to offer their assurance and support to the striking sailors. With his cameramen Eduard Tisse and V. Popov, Eisenstein began filming late in September in 1925; the official premiere took place barely four months later. In those scant four months Eisenstein created what has since become the most renowned film throughout the world. *The Battleship Potemkin* is a film orchestrated by its shots and its editing; it rises and builds with an uncanny tempo toward the devastating climax of the Odessa Steps sequence. Closeups of faces and objects are matched to long shots in a rhythm of increasingly seething unrest. Images, and their visceral and graphic inflections, take on a stark increasing power in *Potemkin,* as if Eisenstein were out to show the world and all of future history what incredible power could be summoned solely through images and their juxtaposition to other images. There is no hero or individual at the center of *Potemkin*; we meet and recognize individuals aboard the ship, and on the steps; but like the objects in the film, they become expressive of larger forces. D. W. Griffith gave film its language in his effort to reconstruct the psychological dynamics underlying the aftermath of the Civil War. Eisenstein, who takes editing to its zenith in *Potemkin,* has achieved something not altogether different, a distillation of history into a classic purity of conflict between spirit and force. No other work of art, of literature or film, expresses so trenchantly the passion and hopes of the Russian revolution.

THE BIRDS

Written by Evan Hunter Directed by Alfred Hitchcock 120 minutes color Universal 1963 With Rod Taylor, Tippi Hedren, Jessica Tandy, Suzanne Pleshette

Hitchcock is known as a practical joker, and if *Psycho* was a harrowing joke played on the audience, the film that followed it, *The Birds*, is a cruel joke, for it raises dark suspicions, as you leave the theater, about the flapping feathery creatures whistling cheerfully overhead. Tippi Hedren plays a society girl from San Francisco who drives north to Bodego Bay, pursuing Rod Taylor. She brings with her two lovebirds that may or may not be the cause of an inexplicable growing attack by the birds on the people of Bodego Bay (and, seemingly, especially upon Tippi Hedren). The tension mounts in the typical Hitchcockian fashion, but here it is a unique, clawingly anxious type of tension: a distinct neurotic sense that in some primeval way the world has gone badly awry. This apocalyptic tenor has no evident explanation within the film; nor is it ever resolved (indeed, the closing shot — of Hedren and Taylor and grandmother and daughter driving slowly through a world blanketed in menacing birds — is one of the most haunting and terrifying images in all of Hitchcock's films). For many reasons — Tippi Hedren and Rod Taylor among them — *The Birds* is not one of Hitchcock's best films. Yet as an experiment in audience terror that in some respects outdoes even *Psycho* (and one can sympathize with Hitchcock's dilemma — how *do* you follow a *Psycho?*), it is surely one of his most interesting films, even though it leaves you shaken and stymied. Distributed by Twyman Films, Inc.

THE BIRTH OF A NATION

Written by D. W. Griffith and Frank Woods Directed by D. W. Griffith Photographed by G. W. Bitzer 195 minutes b/w (silent) U.S.A. 1915 With Lillian Gish, Mae Marsh, Henry B. Walthall, Miriam Cooper, Mary Alden, Ralph Lewis George Sieggmann

To see Griffith's monumental *The Birth of a Nation* today is to be struck — perhaps to a point of being blinded — by its aggressive Southern viewpoint toward the Civil War, its racism, its often heavy-handed melodrama. That movies, so umbilically bound to the manners and styles and tastes of a period, age more rapidly than any other art is a truism. Yet the very fact that we take so much for granted in seeing *The Birth of a Nation* today — its sprawling epic structure, its deft and dramatic cross-editing, its carefully historical use of locales and sets — proves to be an ultimate form of tribute to the movie. With *The Birth of a Nation*, Griffith invented and prodigiously announced the modern motion picture. Its drastic viewpoint made it the raging national controversy he secretly hoped it would become (Griffith was no fool — he knew it needed a promotional edge). And the real force of the film — its organization of disparate shots and scenes and motifs into a powerfully structured whole — was to dominate filmmaking thereafter. Distributed by Macmillan-Audio-Brandon Films.

BONNIE AND CLYDE

Written by David Newman and Robert Benton Directed by Arthur Penn 111 minutes color Warner Brothers 1967 With Warren Beatty, Faye Dunaway, Michael J. Pollard, Gene Hackman, Estelle Parsons

When *Bonnie and Clyde* was first released in 1967, it raised quite a critical stink, largely from reviewers who considered it historically and biographically inaccurate (or worse, romantic and nostalgic). Since then it has been one of the few films of the sixties to lay claim to the status of a genuine classic, and for much the same reason that the original reviewers carped. *Bonnie and Clyde* is a nostalgic reminiscence on gangsters in the thirties; things are presented in the movie less as they probably were than as we'd like to believe they were. The characters are brilliantly etched—Penn's talent for suggesting a personality with a gesture or a slouch has never been so successful as in Clyde's toothpick-roving mouth, or Bonnie's erotic tongue-playing lassitude. The entire film has a dreamily engrossing quality that makes it satisfying after many showings. The lines are beautifully orchestrated with the actions, so that dialogue becomes only another mode of character revelation (a rarity in the sound film) — not the controlling brunt of plot progression. Less a gangster film, perhaps, than an elegy to gangsters, *Bonnie and Clyde* approaches a kind of screen poetry. Even the violence is lyrical, if gut-shattering as well. One of the best-acted, best-written, and most engrossing movies in recent years. Distributed by Twyman Films, Inc.

BRINGING UP BABY

Written by Hager Wilde and Dudley Nichols Directed by Howard Hawks 105 minutes b/w R-K-O 1938 With Katharine Hepburn, Cary Grant, Charles Ruggles, Walter Catlett, Barry Fitzgerald

In wacky comedies, premise is promise, and *Bringing Up Baby* establishes immediately the following: Cary Grant as an absent-minded paleontologist whose life's work has gone into reconstructing a dinosaur, bone by bone; on the critical day he receives the final bone and is to be married the next day; Katharine Hepburn as a thrill-seeking society girl who decides she likes Grant; and her two pets, a dog that buries bones and a leopard. The antics get swiftly out of hand; the essence of wacky comedy may well be a vertiginous movement toward engulfing chaos. But in the best manner of thirties comedy, *Bringing Up Baby* uses sexual warfare as a comic battleground in which Grant is totally swept into Hepburn's alluring madness. The lines are rich, the plot twists are deft and hilarious, and the final climax — when Hepburn sways delightedly on a ladder and collapses the reconstructed dinosaur — is unforgettable. Distributed by Films Inc.

BUS STOP

Written by George Axelrod Directed by Joshua Logan 96 minutes color Twentieth Century-Fox 1956 With Marilyn Monroe, Don Murray, Arthur O'Connell, Betty Field

Bus Stop isn't Marilyn Monroe's best movie. It's not, finally, much of a movie—but it's a splendid example of what her presence could do for an otherwise forgettable film. Marilyn is a dance-hall singer; Don Murray (who's so true to the part that his presence blares at you every time he's on screen) is a rowdy, uninhibited, socially stupefied rodeo rider who decides he wants Marilyn and proceeds to kidnap her and drag her off for marriage as though she were a rodeo calf. It's mostly odd kinds of silliness. One suspects that William Inge's play may have worked better because it gave the audience some distance from the characters. But there are moments of pure magic, transcending the frailties of plot, script, and direction. The moments belong, of course, to Marilyn. Her singing of "That Old Black Magic" is the movie's real high point, a performance so blithe and sensual, so innocent and seductive that it ceases to be a performance, as though every man's dream of a woman had, in these few immortal moments, been bettered. Distributed by Macmillan-Audio-Brandon Films.

THE CABINET OF DR. CALIGARI

Written by Carl Mayer and Hans Janowitz Directed by Robert Wiene 53 minutes b/w (silent) Germany 1919 With Werner Krauss, Conrad Veidt, Lil Dagover, Friedrich Feher

A young man visits a fair and watches as a hypnotist named Caligari opens a coffin-like chamber to reveal what seems to be a cadaver, but is actually his servant Cesare. Cesare tells a student that before dawn he will die, and that night the student is murdered. The young man suspects Caligari. Later Cesare kidnaps the young man's girlfriend from her bedroom; ordered to kill her, he chooses to run away with her instead. Searching for her, the young man visits an insane asylum and asks to speak with its director; that director turns out to be Caligari, who denies everything until Caesare's body is brought to him, at which point he reveals himself as being mad.

Fritz Lang (who was supposed to have directed the film, but didn't) suggested the final ending: that the entire story as described above becomes a lunatic fantasy of the young man, who is trying to organize other inmates to overthrow the director, Caligari. Thus a story frames a story that frames a story. We are caught in a world of shifting illusions and mad fantasies. Further sharpening this sense of imbalance is the manner in which *Caligari* was made. The two scenarists who wrote the script insisted with producer Carl Mayer that the sets be designed after the manner of the expressionist paintings of Alfred Kubin, whose distorted, cubist-like works were very much in vogue. Thus *Caligari* looks unlike any other film made before or since: the walls buckle and angle; shadows are painted onto surfaces; rooftops are squeezed into compressed, paintinglike surfaces. Its bizarre and intwisted narrative structure gives *Caligari* a prominence among horror films and in film history. Not only did *Caligari* give filmic form to Expressionism of the twenties; it gave the film medium new directions and opened new possibilities, new capability for extending inward and for using the surfaces and actions of the world to reflect a distorted psyche. Distributed by Macmillan-Audio-Brandon Films.

CATALOG

Made by John Whitney 7 minutes color/ motion graphics U.S.A. 1971

Made on an analog computer essentially as a promotional tool for his company, Motion Graphics, Inc., John Whitney's *Catalog* is at once an astounding display piece of the range and qualities of graphic motion and a film of extraordinarily rhythmic grace and mutating form. Against a black background shimmering evanescent forms hover, settle, become the word *catalog*, then dissipate; lights, like a slow-motion fireworks display, sputter and burst outward in silence; circular, crescent-rimmed forms spill outward, then fold inward, like flower petals seen in speeded motion; a series of concentric liquid rings undergo color transformations, as though one were watching the birth throes of organic neon; elegant and complex S-shaped figures rotate lazily, then disperse and reconvene. The nature of the movement is so unlike any familiar mode of animation that it seems totally organic. And there is a depth in the movement that forces the eyes into the frame — some moments in *Catalog* have a spellbinding, almost hypnotic optical power. Purity of motion and color and form in *Catalog* impresses the viewer of the awesome potential in computer-generated films for what may well be a wholly new form of cinematic art. Distributed by Pyramid Films.

CHROMOPHOBIA

By Raoul Servais 11 minutes color/ animation Belgium 1968

The theme of oppression is usually treated oppressively. Rarely is it celebrated in as dazzling a range of techniques as in Raoul Servais's extraordinary *Chromophobia*. The film is doubly inventive — not merely for its tour de force of animation ideas (they are here in rare abundance) but for the ways in which these ideas are so consistently, ineluctably matched to the theme. In depicting the goons who take over a European village, Servais uses squalid, squeezing geometric forms: tightening the frame round the goons; lining the goons into a fixed pattern, as when they become a row of triangles watching television (barred lines) on the backs of one another; or, in their movement, squeezing them into flat black triangles to zip up the understructure of a guard tower. The effect is precisely the opposite for the jesters, who upset and ultimately destroy the goons. Their style is playful, hectic, jubilant. And Servais uses extraordinary graphic ingenuity to express that difference. Distributed by International Film Bureau, Inc.

CITIZEN KANE

Written by Herman J. Mankiewicz and Orson Welles Directed by Orson Welles 119 minutes b/w R-K-O 1941 With Orson Welles, Joseph Cotton, Everett Sloane, Ray Collins, Agnes Moorehead

There is something about *Citizen Kane* — both the movie itself and the legends and stories that surround it — that gives rise to whatever urge prods one into filmmaking. Truffaut was absolutely right when he said that *Kane* is the movie "that has started the largest number of filmmakers in their careers." The sense of heightened excitement that *Kane* arouses comes not so much from its dazzling display of virtuosity and technique as from the very transparency of that technique. We can see through the film into the energy and excitement of the talented people who made it — virtually all of them at the height of their powers. As Pauline Kael has pointed out in her superb essay "Raising Kane," the collaboration of actors and technicians, writer and director in *Kane* was of such an unusual and creative pitch that the movie itself suggests nothing so much as the ingenuity and playfulness and exhuberance of those who made it. When one sees *Kane* and dreams of making a movie, he doesn't dream of a finished film; he dreams of somehow matching the reckless, inventive, exuberant atmosphere that must have dominated the set during the filming of *Kane*. *Kane* is more than a movie that proves you *can* draw attention to technique. It goes even further in proclaiming that acting, camerawork, directing, even writing are *fun*: that the very process of making a film can be a venture even more rewarding (is it possible?) than the finished film itself.

Citizen Kane is distributed by Films Inc. (nonadmission showings) and Janus Films (admission showings).

THE CROWD

Written by King Vidor, John V. A. Weaver, and Harry Behn Directed by King Vidor 98 minutes b/w (silent) M-G-M 1928 With James Murray, Eleanor Boardman, Bert Roach, Estelle Clark

During the same period (the late silent era) that Eisenstein was making films that applauded and lionized the masses, King Vidor made this bitter denunciation of the populace. *The Crowd* opens in a crowded city, amid skyscrapers and thick traffic, and gradually focuses on one man. Throughout the film this man is seen up close: his shabby apartment, the birth of his son, the death of another child. Events that link us to him are dramatized sharply. But the pang of the film comes from Vidor's way of returning the man to anonymity, dissolving him back into the midst of the crowd. For example, there is the famous shot in which the camera tilts up toward a skyscraper, then cranes in slowly, finally selecting one of the hundreds of windows, all of which look exactly alike. A subtle cut to the interior shows hundreds of men at hundreds of desks — like the exterior of the building, a repeated geometry of single blocks, suggesting that the workers in this vast office have as much uniqueness and individuality as any of the windows on the skyscraper. The ending is almost optimistic, though obliquely so. The man and his wife go to a vaudeville show and laugh at the clown. The intimation here is that there is at least some manner of delight and joy left. But Vidor's fluid camera (and *The Crowd* makes use of the moving camera in rare and subtle ways) pulls back, revealing the entire audience laughing, and again the man is lost in the mass. Distributed by Films Inc.

DAYDREAMS

Written and directed by Buster Keaton and Eddie Cline 19 minutes b/w (silent) U.S.A. 1922 With Buster Keaton and Renee Adoree

Daydreams is among Keaton's most disturbing works, a film that links him with artists like Kafka and Becket and Brecht in creating a haunting metaphor that conveys the anxieties and emotional futility of our century. The story's structure itself balances on the finest thread of illusion. Keaton, for the hand of a lovely lady, goes forth into the world to make his fortune and prove his manhood. He writes to her and tells of his successes, first on Wall Street, where the girl imagines him as a rising stockbroker, but where he flubs his job as streetcleaner; he describes his success on the Shakespherean stage, where, as an extra, he trips over a spear and throws the play into chaos. But the film's denouement — and one of the most consummate images in film history — takes place when Keaton (as always) is running from a horde of cops. He dashes to the pier, sees a moving ferryboat, and makes an incredible leap, just barely getting on the boat. But he discovers that the boat is coming in, not going out. To escape he flees through the boat and winds up, finally, on the moving paddle wheel, which he races like a treadmill. A staggering athletic feat, a brilliant comic gag, but also an image that rivets itself indelibly in our minds: Keaton flailing desperately on the paddle wheel, oblivious to its stark futility, yet with no other choice. Distributed by Macmillan-Audio-Brandon Films.

DEAD END

Written by Lillian Hellman Directed by William Wyler 93 minutes b/w United Artists 1937 With Sylvia Sidney, Joel McCrea, Humphrey Bogart, Wendy Barrie

Sidney Kingsley's play (on which this movie is based) attempted to show a microcosm of New York — the wealthy and the deprived — squeezed together into a single corner, a dead-end street abutting the East River. The film version achieves more. Wyler's sound direction, Gregg Toland's deceptively gentle cinematography, and Bogart's presence give the film an immediacy and authenticity one suspects the play lacked on Broadway.

On the surface the story seems almost moralistic. A gang of kids (the Dead End kids — Leo Gorcey, Huntz Hall, and the bunch) play a little recklessly while an alumnus from the street, Bogart (now a big-name, wealthy gangster), stands nearby and watches. The story follows a variety of currents: Sylvia Sidney and her kid brother, who seems at the edge of becoming one of the "gang"; Joel McCrea, being wooed by a rich lady but inevitably choosing the poorer Sylvia Sidney; the Dead End kids, who get in their licks (in one scene they tromp a Little Lord Fauntleroy type); and Bogart — whose droll reactions to all this serve as a time compression chamber, suggesting where the street leads after all. Indeed, the two most memorable scenes in the film are those in which Bogart encounters again the two women in his life, his old girlfriend who, to his horror, has become a prostitute; and his mother, who — in one of the most resounding scenes in Bogart's career — slaps him and tells him to go away. A striking, rich film, deftly conveyed. Distributed by UA 16.

DEAD RECKONING

Written by Oliver H. P. Garrett and Steve Fisher Directed by John Cromwell 100 minutes b/w Columbia 1947 With Humphrey Bogart, Lizabeth Scott, Morris Carnovsky

Of the Bogart films we remember best there are those in which he gave a performance in the traditional sense (*The African*

Queen, The Treasure of the Sierra Madre, The Caine Mutiny) — performances of striking force and originality; and there are those in which he was so . . . well, so much Bogart (*Casablanca, To Have and Have Not, The Maltese Falcon*). *Dead Reckoning* is clearly of the latter type. It exists around, for, and by virtue of Bogart. One cannot doubt that the lines were written for Bogart, or that the cinematography and direction and casting (particularly Lizabeth Scott, as a dead ringer for Lauren Bacall) were constructed solely for Bogart. The result is not simply a B-movie elevated considerably by Bogart's presence; it is a kind of tribute to Bogart's presence and style and laconic wit. Therefore it should be no surprise that, despite a wandering plot and some limp scenes, Bogart's presence and acting grip us throughout (and Bogart is present in almost every frame of the film). The story itself seems an ideal vehicle: Bogie as a soldier back from war, discovering that somebody has killed his old army buddy and determined to find out whom. He meets and seems to fall in love with the army buddy's wife (Lizabeth Scott), though she, of course, turns out to be . . . Distributed by Macmillan-Audio-Brandon Films.

DR. STRANGELOVE (OR, HOW I LEARNED TO STOP WORRYING AND LOVE THE BOMB)

Written by Stanley Kubrick, Terry Southern, and Peter George Directed by Stanley Kubrick 93 minutes b/w Columbia 1964 With Peter Sellers, George C. Scott, Sterling Hayden, Keenan Wynn, Slim Pickens

General Jack D. Ripper goes berserk and sends out the order that directs several B-52s toward the interior of Russia to drop H-bombs. The Russians, however, have perfected a "doomsday machine," by which any nuclear bomb would automatically and irretrievably set off total annihilation of the world. The B-52 orders were coded, and the secret code is controlled only by Ripper. Once his base is attacked by U.S. armed forces, he commits suicide. An aide discovers the code, but is prevented from relaying it by a marine colonel now controlling the base. Finally he persuades the colonel, but neither man has a dime for the pay phone (all other phones are out of commission). The aide tells the colonel to shoot a Coca-Cola machine to release a dime. The colonel refuses stoutly, arguing that then he'd be answerable to the Coca-Cola company. At such moments *Dr. Strangelove* verges on that rare peak between unmitigated hilarity and an anguished scream curdled in the throat. Of all Kubrick's films, *Dr. Strangelove* is his most fully realized success, and surely it is the bleakest and funniest of movie black comedy. B-52s sweep into Russia to the tune of "When Johnny Comes Marching Home." The pilot of the one B-52 that escapes the recall whips his hat in the air as he rides the bomb down, as though it were a bronco. When news that the bomb has dropped reaches the Washington, D.C., "war room," a weird ex-Nazi presidential advisor, Dr. Strangelove, describes to the President how a few dozen men can go on living in deep caverns and giggles when he describes the ratio of women to men — and the qualifications of those women — necessary for repopulation. *Dr. Strangelove* relishes in the unthinkable, makes nuclear holocaust the equivalent of a Mack Sennett pie fight. Distributed by Columbia 16.

DUCK SOUP

Written by Bert Kelmar, Harry Rubin, Arthur Sheekman, and Nat Perrin Directed by Leo McCarey 76 minutes b/w Paramount 1933 With Groucho, Harpo, Chico, and Zeppo Marx, Margaret Dumont, Louis Calhern, Raquel Torres

In the mythical nation of Freedonia, a new President is inaugurated, President Firefly, Groucho Marx. Margaret Dumont plays Mrs. Teasdale, the millionaire widow who has chosen Groucho as the new President. ("What about your husband?" Groucho asks Mrs. Dumont. "He's dead." Groucho: "He's just using that as an excuse.") In a song, Groucho informs the assembled guests of his intentions as the new President: "If you think this country's bad off now, just wait till I get through with it." His declaration promises a reign of anarchy, and Harpo and Chico are on hand to provide it.

Rarely have they been in better form, Chico as the minister of war, and Harpo as the President's chauffeur, though both of them secretly work as spies for the opposing nation of Sylvania. Chico's ploys with a sidewalk vendor are enough to drive the vendor to madness. Even as spies they are worse than mischievous. When the man for whom they're spying receives a telegram, Harpo tears it up. Says Chico, "He gets mad because he can't read."

Duck Soup is the only Marx Brothers comedy directed by a man with a strong intuitive sense of comic possibilities, Leo McCarey. It is their purest comedy, not diluted by irrelevant song numbers and minor romances. It is also their most directly political. The Marxes make shambles of the pomp and authority associated with governing a state. The climactic war scene, in which Freedonia battles Sylvania, has at its core a magnificently funny, but sorely relevant, gag in which President Groucho walks around blindly with a pot stuck over his head and his features painted on the pot. Distributed by Twyman Films, Inc.

ERSATZ

Written by Rudolf Sremec Designed and directed by Dusan Vukotic 10 minutes color/animation Yugoslavia: Zagreb 1961

Ersatz depicts a world where everything is inflatable: people, tools, cars, roads, geography itself. But what can be inflated can be deflated; and despite its sleek and superbly maintained comic tone, *Ersatz* contains moments of sheer dread, when characters whom we've come to like or dislike suddenly hiss in a cataclysm of dissolving form as they reduce to tiny scraps, like balloons. This comic idea, developed in a manner that is at once droll and delightful and caustic, compels our attention, gives a nervous edge to our laughter. The central character — who (can any fantasy beat this one?) may choose between little colored scraps to blow up into vivacious, alluring females — finally decides on one; but she prefers a husky muscle-trimmed beach bum. The central character unplugs both of them.

There is a striking graphic ingenuity to *Ersatz*: sharp curves and lines reminiscent of Bauhaus designs give the characters a look unlike any other animation film in memory. The action moves with surprising swiftness, and the gags are graphically inventive. Yet it's style — a blend of pathos and comic richness and dread — that gives *Ersatz* much of its flavor. It was the first film made outside the U.S. to win the Academy Award for animation. Distributed by Contemporary Films/McGraw-Hill.

EXPERIMENTS IN MOTION GRAPHICS

By John Whitney 13 minutes color/motion graphics U.S.A. 1968

John Whitney's *Experiments in Motion Graphics* might be considered an instructional film of sorts. Whitney himself narrates, commenting on the nature and difficulties and potential of computer graphics films, while on the screen we see a dazzling array of examples, culminating in several sequences from the riveting Whitney short *Permutations*. Whitney's commentary is striking. Terse, emphatic, he first explains the principles that guide graphic design on the analog computer. Then he attempts to describe the art itself by comparisons with music and language. Finally he admits to regretting that motion graphics, perhaps the most promising frontier of technological art, remains closed to most because of the inaccessibility of computers, the staggering technical competence still required, and the cost of operating computers.

But underscoring and amplifying Whitney's exposition are the graphics themselves which we see on the screen: geometric figures of three-dimensional contours that rotate, flex, and transform in lucid symmetrical patterns and fluid rhythms. Some of Whitney's most stunning figures and transformations can be seen here. One recommendation in viewing the film (indeed, it virtually proves one of Whitney's points) is to listen to Whitney's commentary and then leave the sound track off and play instead classical guitar or harpsichord; in this way it becomes a different film. Distributed by Pyramid Films.

FELIX MAKES WHOOPEE

By Pat Sullivan 8 minutes b/w (silent)/animation U.S.A. early 1920s

The "Felix the Cat" cartoons were among the first to treat an animal whose actions are identifiably human. Like other early cartoon figures, Felix was characterized less by his neuroses or compulsions (as would, say, the later Disney and Warners cartoon figures) than by the gag situations in which he became involved. These were invariably strong visual gags, normally — again a difference with later animation — without a victim, unless it was Felix. In *Felix Makes Whoopee*, the focus is on a drunken spree, a theme that animator Pat Sullivan uses in playing out a surrealistic allegory about the world's curious mutations when one has imbibed sufficiently. Buildings frolic; cars transform into fish; staircases become mountains and rush in flooding waves beneath his feet as he tries climbing them. A vivid, hallucinatory, nightmarish feeling informs this film. You have a sense of things spinning in and out of other things, transmuting with astounding rapidity, achieving a kind of dizzying swell. If *Felix Makes Whoopee* were shown on television, it would probably arouse protest for being pro-drug or something like that. Yet it clearly shows the sophistication and originality of animated shorts before Disney had even begun doing any animation. Distributed by Creative Film Society.

FLOWERS AND TREES

By Walt Disney and Ub Iwerks 8 minutes color/animation U.S.A. 1932

Flowers and Trees was the first cartoon made to use the tricolor Technicolor process, and even today its colors have a remarkable clarity and strength. But perhaps even more significant, *Flowers and Trees* was one of the first animation shorts to anthropomorphize the entire realm of nature — trees dance, fall in love, and a stumpy, cantankerous tree chases the female and, failing to get her, sets the forest on fire. The theme might sound silly (it belonged to a Disney series called the "Silly Symphonies"), but it would guide much of the animation from Disney's studio, as well as M-G-M and Warners, through the thirties and beyond. In *Flowers and Trees,* for example, the forest fire is extinguished by the combined efforts of flowers, water lilies, and such, a kind of ballet fire brigade The dancelike quality that would hallmark other Disney shorts such as *Skeleton Dance* and *The Old Mill* gives the movements a synchronous flow that we've come to identify with the best of Disney animation. Available from Macmillan-Audio-Brandon Films as part of "Milestones in Animation."

THE FLY

Written, directed, and animated by Vladimir Jutrisa and Aleksander Marks 9 minutes color/animation Yugoslavia: Zagreb 1967

Against a stark background a blank-faced man is distracted by a buzzing fly. The man makes a few efforts to kill the fly, though they are the kind of limp efforts — a movement of his foot — that we suspect characterize this man at his most resolute. When he does finally pin down the fly with his foot, the buzzing ceases momentarily, then rises again, only louder now, more insistent, more aggravating. The man turns his head and sees that the fly has suddenly burgeoned in size: it is half the scale of the man. The man shows only a hint of being disconcerted as the fly gradually continues its growth to an immensity that reverses the earlier scale of fly and man. When the fly finally reaches its full elephantine stature, it begins surrounding the man, shattering the glass-like world around him. Its buzzing has now become a droning roar. The man's world falls away in pieces, till he is left on a tiny sliver of that world in the darkness. Then he begins falling, tumbling down into space. The sliver itself escapes him. When he lands, it is to be joined by the fly — now at his own size — which spreads an arm over his shoulder in — what? A truce, a show of brotherhood, a mockery of equality? The man lifts his arm over the fly's shoulder. Wedding music on the sound track.

The Fly progresses with the dismal and uneasy structure of a nightmare. The slightest of incidents, a frantically buzzing fly, escalates to a literal shattering of the man's entire world. Yet animators Jutrisa and Marks suggest more than a simple nightmare with *The Fly*. At the center, finally, is the man; and his face and movements and doll-like body (it could be hanging from a hook, the way he stands) reflect a complacency that somehow, in Kafka-like logic, brings *on* the horror. Distributed by Contemporary Films/McGraw-Hill.

FOR A FEW DOLLARS MORE

Screenplay by Luciano Vicenzoni Directed by Sergio Leone 130 minutes color Italy United Artists 1967 With Clint Eastwood, Lee Van Cleef, Gian Maria Volente

The "spaghetti Westerns," as they are called, are both a variant upon and a tribute to the classic Hollywood Westerns of John Wayne, Gary Cooper, and Randolph Scott. More precisely, the films of Sergio Leone (*Fistful of Dollars; The Good, the Bad and the Ugly; Once Upon a Time in the West*, etc.) are a kind of nostalgic reminiscence of what he remembered best from those old Hollywood horse epics, set in relief against the bitter, empty landscapes of Spain and southern Italy where he has filmed them. The essence of a Leone Western, someone once remarked, is that every character is out to prove that he's tougher and nastier than the other guys— the old moral conundrum of good vs. bad being resolved to tough vs. not-as-tough. Leone spends much time establishing this toughness: by slow-moving cameras that rove an embittered terrain (whether of bleak, sun-shattered scrub desert or bleak, caustic faces); by a minimum of dialogue and a maximum of buildup to each gunfight (gunfights are to Leone's Westerns what dance numbers are to a Fred Astaire musical); by ignoring plot requirements to the point where action becomes incomprehensible (if you're worried about logical progression). No matter. Movies like *For a Few Dollars More* have at least the virtue of keeping the mythic West alive, even though this time it's a nastier, scroungier, more vicious West, and not exactly the American West at that. Distributed by UA 16.

FORBIDDEN PLANET

Written by Cyril Hume Directed by Fred McLeod Wilcox 98 minutes color M-G-M 1956 With Walter Pidgeon, Leslie Nielsen,, Anne Francis, Robby the Robot

One of the crucial differences between science fiction literature and science fiction movies is that often the literature is characterized by an audacity of imagination that's rarely ever glimpsed in the movies. For the most part science fiction movies threaten us with annihilation but almost never present an astounding idea. *Forbidden Planet* is one of the few exceptions.

A spaceship from earth is sent to investigate a planet where only Walter Pidgeon and his daughter and a robot are living. Pidgeon does not welcome the ship. Indeed, terrible things begin happening to the ship — some invisible monster tears through it at night. Meantime, two of the earthmen discover the secret of the planet. Its entire interior has been hollowed into a vast technological city to provide the energy for a race that had reached a point of controlled evolution at which its inhabitants could transform from bodily into nonphysical creatures. Something went wrong; the race had vanished. And now a dreadful presence haunts the planet, and it centers mysteriously around Pidgeon.

The special effects in *Forbidden Planet* are in some ways more impressive than those in *2001*; they at least tend to stretch the imagination further. There's a lot of the fifties schlock — a tepid romance, crew members talking as though they were hunched over milkshakes — but at its best *Forbidden Planet* reminds us what science fiction film can be if it's done well. In a roundabout manner based on Shakespeare's *The Tempest*. Distributed by Films Inc.

FOREIGN CORRESPONDENT

Written by Charles Bennett and Joan Harrison Directed by Alfred Hitchcock 120 minutes b/w United Artists 1940 With Joel McCrea, Laraine Day, Herbert Marshall, George Sanders

Foreign Correspondent is a chase film in the vein of *The Thirty-Nine Steps* and *North by Northwest*: covering considerable territory both geographically (the U.S., Britain, Holland) and morally. Joel McCrea plays a crack reporter sent to Europe to cover a diplomatic conference that just might avoid the outbreak of war. He stumbles onto a rigged assassination, pursues the villain to a deserted windmill ("That windmill is blowing in the other direction"), and steps into an inferno of intrigue, danger, and assorted audience delights. There are some superb Hitchcockian moments: a seeming murder atop London's Big Ben; a sea of umbrellas wavering as the assassin wends through them; and a convincing crash at sea of the airliner carrying McCrea and his girl and the master spy back to New York. The conclusion is a provocative call to arms, as McCrea stands holding a radio microphone during a German bombing of London: "The lights are going out in Europe! Ring yourself with steel, America!" Distributed by Macmillan-Audio-Brandon Films.

THE FRENCH CONNECTION

Written by Ernest Tidyman Directed by William Friedkin 104 minutes color Twentieth Century-Fox 1971 With Gene Hackman, Fernando Ray, Roy Schneider, Tony LaBianco, Marcel Bozuffi, Frederick De Pasquale

There is a driving, relentless quality to the historically based *The French Connection*, as though the very pulse and fibre of the film were an extension of its violent, compulsive central character, a narcotics cop nicknamed Popeye. It's Popeye, after all, who follows out a few hunches that lead him — and the New York Police Department — to a cache of several million dollars' worth of heroin, at that time the largest single "bust" in the world.

But Popeye is no Joe Friday. In the opening scene we see him dressed as a Santa Claus, chasing and thrashing a black youth. When he goes into a bar for a shakedown, there's no disguising his pleasure at treating the lined-up blacks the way a sadistic SS guard would walk past a row of Jews at Auschwitz. When a sniper shoots at Popeye from atop an apartment building, Popeye's chase after him becomes a savage and private vendetta. in effect, we're given the portrait of the effective cop as a man driven and numbed by a compulsive force that borders on sheer brutality. At the end, when Popeye mistakenly shoots a federal narcotics agent in a chase through a deserted building, he doesn't seem to feel much regret and neither — significantly — do we. Distributed by Films Inc.

THE GENERAL LINE (retitled OLD AND NEW)

Written by Sergei Eisenstein and Grigori Alexandrov Directed by Sergei Eisenstein Photographed by Edouard Tisse 72 minutes b/w (silent) Russia 1929 With Marfa Lapkino, Vasys Buzenkov, Kostya Vailiev

The General Line is Eisenstein's most obscure work, perhaps his least-seen feature film. A pity, because, despite its seemingly fragmentary structure, there is considerable proof of supreme genius here: the introduction of a cream separator to a village co-op, which Eisenstein's intercutting transforms into a moment of shattering triumph; a tortured sequence in which the villagers pray for rain; and a final movement of the tractors, which becomes a virtual dance played out by dozens of tractors on a vast pasture.

Some of Eisenstein's most sophisticated and elaborately orchestrated editing can be found in *The General Line*. His notion of "polyphonic montage" — in which he relates major and minor themes and varying hues of white and black in a rhythmic symphonic whole — is used here to organize sequences which, when seen, have powerful musical rhythm and structure. The theme of *The General Line* is the rural collective, and though this concept would not be realized throughout Russia until several years after the film was made and released, the feeling behind the propogandist thrust is genuine and felt. Distributed by Macmillan-Audio-Brandon Films.

GERTIE THE DINOSAUR

By Winsor McCay 9 minutes b/w (silent)/ animation U.S.A. 1909

There had been animated movement before *Gertie the Dinosaur* — many of the inventions that preceded the movie camera used drawn cartoons, and some practitioners, like Emile Reynaud of France, had developed poignant, sophisticated little shorts. But Winsor McCay's *Gertie the Dinosaur* was the first cartoon that used the modern motion picture camera and projector, and it was a sophisticated venture at that — involving some 10,000 separate drawings. Seeing *Gertie* even today, one is impressed at the fluidity of movement and the use of depth and contours. McCay's dinosaur is no simple two-dimensional figure on a flat surface, but a figure that moves in depth — from a smaller form deep in the frame to a larger form as it approaches the camera. McCay went on to do a series called "Dreams of a Rarebit Fiend," which all began with the premise of a man climbing into bed after eating Welsh rarebit) followed inevitably by a preposterous dream (a house that flies like an airplane, a dog that grows into a canine King Kong and ravages cities). *Gertie the Dinosaur* is distributed by Macmillan-Audio-Brandon Films.

GOLD DIGGERS OF 1935

Written by Manuel Seff and Peter Milne Directed and choreographed by Busby Berkeley 95 minutes b/w Warner Brothers 1935 With Dick Powell, Adolph Menjou, Gloria Stewart, Alice Brady

In the best of Busby Berkeley's musicals — and this is among them — you don't talk about "the film" or the story or the characters; they were as irrelevant for Berkeley as they are for us. You talk about his musical numbers. And *Gold Diggers of 1935* contains one of his most dazzling and outrageous, "The Words Are in My Heart," employing 100 dancing pianos. But even more striking, more memorable, and certainly much darker in its tone and spirit, is the classic "Lullaby of Broadway" number — a number that to this day has never been matched for its immense vitality, its telescoping of time and space, or its cruel, perverse attention to the Manhattan nightclub life — seen invariably in distorted angles, from grim perspectives, and framed in a dream that ends in a kind of giddy suicide. The "Lullaby of Broadway" sequence opens with a totally dark frame, except for a lit, distant face of Wini Shaw singing the song. The camera dollies in on her so slowly that we are unaware of its movement: her head grows larger, and when the camera finished its slow dolly, she finishes the song. The cigarette in her mouth is dead. The camera tilts over her head, and her face dissolves into an aerial shot of Manhattan. This opening suggests the tenor and strange expressionism of the number, which — like all Berkeley's numbers — begin with the everyday and the recognizable and move increasingly toward gigantic spaces and virtual squadrons of dancers. Distributed by UA 16.

GOLDFRAME

Written and directed by Raoul Servais 5 minutes b/w (animation) Belgium 1970

Goldframe explores, with an admirable simplicity and final jarring force, that delicate transition between monomania and paranoiac madness. Jason Goldframe, a movie producer obsessed with the need to be first in everything, stalks from his high-ceiling, award-splashed office after hours and into one of the studios, where he orders a technician to throw a huge spotlight on him. There he enacts a strange, competitive ritual between himself and — yes — his shadow. He dances, pumps himself into a wild frenzy, all to move faster than his shadow. "I must be first, I must be first," he huffs, as he flails in movements that become increasingly spastic, uncontrolled. He flies. He tears off his head. And gradually, as his shadow does lose pace, Goldframe laughs and squats to watch his convulsed shadow whip and wind crazily on the wall. But suddenly it separates from the wall, wedges its hands together into a big impacted fist, and smashes Goldframe over the head.

In its subtle movement from realism to a stunning surrealistic climax, and in its careful buildup of psychological emphasis, *Goldframe* achieves a unique impact. The central metaphor, of a man competing with his very shadow, strikes a resonating, somber note — as though this distorted ritual were rooted in the illusive nature of the movies themselves. And in tearing loose from primal physical laws, Jason Goldframe not only achieves his longing to be first but brings on a vicious, law-shattering revenge. Distributed by International Film Bureau, Inc.

GRAND PRIX

Written by Robert Alan Arthur Directed by John Frankenheimer 179 minutes color M-G-M 1966 With James Garner, Eva Marie Saint, Yves Montand, Toshiro Mifune, Jessica Walter

Grand Prix is symptomatic of that (hopefully) vanishing breed of films in which lavish money and attention and expertise are given to a few visually stunning scenes, while the rest of the movie languishes under a plot so burdened with its own futile intricacies that we never come to know or care about the characters.

This is not to decry the racing sequences in *Grand Prix*. Technically and visually they're often superb. There's a heart-in-the-mouth feeling of outrageous speed, of distances being wiped away by 180-mile-an-hour racing cars shooting like bullets through the streets of Monte Carlo. But because the rest of the film is pure mush — entangled affairs between the drivers and a host of interchangeable women — we don't know or care a thing about any particular driver when we get to the race. So whether a driver wins or loses, is crippled or killed, hasn't any force. We might as well be watching the Grand Prix finals on ABC's "Wide World of Sports." One suspects that the director and the writer and even the stars soon settled down with the decision that they'd make a lot of money and keep the studio happy if only they'd pull off the racing sequences well, which they did. Does this say more about the nature of filmmaking or of audiences? Distributed by Films Inc.

THE GRAPES OF WRATH

Written by Nunnally Johnson Directed by John Ford Photographed by Gregg Toland 128 minutes b/w Twentieth Century-Fox 1940 With Henry Fonda, Jane Darwell, John Carradine, Charlie Grapewin, Doris Dowden

In the mid-thirties, writer John Steinbeck spent considerable time with the "Okies," displaced farmers who had come from the dust bowls of Oklahoma to seek jobs and new homes in California. Instead they found wretched conditions, poverty wages for fruit-picking, and the scars of California's acrimony. Steinbeck's book chronicles these people compassionately and uncompromisingly; but when Twentieth Century-Fox announced the film version, people expected it would be compromised. Then came the rumor that Fox's Darryl Zanuck had bought the book in order to shelve it. "Show me a man who can prove that I spent $70,000 for a book in order to shelve it," Zanuck reportedly said, "and I'll make a picture about *him!*"

Nunnally Johnson's screenplay and John Ford's direction give *The Grapes of Wrath* a humane quality as rich as Steinbeck's novel: the Joad family at the center of the story, setting out from Oklahoma in a claptrap, overburdened truck; looking forward to California with vivid hopes; and being startled and numbed by the hostile reception. When the preacher helps organize labor resistance and is killed, Tom Joad kills a deputy and becomes a hunted criminal. At the center of the film (as she was the center of the novel) is Ma Joad, whose very presence seems a blessing of the highest sort. Photographed with a kind of lingering, gently meditative quality by Gregg Toland (there is but one moving camera shot in the entire film), *The Grapes of Wrath* is as astute in its surfaces and imagery as in the social force of its story. Distributed by Films Inc.

THE GREAT TRAIN ROBBERY

Written and directed by Edwin S. Porter 10 minutes b/w (silent) U.S.A. 1903 With G. M. Anderson, Marie Murray, George Barnes, Frank Hanaway

A gang of bandits attacks a train depot, ties up the telegraph operator, and waits for the train. When it arrives, they rob the mail car and then escape. In the woods they split up the money and celebrate their success. Meantime, a posse forms, chases the bandits, and finally captures them.

If it sounds a mite primitive, that's only because *The Great Train Robbery* was the first Western. It was also one of the first films to break actions down into separate shots, although usually the single shots were depicted with the camera at a single fixed distance. Perhaps the ultimate importance of *The Great Train Robbery* is that it fixed forever the most popular and enduring staples of movie-making: plenty of action, guns, the chase, and the triumph of the good guys over the bad guys. Mythically it is the father of all movies to come later — certainly those from Hollywood (though this film itself was made in a suburb of New York). Distributed by Macmillan-Audio-Brandon Films.

GREED

Written and directed by Erich von Stroheim 114 minutes b/w (silent) M-G-M 1924 With Gibson Gowland, Zasu Pitts, Jean Hersholt, Chester Conklin

James Agee called it the Magna Carta of American films; Denis Marion has compared it, in its tenacious probing of moral decline, with Dostoevsky. *Greed* — in two separate senses — is the supreme tragedy of American movies. As a brilliantly and harshly realistic portrayal of the Frank Norris novel *McTeague*, von Stroheim's work plunges its characters into an abyss of unrelenting avarice and self-contempt. As one of the most ambitious and olympian achievements in film history (von Stroheim's own original cut version was eight hours long), it became a notorious case of studio mutilation; M-G-M's Thalberg ordered studio cutter June Mathis (whom Stroheim claims had read neither book nor script) to trim it down to its present length. What we have of *Greed* today is a fragmentary, albeit consummately powerful, version of von Stroheim's original work.

Greed is the story of McTeague and Trina. McTeague — or Mac — an unlicensed dentist, is blustery, simple, ultimately likable. When he marries Trina, he doesn't realize that her sole and concentrated purpose in life is to amass money, gold coins that she plays through her fingers and hides in her bed. (One of the scenes deleted from von Stroheim's original depicts the naked Trina climbing into bed to caress and fondle her gold). The marriage grows clouded by Trina's greed, ravaging both Mac and Trina till he finally explodes in murder. In the closing sequence Mac flees with Trina's money into the stifling wastes of Death Valley — the figurative and literal hell to which the gold has drawn him.

The characters in *Greed* are etched with psychological precision and telling detail: Trina (Zasu Pitts) scooting her gold into its sack and glaring up at a weary Mac home from work; McTeague (Gibson Gowland) bending nervously, shamefully to kiss the anaesthetized Trina when he first meets her in his dentist's office; Marcus (Jean Hersholt), Trina's cousin, wedging a finger into his ear as he waits nervously with Trina. Von Stroheim also uses his sets and occasions masterfully: during the wedding of Mac and Trina, a funeral procession wends past outside the window; and the sequence in Death Valley is unforgettable — the parched, scabrous land, unbroken to the horizon, becomes the terrain of Mac's inner world, as he sits there with the gold but no water, handcuffed to a dead man. Distributed by Films, Inc.

HALLELUJAH, I'M A BUM! (retitled HEART OF NEW YORK)

Written by S. N. Behrman and Ben Hecht Directed by Lewis Milestone 82 minutes b/w United Artists 1932 With Al Jolson, Harry Langdon, Madge Evans, Frank Morgan, Chester Conklin

At times this delightful Al Jolson musical has the ring of a manifesto, albeit a curiously ambivalent one. For though it depicts most vividly and immediately the realities of the Depression era — brutish, unshaven men who live in Central Park — it seems to celebrate their condition rather than pity it. Jolson plays a fast-talking, gentle tramp called Bumper, who is considered the Mayor of Central Park. He is a good friend of the real mayor of New York City — a cardboard society type with a penchant for booze and a hopeless eye on Madge Evans. A series of twists separates Madge from the mayor. In attempting suicide she is saved by Bumper but has lost all memories. She and Bumper fall in love, and to support her Bumper goes to work — severing himself from the bum's life and becoming part of the mayor's straight, workaday world. When finally Bumper learns that Madge is the mayor's girl, he takes the mayor to her. She recovers her memory and falls into his arms, and Bumper walks away broken hearted — to return to the life of a bum. The musical numbers are rich, stirring, frequent; and they tend to advance, rather than retard, characters and story. But what is unique is the film's warmly sardonic viewpoint, best expressed in a number called "What Do You Want with Money?" in which Jolson tells the other bums that since they're poor, they ought to enjoy it. A Depression movie unlike any others. And the surprise is that director Milestone pulled it off. Distributed by Macmillan-Audio-Brandon Films.

HOBBY

Written and directed by Daniel Szczechura 7 minutes color/animation Poland 1968

Against a grisly-colored, bleak, flat landscape, a woman sits in a chair and knits. Overhead a winged man flies past. The woman rises and, from a starkly photographed angle, is shown lassoing the winged man. Once caught, he becomes a tiny figure in a cage. The woman returns to her knitting until another winged man sails past — whom she captures as well. Gradually we're given the unsettling suggestion that the men are caught less by her intervention than by their own desire to be caught. Finally the woman rises and walks toward a city of cages, where men pound at the bars in futile protest. She adds her new captives and stands staring at her menagerie. Then, inexplicably, she begins opening the cages, releasing the men, and they fly off in vast gathering hordes, a conflagration of winged creatures darkening the sky. The woman returns to her knitting.

A mood of desolation grips this film like a fever. These men — why do they have wings, not the woman? Why so many of them? And the woman who only knits and captures and releases, as in some cycle — what does she want with them, only to release them? Stark and formidable and haunting, and reminiscent of Kafka in its chilling simplicity. Distribution by Contemporary Films/McGraw-Hill.

HOLLYWOOD: THE DREAM FACTORY

Written by Bud Friedgen Narrated by Dick Cavett 52 minutes color M-G-M 1970

It was the studio, beyond all others, that seemed hoisted on the loftiest of dreams. Under the severe "taste tests" of Louis B. Mayer and the mild, but iron, control of Irving Thalberg, M-G-M in the thirties created films that we now identify as the epitome of Hollywood (*Gone with the Wind, The Wizard of Oz, Camille, San Francisco, Meet Me in St. Louis*), films that sought a touch of literary finesse and achieved a production style so lavish and perfect that one cannot discuss them rightly as expressions of anything except, perhaps, the nascent longings of a generation. M-G-M was the studio of expensively mounted daydreams.

It was, after all, the studio that owned Garbo, Gable, the Barrymores, Harlow, Hepburn, Tracy, and — mistakenly — the Marx Brothers. Ah, the rub. There are embarrassing questions to be asked about M-G-M. Why did the Marx Brothers go into decline (ultimately a steep decline) after signing a handsome contract with M-G-M? And why did M-G-M pay Keaton $100 a week in the late thirties as (of all things) a writer, without giving him assignments? What had M-G-M done to von Stroheim's masterpiece, *Greed*, and why did it destroy the footage it chopped out?

Hollywood: The Dream Factory answers none of these questions, at least not directly. Yet there are implicit answers, if simply in the fact that the rush of excerpts — chosen so supremely well to trick that gland of nostalgia in the American brain — makes us lust for the old M-G-M and the kind of movies it made. Exactly. M-G-M knew so well what it was doing that Talent became another production value, like sparkling, lavish sets and exquisite costuming. The last word in the title of this beguiling film is, after all, "factory," and M-G-M was the most supremely well-organized of movie factories. This collection of excerpts, commentary, and perspective (cutting from the "Yellow Brick Road" number in *The Wizard of Oz* to the M-G-M auction at which Dorothy's shoes sold for — yes! — $15,000) makes us aware of what's been missing from movies since television happened. It also suggests much about the nature of M-G-M itself, where Louis B. Mayer's taste became a yardstick — perhaps more powerful than the Production Code — for the entire industry. As a compilation of clips from the features, it's the best, with some marvelous montages of kissing scenes and "The End" shots — ahh, how the formula lived then. Distributed by Films Inc.

I AM A FUGITIVE FROM A CHAIN GANG

Written by Howard J. Green and Brown Holmes Directed by Mervyn LeRoy 93 minutes b/w Warner Brothers 1932 With Paul Muni, Glenda Farrell, Helen Vinson, Preston Foster

The earliest and the most famous of Warners' "social dramas," *I Am a Fugitive* retains, even today, much of the devastating power that shocked audiences in 1932. There is almost nothing cheerful about this movie. It follows the story (based on a real-life incident which, by the way, had a *happy* ending) of a man (Muni) who becomes involved in a robbery against his will, is sent to a chain gang, and escapes. He goes to Chicago and slowly builds a new life for himself. Gradually he becomes a respected, hard-working businessman and looks upon his past as a nightmare that he has finally escaped. A snubbed woman eventually turns him in, and, amid a flurry of controversy ("He's a fine citizen," claim the Chicago newspapers; "States' rights!" shout the Southerners who want him back), Muni finally accepts a deal: ninety days and he'll be given a pardon. But after the ninety days the pardon is forgotten. Muni is forgotten, and the chain gang life becomes even more intolerable for its inequities and deceptions. Muni escapes again, but there is no new life this time: he is a haunted, hunted man eking out some kind of bare existence at the fringes of society. *I Am a Fugitive* strikes hard. The terrors are as deeply felt as they are believable; and the scripting, the direction, and particularly Muni's inward performance give it a strength and intensity that keep it among the handful of best films of social criticism ever made in America. Distributed by UA 16.

THE INFORMER

Written by Dudley Nichols Directed by John Ford 91 minutes b/w R-K-O 1935 With Victor McLaglen, Heather Angel, Preston Foster, Margot Graham

It is ironic that, in the career of a director so attuned to American themes, motifs, and history as John Ford, one of his most lauded films should be set not only geographically away from America (in Ireland during the Irish rebellion), but thematically — and cinematically — at a considerable distance from much of his other work. The John Ford we come to know intimately from *Stagecoach* or *Wagon Master* or *She Wore a Yellow Rib-*

bon or *Young Mr. Lincoln* is not all that present — and certainly not that discernible— in *The Informer*. This is not meant to derogate from the film; only to suggest that it represents Ford's most self-conscious attempt to make a film which is not bound by genre or the standard Hollywood strictures. *The Informer* centers on a stultified, meatish Irishman, Gypo (played by Victor McLaglen), who, following a restless battle with his dim conscience, turns in a friend for twenty pounds, and is forced to live with that knowledge and its effects on others. The story is simple in an almost primitive way, but Ford invests it with a striking psychological power. The fog that mutes all surfaces becomes an active, visual suggestion of Gypo's clouded mind, the use of reflections, of wind, of various characters (such as a blind man who terrifies Gypo) all heighten a sense of psychic ruin, and the frame becomes a visual embodiment of Gypo's mind. The film was a bold and exciting experiment, and if it strikes us today as being too "literary" in its use of symbols and its concentration on emblems and textures, we might well realize that it represents an important break from the genre-dominated, studio-dominated movies of the mid-thirties. Distributed by Films Inc.

JOHNNY BELINDA

Written by Irmgard von Cube and Allen Vincent Directed by Jean Negulesco 102 minutes b/w Warner Brothers 1948 With Jane Wyman, Lew Ayres, Charles Bickford, Agnes Moorehead

This screen adaptation of Elmer Harris' play is at once superbly tactful and tasteful and trenchant in the emotions it arouses. The story seems a sure-fire scenario for a soap opera. A lovely mute girl (Jane Wyman), is befriended by a sensitive local doctor (Lew Ayres) in a small coastal town in rural Nova Scotia; she is raped, and the doctor is implicitly accused. When the rapist comes back to take away her child, she kills him, and goes on trial for murder. Done today, such a film would possibly veer wildly between moments of horrendous violence (the rape, the killing) and ludicrous hysteria (the discovery that she is pregnant, the doctor's reactions, etc.). Yet because of a sensitive script, gentle direction, and — perhaps above all — the softly underplayed and exquisite acting of Jane Wyman (and the performance of Charles Bickford, who has all the tough and feisty naivete of a Bible-belt farmer), the film never loses its focus, never surrenders its characters to the easy route of histrionics. Distributed by UA 16.

K-9000: A SPACE ODDITY

Directed by Robert Mitchell and Robert Swartha 11 minutes color/animation U.S.A.: Haboush Company 1970

In a desert a small befuddled-looking canine sits and listens to an old-fashioned Gramophone, as in the old RCA emblems of "his master's voice." A car approaches. Men get out, grab the dog, and take him off toward a rocket on the horizon. The dog is put in the rocket and sent into the heavens. Among the stars the dog beholds strange marvels, glittering stars that seem to be spilling — in a vast cascade — from a giant salt shaker; an Uncle Sam character pitching dollar bills at a cash register, as though in a horseshoe game. On a barren planet of tiny volcanic pits, little furry creatures stick their heads out to gaze at the dog and giggle. Back in flight, the dog speeds toward a vast Gramophone and seems sucked inside of it. He sees dazzling lights and finally enters a blank, cube-like chamber. Here he meets an older dog, then becomes that older dog — a process repeated till the final dog, a pup, is sent back on the rocket to earth, where he sits and listens to the Gramophone in the desert.

This delightful little animated short manages to spoof *2001* in title and in several of the sequences. Yet it's more than a spoof, a whimsical little fable in which space travel becomes an excuse for a playful surrender to clever graphic fantasies. Distributed by Creative Film Society.

LA JETÉE

Written and directed by Chris Marker 29 minutes b/w France 1963 With Hélène Chatelain, Davos Heinrich, Jacques Ledoux, André Heinrich

World War III. Among the few survivors, huddled in deep catacombs beneath Paris, is a man who relishes a single moment when he stood on the jetty of the Orly airport in Paris and watched a beautiful woman stagger in shock. The survivors are desperate — they have few supplies, little energy, and can turn only to the past or the future for help. The man with the obsessive image is enlisted in an experiment to make contact with past or future as a means of survival.

La Jetée, an extraordinary film, is about the psychological nature of time: nostalgia, the past, the precarious intricacies of the present. Almost as a technique concomitant with his theme, Chris Marker presents not moving images, but frozen images — stop-frames tell the entire story. (There is one moving image in the film; but that's to be caught, not described.) In images that are as stirring as they are resonant, with a first-person commentary as dispassionate as it is poetic, *La Jetée* draws us into a fantasy that becomes all at once a love story, a science fiction horror tale, and a poet's inquiry into the nature of time. Even our memories of the film (and they tend to be vivid) come to reflect the very structure and style of the film, as though Marker were probing those recesses of the mind in which memory and desire and terror mesh.

An astounding, triumphant film; easily one of the best shorts ever made. Distributed by Pyramid Films.

LABYRINTH

By Jan Lenica 15 minutes color/animation Poland 1964

A man wearing a bowler hat and a Victorian suit hovers on wings over a dark, silent city. Entering the city, he discovers monsters and grotesqueries everywhere. For example, an alligatorlike creature is attacking a lady; when the man tries to protect the lady from the monster, she spurns his offer and chooses instead to be dragged off by the monster. A dinosaur skeleton stands in the middle of an empty street, baying mournfully up at the buildings. A man's face, seen between half-closed shutters, undergoes a host of rapid transformations, as though it were made of latex. The man in the bowler is taken, finally, to a special place where his head is fitted for a machine that proceeds to drill, knock, and pump into him whatever fluids will alter his mind. Later, when he tries to escape from the city on wings, he is attacked by a horde of black batlike creatures and falls endlessly through empty space.

Labyrinth invokes images at once chilling and brutal, harsh and authoritative. We are in the zone of the most unsettling forms of nightmares, those that reflect — like glossy, but slightly distorting, surfaces — the face of a world we painfully and immediately recognize, but wish we didn't. The mood of alienation and desultory loss is so keenly established in the film that it haunts the mind long afterward. The best film to date by Jan Lenica, and one of the most profound achievements among recent animated shorts. Distributed by Contemporary Films/McGraw-Hill.

THE LADY FROM SHANGHAI

Written and directed by Orson Welles 87 minutes b/w Columbia 1947 With Orson Welles, Rita Hayworth, Everett Sloane, Glenn Anders

The story goes that Welles, stuck in Philadelphia with baggage and theatrical costumes that he couldn't affort to ship out, got on the telephone with Harry Cohn at Columbia and started describing a fantastic movie project he had in mind. Asked for its source, Welles grabbed a paperback from the drugstore rack near the telephone, and the book became perforce the "origin" of *The Lady from Shanghai*. A wonderful anecdote, though probably not quite true (it does help, at least, to explain the confused, dislocated quality of the film). *The Lady from Shanghai* is a thriller that keeps getting lost. One senses that Welles came to the daily shooting session with new and separate purposes in mind every time. Yet beyond the circumlocutions of plot and even setting, Welles' theatrical drive is everywhere evident, and there are stretches of the film that are as baroque and splendid and visually haunting as anything Welles has done. The fun-house sequence at the end of the film has yet to be matched for its sheer visual bravado and its manner of taking cinematic narrative to new extremes. Distributed by Macmillan-Audio-Brandon Films.

THE LAST LAUGH

Written by Carl Mayer Directed by F. W. Murnau Photographed by Carl Freund 81 minutes b/w (silent) Germany 1924 With Emil Jannings, Maly Deschaft, Max Hiller, Hans Unterkirchen

A middle-aged doorman (Emil Jannings) at an expensive hotel is seen one day by the hotel manager as he lugs a trunk into the hotel. Out of "consideration" for his age, the manager reappoints Jannings as an attendant in the lavatory downstairs. It is a demotion brought home by the transformation in treatment he receives from the guests. As a doorman, Jannings was smiled at, held in regard, tipped well; as an attendant, he's scorned, tricked, derided. Gradually we watch his deterioration: the temptations of suicide, a drunken spree during which people swirl giddily before him. The ending (strictly a concession, and a clumsy one) depicts Jannings suddenly inheriting a great fortune from a man he befriended once in the lavatory. Now Jannings is the hotel's guest and can treat or mistreat doormen and attendants as he pleases.

Carl Mayer, who had co-scripted *The Cabinet of Dr. Caligari*, wrote *The Last Laugh*, but with far more pungency and realism than the earlier film. Jannings' performance is trenchant, pathetic, moving; every slumping step of his body conveys the terrible knowledge of being brought so low. F. W. Murnau made an important technical advance in *The Last Laugh*. Throughout the film the camera tracks with the movement of the characters. The moving camera — till then used only sparingly — became a style for capturing the relationships and spaces in the hotel. It also helped depict the modern city/jungle without soul or mercy — a depiction that would be mirrored four years later in King Vidor's *The Crowd*. Distributed by Macmillan-Audio-Brandon Films.

M

Written by Thea von Harbou Directed by Fritz Lang 90 minutes b/w Germany 1931 With Peter Lorre, Ellen Widmann, Inge Landgut, Gustav Grundgens

In today's movies, psychopaths seem more common and more familiar than normal people. It is illuminating to see *M*, in which Peter Lorre depicts a man whose psychopathic inclinations become evident only slowly, and whose entire personality is as pitiable as it is chilling. The story is based on a series of newspaper accounts and retains a journalistic, near-documentary flavor. Children are found murdered throughout the city of Berlin; as the city grows increasingly terrorized and the police find nothing, our attention is focused on a plump, lonely young man who seems to like children (they certainly like him) and seems obsessed with watching his own image in mirrors or shop windows. We never see the murders. Director Lang chooses instead to concentrate on their repercussions and the frame of mind of the murderer. But as we come to know Lorre, his dismal existence and knotted psyche come to suggest something far more horrifying than direct violence ever could. The city's criminals, dragged into the police net set for Lorre, decide to use their own organization to capture the child murderer. The trial that follows their apprehension of Lorre is stark, solemn, and strangely unsettling — one of the great scenes in all of Lang's movies. Distributed by Films Inc., Macmillan-Audio-Brandon, etc.

MACHINE

By Wolfgang Urchs 11 minutes color/animation Germany 1966

In a two-dimensional world of straight intersecting lines, an inventor is visited by an angel. The inventor designs and makes a machine; and with it he clothes the men below. Goaded by success, the inventor improves his machine, enlarges it, adapts it to destroy a competing machine (and inventor) below, and gradually helps transform it into something more than a simple machine. It becomes a vast, megalithic force, rising monumentally into the air, surrounded by the tiny splinters of the lines it has shattered in its growth. Now the Machine has done everything. It has made products like baby rockers for the families below. It has provided services such as rocking them for the mothers. It has made balls over which men compete and cannons with which to make war; and finally coffins and tolling bells to grieve the dead. The inventor has become obsolete by now. When he tries to escape, the Machine snatches him. Only men, in this mordant fable, are vulnerable in the world of the outsized Machine.

Trenchant in its detail, ineluctable in its progression, *Machine* depicts technology as a force of terrifying growth and power. The inventor soon becomes nothing more than an accessory to his rampant creation. Wolfgang Urchs uses choral music and moments such as the beseeching arms of dead men rolling below in their coffins to imply an almost religious or transcendent dimension to the Machine. Men, it seems, have no choice *but* to worship the monster that seems impervious even to their prayers. Distributed by Pyramid Films.

THE MANCHURIAN CANDIDATE

Written by George Axelrod Directed by John Frankenheimer 126 minutes b/w United Artists 1962 With Frank Sinatra, Laurence Harvey, Janet Leigh, Angela Lansbury

Rarely — even in Hitchcock's films — is a thriller much more than a thriller. Yet *The Manchurian Candidate*, which plunges recklessly forward on the gripping momentum of its own berserk plot, manages to be a stabbing political satire, a brutal attack on "momism" and the matriarchal values of the fifties and, at the same time, the kind of desperate, bleak comedy achieved only rarely in film (Kubrick's *Dr. Strangelove*, for example). The story is far-fetched, improbable. Raymond Shaw, son of an arrogant mother and stepson of a demagogic senator (patterned after Joe McCarthy), returns from Korea a war hero, but only because his entire platoon has been brainwashed into thinking Shaw is a hero. Shaw (played with an acute sense of isolation by Laurence Harvey) is in reality a rigged "mechanism"; and of course his old army buddy, Sergeant Marco (Frank Sinatra) is the first to find out. The dark ironies of cold-war politics, the imminent threat of mind control, and the omniscient presence of the news media give *The Manchurian Candidate*, now over a decade old, a striking contemporary sense. The acting is splendid. Frank Sinatra seems remarkably comfortable in his role; Angela Lansbury turns your spine cold as Raymond Shaw's vicious, dictatorial mother; and James Gregory makes Senator John Iselin into a figure at once comic and terrifying. Distributed by UA 16.

MAN HUNT

Written by Dudley Nichols Directed by Fritz Lang 102 minutes b/w Twentieth Century-Fox 1941 With Walter Pidgeon, Joan Bennett, George Sanders, John Carradine

Walter Pidgeon is a famous sportsman who — "for the sheer sport of it" — slips into Germany and works his way through the most guarded forest in the world, till he lies on a ledge overlooking Hitler's summer palace. He has a high-precision rifle. He aims at Hitler's head and shoots — with no cartridge in the gun (it is, after all, for the sport of it). Next he slips a cartridge in, but guards overtake him before he can shoot. Thus begins one of the most nightmarish man-hunt movies made in Hollywood, a film of strongly delineated characters, places etched so well that their memories become a kind of map to the movie, and tensions underscored by both conflicting personalities and nationalities. As a chase movie, *Man Hunt* is superb. Even the lingering affair between Pidgeon and Joan Bennett adds to — rather than detracts from — the whole, a rarity in good melodrama. As a work of war propaganda, it is one of the best, structured so that Pidgeon's free-spirited gallantry and humane attitudes toward hunting ("It's not the kill; it's the stalk") conflict in basic, yet subtle, ways with George Sanders' feisty authoritarianism and his more rapacious, bloodthirsty attitude toward the hunt. The two men become microcosms of England and Germany. Their war reflects the larger war. As in Geoffrey Household's original novel (*Rogue Male*), the story is encapsulated in the metaphor of the hunt (the film ends, a bit over-patriotically, with Pidgeon returning to Germany). And, again, as in Household's novel, there is always that underlying ambiguity: did he, or didn't he, intend to kill the Fuhrer? Distributed by Films Inc.

MEDIUM COOL

Written, directed, and photographed by Haskell Wexler 110 minutes color Paramount 1969 With Robert Forster, Verna Bloom, Peter Bonerz, Marianna Hill

In the first scene of *Medium Cool*, a television news photographer and his soundman arrive at the scene of a car accident where a woman has been mangled and may be dead. A wheel is still spinning, and no one else has yet arrived. The photographer turns on the camera and directs it at the smashed car. Immediately the theme of *Medium Cool* is struck: the responsibility of the TV cameraman (or, by extension, the media) in a society going steadily mad. The photographer will go on to befriend a woman and her son from West Virginia; to be fired; to become enmeshed in the debacle of the 1968 Democratic convention in Chicago. While structurally and dramatically skittish, *Medium Cool* is a film that blazes with a ferocious inner authority. Haskell Wexler, one of the most astute cameramen in Hollywood, adapted the *cinema verite* style of Godard and other French and Canadian filmmakers to "create" the movie as he was shooting it: thus the rare juncture of documentary and story, giving much of the film a sharp sense of immediacy and of people entangled in the over-powering grip of events.

Wexler's cinematography has never served a film better. Indeed, *Medium Cool* attempts a narrative level of sorts at the surfaces of its images alone — the squeezed mass of the cops' white helmets, seen through a telephoto lens; the shabby character of the tenements that the photographer visits as they contrast with the blank and characterless hallways of the TV station where he always seems to be running, ratlike, through a maze. *Medium Cool* stymied and dismayed the critics when it was released in 1968 and fared poorly at the box office. But it's a film that achieves a unique and powerful hold on one's consciousness. Events become something other than the background of a story; rather, they increasingly impinge on the story, driving into the foreground, till they, more than the characters, become the real focus of the film. Distributed by Films Inc.

METROPOLIS

Written by Thea von Harbou Directed by Fritz Lang 93 minutes b/w (silent) Germany 1927 With Brigitte Helm, Alfred Abel, Gustave Froehlich

One of the earliest (and dourest) of science fiction fantasies, *Metropolis* depicts the world in the twenty-first century — a world of splendid wonders and a comfortable, leisurely existence above ground; and of massive machines tended by an army of dehumanized slaves below ground. As with most later science fiction fantasies about a dehumanized future, there is a robot, a silly love story, and a disaster that threatens to wipe out everything and everyone. Despite a fragile and overacted story, *Metropolis* strikes with force almost unknown in science fiction films. There are images that resonate in the mind, as though director Lang had caught some new vision of hell in the vast machines and their even more mechanized armies of men. This is more than stunning "special effects." Lang, armed with a Marxist viewpoint and a genuine talent for visual melodrama, attacks the machine age head-on, thrusting at us the spectre of machines that in effect become the true masters of men. Distributed by Macmillan-Audio-Brandon Films, Films Inc., etc.

MONKEY BUSINESS

Written by S. J. Perelman and Will B. Johnstone Directed by Norman McLeod 75 minutes b/w Paramount 1931 With Groucho, Chico, Harpo, and Zeppo Marx, Thelma Todd, Ruth Hall

Monkey Business was the first of the Marx Brothers films written expressly for the screen, and partially written by one of the true masters of the throw-away line, S. J. Perelman. (Groucho to Thelma Todd: "Is it true you wash your hair in clam broth? Is it true you used to dance in a flea circus?") There is anarchic savagery of an unmitigated nature in *Monkey Business*: Chico and Harpo shaving the handlebar mustache of a crew member who's come into the barbershop for a shave; Harpo's ploy with the Punch and Judy show, in which he makes of the pursuing captain and mate a hilarious spectacle for the delighted audience of children. Most of the action takes place aboard a ship, where the Marxes are stowaways who manage, by adroit maneuvers, to avoid being caught. The familiar Marxian themes — a firm hostility toward any kind of authority, masterful derailing of pomp and aristocracy, and an enthusiastic plunge into madness — are here in splendid proliferation. Distributed by Twyman Films, Inc.

MY DARLING CLEMENTINE

Written by Sam G. Engel and Winston Miller Directed by John Ford 97 minutes b/w Twentieth Century-Fox 1946 With Henry Fonda, Linda Darnell, Victor Mature, Grant Withers, John Ireland, Walter Brennan, Tim Holt, Ward Bond, Alan Mowbray, Cathy Downs

The battle played out between Wyatt Earp and Doc Holliday against the Clantons at the O.K. Corral is one of the movies' most oft-repeated Western legends. John Ford's version, like other of his Westerns, possesses that classic timeless sense that convinces us that nobody else will ever get quite as close to the legend again.

Henry Fonda's Wyatt Earp is a curious figure; he seems to shun violence unless it becomes inescapable, at which point he enters it with a spartan coolness. Victor Mature, who always seems best cast as a man burdened under the weight of his own sufferings, plays the consumptive, alcoholic Doc Holliday. The wary friendship between the two men — and Fonda's fascination with Holliday's woman (Linda Darnell) that threatens to shatter that friendship — is developed slowly, tenuously by Ford. There are always deeper, subtler drifts in the dialogue between Fonda and Mature that are only hinted at. Throughout the film, Ford concentrates not on a heightening dramatic sense, but on the details of life in Tombstone, Arizona, of the 1880s. Consequently, *My Darling Clementine* reveals Western life with an authenticity and a sense of period style rare even in Ford Westerns. Distributed by Films Inc.

NEVER GIVE A SUCKER AN EVEN BREAK

Story by Otis Criblecoblis (W. C. Fields) Directed by Edward Cline 78 minutes b/w Universal 1947 With W. C. Fields, Edward Cline, Gloria Jean, Leon Errol, Margaret Dumont

In the lunatic world of a W. C. Fields movie, anything goes: Fields chasing a whiskey bottle out of a moving plane and falling to the mountain retreat of a wealthy woman and her lovely daughter; Fields going to Mexico on a mission of selling wooden nutmegs; Fields driving Margaret Dumont — whom he somehow presumes pregnant — to the maternity ward of a hospital and, en route, becoming engaged by the swinging ladder of a fire truck. The plot of *Never Give a Sucker an Even Break* is such a sprawling, confused, incoherent series of weird episodes (connected only sporadically by a story conference at which Fields is trying to sell a script to Esoteric Studios) that in watching it we soon forget just what's happening but focus instead on who it's happening to — and Fields is in fine, fine form. (As a suggested cure to an insomniac: "Get plenty of sleep." Turning down a bromo: "Can't stand the noise.")

Legend has it that one day Fields jotted down the story line of the film hastily on the back of a grocery bill and sold it forthwith to Universal for $25,000. It's not only possible; it's likely. Of all screen comedians Fields was perhaps the one whose life offscreen and onscreen changed the least; one somehow senses that for Fields it didn't matter whether the camera was rolling. Distributed by Macmillan-Audio-Brandon Films.

NINE VARIATIONS ON A DANCE THEME

By Hilary Harris 12 minutes b/w U.S.A. 1966 Danced by Bettie de Jong

A dancer lies on a floor in a side-lit studio. Slowly she rises, flexing arms, then legs. The camera veers closer, then backs slowly away, then encircles her, capturing her dance from a slow, rotating perspective, matching its movement to hers. It is the first of nine dances, in which each time the dance changes, the camera changes, and the style of cutting changes — a transformation so thorough that we're brought into the movement with a striking sense of involvement. The dance belongs not simply to the dancer, but to the camera and the film and the audience.

At first *Nine Variations on a Dance Theme* appears somewhat of an exercise film: the slow, exacting movement of the camera; the speeded montages of arms, torso, legs, hair; the balanced cutting of slow-motion close-ups (as though filmmaker Hilary Harris were demonstrating the potential techniques of camera and editing and light). But as one sees it a second or third time, *Nine Variations* reveals a subtle, cumulative rhythm. Each of the nine dances builds quietly and successfully toward the next; the dancer is transformed from a girl in splendid motion to a series of curved, textured abstractions, and then back into a dancer. There is a sense in which technique does intrude more conspicuously into the dance than, say, McLaren's use of overlapping strobic effects in *Pas de Deux* — but the intrusion amplifies and extends the dance, never severs us from it. Distributed by Film Images.

NORTH BY NORTHWEST

Written by Ernest Lehman Directed by Alfred Hitchcock 136 minutes color M-G-M 1959 With Cary Grant, Eva Marie Saint, James Mason, Jesse Royce Landis

At the climax of *North by Northwest* Cary Grant and Eva Marie Saint are dangling from the immense stone faces of Mount Rushmore, while the evil gunsel (played by Martin Landau) approaches to grab the microfilm and murder them both. Hitchcock has said that what he really wanted to do with the scene was have Cary Grant hiding inside Washington's nose and, unavoidably, go into a sneezing fit. This comment suggests perfectly the spirit of *North by Northwest*, a semi-grim, semi-comic romp over the face of America — Hitchcock's tour de force of the chase film. Throughout *North by Northwest* suspense and comedy intermingle, and Hitchcock's touch has rarely been so sure. When Cary Grant nervously tells his mother that the two men who just got on the elevator are the ones after him, she states out loud to the men: "You gentlemen aren't trying to kill my son, *are* you?" Absolute hilarity sweeps the elevator, but Grant isn't laughing. The film seems to waver and wander and split in a dozen directions, but actually it is superbly structured, building the classic Hitchcockian motif of the normal man being drawn into a chasm of unbalanced moral forces, and extricating himself only by shedding the niceties of his civilized life and summoning instincts and courage. Distributed by Films Inc.

AN OCCURRENCE AT OWL CREEK BRIDGE

Written and directed by Robert Enrico 27 minutes b/w France 1963 With Roger Jacquet, Ann Cornaly, and Anker Larsen

On a bridge in the South during the Civil War, a man awaits hanging at dawn. Soldiers march up and down the bridge; a sentry waits on the hill where the sun finally glowers. And after what has seemed an interminable time — for the victim, for us — the noose is slipped over his head. An officer steps back from the plank, and the man plunges downward into the river and to escape. His relief that he's alive — expressed in a beautifully realized orchestration of camera detail, sound effects, and song — transforms the entire momentum of the drama. By the time he's escaped the soldiers and reached his plantation and sees his wife in the distance, we're jubilant with him; then, as he reaches for his wife's arms, his neck snaps back, his body sags below the bridge, and the dream has ended.

Robert Enrico's drama captures with startling exactness the emotional and psychological intricacies of Ambrose Bierce's story. This may be one of the most successfully faithful film adaptations of a literary piece ever made. Using virtually no dialogue, and with a sound track that gives a stunning polyphonic dimension to the film, Enrico uses the screen to express a doomed man's consciousness, whether in the slow, excruciating extension of time before the dawn hanging, or in the marvel of a dewdrop at the tip of a leaf, suggesting the world as only a man instantaneously saved from death can relish it. Winner of the 1962 Grand Prix at Cannes. Distributed by Contemporary Films/McGraw-Hill.

OLYMPIA (also titled OLYMPIAD)

Directed by Leni Riefenstahl Abridged version: Part I: The Festival of the People (120 minutes) Part II: The Festival of Beauty (85 minutes) b/w Germany released in 1938

The French poet and filmmaker Jean Cocteau once wrote to Leni Riefenstahl: "How could I not be your admirer, when the film genius lives within you and when you have raised the cinema up to the heights where usually it does not ascend." The words are ample: Leni Riefenstahl is surely one of the most original figures in film ever to emerge from Germany, and till now the most prodigiously talented woman ever to guide a movie camera.

Her films reflect at once a simplicity of form and a complexity of feeling achieved as skillfully, only by among other documentary filmmakers, only by Robert Flaherty. In *Olympia*, her four-hour account of the 1936 Olympics that took place in Berlin, she depicts the athletes in a manner that catches their muscular precision, their balanced movement, their tensile energy; but the manner also evokes a mystique of the body that is both rigorous and boldly sensual. In its cumulative impact, the film rouses a fervid Teutonic sense of mythic presence: a subtle awareness that these athletes aren't simply competing on a field or in pools before crowds at one distinct time and place, but that their contests are somehow mythic, godlike, eternal — enacted here and now as no more, perhaps, than a concession to the rest of us.

To what extent her embrace of Nazi ideology (and it was the ideology, not Hitler, she chose) inspired or crippled Leni Riefenstahl may never fully be known. Seemingly, it did both. No other artist, in any field, was able to give expression to the deeper stirrings of the Third Reich with anything like the artistic power of Ms. Riefenstahl, but her connection with Hitler's regime effectively closed her off from future serious film projects after the war. One can only speculate about what documentaries she might have created under different circumstances and with less ideological fervor. In slightly abridged versions, Parts I and II of *Olympia* are distributed by Macmillan-Audio-Brandon Films and Phoenix Films, Inc.

PAS DE DEUX

By Norman McLaren 13 minutes b/w National Film Board of Canada 1967 Performed by Margaret Mercier and Vincent Warren of Les Grandes Ballets Canadiens

Two dancers against a totally black background wend through a slow-motion *pas de deux* in an elaboration of pure, supple movement. The music, the muscular agility, the gentle conquest of that inky space — all are captured by the remarkably restrained camera, which barely moves, barely suggests its own presence. The white figures against black gradually take on a near-hypnotic quality. And when their motions are repeated, strobelike — so that an arching arm continues spilling in a rippling series of white, gentle waves — the technique seems to extend and express the ballet naturally.

It is mainly this delicate grafting of an optical technique to the dance in such a way that the technique never becomes overly conspicuous that makes *Pas de Deux* Norman McLaren's masterpiece to date. The mirrored, cascading movements transform dance and dancers into a flowing continuum in space and time. We see a single action — the sweep of a foot, a pirouette, a spin into space — with each muscular flow visually echoed and visually resounded against other echoes. And as the dance rises and builds, so does McLaren's tactful use of the technique — as though the dancers themselves were, in their control and harmony, giving us this awesome demonstration of the body's mastery over space.

Optical processes as complex and difficult as those McLaren is using in *Pas de Deux* usually overtake the subject matter and reduce it to a splattering of unreal, overlapping colors or a lightshow array of dizzying, distorted movements. The precise, unerring control that McLaren demonstrates in *Pas de Deux* is almost unheard-of among optically processed shorts; it gives *Pas de Deux* a prominence within the genre that (hopefully) will guide other optically designed films of the future. Distributed by Learning Corporation of America.

POINT BLANK

Written by Alexander Jacobs, David and Rafe Newhouse Directed by John Boorman 92 minutes color M-G-M 1967 With Lee Marvin, Angie Dickinson, Keenan Wynn, Sharon Acker

Point Blank is an extraordinary film, and the hindsight of another ten years may well indicate that no other film sums up so well the technical derring-do of sixties filmmaking. Director John Boorman, who makes this film both a celebration of the violent gangster and an elegy to him, draws on every trick in the book and then some: slick, raucous editing; overlapping sound tracks; strong color contrast and compositions structured by colors; reflections and mirrors (especially shattered mirrors) aplenty; and a penchant for violence that is as cinematic as it is symbolic (as in the scene where Marvin demolishes an expensive car belonging to a syndicate flunky, while throttling him in the process). Few films since Fritz Lang's *Metropolis* (1927) have displayed architecture quite so successfully as *Point Blank*. Boorman uses the swept, naked walls and corridors and surfaces of Los Angeles to create a vivid visual projection of the theme, the old-style gangster kicking his way up through a new-style syndicate which is run like a modern corporation. *Point Blank* was made the same year as *Bonnie and Clyde* and is a better and more probing and—yes—more violent gangster film; certainly proof that the genre never truly died. Distributed by Films Inc.

PRETTY POISON

Written by Lorenzo Semple, Jr. Directed by Noel Black 89 minutes color Twentieth Century-Fox 1967 With Tuesday Weld, Anthony Perkins, John Randolph, Beverly Garland

In his best role since *Psycho*, Perkins plays a young man obsessed by engaging fantasies. He has just been released from a mental institution and goes to work at a chemical plant that is spewing tons of garbage into the local small-town river. Enter Tuesday Weld, a high school drum majorette, sprightly, cheery, as clean-cut an American kid as you can find anywhere. She becomes fascinated by Perkins' hushed stories of CIA assignments and coded messages; they become lovers. Then—after Perkins is fired from the plant because of his boss's discovery of his arsonist background — he takes her along to sabotage the chute that carries the plant's sludge into the river. There is a night watchman at the plant who terrifies Perkins; Tuesday Weld murders him with a bravado and delight that has that scalp-itching quality of being absolutely believable.

Pretty Poison is a rare little gem. The acting is superb; the script taut and witty; the direction impeccable. The themes converge well, without intruding into the film's dramatic structure. Pollution — whether in a Tuesday Weld or in the plant's daily excrement — seems an inevitable by-product of America's way of life; and woe to a romantic like Perkins who tries to stop it. Noel Black (who also made *Skater Dater*) uses a skillful, underplayed focus on characters rather than technique which is all too rare in contemporary American films. Distributed by Films Inc.

PSYCHO

Written by Joseph Stefano Directed by Alfred Hitchcock 108 minutes b/w Paramount 1960 With Janet Leigh, Anthony Perkins, Vera Miles, John Gavin, Martin Balsam

"You have to remember," Hitchcock has remarked, "that *Psycho* is a film made with quite a sense of amusement on my part . . . The processes through which we take the audience, you see, it's rather like taking them through the haunted house at the fairground." Indeed. With *Psycho*, not only did Hitchcock make the consummate thriller; he also redirected the genre, paving the way for one decade (and perhaps more to come) of movie shock killings, gushing blood, and exorbitant screen violence. Not that Hitchcock should be blamed. *Psycho* is a triumphant achievement. It includes some brilliantly edited sequences; the story is taut and amazingly well-told; and few other films have guided an audience's response with quite so sure (or perverse) a keenly honed sense of identification. The sense of moral imbalance, usually implicit in Hitchcock's films, becomes downright dizzying in *Psycho*. Once the audience has been shattered by Janet Leigh's grotesque killing, we are left with a sense that *anything* can happen; and Anthony Perkins, at once so "nice" and so psychologically splintered, comes to suggest that anybody we know just might be dangling from that other side of sanity. *Psycho* — like other masterpieces that have been imitated so often that they seem to personify clichés — may lack some of the power it held in its initial release, but it remains unquestionably a harrowing classic of pure filmmaking. Distributed by Twyman Films, Inc.

PULSE

By Peter Spoecker 8 minutes b/w (animation) U.S.A. 1971

The freedom implicit in animation — where the animator can control every figure, every movement, every modification of time and space — is seldom fully recognized, except in the presence of animation shorts that take elaborate advantage of that freedom. *Pulse*, a strangely wrought and curiously compelling little animation short, seems guided by nothing so much as an almost manic sense of potential by the animator. No form or figure has any permanence in this cascading progression of transformations; each new figure surrenders to another figure, then another, creating a kaleidoscopic turmoil of flexing lines and spaces.

Moreover, animator Peter Spoecker does not create his figures in the simple line-drawn or centralized patterns familiar to most animation. They are highly ornate, lacelike, entangled webs that flex in every curve and give way to new, suggestive figures, baroque monsters, strangely disformed hands, tunnels of black rivulets opening onto new figures. This kind of animation, in which movement is spread out over the entire frame and changes constantly, requires an intricacy of sketchwork and such an immensity of effort that it is almost never attempted (Ryan Larkin's *Street Musique* is one rare exception). A visually compelling, strangely engrossing, and sometimes disturbing film. Distributed by Creative Film Society.

RED RIVER

Written by Borden Chase Directed by Howard Hawks 125 minutes b/w United Artists 1948 With John Wayne, Montgomery Clift, Joanne Dru, Walter Brennan

Red River is a magnificent Western, the best Hawks ever directed and one of the best ever made. The story and the characters have an epic quality: Clift as the adopted son of super-rancher John Wayne, who decides he will attempt the treacherous route north to take thousands of head of cattle to the railroad in Kansas. For once Wayne is anything but the good guy; he maltreats men and cattle to the breaking point. It is his stepson (Clift) who rallies the men in a rebellion — sending Wayne off — and continues north with the herd. Wayne, furious, collects a group of men to return and regain his cattle, and an odyssey already fraught with danger becomes electrifying in its tensions. But the real marvel of *Red River* lies in its capturing the soul of the Western: the toughened simplicity of men's lives on the frontier; the grandeur of open spaces; the primal loyalties that both undergird and ultimately ignite the tensions in the plot. Moreover, *Red River* has some of the best lines ever to grace a Western: gunfighter John Ireland strokes a pistol and says, "There are only two things in the world finer than a good gun — a Swiss watch and a woman from anywhere." Distributed by UA 16.

ROAD TO GLORY

Written by Joel Sayre and William Faulkner Directed by Howard Hawks 101 minutes b/w Twentieth Century-Fox 1936 With Fredric March, Warner Baxter, Lionel Barrymore, June Lang, Gregory Ratoff

Like Kubrick's later *Paths of Glory* (1957), *Road to Glory* is set in the trenches of World War I and focuses on the relationships between two French officers. And while *Road to Glory* lacks the vehement anti-war feelings of Kubrick's film (the only anti-war sentiments in Hawks' film are uttered by June Lang in a sloppy little sermon at the end), there is a dramatic tautness here and a remarkable use of characterization, particularly in the first two-thirds of the film. Fredric March plays a captain who lives on aspirin and cognac and a grueling, self-destructive commitment to fight a nasty war "with honor." Warner Baxter — the younger, more humane officer— first takes March's girl (the uncommonly lovely June Lang), then his post. The tensions between the two men are set out well at the beginning, though never fully exploited. Yet the film is touching in a way rare among war movies of any kind. When March's father, a bearded, enthusiastic old French army veteran, shows up as an enlisted private, one can sense March's anguish, and his pride. His father can be both valorous and stupefyingly dense. On one occasion he jumps on a (dud) grenade to save other men's lives; another time he tosses a grenade at his own returning soldiers. The ending slags around in some sentimental movie gimmicks — March's suicidal act to save the troops; Lang's hokey "Why does it have to go on?" But the very end has a brutal ring. Warner Baxter, the new captain, addresses the incoming troops exactly as March had, then turns from them, entering his quarters while tossing down a few aspirin. Distributed by Films Inc.

THE ROARING TWENTIES

Written by Jerry Wald, Richard Macaulay, and Robert Rossen Directed by Raoul Walsh and Anatole Litvak 104 minutes b/w Warner Brothers 1939 With James Cagney, Priscilla Lane, Humphrey Bogart, Jeffrey Lynn

The Roaring Twenties is certainly among the best of a certain mode of gangster film, the documentary-styled gangster-film-as-commentary that would become such a familiar and specious style among "B" melodramas of the fifties. Here, before the style had ossified, Raoul Walsh used it brilliantly to tell and offset in montage perspective the story of a returning World War I veteran who gradually rose to the height of the gangster world in the twenties, then fell back on nothing when the Depression struck.

The Roaring Twenties might well have succumbed to its inherent tendency as moral fable were it not for the presence of Cagney. Even more than Bogart, Cagney makes this gangster film believable, gives it the rough-edged wiliness and the shrewd, blunt energy that we'd like to believe the successful gangsters had. Indeed, Cagney is rarely as fine. Whether organizing and taking over a bootlegging operation, or, down on his luck, gazing up at his old sweetheart, or, finally, meeting and killing Bogart, he always moves with that abruptness and cocky self-assurance that could be generous one minute, spontaneously murderous the next. Distributed by UA 16.

SABOTEUR

Written by Peter Viertel, Joan Harrison, and Dorothy Parker Directed by Alfred Hitchcock 108 minutes b/w Universal Studio 1942 With Robert Cummings, Priscilla Lane, Otto Kruger, Alan Baxter

Alfred Hitchcock's *Saboteur*, made just after America entered World War II, reflects the attempt of Hollywood to instill movies with a kind of "instant propaganda": impassioned, patriotic speeches; a sudden shift to the wartime setting for stories that might have fit a better framework; and an abiding emphasis that what the characters do or don't do matters to the wartime effort. Despite its pro-America sentiments (and this is one of the most patently sentimental of Hitchcock's films) — and even despite Robert Cummings— *Saboteur* is fun. It's a chase film in the vein of Hitchcock's *The Thirty-Nine Steps* and his later *North by Northwest*. It moves across the country from an airplane plant in California to the Statue of Liberty in New York. There are some fine sequences, particularly toward the end: Cummings racing to stop the sabotage of a ship launching; Priscilla Lane trapped in an office building and sending an SOS note fluttering down on the wind; and the breathtaking Statue of Liberty sequence, where the saboteur literally dangles by a thread. Distributed by Twyman Films, Inc.

SAHARA

Written by Zoltan Korda and John Howard Lawson Directed by Zoltan Korda Photographed by Rudolf Mate 97 minutes b/w Columbia 1943 With Humphrey Bogart, Bruce Bennett, J. Carrol Naish, Lloyd Bridges, Don Duryea, and Rex Ingram

A group of Allied soldiers in a tank in the Libyan desert are cut off behind the lines during World War I. They take on a German prisoner of war, and moving through the German patrols, finally locate and control a fortress oasis. Surrounded by Germans — but Germans without water — they hold the fortress, telling the Germans that they'll provide water once they've surrendered. Bogart, as the tough-skinned Allied leader, gives a remarkable performance. He creates the tone for what is something other than a standard war drama: the psychological conflict of man battling a harsh environment, the hostile Germans, and one another.

Director Korda and cinematographer Mate do nothing to romanticize the broiling Libyan desert. The stretching dunes become the motif of outer and inner landscapes, and the dusty men seem to reflect increasingly the desultory terrain. Distributed by Macmillan-Audio-Brandon Films.

SECONDS

Written by Lewis John Carlino Directed by John Frankenheimer Photographed by James Wong Howe 108 minutes b/w Paramount 1966 With Rock Hudson, Salome Jens, John Randolph, Will Geer, Jeff Corey

The premise is as old as the Faustian legend: to trade anything, everything, for a new life, a transformed identity, a world of new and open options. In *Seconds*, an aging, discontented banker named Arthur Hamilton is given that change by a strange, secretive company that guarantees new identities and personalities as though they were face-lifts. He succumbs (it is, after all, the most illusory and compelling of conceivable temptations) and becomes, well, Rock Hudson.

As Rock Hudson, the new Hamilton is sent to a beach studio on Malibu where ladies frolic, and where he proves as uncomfortable at an orgy as at a cocktail party. Never truly happy with his old identity, it's impossible for him to be happy with the new one. When he is recalled to the company headquarters, laid out on a stretcher, and given the brain operation that will make his cadaver useful for the next personality transplant, the viewer's sense of shock and horror mingles with a relief that such a distasteful and somehow wrongly built movie has ended.

What went wrong with *Seconds* is an open question. Rock Hudson, for one: the transition from John Randolph's Hamilton to Hudson's is too far-fetched, even for a science-fiction premise. For another, the transplant company: depicted as an amalgam of old-styled bedside manner and super-efficient business techniques; it seems all conception, without a hint of motivating force (is the kindly faced old country doctor behind all of this out to take over the world, or save it, or what?). And finally, *Seconds* presumes more than it reveals: the characters themselves — Arthur Hamilton (in both identities), the doctor, the wife, and then the girlfriend— seem like walking cadavers; and the notion of personality itself, so crucial to the staggering concept of the story, is given hardly a fragment of dramatic realization. Depersonalization and extreme alienation may be valid themes for film, but only if we're given some yardstick within the film to measure them by. Distributed by Films Inc.

THE SET-UP

Written by Art Cohn Directed by Robert Wise 72 minutes b/w R-K-O 1949 With Robert Ryan, Audrey Totter, George Tobias, Alan Baxter, James Edwards, Wallace Ford

A middle-aged fighter (Ryan), whom critic Manny Farber describes as "one punch away from punch-drunk," tells his woman he can still win, he can still fight, and he waits through a series of bouts at the ring until his fight. Unknown to him, his manager has sold the fight: Ryan is to go down in the third round; the manager, certain that Ryan will lose, doesn't want to share the money. As in other fight films (*The Harder They Fall, Requiem for a Heavyweight, Champion*), the director's focus is not the story, not even the character, but the squalid, dehumanizing nature of the boxing world. Wise's approach seems almost contradictory. He makes us watch the fight in real time (we *see* an entire boxing match), and we cannot help rooting for the hero. Meantime Wise is constantly cutting to the faces of the crowd — and Christians were never thrown to the lions in front of such a crowd: a fat man wedging every conceivable kind of food into his mouth; a woman whose frenzied screams make her hideously ugly; a blind man buffeting the air with his fists, snouting "Go for his eyes!" This is what boxing does to people, Wise seems to be saying; but then, he's forcing us to become that kind of audience too. The ending is predictable, yet it almost comes off perfectly; Robert Ryan's performance is deadly convincing. There is no "best" fight film; this is surely one of the best. Distributed by Films Inc.

SHERLOCK, JR.

Written by Clyde Bruckman, Jean Havez, Joseph Mitchell, and Buster Keaton Directed by Buster Keaton 42 minutes b/w (silent) M-G-M 1924 With Buster Keaton, Kathryn McGuire, Ward Crane, Joseph Keaton, Horace Morgan, Jane Connelly, Ford West

Keaton's art — building as it did on acrobatics, the subtlest twists of a gag, and a sustained sense of irony that can border on the metaphysical — has never been as widely acknowledged as Chaplin's, which is of an altogether different nature. Yet let anyone who considers Chaplin *the* comic genius of the movies see *Sherlock, Jr.*, which is as masterful (and supremely executed) a proof of Keaton's genius as anything he did. J. A. Fieschi has observed that in *Sherlock, Jr.* Keaton "offers one of the most perfect definitions of our art." There's that, yet more. Keaton's comic inventiveness stretches our sense of the movies themselves. We see *Sherlock, Jr.* and laugh crazily at the brilliant gags; but when it's over, we suddenly become aware that we've witnessed a metaphor as complex and engaging as our involvement in movies themselves.

Typically, the story follows Keaton's crazy sense of logic. A projectionist given to fantasies is accused by his girlfriend's father of stealing a watch. He didn't, but plays amateur detective in trying to find out who did, and not too successfully. Later, he falls asleep in the projection booth; his dream figure separates from him to go down and enter the screen. In a brilliant and remarkably disorienting sequence, Keaton steps into the screen but cannot quite relate to the abruptly changing scenes. In the ocean he dives off a rock, but the scene cuts in mid-dive and Keaton is half-buried in desert sand. Later the scene stabilizes, and Keaton's dream figure becomes a detective. In one hilarious episode, Keaton is set up as a murder victim; he's supposed to shoot a pool ball that's really a bomb. (He plays an entire game without ever touching the ball, while the people who set it up huddle in the next room, waiting for the explosion.) In the final sequence Keaton's real self meets his girlfriend in the booth, and he, shy and nervous, doesn't know what to do or say; he glances toward the screen and follows the cues of the leading man in every movement—a superb example of what may be the true psychology of the movies.

Sherlock, Jr. is not Keaton's best-known work. But perhaps better than any other Keaton short — and possibly as much as any of his features — it showcases the range of his talents, the inventive quality of his gags, and the subtle metaphysical insights that this comic could bring to movies. Distributed by Macmillan-Audio-Brandon Films.

SHE WORE A YELLOW RIBBON

Written by Frank Nugent and Laurence Stallings Directed by John Ford Photographed by Winton Hoch 103 minutes color R-K-O 1949 With John Wayne, Joanne Dru, John Agar, Ben Johnson, Harry Carey, Jr., Victor McLaglen, Tom Tyler

John Ford's *She Wore a Yellow Ribbon* has a quality as warm and as stirring as a gentle Irish ballad. A Western in one respect, it is Ford's tribute to the cavalry and, in yet another, to John Wayne. This is certainly one of the most lavishly photographed of Ford's films; its richly formed colors convey much of Ford's deep feelings for the textures and distances and pastels of Monument Valley.

The story seems always secondary to the characters, and the characters seem to have come out of earlier Ford films: John Wayne as the retiring officer, Nathan Brittles; Victor McLaglen as Sergeant Quincannon, the Irish roustabout who chats easily with Wayne, tipples from a bottle he keeps in Wayne's outer office, and destroys half a platoon single-handed in a beautifully realized barroom brawl. The scenes build their cumulative force by the subtle, often nostalgic feelings they evoke: Wayne standing at sunset over his wife's grave; a thunderstorm during which the cavalry patrol moves through Monument Valley (which Ford actually shot in a tumultuous rainstorm); and Wayne's last day with the cavalry, when he receives a watch from the troops, a moment of heightened sentiment that never intrudes on Wayne's persona. The mood of *She Wore a Yellow Ribbon* is tender, nostalgic, elegiac, a film as beautiful as any that Ford has ever made. Distributed by Macmillan-Audio-Brandon Films.

SNOW WHITE (A Betty Boop Cartoon)

By Max and Dave Fleischer 8 minutes b/w (animation) Paramount 1933

The Fleischers and Walt Disney were the competitive forces in animation through the early thirties. Though Disney, with his features and his increasingly slick products, was able to out-distance the Fleischers by the late thirties, it is instructive to compare the Fleischers' *Snow White*—a Betty Boop short they made in 1933 — with Disney's *Snow White and the Seven Dwarfs,* a feature made four years later. For these men represented different approaches to art and style in animation, and one might only wonder where the Fleishers might have gone (say, with features) had *they* been the empire builders, not Disney.

Snow White reveals the Fleischers at their best. The story is richly textured; the backgrounds extraordinary (the Fleischers, like Disney, believed in carefully drawn settings, but the Fleischers preferred a more expressionistic style); the progression of the story curiously unsettling — each step further eases Betty Boop and her companion, Koko, into situations that are increasingly unreal, nightmarish, and capable of becoming even more so. Like a graphic *Alice in Wonderland, Snow White* transforms the fundamentals of geography, so that trees and caves and rivers come to look like worlds summoned from some outrageous dream. And the visual gags — such as the Queen rolling a hoop over Koko and transforming him into a creature of long, elastic legs that circle and knot into chains—have a strange, compelling, surreal force, as though nature itself were caught within this delicately crafted fantasy.

The Fleischers reach for and achieve an effect both subtle and bizarre. To Cab Calloway's rendition of "The St. James Infirmary Blues," a raunchy-edged blues ballad, the clown Kokodances deep in the evil Queen's cave. It is no ordinary dance. At one point his head metamorphoses into a liquor bottle, which he plucks from his torso and pours down his open neck.

A harmless children's fantasy? Certainly a fantasy that children may well follow more successfully than adults. The Fleischer transformations and gags are visual and swift and succinct; reflect momentarily on the brilliance of one and you miss the next. In terms of children, one might well compare this initial *Snow White* with Disney's later feature, with its strangled forest that oozes a premonition of evil, or the Queen herself, a figure of such heightened madness and paranoia that one would sooner expect to find her in a psycho ward than in an animated film. Where the Disney touch is emphatic and ultimately moralistic, the Fleischers' is playful and erratic. Disney will sacrifice everything to a sustained single effect in *Snow White* (as, curiously, he almost never did in his shorts); the Fleischers rush to a punchline, particularly those with a surreal pitch. Children of course will enjoy both, and be frightened some by both; but one suspects that whereas Disney's *Snow White* will leave them with haunted fears of the Queen and her gnarled Kingdom, the Fleischers' *Snow White* will throw their imaginations a little askew, as it does invariably for all of us. Distributed by Creative Film Society.

SOLO

By Mike Hoover 15 minutes color U.S.A. 1971

The feat of climbing a mountain may be one of the precious few frontiers available in which a man's effort is not absorbed and overridden by a complex technology. *Solo*, a graceful and superbly realized short that centers on a single man climbing a mountain, evokes that unique combination of extreme physical exertion and marvel that is a climber's triumph. Mike Hoover stars as the single climber. He made the film with a crew that had never shot film before and most of whom had never climbed before. There are some exceptional moments. In one shot (had he *planned* it?) Hoover is trying to spiderleg his way under an overhanging rock; the metal hook he's pounded into the rock gives, and he swings out on the line over a height of summits that's as breathtaking as it is frightening. There is also a touch of schmaltz. He finds a tiny frog in a rock crevice, gently slips it into his shirt pocket, and later — after he has climbed the mountain and returned — sets the frog into a mountainside stream.

Nonetheless *Solo* does suggest something of the psychology and rewards of a mountain climber, particularly anyone foolish enough to go solo. The nerve, the testing of oneself against a rising rock wall, the apprehension and exultation — they're all here. Nominated for an Academy Award. Distributed by Pyramid Films.

SPELLBOUND

Written by Ben Hecht Directed by Alfred Hitchcock 111 minutes b/w United Artists 1945 With Ingrid Bergman, Gregory Peck, Jean Acker, Donald Curtis, Rhonda Fleming

It would seem that *Spellbound* offered a superb subject for such a clever master of audience manipulation as Hitchcock: the intricacies of the disturbed mind and the world of psychiatry and psychotheraphy. However, Hitchcock chose a straight, traditional approach, and there are only moments that achieve the full complexity and ironic counterpoint we expect of the best Hitchcockian suspense.

Gregory Peck plays a psychiatrist joining the staff of a mental hospital. The previous director has been murdered, and Peck — who has been having spells of dizziness and loss of memory — suspects that he was the murderer and, owing to amnesia, cannot remember any of it. Ingrid Bergman, a psychiatrist at the hospital, falls in love with Peck and gradually comes to believe him incapable of murder — even as Hitchcock is playing shrewdly with audience doubts by setting up potentially murderous situations (as when Peck approaches an older doctor friend of Bergman with a razor in his hand). Ultimately, of course, it's proven that Peck isn't the murderer; another doctor is. When Bergman confronts the other doctor with that knowledge, he kills himself.

Among the most memorable moments of *Spellbound* are the dream sequences. The surrealist artist Salvador Dali helped design the sets, which have a quality of stretched, distorted spaces. Not a major Hitchcock movie, but not a minor one either. Distributed by Macmillan-Audio-Brandon Films.

STEAMBOAT WILLIE

By Walt Disney and Ub Iwerks 10 minutes b/w (animation) U.S.A. 1928

Steamboat Willie was one of the first Mickey Mouse cartoons and the first cartoon to use sound. Though somewhat primitive (Mickey has skinny legs and a generally scrawnier appearance than the later Mickey the world has come to know), *Steamboat Willie* uses a striking variety of comic ideas, particularly in sound, and suggests features of the later evolution of Disney's style. It is probably the first truly important Disney film. It was surely the film that made audiences eager for more of the Mouse.

There is little story to *Steamboat Willie*: an attempted rescue of Minnie from Peg Leg Pete's nasty clutches aboard Peg Leg Pete's steamboat. But what Disney and Iwerks developed was the synchronization of movement and sound. What sound could do to and for a movie was quite problematic in 1928, particularly for animation. Should the characters talk? Should there be music to back up their actions? Disney and Iwerks immediately set a substantial precedent by using music to orchestrate the movement of the characters. While a goat chews on some sheet music entitled "Turkey in the Straw," Minnie winds its tail like a calliope handle and plays that very song. Mickey plays a cow's teeth as a xylophone, tugs at the tails of nursing piglets for an effect, and squeezes the torso of a duck to sound a trombone. The synchronization yields a striking, tap-along involvement; the matchings are often quite clever, though underscoring them all is a subtle note of violence and even sadism. Distributed by Macmillan-Audio-Brandon Films as part of "Milestones in Animation."

STREET MUSIQUE

By Ryan Larkin 9 minutes color/animation National Film Board of Canada 1972

Masterpieces in animation are a curious rarity: the animator, after all, often has a freedom — of expression, of time, of color and form — and a control (he can work by himself, on his own timetable) unavailable to other film artists. Yet, perhaps because animation has been the province of studios for so long and its purposes have been so decidedly commercial, animation has either failed to attract major talent or scared it off. And while there are serious animation artists in Europe, particularly Eastern Europe, there are precious few in North America. Count among them — with the release of *Street Musique* — Ryan Larkin of the National Film Board of Canada.

Larkin had already made *Syrinx,* a beguiling retelling of the Pan fable, using charcoal sketches that dissolve almost imperceptibly one into another, creating a haunting sense of movement. His *Walking* is a classic of observation: touches of caricature are treated with a jaunty grace, urban streets are captured with a droll, fresh eye. But *Street Musique* far outranks either. It is, quite simply, among the most visually alluring and moving films ever created by a single hand.

The title and a few moments of the film's beginning clarify Larkin's premise: animated forms that capture some of the whimsy and playfulness and serendipity of street music. We see black and white cartoon drawings undergoing elaborate transformations. A nodule almost, but doesn't quite, become a man; it returns to a nodule. An ornate eagle squeezes into a fetus, then into a winged mythic man. A rotund head protrudes a long horn, emitting a small dot which grows and itself becomes a rotund head, while the original shrinks and is sucked in by the new horn. The figures and their transformations have a winsome quality; and the movements — invariably involving the total form, unlike the standard localized movements of most animation — follow a course so fresh and unpredictable that the figures seem to wend out of the delicate mandolin and fiddle and guitar score with its subtle, evocative transitions.

But it's with the color that Larkin introduces new techniques and gives *Street Musique* its moments of prescient, haunting magnificence. The figures of two men, back to back, drawn in some manner of dotted chiaroscuro, fusing through a battery of subtly related colors in strobic pulses; a series of splendidly painted suns, dissolving into one another in slow progression up the sky; then a sun setting reminiscent of old country calendar paintings, but so ebullient and evocative in its colors and textures that it seems to have emanated from the distant waftings of a dream. Larkin can transform colors with much the same subtlety and volatility with which he can change forms. No one in animation since Disney in the mid-thirties has used color so lavishly or intricately. Distributed by Learning Corporation of America.

STRIKE

Written by the Proletkult Collective (Eisenstein, Pletnyov, Alexandrov, Kravchunovsky) Directed by Sergei Eisenstein Photographed by Edouard Tisse and Vassili Khvatov 66 minutes b/w (silent) U.S.S.R. 1924 With Grigori Alexandrov, Maxim Strauch, Mikhail Gomarov, Alexander Antonov, Judith Glizer, Boris Yurtsev

Strike was Eisenstein's first film, his first collaboration with his gifted cameraman Edouard Tisse, and — though it's been overshadowed by *The Battleship Potemkin* — the first film to announce a dramatic growth in Russian film. Though it lacks the maturity and control of *Potemkin, Strike* is an astounding achievement, exploding with new techniques and relationships, demonstrating not only Eisenstein's remarkable facility with new forms of cutting, but his genius at what he called the "montage of attractions," fusing images for the heightened dramatic and shock effect. The English critic David Sylvester has compared *Strike* with Eliot's *The Waste Land,* noting, "It is alike in that it operates through the rhythmic relationship of scattered images, each of them precisely concrete yet also symbolic, the juxtaposition of which startles and surprises . . . ."

The suicide of a worker falsely accused of theft in a factory touches off a strike. As the workers grow increasingly hungry, the managers and police and government officials try everything they can to break the strike, finally invading the workers' homes in a massacre climax. Eisenstein used a dazzling range of techniques (some that worked, some that didn't) to develop his themes of the mass as hero and the ineluctable failure of any revolt short of total revolution. In editing alone, the film becomes almost a catalog of later, more polished techniques: thematic intercutting (as between the massacre of the workers at the end of the film and the slaughter of a bull); uses of cutting to expand time; cutting in close-up to emphasize a physical detail; parallel editing: editing constructed around conflicting graphic forces. Many critics argue that *Strike* was Eisenstein's preparation for *The Battleship Potemkin*. But in its exuberance and volatility and its bold experiment with technique, it is more of Eisenstein's *Citizen Kane*. Distributed by Macmillan-Audio-Brandon Films.

TAKE THE MONEY AND RUN

Written by Woody Allen and Mickey Rose Directed by Woody Allen 85 minutes color Cinerama Releasing 1969 With Woody Allen, Janet Margolin, Marcel Hillaire, Jacquelyn Hyde

Made in the lingering popular swell of *Bonnie and Clyde*, Woody Allen's *Take the Money and Run* is at once the best gangster spoof ever made and among Woody's funniest and most fully realized films to date. Woody plays the bank robber as nebbish, a man who cannot even write a holdup note coherently, and who gets into trouble jimmying bubble gum machines. The story has a kind of structure. Using the narrator who *must* have done half the crime-does-not-pay B-melodramas of the early fifties, Woody's sorry foulups as a crook are recounted from his childhood. There is a marvelous bit with his parents — wearing gaudy Halloween mustaches. And there are innumerable unsuccessful holdups: one with a stolen pistol that turns out to be a cigarette lighter; one in a pet store where he dashes out, chased by a gorilla; and finally The Big Heist, which Woody organizes, only to get lost in the confusion of another gang trying to rob the same bank at the same time. As a prisoner, Woody carves a gun out of soap and prods his guard out of the cell and out of the prison — on a very rainy night.

Perhaps because it uses as a springboard the old movies that Woody and his audience know so well, and perhaps because he can localize the comic effects of his (and our) neurosis within the life of a failed criminal, *Take the Money and Run* succeeds brilliantly as a whole. Distributed by Films Inc.

TAMER OF WILD HORSES

Written by Vatroslav Mimica Designed and directed by Nedeljko Dragic 8 minutes color/animation Yugoslavia: Zagreb 1967

A horse tamer with a stern, imperious air seizes on a magnificent stallion and in moments vanquishes it to broken subjection. Searching for another horse, he comes on a vast, metallic, Trojan-size horse. He climbs the horse and proceeds to whip, but it remains stolid, unmoving. Then, surprising the tamer, it begins to move, and it is all the tamer can do to keep a grip. The horse transforms. Its clean, metallic sides give way to a burgeoning of valves and tubes and pistons. And as the mechanical horse steams and gyrates, the tamer is caught and squeezed between the pistons, pummeled and thrashed till his body is crushed. He tries to rise and take hold of the horse, but as it charges forward, he falls and is smashed into the ground by the enormous hooves. The tamer still isn't discouraged. He climbs the horse again, only to discover it undergoing yet another transformation: a creature of white, sleek surfaces, with portals in its sides that open and emit wings. On these wings it slowly rises and, carrying the tamer, wends off into distant clouds.

An allegory about technology? To a point. *Tamer of Wild Horses* begins and develops on a note that seems altogether allegorical. Then, toward the end, it slips into a perhaps-romantic surrealism. What is affecting and convincing about this film, however, is its style. Designer-director Dragic gives the horse an awesome range of graphic moods, drawing on cubism one moment, a pastel expressionism the next — as though in its multifold transformations of color and form the horse were truly revealing the deep complexity of the technological world. Distributed by Contemporary Films/McGraw-Hill.

TEN DAYS THAT SHOOK THE WORLD (originally entitled OCTOBER)

Written and directed by Sergei Eisenstein 103 minutes (abridged: 67 minutes) b/w (silent) Russia 1928 With Nikandrov, B. Livanov, V. Popov

Eisenstein was commissioned to make *October* (later abridged and retitled *Ten Days That Shook the World*) to commemorate the tenth anniversary of the October 1917 Revolution in Russia. In it, Eisenstein takes to almost drastic extremes his intellectual "montage" theory, the idea that two images set in juxtaposition with one another will create a third, "separate" concept for the audience. An example: Eisenstein cuts from the droll, statuesque figure of Kerensky (the temporary dictator) to a fanning peacock — suggesting Kerensky to be a strutting, conceited peacock. In some sequences — notably where there is some dramatic quality to the images and to the montage — this technique works, as in the crumbling of the statue of the Czar, which Eisenstein captures from a variety of angles with a stunning use of low lighting; or in the raising of the bridge, in which a horse strangles — signifying the gross insensitivity of the regime. But often the techniques Eisenstein used left audiences baffled (a major reason for the abridged British and American version).

Ten Days That Shook the World seems almost an exercise piece for Eisenstein — an experiment to test his theories, rather than a film that has emerged organically from dramatic or even persuasive ideas. It lacks the vitality of *Potemkin*, the enthusiasm of *Strike*, the richly textured humanity of *Old and New*. Yet the partial failure of an Eisenstein is vastly superior to many a lesser director's successes; and even in the available abridged version (now the original is available as well), Eisenstein's visual power and editing mastery are apparent. Distributed by Macmillan-Audio-Brandon Films.

THE THIN MAN

Written by Albert Hackett and Frances Goodrich Directed by Willard Van Dyke 93 minutes b/w M-G-M 1934 With William Powell, Myrna Loy, Maureen O'Sullivan, Nat Pendleton, Caesar Romero

Dashiell Hammett's novel *The Thin Man* is a stylish, convoluted mystery story. The filmed version has become quite something else, one of the snappiest-mannered comedies of the thirties — a film shaggily rich in its feisty characterizations, its ebullient movement, and its marvelous double entendres, difficult for even a Mae West to match. (Says Nora, when a plainclothes cop starts digging through her bureau: "What are you doing in my drawers?")

Nick Charles (William Powell) is a reputable detective who has married Nora — and wisely: she's rich and doesn't mind when he reminds her of the fact. (When she presses him to take the case, Nick says, "I don't have any time. I'm much too busy taking care of the money I married you for.") It is an uncommon screen marriage: they bark, tease, upstage one another, but all in a kind of unbroken, alcoholic fun. When an inventor whom Nick knew disappears — and is accused of one, then two, then three murders — Nick reluctantly enters the case. And eventually he solves it. But the mystery story that was the spine of Hammett's novel is compressed and almost set aside here. What interested the writers and the director (and what never fails to intrigue the audience) are Nick and Nora Charles and their splendidly playful banter. The acting is memorable: William Powell as Nick seems, in recollection, never to have been without a martini glass in hand or a slight hiccough in his voice; Myrna Loy can twist her face into a thousand expressions, and Nick (like us) can sense just how seriously to take each one. The minor roles are equally memorable: Caesar Romero, though barely glimpsed, must be the screen's classic gigolo; Minna Combell as Mimi, the inventor's wife, seems all claws. One of the best-written films of the thirties. Distributed by Films Inc.

TOMORROW

Written by Horton Foote Directed by Joseph Anthony Photographed by Allen Green 103 minutes b/w Cine-Art 1972 With Robert Duvall, Olga Bellin, Sudie Bond, Richard McConnell, Peter Masterson, William Hawley, James Franks, Johnny Mask

At a young man's trial for murder, one juror (Robert Duvall) refuses to announce "guilty," despite the furious attempt of the other jurors to sway him. Many years before, when he was living and working on a neighbor's farm, the man met a woman near childbirth and for several days at Christmas took care of her. He came to love her and persuaded her to marry him. Her child, a boy, was born shortly before the woman died. Duvall took the child home and, not caring that it was another man's son, raised him as his own. What happens to the son — and, by extension, to Duvall — explains his stolid refusal on the jury and creates one of film's most emotionally wrenching moments.

Tomorrow is so devoid of the stagecraft of contemporary filmmaking, of spastic vitality, blitzkrieg editing, spurious close-ups, impatient camera movement — that one marvels it was made in 1972, and in America. It is, in effect, surprisingly true to its source, Faulkner's short story "Knight's Gambit," both in its beautifully structured rise of feeling, and in its barren, sometimes chilling use of a winter Mississippi locale. Duvall's performance projects — with stunning conviction — the pale loneliness of a man who has never before known a woman and probably never will again. Allan Green's photography maintains a quiet distance from the characters, as if to let them breathe and move in their own world. Each frame is so carefully and serenely composed that — like Faulkner's rich, evocative language — the images become somehow transparent: we see into the characters from the way they squat and sit and hold their silences. The highest tribute the movies have ever paid Faulkner, *Tomorrow* is a film that stirs feelings we may not suspect are still there. Distributed in 35mm by Filmgroup Productions.

TOUCH OF EVIL

Written and directed by Orson Welles 93 minutes b/w Universal Pictures 1957 With Charlton Heston, Janet Leigh, Orson Welles, Marlene Dietrich

Orson Welles has such an acute theatrical touch that in his films the settings declare and provoke mood and theme often more decisively than script or characters. *Touch of Evil* takes place in a small, sleazy Mexican-border town, and everything about the film comes to reflect that same weary, seedy mood that the town projects. Welles plays a grousing, candy-chewing sheriff with a known penchant for planting evidence whenever he needs to solve a crime. There are some remarkable sequences here: Welles and Marlene Dietrich ("You've been eating too much candy again, baby"); Janet Leigh in a motel room, attacked by a group of young thugs; Welles tromping over a bridge at the end of the film, hearing his voice echoed on a transmitter controlled by Heston, below; and Welles' inevitable death, amidst the floating garbage on the river edge. *Touch of Evil* has the mood and the air of something soiled and left too long in a closed compartment. It is less about guilt, or power, or the law than about the diseases that prey on people in cramped, congealed worlds. Distributed by Twyman Films, Inc.

THE TRIAL

Written and directed by Orson Welles 120 minutes b/w Mercury Production 1962 With Anthony Perkins, Jeanne Moreau, Elsa Martinelli, Orson Welles

Orson Welles' *The Trial*, based on the Kafka novel, is one of the most problematic of Welles' films. Its visual qualities are dense, baroque, sometimes stunning; but its narrative soon strays into a series of convoluted scenes and relationships, and the film becomes all but impossible to follow. As with most of Welles' later films, *The Trial* reflects the prodigious difficulties he encountered in financing. The sets he was originally promised, for example, were lost in a drastic budget cut, and Welles had to shoot the film in a deserted railway station in Zagreb, Yugoslavia. Yet for its camera, its dramatic angles, its harsh and violent lighting, its use of architecture to create a foreboding mood beyond the powers of storytelling, *The Trial* remains a remarkable achievement of recent filmmaking. In some manner it recaptures the haunting, chilling pulse of Kafka's classic beyond what any other contemporary director might have been able to do. Distributed by Macmillan-Audio-Brandon Films.

2001: A SPACE ODYSSEY

Written by Stanley Kubrick and Arthur C. Clarke Directed by Stanley Kubrick 141 minutes color M-G-M 1968 With Keir Dullea, Gary Lockwood, William Sylvester, Daniel Richter, Douglas Rain

Using a triptych structure — the birth of man, the discovery of a signaling device on the moon, and the flight to Jupiter — Stanley Kubrick invests *2001: A Space Odyssey* with a technical sophistication unmatched in any science fiction or fantasy film — and unlikely to be matched for quite some time. Indeed, the substance and subject of *2001* have little to do with its narrative (which reaches its peak in a tense battle between a surviving spaceship member and a monomaniacal computer), but rather with what Kubrick and Clarke presume to be the experience of space flight, the fluid and amorphous lassitude of weightlessness; the ballet of a spacecraft docking in a floating port; the drama of light as planets and moons hover and reveal one another in a choreography of spheres. One suspects that the space-accustomed children of some distant generation might look back on *2001* with much the same tolerant amusement that we have for good melodramas of the early silent era — so conscious of their sentimentality, yet somehow enjoying it all the same. No matter. Whatever its faults, *2001* has broken many barriers and has proven that a film can romanticize even that which is unknown. Distributed by Films Inc.

WALKABOUT

Written by Edward Bond Directed by Nicholas Roeg 95 minutes color Twentieth Century-Fox 1971 With Jenny Agutter, Lucien John, David Gumpilil

A quick montage of modern, urban Australia; a closer look at one home, swimming pool and all. Then the trip — a gloomily preoccupied businessman taking his teen-age daughter and eight-year-old son into the bush for a picnic. There he tries to kill them but ends up killing himself and setting the car afire. The girl and her brother begin wandering through the hot, hostile wasteland, till they chance upon an aborigine youth on his "walkabout" — an endurance test required by his tribe as a manhood rite. The crushing impact of civilization is best felt here. Only the boy can "converse" with the aborigine; the girl remains always suspicious of him, unwilling to make the effort to break through to him. And though the aborigine keeps both the girl and her brother alive long enough to find a road, in a grimly touching scene where the aborigine tries to woo the girl in *his* fashion, her only response is terror and withdrawal. The aborigine commits suicide, but for the girl there isn't a hint of feeling or regret. They had, after all, found a road back to the city.

Walkabout makes its point perhaps a bit too bluntly, but the movie is not without force. The cinematography is superb, capturing the magnificence of the Australian bush and its harsh dangers. Some of the editing is flashy and overdone, but the film is so well conveyed and so visually alive that it manages to absorb its faults. Distributed by Films Inc.

THE WALL

Written, designed, and directed by Ante Zaninovic 4 minutes color/animation Yugoslavia: Zagreb 1966

A little man wearing a bowler and carrying a cane pauses beside a vast rock wall and waits. In a moment another little character comes by, a naked, furry-haired man who attacks the wall with violent force. He tries to climb over it, pole-vault over it, dig under it, smash through it with a cannon — all while the man in the bowler hat watches impassively. Finally, in a crunching last effort, the naked man races to the wall and drives himself bodily into it, smashing out a tunnel, but with his body now piled in the rubble. The man in the bowler gives him a glance, strolls through the hole in the wall, and goes on walking briskly till he reaches another wall, at which point he sits down and waits.

Director Zaninovic treats this mordant little fable in a jauntily pleasant manner. We're so captivated by the gags of the naked man as he tries to conquer the wall that we virtually forget the man in the bowler who's been watching and waiting all along. Which, of course, is the point. Distributed by Contemporary Films/McGraw-Hill.

THE WESTERNER

Written by Jo Swerling and Niven Busch Directed by William Wyler 99 minutes b/w United Artists 1940 With Gary Cooper, Walter Brennan, Doris Davenport, Fred Stone

One of the great and classic Westerns, *The Westerner* concentrates on the complex, evolving relationship of two men, Cole Hardin (Cooper), a canny, poker-faced loner; and Judge Roy Bean (Brennan), the all-time epitome of the hard-drinking, town-choking, hanging judge. The film opens with Cooper coming into town on a stolen horse. In one of his quickly rigged trials, Brennan sentences Cooper to death in the morning, a sentence that (like everything else) hardly fazes Cooper In the best bluffing manner of a tactful poker player (and *The Westerner* is really a game of poker between Cooper and Brennan), Cooper points to a picture of the famous actress Lily Langtry and claims he knows her, that he even has a locket of her hair. This is enough to keep him from hanging, for a while. The film is rich in moments of one-upmanship; for example, a drinking ceremony between Cooper and Brennan, which Brennan wins, but which enables Cooper to make a getaway next morning. Distributed by Macmillan-Audio-Brandon Films.

WHITE HEAT

Written by Ivan Goff and Ben Roberts Directed by Raoul Walsh 114 minutes b/w Warner Brothers 1949 With James Cagney, Virginia Mayo, Edmond O'Brien, Margaret Wycherly

One of the toughest and most unrelenting of gangster films, *White Heat* depicts James Cagney as Cody Jarrett, a hoodlum who verges on the psychopathic. As a way of providing an alibi for one major crime, for example, Jarrett turns himself in for a lesser crime committed at the same time in another city. A suspicious federal agent, Edmond O'Brien, is set up in prison to get close to Jarrett; he does, and that proves, finally, to be Jarrett's undoing. Director Walsh has an acute feeling for the genre and particularly for Cagney's character. Cagney is always killing people through doors—an apartment door, the door of a car trunk — as if to mask and further simplify the act of murder, which to him is no more immoral than grabbing a bite of somebody's cake. Cagney's character here is one of his best developed: his moods fluctuate from morose to ecstatic; he is supremely confident of himself and moves with the economy of expression one would expect to find in such a man. Much of the film is framed amid machinery — the machine shop in the prison, the machines that go berserk in Cody's head during a seizure, the oil refineries at the close of the film — as if to intimate that the gangster is perhaps a product of the machine age, the victim of his own inability to fit the cogs and sprockets of the modern dynamo. Distributed by UA 16.

WILD BOYS OF THE ROAD

Written by Daniel Ahearn Directed by William Wellman 68 minutes b/w Warner Brothers 1933 With Frankie Darro, Dorothy Coonan, Edwin Phillips, Rochelle Hudson

Of the thirties films that attempted social realism, *Wild Boys of the Road* remains — despite undeserved obscurity — one of the best. Two boys, good friends, realize that they have become an unnecessary burden on their out-of-work parents. They take to the railroad in an attempt to find work in some distant, bigger city. But each city already has large bands of similarly unemployable youth — good-hearted, decent kids who, like moving armies, ride the freight trains. Coming into one city, the boys are forced to jump off the train while it's still moving; one of the heroes falls and cannot quite pull himself from the track when a train pulls into the yard. He loses his leg. The situation could have led to a kind of pathetic soap opera. Instead the boy's missing leg comes to signify the crippled social condition of the kids. When they construct a city-camp out of huge pipes and other makeshift material, the authorities come to clear them out (a scene reminiscent of the Italian neo-realistic fantasy, *Miracle in Milan*). The ending is a bit forced, but the film has enough fine touches — the opening sequence, the stolen plastic leg that won't fit, the kids on the trains — that the veneer of sentimentality doesn't obscure the sound acting or forthright direction. Distributed by UA 16.

THE WILD BUNCH

Written by Walon Green and Sam Peckinpah Directed by Sam Peckinpah 145 minutes color Warner Brothers 1969 With William Holden, Ernest Borgnine, Robert Ryan, Edmond O'Brien, Warren Oates, Ben Johnson, Strother Martin, L. Q. Jones

Early in *The Wild Bunch*, a battered, hair-trigger-tempered group of middle-aged outlaws try to "take" the bank in some Southwestern town. On the street outside, a temperance union rally parades proudly, singing confected religious hymns. Gunfire cracks from atop a building; a small army of bounty hunters has circled on Pike Bishop's gang like vultures. And soon director Peckinpah indulges in a blood-spattering massacre—with outlaws, bounty hunters, and mostly the temperance union bystanders pitching and exploding with blood. The scene becomes a spectacle. We are shown more violence and killings than we may want (or than the film may need) — for example, the even more extravagant massacre at the end, in which Pike's gang takes on an entire regiment of Mexican soldiers.

Yet *The Wild Bunch* manages somehow to be better than its exorbitant violence would suggest. There are refrains, moods, tensions, reverberations just below the surface of the movie, bringing back to us all the Westerns we've seen, and *The Wild Bunch* takes on the quality of a dark elegy to a genre, a myth, a character type. Peckinpah has cast the film for precisely that effect, and the dialogue — spare, masculine, vivid, even archaic ("You're not gonna get a chance to dry-gulch me, old man") — only heightens our sense of *déja vu. The Wild Bunch* is probably about the death of the Westerner, though that is less dramatically or symbolically presented than instinctively felt. Distributed by Warner Brothers 16.

THE WIND

Written by Frances Marion Directed by Victor Sjöström 120 minutes b/w (silent) M-G-M 1927 With Lillian Gish, Lars Hanson, Montagu Love, Dorothy Cummings

Victor Sjöström was in the first wave of major European directors who came to Hollywood: Sjöström from Sweden, Lubitsch, F. W. Murnau and Fritz Lang from Germany. Such men invested the Hollywood films of the twenties and the thirties with a vitality and artistic ambition only rarely achieved by American-born directors. (It is an interesting comment that several other major directors of that period — Erich von Stroheim, Joseph von Sternberg, for example — began their careers in Hollywood but were born in Europe.)

The Wind, Sjöström's best American film, is replete with the vivid sense of nature that has always underscored Swedish films, from Sjöström to Bergman. Indeed, one could argue that the central character in the film is not Lillian Gish (who plays a timid Eastern girl come West to be a schoolteacher, and who marries a cowhand she dislikes) but the wind that howls and sweeps relentlessly throughout the film. The sandy, grainy, ubiquitous wind at once organizes and unifies the film. We best know Gish through her reactions to the wind; and the climactic scene in which Gish kills a man who tries to rape her includes, almost as a scoring accompaniment, the peak of a severe windstorm. Sjöström's camera and Gish's exquisite acting give *The Wind* a fierce, real power. Watching it even today, you can feel the gritty textures, the harsh rush of blown sand. Distributed by Films Inc.

Film Distributors

Columbia (16) Cinematheque
711 Fifth Ave.
New York, N.Y. 10022

Contemporary Films/McGraw-Hill
Princeton Rd.
Hightstown, N.J. 08520

828 Custer Ave.
Evanston, Ill. 60202

1714 Stockton St.
San Francisco, Calif. 94133

Creative Film Society
7237 Canby Ave.
Reseda, Calif. 91335

Film Images
17 W. 60th St.
New York, N.Y. 10023

1034 Lake St.
Oak Park, Ill. 60301

Films Inc.
277 Pharr Rd. N.E.
Atlanta, Ga. 30305

161 Massachusetts Ave.
Boston, Mass. 02115

1414 Dragon St.
Dallas, Tex. 75207

98 W. Jackson St., Suite 1
Hayward, Calif. 94544

5625 Hollywood Blvd.
Hollywood, Calif. 90028

35-01 Queens Blvd.
Long Island City, N.Y. 11101

4420 Oakton St.
Skokie, Ill. 60076

International Film Bureau, Inc.
332 So. Michigan Ave.
Chicago, Ill. 60504

Ivy Films
120 E. 56th St.
New York, N.Y. 10022

Janus Films
745 Fifth Ave.
New York, N.Y. 10022

Learning Corporation of America
711 Fifth Ave.
New York, N.Y. 10022

Macmillan Audio Brandon Films
34 MacQueston Parkway So.
Mount Vernon, N.Y. 10550

406 Clement St.
San Francisco, Calif. 94118

1619 No. Cherokee
Los Angeles, Calif. 90028

8615 Directors Row
Dallas, Tex. 75247

512 Burlington Ave.
La Grange, Ill. 60525

Phoenix Films, Inc.
267 W. 25th St.
New York, N.Y. 10001

Pyramid Films
Box 1048
Santa Monica, Calif. 90406

Twyman Films, Inc.
329 Salem Ave.
Dayton, O. 45401

United Artists 16 (UA 16)
729 Seventh Ave.
New York, N.Y. 10019

Walter Reade 16
241 E. 34th St.
New York, N.Y. 10016

Warner Brothers 16
Non-theatrical Division
4000 Warner Blvd.
Burbank, Calif. 91505

Index

Page numbers in parentheses indicate photographs. Book titles are in bold type.